Cases in
Advertising
and
Communications Management

Cases in Advertising and Communications Management

Stephen A. Greyser
HARVARD UNIVERSITY
GRADUATE SCHOOL OF BUSINESS ADMINISTRATION

PRENTICE-HALL, INC., Englewood Cliffs, New Jersey

ISBN: 0-13-118497-0

Library of Congress Catalog Card Number: 74-158911

Printed in the United States of America

10   9   8   7   6   5

All of the case material in this book, with the exception of
*Exercise in Television Commercial Analysis, On Exposure to
Advertisements,* and *What Americans Think about Advertising,*
is copyrighted by the President and Fellows of Harvard College
and is used with their permission. Case material is made possible
by the cooperation of business firms who may wish to remain
anonymous by having names, quantities, and other identifying
details disguised while maintaining basic relationships. Cases are
prepared as the basis for class discussion rather than to illustrate
either effective or ineffective handling of administrative
situations.

Prentice-Hall International, Inc., *London*
Prentice-Hall of Australia, Pty. Ltd., *Sydney*
Prentice-Hall of Canada, Ltd., *Toronto*
Prentice-Hall of India Private Limited, *New Delhi*
Prentice-Hall of Japan, Inc., *Tokyo*

Contents

PART III

Developing
and
Appraising
Advertising Messages   **233**

PART IV

Evaluating Promotional Programs 387

PART V

Advertiser-Agency Relationships 585

PART VI

Promotion and Social Issues 597

Preface

This is a casebook in *advertising and communications management.* Its principal orientation is toward those individuals responsible for planning, developing, appraising, and administering advertising and promotional activities. Its principal focus is that of *managing the advertising function,* whether in the role of a company product or advertising manager, an advertising agency executive, or in some other capacity. Thus, it is addressed to managerially-oriented students and teachers.

OVERARCHING MANAGERIAL PERSPECTIVE

One can look at advertising from a variety of perspectives. For example, many advertising problems can be seen as calling for the capability of creative experts, of media specialists, and the like. Or one may consider overall advertising planning to be the bailiwick of the behavioral marketing communications specialist or quantitative model-builder.

Certainly the cases in this volume treat issues where such expertise can make a significant contribution, such as preparing a media plan, devising a communications strategy that considers behavioral research findings, creating sparkling advertising themes and copy, or building a research model to evaluate an overall advertising-marketing program. Although such capabilities are obviously relevant in their own terms to the advertising executive, his true job lies in pulling them together into a coordinated advertising program. Thus throughout the book, the overarching perspective remains that of the manager responsible for planning and developing advertising strategy.

PRACTITIONER PROBLEMS

Because of this major concern with the manager, practitioner problems provide the primary context for the book's cases. These problems cover a wide variety of different kinds of advertising: advertising in behalf of products, services, and ideas; advertising directed at end-consumers (the bulk of the cases) and that aimed at producers or prescribers; advertising to mass markets and to segmented markets, for large companies and small ones, to national markets and to regional-local ones; campaigns for established products and for new products, for frequently-purchased items and infrequently-purchased items; and the advertising programs of the international advertiser.

CONTENT AREAS

The major content areas of the book are deliberately sequenced to follow a typical pattern of how advertising management considers, plans, and develops advertising programs. First is the assessment of the *role of and opportunities for promotion.* This section is followed by problems of *market identification and media strategy,* and in turn leads to the third area, namely *developing and appraising advertising messages.* The fourth part deals with the broad and thorny issues of *evaluating promotional programs.* This four-stage sequence on advertising programs is followed in the fifth section by cases that treat the *relationships between advertisers and advertising agencies.* The final part of the book presents cases that address *social and ethical issues in advertising.*

Let us look at each of these more closely.

1) Promotion's Role and Opportunities—The initial section of the book looks at overall advertising management issues, particularly those involving the role of and opportunities for advertising under various industry and competitive situations. Among the key elements of advertising management treated in the cases in this section are:

— the relationship of advertising to other elements of the firm's marketing mix, i.e., the role and interrelationship of advertising considerations within the company's overall marketing strategy;

— the opportunity for advertising (and/or other company-controlled activities) in given consumer and competitive situations, i.e., whether and to what extent advertising can make a contribution;

— the importance of environmental factors (cultural and behavioral) in this assessment;

— the implications of various roles and opportunities for the ways in which advertising should most appropriately be evaluated.

2) Market Identification and Media Strategy—The second section centers on market and media issues. Among the questions posed are:

— Just what population groups are the target(s) of the advertising program?

— What general media strategies are most appropriate to reach mass and/or specialized audiences? How should one best identify (stratify) the audience?

— Under what conditions should companies consider changes in their basic media strategy?

— Are there particular media environments and/or use patterns that offer distinctive opportunities in given situations?

— How does one analyze the "fit" between a company's advertising situation and a particular media vehicle?

— What is it like to build an actual media schedule from budget and cost information?

— What are the relevant questions to ask in trying to evaluate media?

3) Developing and Appraising Advertising Messages—Linked to market and media strategy is the creative strategy—conceiving and executing advertising platforms, themes, and individual advertisements. This includes such matters as:

— the relationship of overall advertising objectives to creative objectives;

— "positioning"—the development of creative platforms in light of market and competitive information;

— the role of research studies as a guide to creative strategy;

— translating basic creative strategy into the execution of specific advertisements;

— "What makes for a good ad?"—preparing and critiquing individual ads and their rationales (exercises);

— copy testing—methods and criteria for appraising individual print and TV ads;

— pretesting and post-testing advertising messages;

— consumer receptivity to advertising messages: exposure to advertising vehicles and to specific ads within a vehicle.

4) Evaluating Promotional Programs—Beyond the problems of assessing advertising themes and individual advertisements are broader issues of evaluating entire advertising campaigns and programs. Among the areas included are:

— the appropriateness of *communications* measures vs. *sales* measures of advertising effectiveness;

— experimental design in advertising effectiveness studies;

— differences in assessing product advertising campaigns and institutional advertising campaigns;

— how much to spend on advertising;

— when to change a campaign;

— taking a regional program onto a national basis;

— developing an overall advertising evaluation system and model for all facets of an advertising program.

5) Advertiser-Agency Relationships—A major aspect of administering advertising activities is the way in which advertisers and their advertising agencies work together. Involved are such questions as:

— Under what conditions are different kinds of agencies—e.g., full-service, "boutique"—more or less likely to work better for a company?

— How should the client-agency relationship be evaluated? What roles and responsibilities does each party have in the relationship?

6) Promotion and Social Issues—In recent years especially, broader issues involving advertising have emerged as important considerations for advertising executives. These social and ethical aspects of advertising impinge on the daily practice of advertising management . . . and its future practice. Topics addressed in the cases in this area include:

— the public's overall attitudes toward advertising (as an institution in our society) and toward advertisements themselves;

— truth and exaggeration in ads; "how far" ads should go under what conditions;

— the government's role in regulating advertising;

— the practice and implications of political advertising;

— pragmatic problems and changing criteria for advertising acceptability by the media;

— the response to consumerism.

CASE FEATURES

Students (and instructors) may find it helpful to know about several particular aspects of the entire case collection. First, in addition to the usual case series intended for consecutive study, there are some case series that are intended for study at several different (i.e., *non*-consecutive) points. These case situations—the Weyerhaeuser Company, the American Sheep Producers Council, and the Beech Aircraft Company—provide an opportunity to observe and participate in a variety of related advertising issues *as they develop.* Thus, one is afforded an insight not only into different facets of the same situation, but also into the overall company advertising strategy as it evolves. In addition these cases allow previous preparation to serve as a foundation for examining still further steps in the company's advertising process.

Another element of relevance concerns matters of research. Although there are cases that explicitly focus on advertising research problems in their own terms, a strong undercurrent of research runs through the entire book. For, after all, it is the advertising manager's task not so much to *undertake* research as it is to *understand* it. Thus a managerial consideration of advertising research calls not for "pigeon-holing" it in a separate box, but grasping its application *throughout* the advertising process. As a result, behavioral and quantitative data appear for use in case analysis whether the problem is one of market identification, media strategy, message development, or building and evaluating advertising programs. In this way, research fits into an overall context of aiding management judgment and decision-making.

There is a further common element in the cases—each case is preceded by a brief synopsis and followed by suggested study questions. The purpose of both is to aid, rather than to restrict, preparation and classroom discussion. Via the synopsis, an overview of the case situation is quickly taken; via the questions, attention is concentrated on key issues, albeit not necessarily for discussion in the same order, nor to the exclusion of ideas for additional exploration.

TO ANALYZE THE SUBJECTIVE

By its very nature advertising is a highly subjective field, often characterized by great flights of intuition. Since intuition is a skill not easily learned (or taught!), a major task of the incipient advertising executive is to develop objective, analytic means of considering advertising problems. The intent of the cases in this book is to provide an opportunity for such reasoned analysis to be applied. Toward this end, the first four sections of the book, as noted above, follow the logical sequence of events in planning and developing advertising programs. These four fundamental steps in advertising management can be seen as a series of "four M's"—

- *markets* (whom—what publics—are we trying to reach?)
- *media* (how do we reach them?)
- *messages* (what do we want to say—themes and copy—to each of them?)
- *measurement* (making evaluations against market-media-message objectives.

The above makes no claims to be a model or a theory of advertising. Rather it seeks only to help provide a foundation for analyzing company advertising programs and problems. For it is through careful study and analysis of a wide *variety* of such situations that we all can gain greater insights into the answers to essential, and permanent, questions about advertising: what constitutes good advertising planning, what should be advertising's goals, how does advertising work, what are the characteristics of effective ads, what are the best ways to evaluate individual ads and campaigns, and—most important—under what conditions and in what situations do the answers to these questions vary.

"Conditions" and "situations" bring us back to "cases." Cases, of course, are descriptions of business situations. Students are asked to appraise past company actions, consider future ones, and decide what route to follow and how. As students attempt to perform the aforementioned kinds of analysis and decision-making, they must put themselves in the executive's chair; they must sift the evidence; they must weigh and pose alternatives; *they must decide.*

Some suggestions are in order here regarding these tasks of case study and preparation. Case appraisals typically should start with an attempt to understand *what* current company objectives, policies, and practices are, and *why*. In this effort, it is important to separate what the company's intended aims and policies *are* from one's own view of what they *should be.*

A further delineation to be made is that between *aims* and *execution;* a well-conceived advertising program may have been executed poorly, and vice versa. At this point, having understood and critiqued existing company strategy and/or practice, alternatives can be considered. Alternatives posed in the case should be treated first, after which one's own ideas and alternatives can be presented. In presenting a fresh program, it is important that the premises on which it is based be set forth carefully, and not be overwhelmed by enthusiasm over one's personal approach.

Some further words are in order concerning class participation. Obviously careful case study and preparation are a precursor to effective class participation. But in addition, there must be present a strong willingness on the student's part to commit his thoughts into words, to share them with and defend them against fellow students and faculty, and to argue for them in the face of opposing viewpoints. Sharing one's insights in these ways is particularly meaningful in an advertising course, since verbal facility and presentation contribute to success in advertising jobs.

Whether one is preparing for oneself, for oral presentation in class, or for a written case assignment, some additional thoughts may be of help. More specifically:

— Avoid rehashing case facts. *Interpret them* . . . the other students (and the instructor) have read the case!

— Let the listener or reader know at the outset what you are trying to do, where you are headed, and (if appropriate) why.

— If a decision is called for, be sure to make it. Deal with stated alternatives before posing your own new ones, however good the latter may be. When rejecting all alternatives, there is an obligation to develop a substitute.

— If you recommend research, discuss *what* and *why*. Try to show how the information would help, indicating where possible the decision avenues you would take if particular research results were to be found.

— Face up to the operational ramifications (e.g., risks, feasibility) of your own plans and those of others.

— *Think* before you talk or write. Remember that the order of presentation often differs from the process of analysis.

The foregoing has sought to define what this book is all about, to sketch its principal perspectives and orientation, to describe its general and specific contents in some detail, and to provide some framework and guidelines for case preparation and analysis. Obviously the hope, the intent, is that this introductory material—and the cases themselves—will serve the purposes of the advertising executives-to-be to whom it is directed.

ACKNOWLEDGEMENTS

This book owes its existence to a number of people whose inspiration, ideas, efforts, and support have helped make these cases a reality.

My largest debt is to those who have preceded me in teaching the advertising course at the Harvard Business School. Of particular importance in this regard are two well-known HBS professors:

— *Neil H. Borden,* the beloved and respected "Advertising's Mr. Chips," who imparted to the advertising course its managerial character, and who developed the nation's first extensive collection of advertising management cases during the more than 30 years that he was associated with the course; it has been a personal pleasure and professional privilege to know him, to exchange views with him, and to benefit from his wisdom.

— *Martin V. Marshall,* who over a 15-year period reinforced the managerial orientation of the course, produced numerous cases covering the full range of advertising practitioner problems, and maintained a truly "real world" flavor in the advertising classroom; he continues to be involved with course development and teaching in the marketing management and advertising areas, and has been a valuable personal guide through the sometimes labyrinthine paths of course development.

My early interest in advertising was nurtured by *Jerome M. O'Leary,* under whose tutelage and in whose agency I spent seven formative years, and by the late *James T. Chirurg,* whose Advertising Fellowship provided tangible support in my MBA student years at Harvard.

Whatever crafts one develops in case development typically grow from the patience and experience of senior faculty members. Several HBS professors warrant special mention for their roles both in honing my casewriting abilities and in fostering a conceptual approach to the development of a course. *Thomas C. Raymond* and *John B. Matthews* early sensitized me to the pedagogical verities of effective classroom material. *Harvard Business Review* Editor *Edward C. Bursk* gave me the benefit of his extensive experience in building courses, writing cases, and presenting ideas in print clearly and succinctly; he also initially developed the *Saturday Evening Post* cases. *Raymond A. Bauer,* mentor and friend, taught and trained me to recognize quality research and information-gathering, and to try to emulate it.

The conception, field research, preparation, and writing of a case are intellectually challenging and time-consuming activities. In the work leading to these cases, I have been blessed with research assistants of great competence, unflagging energy, and sunny disposition. Both are Harvard MBA's, and my former students in the Advertising course. To *George Leighton,* who prepared the American Sheep Producers Council, Beech, and Weyerhaeuser series, as well as the Abex, Irish Tourist Board, and Brown-Forman cases, I am particularly grateful for his consummate writing facility, creative approaches to pedagogy, and willingness to share the peculiarities of my frequent evening and weekend schedules. To *Bonnie Reece,* who prepared the Consumer Value Stores, Abbott Steel, Lake Michigan, and Cramer Food cases, and whose editorial talents are reflected in many others, I'm especially thankful for her delicate blend of advertising knowledge, teaching capability, and student orientation that manifests itself in the continued salutary reshaping of the course, in beneficial editorial and administrative aid in case preparation and production, and in a pleasant firmness that guides the necessary work to completion amidst my daily calendar crises.

In addition to George and Bonnie, credit should also be given to three former and present Harvard Business School doctoral candidates whose efforts contributed to the casebook. To Alice E. Courtney (Nassau County Election), Wallace Feldman (FTC and Aspirin Advertising), and Ulrich Wiechmann (Whirlpool) go my appreciation for their labors and for three pleasant working experiences.

To the smiling faces and willing fingers who helped translate written and dictated notes into legible text also go my thanks. Terry Eger, who has been midwife

xvi   *Preface*

to much of the book, deserves special thanks for contending with my eleventh-hour editorial revisions.

As is true with any case collection, incalculable thanks are owed to the many firms whose experiences *are* the book. These companies, whether their names be disguised herein or not, contribute their experiences for the improvement of *all* advertising practice, and we all are in their debt. In this regard, special contributions of time and effort were made by the American Sheep Producers Council, the Beech Aircraft Corporation, and the Weyerhaeuser Company. In addition, for permission to draw on their original materials we are grateful to the Leo Burnett Company and the Columbia Broadcasting Company.

At the Harvard Business School, support for course development activities and case-writing has been an institutional tradition. Time and budget assistance for my efforts have been generously provided by Senior Associate Dean George F. F. Lombard and Associate Dean Thomas A. Graves. Andrew R. Towl, whose experience in case development and distribution spans over 30 years has offered many useful insights into the case development process.

Finally I would like to thank Jeffrey A. Barach, Associate Professor at Tulane University, S. Watson Dunn, Chairman of the Department of Advertising at the University of Illinois, and Lyman E. Ostlund, Associate Professor at the Graduate School of Business at Columbia University, for their helpfulness in reviewing this book.

Despite the many contributions of others mentioned here, it is to my failings that readers and users should attribute any errors or omissions in the book. Not in the energies behind its inputs, but in the perceived value of its outputs, should lie the reader's criterion of the volume's usefulness.

Stephen A. Greyser

Boston, Massachusetts

Cases in
Advertising
and
Communications Management

Promotion's Role and Opportunities

PART I

American
Sheep Producers Council (A)

The trade association attempts to increase national consumption of lamb, a meat which a major attitude study found to have serious image problems. This case outlines the industry marketing situation, with a focus on various lamb advertising themes directed at important target groups.

In early 1969, executives of the American Sheep Producers Council (ASPC) were reviewing their efforts to promote the consumption of lamb in the United States. Their attention was focused particularly on a number of research studies which ASPC had commissioned since 1964. These studies had sought to obtain consumer information which would make possible more specific copy and media direction in the Council's national lamb advertising campaign. Executives believed that the rising cost of promotion had made a "rifle-shot" approach—aimed at specific objectives and preferences of certain consumer groups—increasingly imperative in ASPC's advertising and promotional effort.

ASPC—FORMATION AND SCOPE OF OPERATIONS

The National Wool Act, passed by Congress in 1954, authorized the sheep industry to conduct a self-help program of promotion of its two principal products: lamb and wool. In 1955, the American Sheep Producers Council was designated as the body to implement and coordinate the various programs of wool and lamb promotion.

ASPC drew its promotion funds from the incentive payments which American sheep producers received from the government. ASPC deductions from these payments were automatic—1½ cents per pound of shorn wool and 7½ cents for each 100 pounds of unshorn lamb. As such, nearly every sheepman in the U.S. contributed to ASPC in an amount varying with the size of his operation. Some were unaware that they were "contributing" to the Council's programs since the ASPC deductions came before sheepmen received the incentive payments. ASPC's

3

continued existence was approved in 1959, 1962, and 1966 by means of national referenda of sheep producers.

Lamb promotion received a somewhat greater portion of the Council's total budget than did wool promotion (in 1968-1969 the lamb/wool balance was roughly 56/44). This case is concerned only with ASPC's efforts on behalf of lamb.

Promotion of lamb encompassed four major activities:

1) *Advertising*—Advertising was directed to consumers and the trade, primarily in newspapers, magazines, and radio. Advertising was by far the largest single cost item in lamb promotion, totaling over $1 million annually in the late 1960s.

2) *Merchandising*—Merchandising activities aimed at enlisting the coopera- of packers and retailers in displaying and promoting lamb to its best advantage as well as providing them with posters and banners for meat-department displays.

3) *Publicity*—Publicity efforts provided food editors of newspapers, magazines, and the broadcast media with stories about lamb cookery and photographs showing lamb dishes.

4) *Education*—Education activities focused on providing educational materials on lamb cookery and preparation—in the form of reading matter, motion pictures, and film strips—to schools, colleges, women's clubs, and other organizations. In addition, ASPC considered much of its consumer advertising to be educational in nature.

PROBLEMS FACING ASPC

One major problem facing the Council in 1969 was the limited supply of lamb and the resulting limitations in its distribution. The nation's sheep population declined 35% during World War II, and continued to drop further at a rate of approximately 6% annually through the 1960s. This served to intensify the then already-acute lamb availability problem. In 1969, lamb was consistently available primarily only in the Great Lakes region and on both coasts. It accounted for roughly 2% of total U.S. meat consumption. Exhibit 1 contains production data for lamb and other leading meats for the years 1958-1966.

The falling lamb population within the industry was in a large part believed to be the result of the many risks and adverse influences facing the American sheepman. For example, individual sheepmen occupied a relatively weak power position as compared with other segments of the industry distribution system. An ASPC executive identified problems at both the supermarket chain and the meat packer levels:

a) *Supermarket chain*—Since lamb represents only about 2% of total meat sales, the meat buyer for a chain may easily decide simply not to carry it, especially if he has reason to believe that lamb may not be available whenever he wants it in the future. This is unfortunately a justifiable fear in some of the more remote areas of the country. The buyer doesn't want to establish a consumer demand for lamb which he will be unable to meet at some later date. In addition, supermarket meat-cutters tend to discourage buying lamb because their training and experience is mainly with different cuts of *beef*; a lamb carcass is often a little unfamiliar to them.

b) *Meat packers*—Only three large packers dominate the bulk of all lamb purchasing from sheepmen. Thus each packer wields considerable power when dealing with sheepmen. Furthermore, the rising labor costs facing the packers over the past several years have forced them to consolidate operations and shut down several plants. This has resulted in higher shipping costs to many sections of the country—particularly mid-America—intensifying the availability problem in these areas.

"HEAVY LAMB" AND THE BREEDING CYCLE

One of ASPC's most pressing problems, the retail ceilings on "heavy lamb," resulted directly from the immense power possessed by supermarket chain meat buyers and lamb packers. Chain buyers traditionally preferred lamb carcasses of no more than a certain weight, believing that the extra weight of a larger carcass was composed largely of fat, bones, and other waste material. As a result, retailers imposed a ceiling—usually 55 pounds—on the carcasses they would consider for purchase at the full market price. Any carcasses of above 55 pounds ("heavy lamb") would be bought only at a reduced "penalty" rate.

This practice caused serious problems when compounded by the nature of the sheep-breeding cycle. Sheep were traditionally bred in the fall, and became ready for market in roughly one year. Thus the heaviest sheep slaughtering activity typically took place in the September-November period, and the April-June months were the lightest. A number of factors, such as the need to use high-priced artificial feed, combined to make breeding out of the cycle considerably more expensive.

The fact that the greatest number of sheep reached market at the same time each year resulted in a significant decline in the prices paid to sheepmen for carcasses during that period. Breeders reacted by holding on to their herds overlong, waiting for price levels to rise, causing an eventual glut in the marketplace of heavy lamb carcasses. A large number of breeders every year were finally forced to dispose of their heavy lamb at distress prices. (An ASPC executive noted, as an example, that in 1967 the price paid by packers for lamb carcasses varied from $14 to $30 per hundredweight, compared with a breeder's breakeven price of about $22.) This widespread price instability was then passed on to the consumer, causing considerable fluctuations in the supermarket price for lamb cuts even in areas of the country where lamb was in adequate supply throughout the year.

An ASPC executive summarized the way in which the lamb distribution system posed extremely difficult problems for the Council in its efforts to aid the sheepman:

> Our efforts are directed at all levels of the distribution system—we attempt simultaneously to stimulate demand at the consumer level as well as to assure that the lamb will be available in the supermarket meat department when the

consumer goes looking for it. But look at what happens. It is uncertain—even if we significantly stimulate demand—that this demand will filter all the way through the system to the breeder because of a vicious circle at play. The supermarket meat buyer waits for a definite consumer demand for lamb before he buys it; whereas the housewife's interest in lamb dies off after repeatedly finding no lamb available in her market's meat department.

PROBLEMS AT THE CONSUMER LEVEL

In addition to the above issues, ASPC faced two problems at the consumer level:

a) *Consumer preference for a small number of lamb cuts*—Of the 54 different cuts of lamb which a lamb carcass provided, only two—leg and loin cuts—accounted for the great bulk of total lamb sales. As a result, a supermarket would generally be unable to utilize the greater part of the lamb carcass and, to break even on the total carcass, would be forced to raise prices on the few cuts for which consumer-demand existed. This practice was viewed by ASPC executives as largely responsible for lamb's "high-cost" image.

b) *"Mutton stigma" from World War II*—As an executive on the lamb account team at the Council's advertising agency of Frye-Sills & Bridges explained:

A great deal of antilamb feeling originated during World War II, when strongly flavored mutton dominated the domestic market. Overseas, our troops also reacted strongly against mutton. These people associated the mutton which they disliked *during* the war with the lamb which has been available *since* the war. The result has been that they have continued to resist trying lamb to this very day, which is particularly unfortunate for us since their children, who are the young homemakers of today, have never been exposed to lamb in their parents' home.

LAMB MARKETING/ADVERTISING PROGRAMS

Faced with the problems resulting from the industry structure and overall marketing environment as discussed above, the Council divided the bulk of its promotional efforts among the three different "buyer" groups in the lamb distribution system: packers, retailers, and the ultimate consumers.

a) Packers This group bought live sheep from the breeders, slaughtered the sheep, and then sold the carcasses to retail outlets. Council representatives, through concentrated personal contacts, attempted to develop close-working relationships with every packer in the U.S. The joint development by the Council and packers of the Cryovac packaging process is a representative example of the

Council's work with packers. This new vacuum-film packaging process allowed greater flexibility in shipping from the packer to the retailer because it permitted shipment of either the entire carcass or only the particular cuts desired by a retailer. Furthermore, the Cryovac process protected its contents considerably longer than did previous shipping methods, a development regarded by industry leaders in the late 1960s as especially timely due to the recent consolidation of packer operations which resulted in generally more lengthy shipments from packer to retailer. Industry leaders anticipated that the process would ultimately result in a lower retail price for lamb because it entailed less shipment of fat and bone.

b) Retailers Council efforts with retailers took a number of forms. Merchandising calls to the trade covered over 60,000 major volume supermarkets annually. In addition, new product research was undertaken as much with the *retailer* in mind—to provide him with higher volume, faster moving items—as to stimulate consumer demand with quicker cooking, easier-to-prepare lamb products. Cryovac packaging gave the retailer increased purchasing flexibility, and also significantly cut down the degree of "breaking down" labor required to reduce the carcass to various cuts for the meat cases.

In other areas of product development, the Council played a leading role during the 1960s in the development of boneless leg and shoulder roasts as well as the investigation of the possibility of marketing frozen lamb cuts.

Advertising and literature aimed at retailers generally featured tips on how to prepare, display, and promote lamb in such a way as to maximize profits. Exhibit 2 contains excerpts from an ASPC brochure to retailers.

c) Ultimate Consumers This group included those who bought lamb in retail outlets for home consumption, institutional purchasers, and the military. The first of these was the largest subgroup, with over 80% of all lamb sold in the United States in 1968 accounted for by supermarkets and other retail outlets. However, lamb sales to hotels, restaurants, schools, and other institutional sources had increased significantly as a percentage of the total during the 1960s, and Council executives anticipated that this proportion would continue to increase in the near future as the national economy prospered and provided increasing levels of discretionary income. Meanwhile the military market had been pursued by ASPC for a number of years, with success finally coming in 1968 when the Army and Air Force agreed to place lamb on their menus twelve times a year. This breakthrough resulted in an increase of about 8% in the demand for lamb annually.

ADVERTISING THEMES BY TARGET GROUP

Council executives pointed out that success with each of the above ultimate consumer groups was based on different weightings of selling factors. They thought, for instance, that pursuing the military opportunity largely depended on a personal sales strategy emphasizing availability and economy. Demand among housewives was seen as being stimulated through advertising and educational approaches supplemented by colorful point-of-purchase displays. Institutional approaches were usually planned as a combination of personal sales efforts and advertising in trade journals. Insertions in these journals (which included *Nation's Restaurant, Club Management, Metropolitan Restaurant News,* and others) generally emphasized how the Council's "Order Lamb When You Eat Out" advertisements—placed in such *consumer* publications as *Sunset, Holiday, Gourmet,* and *New Yorker*—worked to the benefit of the hotel/restaurant trade by urging people to dine out. The trade campaign was intended to ultimately influence institutions to include lamb as a featured item on their menus. Exhibit 3 contains a representative ad to the institutional trade.

Various advertising approaches combined appeals to retailers and end consumers. The "Today's New Lamb" advertising theme was instituted in 1966 in response to the previous winter's particularly extreme glut of heavy lamb. This theme's message to consumers and retailers was that "Today's New Lamb" was a bigger, better-fed, more tender animal than ever before. These claims were all made more credible to retailers as a result of a 1967-68 study conducted by six universities. This study concluded that heavy lamb carcasses were as desirable as—or, in many respects, more desirable than—the carcasses in the under-55-pound weight range which previously had been preferred by retailers. Following personal visits by Council representatives which supplemented the "Today's New Lamb" advertising appeals, 92 separate chain headquarters, representing over 4,000 retail stores, agreed during the 1967-68 winter promotional program to raise their lamb-buying (i.e., carcass weight) specifications by 5 to 10 pounds. (See Exhibits 4-A and 4-B for examples of ads to consumers and retailers featuring the "Today's New Lamb" theme.)

As a further tactic in this area, the Council offered 30- and 60-second cooperative radio commercials to supermarkets at the Council's expense. The commercials were split, with one-half required to feature lamb advertising and the other half containing any nonmeat sales appeal desired by the supermarket. In return the supermarket agreed either to carry lamb for the first time, or to raise its lamb-buying specifications. Due to limited availability of lamb from the packers, the Council's use of these cooperative radio offers as a means of expanding the availability of lamb at the retail level had remained fairly limited geographically through 1968.

Another advertising approach that combined appeals to end consumers and retailers consisted of ads featuring little-known cuts of lamb. These ads attempted to combat the problem of underutilization of the entire lamb carcass and the resulting necessity for a few cuts, such as leg roasts and chops, to carry the entire cost burden of the carcass at the retail level. It was believed that educating the consumer on how to use as many of the 54 lamb cuts as possible would eventually pay a triple dividend in the form of greater profits to the retailer, lower consumer prices on *all* cuts of lamb, and enhance status of lamb as a "regular" meat in American households. Exhibit 5 contains an ad featuring use of little-known lamb cuts.

CONSUMER ADVERTISING: MEDIA

About half of ASPC's total media budget of roughly $1 million was traditionally allocated to newspapers. The remainder was split between radio spots and magazine insertions, with an occasional minor expenditure approved for outdoor displays and subway cards. Full- and half-page newspaper placements were both black-and-white and four-color. Exhibit 6, which summarizes the ASPC budget for lamb advertising in the 1961-62 fiscal year, shows how newspaper and radio totals were broken down by major metropolitan areas. As seen, the radio total was split between local commercials (60-second announcements) and national sponsorship of "Breakfast Club." The magazine expenditure represented insertions in regional editions of national women's magazines such as *Woman's Day* and *Family Circle.* Advertising in all media was concentrated during periods of the year when lamb was in peak supply.

Television was rejected as a prospect for a major budget allocation for various reasons over the years. According to ASPC executives, these included the following:

–TV's appeal lies predominantly among low-income families.

–The "taste appeal" of lamb commercials on TV is limited as long as the proportion of color TV receivers remains in the minority.

–"Since our target is the adult female, logic would point to daytime television. Daytime TV housewives participate largely in the audio portion of the programs, leaving the video portion of the program unwatched in many cases." (Excerpt from advertising agency media recommendations for 1965-66.)

CONSUMER ADVERTISING THEMES

During the 1950s and early 1960s lamb-consumer advertising themes varied only moderately. The 1959 print campaign featured a "Taste Adventures with Lamb" theme. Individual ads stressed lamb's variety and contained recipes for economical, unusual, and outdoor lamb "taste adventures." (See Exhibit 7-A.)

In the 1960 campaign, lamb was presented as "America's Number One Meal." In these ads special copy attention was paid to lamb as a changeover meal which adds variety to the dinner table. (See Exhibit 7-B.) Beginning in the early 1960s, occasional ads featured the theme "Once A Week . . . Every Week . . . Lamb–The Tender Surprise" as a direct attempt to increase the frequency of lamb consumption among lamb users. (See Exhibit 7-C.)

As a further development of the early 1960s, the annual lamb advertising and promotion campaign began to feature four separate seasonal themes: Outdoor Cookout, Autumn Harvest, Winter Wonder, and Milk-fed Spring Lamb. (See Exhibit 7-D.) This move was instituted primarily for the purpose of providing retailers with definable themes to serve as a basis for different in-store promotions during the course of a year. It was also hoped that these themes would increase lamb consumption during the traditional non-peak periods of the year.

Despite the above variations, the major thrust of lamb advertising during this period continued to focus on taste appeal. Recipes were heavily employed to educate the consumer on how to prepare a number of different lamb cuts for a number of different settings.

CONSUMER TARGET GROUP CONSIDERATIONS

In view of what was regarded as a quite limited budget, the account team from the Council and its advertising agency attempted to direct ASPC advertising at certain population groups. The following statements were made by ASPC and agency executives in late 1968:

> It's always easier to increase consumption among present users than to try and convert nonusers. However, we must appeal to both of these groups. Recipes in ads are the key to both converting nonusers and showing present users new and different ways of using lamb—hopefully, more often.

> The best place for a nonuser to try lamb for the first time is in a restaurant, where the atmosphere is relaxed and the meat is prepared as it should be. This is the reason for our "Eat Lamb When Dining Out" campaign, not to mention the side benefits this campaign brings us in terms of good relations with the institutional trade.

> Most of our "rifling" comes in with media selection—we pretty much concentrate our newspaper and radio push, for instance, in areas where lamb has already gained some acceptance.

> We try to reach the well-educated, upper-income, active consumer. We also try for the *younger* housewife—if we can convert her into a moderate or heavy lamb consumer at an early age, we've gained many extra years of lamb consumption. Due to these sorts of demographic considerations, we've shifted a lot of our newspaper placements out of inner city papers in favor of suburban papers.

ADVERTISING RESEARCH: THE 1964 CONSUMER ATTITUDE STUDY

In 1964 ASPC commenced a series of research studies designed to ultimately determine which specific advertising appeals to which consumer groups would offer the greatest return to ASPC in terms of increased lamb consumption. In other words, it was hoped that detailed analysis of the attitudes and purchasing habits of American meat-consumers would allow ASPC to more effectively "rifle" its advertising at certain key consumer groups within the total population.

A major study sponsored by the Council in cooperation with the U.S. Department of Agriculture was conducted in 1964 by National Analysts, Inc. to provide more information about the image of lamb and competitive meats in the United States. The format and findings of this study are summarized in Appendix A.

The National Analysts' report analyzed and appraised the results of the study in terms of possible implications for the future directions of lamb advertising. Among the issues treated by this report were the following:

—Should the primary target group for lamb advertising be current *users* or *nonusers*?

—Should lamb be presented as a *specialty* or *regular* meat?

—Should lamb advertising contain *sensory* or *rational* appeals?

—Which demographic groups should be appealed to? With what appeals?

—By what means, demographic or otherwise, can the total consumer population be broken down into meaningful subgroups to allow greater direction in future lamb advertising?

STUDY FINDINGS

In a number of specific areas, the 1964 study results provided insights into the public's views of lamb. Some highlights are treated below.

Seasonal Themes Vague The seasonal identification featured in lamb advertising and promotion was cited in the National Analysts' report as causing two different kinds of problems. First, the different seasonal themes held no meaning to significant percentages of respondents, ranging from 82% of respondents who said that "Winter Wonder Lamb" had no meaning to them to 22% who gave this response for the "Spring Lamb" theme. Second, to the 78% of respondents to whom "Spring Lamb" *had* meaning, the dominant beliefs were that Spring Lamb is young and tender, which, although favorable, the study noted as implying ". . . that the other types of lamb are inferior to Spring Lamb."

Lamb's "Narrow Image" The report emphasized the "narrow image" of lamb by interpreting the responses to selected semantic differential questions from the complete list presented here in Exhibits A-2 and A-3. The consumer's need for more information on lamb was seen by National Analysts as not being met, based on findings such as the following:

—Of the five basic meats (lamb, beef, pork, veal, and chicken) lamb rated the poorest on "Makes many different good dishes."

—Of these five basic meats, lamb and veal rated the lowest on "Many different cuts."

—Of the five basic meats, lamb rated the poorest on "Good for left-overs."

Additional findings were presented to support the contention in the report that, due to lack of information about the various ways in which lamb can be prepared, consumers tend ". . . to think of lamb in very traditional and unimaginative terms." For instance, when asked which of a list of thirteen items would cause them to serve or increase their use of lamb, respondents selected the following two items most frequently:

Offering interesting recipes with the lamb (37%).

Offering exact cooking directions with the lamb (19%).

[Other responses drawing considerable support were: canned lamb (26%); premium coupons (21%); and special kinds of lamb—barbecue, kabobs, etc. (20%). None of the 13 choices involved changes in either the price of lamb or any of lamb's sensory qualities.]

On the other hand, when nonusers were presented with a list of eight possible reasons why they did not use lamb, over two-thirds of them selected the reason that "someone in the family does not like it," while only 8% selected "too hard to cook." (See Exhibit 8 for a complete breakdown of these responses.)

Expensive Image   The report cited a number of findings to support the belief that "... the single most pronounced aspect of the image of lamb is that *'lamb is expensive.'"* Among the findings cited were the following:

—52% of lamb users said that lamb, compared with the same cuts of other meats, generally has a higher price per pound. (11% answered "lower," and 30% answered "no difference.")

—18% of all respondents said that the way to change lamb so that they will serve it or serve it more is to "make it less expensive." (See Exhibit 9.)

—Lamb's score on a seven-point economy sale (7.0 = not economical) was 4.7, compared to veal (4.2); pork (3.0); beef (2.6); and chicken (1.3).

The Specialty Meal Dilemma   As a final issue the report explored the "specialty image" of lamb, a consumer perception regarded as second in importance only to the expensiveness of lamb. National Analysts noted this specialty image as "a particularly distressing dilemma" since there appeared to be "... very few applications for which the consumer feels this specialized food is suitable." When compared directly with beef, lamb was indicated by only a small minority of respondents as a first choice for any variety of meal situations ranging from holiday dinners to dinner for important guests to a warm-weather outdoor meal. (See table below.)

Occasion	% Prefer Beef	% Prefer Lamb
Family dinner at home	63	3
Meal prepared for person with unknown meat tastes	60	-
Important guests to dinner	54	2
Inexpensive meal	53	1
Dinner in a hurry	51	2
Warm weather outdoor meal	46	-
Lunch out in a restaurant	45	1
Lunch at home	31	1
Easter dinner	6	3
Christmas dinner	3	-
Special breakfast	2	-

At the time that ASPC advertising executives examined the results of the 1964 attitude study, their main concern was to translate the findings and conclusions of these studies into action alternatives. Of primary concern was to determine which messages seemed to be called for in future lamb advertising. In addition, they discussed possible directions for further consumer research.

American Sheep Producers Council (A)
LIST OF EXHIBITS AND APPENDIX EXHIBITS

Exhibit 1

COMMERCIAL MEAT PRODUCTION BY CLASS OF SLAUGHTER, 48 STATES: 1958-1966
(FIGURES IN MILLIONS OF POUNDS)

Year	*Total Meat*	*Beef* Pounds	%	*Veal* Pounds	%	*Pork (excluding lard)* Pounds	%	*Lamb and Mutton* Pounds	%
1958	24.4	13.0	53.3	1.10	4.5	9.62	39.4	0.674	2.8
1959	26.0	13.2	50.8	0.929	3.6	11.1	42.8	0.724	2.8
1960	27.0	14.4	53.3	1.02	3.8	10.9	40.1	0.754	2.8
1961	27.4	14.9	54.4	0.960	3.5	10.7	39.1	0.818	3.0
1962	27.9	14.9	53.4	0.936	3.4	11.2	40.3	0.795	2.9
1963	29.6	16.0	54.1	0.847	2.9	11.9	40.4	0.757	2.6
1964	31.7	18.0	56.8	0.928	2.9	12.0	38.1	0.703	2.2
1965	30.6	18.3	59.8	0.936	3.1	10.7	35.0	0.639	2.1
1966*	32.1	19.5	60.8	0.862	2.7	11.1	34.5	0.639	2.0

*Data for 1966 not consistent with previous years due to change in definition between commercial and lamb slaughter.

Source: United States Department of Agriculture, "Livestock and Meat Statistics," *Supplement for 1966 to Statistical Bulletin No. 333,* p. 80.

Exhibit 2

EXCERPTS FROM ASPC BROCHURE TO LAMB RETAILERS

6 ideas to help you merchandise high profit LAMB all year 'round

Here's how you can boost volume of LAMB sales to 15 PERCENT OF TOTAL MEAT SALES...5 TIMES THE NATIONAL AVERAGE.*

1. ORGANIZE YOUR MEAT CASE BETTER.

Give lamb 15% of red meat space... it can make your meat department far more profitable.

Add more LAMB to your product mix. You can now merchandise with more than 40 Lamb cuts! Be sure to include the new boneless netted ROLLED ROASTS.

2. FEATURE AND PROMOTE LAMB ALL YEAR 'ROUND

SPRING—Beginning in March and continuing through June, it's MILK-FED SPRING LAMB time, recognized by your customers as a prime time of the year to enjoy the tender, succulent goodness of young lamb. Lamb is the traditional feast at Easter, a time to feature legs, racks and a showy crown roast.

*Progressive Grocer, March 1965

SUMMER—It's cookout time in America. Give generous space to the new netted legs and shoulders for the spit, lamb cubes for kebabs, lamb riblets, spareribs and chops for the grill. There are 30 different lamb cuts just right for outdoor cooking.

AUTUMN—Lamb goes so well with all the fruits and vegetables of the harvest it makes good sense to make a special effort to sell it. Step up your profits by featuring the new netted products — the boneless leg, shoulder and Scotch roast. The football crowd will respond to lamb cuts that can be barbecued.

WINTER—It's Winter Wonder Lamb time when hearty appetites respond to the appeal of thick lamb chops, lamb for zesty stews, and a fine leg of lamb. The new netted products will create additional lamb sales for you. Gourmet cuts — the racks and regal crown roasts — are holiday favorites.

3. RECIPES PULL GREAT AT THE MEAT CASE

Suggest Lamb specialties to your customers as an intriguing change of pace from everyday meals. Develop a variety of lamb cuts exclusive to your store. It's a great way to make your store stand out against competition. Spring, summer, autumn, winter—lamb comes through for you with take-one recipe holders and folders that illustrate and describe exciting new ways to prepare and serve the varied cuts of lamb. Give recipes a good spot. They'll trigger lamb sales for you as they encourage new users to try lamb, regular users to serve it more often.

4. TIE-IN RELATED ITEMS AND SELL A WHOLE MEAL WITH LAMB

To capture consumer interest, exploit natural tie-ins with lamb. Build unique meat case displays with canned pears, sauces, jellies, salads, barbecue products, marinades, stuffings, peppers, avocados, onions, tomatoes, juices, seasonings, raisins and prunes. Lamb looks for such natural "go-togethers" and invites their participation in joint promotions that have storewide significance. Case in point: the current Springtime marriage of LAMB and AVOCADO. Don't overlook products of special appeal to ethnic groups in your neighborhood.

5. FOR IN-STORE MERCHANDISING LAMB IS BACKED WITH A GREAT ARRAY OF DAZZLING, COLORFUL, YEAR 'ROUND DISPLAY MATERIALS

Each new promotional period in the Lamb year brings you a raft of beautiful full-color promotional materials: overwire theme banners, window and meat department posters, channel strips, stack cards, shelf talkers and recipe folders. Use this power at the point-of-purchase to good advantage.

6. FEATURE LAMB IN YOUR RETAIL ADS

Drop-in ad mats and radio commercials are available... FREE! So are glossy photos of the new boneless netted ROLLED ROASTS. Tie in with LAMB'S heavy consumer advertising campaign. Big ads, good ads, multiple insertions throughout the year pre-sell and re-sell your customers and build LAMB traffic. IDEA... Lamb, as a co-feature with other meats, will give you added profits.

Exhibit 3

1967 BLACK-AND-WHITE MAGAZINE AD TO HOTEL-RESTAURANT INSTITUTIONAL MARKET

DISTINCTIVE

GOOD TASTE

Good ta...
choice o...
where la...
cuisine. L...
ferent. It's...
own good...
dining ro...
ner. And...
sented by...
In the cir...

america...

departme...
909 Seve...
Denver, C...

different

As the gourmet differs from the gourmand, so too is lamb different. Lamb has a gentle yet sturdy flavor; distinctive, remote, elegant. Pleasing. Different. Delicious. Chefs in finer restaurants everywhere are featuring lamb for its difference. For the way it says, "let's dine in elegance tonight..."

...can **lamb** council
...ment LCFS-267A
...venteenth Street
...olorado 80202

ELEGANCE

Elegance is the quiet room, the ornate candelabrum, the distinctive presentations of the chef, your own selection of lamb from his list of entrées. Lamb is artful in its look, musical in its flavor. Come to know the elegance of today's new lamb. Ask for lamb... in the finest restaurants everywhere.

american lamb council

department LCFS-167B
909 Seventeenth Street
Denver, Colorado 80202

these ads will
SELL MORE
LAMB
for you

...all year long in some of America's best magazines... the ones that are read by sophisticated people who can afford to dine out more often. People who appreciate a restaurant like yours and the artistry of your chef know good dining when they taste it. Gourmets who know and love lamb as a distinctive, elegant, different meat... in the circle of good taste. Be sure they can *get* lamb when they come to dine with you! Have lamb on your menu often. It makes profits.

Here are the publications where these ads appear all year long:

TIME
NATIONAL OBSERVER
LOS ANGELES MAGAZINE
TOWN & COUNTRY
SAN FRANCISCO MAGAZINE
NEW YORKER
HOLIDAY
GOURMET
VENTURE

AMERICAN LAMB
in the circle of good taste

For a free set of delicious lamb recipes, write:

american lamb council
Dept. LFS-267A, 520 Railway Exchange Bldg.
909 17th Street • Denver, Colorado 80202

FRYE-SILLS & BRIDGES, INC.
Trade Ad LFS-267
Black & White
7 x 10

Catering Executive, May-June	LFS-267	Metropolitan Restaurant News, June	LFS-267D
Chuck Wagon, May-June	LFS-267A	Pacific Coast Record with Western Restaurant, June	LFS-267E
Cirascope, June	LFS-267B	Nation's Restaurant News, June 3	LFS-267F
Florida Restaurateur & Purveyor News, June	LFS-267C	Club Management, June	LFS-267G

Exhibit 4-A

1968 "TODAY'S NEW LAMB" COLOR AD TO CONSUMERS

there's a
new kind of lamb
these days!

TODAY'S NEW LAMB

with bigger chops, more lean meat, and a wonderfully tasty tenderness, is showing up in more and more meat cases these days. It's a delicious full flavored meat from a bigger, more carefully-fed lamb.

Take the famous leg o' lamb. Buy a full leg and have your meat man cut several delicious steaks off the sirloin end before you roast it. Two meals for a hungry family!

Remember too, the tasty, tender fore-quarter cuts. Shanks. Riblets. Shoulder roasts and chops – every bit as good.

If you haven't tried Today's New Lamb lately, you're missing something special. At better markets everywhere. Restaurants, too.

Try this easy recipe today!

ONION-ORANGE LAMB ROAST (makes 8 servings)

¾ leg of lamb	2 tablespoons prepared mustard
¼ cup chopped onion	¾ teaspoon rosemary
½ cup orange juice	Salt and pepper to taste

Place lamb on rack in shallow roasting pan. Roast in 325° (slow) oven 30 to 35 minutes per pound, or until meat thermometer registers 175° for medium doneness. Combine onion, juice, mustard, rosemary and seasoning and spoon over the lamb during the last hour of roasting time.

For more FREE lamb recipes, write:

american lamb council

*Dept. LC-268A, 520 Railway Exchange Bldg.
909 17th St., Denver, Colo. 80202*

AMERICAN
LAMB
in the circle of good taste

MAGAZINE	SIZE	KEY DEC.	JAN.	FEB.	MAR.	APR.	JUNE
Family Circle	½ p	LC268	LC268B		LC268I		
Ladies' Home Journal	½ p	LC268A		LC268H			
McCall's	½ p		LC268C		LC268J		
National Geographic	1 p		LC268D				
Woman's Day	½ p			LC268E		LC268K	LC268N
Sunset	⅔ p			LC268F		LC268L	LC268O
Redbook	½ p			LC268G		LC268M	LC268P

Exhibit 4-B

1967 "TODAY'S NEW LAMB" AD TO RETAILERS

"It works for me"... says a meat department manager in a midwest city who buys heavier lambs and markets them profitably.

Today's New Lamb, bred and fed to produce bigger chops and better cuts of all kinds, can produce bigger profits, too.

Buy · Display · Sell Today's New Lamb

Put something new in your meat case....

Play catch-up with the other departments in the store that are always turning up with new products. There's a fresh idea in fresh meats and it's Today's New Lamb. Big-eye chops. Thick steaks cut from the sirloin end of a bigger leg of lamb. New boneless, netted lamb roasts that are catching on all over the country. Lamb spareribs, stew meat, ground lamb.

We're telling your customers about Today's New Lamb · In national magazine ads · In newspaper ads in principal lamb markets from coast to coast · On radio and billboards

Ask how you can participate. Get in touch with your American Lamb Council representative. Or write:

american lamb council

Dept. LT-367, 520 Railway Exchange Bldg.
909 17th St. Denver, Colorado 80202

TODAY'S NEW LAMB...

AMERICAN LAMB in the circle of good taste

"Happiness is the profits you make tomorrow on TODAY'S NEW LAMB."

2-Page Spread, B & W, Progressive Grocer LT-367, Food Topics LT-367.

Exhibit 5

1959 AD FOR LITTLE-KNOWN LAMB CUTS

One in a series of "Taste Adventures with Lamb" by American Sheep Producers Council

Exhibit 6

1961-62 FISCAL YEAR MEDIA BUDGET FOR LAMB ADVERTISING

Market	Newspaper	Radio	Total
Boston	$ 6,869.00	$ --	$ 6,869.00
New York	8,120.00	--	8,120.00
Albany	7,055.00	380.00	7,435.00
Philadelphia	8,736.00	--	8,736.00
Baltimore	6,055.00	--	6,055.00
Washington, D.C.	6,500.00	--	6,500.00
Atlanta	14,788.00	--	14,788.00
Jacksonville	10,053.00	792.00	10,845.00
Tampa/St. Petersburg	10,730.00	--	10,730.00
Miami	11,539.00	1,104.00	12,643.00
Cincinnati	9,081.00	2,688.00	11,769.00
Indianapolis	10,397.00	2,717.00	13,114.00
New Orleans	12,376.00	589.00	12,965.00
Houston	11,810.00	--	11,810.00
Dallas/Ft. Worth	19,578.00	1,200.00	20,778.00
Memphis	10,788.00	820.00	11,608.00
St. Louis	22,280.00	3,000.00	25,280.00
Pittsburgh	16,318.00	3,075.00	19,393.00
Cleveland	23,867.00	--	23,867.00
Detroit	31,459.00	--	31,459.00
Chicago	53,462.00	--	53,462.00
Milwaukee	17,403.00	2,926.00	20,329.00
Minneapolis/St. Paul	25,504.00	4,320.00	29,824.00
Omaha	7,613.00	--	7,613.00
Kansas City	15,471.00	1,848.00	17,319.00
Des Moines	6,868.00	1,666.00	8,534.00
Denver	11,062.00	--	11,062.00
Salt Lake City/Ogden	5,005.00	--	5,005.00
Phoenix	7,057.00	744.00	7,801.00
Seattle	8,523.00	1,341.00	9,864.00
Tacoma	340.00	212.00	552.00
Portland	9,153.00	1,543.00	10,696.00
Northern California*	21,326.00	5,810.00	27,136.00
Southern California**	25,106.00	15,456.00	40,562.00
Total	$472,292.00	$52,231.00	$524,523.00
Base Radio (Breakfast Club)			$ 71,994.00
Magazines			$ 49,900.00
Contingency			$ 58,583.00
		Grand Total	$705,000.00

*   Includes San Francisco, Oakland, and Sacramento.
** Includes Los Angeles and San Diego.

Exhibit 7-A

1959 "TASTE ADVENTURES WITH LAMB" COLOR MAGAZINE AD

Patio **Taste Adventures** with
Lamb

Along with the fun of outdoor cooking, enjoy the fun of good eating, too. You're in for a new adventure when you highlight your barbecue or "cookout" with LAMB. Lamb is so tender, so distinctive in flavor, so easy to prepare . . . no wonder lamb is "the meat most ideal for outdoor cookery". And the abundant protein, vitamins and minerals in lamb meet a nutritional "must" in joyous, energetic living!

Paula Owen

"Enjoyable Meals with Lamb"—a 32 page recipe book now yours for only 35c. Send 35c in coin to LAMB, Dept.FC-7, 18 E. 2nd Ave., Denver 3, Colorado.

American Sheep Producers Council
Denver 2, Colorado

SHISH KEBAB — Marinate 1½" cubes of lamb (from shoulder or leg) in barbecue sauce. Skewer and partially broil. Alternate with mushrooms and chunks of pineapple and green pepper. Finish broiling.

LAMB LOIN AND RIB CHOPS —A sure hit for any occasion! Broil to suit individual preference. Season with pepper and a sprinkle of garlic salt.

LAMBURGERS — Mix 1 teaspoon salt and 1 tablespoon finely chopped onion with each pound of ground lamb. Shape into patties and broil on squares of aluminum foil.

ROAST ROLLED SHOULDER—Wonderful flavor — rotisserie barbecued indoors or **out!** Baste with barbecue sauce. Roast until meat thermometer registers 175°.

Lamb is delicious so many different ways

Exhibit 7-B

1960 "AMERICA'S NUMBER ONE MEAL" NEWSPAPER AD

new!
tender
Lamb
in rolled, boneless
roasts

sweet and sour
Shoulder of Lamb
(8 SERVINGS)

New look for lamb

Right here, right now, leading markets are featuring lamb processed a new way. Lamb legs and shoulders are boneless, rolled and netted for roasting. No waste. It's all meat and marvelous. Easy to carve into firm, uniform slices for serving. Take one of these new lamb roasts home from your store today!

Good lamb cooks

invariably have at hand Paula Owen's popular Lamb Cookbook. Now it's available in a paperback edition. To get your copy, send 50¢ in cash (no stamps) to American Lamb Council, Dept. L-966, 520 Railway Exch. Bldg., Denver, Colo. 80202. Allow four weeks for delivery.

Waffle-baked lambwich

Run a pound or so of leftover lamb roast through a grinder. Add ⅓ cup pickle relish, drained, and 1 tablespoon prepared mustard. Mix well. Spread, sandwich-fashion, between 12 slices of light or dark bread, or 6 round buns which you've buttered on the outside. Toast in a heated waffle iron until golden brown. Makes 6 servings. Serve piping/hot with salad and a beverage for a quick supper.

Place on a rack in a roasting pan one of the new net-wrapped boneless lamb shoulders. Combine ¾ cup cider vinegar, ¾ cup water, ¼ teaspoon salt, 3 tablespoons brown sugar, a medium-sized onion, sliced, and two sprigs of parsley. Mix well.

Pour the sweet and sour sauce over the lamb.

Bake in slow oven (325°) 3 to 4 hours or until meat thermometer registers 170° to 180° F...165° if you like your lamb rare-pink. Baste lamb frequently as it roasts.

When roast is done, let it "set" 10 minutes. Turn roast over; slit netting on underside and pull off in one piece.

Carve. No experience needed. Beautiful slices every time.

Lamb for me, please.

Ever-so-many people order lamb when they dine out. It's one of the more popular choices on the menu. Good chefs take special pride in the way they prepare it, whether it's a succulent leg of lamb, flaming shish kebabs or tender chops. Next time you dine out, order lamb. You'll be glad you did.

Rosy glow

Glaze your boneless, rolled lamb roast with currant jelly or jellied cranberry which you've melted in a double boiler. Gives lamb a special tang, a bright touch of color!

The perfect diet meat

If you're on a lean meat diet, lamb's your dish. Lamb isn't marbled with fat as most meats are. You can easily trim away any fat that rims the cut before you cook it.

Why is it

that lamb is so tender? Hear, hear. Lamb is young meat, seldom more than 9 months old. Young—tender. It follows. Cook lamb according to cut—there are 44 in all. Roast always at a low temperature, 325°, for an extra-tender treat.

Rotisserie roast

The new netted, rolled and boneless lamb cuts are perfect for roasting on the spit—indoors on your rotisserie, out-of-doors over charcoal. For extra zing, marinate the lamb before roasting in your favorite Italian dressing.

Free lamb recipes! Write

american lamb council

**Dept. L-966, 520 Railway Exchange Bldg.,
909 17th Street, Denver, Colorado 80202**

once a week...every week...lamb–the "tender surprise"

Ad No. L-966, 5 col. x 200 lines, Newspaper b & w.

Exhibit 7-D

1964 "WINTER WONDER LAMB" COLOR MAGAZINE AD

Ad No. C-663, Sunday Supplements, 1964 Campaign.

Exhibit 8

NONUSERS' REASONS WHY LAMB IS NOT SERVED

Classification of Respondents	Some Don't Like It	Don't Like Smell	Not Economical	Too Greasy	Not Easily Available	Don't Like Texture	Too Hard to Cook	Not Healthy
Total respondents	67.6%	50.9%	26.8%	23.5%	21.6%	17.9%	8.2%	2.1%
By regions:								
Mid Atl. & New Eng.	75.8	60.6	20.9	41.2	7.3	25.8	5.8	2.1
East-North Central	71.5	49.7	24.9	19.9	14.9	18.1	10.2	1.6
West-North Central	62.9	40.0	21.1	12.0	36.6	8.0	10.3	1.1
East-South Central & S Atl.	60.7	43.1	30.0	17.0	28.6	17.8	3.9	3.1
West-South Central	61.0	53.7	33.3	15.3	37.3	11.9	15.3	.6
Mtn. & Pacific	73.7	63.8	31.0	34.3	13.6	19.2	11.3	2.3
By age:								
Under 25	67.8	43.2	28.6	26.6	20.1	20.1	12.6	---
25-34	74.8	51.2	27.7	25.8	13.3	17.2	7.2	2.2
35-44	71.7	57.3	22.6	23.1	18.2	19.8	6.6	1.4
45 and over	62.3	49.3	28.1	22.0	27.5	16.7	8.5	2.9
By income:								
Under $3,000	60.6	43.8	30.3	22.7	25.9	13.3	5.5	2.7
$3-5,999	68.7	50.1	28.4	23.8	22.2	18.7	9.3	1.4
$6-9,999	72.2	54.6	23.0	23.8	17.2	20.5	9.0	2.7
$10,000 and over	72.8	64.0	22.1	22.8	18.4	15.4	11.0	---
By family type:								
Adults only	62.2	50.4	30.2	24.5	24.5	17.7	10.0	2.6
With children	72.4	51.7	23.9	22.6	18.6	18.2	6.6	1.6
By location:								
City center	70.5	60.2	26.3	34.9	10.5	23.0	9.5	3.0
Suburban	71.1	53.9	25.1	27.7	10.3	20.6	9.4	2.9
Non-metropolitan	64.0	44.0	28.0	14.5	34.0	13.6	6.8	1.1

Reasons

Exhibit 9

SUGGESTED LAMB PRODUCT CHANGES FOR INCREASED CONSUMPTION

Given reasons*	Total Respondents	Total Users	More Frequent Users	Less Frequent Users	Nonusers	Adults Only	With Children
Make less expensive	17.6%	30.9%	30.7%	31.1%	9.9%	15.3%	19.8%
Change flavor	10.2	7.4	5.1	9.4	11.9	9.6	10.8
Change odor	9.9	6.5	3.5	9.2	11.8	7.5	12.1
Make available	8.2	10.6	10.0	11.1	6.7	7.7	8.6
Make less greasy	5.9	9.5	11.1	8.0	3.8	5.7	6.1
Education on preparation	5.7	4.2	2.3	5.9	6.5	6.1	5.3
Publicize	2.5	1.8	.4	3.1	2.9	2.5	2.5
Cut waste	2.2	4.7	6.3	3.3	.7	1.4	2.9
Package better	1.2	2.8	3.7	2.1	.3	1.3	1.1
Change texture	1.0	1.0	.8	1.2	1.1	.8	1.2
Precook	.8	.6	.2	1.0	.9	.6	.9

* Reasons were volunteered rather than selected from a predetermined list.

APPENDIX A

Excerpts from 1964 Study "Lamb and the Consumer . . . Preferences, Attitudes, and the Image of Lamb in the United States"

STATED OBJECTIVES:

    1)　To determine the consumers' preference for the different qualities and cuts of lamb;

    2)　To determine the consumers' image of and attitudes toward lamb; and

    3)　To determine the product competition of lamb.

PROCEDURE:

A qualitative study of 14 groups of consumers was conducted prior to the development of the questionnaire. Group depth interviews, led by trained psychologists, provided many insights which were incorporated into the study.

The questionnaire was developed, pre-tested, and revised prior to the national field survey. On the basis of area probability sampling procedures, the respondent sample of 3,117 consumers was considered to represent the entire U.S. consumer population within an accuracy range of plus or minus two percentage points.

COMMENTS:

Findings grouped respondents according to various demographic variables as well as frequency of lamb use. Exhibit A-1 contains a representative breakdown of this kind. Persons who did not serve lamb in their homes (63% of all respondents) were classified as nonusers. However, 10% of these respondents reported that they did eat lamb outside the home. Reasons quoted were:

—No one else in the family likes it	(52.4%)
—Will eat it when it is served	(25.9%)
—Tastes better when prepared by someone else	(17.3%)
—Available in restaurants	(7.0%)
—Too expensive to serve to the family	(5.6%)
—Other	(2.2%)

Thus over half (52%) of all respondents stated that they "do not eat" lamb either at home or elsewhere. In contrast, only 23% claimed to "really enjoy eating" lamb. These responses, as shown in the following table, indicated that lamb was the least popular of all major meats.

Table A-1

POPULARITY OF SELECTED MEATS

Meat	% Really Enjoy Eating	% Sometimes Eat	% Do Not Eat
Beef	91	8	1
Chicken	85	14	1
Ham	68	31	1
Pork	57	38	5
Fish	57	40	3
Turkey	53	46	1
Shellfish	30	28	42
Veal	25	44	31
Lamb	23	25	52

Of those respondents who served lamb at home, the average frequency of serving was roughly once every three weeks. Less than one-third of this group served it as often as once per week. Another third served it once a month, and the remainder served it less than once per month. Consumption was highly peaked in certain metropolitan areas. For instance, in New York and San Francisco over four out of five respondents indicated that they served lamb weekly. In other major markets, such as Boston, Washington, Los Angeles, Chicago, and Cleveland, well over half of all respondents served lamb at least once every two weeks.

Exhibit A-2, which details ratings by all respondents regarding lamb's image against chosen polar adjective pairs, was followed by three additional tables which broke down these responses according to income, age, and user/nonuser groups. These tables showed that the most favorable responses tended to come from the older, higher income respondents and lamb users. Exhibit A-3 contains the user/nonuser response breakdown.

Exhibit A-4 contains responses by users regarding the following issues: cookery of lamb outdoors; lamb as a substitute meat; seasonality of lamb use. Exhibit A-5 contains answers from *all* respondents to the following questions: Was lamb served in your parental home? Are the lamb cuts you want available? Have you heard or seen lamb advertising? Which advertising media affect your food purchases most?

Exhibit A-1

CLASSIFICATION OF RESPONDENTS ACCORDING TO LAMB USE

Classification of Respondents	Total Users	More Frequent Users	Less Frequent Users	Nonusers
By region:				
Mid Atl. & New Eng.	54%	29%	25%	46%
East-North Central	32	N.A.	N.A.	68
West-North Central	17	7	10	83
East-South Central & S Atl.	23	8	15	77
West-South Central	25	9	16	75
Mtn. & Pacific	52	29	23	48
By type of family:				
Adults only	37	20	17	63
With children	37	16	21	63
By age:				
Under 25	30	9	21	70
25-34	33	15	18	67
35-44	37	17	20	63
45 +	40	20	20	60
By income:				
Under $3,000	23	11	12	77
$3-5,999	32	14	18	68
$6-9,999	42	18	24	58
$10,000 +	60	35	25	40
By location:				
City Center	48	27	21	52
Suburban	43	19	24	57
Non-metropolitan	23	8	15	77
By educational level:				
Grammar school	29	14	15	71
High school	36	16	20	64
College	51	26	25	49
Total respondents	37	17	20	63

Source: The American Sheep Producers Council, Inc., "Lamb and the Consumer," 1964.

Exhibit A-2

CONSUMERS' IMAGE OF LAMB

Semantic Scale

Classification of Adjectives	Mean	1	2	3	4	5	6	7
Healthful / Not Healthful	2.3	54.9%	9.7%	7.1%	20.2%	2.8%	1.4%	3.9%
Most people enjoy eating it / Most people do not enjoy eating it	4.8	14.3	3.5	5.5	22.9	9.2	10.1	34.5
An economical meat / Not an economical meat	4.7	13.9	4.8	7.8	23.5	8.8	7.9	33.4
Many different cuts you can buy / Only few different cuts you can buy	3.6	28.3	8.7	10.0	22.3	6.2	6.0	18.4
Good for older people / Not good for older people	2.4	53.3	9.3	6.7	20.7	3.0	1.6	5.5
Good for young people / Not good for young people	2.3	53.7	9.2	7.3	21.5	2.6	1.2	4.5
Easy to cook / Hard to cook	2.9	44.2	9.7	6.5	19.6	4.6	2.9	12.5
Has about the right amount of fat / Has too much fat	4.0	23.1	7.0	8.2	25.2	6.4	6.5	23.5
Can make many different & good dishes / Cannot make many different & good dishes	4.1	22.5	6.7	7.3	24.9	6.8	6.6	25.2
Easy to eat in a public restaurant / Hard to eat in a public restaurant	2.9	43.7	7.7	7.1	22.4	4.1	2.5	12.5
Smells good when cooking / Does not smell good when cooking	4.4	25.6	4.8	5.3	16.1	4.5	5.8	37.7
Tender / Not tender	2.4	51.7	10.8	7.9	17.4	3.6	2.5	6.1

Exhibit A-2 (cont.)

Classification of Adjectives	Mean	1	2	3	4	Semantic Scale 5	6	7
Appetizing / Not appetizing	3.8	35.2	6.7	6.7	13.5	3.5	4.2	30.3
Easy to digest / Hard to digest	2.7	48.0	8.8	6.7	21.4	3.0	2.8	9.2
For a reducing diet / Not for a reducing diet	3.2	36.1	7.1	7.5	29.9	4.1	3.5	11.7
Lean / Greasy	3.8	27.2	8.2	9.0	20.5	6.4	7.2	21.5
Always available at stores / Not always available at stores	4.0	28.1	6.5	6.3	16.9	7.1	6.6	28.6
Good for leftovers / Not good for leftovers	4.6	16.8	3.9	5.9	25.7	7.1	7.1	33.7
Makes good gravy / Does not make good gravy	4.2	23.9	4.3	5.6	24.9	6.2	5.3	29.9
Suitable for any meal / Suitable only for special meals	4.5	18.4	3.8	6.5	23.4	8.0	8.1	31.7
You don't get tired of it / You do get tired of it	5.1	12.0	3.1	5.3	20.1	7.0	8.3	44.2
Clean / Not clean	2.4	53.2	8.5	5.7	20.8	4.0	2.4	5.3
Nice color when cooked / Not a nice color when cooked	2.8	42.3	9.4	7.7	23.9	4.8	3.0	8.9
Smells good when you're eating it / Doesn't smell good when you're eating it	4.0	30.0	6.5	5.1	17.6	5.7	5.7	29.4
Very rich / Not very rich	3.6	24.6	8.1	10.1	32.7	6.8	4.7	13.0

Exhibit A-2 (cont.)

Semantic Scale

Classification of Adjectives	Mean	1	2	3	4	5	6	7
Tastes good	3.6	38.3	6.7	5.5	13.7	3.9	3.4	28.4
Doesn't taste good	3.5	29.0	7.0	8.0	30.3	6.4	5.1	14.3
Keeps well after cooking								
Does not keep well after cooking	2.6	43.9	9.3	8.4	28.6	3.4	1.2	5.1
High protein								
Low protein	4.0	18.5	5.7	8.2	37.5	7.1	5.6	17.3
High calorie								
Low calorie	4.6	19.0	4.3	5.4	22.9	5.1	6.5	36.9
Is good cooked & cold								
Is not good cooked & cold	4.4	22.0	5.0	5.4	21.3	6.4	6.4	33.5
A regular meat								
A variety meat	2.8	42.3	9.2	6.8	28.0	4.5	3.0	6.2
Easy to carve								
Hard to carve								

Source: The American Sheep Producers Council, Inc., "Lamb and the Consumer," 1964.

Exhibit A-3

LAMB USERS' AND NONUSERS' IMAGE OF LAMB

Classification of Adjectives	Users			Nonusers		
	Mean	1-3	5-7	Mean	1-3	5-7
Healthful Not healthful	1.6	88.7%	1.6%	2.7	59.6%	12.6%
Most people enjoy eating it Most people do not enjoy eating it	3.9	38.2	38.2	5.4	13.0	64.6
An economical meat Not an economical meat	4.4	35.3	46.7	4.9	20.3	42.4
Many different cuts you can buy Only few different cuts you can buy	3.1	59.8	23.9	4.0	38.0	35.3
Good for older people Not good for older people	1.7	85.8	3.6	2.8	57.6	14.6
Good for young people Not good for young people	1.7	87.4	2.3	2.8	58.1	12.6
Easy to cook Hard to cook	1.9	85.2	6.8	3.6	42.8	29.6
Has about the right amount of fat Has too much fat	3.5	50.8	32.5	4.3	29.5	39.2
Can make many different & good dishes Cannot make many different & good dishes	3.5	52.2	30.8	4.5	26.2	44.1
Easy to eat in a public restaurant Hard to eat in a public restaurant	2.3	74.6	12.2	3.4	47.3	23.9
Smells good when cooking Does not smell good when cooking	3.1	61.5	28.1	5.2	18.1	61.7
Tender Not tender	1.7	90.3	2.8	3.0	57.4	18.8

Exhibit A-3 (cont.)

Classification of Adjectives	Users			Nonusers		
	Mean	1-3	5-7	Mean	1-3	5-7
Appetizing / Not appetizing	2.1	81.9	11.2	4.9	26.2	56.5
Easy to digest / Hard to digest	1.9	83.9	6.6	3.2	49.1	21.0
For a reducing diet / Not for a reducing diet	2.7	64.6	14.2	3.5	41.0	22.9
Lean / Greasy	3.5	50.9	32.0	4.0	39.9	27.2
Always available at stores / Not always available at stores	3.2	57.9	30.3	4.6	29.0	50.6
Good for leftovers / Not good for leftovers	4.1	39.7	42.5	4.9	17.2	52.6
Makes good gravy / Does not make good gravy	3.5	51.4	33.2	4.7	21.1	47.2
Suitable for any meal / Suitable only for special meals	3.7	46.7	36.5	5.0	16.1	55.8
You don't get tired of it / You do get tired of it	4.2	38.5	44.7	5.7	7.7	69.9
Clean / Not clean	1.8	83.6	4.7	2.8	56.3	16.5
Nice color when cooked / Not a nice color when cooked	2.0	81.7	6.3	3.5	43.5	24.2
Smells good when you're eating it / Doesn't smell good when you're eating it	2.6	71.3	18.4	5.0	20.9	56.4
Very rich / Not very rich	3.4	52.4	23.8	3.7	36.0	25.1

33

Exhibit A-3 (cont.)

Classification of Adjectives	Users			Nonusers		
	Mean	*1-3*	*5-7*	*Mean*	*1-3*	*5-7*
Tastes good	1.9	84.9	8.5	4.8	26.5	54.8
Doesn't taste good						
Keeps well after cooking	2.8	64.7	16.4	4.0	28.9	32.6
Does not keep well after cooking						
High protein	2.1	75.3	4.8	3.0	52.1	13.3
Low protein						
High calorie	3.9	38.3	30.2	4.0	28.2	29.9
Low calorie						
Is good cooked & cold	4.0	44.4	41.9	5.0	17.6	53.0
Is not good cooked & cold						
A regular meat	3.6	50.7	34.5	5.0	19.8	54.4
A variety meat						
Easy to carve	2.2	75.7	9.8	3.2	46.0	16.4
Hard to carve						

Source: The American Sheep Producers Council, Inc., "Lamb and the Consumer," 1964.

Exhibit A-4

USERS' ATTITUDES ON SELECTED ISSUES

*Classification
of Respondents*

A. OUTDOOR COOKERY

	Cook Lamb Outdoors	Cook Out Not Lamb	Don't Cook Out	Don't Know
Total users	14.8%	49.2%	35.6%	.4%
More frequent users	20.4	37.6	41.7	.4
Less frequent users	9.8	59.6	30.1	.5

B. LAMB AS A SUBSTITUTE MEAT

	Good Sub- stitute	Poor Sub- stitute	Not Sure
Total users	66.0%	28.7%	5.3%
More frequent users	77.7	19.0	3.3
Less frequent users	55.6	27.3	7.1

C. SEASONALITY OF LAMB USE

	Less Often Summer	Less Often Winter	Less Often Other Times	Same Throughout Year	Don't Know
Total users	14.2%	3.0%	11.4%	66.9%	4.3%
More frequent users	15.3	3.3	8.7	71.6	1.3
Less frequent users	13.2	2.8	13.9	62.7	6.9

Source: The American Sheep Producers Council, Inc., "Lamb and the Consumer," 1964.

Exhibit A-5

SELECTED ISSUES BY LAMB USE

*Classification
of Respondents*

A. WAS LAMB SERVED IN YOUR PARENTAL HOME?

	Respondent			Respondent's Husband		
	Yes	*No*	*Don't Know*	*Yes*	*No*	*Don't Know or No Answer*
Total respondents	47.1%	47.7%	5.2%	32.2%	33.3%	34.4%
Total lamb users	72.3	23.7	3.9	48.5	20.9	31.6
More frequent users	79.9	17.1	2.9	55.6	14.9	29.5
Less frequent users	65.6	29.7	4.8	42.2	26.3	31.4
Nonusers	32.4	61.7	5.9	22.7	40.6	36.7

B. ARE THE LAMB CUTS YOU WANT AVAILABLE?

	Yes	*No*	*Don't Serve*
Total respondents	39.3%	35.8%	24.8%
Total lamb users	71.3	27.7	1.0
More frequent users	76.4	23.6	–
Less frequent users	66.7	31.4	1.8
Nonusers	19.4	40.9	39.7

Exhibit A-5 (cont.)

C. HAVE YOU HEARD OR SEEN LAMB ADVERTISING?

	Yes	No
Total respondents	25.9%	74.1%
Total lamb users	36.7	63.3
More frequent users	40.5	59.5
Less frequent users	33.3	66.7
Nonusers	19.6	80.4

D. WHICH ADVERTISING MEDIA AFFECT YOUR FOOD PURCHASES MOST?

	Newspaper	In Store	TV	Magazines	Sunday Supplement	Radio	Outdoor	Bus & Subway Cards
Total respondents	61.5%	45.3%	39.3%	38.8%	12.3%	12.3%	4.7%	.9%
Lamb users	63.2	46.3	33.5	41.2	15.9	11.5	6.0	1.6
More frequent users	61.9	46.8	26.8	36.8	17.9	7.8	6.5	1.7
Less frequent users	64.3	45.9	39.5	45.1	14.1	14.9	5.6	1.5
Nonusers	60.6	44.7	42.7	37.4	10.2	12.7	3.9	.5

Source: The American Sheep Producers Council, Inc., "Lamb and the Consumer," 1964.

QUESTIONS

1.   *What target groups is ASPC trying to reach? Whom should they be trying to reach? (Be sure to consider the size of each consumer segment and the probability of "success.")*

2.   *What copy appeals are most likely to work best for these groups?*

3.   *What basic media strategy should ASPC follow?*

Beech
Aircraft Corporation (A)

A light-aircraft manufacturer examines all aspects of its advertising policy, including historical approaches to advertising, the role of advertising within the overall company strategy, market segmentation, and advertising evaluation.

In mid-July 1968, Mr. James Yarnell, Manager of Advertising and Sales Promotion at Beech Aircraft Corporation, and Mr. Jack Dick-Peddie, Account Executive in charge of the Beech account at the Bruce B. Brewer advertising agency, prepared their final recommendations to Beech top management regarding Beech's fiscal 1969 advertising strategy. They hoped to gain approval for two significant departures from the strategy of the last several years. First, a sizable portion of the proposed budget was devoted to single-page print advertisements rather than to the two-page spreads which had been heavily employed since 1965. Second, a common theme was developed to promote a unifying "look" to all Beech advertisements in the many different markets toward which Beech advertising was directed. Basically unchanged, however, was the segmented advertising approach which company and agency advertising executives believed best served the specific and widely varying needs of these numerous markets.

COMPANY BACKGROUND

Since its founding in 1932 by Walter and Olive (Mrs. Walter) Beech, Beech Aircraft Corporation of Wichita, Kansas, was one of the leading general aviation manufacturers in the world. By 1967 total sales had reached nearly $175 million, of which some $70 million came from the company's military and aerospace activities. Export sales totaled nearly $25 million, reflecting a 168% increase in five years. (See Exhibit 1 for selected financial data for the years 1958-1967.)

In September of 1968 Beech offered a product line of 20 business and utility aircraft, from the three-model single-engine Musketeer series, including a two-place trainer, to a family of twin-engine corporate transports and third-level airliners (i.e., for use by scheduled commuter and air-taxi operators). The company was perhaps

39

best noted for its Bonanza models featuring the distinctive V-tail; Beech had sold over 8,800 Model 35 Bonanzas in 23 years of production. The Model 18 series, represented in 1968 by the Super H18, had been in continuous production longer than any other airplane in the world. Since 1937 over 9,000 units of this model had been delivered. The top-of-the-line King Air, introduced in late 1964, had by mid-1968 achieved sales in excess of $128 million. The complete Beech product line is presented in Exhibit 2.

The company operated facilities in four separate locations. Wichita housed the corporate offices as well as two commercial production facilities. In addition, the Aerospace Division manufacturing capabilities were located in Wichita. The Liberal (Kansas) Division, opened in 1951, served as the production center of the Musketeer line. The Salina (Kansas) plant, opened in 1966, provided manufacturing capacity for commercial, aerospace, and military programs. The Boulder (Colorado) Division, since its establishment in 1956, had specialized in research and development of sophisticated aerospace programs. All facilities combined to provide jobs for over 11,000 employees.

THE GENERAL AVIATION INDUSTRY

"General Aviation" is a term which applies to all U.S. aviation other than military and scheduled airlines. In 1968, scheduled airlines served only 542 of the nation's 10,015 airports, boarding more than 60% of their passengers at only 21 cities. All scheduled airlines combined operated with only 2,000 aircraft. By contrast, general aviation operated 110,000 aircraft in the U.S., carrying as many people each year as were carried by all airlines combined. Moreover, general aviation pilots logged four times as many aircraft hours in 1967 as all commercial airlines, representing over twice as many air miles flown.

General aviation aircraft served four major purposes:

a) *Business*—aircraft used by a company for transportation required by its business, flown either by a professional pilot or by a company executive holding a pilot's license.

b) *Commercial*—primarily including air-taxi operations, argicultural applications, and certain specialized industrial applications such as aerial advertising photography.

c) *Personal*—pleasure uses not associated with a business and not for hire.

d) *Instructional.*

Of these four categories, business aviation had always ranked first in terms of actual use, according to rough FAA estimates. In 1966 the 1.5 billion miles flown by business aircraft constituted 46% of total miles flown by general aviation. Of the 11,977 multiengine aircraft in the general aviation fleet, 68% were used primarily for some phase of business flying. Furthermore, the FAA predicted in late 1966:

Because of the increased use of aircraft as a mode of transportation for business, business aviation now constitutes the most promising and fertile segment for the future growth of civil aviation. The attractiveness of the aircraft as a business transportation vehicle, coupled with the introduction of more and less expensive smaller-type turbine aircraft, substantiates the premise that the more significant areas of growth in civil aviation will emanate mainly from the business aviation segment.[1]

Exhibit 3 shows the general aviation breakdown for 1966 by types of aircraft use in terms of miles flown, hours flown, and number of aircraft in use.

As seen in Exhibit 4, the great majority of general aviation aircraft were single-engine planes, although the largest single category—single-engine planes of four places and above—demonstrated the least growth of any category from 1965 to 1966 with a 6% increase. In 1966, over half of all general aviation aircraft were still in this category. An additional one-third of the general aviation fleet consisted of single-engine planes of three places and less; this category was up 14% from its 1965 total. Meanwhile, multiengine piston aircraft represented 12% of the total (up 11%); and turbine-powered craft, of which over 95% were multiengine planes, increased 59% from a total of 574 in 1965 to 915 in 1966.

FAA pilot statistics demonstrated the significant growth in popularity enjoyed by flying during the mid-1960s Total pilot certificates held increased by 29% from 1963 to 1965 (378,700 in 1963 to 479,770 in 1965) as compared with the 21% increase of 1957-1963. Primarily responsible for this 1963 growth were student licenses (up 32% from 105,298 in 1963 to 139,172 in 1965) and private licenses (up 29% from 152,209 in 1963 to 196,393 in 1965). This surge of interest among new flyers is further highlighted by 1966 figures which show the "Instructional" category increasing from 20% of all general aviation hours flown in 1965 to 27% in 1966, and from 14% to 19% of all miles flown. Meanwhile the share of the total held by all other general aviation categories (business, commercial, and personal) had declined from 1965 to 1966.

In spite of the rapid growth of general aviation, in aircraft and in pilots, industry sources felt that this potential had been only barely tapped thus far. Market research studies indicated that the business aviation market was at a 15% saturation point; approximately 400,000 companies in the United States thus had some prospective need for and ability to own and operate a business airplane, but were yet to be convinced of the advantages of corporate flying.

THE AIR-COMMUTER MARKET

The mid-1960s witnessed the continuing decline of rail passenger service, combined with the rapid conversion of domestic trunk airlines to 100% pure jet aircraft and supersonic transports in order to concentrate on high-volume stops in high-density markets. As a consequence, wide sections of the country were left

[1]*FAA Statistical Handbook of Aviation*, 1966 Edition, pp. 92-93.

without scheduled service. To fill this transportation void, the small number of U.S. light-plane manufacturers geared up to meet expanding demand from the rapidly increasing number of air taxis and commuter airlines for modest-size, single- and twin-engine propeller-powered airplanes selling for $20,000 up to $500,000. The commuter airline business, which did not exist before 1960, had expanded to 175 operators by 1968. Commuter airlines, by common definition, flew according to a fixed schedule, as distinct from the 3,000 air-taxi operators who were available for business on a "call us when you want us" basis. The latter operators were expected (by the aircraft industry) to continue with their policy of purchasing primarily used rather than new aircraft.

The National Air Taxi Conference, a growing trade association representing charter and scheduled operators, had 248 members in early 1968. Passengers reported by NATC members totaled 553,000 for 1967, an increase of 69% over 1966. This traffic was evenly divided between scheduled and charter operators. The scheduled operators drew a sizable portion of their business through service agreements with 23 domestic scheduled airlines, allowing the airline passengers to through-ticket on commuter flights.

BEECH'S POSITION IN THE INDUSTRY

The Big Three of general aviation—Cessna, Beech, and Piper—accounted for over 90% of units sold, and over 80% of industry dollar volume in 1967. Exhibit 5, containing the industry sales breakdown among leading manufacturers for the years 1962-67, demonstrates the trend on the part of most manufacturers toward larger, faster, more expensive aircraft. The more expensive King Air was largely responsible for the significant hike in average Beech sales since the model's 1964 introduction.

Until the early 1960s, Beech had chosen to concentrate its efforts in the twin-engine and high-performance single-engine markets leaving Cessna and Piper to compete for the lower-price segment of the single-engine market. Until that time it had faced virtually no competition in the twin-engine market. However, the mid-1960s found the three major manufacturers moving into each other's marketing areas to bring about an increasingly competitive situation. Beech introduced the Musketeer in 1962 at $13,300 to enter into direct competition with the low-price models where the bulk of Cessna and Piper sales were concentrated. The latter two firms, meanwhile, were extending their lines upward into a more competitive position with Beech through twin-engine model introductions. In addition, the Beechcraft King Air faced competition from more expensive aircraft in the form of the new business jets.

Beech's reputation as "Rolls Royce of the Air" was indicative of the high esteem in which Beechcrafts were held by the pilot community. Beech sold on the basis of quality, offering what it considered superior construction features, finer appointments, and superior performance characteristics than competitive models. This, however, resulted in a premium price, as exemplified by the following directly comparative models:

Twins:	Beechcraft Baron	$79,775
	Cessna 310	68,400
	Piper Aztec	64,000
Single-Engines:	Beechcraft Bonanza	37,200
	Piper Comanche 400	34,500
	Cessna Centurion	29,950

Whereas a large portion of Cessnas and Pipers were bought for personal use, the high Beechcraft unit price put most models out of reach of the pleasure flyer; over 95% of all Beechcrafts were sold to companies.

BEECH MARKETING AND MARKET RESEARCH

Beech sold its aircraft solely through a highly selective network of 24 domestic distributors serving 140 Beech dealers. This compared with the broader Cessna and Piper networks of over 500 dealers each. Beech officials indicated that the limited dealership policy resulted from the heavy corporate emphasis on marketing and serving the customer needs. Only through carefully scrutinizing every prospective dealer could the company assure that every authorized dealer would remain financially sound and, therefore, generally stable and able to service the customer well; no dealership would be authorized until Beech analysis indicated that sufficient potential existed in a particular market area to merit a new dealer. Beech dealers were reputed to be primarily sales-oriented, as opposed to many Cessna and Piper dealers who were generally noted within the industry as being in business primarily for maintenance, instruction, or other activities related to airplane sales.

Beech manufactured nearly every component of its aircraft within its own facilities to assure the highest possible quality. It manufactured on distributor demand only, producing no aircraft for inventory. Dealers rarely had available any models other than the necessary number of demonstrators and trainers. Thus nearly all aircraft manufactured were in essence custom-made, fitted to the specifications of a particular customer order, and relayed to the manufacturing facilities through a dealer and distributor.

The Beech product line had expanded from nine models in early 1964 to some twenty models in 1968. Each new model was introduced to meet what Beech saw as an unfilled customer need, manufactured in the "quality Beech tradition," and then priced. One Beech official noted that this policy of postponing pricing until after the model had been manufactured rather than manufacturing in such a way as to meet a given competitive price was responsible for Beech's premium prices. Some officials expressed mixed feelings about the policy, especially as it applied to the Musketeer series which had been introduced in late 1962 to provide dealers with a trainer matched to the needs of the beginning flyer. Brand loyalty was known to be strong among flyers, leading a flyer who learned in a particular make of aircraft to tend to continue flying in that brand, and to purchase that brand eventually.

As evidence of this phenomenon, Beech records indicated that over 50% of all Beechcrafts sold above the Model 33 Bonanza price level were purchased by former Beechcraft owners. Meanwhile, approximately 50% of the companies and individuals purchasing a Model 33 or Musketeer had never before owned an airplane of any make. This percentage of first-time purchases decreased to 10-20% among buyers of the more expensive models. Thus, before the Musketeer introduction, the great bulk of Beech sales had gone to former aircraft owners who had had no choice but to learn to fly in a competitive model, due to Cessna's and Piper's predominance in flying schools with their low-price, single-engine models. Beech hoped that the Musketeer would serve to introduce future generations of beginning flyers to flying in a Beechcraft and thereby indirectly enhance the sales of Beech higher-priced models through the brand loyalty influence. However, the Musketeer had failed to make sizable inroads in the beginner market, due in large part to its price (about $13,000 versus competitive models priced at about $8,000) which was a direct result of the "price-last" policy.

Other factors to which executives attributed the limited success of the Musketeer included inadequate advertising support and lack of aggressive dealer effort. Selling a Musketeer often entailed convincing a nonflyer of the benefits of flying as a concept, a process Beech had traditionally found difficult (83% of total company sales were to those who had already owned some make of aircraft). It was believed that company dealers and salesmen much preferred to concentrate their efforts on prospects who had already been sold on flying as a concept, since detailed information was available on such individuals and firms, and the generally higher unit price also made these sales more attractive.

This detailed analysis of company sales was handled entirely by Beech's two- to three-man market research team. The group concentrated primarily on arriving at a variety of sales breakdowns to pinpoint exactly what sort of people or corporations were purchasing Beechcrafts, such as the former owner/first-time purchaser data discussed above. In addition, sales data were organized according to geographical area, model, SIC heading,[2] type of plane being traded in, size of company purchasing, and so forth, to provide Beech dealers and marketing executives with tangible information to help guide their marketing thrusts. Examples of this sort of research are found in Exhibit 6.

In general, research discovered that sales were quite evenly distributed among all sizes and types of companies. In 1966 Beechcrafts were sold to companies in 180 different SIC categories, with only 6 SIC categories accounting for more than 20 airplane sales apiece. A 1966 study of Beech corporate twin sales (airplanes selling for over $150,000) produced the following findings:

a)   161 corporate twins were purchased in 75 different SIC categories.

b)   Less than 15% of these were purchased by companies listed in "Forbes Top 125 Industrialists."

c)   Only 27.2% were sold in cities of over 500,000 population.

d)   63.3% were sold in cities with less than 250,000 population.

[2] Standard Industrial Classification; major industry classifications included Manufacturing, Government, Mining and Petroleum Extraction, and ten other major categories.

Corporate purchases were found to be influenced actually by three separate groups:

a) *Pilots*—who do not own an airplane but professionally fly the company plane (professional pilots generally flew the large corporate Queen Air and King Air twins).

b) *Pilot-Executives*—who fly company-owned airplanes (70% of Beech single-engine and light twin models were owner-flown and used in large part by smaller companies).

c) *Executive-Owners*—nonpilots who make the ultimate decision on what company plane to buy.

More detailed research was not attempted in an effort to pinpoint the relative influence of each of these groups, actual usage of Beechcraft for business or pleasure purposes, or attitudes of flyers/nonflyers. Jack Dick-Peddie gave three reasons for this lack of more rigorous research:

a) *The great diffusion of the decision process within a company* (". . . the actual decision-influencer is impossible to determine . . . we can only vaguely relate an inquiry from Mr. X of the XYZ company in 1964, and the eventual sales of a Beechcraft to this company in 1965 . . . the name that signs the check may not be of the same person who started the inquiry process—or the airplane might be purchased under the name of a subsidiary company.")

b) *The difficulty in determining the true reasons for purchase* ("Many studies have attempted to determine why people buy airplanes, but they're mostly invalid. Many are bought for hardheaded business reasons only, yet the factor of emotion also plays an important part in the decision to buy a particular aircraft in many cases. So, although there may always be a business justification in the purchase of an airplane, it has a natural appeal for the pleasure-seeking side of the individual. The business/pleasure mix isn't easily measured because they overlap.")

c) *The unmentionable fear of nonflyers* ("Many people resist flying or purchasing a small plane simply because they're afraid. If not actually afraid to fly, many are afraid they can't master the 'mysterious, complicated' procedures. In other words, a fear of the unknown. Rather than admit it, though, they'll give any of a number of rational reasons to cover up the truth.")

ADVERTISING AT BEECH

James Yarnell commented on the role of advertising at Beech:

Our advertising has to inform, educate, and persuade. We are continually communicating with a given audience who are themselves progressing and becoming more affluent. We bring them along step-by-step up to the point where we *activate* them to contact us with an inquiry; this is *the* big day, but all the days in preparation were invaluable. Much of our job is a matter of developing confidence—developing a relationship with our readers through steady, continuous messages with a relatively constant mood and tone.

Advertising cannot sell an airplane; going out and ringing doorbells and getting people into the planes is what sells them . . . once we have someone sitting in a Beechcraft we're half the way home. The real sale is in the plane itself. This is why *promotions* are so important in this business—they get people into the plane. However, advertising serves the vital function of providing the interested reader with the information he needs to know about our product.

Mr. Yarnell noted the recently-completed "Bonanza Bonanza" promotion as typical of those undertaken by general aviation manufacturers, since its primary attraction for participants was the free use of a Bonanza for a specified time (up to two weeks).

Mr. Yarnell then proceeded to relate copy philosophy to this recognition of advertising's role at Beech:

We use fairly long copy—we don't play with cute one-line gimmicks since we feel that our prospects go through a more lengthy decision process and need to be educated about our product. Our advertising must be serious, as a result. The farthest thing from our minds is to win art directors' awards—they're nice, and we've certainly got the creative talent that could win them, but above all we want readership. We will gladly sacrifice glamour for good, hard-hitting informative copy that answers readers' questions about air travel. We must somehow overcome all the misconceptions, ignorance, and fears held by the general public with regard to small-aircraft travel.

The corporate executive doesn't realize that he's scheduling his business and his life to the schedule of the airlines. He equates speed with a jet airliner, without realizing that a small plane actually buys him time and convenience. You know, it's funny . . . the American executive is a very unselfish fellow. He takes great pains to enhance the comfort and efficiency of everyone in his firm, but he doesn't do much for himself. He'll buy all the latest time and labor-saving gimmicks for his secretary, and then turn around and think nothing of sitting one or two hours in a plane terminal. He thinks of himself last; all we're trying to do is to get him to think of *himself* for a change.

Mr. Yarnell noted the difficulty in experimenting with various campaign themes on expenditure levels due to the diffusion and length of the purchase decision, which he thought rendered impossible any attempts to relate sales changes to some particular advertising approach. Beech advertising expenditures for the period 1959 to 1969 are presented in Exhibit 7. He commented on the level of advertising expenditures:

Every year we set our advertising budget at 1% to 1½% of projected sales for the upcoming year. This establishes us as the leading advertiser in our industry. [Note: Available figures verified that Beech generally led the industry in total advertising expenditures and advertising as a percentage of sales.] More than that, though, we feel that consistency in both the amount and content of our advertising is a goal in itself. New prospects are arriving on the market every year; only through a continuous, consistent ad push can we catch each of them as they come. Furthermore, this approach imparts a solid, dependable, quality image to the company which would not be possible if we were changing themes and varying expenditure levels drastically from year to year.

The budget was divided fairly evenly among product lines except for the Musketeer line, which received substantially less advertising support than other Beech product groups (Bonanza, Light Twin, and Corporate Twin groups). Mr. Dick-Peddie explained that this even allocation was followed rather than dictating a product line's allocation on the basis of the line's dollar sales volume since Beech attached such great importance to every sale and refused to neglect any potential customer.

In addition to the space advertising budget, Beech sales-promotion expenditure averages roughly 25% of this total, although Mr. Yarnell emphasized that this relationship was coincidental rather than planned. Sales-promotion activities financed brochures, dealer aids, shows, exhibits, and a variety of promotions designed to urge prospects into a Beechcraft. Furthermore, a relatively minor sum $20,000-$50,000) was allocated each year to serve as a contingency fund.

EVALUATING BEECH ADVERTISING

Beech executives relied heavily on Starch Readership Reports to evaluate the performance of company advertisements. As previously noted, executives held grave doubts regarding the relevance of sales results as measures of advertising effectiveness, and attitude studies were believed to be invalid. Thus Beech officials thought that the best single measure of the performance of their long-copy advertisements was simply the extent to which people read through the ads and retained the messages. Extended study of Starch readership scores showed that a number of factors produced increased readership of Beech ads:

a) Size—the larger the ad, the more readers.

b) Photos of people with (or in) airplanes.

c) Multiple illustrations.

d) Long copy—the more information, the more readers.

e) Color—over a seven-year period, color ads attracted 54% more readers than black-and-white ads.

f) Frequency—over a seven-year study of ads in *Time,* the year in which the most ads were run resulted in 84.3% more readers per ad than the year in which the least number of ads were run.

In recent years Beech ads had consistently been among the best-read ads in all publications in which Beech advertised; Beech officials looked particularly at the "Read Most" score due to the lengthy and serious Beech sales message.[3] Executives believed that the consistently high Starch scores inherently served to discourage further in-depth research because they thought these scores gave strong indication that "we're doing something right." Priorities in other marketing areas served as further constraints on additional research efforts.

Despite the satisfaction with Starch readership scores as evaluative indicators, periodic additional advertising research of various types did take place. About once a year an in-depth Starch Impression Study was commissioned (a description of this type of study is contained in Appendix A) although Mr. Yarnell noted that "the answers never surprise us." Occasional special media studies had been undertaken, often to justify a certain media selection policy to a questioning top executive or to a skeptical Beech distributor. The advertising executives expressed favorable reactions to such inquiry; they thought it demonstrated a healthy interest in Beech's advertising by others within the firm. One such inquiry by a company distributor in 1965 questioned the heavy emphasis of Beech advertising in general business publications rather than in vertical trade journals—publications directed at a particular industry such as the steel, chemical, or construction industry. (See Appendix B for a summary of the advertising group's response to this distributor.)

Then in 1967, a top Beech executive questioned why more company ads were not placed in unique media environments, that is, in publications having no other advertisements for aircraft or even vaguely similar products. He believed that Beech advertisements in these publications would achieve great impact through an inherent distinctiveness not possible in publications such as *Time* or *Business Week*, in which advertisements of business products were dominant. In response, the advertising team decided to run advertisements in the top two vertical trade publications of six different industries as well as in the top two publications in two special interest fields (golf and yachting). None of these publications contained any advertising for products other than those directly related to the specific field of interest. Despite ads, which were thought to be quite inquiry-provoking, the inquiry rate was extremely low (cost per inquiry was $43 as compared with the average of $2-3 in traditional publications). However, one industry (construction) did show sufficient promise in this trial to warrant continuing advertising in construction trade journals through 1968.

Inquiries in general were constantly studied by the Beech-Brewer advertising team as a measure of the performance of either a particular advertisement or of a publication as an advertising vehicle.

COPY AND MEDIA: 1957-1968

The Bruce B. Brewer advertising agency of Kansas City took over the Beech account in 1957. At that time, Beech advertisements were primarily of a short-copy

---

[3]Starch scores came in three categories: "Noted," "Seen-Associated," and "Read-Most." A Starch score of 60-30-10 indicates that 60% of the test audience recalled seeing the ad; 30% associated the ad with the product or advertiser; and 10% read 50% or more of the ad's reading matter.

"gimmick" variety presented in vertical trade vehicles. Exhibit 8 demonstrates one of these pre-Brewer ads. The first change instituted by the Brewer account team was to forsake the vertical magazines in favor of a broad, horizontal push in general business publications such as *Time, Newsweek,* and *U.S. News & World Report.* This shift was brought about by sales data which indicated that sales were coming from a more diverse population than executives believed could be effectively reached by vertical publications. An analysis of media data (as in Appendix B, for an example) led Brewer and Beech to believe that a horizontal approach could economically reach the most men with a need for and ability to buy an airplane. This horizontal attack, in which *Time* received the bulk of Beech's media expenditures, carried through to 1968. The bulk of the remainder of the media budget through 1967 was allocated to flying journals aimed at the pilot market.

Jack Dick-Peddie elaborated on *Time* as the "perfect" publication for Beech advertising:

> *Time* is great. It strikes directly at the businessman market we're after. The mood of the magazine is ideal—the reader is serious and thinking business when he reads it. It reaches the college-age reader better than any other publication and these are the future decision-makers we must reach now. It also has a high readership among women, who are not decision-*makers* but have *influenced* many purchase decisions by discouraging their husbands from flying in a small plane. On a pure cost-per-thousand basis, *Time* can be beaten. But we're more interested in the raw numbers . . . with relatively low unit sales we simply don't want to miss anybody.

During their first few years with the Beech account the Brewer team emphasized a copy approach selling flying as a concept rather than Beech specifically. Beech sales were less than 1,000 units annually during this period, and the education job needed for the vast untapped market seemed most compelling even though it was recognized that competitive manufacturers were profiting somewhat from advertising of this sort in which a minimum of Beech product superiority received mention.

As previously noted, however, during this period there was little direct competition between the strong Beech lines—Bonanza and the twin-engine models—and the lower-priced lines in which the Cessna and Piper strength was centered; therefore Beech officials felt a minimum of concern for any possible boost that Beech advertising was giving to competition. Exhibit 9 contains an advertisement from this period. By 1964 the Beech line had expanded from 5 to 10 models, and it was decided that more product exposure was needed. In addition to shifting the copy emphasis somewhat in the direction of explaining Beech product superiority, ads attempted to convey a variety of other messages such as:

Flying is fun.

Flying is safe.

Learning to fly is easy.

Beech is a competent aerospace contractor.

A small plane is a sound business investment.

The desire to employ such a multipronged selling approach led to the first consideration of two-page spreads which were first used in quantity in 1965. Spreads had been planned for use in 1964, but a last-minute budget cut forced the continued dependence on single-page ads through 1964, with the result that Jack Dick-Peddie described as "... a mishmash ... we tried to say too much at once. These ads got terrible readership [see Exhibit 10] but evolved into the same principles of segmented advertising that are so relevant today." Exhibit 11 contains an example of a 1964 advertisement.

In 1965, the ad budget expanded to allow use of spreads. Beech was anxious to move in this direction for a variety of reasons:

> a) *Cost effectiveness*—numerous studies justified the extra expense of color spreads in pure economic terms of the greater readership they attracted.
>
> b) *Prestige*—the light aircraft industry was still regarded as a somewhat infant industry, especially in comparison with most of the advertisers in a publication such as *Time*. Color spreads conveyed the impression of product leadership, corporate success, and bigness.
>
> c) *Uniqueness*—it bothered agency executives that Beech ads looked the same as other airplane ads; they felt that distinctive-appearing ads would reflect Beech's "Rolls Royce of the Air" image.
>
> d) *Neat, uncluttered appearance*—spread ads allowed extensive product exposure, multiple illustrations, and long copy without the cluttered effect of the 1964 single-page ads.

The 1965-68 color spreads achieved the highest *Time* readership in Beech history. (See Exhibit 10.) It constantly ranked among the five best-read ads in each issue. Exhibit 12 contains a spread advertisement from this period.

By 1968 Beech found that its marketing environment had reached such a state of complexity that, on analysis, they discovered that some 12 separate market segments had come to merit special advertising attention. A variety of media/ message combinations were used to reach these different segments. Color spreads continued as the dominant means of presentation. Exhibit 13 outlines these 12 markets, and how Beech approached them in 1968. (See Beech Aircraft Corporation (B) for a detailed presentation of the 1968 Beech 12-pronged market-segmentation approach.)

PLANS FOR 1969

Despite their belief that the 1965-68 spreads had been a great success, Beech and Brewer advertising executives were considering returning to single-page ads in 1969, primarily for reasons of product exposure and advertising frequency. First, single-page ads would allow more comprehensive and explicit product exposure than the cost of the spreads allowed. Especially with the Beech product line continuing to expand, particularly into totally new markets such as the commuter airline market, Beech executives felt the compelling need for greater model exposure. Second, spreads allowed only limited frequency within each vehicle, especially in high-cost publications such as *Time*. Executives thought that greater frequency and product exposure could now be higher-priority goals since the four years of color spreads had successfully achieved for Beech the desired quality image of leadership and corporate strength. Executives' confidence was also bolstered by the high Starch readership scores attained by single-page ads run in *National Geographic* and *Fortune* on a trial basis during 1968.

For 1969, executives believed that a Beech logo importing a unifying theme to all ads would also achieve a synergistic effect. They intended to employ a "Be there" logo in every Beech ad to convey that a Beechcraft allows a businessman greater flexibility and permits him to conduct business on a face-to-face basis rather than by letter or over the phone.

Beech Aircraft Corporation (A)

LIST OF EXHIBITS

Exhibit	*Contents*
1	Selected Financial Data: 1958-1967
2	The Beechcraft Product Line—1968
3	General Aviation Data: Aircraft Miles Flown, Hours Flown, and Number of Aircraft in Use According to Use of Aircraft—1966
4	General Aviation Aircraft by Size of Aircraft by Aircraft Use—1965
5	The Leading Manufacturers and Industry Sales: 1962-67
6	Examples of Beech Market Research
7	Beech Advertising Budgets: 1959-1969
8	Pre-Brewer Ad: "Disraeli Went out on a Limb . . . " (1949)
9	1962 Twin-Bonanza Ad: "Your Treasurer Would Be Quick to Say, 'Yes.' "
10	Starch Readership Scores in *Time* and *Business Week:* 1963-68
11	1964 Ad: "How much can you earn *here* for your company?"
12	1965 Spread: "Wherever in the world V.I.P.s fly—the famous 'Twin Beech' has been there!"
13	The Twelve Beech Markets for 1968

Exhibit 1

SELECTED FINANCIAL DATA: 1958-1967

(figures in millions)

	1967	1966	1965	1964	1963	1962	1961	1960	1959	1958
Total sales	174.1	164.6	122.5	107.2	73.9	67.7	72.0	98.9	89.5	95.9
Commercial	103.9	100.7	74.3	54.3	45.3	40.3	43.1	46.6	37.9	32.1
Aerospace and Military	70.2	63.9	48.2	52.9	28.6	27.3	28.9	52.3	51.6	63.8
Net income after taxes	9.0	8.8	5.5	3.4	2.0	3.0	2.6	4.9	4.0	3.3
% of sales	5.2	5.3	4.5	3.2	2.7	4.4	3.6	4.9	4.4	3.5

Source: Annual Report, 1967.

Exhibit 2

THE BEECHCRAFT PRODUCT LINE – 1968

Model	Seating	Cruise Speed	Avg. Equipped Price	1967 Sales	1968 Sales to June 30***
* King Air B90	6-10	256 m.p.h.	$442,000	134 units	72 units
* Model 99	17	254	415,000	**	14
* Queen Air 88	6-10	221	259,500	6	2
* Queen Air B80	6- 9	224	194,000	40	35
* Super H18	7-11	220	179,500	9	6
* Duke	4- 6	278	166,500	**	**
* Queen Air A65	6- 9	214	144,500	31	27
* Turbo Baron 56TC	4- 6	290	95,950	11	47
* Baron D55	4- 6	230	73,950	220	148
* Baron B55	4- 6	225	59,950	26	76
* Travel Air D95A	4- 5	200	53,500	30	15
Bonanza V35TC	4- 6	230	40,950	43	21
Bonanza 36	6	195	40,650	**	35
Bonanza V35A	4- 6	203	35,750	256	212
Bonanza E33A	4- 5	200	34,150	80	39
Bonanza E33	4- 5	185	30,750	69	61
Musketeer Super III	4- 6	150	17,950	135	70
Musketeer Custom III	4	143	16,450	77	62
Musketeer Sport III	2- 4	131	13,750	146	68

* Twin engine models.
** New model.
*** Represents nine months of fiscal year.
Source: *Beech Aircraft Corporation Preliminary Debenture Prospectus*, July 22, 1968.

Exhibit 3

GENERAL AVIATION DATA: AIRCRAFT MILES FLOWN, HOURS FLOWN,
AND NUMBER OF AIRCRAFT IN USE ACCORDING TO USE OF AIRCRAFT — 1966

(miles and hours in thousands)

Category	Miles Flown	% of Total	Hours Flown	% of Total	Aircraft in Use*	% of Total*
Business	1,536,158	46	7,057	33	21,650	23
Commercial	515,730	16	3,555	17	11,355	12
Instructional	646,169	19	5,674	27	8,034	8
Personal	605,912	18	4,540	22	51,093	54
Other	32,169	1	197	1	3,310	3
Total	3,336,138	100	21,023	100	95,442	100

Source: *FAA Statistical Handbook of Aviation*, 1967 Edition, except where noted by *, in which case the source is the 1966 Edition.

Exhibit 4

GENERAL AVIATION AIRCRAFT BY SIZE OF AIRCRAFT BY AIRCRAFT USE – 1965

Type of Aircraft	Total	Aircraft Use Code*							
		1	2	3	4	5	6	7	8
Total, all aircraft	95,442	7,215	14,435	51,093	5,041	8,034	5,215	1,099	3,310
Single-engine, total	81,153	3,140	10,120	48,749	4,772	7,628	3,344	819	2,581
1-3 places, up to 100 hp	21,842	102	512	16,559	405	3,487	80	217	480
1-3 places, over 100 hp	9,522	91	332	3,598	4,243	334	145	301	478
4 places and over, up to 200 hp	26,796	753	2,831	17,790	37	3,427	1,109	83	766
4 places and over, over 200 hp	22,993	2,194	6,445	10,802	87	380	2,010	218	857
Multiengine, total	11,977	3,915	4,180	1,585	90	145	1,419	86	557
Up to 800 hp	8,868	2,472	3,482	1,425	10	113	1,025	35	306
801-2,000 hp, under 12,500 lbs	1,641	647	396	120	13	6	341	20	98
801-2,000 hp, 12,500 lbs. and over	74	30	24	—	—	—	11	3	6
Over 2,000 hp, under 12,500 lbs	29	3	2	—	6	—	13	—	5
Over 2,000 hp, 12,500 lbs. and over	1,365	763	276	40	61	26	29	28	142
Rotorcraft	1,503	160	135	163	179	104	447	193	122
Gliders, balloons, and blimps	809	—	—	596	—	157	5	1	50

* Column 1: Executive transportation (professionally flown)
  2: Business transportation (owner flown)
  3: Personal
  4: Aerial application
  5: Instructional
  6: Air taxi
  7: Industrial/special
  8: Other

Source: *FAA Statistical Handbook of Aviation*, 1966 Edition.

Exhibit 5

THE LEADING MANUFACTURERS AND INDUSTRY SALES: 1962-67

Manufacturer	Units	Share of Total	$ Volume	Share of Total	Average Price
1962					
Cessna	3026	49%	$ 58,127,505	39%	$ 19,200
Beech	803	13	39,283,525	27	49,200
Piper	2199	36	38,148,400	26	17,300
Aero Commander	110	2	11,043,000	8	100,000
Total	6138	100%	$146,602,430	100%	$ 24,000
1963					
Cessna	2873	44%	$ 55,426,220	37%	$ 19,200
Beech	1038	16	39,230,950	26	37,800
Piper	2047	31	38,909,170	26	19,000
Aero	103	2	10,972,500	7	106,000
Mooney	430	7	7,073,500	4	16,400
Total	6491	100%	$151,612,340	100%	$ 23,300
1964					
Cessna	3985	46%	$ 75,897,945	36%	$ 18,900
Piper	2911	34	58,724,135	27	20,000
Beech	999	12	49,740,850	23	49,700
Aero	121	1	15,921,700	8	132,000
Mooney	611	7	12,030,590	6	19,700
Total	8627	100%	$212,315,220	100%	$ 24,600

Exhibit 5 (cont.)

Manufacturer	Units	Share of Total	$ Volume	Share of Total	Average Price
1965					
Cessna	5037	46%	$ 97,033,445	31%	$ 19,200
Piper	3838	35	74,641,580	24	19,400
Beech	1220	11	70,431,750	23	57,800
Lear Jet	56	-	32,200,000	10	577,000
Aero	108	1	22,561,100	8	209,000
Mooney	750	7	13,080,315	4	17,400
Total	11009	100%	$309,948,190	100%	$ 28,100
1966					
Cessna	7922	54%	$167,973,155	33%	$ 21,200
Beech	1422	10	119,827,745	23	84,500
Piper	4256	29	100,965,790	20	23,800
Aero	201	1	65,636,475	13	327,000
Lear	70	1	42,950,000	8	617,000
Mooney	782	5	18,022,990	3	23,100
Total	14572	100%	$515,376,155	100%	$ 35,100
1967					
Cessna	6187	48%	$140,098,490	31%	$ 22,700
Beech	1313	10	120,468,200	27	92,900
Piper	4276	34	98,267,200	22	22,800
Aero	330	3	43,977,925	10	132,000
Lear	32	-	20,768,000	5	650,000
Mooney	650	5	20,355,500	5	31,400
Total	12788	100%	$443,935,315	100%	$ 34,800

Source: Company records.

Exhibit 6

EXAMPLES OF BEECH MARKET RESEARCH

National and Regional Retail Beech Markets
Calendar Year – 1967
(percentage distribution of retail sales within each region: models: 33-35)

Major Industry Classifications	Pacific	North Central	South Central	Great Lakes	Southeast	Northeast	National
	%	%	%	%	%	%	%
Agri., forestry, fisheries	10	2	8	3			5
Mining & petroleum extract.		2	10			1	3
Contract construction	8	15	14	6	15	14	12
Manufacturing	22	15	7	31	23	18	17
Trans., communi., pub. util.	3	4	10	6		4	5
Wholesale trade	3	17	11		15	6	8
Retail trade	13	17	15	18	7	13	14
Finance, ins., real estate	5	6	13	9	4	7	8
Service firms	15	6	7	12	4	7	9
Medical	17	6	4	6	12	7	8
Government	2						
Miscellaneous (retired, mfg. rep. & fly club)		2		6	8	4	3
Not classified	2	8	1	3	12	19	8
Total percentage	100%	100%	100%	100%	100%	100%	100%

Exhibit 6 (cont.)

Aircraft by BMA-State & County by Class: YR MFG 65-66

BMA*	State	County	CL** 01	CL 02	CL 03	CL 04	CL 05	CL 06	CL 07	CL 08	CL 09	CL 10	Total
113	20	001	1	3			1						5
113	20	005	10	5	4	3	2			1			25
113	20	009	20	12	7	4	3	1		1			48
113	20	017	27	15	18	4	7				1	1	73
113	20	019			1								1
113	20	021	18	13	7	5	5						48
113	20	023	2	1	2		2						7
113	20	025	1	3	3	3	4		3	2	5	3	27
			79△	52△	42△	19△	24△	1△	3△	4△	6△	4△	234△
113	38	001	1										1
113	38	003		1	1								2
113	38	005			1			1		1			3
113	38	007	7	4									11
113	38	009				1							1
			8△	5△	2△	1△		1△		1△			18△
			87□	57□	44□	20□	24□	2□	3□	5□	6□	4□	252□

*BMA = Beech Marketing Area (e.g., 113 representa a particular metropolitan area).

**CL = Beech General Aviation Class; Beech grouped all general aviation aircraft into ten arbitrary classifications for the sake of data compilation.

Casewriter's note: Data represent general aviation aircraft of *all* makes registered in BMA 113 during 1965-66.

Exhibit 7

BEECH ADVERTISING BUDGETS: 1959-1969

(space only)

1959	$ 435,000
1960	885,000
1961	588,000
1962	678,000
1963	736,000
1964	522,000
1965	844,000
1966	1,144,600
1967	1,336,000
1968	1,614,400
1969 (proposed)	1,967,400

Source: Company records.

Exhibit 8

PRE-BREWER AD: "DISRAELI WENT OUT ON A LIMB . . . " (1949)

Disraeli went out on a limb... £4,000,000 worth!

A 100-mile ditch was dug across the Isthmus of Suez . . . and the world was made 5000 miles smaller. Prime Minister Disraeli realized the vast importance of the Suez Canal—a *faster* way to reach the markets of the East. So in the name of the Cabinet, he bought part of the Canal . . . to the tune of £4,000,000! Parliament, fortunately for him, backed up his wisdom with hard cash.

Disraeli, like any man with vision, knew that markets are most productive when you utilize the fastest way of getting at them.

To the aid of today's businessman comes a superior method of getting places fast, *and frequently:*

company ownership of the twin-engine Beechcraft Executive Transport. Because of its 200-mph speed, executives are no longer desk-bound; business travel time is cut 75%. Personal attention to distant markets is again possible, and the profit side of the ledger reflects such increased activity. Travel in this 7- to 9-place luxuriously comfortable Beechcraft is travel as it should be—fast, relaxing and free of fatigue. And it is particularly economical transportation as well.

● A note on your company letterhead will bring you an informative 60-page brochure on "The Air Fleet of American Business." Write today to Beech Aircraft Corporation, Wichita, Kansas, U. S. A.

BEECHCRAFT
EXECUTIVE TRANSPORT
MODEL 18

BEECHCRAFTS ARE THE AIR FLEET OF AMERICAN BUSINESS

61

Exhibit 10

STARCH READERSHIP SCORES IN TIME AND BUSINESS WEEK: 1963-68

Year	No. Ads	Space	Average Readership

A. STARCH AVERAGES 1963 THROUGH 1968: TIME MAGAZINE

Year	No. Ads	Space	Average Readership
1963	7	Pg 2C + 1/3 Pg B/W	33-30-6
	3	Pg 2C	32-30-7
1964	5	Pg B/W	25-20-4
	2	Spd B/W	36-30-4 1/2
1965	6	Spd B/W	37-32-7
	1	Spd 4C	61-54-9
1966	2	Spd B/W	44-40-8
	6	Spd 4C	53-45-9
1967	2	Spd B/W	44-37-8
	7	Spd 4C	57-50-10
1968 (partial)	2	Spd B/W	55-44-11 1/2
	2	Spd 4C	68-60-13

B. STARCH AVERAGES 1966 THROUGH 1968: BUSINESS WEEK

Year	No. Ads	Space	Average Readership
1966	6	Spd B/W	44-41-14
1967	6	Spd B/W	43-39-12
1968 (partial)	2	Spd B/W	49-44-11

Source: Company records.

Exhibit 11

1964 AD . . . "HOW MUCH CAN YOU EARN HERE FOR YOUR COMPANY?"

How much can you earn here for your company?

This top man can't make a nickel for his company when he's "sitting it out" somewhere on a trip. Think of the hours *you* have lost this way. Think, too, of your firm's investment in electric typewriters, automatic calculators, automated machinery, air conditioning, background music and other things to help your office and plant employees accomplish *more.* Your key executives, on the other hand, may be *losing* endless hours just trying to get from one place to another. The answer for many companies is a Beechcraft—the business machine that multiplies key management people. Think what a Beechcraft could mean to your firm in extra executive accomplishment and better-looking Profit & Loss statements. Get more facts now.

Beechcraft Queen Air 80 seats 6 to 9 in quiet comfort, surrounded by rich leathers, luxurious fabrics, fine-grained woods and deep-pile carpeting. Supercharged fuel injection engines give it a top speed well over four miles per minute. Span the continent with only one fuel stop. Airstair door provides easy entrance, one of many airliner-type features.

Wide choice of newest electronic equipment for navigation and communication, including radar, for "on schedule" operations, day or night.

In your Queen Air 80 you and other executives can work and plan in quiet and comfort. Folding doors to lavatory and flight deck give complete privacy.

FREE: Write today for "Answers to the 19 Most-Asked Questions about Business Flying." Address **Beech** Aircraft Corp., Public Relations Dept., 9709 E. Central, Wichita, Kansas 67201, U. S. A.

The World Is Small When You Fly A **Beechcraft**

Beechcraft Travel Air carries 4 or 5 and bags at over 3 miles a minute. Easy-to-fly twin. 1,000-mile range.

5-seat Beechcraft Bonanza flies at speeds to 212 mph. Many executives in their 50's learned to fly in it.

Beech "Imaginuity" in research, development and technical fabrication plays a vital part in many of today's AEROSPACE and MILITARY projects, as well as in building better business airplanes. For example: Beech developed today's most successful, most sophisticated supersonic operational missile target weapons system, the Navy's AQM-37A—another example of the broad range of Beech capabilities.

Exhibit 12

1965 SPREAD: "WHEREVER IN THE WORLD V.I.P.s FLY— THE FAMOUS 'TWIN BEECH' HAS BEEN THERE!"

Exhibit 13

THE TWELVE BEECH MARKETS FOR 1968

Market	Copy Thrust	Publications Used	Dominant Presentation	Frequency	Cost
1. Business Executive	Beechcraft is a wise investment for a company.	*Time, Business Week, Newsweek, Wall Street Journal*	Color spread B & W spread	36 insertions	$ 790,248
2. Executive Prestige	Corporate image directed at business executive audience.	*National Geographic, Fortune*	Color page	8	163,075
3. Corporate	Corporate image directed at financial community.	*Forbes*	B & W spread	4	47,240
4. Commuter Airline	Model 99 is the first aircraft designed specifically to meet the needs of the commuter airline industry.	5 airport management and flying journals, *Wall Street Journal*	B & W spread	18	55,572
5. General Aviation	Beechcraft high-performance product characteristics emphasized to owner/pilots.	6 general aviation journals	Sell-O-Chrome (4-page color insert)	59	134,059
6. Sportsman	Good times come easy and more often in a Beechcraft; emphasizes pleasure uses of Beechcrafts.	*Sports Illustrated*	B & W page	5	53,245
7. Professional Pilot	Heavy emphasis on technical superiority of Beech corporate twins.	*Business/Commercial Aviation, Professional Pilot, Flight*	Sell-O-Chrome B & W spread	38	75,180
8. Special Industries	Specialized uses for Beechcrafts within the construction industry.	*Engineering News Record, Construction Methods and Equipment*	B & W page	8	13,300

Exhibit 13 (cont.)

Market	Copy Thrust	Publications Used	Dominant Presentation	Frequency	Cost
9. Women's Prestige	Corporate image; the prestige of Beech ownership.	*Harper's Bazaar, Vogue, Town & Country*	B & W page	12	56,352
10. Aerospace and Military	Beech is a skilled defense and aerospace contractor.	9 military/aerospace journals	Sell-O-Chrome B & W page	57	241,906
11. International Business	Beech is a wise investment for a company.	Various overseas general business publications	B & W page	86	146,608
12. International Pilot	Beechcraft high-performance product characteristics emphasized to owner/pilots.	Various overseas flying journals	B & W page	62	28,005
TOTAL 1968 AD SPENDING					$1,804,790

Source: Casewriter's reconstruction from company records.

APPENDIX A

Description of Starch Special Audience Impression Studies[4]

The Starch Impression Program, established in 1954, is basically a qualitative service that tells advertisers what meanings people find in advertisements and how much importance they attach to these meanings. The Starch impression technique is adaptable to pre-test and post-test needs. The emphasis in an Impression Study falls on the study advertisement itself, not on the media or the relative performance of other advertisements in the same product category and issue.

The Starch Impression Studies have demonstrated value for answering such important questions as these:

> —What image of our company and our product does the advertisement communicate?
>
> —Do illustration and copy work together or clash?
>
> —Do the product features which we are highlighting give us a competitive advantage? Are these features important to readers?
>
> —Do most readers find the same meanings in our advertisement—the meanings we want them to find?

In the Special Audience Impression Studies, the sample is designed to meet the requirements of a particular advertiser. The title page describes the kind of audience used in the study. Throughout the interview the reader has the advertisement before him, and a semistructured questioning procedure is used to channel the reader's thoughts into four general areas of the advertisement—the total advertisement, the product, service or company, the illustrations, and the written material. The reader tells in his own words what the advertisement said to him, and what personal meanings he saw in that message.

The Starch Impression Program represents an optimal combination of flexibility and standardization. Although the Impression interview is standardized to guarantee maximum reliability, the Impression analysis, prepared by trained psychologists on the Starch staff, is tailored to the needs of the individual advertiser and to his specific advertising objectives.

INTERVIEWERS

The specially trained interviewers who carry out the field work for the Impression program have demonstrated ability in establishing and maintaining rapport with respondents. Throughout their association with the Impression program, interviewers must sustain high quality performance. Interviewer performance is checked by Field Supervisors and by quality control procedures in the home office.

[4]From introduction to Starch Impression Study prepared for Bruce B. Brewer & Company, November 25, 1966, by Daniel Starch and staff.

HOW THE INTERVIEW IS CONDUCTED

In Special Audience Impression Studies the advertisement is placed before the respondent, and he is asked to read the ad as much as he likes. There is no forced reading. Then the standardized Impression questions and probes are employed.

They are as follows:

1. When you first looked at this advertisement, what was outstanding to you? Tell me more about it. (The answer is read back to the respondent followed by:−

WHAT DOES THAT MEAN TO YOU?

2. In your own words, what did the advertisement tell you about the product (service, company)? Tell me more about it.

WHAT DOES THAT MEAN TO YOU?

3. What did the picture tell you? Tell me more about it.

WHAT DOES THAT MEAN TO YOU?

4. In your own words, what did the written material tell you? Tell me more about it.

WHAT DOES THAT MEAN TO YOU?

In questioning the respondent, the interviewer does not ask: "Do you like the product?" "Do you believe the claims?" "Would you buy the product?" "What do you think of the company?" Or even "Did you understand what you read?" Comments that reveal the answers to these important questions must come from the reader on his own and in his own words.

PREPARATION OF THE STARCH IMPRESSION STUDY

In the interview, the questions about "what was outstanding," "what the advertisement said about the product," "what the picture said," and "what the written material said," are asked to refocus the respondent's attention on the content of the advertisement. This refocusing is a necessary preliminary to asking the "what does it mean to you" question which brings out the range of meanings. These "meaning" responses are the raw material of the Impression analysis and indicate the degree of the reader's involvement.

Complete verbatim transcripts of all interviews conducted on an advertisement are analyzed by Starch staff psychologists, each of whom has had extensive training and experience in the qualitative analysis and evaluation of response to printed advertising.

The Impression Study tells Starch clients how many readers revealed positive, neutral, or negative attitudes toward: the advertisement as a whole, the illustration, major copy points, the company, and the product. The qualitative section of the report explains how and why readers interacted with the advertisement to produce these attitudes. Findings are illustrated and supported by verbatim quotations from the readers themselves.

APPENDIX B

A Comparative Study of Vertical Trade Journals and General Business Publications[5]

For this investigation, Beechcraft sales by industry were studied. Hundreds of trade books in a wide variety of fields were analyzed for advertising content. Thirty-six specific trade publications were asked for presentations and audience breakdowns. These, too, were studied. The following facts and figures are from these sources, plus Publisher's Index Bureau (PIB); Starch Consumer Magazine Report; Standard Rate and Data Service (SRDS); Simmons Report 1965; and 1964 Beechcraft Industry Breakdown.

GENERAL COMMENTS [6]

Last year Beech sold airplanes within 167 different SIC (Standard Industry Classification) categories.

SRDS lists 172 different business publication (trade book) categories. A good parallel.

If Beech were to direct its advertising vertically in trade books, and attempt to reach the full range of industries that constitute the known market:

One page, B/W, in just the one leading trade book in each field would cost $208,279.

This would reach 11,481,180 people at a CPM of $18.14.

One page, B/W, in *Time* cost $16,895. It reaches 3,100,000 homes at a CPM of $5.45.

For less than the same cost of the one-time shot in trade publications, Beech could run 12 pages in *Time* and make 37,200,000 impressions—over 3 times the number of impressions, but with 12 times the impact.

Even McGraw-Hill, the nation's leading trade-book publisher, states that it takes more than one trade book to cover a given field. Thus, in the above example, we are not penetrating the various markets to any great extent.

Of course there is "waste circulation" in any consumer magazine. But if "top management" is the ultimate target for Beech, trade books deliver even greater "waste circulation" than carefully selected consumer magazines . . . and at a fantastically higher cost per thousand.

In media selection, there are practically no guideposts for trade publication buying. In almost every case, the media buyer must take the trade book's own word for the quality of its circulation. The methods for arriving at circulation-analysis figures are highly suspect.

[5]From Bruce B. Brewer & Company records, 1965.

[6]Casewriter's note: This section summarized the study, the bulk of which consisted of detailed analysis of vertical publications serving a number of different industries.

On the other hand, there are many guideposts to use in the selection of consumer media—Starch, Simmons, PIB, Politz, etc., all highly respected and accepted research organizations that measure all major consumer publications by like standards.

In short, the media buyer hopes he is reaching X thousand "management" people when he schedules his client's advertising in *Textile World.*

On the other hand, he *knows* that *Time* covers:

*37% of all American households headed by professional/managerial men . . .

*39% of all American households owning homes valued at $40,000 or more . . .

*39% of all American households headed by a college graduate . . .

*45% of all American households with incomes of $25,000 or more . . .

*55% of all top management of large companies . . .

*35% of all top management of middle-size companies . . .

*1,000,000 farmers . . .

*A minimum of 75,000 doctors . . .

And he *knows* that no other publication in the world directed to top management even comes close to equaling *Time's* coverage of this market.

He *knows* that the major advertisers of considered purchase items select *Time*. *Time* leads all other consumer publications in advertising directed to:

*Business and Industry.

*Travel, Hotels, and Resorts.

*Corporate Promotions.

*Aviation, Accessories & Equipment.

*Financial.

*Office Equipment.

*Industrial Building Materials.

No other manufacturer of universal-use products advertises regularly in trade publications.

Time circulation spans the entire spectrum of the Beech market more efficiently and economically than any other publication or a combination of publications in the world.

Other industry leaders seem to feel the same way. To paraphrase a famous slogan: Beech is in good company when it invests in *Time*.

Among the giants of the business-machine industry who, this year, are choosing *Time* as their No. 1 media investment are IBM, NCR Computers, Pitney-Bowes, Burroughs Corporation, Dictaphone Company, and Xerox Corporation. Among the giants of the industrial machinery industry who, this year, are choosing *Time* as their No. 1 media investment are Bendix, Clark, GE, Hughes, and Rockwell-Standard.

This year, through June, the five leading magazines for business and financial advertisers are:

Time	$14,936,146
Business Week	13,177,356
Life	8,921,061
Newsweek	7,127,747
U. S. News	6,741,478

QUESTIONS

1. *What is the role of advertising at Beech? What should it be?*
2. *What measures of advertising effectiveness are appropriate for this company?*
3. *Should the changes in advertising planned for 1969 be approved?*

Abbott
Steel Corporation

The staff of the marketing department must determine the meaning and implications for promotional policy of the results of a research study conducted among purchasing agents. The study dealt with relative evaluations of company advertising and sales force.

In the summer of 1970, the sales and advertising managers of Abbott Steel Corporation met to discuss the meaning and the implications for promotional policy of the results of a recent research study of purchasing agents. The study concerned reactions to the advertising and personal selling activities of four leading steel firms, and was based on a national sample of purchasing agents who had been prescreened to determine that they were specifiers of steel products.

Abbott, one of the major steel companies in the country, manufactured a wide line of steel products for fabricators and other industrial firms. Abbott's products were sold direct and through a national warehouse distribution system, with the latter accounting for over half of Abbott's sales. In its direct sales effort, like most of its competitors, Abbott had a sizable field force of several hundred sales engineers operating from offices in principal cities. These men called on purchasing agents, and also worked on special applications with development engineers and design people in the plants of customer companies.

In the same way that all the major firms employed extensive sales forces, Abbott also undertook advertising campaigns in vertical and horizontal trade magazines. So in addition to maintaining its sales force Abbott spent over $2-1/2 million in advertising, almost all of it in trade magazines.

Thus it was with considerable interest that Abbott's marketing staff perused the results of a research study conducted by a major trade-publication firm. The study had been conducted with over 2,000 purchasing agents, and focused on their ratings of major steel manufacturers along three specific dimensions: overall preference for the company, preference for the company's salesman, and preference for the company's advertising. The specific questions were:

a)　All things considered, based on their overall performance, in what order would you rank these companies?

b)　In terms of the performance of the salesmen representing these companies, how would you rank these companies?

c)　In terms of the usefulness of the advertising of these companies, how would you rank these companies?

The research was part of a broader study of purchasing-agent preferences, and respondents to the questions about steel companies had been prescreened as to their actual involvement in specifying steel products. The trade magazine considered the study to be a rather accurate reflection of the purchasing-agent population. The Abbott people, although recognizing that there was no way of knowing which P.A.'s bought direct and/or through warehouses, nevertheless thought that the data could provide some vital insights to aid in understanding the impressions made by Abbott's sales force and its advertising. They were also impressed with the rather close correlation between Abbott's own share of market data and the overall company preference ratings in the trade publication's study.

As the sales manager and advertising manager reviewed the key data (summarized in Exhibit 1) they wondered what the results meant, especially in terms of implications for Abbott and for its major competitors. The latter, of course, presumably were also seeing the results of the study.

Exhibit 1

PERCENTAGE OF PURCHASING AGENTS PREFERRING COMPANY UNDER VARIOUS CONDITIONS*

Brand	Condition 1	Condition 2	Condition 3
Grant	43%**	28%	9%
Abbott	43	38	28
Duluth	58	50	45
Fletcher	19	13	9
Combined "Big 4"	42	34	19

*Conditions:

Condition 1–Purchasing agent prefers *both* the company's advertising and its salesman.
Condition 2–Purchasing agent prefers the company's salesman but not its advertising.
Condition 3–Purchasing agent prefers the company's advertising but not its salesman.
**To be read: When the purchasing agent prefers *both* the company's salesman and its advertising, the probability is .43 that he ranks the company No. 1 overall.
Note: The percentages should not add in either direction.

QUESTIONS

1.　What are the implications of the research results for Abbott's promotional policy?

2.　What does the study suggest regarding the other major manufacturers?

Wolff
Drug Company

Sources of Drug Information

The marketing research director examines the results of four related research studies in order to determine the implications for promotional strategy and the direction of future research.

After studying the results of two recent surveys on physicians' sources of drug information, the marketing research director of the Wolff Drug Company looked for further studies of doctors' feelings on the subject. Although he had reached some tentative conclusions about the ways in which drugs are discovered and prescribed by doctors, there had been apparent conflict in the results shown by the initial reports. The marketing research director was convinced that gaining additional information would be of help to him in planning where among the several available channels company promotional funds might best be spent. By the end of 1958, four related studies were under examination.

The first of these was a research study by Professors Ferber and Wales, entitled *The Effectiveness of Pharmaceutical Promotion,* published in 1958 by the University of Illinois. Conducted in 1956, the research involved a structured questionnaire given personally to 421 doctors in and around Chicago. The doctors were identifiable as general practitioners or specialists in one of seven fields.

Drug adoption was one area covered in the study. After being asked to name several drugs recently adopted, the physician was further questioned as to where he had initially heard about the **product** and what source(s) had convinced him to adopt it. Replies to these questions follow:

CAN YOU TELL ME WHAT FIRST BROUGHT _____ TO YOUR ATTENTION?

DO YOU RECALL READING ABOUT OR SEEING THE SAME PRODUCT SOMEWHERE ELSE?

	First Notice	Other Notices	All Notices
Detailman	38%	14%	28%
Journal	25	41	32
Direct Mail	19	22	21
Colleague	6	7	6
Convention, meeting	4	4	4
Sample	2	3	2
Hospital	2	3	2
Other	4	6	5
Total	100%	100%	100%
Total first mentions (products)	902		
Total other mentions		669	
Total mentions			1,571

WHAT FINALLY CONVINCED YOU TO MAKE USE OF THIS PRODUCT?

	Convincing Source
Journal	28%
Detailman	21
Direct Mail	15
Colleague	10
Convention, meeting	4
Hospital	3
Sample	2
Other	17
Total	100%
Total mentions	814

A cross-tabulation by the researchers of "sources of first notice" and "convincing sources" revealed that when journals were recalled as the initial sources of notice, 64% of the time they were also given as the convincing source. For detailmen this figure was 51%, for direct mail 45%, and for all other sources combined 83%.

The researchers secured the cooperation of 210 of these doctors in keeping a diary of their prescriptions, and filling out a questionnaire similar to the foregoing for a number of drugs prescribed. Many of these drugs, in contrast to those reported above, were established products. Tabulations of diary replies follow:

WHERE DID YOU FIRST HEAR ABOUT THIS PRODUCT? (sources were listed.)

	Most Frequently Mentioned	Second Most Frequently Mentioned
Detailman	44%	24%
Journal	31	27
Direct mail	16	11
Colleague	15	19
Convention	3	9
Other	3	2
Total	112%*	92%**
Total diaries kept	210	

*Percentages add to more than 100 because on a number of diaries two or more sources were checked with equal (highest) frequency.

**Percentages add to less than 100 because on some diaries no second choice was checked for any category.

DID YOU START USING IT AS A RESULT OF (sources were listed.)?

	Most Frequently Mentioned	Second Most Frequently Mentioned
Detailman	35%	24%
Journal	27	30
Colleague	23	24
Direct mail	10	17
Other	5	4
Total	100%	100%
Total diaries kept	232	181

A second study which the marketing research director examined was a survey of 256 physicians performed by the Audits and Surveys Company. Two-thirds of these were general practitioners, with the remainder widely scattered among several specialties. Although the study was primarily designed to gather information on the audiences of several medical magazines, it did supply data on the comparative effectiveness of three commercial sources of drug information on new products. In addition, specific aspects of drug information—indications, dosage, and side effects—were probed. Results of these questions follow:

ALTHOUGH WE REALIZE THAT YOU OFTEN HEAR OF NEW DRUGS FROM A GREAT MANY SOURCES, FROM WHICH ONE OF THE FOLLOWING THREE—DETAILMEN, MAGAZINE ADVERTISING, OR DIRECT MAIL—ARE YOU MOST LIKELY TO LEARN FIRST THAT A NEW DRUG HAS BECOME AVAILABLE FOR GENERAL USE?

Detailmen	66.8%
Magazine advertising	16.4
Direct mail	16.8
Total respondents	100.0%

WHICH <u>ONE</u> OF THE THREE HAVE YOU FOUND MOST USEFUL AS A SOURCE OF INFORMATION REGARDING <u>INDICATIONS</u> OF NEW DRUGS?

Detailmen	65.5%
Magazine advertising	16.5
Direct mail	18.0
Total respondents	100.0%

WHICH <u>ONE</u> OF THESE THREE HAVE YOU FOUND MOST USEFUL AS A SOURCE OF INFORMATION REGARDING <u>DOSAGE</u>?

Detailmen	57.7%
Magazine advertising	15.4
Direct mail	26.9
Total respondents	100.0%

WHICH <u>ONE</u> OF THESE THREE HAVE YOU FOUND MOST USEFUL AS A SOURCE OF INFORMATION REGARDING <u>SIDE EFFECTS</u>?

Detailmen	52.8%
Magazine advertising	19.3
Direct mail	27.9
Total respondents	100.0%

A third study consulted was a 1954-55 AMA sponsored report on the promotion, marketing, and acceptance of five new drugs in a single community. All 55 physicians in the locality were interviewed. Somewhat different promotional strategies were employed for each product, but a grouping of information sources for all five drugs was nevertheless compiled. These figures follow:

WHERE DID YOU HAPPEN TO GET THE INFORMATION ABOUT_____WHICH LED YOU TO PRESCRIBE IT?

Total Physicians Interviewed: 55*	
Detailmen	46%
Medical journal articles	31
Medical journal advertising	12
Direct mail	10
Other doctors	8
County meetings, staff meetings	6
National conventions	5
Other sources	3

* Percentages add to more than 100 because of multiple answers.

Breaking out only the major commercial sources from these data, detailmen were given as the information source in 67% of the cases, medical journal advertising in 18%, and direct mail in 15%.

The final study which the Wolff Drug Company's marketing research director examined was an article published in *Public Opinion Quarterly* by Menzel and Katz. The article, entitled "Social Relations and Innovation in the Medical Profession," was an intensive view of the social structure of the medical community in a New England city of about 30,000. Thirty-three of the city's 40 doctors were interviewed, and a prescription audit of a new drug was made at local drugstores to note the adoption pattern. Questions were asked concerning how the physician had learned about two drugs he had recently adopted. The researchers cross-tabulated these responses with information on the physician's popularity among his fellow doctors. This tabulation follows:

Respondents' Information Source	Number of Physicians Who Turned to Respondent for Advice:			All Respondents
	None	One, Two	Three or More	
Detailmen	40%	25%	21%	29%
Mail & periodicals from drug houses	30	18	21	22
Colleagues	15	15	16	15
Articles in journals	10	39	32	29
Meetings	0	0	11	3
Other sources	5	3	0	3
	100%	100%	100%	100%
Number of sources mentioned (Exceeds number of physicians)	20	34	19	73

Another question pertained to possible differences in information sources based on whether a drug was generally applicable to acute or chronic conditions. These replies follow:

	Percent of Total Sources Mentioned	
	Acute Conditions	Chronic Conditions
Detailmen	33%	27%
Articles in journals	26	27
Mail & periodicals from drug houses	23	17
Colleagues	7	22
Meetings	0	5
Other sources	10	2
	100%	100%
Number of sources mentioned (Exceeds number of physicians)	30	41

The marketing research director realized that the four studies were not conceived with the same objective, nor had the information in them been gathered uniformly. However, he felt that an overall view of the data would reveal to him underlying patterns in drug adoption. In addition, he felt that the information could provide new avenues of research inquiry for Wolff.

QUESTIONS

1. What are the marketing implications of the results of the four studies?

2. What additional research data would you like to see before making promotional decisions?

Weyerhaeuser Company (A)

A national institutional print advertising campaign establishes a distinctive corporate identity for the company. Because of corporate growth and diversification, the appropriateness of this identity is questioned. As a result, different copy and media directions are considered.

"It's not easy," exclaimed Carroll O'Rourke, Director of Public Relations and Advertising for the Weyerhaeuser Company, "to give up something as good as our forestry campaign has been to us. Over the last fifteen years the campaign has done a real job in establishing a distinctive corporate image for Weyerhaeuser. All indications point to the fact that the campaign, in its present form, is continuing to win friends for the company and hold the old ones too. However, we have reached a point where we have so many new and exciting things to say about Weyerhaeuser that in fact the campaign is simply not conveying a *true* picture of the company as it actually is today."

In early 1967, Mr. O'Rourke, and Mr. B. L. Orell, the company's Vice-President of Public Affairs to whom he reported, were reviewing the 15-year history of Weyerhaeuser's corporate advertising campaign. The campaign, consisting entirely of full-page insertions in leading national publications, had won a number of awards for its tasteful presentation of forestry wildlife scenes. However, as the nature of the company had changed considerably during the life of the campaign, Mr. O'Rourke believed it necessary to re-examine the copy and media components of the existing advertising approach to determine the extent to which they were serving the needs of the company in 1967. As part of this re-examination, he was weighing the implications of shifting the campaign, in whole or in part, to television. He was hoping, in this regard, for meaningful results from a recent research study testing the effectiveness of television as a medium for the Weyerhaeuser corporate message.

BACKGROUND OF WEYERHAEUSER CORPORATE ADVERTISING

Weyerhaeuser, a leading forest products firm, had long considered its extensive holdings in forest lands to be its most valuable asset. Some 3.8 million acres of land, an area about the size of Connecticut, were owned by the company, and harvesting rights were held on another 9.5 million acres around the world.

Since its corporate existence was dependent on the long-term productivity of its forests, the company placed a high premium on the responsible management of its lands. It achieved early fame within the industry for pioneering the tree-farm movement which, for the first time, treated timber as a crop to be harvested and replanted for the purpose of assuring a permanent supply of timber. This movement was unique at the time because throughout the westward expansion and development of the country, trees had traditionally represented a *hindrance* to development of land and had been cut down to allow for farms, roads, and communities. Not until the 20th century did the first fears arise regarding the permanence of the nation's timber supply.

Thus, in 1941, Weyerhaeuser initiated the private tree-farm movement by dedicating the first of its tree farms—143,000 acres in the state of Washington. The company continued to be regarded as a leader in the forest conservation movement over the next quarter century. Then, in 1967, it instituted its High Yield Forestry Program on its U.S. land holdings. This scientific program of forest management allowed the company to grow about a third more wood on the same land base than natural growth would provide.

In the light of this long-time commitment to what they saw as ethical forest management, Weyerhaeuser executives were extremely sensitive to the mounting concern among the general public during the post-World War II years that the nation's forest lands were being seriously depleted. This perceived problem was believed by the public to be due largely to wasteful management of timberlands by *private* landholders, whereas government-held forests were thought to be more ethically managed. A nationwide study sponsored by the American Forest Products Institute, and conducted by Opinion Research Corporation, in 1952, uncovered the following:

— 44% of interviewees believed that the amount of standing timber in the U.S. was being reduced at a "serious" rate, compared with 25% who held this opinion in 1941.

— Although a majority of people (56%) did not anticipate exhaustion of our forest resources within the next 50 years, over one-fourth (26%) *did* think that this danger exists.

— Lumber and paper companies were credited by only 25% of the public for "doing enough" to assure an adequate supply of timber for the future. Asked what more companies should be doing, most frequently people mentioned *reforestation* and *selective cutting*.

— Although over half (56%) of the people were aware of programs to plant seeds and seedlings to grow forests, only 6% attributed sponsorship of these programs to the lumber and paper companies compared with 40% who attributed sponsorship to either a state or national government.

THE NEED FOR A NATIONAL ADVERTISING CAMPAIGN

Weyerhaeuser executives, fearing that further intensification of such sentiment could lead to eventual legislation to nationalize *all* large forest holdings, believed that the public should be informed of the numerous ways in which the company managed its forests ethically and responsibly. Even apart from any prospective legislation threat, many executives believed it necessary simply in the name of sound public relations to correct what they saw as a serious public misconception which appeared to be held by a significant portion of the nation's population.

Thus, in 1952, the company commenced a national print advertising campaign which, despite occasional minor variations, would maintain the same basic thrusts through 1967. A Weyerhaeuser executive recalled the four major objectives that served to guide the campaign from its inception:

> 1) To inform the public of the steps taken by private landowners in general, and Weyerhaeuser in particular, not only to assure a perpetual timber supply, but also to perpetuate watersheds, wildlife, recreational facilities—and payrolls.
>
> 2) To emphasize that Weyerhaeuser's land, manufacturing, and marketing policies are sound, progressive, and in the public interest. . .thus maintaining and broadening respect for the company's business ethics and leadership.
>
> 3) To make known the progress that was being made toward complete utilization and conversion of the forest crop.
>
> 4) To build a favorable business climate in which the company could market its increasingly diversified line of products.

An executive of the company's advertising agency, Cole and Weber, retrospectively described the thinking that had determined the format and means of presentation of the ads:

> To accomplish the Weyerhaeuser objectives, it was decided to institute a campaign which, like the company's long-range forestry programming, would continue on a year-in, year-out basis.
>
> The tenor of the campaign was established when someone suggested that "the way to get people interested in trees is to get them into the woods." Since that was hardly possible, we decided instead to bring the woods to the people by using a series of advertisements featuring wildlife in forest settings.

Over the years the company had commissioned more than 150 full-color paintings of wildlife scenes. These paintings, which typically featured the tranquility and serenity of forest animals in their natural settings, usually covered the greater part of a full-page ad, and the accompanying copy emphasized the ethical and responsible manner in which Weyerhaeuser managed its timber holdings. Exhibits 1-4 contain representative ads from selected years of the campaign.

Media selection for the campaign was based on the desire to reach active, influential opinion leaders—well-educated professional people—among the business, government, and general public. In addition, a tasteful and conservative mood in the magazine was preferred. Through the years, publications such as *Look, Time, U.S. News and World Report, Saturday Evening Post, Harper's, Atlantic,* and *Saturday Review* featured Weyerhaeuser insertions. Exhibit 5 contains a typical Weyerhaeuser media schedule.

THE FORESTRY CAMPAIGN: 1952-1967

Despite the overall continuity provided by the wildlife paintings the forestry campaign did pass through a number of stages from 1952 to 1967. The first ads, designed primarily to justify private ownership of forest lands, emphasized the ethical management practices of the lumber and paper industry as a whole with little or no mention of Weyerhaeuser except for the corporate signature. (See Exhibit 1.)

Within a year, the campaign began to focus more specifically on Weyerhaeuser and its efforts directed in the public's best interests. This emphasisis continued throughout the bulk of the campaign. (See Exhibits 2 and 3.)

Beginning in 1954, certain ads included subillustrations featuring Weyerhaeuser products. Typically the smaller illustration in this type of ad carried its own explanatory caption, and the main copy thrust of the ad continued to focus on the company's ethical forest-management policies. (See Exhibit 4.)

For two years, 1955 and 1956, the campaign format changed markedly. This period marked the span of the "Men in Forestry" campaign which presented biographical sketches of a number of historical figures who in some way had contributed importantly to early-day forest conservation. (See Exhibit 6.) These ads proved highly popular within the lumber-and-paper industry, and were believed by company executives to have been particularly notable in enhancing Weyerhaeuser's image in the recruiting market. The wildlife scenes, however, were regarded (on the basis of Starch readership scores and other measures) as having broader public appeal, especially to women. For this reason the wildlife format was resumed in 1957, and continued with little change through 1967.

During the first 15 years of its existence the wildlife campaign won over a dozen awards and commendations. Three times it was ranked first in the nation by *Saturday Review* for "distinguished advertising in the public interest." The full-color paintings of wildlife scenes became a virtual trademark of the company. Unsolicited requests for reprints and calendars of these paintings consistently totaled over 1,500 per month. A 1964 *Printers' Ink* article proclaimed, "It is possibly one of the most successful institutional campaigns ever run by any company."[1]

---

[1]*Printers' Ink,* April 10, 1964, pp. 40-41.

UPDATING THE CORPORATE IDENTITY

The decade from the mid-1950s to the mid-1960s was one of extreme change and growth for Weyerhaeuser. In 1956 the company's production was limited primarily to lumber, plywood, and pulp. But by 1966, lumber accounted for less than 25% of total sales and the company had established marketing strength in such areas as packaging (entered in 1957); hardwood (1960); laminated beams and arches (1960); and paper (1961-62). An extensive research effort was actively investigating further product-development areas and diversification possibilities. Despite this diversification, the company remained the world's leading lumber marketer and third leading producer of pulp. By 1966 company sales totaled $838 million, which roughly doubled the 1957 figure.

Changes were instituted in all facets of the company's operations to recognize the revised nature of its business. To the general public, two changes were most apparent. First, in 1959 the corporate name was changed from "Weyerhaeuser Timber Company" to simply "Weyerhaeuser Company"; accompanying the name change was a new corporate symbol (see, for example, Exhibit 3) which was intended to connote forward-looking and dynamic impressions of the company. Second, new advertising approaches attempted to convey this "new look" of Weyerhaeuser. In the early 1960s, ads occasionally contained a subillustration featuring "new ideas in wood," and the main copy of the ad described this new Weyerhaeuser product or research breakthrough. (See Exhibit 7.)

In 1965 the company sponsored opinion studies in nine high-income U.S. communities containing a high proportion of the "decision-influencers" at whom the corporate advertising was directed. The survey results showed that this audience had a distinct image of Weyerhaeuser as an ethical, responsible company. However, somewhat less was known about the firm's recent growth and diversification. The corporate identity as shown in these studies contrasted significantly with the success achieved by some of Weyerhaeuser's competitors in establishing dynamic, forward-looking corporate identities. As one executive noted: "People knew what we were doing to *grow* trees, but they had no idea how we were *using* them."

In response, the corporate campaign moved in a number of new directions to create an identity with the public which company executives believed to be more congruent with the "real" Weyerhaeuser. In the 1965 campaign, the wildlife paintings, although still featured, were slightly reduced in size, and the headline and copy hit more directly at the company's broad product line and commitment to research. (See Exhibit 8.) This format was designed to maintain the serenity and tastefulness for which the forestry campaign was noted, and, in addition, to convey meaningful messages about "Weyerhaeuser on the move."

This broadened emphasis was continued through 1966 and 1967. During this period, for the first time "man" entered the main illustration wildlife setting of a Weyerhaeuser ad in the form of a helicopter conducting a reseeding operation. (See Exhibit 9.) This ad resulted in a number of letters of protest from readers who feared that the helicopter was a detrimental influence on the tranquility of the wildlife scene, and, specifically, the nesting eagles.

THE CAPABILITIES CAMPAIGN

In addition, in 1966 the company decided that a separate and unique copy and media strategy was needed to tell the "Weyerhaeuser on the move" story to the increasingly important target audiences of business executives and the financial community. To accomplish this, a parallel campaign was instituted (in 1966) in *The Wall Street Journal* to augment the continuing forestry campaign. Twenty-five full-page ads in what the company called the "capabilities" campaign presented some specific aspect of the company's new capabilities, covering subjects which ranged from new research ideas to the high caliber of Weyerhaeuser management. The wildlife style was forsaken in the capabilities campaign in favor of an entirely new format (shown in Exhibit 10) which expanded to include seven *Business Week* insertions in 1967, in addition to *The Wall Street Journal* series.

DOUBTS ABOUT THE FORESTRY CAMPAIGN

In mid-1967 the forestry campaign appeared to be gaining rather than diminishing in popularity. Meanwhile the capabilities campaign was credited by executives as having attained readership levels at least equal to company anticipation. Yet Mr. O'Rourke had serious doubts as to whether to continue either campaign in its existing form. Commenting on the forestry campaign, he noted:

> We've known all along that the wildlife illustrations create most of the impact in these ads. We can look at the detailed Starch breakdown for any ad [see Exhibit 7] and see that registerability declines drastically from the illustration to the copy. Of course this is to be expected in *any* ad, but in our ads the fall-off is particularly pronounced. What really hurts us is when we try to convey some *new* messages, such as we've done in the past few years with our "Weyerhaeuser on the move" campaign. The illustration registers just as it always has, but this new message just doesn't come through. For the most part, people seem to assume that it's the same forest management message. The Gallup and Robinson reports[2] back this up for the most part; people can play back the illustration in great detail, but they're usually at a loss when asked what the major thrust of the ad was. [Exhibit 11 contains selected verbatim comments from a Gallup and Robinson playback study of the 1966 ad shown in Exhibit 3.] I really wonder if it's possible to maintain *any* link with the past through continued use of the wildlife illustrations and still have any luck in creating a forward-looking corporate identity for the company.

With regard to the capabilities campaign in *The Wall Street Journal* and *Business Week,* he remarked:

> This campaign has achieved generally great readership and many favorable

[2]Gallup and Robinson Magazine Impact Reports include a major section which contains verbatim comments by interviewees on the ad in question.

comments, which is significant to us since it represents such a sharp departure in format from the wildlife settings of the forestry campaign. However, the question *here* is: "How do we achieve the same distinctiveness with these ads as we have with the forestry campaign?" I can pick up any ad from our forestry campaign, cover the corporate signature, and you'll still recognize it as a Weyerhaeuser ad. I don't think the same would hold true with one of the capabilities ads. Furthermore, since we began *The Wall Street Journal* series, two of our competitors have entered the *WSJ* with corporate campaigns of their own. . . . I wonder if it's getting too cluttered there for *any* of us to make much of an impression.

This "cluttering" is a problem in *Business Week* as well, and in just about all top publications directed at the business executive audience. There are a lot of companies that are growing and diversifying and want to tell this audience about their "new look"; they all are anxious to tell their story in publications with a proven track record in reaching the business executive. If we accept the fact that the identity of Weyerhaeuser needs updating to bring it into line with the company as it actually is, then we must determine some way to do this *distinctively* so that we don't become "just another one of those growing, diversified, research-minded companies."

We know that our forestry campaign has developed an extremely loyal and sensitive following. We have learned to tread lightly here as a result of such experiences as the storm of protest which we raised quite unsuspectingly by running the helicopter ad. This was partially responsible for the decision to run the capabilities campaign in entirely new publications. We believed that a radical new format in the old publications would have antagonized the large audience which continues to enjoy the wildlife scenes.

TELEVISION ENTERS CONSIDERATION

Beginning in the early 1960s, the Weyerhaeuser account team at the Cole and Weber agency periodically suggested that television merited consideration as a suitable medium for the corporate campaign. At about the same time, one of the company's major competitors ran a number of spot TV commercials which caused several top Weyerhaeuser executives to take interest in this issue and inquire of the advertising team if this medium had been investigated.

For a number of years the ad team had cited three main reasons why television was not considered "right" for Weyerhaeuser. First, it was believed that color was a vital element of the corporate campaign; and color television was not considered sufficiently widespread during the early 1960s to justify a color national TV campaign. Second, most advertising industry rules-of-thumb indicated that the minimum expenditure necessary to achieve significant impact and frequency in a national TV campaign was beyond the $700,000–$1 million that Weyerhaeuser had traditionally budgeted for its print campaign. Finally, many in the company pointed to the continuing success of the print campaign and maintained that a move to TV would require the company to abandon the equity which had accrued during the lifespan of the print campaign.

For these reasons the television question remained only a subject of debate within the company and agency, and no action took place. However, various developments combined to eliminate these barriers preventing serious consideration of television. The mid-1960s witnessed a sharp increase in the acceptance of color TV, especially among the upper-income audience toward whom the corporate campaign was primarily directed. In addition, advertising rules-of-thumb had shifted to the extent that by 1967 it was generally believed that a TV investment of the magnitude which Weyerhaeuser was willing to spend *could* prove effective, with careful program selection. Finally, as the company grew increasingly diversified and the advertising team experienced increasing frustration in presenting the "real" Weyerhaeuser through the forestry campaign, ultimately the decision was made to re-examine *all* aspects of the corporate advertising effort including the commitment to print media.

Mr. O'Rourke commented:

> The difficulties we have encountered in establishing a new identity in print media appear to be in large part due to the equity developed in these media by the dominant conservation theme. Many of us believe that only by moving boldly into a totally *new* medium, such as TV, will we finally be able to convince people that we really *are* a different company from what we were ten or twenty years ago. At the same time this would, hopefully, minimize the direct antagonization of the admirers of the wildlife campaign.

In early 1967, the company conducted a six-week test to determine the extent to which the Weyerhaeuser corporate story could be told on television. (See Appendix A for a description of the test, including objectives, method, and different means by which findings were to be presented. Weyerhaeuser Company (B) presents the test and its findings in detail.)

ROLE AND OBJECTIVES OF
WEYERHAEUSER CORPORATE ADVERTISING

As Mr. O'Rourke and Mr. Orell awaited the results of the TV test in the spring of 1967, they pondered the entire corporate advertising effort and its role within the company. Mr. O'Rourke summarized:

> As a forest products firm, most of our products are essentially commodities sold through industrial channels. Paneling is our only real consumer product. Although our Wood Products division does considerable product advertising [Wood Products advertising and promotional expenditures were generally of the same magnitude as those of the corporate campaign] none of our other products actually has a purchasing audience of sufficient size to justify its own product advertising support. As such, the corporate identity campaign must create a favorable corporate identity for Weyerhaeuser among purchase-influencers in a wide variety of industries.

We're following a basic public-relations axiom that you've got to sell the company before you can sell the product. . .the easier we can make it for a purchasing agent to justify a Weyerhaeuser purchase to his top management, the better off we are.

Of course we're also trying to enhance ourselves in the recruiting market, in the financial community, and with our employees and stockholders, which all adds up to a pretty broad target audience for the corporate campaign.

In view of the broad nature of the target audience, Mr. O'Rourke noted that the corporate campaign had thus far been directed at individuals who are influential in general, whatever their occupation or interest. "Influence" was believed to be correlated with four factors:

−Income (over $15,000);
−Age (25-45);
−Education (College);
−Social Position (Leadership in civic and community groups, etc.).

Women were appealed to as strongly as men.

Mr. O'Rourke commented that although television was not generally regarded as the ideal medium to reach people satisfying the above criteria, he believed that careful program selection could possibly serve as a solution. For instance, he mentioned that programs such as *Wide World of Sports* and *Meet the Press* would possibly be appropriate in terms of climate and audience for Weyerhaeuser's corporate message. He intended to investigate the sponsorship availabilities of these and other programs in the event that the TV test justified television as a medium for the Weyerhaeuser corporate campaign.

Weyerhaeuser Company (A)
LIST OF EXHIBITS

Exhibit	Contents
1	1952 Forestry Ad
2	1952 Forestry Ad
3	1966 Forestry Ad
4	1954 Forestry Ad with Product Subillustration
5	1966 Forestry Campaign Magazine Schedule
6	1955 "Men in Forestry" Ad
7	1963 "New Ideas in Wood" Ad
8	1965 "Weyerhaeuser on the Move" Ad
9	1967 Helicopter Forestry Ad
10	1966 "Capabilities" Ad
11	Selected Verbatim Comments from 1966 Gallup and Robinson Impact Report
A-1	Print Ad used in 1967 TV Test
A-2	Description of Commercial Used in 1967 TV Test
A-3	Questionnaire for the 1967 TV Test
A-4	Format of Selected Tables for Presentation of TV Test Findings

Exhibit 1

1952 FORESTRY AD

GOLDEN-MANTLED GROUND SQUIRREL on a western tree farm

tomorrow's trees from cones like these...

On tree farms nature is chief forester and the tree farmer her assistant. In most cases, to reforest harvested timberlands the tree farmer plans to leave properly located seed trees and nature does the rest. One warm fall day the cones on these trees will open and the winds will scatter their winged seeds across the harvested lands. During the next few months this seed will germinate and a new industrial forest will have taken root. There will be many thousands of seedlings on each acre . . . and there will be keen competition among them to reach upward toward the sunlight. Under reasonably favorable conditions a growing Douglas fir will be as high as a 2-story house in 20 years and reach sawlog size in about 30 years. Millions of acres of rain-drenched rugged mountain country in the Pacific Northwest are better suited to growing timber than any other type of crop. In this and other tree-growing areas all across America, several thousand tree farmers are growing their full share of the nation's future wood supply.

However, regeneration is only one of the many aspects of tree farming, for young forests must be cared for . . . protected from fire, insects and disease until they reach harvestable age. If you would like to learn more about the growing movement of tree farming, and how it can assure our nation of a permanent supply of forest products, our free booklet on tree farming is available for the asking. Just write us at Box A, Tacoma, Washington.

Weyerhaeuser Timber Company

Timber is a crop

The forest industry is making steady progress toward complete use of the forest crop. Today we manufacture this variety of products: *4-SQUARE LUMBER, PLYWOOD and fabricated products for home, farm and industrial construction and for varied manufacturing uses . . . SULPHITE and SULPHATE pulps for paper, paperboard and other wood cellulose products . . . *SILVACEL, *SILVAWOOL and *SILVALOY fiber products for insulation, paper making, oil well drilling, compression molding and other uses . . . *SILVACON from bark for plastic, adhesives, insecticides, composition flooring . . . *TREES-TO-LOGS for fuel. *Registered Trademarks.

This advertisement appears in *The Saturday Evening Post* issue of July 19; *U.S. News,* July 18; and *The Farm Journal* for August, 1952.

Exhibit 2

1952 FORESTRY AD

BLUE GROUSE thrive on tree farms of the Pacific Northwest

nature's way...new trees follow the old

Blue Grouse and other wildlife find food and shelter among new trees on a western tree farm. This forest of young trees was replanted naturally by wind-borne seed from the cones of older Douglas firs left standing for this purpose...the new naturally follows the old. As the seasons pass these young firs will grow tall and straight...protected from fire and guarded from insects and disease. New forests such as these are common sights in the nation's tree-growing areas.

On more than twenty-three million acres of privately owned forestlands, men are growing and harvesting timber as a crop. They are farming the forestlands—operating tree farms—to grow a continuous supply of forest products for you, your children and your grandchildren.

In Alabama, a farmer watches the growth of his pine forest. In Maine,

a far-seeing Yankee tends his timber crop. In Michigan, a father and son proudly post their tree farm sign in a stand of maple. In nearly every forest region of America, farmers and pulp and lumber companies are joining in a great voluntary movement to grow new crops of timber following every log harvest.

Today, forestry leaders agree that timber growth and timber harvest are approaching a balance. Only through tree farming can this balance be achieved and maintained.

All Weyerhaeuser Timber Company operating forestlands are tree farms, managed by skilled foresters. They are located in Washington and Oregon. An interesting booklet about tree farming is yours for the asking. Write us at Tacoma, Washington, for your copy.

Weyerhaeuser Timber Company

Timber is a crop

The forest industry is making steady progress toward complete use of the forest crop. Today we manufacture this variety of products: *4-SQUARE LUMBER, PLYWOOD and fabricated products for home, farm, and industrial construction and for varied manufacturing uses...SULPHITE and SULPHATE pulps for paper, paperboard and other wood cellulose products...*SILVACEL, *SILVAWOOL and *SILVALOY fiber products for insulation, paper making, oil well drilling, compression molding and other uses...*SILVACON from bark for plastics, adhesives, insecticides, composition flooring...*BARK-TO-LOGS for fuel. *Registered Trademarks

WEYERHAEUSER FOREST PRODUCTS

This advertisement in *The Saturday Evening Post*, February 23, *U.S. News*, February 22; and *The Farm Journal* for March, 1952.

Exhibit 3

1966 FORESTRY AD

A computer is baby-sitting these young trees

Red fox in a harvested area which was reforested by helicopter seeding

Keeping track of millions of trees growing on Weyerhaeuser lands used to be a laborious job. Today it's a different story. Our computers play back the answers we need at the flick of a button.

How much wood we're growing. How fast. Where to re-seed or hand plant new crops. How much we can safely cut without eventually running out of trees.

This is up-to-date tree farming at work for you and your children. For their children. And their children.

It's the kind of scientific forestry that means there will be trees on our lands, always. Trees to make the lumber, plywood, paper, cartons and scores of other products you use. Trees, too, to protect watersheds, shelter wildlife and beautify recreation areas.

Yes, America can have trees and still enjoy their products. To learn more, write us at Box A-2, Tacoma, Washington 98401, for a free booklet. Printed, of course, on paper from our tree farms.

Where the future grows... **Weyerhaeuser**

Exhibit 4

1954 FORESTRY AD WITH PRODUCT SUBILLUSTRATION

CANADIAN GEESE over a Pacific Northwest tree farm . . . where timber is grown and harvested in repeated crops. Douglas fir forest lands are scientifically harvested in scattered patches to permit natural reseeding of the cutover areas by mature trees left standing.

more wood for everyone from industrial tree farms...

The natural beauty and warmth of Douglas fir adds distinctive charm and friendliness to this combination living room and den. Economical, versatile wood can give individuality to any home.

More and more wood is being used every day to supply America's growing demand for lumber, pulp, paper, chemicals, fibers and other forest products. Today, much of this wood comes from industrial tree farms. However, to assure a future supply, all the nation's timberlands must be managed by modern forestry methods.

Tree farms are privately owned, tax-paying forestlands certified by regional timber associations. The owners voluntarily agree to protect their forests from fire, insects and disease. They also must harvest under a long-range plan which provides for natural and artificial reforestation of cutover lands. Such commercial forests can be perpetuated by maintaining a favorable ratio between the trees grown and the amount of wood harvested.

The tree farm movement was officially recognized in June, 1941 with dedication of the Clemons Tree Farm, owned by Weyerhaeuser Timber Company. All Company forestlands are now certified tree farms...as are more than 30 million acres operated by about 5,100 other private owners throughout America. *Write to us at Box A, Tacoma 1, Washington for your free copy of our interesting and colorful booklet, Tree Farming in the Pacific Northwest.*

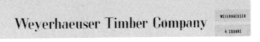

Weyerhaeuser Timber Company

This advertisement appears in *The Saturday Evening Post*, issue of May 15; *U.S. News*, May 14; and *The Farm Journal* for June, 1954.

Exhibit 5

1966 FORESTRY CAMPAIGN MAGAZINE SCHEDULE

Publication	Insertions	Cost
Atlantic	6	$ 22,950
Harper's Magazine	6	22,950
Look	9	432,990
Saturday Review	6	29,400
Scholastic Magazines	8	65,280
Time	9	223,750
Total		$797,320

Source: 1966 Publisher's Information Bureau records

Exhibit 6

1955 "MEN IN FORESTRY" AD

This advertisement appears in *The Saturday Evening Post*, issue of September 24; *U.S. News*, September 23; and *The Farm Journal* for October, 1955.

Exhibit 7

1963 "NEW IDEAS IN WOOD" AD

COYOTE FAMILY on a Weyerhaeuser tree farm. These lands will provide wood, water, & other benefits in endless supply—and an expanding variety of products developed b

A new idea in wood from Weyerhaeuser tree   s...

Kraft honeycomb in unlimited lengths is the result of an exclusive Weyerhaeuser   s. The availability of any desired continuous l   w uses for honeycomb. This versatile product is   vidths, thicknesses and cell sizes, too. All dimens   lerances.

Combined with its ability to furnish great strength without weight, Weyerhaeuser kraft honeycomb offers exceptional advantages as a core material for wall and roof panels, doors, furniture and other products. It is also an excellent material for packaging dividers.

The new dimensions added to honeycomb are typical of our continuing effort to make Weyerhaeuser products — and forests — more useful to people everywhere. For additional information, write for a free folder: Weyerhaeuser Company, Box A, Tacoma 1, Washington.

Symbol of quality in the world of wood   Weyerhaeu

Exhibit 8

1965 "WEYERHAEUSER ON THE MOVE" AD

Osprey on a Weyerhaeuser tree farm where trees are grown in repeated crops

Some people think our business is trees
(that's only half the story)

Ask almost anybody what Weyerhaeuser does and he's apt to tell you we grow trees for lumber. Right. We're producing more lumber than ever. Yet we make so many other things from wood that they account for nearly 75% of our business. Today we're literally taking the trees apart and transforming the wood fibers into products many people never dreamed would come from wood. Capacitor papers for satellites.

Molded parts as hard as many metals for cars. Industrial chemicals. Business and specialty papers. Plastic coated paperboard milk cartons. Frozen food containers. Exotic plywoods.

The list of Weyerhaeuser wood products now numbers into the thousands.

And new products are coming so fast we can't even imagine what we'll be making 100 years from now. But thanks to our policy of growing trees in perpetual crop cycles we *do* know this.

Whatever our researchers *do* develop in new products, we'll always have the wood fiber to make them.

If you would like additional information about the new things that come from wood, send for our free booklet, "From Weyerhaeuser tree farms to you." Write Weyerhaeuser Company, Box A2, Tacoma, Washington 98401.

A full range of paneling to fit any budget

Colorful cartons for almost every product you eat, use or wear

Weyerhaeuser paper serves you wherever you are

Weyerhaeuser
Pulp, paper, chemicals, packaging, lumber, plywood

This advertisement will appear in: *Look*, June 15; *Time*, June 11; *Saturday Review*, June 19; *Harper's*, July.

Exhibit 9

1967 HELICOPTER FORESTRY AD

"High Yield Forest" is a service mark of Weyerhaeuser Company.   Orange balloons mark a Weyerhaeuser timber area for helicopter fertilizing.

Helicopter fertilizing is just one way we're making our lands 33% more productive.

This is the new Weyerhaeuser High Yield Forest in action. Its purpose: grow more wood, faster, year after year on our 3.7 million acres of timberland.

Besides aerial fertilizing, High Yield Forestry involves special seed orchards and nurseries. Thinning. And thorough analysis of the soil to determine its tree-growing qualities. Also new planting and harvesting techniques.

High Yield Forestry didn't happen overnight. This revolutionary program took twenty years of research. And the processing of mountains of data through our computers to perfect the right mix of factors to grow, ultimately, 33% more wood on the same land.

Already High Yield Forestry is considered by many to be the most significant improvement in forest manage-

ment since we introduced tree farming 26 years ago. The results will be far reaching. More wood. Better use of land. And a continuous supply of raw material for thousands of wood and paper products.

For more information on the High Yield Forest, write us at Box A-46, Tacoma, Washington 98401. Include *your* zip code.

Weyerhaeuser

Ad No. 223: *Saturday Evening Post*, Sept. 9, 1967; *U.S. News & World Report*, Sept. 11, 1967; *Newsweek*, Sept. 25, 1967; *Saturday Review*, Oct. 21, 1967; *Harper's*, Oct. 1967; *Atlantic*, Oct. 1967; *The Reporter*, Nov. 16, 1967.

Exhibit 10

1966 "CAPABILITIES" AD

The sun never sets on Weyerhaeuser operations.

Around the world and around the clock, Weyerhaeuser is on the move. Only yesterday, we were a Pacific Northwest lumber, plywood and pulp company. Now we're worldwide, making more things out of trees than any other company anywhere. We have 98 plants at home turning out everything from milk cartons to movable partitions. And investments in 25 abroad, making (for example) lingerie boxes in Italy, perfume cartons in France, shipping containers in Guatemala, pulp in Canada and electrical papers in Scotland. We sell more and more of our domestic products abroad, too. Last year one twelfth of our total sales were export. We're opening new distribution centers all over the globe—the latest was in Sydney, Australia. If you'd like to know more about the dynamic, on-the-go Weyerhaeuser, send for our brand-new annual report. Printed on Weyerhaeuser paper, of course. Write us at Box A-71, Tacoma, Washington 98401.

Weyerhaeuser

Exhibit 11

SELECTED VERBATIM COMMENTS FROM 1966 GALLUP AND ROBINSON IMPACT REPORT

"There was a picture of a fox in the forest. It was a typical Weyerhaeuser ad. I didn't read it all, but it must have said something about replacing the trees that they cut down. I always like their ads. Their purpose was to show that the Weyerhaeuser Company is interested in the conservation of the forests— not just destroying the trees that they use. I learned it's a good, reliable company. I think they made a strong case. They are also looking out for the public interest."

"That was a real pretty colored ad. It showed about a million pine trees and a little red fox sitting on a stump right in the foreground. That's all there was—the green trees and the red fox. Oh, it just said something about a computer telling them when to plant trees, I think. That's all I can remember. I don't know any more. I thought it was a real pretty picture. What was the purpose? Beats me. I just got the pleasure of looking at the picture. A strong case for what?"

"It was another pretty, colorful, conservation-type ad. It showed a rolling countryside with young green pine trees and a laughing young fox sitting on a stump. They were talking about replanting and reforesting. I thought that this is progressive lumbering. Their purpose was primarily to sell Weyerhaeuser lumber. Well, we are a conservation-minded family and, of course, I liked it. I think they did make a strong case. They are replacing the normal resource which is their primary product so they can keep in business indefinitely and that, of course, helps the general economy."

APPENDIX A

The 1967 Corporate Advertising TV Study

OBJECTIVES

The TV test had four specific objectives:

— To measure the increase in recognition over the regular print schedule caused by a program-oriented television schedule.

— To measure the increase in recognition over the regular print schedule caused by a spot-oriented television schedule.

— To measure the increase in recognition over the regular print schedule caused by a magazine schedule raised to the dollar expenditure level of the television tests. (Both program and spot TV schedules assumed a $1.5 million annual level of spending, or roughly a 50% increase over the existing level of spending in the print campaign.)

— To evaluate the results of each of the above tests in relation to the regular print schedule and in relation to each other.

METHOD

The findings from the test resulted from before-and-after recognition measures among the adult population in eight metropolitan areas. For the test, these markets were broken down into four pairs. The first market pair viewed Weyerhaeuser commercials only in regularly scheduled programs. The second pair received only spot commercials. The third received the increased magazine exposure, and the fourth pair of markets had only normal print exposure and served as the test control.

The print ads and TV commercials featured Weyerhaeuser's replanting of forests by helicopter seeding and hand planting. The agency creative team attempted to make the print and TV versions as identical as possible. (See Exhibits A-1 and A-2 for the print ad and storyboard of the TV commercial used to convey the helicopter seeding message.)

Matched samples of the adult population were given identical questionnaires immediately prior to and following the six-week test period. Exhibit A-3 contains the questionnaire used in all interviews. The findings were to be presented along a number of recognition and demographic dimensions. (See Exhibit A-4 for the format of selected tables which would present the test findings.)

PRINT AD USED IN 1967 TV TEST

Some days we seed a million trees before your morning coffee break.

Elk flee as a helicopter seeds a new forest on a Weyerhaeuser tree farm

The pages in this magazine came from a harvested tree. So did the milk cartons in your kitchen, the lumber in your home and the beautiful paneling in your den.

Replacing the trees you use is a man-size job. For you consume wood at an incredible pace.

Sometimes we sow seed from helicopters to speed the work along. In other cases, we leave seed trees close by to restock an area naturally. Or set out millions of young trees by hand.

We call it reforestation — restoring the trees on the scattered spots we harvest every year. This prompt reforestation keeps our land constantly covered with trees of all ages, from tiny seedlings to large, mature timber.

As a result, there always will be beautiful forests, water, wildlife and recreation for you and yours on our tree farms. Today. Tomorrow. Generation after generation.

If you'd like to know more about what we're doing to help keep America beautiful and still meet today's demand for forest products, just write us. Ask for "Tree Farm to You." It's free. Box A-36, Tacoma, Washington 98401.

▲ Weyerhaeuser . . . *where the future grows*

Ad No. 209: *Look*, Sept. 20, 1966; *Time*, Sept. 9, 1966; *Saturday Review*, Sept. 10, 1966; *Harper's Magazine*; and *Atlantic*, October, 1966.

Exhibit A-2
DESCRIPTION OF COMMERCIAL USED IN 1967 TV TEST

Video	*Audio*
Forest scene with deer grazing.	*Quiet of woods broken by calls of birds.*
Close-up of deer alert to sound. Deer bound away as helicopter draws near.	*Sound of helicopter first softly, as from a a distance, then louder and louder.*
Close-up of helicopter with foresters inside.	*Announcer*: These men are farmers of the forest. Their job . . . growing continuous crops of timber on Weyerhaeuser tree farms.
Camera closes in on seeds spewing from helicopter	They sow the seeds of tomorrow's trees with the promise of . . .
As helicopter pulls away, the lush forest below is revealed.	a harvest more bountiful than nature alone could ever produce.
Logging truck snakes down a mountain road.	[*Sound of helicopter fades into truck sound.*] These modern tree farms provide an endless supply of raw materials . . .
Shots of sawmill with slab being cut from giant log.	for Weyerhaeuser Mills . . . world wide producers of . . .
Carpenter putting exterior plywood on skeleton of house.	lumber and plywood . . .
School room scene.	paper . . .
Containers being loaded at dock.	packaging . . .
Arched beams at a construction site.	more than five thousand useful products made from trees.
Forest scene with tree farm sign.	Weyerhaeuser – the company that grows today's forests for tomorrow's needs.
Weyerhaeuser logo and name.	The mark of quality on products made from wood.

Exhibit A-3

QUESTIONNAIRE FOR THE 1967 TV TEST

MARKET DYNAMICS, INC.
Princeton, New Jersey

Hello. My name is _____ . I'm an interviewer for Market Dynamics Research
Company of Princeton, New Jersey. We're conducting a survey throughout the country and
we'd like to ask you just a few questions. First...

		U.S. PLYWOOD	GEORGIA PACIFIC	WEYERHAEUSER (Pronounced "Wear-Houser")	OTHERS (Specify)
1a.	Would you please name as many companies as you can in the forest products industry? (PROBE: Any others?)	1	2	3	_____ _____ _____ _____
(FOR EACH NOT MENTIONED, ASK):					X NONE
b.	Have you ever heard of a company called _____?				
	YES	1	5	9	
	NO	2	6	0	
	DON'T KNOW	3	7	X	

(FOR EACH CIRCLED IN BOX ABOVE, ASK):

		U.S. PLYWOOD	GEORGIA PACIFIC	WEYERHAEUSER
2.	What are the principal products you associate with (COMPANY)? (PROBE: What others?)	_____ _____ Y DON'T KNOW	_____ _____ Y DON'T KNOW	_____ _____ Y DON'T KNOW

3.	How involved would you say (COMPANY) is in programs of forest conservation? Would you say (COMPANY) is...		U.S.PLYWOOD	GEORGIA PACIFIC	WEYERHAEUSER
		DEEPLY INVOLVED------	1	1	1
		SOMEWHAT INVOLVED----	2	2	2
		SLIGHTLY INVOLVED or-	3	3	3
		NOT AT ALL INVOLVED--	4	4	4
		DON'T KNOW-	5	5	5

(ASK EVERYONE)

4a.	Do you recall having recently seen or heard any advertising about forest products companies?	1 YES ⟶ GO ON TO Q. 4b 2 NO ⟶ SKIP TO Q. 6

b. What firm or firms was this advertising for? _____
   (PROBE: Any others?)

(FOR EACH FIRM MENTIONED, ASK):

c.	Where did you see or hear the advertising for (COMPANY)?			
		TELEVISION	1	1
		NEWSPAPERS	2	2
		MAGAZINES	3	3
		RADIO	4	4
		OTHER (Specify) _____		

d.	What did the advertising for (COMPANY) say or show? (PROBE: What else?)	_____ _____ _____ _____	_____ _____ _____ _____

Continued.....

Exhibit A-3 (cont.)

(IF WEYERHAEUSER NOT MENTIONED IN Q. 4b, ASK):

5a. Do you recall seeing or hearing any advertising for the Weyerhaeuser Company?

    1 YES ⟶ GO ON TO Q. 5b

    2 NO ⟶ SKIP TO INSTRUCTIONS
    3 DON'T KNOW ⟶ PRECEDING Q. 6

b. Where did you see or hear the advertising for Weyerhaeuser?

    1 TELEVISION   4 RADIO
    2 NEWSPAPERS   5 OTHER (Specify)
    3 MAGAZINES _____

c. What did the advertising for Weyerhaeuser say or show? _____

> IF "REFORESTATION BY HELICOPTER SEEDING OR BY HAND PLANTING" MENTIONED ANYWHERE, SKIP TO Q. 7. IN <u>ALL OTHER CASES</u>, GO ON TO Q. 6.

6a. Do you recall seeing or hearing any advertising that talked about the replanting of forests by hand planting or by helicopter seeding?

    1 YES ⟶ GO ON TO Q. 6b   2 NO
    3 DON'T KNOW ⟶ SKIP TO Q. 7a

b. Where did you see or hear this advertising?

    1 TELEVISION   2 NEWSPAPERS   3 MAGAZINES
    4 RADIO   5 OTHERS (Specify) _____

c. Can you recall whose advertising this was?

    1 YES ⟶ Whose advertising was it? _____
    2 NO

d. What can you tell me about this advertising? (PROBE: What else did the advertising say or show? _____

Now just a question or two for classification purposes only.

7a. Into which of these age groups do you fit? Are you...

    1 UNDER 20   2 IN YOUR 20'S   3 IN YOUR 30'S
    4 IN YOUR 40'S <u>or</u>   5 50 OR OVER

b. What is the occupation of the head of this household? (BE SPECIFIC)

_____ (JOB)   _____ (INDUSTRY)

c. Is your family's total yearly income...

    6 UNDER $7,500 ⟶ Is that..........   1 UNDER $5,000, <u>or</u>
    2 OVER $5,000

    <u>or</u>

                             3 UNDER $10,000,
    7 OVER $7,500 ⟶ Is that..........   4 BETWEEN $10,000 AND $15,000, <u>or</u>
    5 OVER $15,000

d. INDICATE: 1 MALE   2 FEMALE

8a. May I have your name please? _____
b. And your telephone number? _____
c. City _____ State _____

THANK YOU VERY MUCH FOR YOUR COOPERATION

INTERVIEWED BY: _____ DATE: _____

Exhibit A-4

FORMAT OF SELECTED TABLES FOR PRESENTATION OF TV TEST FINDINGS

Table 1

Awareness of Forest Products Companies — Weyerhaeuser

	TV Program			TV Spot			Magazine			Control		
	Pre	Post	Diff	Pre	Post	Diff	Pre	Post	Diff	Pre	Post	Diff
Total No. Interviews: %	%	%		%	%		%	%		%	%	
Total												
Men												
Women												
Under 30												
30-39												
40-49												
50 & over												
Under $6,000												
$6 - $7,999												
$8 - $9,999												
$10,000+												

QUESTION: WOULD YOU PLEASE NAME AS MANY COMPANIES AS YOU CAN IN THE FOREST PRODUCT INDUSTRY? ANY OTHERS? HAVE YOU EVER HEARD OF A COMPANY CALLED _____ ?

Exhibit A-4 (cont.)

Table 2

Extent of Weyerhaeuser Involvement in Forest Conservation

	TV Program			TV Spot			Magazine			Control		
	Pre	Post	Diff	Pre	Post	Diff	Pre	Post	Diff	Pre	Post	Diff
Total Aware of No. Weyerhaeuser: %	%	%		%	%		%	%		%	%	
Weyerhaeuser is:												
Deeply involved	%	%		%	%		%	%		%	%	
Somewhat involved												
Slightly involved												
Not at all involved												

QUESTION: HOW DEEPLY WOULD YOU SAY WEYERHAEUSER IS IN PROGRAMS OF FOREST CONSERVATION? WOULD YOU SAY IT IS DEEPLY INVOLVED, SOMEWHAT INVOLVED, SLIGHTLY INVOLVED, OR NOT AT ALL INVOLVED?

Exhibit A-4 (cont.)

Table 3
Recalled Weyerhaeuser Advertising

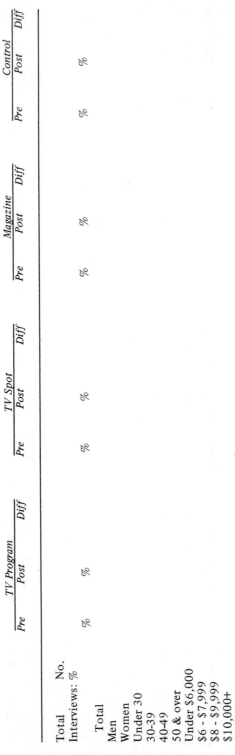

	TV Program			TV Spot			Magazine			Control		
	Pre	Post	Diff	Pre	Post	Diff	Pre	Post	Diff	Pre	Post	Diff
Total No. Interviews: %	%	%		%	%		%	%		%	%	
Total												
Men												
Women												
Under 30												
30-39												
40-49												
50 & over												
Under $6,000												
$6 - $7,999												
$8 - $9,999												
$10,000+												

QUESTION: DO YOU RECALL HAVING RECENTLY SEEN OR HEARD ANY ADVERTISING ABOUT FOREST PRODUCTS COMPANIES? WHAT FIRM OR FIRMS WAS THIS ADVERTISING FOR? DO YOU RECALL SEEING OR HEARING ANY ADVERTISING FOR THE WEYERHAEUSER COMPANY?

QUESTIONS

1.   Was the decision to develop the new campaign wise? Why? Why not?

2.   Appraise the specific elements of the new program—target audience, copy theme, media, and the like.

3.   Appraise the test design. What other evaluation, if any, would you recommend? What criteria would you use for "success"/"failure"?

Market Identification and Media Strategy

PART II

Beech
Aircraft Corporation (B)

A light aircraft manufacturer looks at the specific advertising programs (markets, media, messages) that it has developed for twelve separate target groups.

In 1968 Beech Aircraft Corporation, a leading light-aircraft manufacturer, employed a 12-pronged segmented advertising approach to reach the various market groups influential in the purchase of the company's aircraft. [See Beech Aircraft Corporation (A) for background information on the company, its advertising, and the general aviation industry.] Mr. Jack Dick-Peddie, Account Executive of the Beech account for the Bruce B. Brewer Advertising Agency of Kansas City, commented on this approach:

> This segmented idea has evolved for two reasons. First, we're trying to service the specific needs of each specific market by directing each program straight at the heart of the market. This means a carefully thought-out copy approach for each market, presented in the media which best reach each market. Second, as Beech introduces new products over time, we find ourselves in new markets with new needs which we haven't had to hit previously. For instance, the air-commuter market and the aerospace market are both quite new for us, and they dictate an approach completely different from anything we've ever used to sell executive aircraft.

The 1968 Beech advertising budget of roughly $1.8 million was devoted entirely to national print media. In addition, the company spent approximately 10% of this sum to produce sales-promotion aids and literature, along with another 15% for various trade shows, exhibits, and sales-promotion meetings; the annual Beech International Sales Spectacular alone was budgeted at $110,000. Furthermore, as in most years, a contingency fund of $20,000–$50,000 was budgeted to instill some degree of flexibility into the schedule and to allow for unforeseen needs arising during the year.

The 1968 segmented advertising program was first presented on October 24, 1967, at the International Sales Spectacular, where a presentation was made by company and agency executives to Beech sales representatives. Exhibit 1 summarizes the media plans and budget allocations for each of the 12 markets.

Each of these markets is discussed here in some detail, based on the company-agency presentation.

THE TWELVE BEECH AUDIENCES

    1. Business Executive Market Since 95% of Beech sales went to companies rather than individuals, this was regarded as the single most important market segment for Beech advertising. Mr. William Alexander of the Brewer agency spoke of this audience to the Beech sales representatives:

> This is the audience that represents the greatest sales potential in your marketing area. These are the corporate executives—the company presidents and administrative officers—the top-income people who guide the affairs and destinies of their companies.
>
> Our largest advertising program is directed specifically to these key businessmen in your own particular area . . . the decision-makers of commerce and industry.
>
> We know how to reach these people with advertising because research shows us which publications they read. By far the best-read publication by business executives is *Time*. And so we use *Time* not just once or twice. . .but throughout the year.
>
> In addition, we use extensively the next three leading publications: *Newsweek, Business Week,* and *Wall Street Journal.* The combination and overlap of these publications covers *every* key business prospect in your market.
>
> These people have a variety of interests and a great variety of experience. Some are very sophisticated about airplanes. They own and use them in their business. Some even have fleets of corporate aircraft. But others have never owned an airplane in their business and know very little about them.
>
> So our advertising must talk to both groups . . . telling them how a Beechcraft will solve their own particular problems.

    See Exhibit 2 for a representative *Time* advertisement directed toward the Business Executive market.

    2. Executive Prestige Market This campaign, first instituted in 1968, carried a corporate image message to basically the same business executive audiences. Whereas the Business Executive ads emphasized product features of specific Beech models, the Executive Prestige ads spoke of the company in general. Bill Alexander elaborated on this distinction:

> *Fortune! National Geographic!* Magazines that are synonymous with quality and success. What better place for the airplanes that also stand for quality and success.
>
> Exciting and colorful . . . these publications command the respect of all of us. Beechcraft advertisements here are written and tailored to the magazine and to the audience . . . thoughtful, prosperous people who read the magazines to learn how to do things right.
>
> When it comes to flying—owning a Beechcraft is doing it right! And while

these ads bear a strong family resemblance to other messages directed to executives, they have slight and subtle differences to make them more campatible with the editorial content of the magazine and the readers' mood. The ads point out the craftsmanship and quality of all Beechcrafts and the leading role the company plays in the field of general aviation. There is a slight softening of product sell so that we can strengthen our corporate story.

We'll have a total of 8 four-color pages in *Fortune* and *National Geographic.* And along with this healthy frequency is another important fact. These magazines are often filed for future reading and reference . . . so the ads work for a long, long time! And the *National Geographic* ads present another nice bonus . . . they will be read by over a quarter of a million important prospects in countries overseas.

Exhibit 3 is an Executive Prestige ad.

3. Corporate Market   This campaign had three primary purposes. First it sought to impress the financial community with Beech's corporate strength and reputation, and thereby increase "Wall Street's" willingness to finance corporate ventures in which Beechcrafts figured predominantly. This approval by the financial community was considered to be particularly crucial in aiding the formation of new commuter airlines. [See Beech Aircraft Corporation (A) for details on the air-commuter market.] In addition, many individuals instrumental in establishing commuter airlines did not have an extensive background in aviation. Beech executives thought that familiarizing these entrepreneurs with Beech through corporate image advertising would maximize the probability of selecting Beech-crafts for the new airlines. Finally, image advertising of this sort was believed to have a favorable effect on the price of Beech common stock.

Jack Dick-Peddie commented on these ads:

> The Corporate audience overlaps and augments the business-executive market. It includes the executives, but it adds another group that are key and important people in your community . . . your bankers, the finance people, the stockbrokers, the CPA's, the investors, the corporate treasurers.
>
> We use a leading national magazine specifically designed to appeal to this particular market—*Forbes.* This is a magazine of business, finance, and investments. And to this particular audience we tell a different story. We talk about Beech Aircraft Corporation—the company itself rather than the product.
>
> Our special series of ads to this audience tells the story of Beech diversi-fication—Beech integrity—Beech capabilities—Beech pioneering and, most of all, Beech leadership. We leave no doubt in the minds of this audience that the people who make Beechcrafts—or any other Beech products, whether they operate on land or in the air or in outer space—are the finest products that man can make or money can buy. Even though the ads in *Forbes* are not Beechcraft product ads, they are working for you [salesmen] con-stantly. . .impressing the key people in your community you deal with, or the people who are influential advisors to your customers and prospects.

See Exhibit 4 for an example of an ad from this campaign.

4. Commuter Airline Market   Beech had sold a number of Queen Airs to this growing market; and in 1968 introduced the Model 99, specifically designed to meet the needs of commuter airlines. Jack Dick-Peddie explained the Beech approach:

> We've had to learn a brand-new language to properly address this new and different audience with Beechcraft advertising. Beech is now in the airline business—impressively—with a brand-new model that solves commuter airline problems as they have never been solved before. The new world the Beechcraft 99 opens up staggers the imagination.
>
> Our audience for this new product includes air-taxi operators, feeder-airline companies, and major airlines, as well as investors and businessmen who probably never thought of going into the airline business.
>
> We'll talk *their* language in *their* major publications . . . *Air Transport World* . . . *Airport Services Management* . . . special sections of *B/CA* [Business & Commercial Aviation] . . . *American Aviation* . . . *Airline Management and Marketing* . . . and to the investors and unknown prospects, in the *Wall Street Journal*.
>
> The benefit of this advertising goes to every Beechcraft salesman directly and indirectly. You know the direct benefit. And the indirect one is of equal importance. The more airlines using Beechcraft airliners, the more thousands of corporate executives "sampling" Beechcraft travel in Beechcraft airliners. That means greater endorsement for Beechcrafts—above all other brands—for private or corporately owned aircraft. . . .
>
> So again, this specialized advertising to specialized market audiences has a direct benefit in the marketplace of your town, your trading area, the place where you do your business.

Exhibit 5 contains an ad to the commuter airline audience.

5. General Aviation Market   This audience consisted of private pilots and individuals who personally owned airplanes. Jack Dick-Peddie commented:

> Those wonderful guys who love flying so much that it becomes a major hobby . . . they are the lifeblood of our industry.
>
> The young guy who learns to fly, and then buys his own new or used airplane, is also the aggressive, pioneering type of person who quite often winds up on the management level of his company . . . and thus becomes a key influence in the purchase of a company airplane. As we all know, the list of private pilots and airplane owners is growing by leaps and bounds. Today, there are more than half a million pilots in America . . . that's one pilot in every 100 families in your own city. This huge and growing audience constitutes our basic growth potential for the next 10 to 20 years. And rest assured . . . we're not missing one single member of that important audience!
>
> We reach them with a combination of the leading magazines devoted to the world of flying. We're in every single issue of the biggest publication in the field . . . *Flying Magazine.* In addition, we're in *American Aviation* and *Air Facts.* We're also in the special-interest flying magazines such as *Flying Farmer* . . . *Flying Physician* . . . *Flying Dentist.* We're in the important annuals such as the *Travelguide* and the *Flying Annual & Pilot's Guide.*

But the really *big* point is that we're not just *in* these leading publications—*we dominate them!*

In these flying publications Beech primarily employed four- and six-page color inserts called Sell-O-Chromes which had been highly successful.

Exhibit 6 contains a spread advertisement to this market.

6. Sportsman Market Bill Alexander discussed this market with the Beech sales representatives:

> This is our chance to talk to the top sportsmen in your market—the action crowd—the people who get out and do things. An audience that likes a good time . . . to go places . . . this crew likes sports and travel and they have the money to do it.
>
> They are the readers of *Sports Illustrated* magazine. We think so much of this market's potential that we prepare special full-page ads just for them.
>
> These are exciting ads. We tell the reader that good times come easy and more often in a Beechcraft, and we use big pictures showing pilots and friends on their way to a favorite resort . . . a golf tournament . . . scuba diving . . . hunting . . . a college football game . . . if you think this isn't a growing market, try to land some Saturday in the Fall at a town like Norman, Oklahoma . . . it makes JFK [Airport] look like a deactivated Air Force base.
>
> There's also a serious side to these ads. We point out that the same plane that means so much fun can also mean business profit during the week.

See Exhibit 7 for a "good times come easy and more often in a Beechcraft" ad.

7. Professional Pilot Market These ads were directed toward the non-company executives who flew corporate aircraft professionally. Bill Alexander explained:

> This is an exclusive pilot group. They are a sophisticated group. They are knowledgeable. And they have top influence with their managements when it comes to deciding which corporate airplane to buy.
>
> To the pro pilot audience you talk a different language. And so do your advertisements.
>
> Our Beechcraft messages reach this special group in such publications as *Business & Commercial Aviation* and *Professional Pilot* magazines. We put heavier advertising emphasis on our larger corporate aircraft.
>
> And in addition to the special ads we run the most appropriate 4-page and 6-page Sell-O-Chromes. The 1968 campaign—with the addition of totally new airplanes such as the Duke, the 99 executive version, and the B90—makes our program bigger, stronger, and more powerful than ever.

See Exhibit 8 for an ad directed to the professional pilot.

8. Special Industries Market Jack Dick-Peddie explained Beech's return to this market, based on the result of a 1967 study described in Beech Aircraft Corporation (A):

We are constantly searching for new fields to conquer, new audiences to play to that might prove to be better than average prospects for Beechcrafts. We know—statistically—that our other programs reach the leaders in *all* industries. We know, for example, that *Time* magazine by itself reaches more contractors, bankers, doctors, lawyers, and merchants than a combination of the two leading trade journals in any industry.

But why not try a direct approach? Why not probe some industries that are especially important to Beech, talk to them in their own languages in their own industry publications to see if we *can* uncover some new fields to conquer?

Last year we did just that with ads to the insurance, banking, construction, lumber, petroleum, and textile industries. We checked the fan mail and learned that one industry in particular—the construction industry—showed a remarkable interest in Beechcrafts.

This year, we're going to take this program one step further to this industry. Using the two leading trade magazines, *Engineering News Record* and *Construction Methods and Equipment,* we will run special ads talking this industry's special language, closely identifying Beechcrafts with their specialized uses within the industry.

Exhibit 9 contains an ad directed to the construction industry through a vertical trade publication.

9. Women's Prestige Market   These ads were directed toward the woman, not as a decision-*maker,* but as a decision-*influencer.* Bill Alexander elaborated:

No one knows better than you [salesmen] the importance of women in today's marketplace. Women are not only important in influencing the purchase of a Beechcraft—either for business or pleasure—but they can also be influential in preventing the sale of a Beechcraft. Many years ago we found it of vital importance to contact the feminine audience—the leaders among women in America—the top women in their fields in industry, in the arts, in social affairs.

And the combination of magazines that best reaches this particular audience is *Vogue, Harper's Bazaar,* and *Town & Country.* Every single month we talk to these influential women about Beechcraft ownership—the joy, the pleasure, the fun, the prestige, the utility that comes with the ownership of a Beechcraft.

We point out that Beechcraft ownership is not only a money-making proposition for business executives but a badge of success—a mark of distinction—and the vital and timesaving utility it offers in the furtherance of important activities whether business, civic, social, or personal. Our messages are read every month by the women in your community, and the top women in business throughout your market.

Exhibit 10 contains a Women's Prestige ad.

10. Aerospace and Military Market   This campaign began in 1965 to convince the defense/aerospace market of Beech's technical competence in areas other than light commercial aircraft design and manufacture. Beech employed Sell-O-Chromes in this market in much the same manner as it did in the General

Aviation market. By 1968, these ads were serving a variety of purposes as noted by Bill Alexander:

> To talk to the very sophisticated and diversified audience of military and aerospace people, we will use a total of 9 different publications in 1968.
>
> The combination of these publications blankets *all* the military services, the scientists, engineers, and technicians of the vast NASA complexes . . . the Department of Defense, and the key corporations that are suppliers to military and aerospace services.
>
> *How does this advertising benefit you as a Beechcraft salesman?* This is a long-range program that benefits you in many ways.
>
> Every year thousands of military pilots who have flown Beechcrafts in the service become civilians and enter into business. Many of these become corporation pilots and influential in the designation of the aircraft their companies will own.
>
> Other key military and civilian personnel in these services at *administrative* levels leave and become key *administrative* personnel in industry and commerce in your market. And the more they have been presold on Beechcraft contributions to the military services, the more Beechcraft influence they will exert in commercial decisions.
>
> And still further, Beech pioneering and experience in the sophisticated fields of aerospace—its advertised reputation in missiles and rockets, cryogenics, the Gemini and Apollo programs, and other highly skilled technologies in probing outer space—add extra intrinsic value to every Beechcraft airplane you sell. Our messages make it clear to prospects that if Beech can do all those sophisticated things, "no wonder they build better airplanes!"
>
> And, of course, the military endorsement of Beechcrafts should be one of your strongest selling points. It should be an especially important competitive point in such models as the *Baron,* and the *King Air* and *Queen Air* category planes, all of which are bought in quantity by the military services in virtually off-the-shelf configuration—chosen by these experts against the strongest kind of competition!

See Exhibit 11 for an ad directed to the Aerospace and Military market.

11. International Business Market Overseas, Beech used a simplified segmentation approach similar to its domestic market segmentation. Owing to internal constraints on the advertising budget, however, the segmentation was limited to a businessman/pilot distinction. Jack Dick-Peddie explained how Beech approached the international businessman:

> To a certain degree, we approach this businessman the same way. But there are subtle differences. The psychological approach is different. Selling techniques are different. There are different reasons—or justifications—for buying Beechcrafts. And our new 1968 international campaigns will reflect these differences.
>
> The major difference, of course, is in language. So we play to each international audience in its native tongue. In Deutschland, for instance, our ads appear in *Der Spiegel.* This is the German equivalent of *Time* and is the number one medium for reaching the German businessman.

For the same reason, *L'Express* carried the Beechcraft message in France. In Brazil, it's *Visao*. And in the remainder of Latin America we use a special Spanish-language edition of *Life, Life en Español*. For the Australian audience, and the thousands of European executives who use English as their business language, we also run impressive campaigns in special international editions of *Time*. In addition, many of the fine publications we use domestically have important and significant distribution to English-speaking businessmen throughout the world.

In keeping with the tremendous sales potential in our overseas markets, the advertising budget that Beech management has set aside for its international effort in 1968 is by far the largest in history. This means that we'll be able to play to *new* audiences in *new* markets and increase our impact on the markets we are now in.

See Exhibit 12 for an English-language version of an international ad. Beech traditionally let overseas agencies translate the Beech ads into the language of each local country.

12. International Pilot Market This final Beech market was the international version of the domestic general aviation market. Jack Dick-Peddie commented:

Pilots are pilots the world over. We talk the same pilot language internationally that we do domestically. But we try to do it in their native tongue.

Interavia is one of our most important international aviation magazines. It is distributed throughout the free world and printed in the language of the country. We also use other foreign-language publications such as *Flug Revue* and *Revista Aerea*. In England and Australia, we use *Flight International*. This year we plan to expand our efforts in Canada beyond the reliable *Canadian Aviation*. Also it should be noted that many of our domestic magazines such as *Flying* have important distribution in English-speaking overseas markets.

Exhibit 13 is an English-language version of an ad to this market.

CAMPAIGN EVALUATION

The Beech advertising team relied heavily on Starch Readership scores to evaluate the effectiveness of the company's advertisements. [Further details on Beech's evaluation of its advertising program appear in Beech Aircraft Corporation (A).] Exhibit 14 includes Starch scores for ads run in general business publications during 1967-68. Executives were especially pleased with the performance of the *Time* ads, which consistently pulled higher "Read-Most" ratings than the great majority of ads by other *Time* advertisers, many of whom were regarded by these executives as very sophisticated advertisers. Exhibit 15 highlights the performance of the company's Sell-O-Chrome inserts in flying journals.

PRIORITIES AMONG THE MARKETS

When asked to assign priorities to Beech's different markets, Mr. Dick-Peddie commented that the top priority markets would have to be the Business Executive and General Aviation Markets, in that order. Expanding on this comment, he noted:

> The Business Executive Market includes over 350,000 firms with the need for and ability to buy a corporate plane. Our future growth has simply got to come from here. It's all a matter of how effectively we can educate them and convince them of their need. Meanwhile, the great bulk of our present sales are going to the flyers and present owners represented by the General Aviation group. Thus we certainly can't slack off here one bit.

When asked what areas would be cut first in the event of a budget slice, he expressed the difficulty of the proposition:

> It's pretty tough to drop anything. I guess the first thing to go would be our contingency special budgets which we reserve for problems that arise with a particular line, or other things that come up unexpectedly for which we want a quick boost. This would be the first thing to get the ax simply because it can be dropped the most easily.

Beech Aircraft Corporation (B)

LIST OF EXHIBITS

Exhibit	Contents
1	The Twelve Beech Markets for 1968
2	Business Executive Market Ad: "Why does this airplane outsell its nearest competitor 5 to 1?"
3	Executive Prestige Market Ad: "Try the hotel . . . the fried chicken is great!"
4	Corporate Market Ad: "Controlled Rate-of-Climb is important in a company's growth . . . just as it is in airplanes and missiles."
5	Commuter Airline Market Ad: "Today's newest airliner is already indispensable."
6	General Aviation Market Ad: "Introducing the exciting new 6-place Beechcraft Bonanza 36!"
7	Sportsman Market Ad: "Good times come easy and more often in a Beechcraft Musketeer."
8	Professional Pilot Market Ad: "The new King Air B90 now 15 ways better!"
9	Special Industries Market Ad: "Hard-working construction men speak out for the workingman's airplane!"
10	Women's Prestige Market Ad: "Easy Street"
11	Aerospace/Military Market Ad: "Six reasons why Beech was selected for this important Apollo assignment."
12	International Business Market Ad: "Why have so many important people been waiting for the Beechcraft Duke?"
13	International Pilot Market Ad: "Why do so many flying schools use Beechcraft?"
14	Starch Readership Scores for Beech Ads in General Business Publications
15	Starch Scores for Beech Sell-O-Chrome: 1966-68

Exhibit 1

THE TWELVE BEECH MARKETS FOR 1968

Market	Copy Thrust	Publications Used	Dominant Presentation	Frequency	Cost
1. Business Executive	Beechcraft is a wise business investment.	Time	Color spread	8	$ 501,837
			B&W spread	7	
		Newsweek	Color spread	1	116,288
		Business Week	B&W spread	3	
			Color spread	1	100,728
		Wall Street Journal	B&W spread	5	71,395
			B&W ½-page	11	$ 790,248
2. Executive Prestige	Corporate image directed at business executive audience.	National Geographic	Color page	4	$ 112,855
		Fortune	Color page	4	50,220
					$ 163,075
3. Corporate	Corporate image directed at financial community.	Forbes	B&W spread	3	47,240
			B&W page	1	$ 47,240
4. Commuter Airline	Model 99 is the first aircraft designed specifically to meet the needs of the commuter airline industry.	Wall Street Journal	B&W ½-page	3	$ 28,558
		Airline Management and Marketing	B&W spread	3	7,890
		American Aviation	B&W spread	3	6,459
		Air Transport World	B&W spread	3	6,163
		Airport Services Management	B&W spread	3	3,277
		Business/Commerical Aviation	B&W spread	3	3,225
					$ 55,572

Exhibit 1 (cont.)

Market	Copy Thrust	Publications Used	Dominant Presentation	Frequency	Cost
5. General Aviation	Beechcraft high-performance product characteristics emphasized to owner/pilots.	Flying	Color spread	1	
			SOC*	8	
			B&W page	9	$ 91,101
		American Aviation	Color spread	1	
			SOC	5	
			B&W spread	7	
			B&W page	1	$ 32,509
			B&W spread	12	5,400
		Air Facts	Color spread	1	
		Flying Farmer	SOC	4	
			B&W page	1	3,968
		Flying Physician	B&W spread	4	720
		Flying Dentist	B&W spread	4	360
					$ 134,058
6. Sportsman	Good times come easily and more often in a Beechcraft; emphasizes pleasure uses of Beechcraft.	Sports Illustrated	B&W page	5	$ 53,245
7. Professional Pilot	Heavy emphasis on technical superiority of Beech corporate twins.	Business/Commercial Aviation	Color spread	2	
			SOC	6	
			B&W spread	5	
			B&W page	1	$ 44,320

Exhibit 1 (cont.)

Market	Copy Thrust	Publications Used	Dominant Presentation	Frequency	Cost
		Professional Pilot	SOC	2	
			B&W spread	4	6,708
		Flight	Color spread	2	
			SOC	6	
			B&W spread	9	
			B&W page	1	24,153
					$ 75,181
8. Special Industries	Specialized uses for Beechcrafts within the construction industry.	*Engineering News Record*	B&W page	4	$ 7,260
		Construction Methods and Equipment	B&W page	4	6,040
					$ 13,300
9. Women's Prestige	Corporate image; the prestige of Beech owner- ship.	*Harper's Bazaar*	B&W page	4	21,840
		Vogue	B&W page	4	21,840
		Town & Country	B&W page	4	12,672
					$ 56,352
10. Aerospace and Military	Beech is a skilled defense and aerospace contractor.	9 military/aerospace journals	SOC	57	$ 241,906
11. International	Same as 1 to overseas audience.	14 international business publications	B&W page	86	$ 146,608
12. International Pilot	Same as 5 to overseas audience.	9 international flying journals	B&W page	62	$ 28,005
Total					$1,804,790

*Sell-O-Chromes: 4- and 6-page color inserts produced by Beech both for insertion in flying journals and for distribution as promotional leaflets.

Exhibit 2

BUSINESS EXECUTIVE MARKET AD:
"WHY DOES THIS AIRPLANE OUTSELL ITS NEAREST COMPETITOR 5 to 1?"

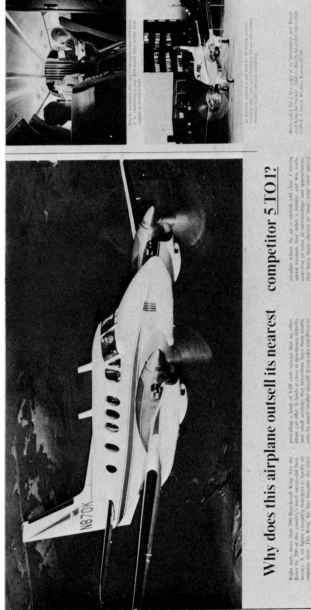

Exhibit 3

EXECUTIVE PRESTIGE MARKET AD:
"TRY THE HOTEL . . . THE FRIED CHICKEN IS GREAT!"

As advertised in *Fortune* and *National Geographic*.

Exhibit 4

CORPORATE MARKET AD:
"CONTROLLED RATE-OF-CLIMB IS IMPORTANT IN A COMPANY'S GROWTH . . . JUST AS IT IS IN AIRPLANES AND MISSILES."

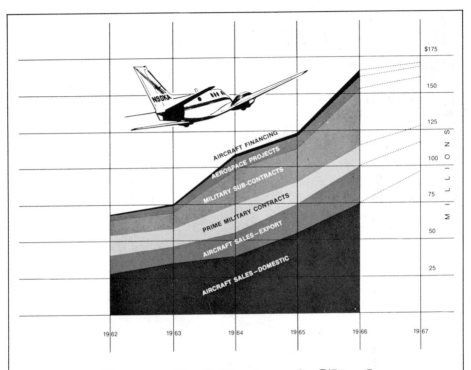

Controlled Rate-of-Climb

is important in a company's growth...just as it is in airplanes and missiles:

There are many advantages in diversified sources of corporate income. Especially true if they are growth incomes. And even better if they can grow in healthy relationship to each other. *Long-range planning by its management* has helped Beech to maintain its various incomes in continuously orderly proportions.

The soundness of Beech's long-range programming is reflected in the above chart. Not only has Beech grown at a rapid rate, in each of its rapidly growing fields, but each income volume, as it grows, has maintained its own proper ratio to the total.

This is a major reason why Beech growth is a healthy growth—and why Beech has provided its stockholders with a continuous high earnings ratio, as well as increased sales.

And the future looks bright in each of Beech's operating areas. General Aviation continues to grow. Business flying, in which Beech is the pioneering leader, has more than doubled its mileage in the last 10 years—and based on current growth rate, should double again in the next 5 years! (World wide as well as domestically.)

In the new rapid development of third level airlines Beech, again, is a pioneer and industry leader with its profitable Queen Airliners, and its new 17-place turboprop 99 Airliner. These planes today are opening a new era in rapid transportation between smaller cities and the smaller "downtown" airports of large metropolitan centers.

Beech Aircraft Corporation's military products are primarily "off-the-shelf" products which are required in times of peace as well as times of war.

The company's aerospace projects are those involved with the next 30 years of space exploration...and in its field Beech is both a pioneer and a leader in such sophisticated areas as space cryogenics and rocketry.

Beech's growth continues at a healthy "controlled rate-of-climb" into the exciting era ahead!

FREE: Write today for descriptive Beech folder about
☐ Beech aircraft for business or pleasure
☐ Beech aerospace activities
☐ Beech manufacturing capabilities
Address: Beech Aircraft Corporation
Wichita, Kansas 67201 U.S.A.

Beech Aircraft Corporation

As advertised in *Forbes*.

Exhibit 5

COMMUTER AIRLINE MARKET AD:
"TODAY'S NEWEST AIRLINER IS ALREADY INDISPENSABLE."

Today's newest airliner is already indispensable:

the all-new 17-place Beechcraft 99

Now, as the first Beechcraft 99 Airliners roll off the production line in Wichita, the whole complexion of commercial aviation stands on the threshold of a new and exciting era.

The Beechcraft 99 comes as two very importa[nt] changes are taking place in air travel.

First, the major airline emphasis continues to shift [to] bigger, faster jet aircraft and nonstop transcontinen[tal] flights. Smaller cities are being bypassed, creating [a] serious "service gap" at important population cente[rs] where the airports are just too small to accommoda[te] large jet transports.

And second, there is a growing trend for business a[nd] industry to locate in smaller cities—ones not served b[y] the new jets. There has long been a need for air trav[el] to and from smaller cities, and this need is increasing a[t] a time when major airline service is being concentrate[d] in major metropolitan areas.

The result is that third-level commuter airlines connectin[g] smaller cities with major ones—and with other sma[ller]

cities — are doing a land office business all over the country. Until the Beechcraft 99 was introduced, this vital new breed of airlines had to "make do" with modified corporate airplanes and rebuilt airliners from a bygone era.

Now comes the modern, 17-place Beechcraft 99 Airliner — the first high-performance, retractable gear airplane expressly built to meet the needs of the nation's fast growing commuter airlines. It was specifically designed and approved for operation under new FAA regulations for third-level carriers.

It is the *only* airplane providing such an exceptional combination of:

- Speed (to 250 mph).
- Seating capacity (room for fifteen passengers and a two-man crew).
- Short field ability (lands over a 50-foot obstacle in a mere 1,810 feet).
- Useful load capability (carries more than 2 tons).
- Economy of operation (less than 3c per seat mile).
- Versatility (movable bulkhead and removable seats make it 3 planes in one — passenger, cargo or a combination).

No other airplane combines the remarkable features of this great new Beechcraft. In addition, Beech provides a broad spectrum of computerized consulting services to help in the establishment, operation and expansion of commuter airlines.

For more information about the new Beechcraft 99 Airliner, write Beech Aircraft Corporation, Airline Department, 9739 East Central, Wichita, Kansas 67201.

Beech Aircraft Corporation, Wichita, Kansas 67201

The same features that make the Beechcraft Model 99 so well suited to commuter airlines also make it ideal for use as a corporate aircraft. Its low operating costs, high seating capacity and short field capability enable companies to transport large and small groups economically to thousands of airports of all sizes. Write today for details of corporate uses of this great new Beechcraft 99.

Exhibit 6

GENERAL AVIATION MARKET AD:
"INTRODUCING THE EXCITING NEW 6-PLACE BEECHCRAFT BONANZA 36!"

Introducing the exciting new 6-place

The only high-performance, single-engine airplane ever specifically designed for 6 big people.

The biggest Bonanza ever built! Yet, with all its new roominess and useful load capacity, the Bonanza 36 is every inch a Bonanza. Fast. Easy to fly. Comfortable. *Built even better than it has to be!*

The amazing Bonanza 36 is the only airplane in its class that can carry six 170-pound people...and standard fuel...avionics equipment and baggage.

Fully loaded, it can travel as far as 980 nonstop miles with a 45 minute reserve. Top speed exceeds 200 mph. Moves up and out fast with a 285 hp fuel injection Continental engine.

The Bonanza 36 with utility interior can't be beat for carrying heavy, bulky, oddly-shaped cargo. The huge double door takes the chore out of loading. Spacious interior. Hefty 1,620 pound useful load

capacity. You may find you're making one trip to carry loads that used to call for two trips.

The roomy Bonanza 36 is a station wagon on wings. Family air travel takes on a new dimension in its big, comfortable interior. Plenty of leg room, elbow room and head room. Traditional Beechcraft comfort and new stretch-out room turn those long, tiring trips into refreshing family outings.

And think what the Bonanza 36 can do for air taxis. Single-engine economy and high-cruise speeds bring expenses down. Six seat capacity boosts profits.

Air ambulance services find the big, double door easily admits stretcher and patient to the huge cabin. And with stretcher aboard, there is still ample room for doctor, nurse or members of the family.

The Bonanza 36 is in full production *now.* Ask your nearby Beechcraft dealer to arrange a flight. After you've flown it, you'll agree: Bonanza 36 is destined to make flying more fun, more practical and more profitable for thousands...including you!

Stretch-out room for 6 big people. Reclining seats and tinted windows for all.

People or cargo...big double door (almost 4 ft. wide) means easy loading.

Beechcraft Bonanza 36!

Here are *just a few* of the *many* special features of the Bonanza 36...

■ FAA certified in the "big muscle" utility category at full gross weight; built 15½ per cent stronger than required in normal category.

■ Rugged landing gear. Same as Beechcraft Baron gear.

■ Slotted flaps move back and down, increasing wing chord. Lower stall speed; better short field operation.

■ Complete avionics package included as standard equipment.

■ "T" formation flight instrument grouping simplifies scanning during instrument flight.

■ Reliable, efficient pressure system operates gyros.

■ Exclusive Beechcraft "throw over" control wheel does the work of two; gives more room up front.

■ Air intake aft for quieter cabin.

■ Center windows open for greater comfort on the ground during hot weather.

FREE! Write today for an illustrated brochure on the new Beechcraft Bonanza 36, or any other Beechcraft. Address Beech Aircraft Corporation, Marketing Services, Wichita, Kansas 67201.

Exhibit 7

SPORTSMAN MARKET AD:
"GOOD TIMES COME EASY AND MORE OFTEN
IN A BEECHCRAFT MUSKETEER."

Good times come easy and more often in a Beechcraft Musketeer

Fill a thermos with hot coffee, gather a group of fans, and take off for homecoming kick-off in your own Beechcraft Musketeer. It's the low price, low wing airplane with the high-performance, high-style Beechcraft way about it!

A big part of the fun is flying there. Look down with sympathy at those long lines of creeping cars, bumper to bumper for miles. *You* arrive relaxed, with no "traffic jam jitters".

Your Musketeer replaces long, dreary drives with short, cheery flights. Cruising speeds up to 150 mph and nonstop range over 800 miles make traveling with the team an easy, fun-filled Autumn outing...even for a family of six.

Between gridiron weekends, combine flying pleasure with business. That same Beechcraft Musketeer can be a time-saving, profit-making member of your *business* team.

See your Beechcraft dealer today.

 FREE! Write today for informative illustrated brochures on the Beechcraft 3 Musketeers, or other Beechcrafts. Address Beech Aircraft Corp., Marketing Services, 9759 E. Central, Wichita, Kansas 67201.

If you're not a pilot yet, write for your free "Win Your Wings" booklet; a step-by-step guide to your Private Pilot's license. Tells what you learn, how you learn it, how to get started right.

Beech Aircraft Corporation, Wichita, Kansas 67201

As advertised in: Sports Illustrated

Ad No. 8-2302N

132

Exhibit 8

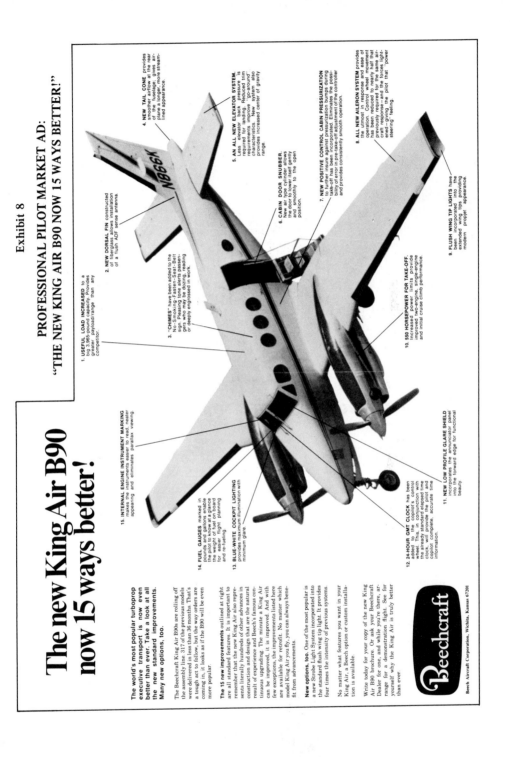

PROFESSIONAL PILOT MARKET AD:
"THE NEW KING AIR B90 NOW 15 WAYS BETTER!"

The new King Air B90 now 15 ways better!

The world's most popular turboprop executive transport is now even better than ever. Take a look at all the new standard improvements. Many new options, too.

The Beechcraft King Air B90s are rolling off the assembly line. 317 of the previous models were delivered in less than 36 months. That's a tough act to follow, but the way orders are coming in, it looks as if the B90 will be even more popular.

The 15 new improvements outlined at right are all standard features. It is important to remember that the new King Air also represents literally hundreds of other advances in construction and design that are the natural result of experience and Beech's famous continuous upgrading. The minute a King Air can be improved, it is improved. And with few exceptions, the improvements listed here are available for retrofit. No matter which model King Air you fly, you can always benefit from advancements.

New options, too. One of the most popular is a new Strobe Light System incorporated into the standard flush wing tip light. It provides four times the intensity of previous systems.

No matter what features you want in your King Air, a Beech option or custom installation is available.

Write today for your copy of the new King Air B90 brochure. Or ask your Beechcraft Dealer for one, and while you're there, arrange for a demonstration flight. See for yourself why the King Air is truly better than ever.

1. USEFUL LOAD INCREASED to a big 3,965-pound capacity. Provides greater payload/range than any competitor.

2. NEW DORSAL FIN constructed of fiberglass allows installation of a flush ADF sense antenna.

3. "CHIMES" have been added to the No-Smoking Fasten-Seat-Belt sign. Pleasing tone alerts passengers who may be dozing, reading or deeply engrossed in work.

4. NEW TAIL CONE provides smoother airflow at the rear of the fuselage, gives airplane a longer, more streamlined appearance.

5. AN ALL NEW ELEVATOR SYSTEM. Less elevator "back pressure" is required for landing. Reduced trim requirements improve "go-around" characteristics. New system also provides increased center of gravity range.

6. CABIN DOOR SNUBBER. New air type cylinder allows the door to lower itself gently and smoothly to the open position.

7. NEW POSITIVE CONTROL CABIN PRESSURIZATION to further insure against pressurization bumps during take-off has been incorporated. Eliminates the possibility of error in pre-take-off adjustment of the controller and provides consistently smooth operation.

8. ALL NEW AILERON SYSTEM provides the utmost in response and ease of operation. Control wheel movement has been reduced so that half that previously required for the same aircraft response—and the forces lightened—giving the pilot that power steering "feeling".

9. FLUSH WING TIP LIGHTS have been incorporated into the extended wing tips providing modern projet appearance.

10. 550 HORSEPOWER FOR TAKE-OFF. Increased power limits provide improved two-engine, single-engine and initial cruise climb performance.

11. NEW LOW PROFILE GLARE SHIELD incorporates the annunciator panel into the forward edge for functional beauty.

12. 24-HOUR GMT CLOCK has been added to the copilot's control wheel. This, in conjunction with the already standard elapsed time clock, will provide the pilot and copilot complete, accurate time information.

13. BLUE-WHITE COCKPIT LIGHTING provides maximum illumination with minimum glare.

14. FUEL GAUGES marked in pounds and gallons enable the pilot to know at a glance the weight of fuel on board for easier flight planning and re-fueling.

15. INTERNAL ENGINE INSTRUMENT MARKING makes the instruments easier to read, neater appearing and eliminates parallax viewing.

Beechcraft

Beech Aircraft Corporation, Wichita, Kansas 67201

133

Exhibit 9

SPECIAL INDUSTRIES MARKET AD:
"HARD-WORKING CONSTRUCTION MEN SPEAK OUT
FOR THE WORKINGMAN'S AIRPLANE!"

Beechcraft Bonanza V35A. 203 mph cruise. Seats 4 to 5 people.

Hard-working construction men speak out for the working man's airplane!

Top people are scarce. *Expensive.* So what do you do when your operations are scattered? How do you avoid the cost of additional supervisors? How can you crowd more jobs into the workdays of experienced people?

Invest in a working man's airplane. A rugged, efficient Beechcraft Bonanza. It's a profitable solution used by firms across the nation.

THESE MEN KNOW: A California man whose firm works at scattered missile bases explains..."tight schedules and coordination with other contractors make close supervision necessary." Yet this man actually *reduced* the number of supervisors at each base by using two Beechcrafts.

A New York businessman-pilot in road and pipeline construction personally supervises a statewide operation. His enthusiasm for business flying is even greater since he moved up to a Beechcraft. He likes the low wing particularly because..."visibility is mighty important around New York's busy airports."

A Fresno man who makes frequent trips to San Diego says..."That 12-hour drive is now just a 3½-hour flight in our Bonanza. We wouldn't fly anything else."

LOTS OF MUSCLE. Time after time, construction men invest in Beechcrafts. They know that Beechcraft "extra muscle" means low overall maintenance costs. Minimum down-time for repairs. And it means a Beechcraft is worth more when you buy it—worth more when you trade.

PROOF OF PROFIT. Many construction men credit company Beechcrafts for a large measure of their success. We will send you complete case histories that tell how these men put Beechcrafts to work. You may discover that *you* can profit by using a working man's airplane.

WRITE—OR USE THIS CONVENIENT FORM:

Beech Aircraft Corporation
9711 E. Central
Wichita, Kansas 67201

PLEASE SEND THE FOLLOWING INFORMATION AT ONCE!

☐ Construction Industry Case Histories

Illustrated brochures on the following aircraft: (Check as many as you like)
☐ BONANZAS — (4-5 place high performance single engine airplanes)
☐ BARONS — (4-6 place light twins)
☐ QUEEN AIRS — (6-10 place medium twins)
☐ KING AIR — (Turboprop, pressurized corporate transport)

Name_____Title_____

Company_____

Address_____

City_____State_____Zip_____

As advertised in *Engineering News Record; Construction Methods & Equipment.*

134

Exhibit 10

WOMEN'S PRESTIGE MARKET AD:
"EASY STREET"

Easy street.

That's having your own Beechcraft and getting above the honking, hurrying, train catching and plane switching. Your days aren't carved up by relentless timetables. You don't have to be anywhere at 9:02 or 10:13 or 3:08! No ticket punching. No tickets, period. No loudspeaker tells *you* where to go.

Your magnificent 'Beechcraft King Air is pressurized, with three-compartment privacy, center aisle room, and wall-to-wall comfort. When and where it takes off is for *you* to say. So business and pleasure get mixed up exactly the way it suits you.

Beechcrafts are for people who insist on running their own lives.

Accustomed to the finest...you'll find it in a Beechcraft

Beech Aircraft Corporation, Wichita, Kansas 67201, U.S.A.

Exhibit 11

AEROSPACE/MILITARY MARKET AD:
"SIX REASONS WHY BEECH WAS SELECTED FOR THIS IMPORTANT APOLLO ASSIGNMENT."

R & D

Engineering

Manufacturing

Testing

Versatility

Management

6 reasons why Beech was selected for this important Apollo assignment

The problem: store 11,000 cubic feet of hydrogen in fourteen cubic feet of space and 7,000 cubic feet of oxygen in nine cubic feet of space.

The solution: do it with cryogens. And to do it in the lightest, most reliable manner required experts in the field of cryogenics. This is why North American selected Beech.

The fluids perform two functions vital to the success of the Apollo mission: Oxygen will be furnished to the environmental control system in the command module...oxygen and hydrogen will be fed to fuel cells which produce electrical power for the command and service module systems.

Take a look at the 6 reasons why North American assigned these important jobs to Beech:

1. **R & D!** — Beech is a pioneer in cryogenics R & D, with many contributions to cryogenic technology during the last 12 years.
2. **Engineering!** — Engineering goes hand in hand with R & D. When you pioneer, you must be capable of converting nebulous concepts into reliable, functional hardware.
3. **Manufacturing!** — Beech has been a pioneer in the development of methods and techniques for fabrication of titanium. (Beech discovered — and proved — titanium

"creep.") But this is only a highlight of Beech capabilities-in-depth for fabrication of the exotic metals and materials required to contain and control cryogenic hydrogen, oxygen, helium and nitrogen.

4. **Testing!** — Complete, under-one-roof testing capability is important for economy and on-time production. What Beech produces, Beech can qualify.
5. **Versatility!** — Bench Maintenance Equipment systems to test and functionally certify components and modules of the Beech-built cryogenic storage subsystems were required. Beech designed and built them — thus providing additional dramatic proof of complete Beech capabilities.
6. **Management!** — Capabilities have been developed through the successful Management of over 50 cryogenic programs. These have contributed to such major programs as Centaur, Atlas, Titan, Saturn, and Gemini.

Beech facilities, people, and experience are ready **now** for you to use as your own on vital projects of any size. Write, wire or phone Contract Administration, or Aerospace Marketing, Beech Aircraft Corporation, Wichita, Kansas 67201, U.S.A., for complete information about Beech capabilities in your area of interest.

Beech Aerospace Division
BEECH AIRCRAFT CORPORATION ● WICHITA, KANSAS 67201

HELPING BUSINESS GROW FASTER: Only Beechcraft offers such a complete line of planes with so much speed, range, comfort and quiet to help business multiply the money-making decisions that each top man can make. That's how thousands of Beechcrafts have paid for themselves.

EXECUTIVES: *Write today* for free booklet, "Answers to the 19 Most Asked Questions About Business Flying." It could point the way to major new profits for your company. Address Beech Aircraft Corp., Marketing Services, Wichita, Kansas 67201, U.S.A.

Exhibit 12

INTERNATIONAL BUSINESS MARKET AD:
"WHY HAVE SO MANY IMPORTANT PEOPLE BEEN WAITING
FOR THE BEECHCRAFT DUKE?"

Why have so many important people been waiting for the Beechcraft Duke?

The new Beechcraft Duke is here. It's the answer to the need for a high-performance "light twin" that would offer pressurized comfort and high altitude capabilities.

The Duke speeds through the sky at over 260 mph and has a nonstop range of over 1000 miles. Wide center aisle with deep-cushioned seats for four. (Fifth and sixth-place seating available.) Wall-to-wall carpeting, and a flight deck designed to accommodate all the avionics — including radar — you'll ever want. Powered by twin 380 hp turbocharged engines that enable you to cruise up where the air is smooth and clear — high over any mountain range in the world.

The Duke joins 17 other members of the distinguished family of Beechcraft airplanes. From 2-place Musketeer trainer to 17-place 99 Airliner — each is the tops in its class. No matter what your aircraft requirements, there is a Beechcraft to do the job.

Because Beechcraft owners travel far and wide, they need a plane with service facilities that match its performance. They find it with Beech. Around the world are dealers with outstanding service — with mechanics trained at the Beech factory — with a complete inventory of parts and accessories.

The finest airplanes in their class, plus the finest world-wide service — that's why important airlines, governments, military forces, and individuals select a Beechcraft. To learn why you should join them, visit your nearest Beechcraft Dealer or write Beech Aircraft Corporation, 9799 E. Central, Wichita, Kansas 67201, U.S.A., for information. There is no obligation.

138

Exhibit 14

STARCH READERSHIP SCORES FOR BEECH ADS IN GENERAL BUSINESS PUBLICATIONS

Publication	Date	Space	Feature	Starch Scores*	"Read-Most" Ranking**
Time	12/1/67	Spd B/W	Queen Airs	39-31-5	T5/41
	12/15/67	Spd 4C	Light Twins	63-54-9	T3/60
	1/26/68	Spd 4C	Bonanzas	80-71-16	2/29
	3/22/68	Spd 4C	King Air	56-48-10	T2/31
	4/26/68	Spd B/W	Queen Airs	54-43-11	T4/51
	5/24/68	Spd B/W	Bonanza	57-45-12	T3/51
Business Week	10/28/67	Spd B/W	Queen Airs	39-37-10	T27/91
	12/16/67	Spd B/W	King Air	38-36-9	T15/88
	2/17/68	Spd B/W	Light Twins	47-42-10	T9/90
	4/13/68	Spd B/W	King Air	51-46-12	4/76
*Newsweek***	11/27/67	Spd B/W	King Air	50-45-12	T5/50
	5/6/68	Spd B/W	Light Twins	57-46-16	T2/83

* Starch readership scores came in three categories: "Noted," "Seen-Associated," and "Read-Most." A Starch score of 39-31-5 indicates that 39% of the test audience recalled seeing the ad; 31% associated the ad with the product or advertiser; and 5% read the majority of the ad's reading matter.

**Indicates "read-most" ranking of Beech ads in magazine. Example: T5/41 means Beech ad was tied for fifth place out of 41 ads in magazine.

***Not Starched until recently—not every issue Starched.

Exhibit 15

STARCH SCORES FOR BEECH SELL-O-CHROME: 1966-68

Date	Company	Space	Starch Scores	"Read-Most" Ranking
May 1966	Beech	4 Pg S-O-C	62-60-35*	1/73
	Cessna	Spd 4C	66-64-24	
October 1966	Beech	4 Pg S-O-C	63-60-33	1/36
	Cessna	3 Pg 4C	56-52-21	
	Cessna	Spd 4C	64-61-28	
May 1967	Beech	4 Pg S-O-C	57-56-25	3/52
	Piper	Spd 4C & B/W	65-64-20	
	Cessna	Pg 4C	59-56-21	
February 1968	Beech	4 Pg S-O-C	69-61-26	1/44
	Cessna	Spd 4C	62-60-16	
	Piper	4 Pg S-O-C	68-56-19	
March 1968	Beech	4 Pg S-O-C	70-65-27	1/54
	Cessna	8 Pg S-O-C**	64-60-26	
April 1968	Beech	4 Pg S-O-C	61-58-23	3/53
	Cessna	3 Spds 4C	65-62-28	
	Piper	Spd 4C	55-51-22	

*Average of space.
**Including gatefold and split in magazine.

QUESTIONS

1. *Appraise the segmented advertising approach used by Beech in 1968.*
2. *What changes, if any, would you make?*

Shell's 1961 Media Strategy

Company officials review a decision, made at the recommendation of its advertising agency, to concentrate 1961 advertising expenditures in a single medium.

In late 1960, the Shell Oil Company and its newly-appointed advertising agency—Ogilvy, Benson, and Mather—startled the advertising world with the announcement of Shell's 1961 media strategy. The oil company, which had spread its more than $13 million advertising budget over all eight measured media in 1959, was going to put virtually all its media advertising dollars into newspapers.

Several weeks later, *Advertising Age* reported[1] on the story behind the all-newspaper campaign and related some of the details of the proposed Shell advertising schedule. The article included a report on Ogilvy, Benson, and Mather's view of Shell's problems, the OBM outline of the defects of Shell's past advertising and media approach, and the OBM suggestions for 1961. (In addition, a six-part program for research on consumers, dealers, brand, internal data, and advertising was described along with an extensive plan to merchandise the new advertising and media program.)

After outlining what it saw as Shell's problems, and particularly calling attention to the increasingly competitive nature of the gasoline business in light of the leveling-off of industry growth, the agency pinpointed marketing and advertising objectives.

Marketing objectives—Increase share of market; build total sales; build sales in areas most profitable to company.

Advertising objectives—Build greater preference for Shell products by improving the public's image of Shell products and of the company itself, and convert that preference into buying action by means consistent with the image being projected.

---

[1] "How and What Ogilvy Sold Shell," *Advertising Age,* December 12, 1960. Portions of the article are reprinted with permission of *Advertising Age.* Copyright © 1960 by Advertising Publications Inc. Indentations are *Advertising Age* extracts; quotations are from the *Advertising Age* report of Ogilvy, Benson, and Mather's presentation.

In presenting his agency's creative approach to Shell's advertising, Mr. Ogilvy was said to have described the job as one of "making the voice of Shell heard above the crowd."

Shell is one of 30,000 brand names now fighting for consumer recognition . . . $11 billion in advertising is hitting the consumer a year, including 10,000 TV commercials. Shell advertising represents only one-tenth of 1% of all advertising. It is only 6% of all gasoline advertising. Shell spends $13,000,000 a year on advertising, but "it is now being dispersed into too many different campaigns, appearing in too many media. Dispersion has made the voice of Shell inaudible . . . the less you splinter your advertising into different campaigns, for different purposes, the stronger it will be."

The new campaign was described as selling products and building prestige. The focus was to be on "the real truth about gasoline," telling about the ingredients in Shell. The campaign was to be serious in nature rather than entertaining; its long-copy advertisements were to be factual, sell-hard, and look important.

An explanation of the decision to shift media advertising into newspapers was preceded by extensive analysis of the media situation. Expenditures of Shell's major competitors were analyzed and found to be quite varied. For example, Gulf spent 61% in TV, only 9% in radio; Sinclair spent 5% in TV, 58% in radio. This pattern of concentration in a medium was thought by OBM to be a good one. Shell's divisions had varied in their media plans, whereas Detroit had spent 19% in TV and 17% in radio; New Orleans spent 50% in TV and 2% in radio. The result was "fragmentation." For a specific example, the New York television situation was examined. Texaco sponsored the 15-minute daily Huntley-Brinkley news program. "What does Shell sponsor in New York. Can you name the programs?" (Shell had sponsored various news and feature programs scheduled at scattered intervals during the year, and 1/4 of the New York Giants pro football telecasts.)

Against this dispersion it was proposed that three media criteria be set up:

1) Media must reach the prime markets in depth, with ad dollars allocated in relation to sales opportunity and objectives.

2) Media usage must be concentrated rather than fragmented on the principle that Shell need not only meet its competitors' advertising, but all advertisers.

3) Media must be suited to the creative approach of the selling message. Here it was said that the simple "Cars love Shell" campaign would have been better in outdoor than in newspapers.

Shell's markets were broken down into three groups: primary—128 cities, 85%

of "standard market gallonage"; secondary—98 cities, 15% of SMG; tertiary—other areas with small gallonage and population. To reach these markets, a large-space very high-frequency newspaper campaign was recommended at a reported cost of over $13 million, almost the entire advertising budget. The money represented Shell's 1960 newspaper, outdoor, radio, television, magazine oil, and magazine institutional expenditures, plus the advertising reserve fund, the "station decoration" budget, and a planned 3% increase in overall advertising dollars. (See Exhibit 1 for a breakdown of these expenditures.)

The newspaper program planned for 1961 included 78 full-page advertisements, in every important paper. For example, all seven major New York dailies were to be covered, plus campaigns in Long Island and other suburban papers. The *Wall Street Journal* was to get 26 full page ads, giving national management coverage. Five Los Angeles dailies and sixteen Los Angeles suburban papers were scheduled for full and half campaigns (78 and 39 insertions, respectively). Four Chicago papers were to get the full schedule.

OBM recommended that Shell encourage jobbers, whose advertising also had been fragmented into several media, to concentrate in newspapers along with Shell. The media analysis had shown that only four petroleum companies were among the 75 largest spending newspaper advertisers (Shell—29th; Phillips—37th; Socony—46th; Sun—49th). Under the all-newspaper plan, including the jobber program, Shell would receive more newspaper advertising in its market areas than all other gasoline brands combined. "No oil company has ever mounted such an overpowering barrage. [Shell] will seem to *own* the newspapers."

In the industrial products area the agency also tried to avert fragmentation. For example, it was recommended that the list of the 49 publications carrying Shell industrial lubricant advertising be halved (in more than half of these magazines, only three ads a year were run) with concentration on the most important ones "to give the impression of leadership, to build dominance and impact."

One reported agency comment gave an indication of possible future Shell media strategy: "The policy of concentration dictates giving up many things which are in themselves desirable. It may be that in 1962 we will concentrate on television—and make more telling use of it than Shell has in the past."

QUESTION

1. Appraise Shell's 1961 plan and its media analysis (Exhibit 1, page 144).

Exhibit 1

1960 SHELL ADVERTISING BUDGET*

Medium	1960 Expenditures (000)	Comment** re 1961 Campaign
Newspaper	$1,916	
Outdoor	2,798)	Media do not allow full-selling story to be told
Radio	1,374)	
Television	3,612	
Production	63	Production budget for radio – TV – outdoor ads.
Magazines (Oil)	530	Inadequate for a magazine campaign of consequence
Magazines (Institutional to Management)	325	Management readership not concentrated; will be hit via newspaper ads in major cities and in *Wall Street Journal*.
Advertising reserves	600	
Station decoration	881	

* Partial listing; excludes business publications budget, and miscellaneous expenditures. Does not include jobber advertising.
** Ogilvy, Benson, and Mather comment as reported by *Advertising Age*.
Source: *Advertising Age*, Dec. 12, 1960. Reprinted with permission.

Gulf Oil's
News Specials

Company executives review a recently announced decision that Gulf would sponsor NBC-TV's "instant news specials."

In late 1960, the Gulf Oil Company and NBC-TV announced that henceforth the company would sponsor the network's unplanned news specials. In an unusual television programming arrangement, the network found a sponsor for its "instant specials," i.e., unscheduled coverage of important news events, and the oil company found a framework for its corporate image advertising.

Gulf set aside $1.2 million in a fund for the programs[1] against which were to be assessed time charges on the news specials which NBC-TV would present. In addition, Gulf received first refusal rights on NBC-TV's so-called planned news specials—usually longer news-feature programs produced somewhat further in advance than the "instant specials" which often were readied on less than a day's notice. Planned news specials, for example, included the "Projection 61" hour-long news report December 30, 1960; and early 1961 "instant specials" included Laotian reports, Cuban invasion coverage, and the astronaut flight.

The purchase marked a return of Gulf to television program sponsorship for the first time since 1957, when the company sponsored "The Life of Riley." Network television expenditures since that time had been for participations, i.e., announcements within programs rather than direct sponsorship. Gulf's major media expenditures in recent years are given in Exhibit 1, page 147.

Commercials for the programs were made in advance and kept at NBC-TV. When apprised of a forthcoming special, Gulf officials scheduled the commercials considered most appropriate. Gulf advertising executives and the company's advertising agency representatives, quoted in *Sponsor* magazine[2], considered the purchase a

---

[1] According to *Advertising Age* (December 12, 1960) the cost formula was based on past experience with the network's news preemptions. (The networks have the right to preempt regular programs for special events.) The $1.2 million cost was reportedly based on network time charges (Gulf did not pay for production costs of the programs) for what usually were half-hour programs, and an experience estimate of about twenty news specials per year.

[2] *Sponsor*, May 15, 1961, p. 43.

desirable one for "impressing the public with Gulf's position." Executives described the Gulf commercials inserted in the programs as trying to picture Gulf as a "dynamic growing company in the dynamic growing energy industry."

QUESTION

1.   *Appraise Gulf's strategy with regard to this media buy.*

Exhibit 1
GULF'S MAJOR MEDIA EXPENDITURES – 1954-59
(000's)

	Magazines	Newspapers	Farm	Spot Radio	Network TV	Spot TV	Bus. Papers	Outdoor	Nat'l Farm*	Total
1959	$1,135	$ 478	$ 62	$ 415	$1,492	$ 857	$400	$ 704	$62	$5,546
1958	1,511	2,854	88	1,000	549	1,916	344	671	88	8,919
1957	1,082	3,366	129	-	1,100	179	310	1,608	81	7,777
1956	237	2,218	190	n.a.**	2,268	89	348	1,178	94	7,132
1955	359	2,495	187	87***	2,162	-	365	1,878	99	7,534
1954	290	2,048	108	- **	1,701	-	360	1,983	35	6,493

* National Farm figures are not included in totals; these investments are duplicated in Newspaper Farm listings.
** Network radio expenditures; spot radio not available.
Source: *Printers' Ink Advertisers' Guide to Marketing*, 1960 and 1961.

Saturday Evening Post (A)

Advertising sales executives at the *Saturday Evening Post* reappraise past and present efforts to sell magazine space to a major beer company (Schlitz).

In June 1966, advertising sales executives of the *Saturday Evening Post* were reappraising the magazine's efforts to sell advertising to the Joseph Schlitz Brewing Company. Management wanted to assess what had happened to the *Post's* relationship with Schlitz, and to make plans for the future, hoping to get Schlitz back into the *Post* in a substantial way. In 1962 Schlitz had spent $464,000 with the *Post* but only $64,000 in 1963, and since then virtually nothing.

THE BEER INDUSTRY AND SCHLITZ

Appendix A contains information on beer consumption in the United States in 1960 and 1965 along with certain projections for the 1970s. During the early 1960s Schlitz ranked number two in the industry, behind Anheuser-Busch and ahead of Pabst. During the 1961-65 period, Schlitz sales increased about 50% although some of this increase represented minor brands. In contrast, the industry gained not much more than 10%. However, Anheuser-Busch gained about 40%, and Pabst 60%. For the ten years prior to 1962, Schlitz's sales trend had been relatively stagnant. Schlitz's sales—barrels and dollars—in the 1961-65 period are shown below:

Year	Millions of Barrels	Millions of Dollars
1961	5.8	$155.3
1962	6.9	184.4
1963	7.8	226.4
1964	8.3	238.7
1965	8.6	248.8

There had been a sharp change in Schlitz's top management in 1961. The new management, headed by Utah, was dedicated to the notion of bringing new life into the company and to its major brand (Schlitz). As a corollary there was a series of changes in the marketing, advertising, and brand management ranks from that time up through 1966. (Appendix B is an *Advertising Age* article about Schlitz's marketing.) According to a *Fortune* article:

> Perhaps the most vivid difference between old and new lies in the realm of marketing. The old Schlitz was an efficient beermaker but a backward beer marketer. With its mixture of the modern and the archaic, the company resembled, in a way, its own main brewery in Milwaukee; sleek, highly automated beermaking equipment housed in multistoried old buildings. Marketing coasted on Schlitz beer's established reputation and its enviably well-known slogan, "The Beer That Made Milwaukee Famous." Virtually no use was made of marketing research. The new Schlitz has a marketing vice-president, Hogan, who is committed to what he calls "the objective study of facts." Hogan has assembled a marketing-research team that averages two college degrees per man. "We've got genius-IQ types working here who wouldn't even have been interviewed before," he says happily. The marketers consult their own IBM 1620 computer, said to be the first computer in the U.S. devoted entirely to marketing research.

BEER ADVERTISING

Schlitz was the industry's highest spender in advertising in total dollars as well as in dollars per barrel. Schlitz spent around $2 per barrel; Anheuser-Busch $1.50; and Pabst $1.25. Schlitz advertising had for some years featured the slogan "The Beer That Made Milwaukee Famous." However, the new (1961) company management was said to think that the slogan was tired. In September 1961, the Schlitz account moved from Brush Advertising to the Benson agency, which developed a new slogan, "Real Gusto in a Great Light Beer," that was used during the succeeding years.

In 1965, the two leading brands were spending their magazine money as shown in Exhibit 1. (Pabst Blue Ribbon, the No. 3 brand, spent no money for magazines except a nominal amount in *Ebony.*) In addition to what is spent in magazines, Schlitz typically spent, per year, almost $11 million for TV and about $2½ million for spot radio.

Other beer advertising carried by the *Post*, in addition to Schlitz and Budweiser, was negligible. There was, for example, a scheduled total of only 6 pages from eight brands in 1966.

PAST POST EFFORTS

The following is a condensed account, drawn from *Post* files, of some of the relevant events in the history of the *Post*'s effort to sell advertising space to Schlitz. (For Cast of Characters, see Exhibit 2.)

1958   When the *Post* decided to revise an old policy and accept alcoholic beverage advertising during 1958, it "automatically received" about 5 pages of Schlitz advertising to finish out the year. Abbott was assigned to the Schlitz account, then being served by Brush Advertising, and its agency. According to Abbott, it was the kind of account that "required more work at the company than at the agency."

1959   The *Post* did a "This Is Your Life" at Schlitz's national sales meeting, which gave *Post* personnel a chance to develop contacts with Schlitz top management—particularly Utah (who became president of the company in 1961) and Mason (who became director of marketing for the Schlitz brand in November 1963). Schlitz scheduled 13 pages in the *Post* in 1959.

1960   Gibson, who had worked for a cigarette company, joined Schlitz as advertising director for the Schlitz brand. He was heralded as a great friend of the *Post*. The contract for 13 pages had been renewed for 1960, but only after a "hassle."

Schlitz objected to *Post's* acceptance of regional advertising on the ground that it helped Schlitz's regional competitors. However, Abbott felt that relationships were good at all levels; even Utah attended an occasional presentation, and Mason was "always a good friend" and a source of helpful information. Abbott was transferred east during the year, and Vincent was assigned to the account.

1961   At the suggestion of Brush Advertising, Vincent was removed from the account. Apparently there was dissatisfaction with the way he had explained the *Post's* regional advertising, and also because of his attitude of not caring one way or the other. (He was independently wealthy.) Kelly replaced him on the account just before Gibson "personally and without any solicitation" announced that Schlitz's advertising was being switched to the Benson agency. In 1961, the *Post* carried 4 pages; Schlitz's attitude toward regional advertising "was subordinate but still an element."

1962   This year the *Post* was up again to 9 pages ($464,000). Throughout most of 1962, Michaels was handling the Schlitz account for the *Post*. After making some distribution calls he informed Gibson that their distribution pattern was "not the greatest," and that in fact they did not have a nationally distributed beer. According to one comment, "Of course no brand has complete distribution, but Michaels argued that Schlitz did lack national distribution [as a reason for using the Post] and Gibson wasn't disposed to argue the point."

1963   This year Schlitz spent only $64,000 in the *Post*, all of it regionally. The agency appeared to be the stumbling block—in the opinion of the *Post* people concerned. In June, Kelly was again assigned to the account. On June 12, Madison and Kelly lunched with Gibson, Mason, and Peters (organizationally Gibson's boss as Brand Director). Mason, at that time, was "beginning to emerge as a real power" at the expense of Gibson. Madison "really clicked with Mason." On October 17, Madison met with Jackson, the No. 1 man on Schlitz at Benson, and again did a "damn good selling job." It looked as if the *Post* would be on the schedule for 1964.

However, there were a few "intermediate flies in the ointment." On October 16, Lenox had made a presentation to the entire Benson Media Department; 35 Benson people were present. The presentation dealt with the comeback of the *Post*—"The *Post* Is Being Recognized"—and with its new editorial vitality and readership. Much was made of the fact that the *Post's* circulation (6,500,000 versus 7,000,000 for *Life* and 7,400,000 for *Look*) was concentrated more highly than *Life's* and *Look's* in the quality segments of the market in terms of income, education, occupation (managerial, professional, white-collar), social class, and buying power (ownership of cars, boats, etc.). Apparently this failed to impress the Benson people; if anything, it alienated them. Then, on December 7, Victor also made a poor impression in a meeting with Jackson.

1964 On March 10, Kelly took Benton (transferred from Pittsburgh) to introduce him to Gibson as the new *Post* representative. Benton had known Gibson before through summering at the same place. After a two- or three-hour meeting Gibson seemed "110% sold on the *Post.*" One week later, Benton resigned. Gibson seemed unwilling to accept the explanation of his sudden departure.

On April 27, Walters was assigned to the Schlitz account (though Kelly still maintained his interest in it). In a call at Schlitz, Gibson commented on the *Post's* personnel problems and was generally uncomplimentary to the *Post.* (For example, he indicated his complete dissatisfaction with Lenox, and praised Madison who had just resigned.) During July and August a presentation was prepared under Walter's direction and given to the agency on September 1, and again on September 2, and to the Schlitz people on September 10. It was well received. Schlitz even made a position commitment for the Saint Patrick's Day issue of 1965. The presentation contained: (a) an editorial "sell"; (b) evidence of *Post* as a communications vehicle (reading magazine); (c) advantages of combined advertising in both *Post* and *Life* over *Look* and *Life.*

Unfortunately an editorial castigating Goldwater in the September 19 issue of the *Post* considerably antagonized the Schlitz people. Whether that had anything to do with it or not, Schlitz decided not to use the *Post* in 1965. According to a status report of January 11, 1965:

> The Benson agency originally recommended the use of *Life, Look* and *Post* for 1965. Based on client's feeling that *Life* magazine was receiving too much money from Schlitz, *Life's* schedule was decreased for 1965. *Post* and *Look* were to be used exclusively on a regional basis in states contributing approximately 60 to 65% of Schlitz's national sales.
>
> After the first recommendation *TV Guide* presented a rather strong case to

the client, recommending the elimination of *The Saturday Evening Post* in favor of *TV Guide* in partnership with *Look* and *Life*. (The *TV Guide* presentation in its entirety was provided to the *Post* by Benson's media department for analysis and rebuttal.) The agency successfully eliminated *TV Guide* from contention.

Just about the time the agency eliminated *TV Guide*, the Marketing Committee of Schlitz informed Schlitz Brand Director Peters that his brand would be cut back $1,600,000 under his budget recommendation for 1965. The agency then went back to redo their media proposals for 1965, which called for the use of *The Saturday Evening Post* and *Life* in the general mass-field. The Advertising Director of Schlitz at that time (Gibson) would not concede that the *Post,* statistically a better buy than *Look,* should be on the schedule. This led to many more meetings on the subject, and during the interim Gibson was taken off Schlitz and replaced by Allison.

The final determination on this situation was resolved on Tuesday, January 5, when Peters, Brand Director, and Allison, Advertising Manager on Schlitz, consulted with Gibson who stated: "The statistics prove that the *Post* in combination with *Life* magazine is marginally more effective and efficient than *Look* in combination with *Life* magazine. [See Appendix C.] However, based on the personnel and financial trouble which Curtis is facing, I would not invest $270,000 of my brand's money in a magazine whose future seems to be in jeopardy."

1965 On January 20, Campbell and Centurion called on Schlitz. The purpose was to reassure Schlitz of the stability and continued existence of the *Post*. However, the Schlitz people apparently expected a presentation that dealt with the advertising power of the *Post* and what that could do for Schlitz, and were not reassured in any way about its future. Much of the same thing happened at the agency on March 5—which by coincidence was the day that the newspapers carried the story of the *Post's* corporate losses in 1964.

During the balance of 1965 Walters concentrated on the agency, where he had good connections, especially with Timberly and Paulson. Kelly's strong contacts were with Jackson, Edison, and Rogers (who had been Account Supervisor before Timberly). This resulted in $13,000 of remnant[1] business in July and September, but the remnants were not satisfactory to Schlitz.

In the *Post* ranks, considerable frustration had developed. No real progress seemed to have been made despite what had originally been considered goodwill on the part of Gibson and what was still supposed to be a close friendship between Mason and Kelly. Moreover, there now appeared to be support for the *Post* on the

---

[1] "Remnants" are very small space units that become available in a particular magazine issue when the total advertising and editorial content are laid out. These are sometimes offered at bargain rates to particular advertisers or prospective advertisers.

part of the Benson agency—which had been one of the first agencies to "jump on the bandwagon" when the *Post* announced its new reduced rates on July 30, 1964.

One possible explanation advanced was that basically Schlitz was interested in "reach" and "frequency" rather than in "atmosphere" and "efficiency."

Another explanation was given confidentially to a member of the Chicago office by one of the lower-level advertising people at Schlitz: "Your problem isn't the Campbell meeting, or anything like that. The trouble is that our company has very bad internal problems, too, and until these are unwound there will be little change in our media buys, little intelligent planning in media and other marketing problems. Our problems make the Curtis upheaval look like a kindergarten, but we ought to be in better shape soon." To emphasize the point, this person then got out a book containing information about company personnel and showed how many pictures had been crossed out because of people who had changed jobs or left the company.

1966   During the first half of 1966, the status quo in Schlitz-*Post* relations remained about the same. According to another report:

> In the years we have not had any Schlitz business, Mason has had a hand in directing the advertising course of the Schlitz brand. He was sold to the teeth on *Look* Kromatic, and he single-handedly changed the program from the use of *Life* on a national basis and *Look* on a regional basis to *Look* nationally (to take advantage of Kromatic processing) and *Life* regionally. Our argument with him was that he should instruct or order the agency to put the *Post* on the list. He was very upset with *Life* magazine, and in all probability would have knocked *Life* off the schedule. But he had put himself in the precarious position of dictating sales policy to the Sales Manager, and as a result found it necessary to fire him and assume the responsibilities of the Sales Manager himself. He said that if he directed the Schlitz Brand Ad group to knock *Life* off the schedule, then he would inherit the ad function too and the whole operation would eventually disintegrate into a one-man show.

Apparently the trouble with *Life* arose out of poor color reproduction, poor positioning, and refusal to make adjustments.

PRESENT SITUATION

This was the situation when Walters was transferred to Omaha in June 1966, and Kelly was again given responsibility for the Schlitz account. The *Post's* advertising sales executives deeply believed that the magazine represented a solid buy for Schlitz and wondered what route they now should try.

Exhibit 1

MAJOR ADVERTISING EXPENDITURES IN MAGAZINES
BY THE TWO LEADING BRANDS OF BEER*

(Dollars in Thousands)

	Life		Look		Sat. Eve. Post		Playboy		Sports Illustrated		Time		Newsweek		Total Magazine Expenditures	
	Pages	Amount	Pages	Amount	Pages	Amount	Pages	Amount	Pages	Amount	Pages	Amount	Pages	Amount	Pages	Amount
1961																
Budweiser	12	$ 595	8	$ 388		$		$		$	8	$ 197	10	$ 506	62	$1,931
Schlitz	14	679	10	422	4	132			14	133	10	212	10	119	94	1,938
1962																
Budweiser	12	678	7	380	9	449			9	103	6	159			55	1,892
Schlitz	16	868	10	564	9	464			7	55					64	2,069
1963																
Budweiser	12	705	9	526	10	509			9	106	8	212	9	143	73	2,336
Schlitz	26	1,360	6	381	1	64	7	75	1	15					55	2,001
1964																
Budweiser	13	633	11	557	11	490			7	160	7	160			69	2,082
Schlitz	25	1,324	6	369			9	125	13	131					77	2,128
1965																
Budweiser	14	666	12	561	12	439			12	122			12	170	106	2,563
Schlitz	22	1,170	3	177			9	179	9	101					67	1,842
*1966***																
Budweiser	15	725	11	529	8	273			13	178					77	2,035
Schlitz	19	1,144	12	310			10	196							49	1,947

* In general, amounts less than $100,000 omitted, so media figures do not add up to Total Magazine Expenditures.
** Estimated on basis of schedules to date of case.

Exhibit 2
CAST OF CHARACTERS

Post

Campbell	President
Madison	Ex-Publisher
Victor	Ex-Senior Vice President in Charge of Magazines
Lenox	Ex-Advertising Director
Centurion	Vice President—Advertising Director
Abbott	Advertising Salesman (new Branch Office Manager)
Vincent	Advertising Salesman (Ex)
Michaels	Advertising Salesman (Ex)
Kelly	Advertising Salesman (now Associate Branch Office Manager)
Walters	Advertising Salesman (now Omaha Manager)
Benton	Advertising Salesman (Ex)

Schlitz

Utah	President of Company
Hogan	Marketing Vice President of Company
Peters	Brand Director—Schlitz Brand
Mason	Marketing Director—Schlitz Brand
Gibson	Ex-Advertising Director—Schlitz Brand
Allison	Advertising Director—Schlitz Brand

Benson

Jackson	Vice President, Client Service
Rogers	Ex-Account Supervisor
Timberly	Account Supervisor
Edison	Media Supervisor
Paulson	Account Executive (Malt)

APPENDIX A

Table 1

BEER INDUSTRY STATISTICS

Growth of Beer-drinking Population
(20 years and over)

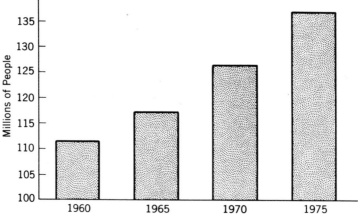

Per Capita Consumption

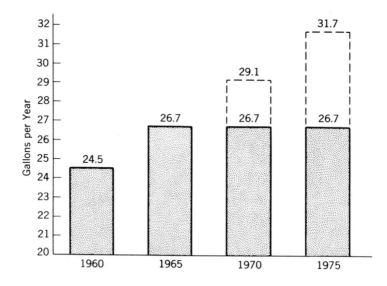

(Figures for 1970 and 1975 based on extrapolation of current trends.)

Table 2

BEER INDUSTRY STATISTICS

Beer Consumption Data Sheet

All Data in Thousands (May Not Add Due to Rounding); Per Capita Gallons in Parentheses

	1960	1965	1970	1975
Beer consumption:				
Barrels	87,495	100,600	108,700/118,300	118,800/139,800
Gallons	2,712,345	3,118,600	3,666,600	4,334,000
Total population	179,984	194,044	208,368	225,283
Pop. 20 & Over Total	110,539 (24.54)	116,936 (26.67)	126,176 (29.06)	136,745 (31.69)
Male	53,423	56,052	60,330	65,245
Female	57,116	60,884	65,846	71,500
20-34 Total	33,567 (32.80)	35,459 (35.90)	41,923 (39.02)	49,889 (42.24)
Male	16,428	17,402	20,734	24,814
Female	17,139	18,056	21,189	25,075
35-44 Total	24,122 (30.64)	24,333 (33.53)	22,888 (36.44)	22,308 (39.45)
Male	11,772	11,845	11,192	10,908
Female	12,350	12,488	11,696	11,399
45-54 Total	20,567 (24.14)	22,033 (26.42)	23,328 (28.72)	23,533 (31.09)
Male	10,125	10,711	11,279	11,340
Female	10,442	11,322	12,049	12,194
55 & Over Total	32,283 (11.64)	35,111 (12.74)	38,037 (13.85)	41,016 (15.00)
Male	15,098	16,094	17,125	18,183
Female	17,183	19,017	20,912	22,833

Note: (1) Per capita figures for 1970 and 1975 are based on continuation of 1960-65 trend.
(2) Total Barrelages are shown in a range: at 1965 per capita/continuation of trend.

157

Table 3

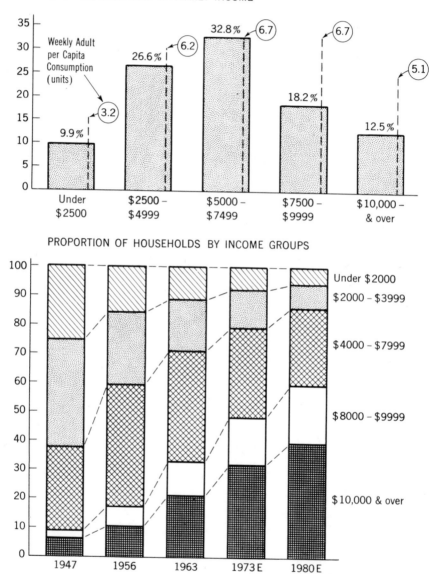

BEER CONSUMPTION BY FAMILY INCOME

PROPORTION OF HOUSEHOLDS BY INCOME GROUPS

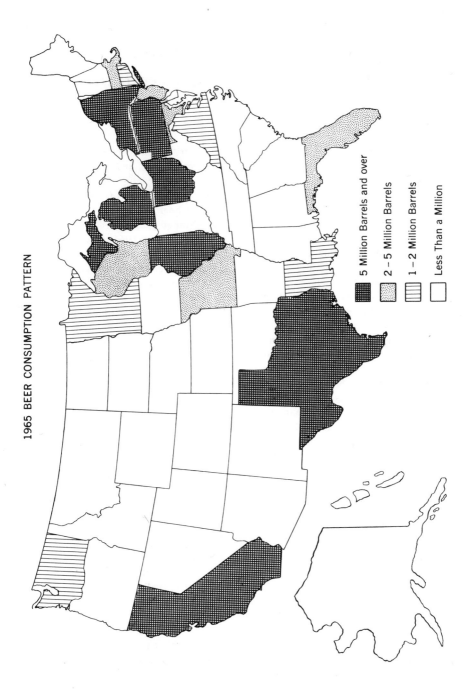

1965 BEER CONSUMPTION PATTERN

5 Million Barrels and over

2 – 5 Million Barrels

1 – 2 Million Barrels

Less Than a Million

APPENDIX B

Excerpts From Advertising Age Article About Schlitz

COMPUTER HELPS SCHLITZ BREW MARKET STRATEGY

Scientific Management Given Simultaneous Data on Host of Alternatives

By Rance Crain

MILWAUKEE, March 10—An era of scientific management has dawned at Jos. Schlitz Brewing Co., and the brewer's IBM 1620 computer—used exclusively for marketing problems—is busy spewing out a myriad of alternative courses of action for the company's new breed of executives.

Provider of this data, which ranges from beer sales projections and sales promotion effectiveness studies to beer drinker profiles, is the company's business research division. The division was set up in 1961, when the Schlitz marketing department was established, and it now has a staff of 23.

Objectives of the business research division, according to 29-year-old Gene Richmond, its manager, "are mainly to supply information to management to enable them to make better decisions. The computer is our No. 1 tool, I would say, because the mass of data which we have accumulated through various surveys, and reports that our field people and wholesalers send in is almost impossible to use unless you can reduce it to some form that management can look at and base decisions on."

In order for the computer to be a basic tool, however, two conditions must be met, Mr. Richmond said: "First, a company must have a management that insists on using facts in its decision making. Second, the company must be able to anticipate its data needs far enough in advance so that the computer can be properly programed."

Mr. Richmond's boss, Fred Haviland Jr., exec vp of marketing, considers the computer one muscle among many in the corporate body.

"It just extends men's ability to more closely fulfill the requirements imposed by a management that really subscribes to the essence of the science of managing its business," he told *Advertising Age*.

And the essence of scientific management, to Mr. Haviland, is "an understanding and an appreciation of what managing is. No marketing department previously existed at Schlitz. There were scattered pieces reporting to general management. The marketing department was created in December, 1961, and today I think we have a classical example of a multiple brand marketing organization in that it is conceptually completely capable of carrying out business in this new way and increasingly capable of implementing it by the use of the biggest management tool available, and that's research.

"Each of our brand directors, if his was the only brand, would be the marketing director. While obviously we have total corporate staff marketing facilities, we have five brand teams (one for Schlitz, Burgermeister, Old Milwaukee, Primo and the new Schlitz malt liquor) in which we have invested in the brand director total authority, as well as complete responsibility for sales and profits.

"We have matched the assignment and the delegation of responsibilities of these people with authority, and they are total marketing men, not essentially advertising men, as is frequently found. They are as whole cloth marketing management people as we have been able to develop.

"If these guys really function, I will have organized myself out of a job."

One of the things a computer allows a marketer to do, Mr. Haviland explained, is to "manipulate these data in greater detail at allowable costs, so that explorations of the observations, made through relatively conventional research methods, increase their utility."

Data of one kind developed from one source can be programed into a more sophisticated problem, he said, using data from other sources and additional estimates of consumer behavior.

"We have increased our marketing efficiency per dollar," Mr. Haviland said, "and it doesn't make any difference where the money is used—whether for a new automatic keg line, for advertising in a highly competitive market for a more sophisticated package that will attract samplers to a Schlitz brand or for salaries of half a dozen researchers."

To forecast the potential of beer, for instance, Schlitz has set up what it calls Media Coverage Areas (as opposed to the usual wholesaler trade areas). Each media coverage area is a small geographical unit encompassing the range of a television station, since most of Schlitz's advertising dollars are allocated to that medium.

"Although we don't have direct responsibility for the allocation of advertising dollars," Mr. Richmond explained, "we supply the various brand directors with beer potential by media coverage area.

"We will rank these areas according to, let's just say, estimated potential volume for one to five or ten years in the future. And we give him rates of growth of these areas and data on the competitive hardness or softness of the market," Mr. Richmond said.

Media coverage areas are the geographical units used in other Schlitz research activity, too. For example, Schlitz constructed a grid of 16 test markets for its malt liquor, plus four control markets. Four variables were measured: Regular Schlitz beer share of market; the share of existing malt liquor brands; the price level; and the advertising level. Schlitz selectively introduced the malt liquor in each market as the product became available. The company kept weekly reports on sales and shipments; at the end of 13 weeks it analyzed sales and did some market research on moods and attitudes and image.

Although the product is now in national distribution, Schlitz is keeping the 16 original cities as test markets to introduce a fifth variable—time. And the company has established still other markets to extract data on new packages.

Mr. Richmond is of the opinion that "research, obviously, will never create a campaign.

"All research will do is indicate direction," he said. "The execution, of course, is a function of the advertising agency and its creative people. A lot of times this is misinterpreted by creative people. We're not trying to develop ads. What we're trying to do is develop directions which will narrow the parameters down, so that creative people can point all their efforts in one direction.

"The biggest mistake you can make is to say, 'Gee, here's something that's successful; now let's run it for ten years.' Hamm's has had some of those problems, which they're changing now. Their campaign showing those little bears was perhaps the best liked of any campaign in the country. But having the best liked campaign doesn't necessarily mean that people are going to be induced to buy the product.

"Action inducement is one of the biggest objectives of an advertising campaign. Likability is, too, but it's not as important as action inducement. So campaigns have to change to keep up with the times. And in order to find out what's changing you have to do research."

One of the most important things that's changing is the tastes of the nation's beer drinkers, Mr. Richmond said. "This is what's really fascinating about the beer business today. The population is so varied and so segmented that the opportunities to get into this market and be successful are just enormous, if you know what your segments are and you take advantage of them."

A strike last summer in California pointed up one of the major shifts in taste toward lighter beers. The only brands which were available on the West Coast during that period were the three lightest brews—Coor's, Miller's and Olympia. For a three-month period beer drinkers in the area could buy nothing but light beers.

"So what happened after the strike was that the taste in the entire market changed—overnight, almost. It never happens that fast. We have the problem now of getting back to where we were before."

The California situation is a good example of the trend toward lighter, milder beers, Mr. Richmond said.

"However, there's still a segment of the population that likes a heavier, more full-bodied product. So you don't want to have one brand of beer that will be all things to all people—that's the whole idea of multiple brand strategy.

"One segment might prefer a very light beer," Mr. Richmond said. Another might enjoy a darker, heavier brew, as represented by imports, which now account for about 0.5% of the market (about 500,000 bbls.)—and could account for 1% of the market by 1970. Mr. Richmond said malt liquor might satisfy this segment, or perhaps Schlitz will be forced to market a brew similar to Hamm's Waldech or Anheuser-Busch's Michelob.

"We also have a premium segment that wants quality and is willing to pay for it. The image, the reputation of the brewer is important to these people. We sell Schlitz for them. Other people want something not heavy but just an average-type beer. This is Burgermeister. We could sell Primo as an exotic Hawaiian type, which appeals to another segment of the population. There's no reason why we couldn't have national distribution for all these products."

Mr. Richmond said Schlitz couldn't have put its multiple brand strategy into gear without computers.

"We couldn't get the information together; we couldn't develop the information," he said. "We make decisions on what I consider a very limited amount of information, even though it's vastly more than we've ever had before. It doesn't exhaust all the possibilities by any means."

Source: *Advertising Age*, March 15, 1965.

APPENDIX C

Table 1

STATISTICS ON THE POST'S "EFFICIENCY"

Post Reaches Beer Drinkers More Efficiently
(1965 Starch)

Primary Households	% of Households Serving or Consuming Beer	(4-C Page: Bld. CPM)
Post	57.7%	$12.24
Look	56.8	14.50
Life	58.6	15.14
In Combination	*Post + Life*	*Life + Look*
Net Households	7,551,000	7,590,000
% Unduplicated	88.1	84.2
CPM—4-Color Page Unduplicated Households	$12.08	$13.88

Table 2

STATISTICS ON THE POST'S "EFFICIENCY"

Post/Life - The Most Efficient Combination for Schlitz
Household Serving Alcoholic Beverages in Past Week

(1965 Simmons)

	Any Alcoholic Beverage Served (000)	(4-C Page: Bld. CPM)	Domestic Bev. & Ale Served (000)	(4-C Page: Bld. CPM)
Post/Life	14,152	$7.49	10,489	$10.11
Look/Life	14,685	8.26	10,963	11.06
Post/Look	13,217	7.94	9,877	10.62

Table 3

STATISTICS ON THE POST'S "EFFICIENCY"

Beer and Ale Advertiser Gets Better Readership
in the *Post*
(Starch Adnorms, 1965; % "noting")

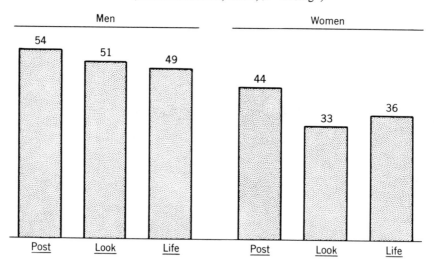

Table 4

STATISTICS ON THE POST'S "EFFICIENCY"

Market Profile — Beer Drinkers
(1964 B. R. I.)

Men Readers	All Beer Drinkers		Regular Beer Drinkers	
	50.7% of U.S. Men (Index)	100% of U.S. Consumption (% Comp.)	19.4% of U.S. Men (Index)	78.2% of U.S. Consumption (% Comp.)
Age:				
Under 25	99	50.2%	100	19.4%
25 - 49	120	61.0	115	22.4
50 - 64	84	42.5	93	18.1
Income:				
Households				
Under $5,000	79	40.2	89	17.2
$5,000 +	111	56.1	107	20.7
Education:				
Grade School or Less	74	37.7	91	17.7
High School or Better	111	56.3	104	20.2
County size:				
A & B	115	58.5	118	22.8
C & D	68	34.3	64	12.4

Table 5

STATISTICS ON THE POST'S "EFFICIENCY"

Combination Coverage of Marketing Targets
(1965 Simmons)
Net Unduplicated Audience, Average Issue — 4-C Page Bld., Open Rates

Men Readers	Post/Life (000)	CPM	Post/Look (000)	CPM	Life/Look (000)	CPM
All	22,442	$4.72	21,063	$ 4.98	23,276	$ 5.21
Age 25 - 49	11,289	9.39	10,183	10.30	11,551	10.50
In households with income $5,000 +	17,311	6.13	15,951	6.58	17,838	6.80
Education — some high school or better	18,638	5.69	17,032	6.16	19,111	6.34
Living in metro areas	15,029	7.06	13,277	7.90	15,371	7.89

Table 6

STATISTICS ON THE POST'S "EFFICIENCY"

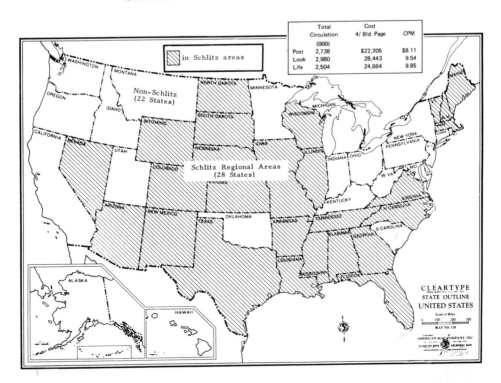

	Total Circulation (000)	Cost 4/ Bld. Page	CPM
Post	2,738	$22,205	$8.11
Look	2,980	28,443	9.54
Life	2,504	24,664	9.85

QUESTIONS

1. *As Schlitz, what criteria would you use to assess the* Post *as an appropriate media buy?*
2. *How does the* Post *measure up on these criteria? Is the* Post *a good media buy for Schlitz? Why? Why not?*
3. *Appraise the* Post's *efforts to sell the Schlitz account.*

Saturday
Evening Post (B)

Advertising sales executives at the magazine wonder how some additional market data they have received can be used to further their efforts to sell advertising space to Schlitz.

In August 1966, additional information became available to the advertising sales department of the *Post*. This material, which appears in Appendix A, included:

— Demographic profiles of male beer drinkers, including all beer drinkers, regular (one or more glasses daily) and heavy (three or more glasses daily) beer drinkers, and nonbeer drinkers. (See Table 1.)

— Beer consumption (Table 2) and Schlitz preference (Table 3) analyzed by readership of various magazines.

— Usage profile of male and female beer usage (i.e., served in home) and Schlitz usage. (See Table 4.)

— Beer usage and brand preference related to magazine readership, and magazine advertising costs for all adults (Table 5); for men (Table 6); and for women (Table 7).

Post advertising sales executives wondered how best to use this information in their efforts to sell space to Schlitz.

QUESTIONS

1. *With the additional information from Saturday Evening Post (B), what further thoughts do you have on the suitability of the* Post *as an advertising medium for Schlitz?*

APPENDIX A

Table 1

PROFILE OF TOTAL ADULT MEN BEER DRINKERS: PERSONAL CONSUMPTION OF BEER, 1966

	Total Beer Drinkers	Total Regular Beer Drinkers	Heaviest Beer Drinkers	Don't Drink Beer
U.S.	100	100	100	100
Age of individual				
Under 25 years	96	97	90	105
25-34 years	125	125	116	72
35-49 years	113	107	118	86
50-64 years	91	99	97	110
65 & over	59	61	61	145
Household income				
Under $5,000	85	101	111	116
$5,000 to $7,999	99	101	100	101
$8,000 to $9,999	112	103	92	87
$10,000 & over	117	95	88	81
Education of individual				
Grade school or less	79	83	84	123
High school but not beyond	104	113	123	95
College	118	97	80	80
County size				
A	115	120	124	83
B	100	95	96	100
C & D	82	81	77	120
Region				
North East	115	128	122	83
North Central	106	107	119	94
South	78	73	66	124
West	109	97	101	91

	Total Beer Drinkers	Total Regular Beer Drinkers	Heaviest Beer Drinkers	Don't Drink Beer
Occupation				
Professional and technical	119	91	90	79
Manager, official, execu- tive, & proprietor	113	100	89	86
Clerical and sales	113	103	113	86
Craftsman and foreman	110	114	110	89
Unskilled-service, labor, farm	98	110	114	102
Not employed, student, etc.	75	78	76	128
Household head				
Male head	103	101	99	97
Not male head	88	97	106	113
Race				
Negro	106	119	98	94
White and other	99	98	101	101
Presence of children by household income				
No children under 18				
Hld. income under $5,000	77	96	108	125
$5,000 to $7,999	93	100	95	108
$8,000 or more	107	100	94	93
Youngest child 6-17				
Hld. income under $5,000	83	77	77	118
$5,000 to $7,999	90	93	82	111
$8,000 or more	109	89	73	90
Youngest child under 6				
Hld. income under $5,000	107	133	145	93
$5,000 to $7,999	116	111	125	83
$8,000 or more	132	109	106	65

Definitions: Total Beer Drinkers - All men who drink beer
Total Regular Beer Drinkers - One or more glasses a day
Heaviest Beer Drinkers - Three or more glasses a day
Don't Drink Beer - Nonusers

Source: 1966 Brand Rating Index on total adult men (18 years and over).

169

Table 2
BEER—PERSONAL CONSUMPTION: HEAVINESS OF PRODUCT USAGE AMONG TOTAL ADULT MEN, AVERAGE-ISSUE AUDIENCE

Beer—Personal Consumption	U.S. (total)	Post	Life	Look	Sports Illustrated	Newsweek	Playboy
Heaviest beer drinkers							
%	9.3	11.0	8.7	9.6	11.0	9.6	12.8
Index	100	118	94	103	118	103	138
No. (000)	5,517	1,218	1,359	1,456	595	620	1,034
CPM-P4C, open rate	—	$32.98	$39.92	$36.35	$20.28	$26.18	$22.68
Total regular beer users							
%	23.2	27.1	25.3	25.6	30.9	29.5	34.3
Index	100	117	109	110	133	127	138
No. (000)	13,762	3,000	3,951	3,882	1,671	1,905	2,770
CPM-P4C, open rate	—	$13.39	$13.73	$13.63	$ 7.22	$ 8.52	$ 8.47
Total beer drinkers							
%	52.3	62.3	60.7	58.9	64.4	63.1	71.8
Index	100	119	116	113	123	121	137
No. (000)	31,025	6,897	9,480	8,931	3,482	4,074	5,799
CPM-P4C, open rate	—	$ 5.82	$ 5.72	$ 5.93	$ 3.46	$ 3.98	$ 4.04
P4C, open rate	—	$40,170	$54,250	$52,920	$12,065	$16,230	$23,450

Definitions: Heaviest Beer Drinkers - Three or more glasses of beer a day.
  Total Regular Beer Users - One or more glasses of beer a day
  Total Beer Drinkers - All beer drinkers
Source: 1966 Brand Rating Index on total adult men (18 years and over).

Table 3

CONSUMER BRAND PREFERENCES AMONG TOTAL ADULT MEN, AVERAGE-ISSUE AUDIENCES 1966

Schlitz Beer	U.S. (total)	Post	Life	Look	Sports Illustrated	Newsweek	Playboy
Total marketing targets							
%	16.3	21.5	20.5	20.7	24.3	24.9	26.8
Index	100	132	126	127	149	153	164
No. (000)	9,655	2,380	3,201	3,139	1,314	1,608	2,164
CPM-P4C, open rate	---	$16.88	$16.95	$16.86	$ 9.18	$10.09	$10.84
Total prime marketing targets							
%	9.1	11.8	10.3	11.3	12.9	12.4	13.2
Index	100	130	113	124	142	136	145
No. (000)	5,390	1,306	1,609	1,713	698	801	1,066
CPM-P4C, open rate	---	$30.76	$33.72	$30.89	$17.29	$20.26	$22.00
The (A) brand I buy most often							
%	4.0	6.0	5.2	5.4	7.5	6.3	6.4
Index	100	150	130	135	188	158	160
No. (000)	2,369	664	812	819	406	407	517
CPM-P4C, open rate	---	$60.50	$66.81	$64.62	$29.72	$39.88	$45.36
Page 4C, open rate	---	$40,170	$54,250	$52,920	$12,065	$16,230	$23,450

Definitions: Total Marketing Targets - Bought in last six months or better
Total Prime Marketing Targets - Second choice or better
The (A) Brand I Buy Most Often - First choice

Source: 1966 Brand Rating Index on total adult men (18 years and over).

Table 4

PROFILE OF ADULT BEER DRINKERS*: USAGE AND BRANDS, 1966

	Served Domestic Beer in Past Month	No. of Glasses Used in Past Week			Total Users	Nonusers	Schlitz Beer Used Most Often in Past Week
		Heavy	Medium	Light			
U.S.	100	100	100	100	100	100	100
Age respondent							
*Men**							
18-34 years	120	102	120	119	116	140	151
35-49 years	105	119	106	106	109	88	74
50 years & over	77	83	77	78	78	73	74
*Women**							
18-34 years	130	124	130	123	127	146	126
35-49 years	119	146	125	118	126	88	138
50 years & over	58	42	54	66	56	68	48
Household head—occupation							
Professional/managerial	121	95	115	120	112	158	111
Clerical/sales	110	113	116	112	114	93	140
Other employed	100	109	102	100	103	89	103
Not employed	66	72	65	68	68	62	51
Household head—education							
Attended/graduated college	119	108	100	127	112	147	114
Graduated high school	107	110	110	106	109	102	93
Did not graduate high school	86	89	93	82	89	75	97
Marital status							
Married	105	107	103	106	105	106	102
All other	86	81	92	85	87	83	96

Table 4 (cont.)

	Served Domestic Beer in Past Month	No. of Glasses Used in Past Week			Total Users	Nonusers	Schlitz Beer Used Most Often in Past Week
		Heavy	Medium	Light			
Household Income							
$15,000 & over	132	95	136	126	125	164	181
$10,000 - $14,999	129	105	123	136	124	151	121
$ 5,000 - $ 9,999	111	135	109	105	113	105	127
Under $5,000	66	55	70	72	68	57	39
Individual income							
$8,000 and over	122	127	94	128	113	160	109
No. of people in household							
1 - 2	77	79	78	73	77	81	81
3 - 4	110	109	113	109	111	109	120
5 or more	115	115	112	122	116	112	98
Geographic region							
Northeast	127	118	141	120	129	120	88
Central	110	129	102	103	108	122	143
South	59	45	58	71	60	54	75
West	115	122	110	117	115	116	90
Locality type							
Metro central city	118	122	131	113	123	100	128
Metro suburban	116	124	105	119	114	126	95
Non-metro	68	58	66	70	66	76	78

*Beer served in the home.
**Based on total U.S. men and total U.S. women.
Source: 1966 Simmons.

Table 5

AVERAGE-ISSUE ADULT AUDIENCES
(SIMMONS 1966)

B-1 - Beer - Domestic - Served in the Home - Usage and Brands

	U.S.		Post		C/M
	%	(000)	%	(000)	P4C
Total adults	100.0	121,961	100.0	22,322	$ 1.80
Served — past month					
Beer — domestic	44.5	54,319	47.8	10,670	3.76
Number glasses used in past week					
Heavy	7.1	8,683	7.0	1,561	25.73
Medium	15.8	19,294	16.4	3,661	10.97
Light	12.9	15,781	13.2	2,948	13.63
Total users	35.9	43,758	36.6	8,170	4.92
Nonusers	8.7	10,561	11.2	2,500	16.07
Brand used most often					
Ballantine	1.2	1,430	1.9	*415	96.80
Budweiser	4.3	5,194	4.7	1,048	38.33
Carling	1.8	2,141	1.4	319	125.92
Coors	1.9	2,337	2.7	592	67.85
Falstaff	1.9	2,313	1.9	432	92.99
Hamms	2.1	2,611	2.7	594	67.63
Miller	2.9	3,509	2.6	579	69.38
Olympia	1.8	2,219	2.9	657	61.14
Pabst	2.2	2,704	2.9	657	61.14
Rheingold	0.9	1,153	0.7	*157	
Schaefer	0.9	1,081	0.7	*153	
Schlitz	2.6	3,127	2.8	620	64.79
Other	18.5	22,602	18.1	4,042	9.94
Do not remember	1.7	2,129	2.1	466	86.20

Definitions: Heavy - 15 or more glasses in past week
             Medium - 5 to 14 glasses in past week
             Light - 1 to 4 glasses in past week
* Projection relatively unstable because of small sample base.
**Number of cases too small for reliability; shown for consistency only.

	Look			Life			Sports Illustrated	
%	*(000)*	*C/M P4C*	*%*	*(000)*	*C/M P4C*	*%*	*(000)*	*C/M P4C*
100.0	29,915	$ 1.77	100.0	33,272	$ 1.63	100.0	6,520	$ 1.85
48.4	14,468	3.66	51.1	16,984	3.19	61.7	4,021	3.00
8.9	2,673	19.80	8.5	2,828	19.18	10.0	654	18.45
16.6	4,961	10.67	18.1	6,020	9.01	21.9	1,427	8.45
13.7	4,097	12.92	14.7	4,904	11.06	15.9	1,039	11.61
39.2	11,731	4.51	41.3	13,752	3.94	47.9	3,120	3.87
9.1	2,736	19.34	9.7	3,232	16.79	13.8	902	13.38
1.4	404	130.99	1.7	575	94.35	1.3	**83	145.36
3.9	1,181	44.81	4.6	1,546	35.09	8.6	562	21.47
1.6	481	110.02	2.3	749	72.43	1.7	*113	106.77
2.3	684	77.37	1.9	636	85.30	3.5	*228	52.92
1.9	581	91.08	1.9	640	84.77	2.9	*190	63.50
2.6	775	68.28	2.0	671	80.85	3.2	*209	57.73
3.2	964	54.90	4.5	1,501	36.14	5.3	347	34.77
2.4	709	74.64	2.5	825	65.76	2.7	*175	68.94
2.3	689	76.81	2.0	655	82.82	3.6	*234	51.56
0.9	*258		0.9	291	186.43	0.3	**22	
1.1	321	164.86	1.1	380	142.76	1.2	**81	148.95
2.7	804	65.82	3.6	1,187	45.70	2.6	**170	70.97
20.2	6,046	8.75	19.9	6,629	8.18	23.5	1,534	7.87
2.1	638	82.95	2.3	762	71.19	1.5	*95	127.00

Table 5 (cont.)

	Newsweek			Playboy		
	%	(000)	C/M P4C	%	(000)	C/M P4C
Total adults	100.0	10,124	$ 1.60	100.0	9,000	$ 2.61
Served — past month						
Beer — domestic	53.2	5,383	3.02	65.0	5,847	4.01
Number glasses used in past week						
Heavy	8.6	872	18.61	13.3	1,197	19.59
Medium	18.8	1,906	8.52	23.7	2,132	11.00
Light	16.4	1,660	9.78	14.9	1,341	17.49
Total users	43.8	4,438	3.66	51.9	4,670	5.02
Nonusers	9.3	946	17.16	13.1	1,177	19.92
Brand used most often						
Ballantine	0.8	*84	193.21	1.6	**146	160.62
Budweiser	7.0	708	22.92	9.3	836	28.05
Carling	0.8	*79		2.5	*224	104.69
Coors	2.8	280	57.96	4.3	383	61.23
Falstaff	2.7	*271	59.89	2.7	*242	96.90
Hamms	2.1	*214	75.84	2.0	*178	131.74
Miller	4.2	428	37.92	7.8	703	33.36
Olympia	2.9	*294	55.20	3.2	288	81.42
Pabst	4.3	436	37.22	4.6	416	56.37
Rheingold	1.1	**111	146.22	1.1	**96	
Schaefer	0.6	**57		1.9	*167	140.42
Schlitz	3.1	*313	51.85	3.5	*316	74.21
Other	19.3	1,949	8.33	18.7	1,682	13.94
Do not remember	1.9	*188	86.33	2.2	*199	117.84

Definitions: Heavy - 15 or more glasses in past week
             Medium - 5 to 14 glasses in past week
             Light - 1 to 4 glasses in past week
* Projection relatively unstable because of small sample base.
**Number of cases too small for reliability; shown for consistency only.

Table 6

AVERAGE-ISSUE ADULT MALE AUDIENCES
(SIMMONS 1966)

B-1M - Beer - Domestic - Served in the Home - Usage and Brands

	U.S.		Post		C/M P4C
	%	(000)	%	(000)	
Total Adult Males	100.0	58,995	100.0	11,190	$ 3.59
Served − past month Beer − domestic	48.9	28,825	51.0	5,708	7.04
Number of glasses used in past week					
Heavy	8.2	4,867	6.9	769	52.24
Medium	17.1	10,061	18.3	2,047	19.62
Light	13.8	8,145	14.3	1,595	25.18
Total users	39.1	23,073	39.4	4,411	9.11
Nonusers	9.7	5,752	11.6	1,297	30.97
Brands used most often					
Ballantine	1.2	717	0.8	**93	
Budweiser	4.7	2,762	5.3	590	68.08
Carling	2.1	1,268	1.4	*153	
Coors	2.4	1,391	3.2	355	113.15
Falstaff	2.2	1,289	1.8	*202	198.86
Hamms	1.9	1,146	3.2	356	112.89
Miller	3.1	1,810	2.5	277	145.02
Olympia	1.8	1,082	3.1	348	115.43
Pabst	2.9	1,732	4.1	*462	86.95
Rheingold	0.9	553	0.9	**96	
Schaefer	1.0	566	0.8	**84	
Schlitz	3.0	1,786	3.4	*375	107.12
Other	20.0	11,818	19.4	2,173	18.49
Do not remember	1.8	1,043	1.7	*190	

Definitions: Heavy - 15 or more glasses in past week
                Medium - 5 to 14 glasses in past week
                Light - 1 to 4 glasses in past week
 * Projection relatively unstable because of small sample base.
**Number of cases too small for reliability; shown for consistency only.

Table 6 (cont.)

	Look			Life		
	%	(000)	C/M P4C	%	(000)	C/M P4C
Total Adult Males	100.0	14,989	$ 3.53	100.0	16,925	$ 3.21
Served — past month						
Beer — domestic	52.6	7,883	6.71	55.5	9,388	5.78
Number of glasses used in past week						
Heavy	9.1	1,366	38.74	9.2	1,551	34.98
Medium	18.4	2,761	19.17	20.1	3,401	15.95
Light	16.2	2,421	21.86	15.7	2,655	20.43
Total users	43.7	6,548	8.08	44.9	7,607	7.13
Nonusers	8.9	1,335	39.64	10.5	1,781	30.46
Brands used most often						
Ballantine	1.1	*171		1.6	*275	
Budweiser	4.5	668	79.22	6.1	1,039	52.21
Carling	1.7	*262		2.5	420	129.17
Coors	2.7	405	130.67	2.0	335	161.94
Falstaff	2.2	328	161.34	2.4	405	133.95
Hamms	2.4	361	146.59	2.1	348	155.89
Miller	3.7	556	95.18	5.4	914	59.35
Olympia	2.7	412	128.45	2.4	409	132.69
Pabst	2.9	436	121.38	2.3	383	141.64
Rheingold	1.1	**166		1.1	*183	
Schaefer	1.4	*210		1.2	*209	
Schlitz	3.0	444	119.19	3.8	650	83.46
Other	21.7	3,256	16.25	20.8	3,513	15.49
Do not remember	1.7	*248		2.1	351	154.56

Definitions: Heavy - 15 or more glasses in past week
Medium - 5 to 14 glasses in past week
Light - 1 to 4 glasses in past week
* Projection relatively unstable because of small sample base.
**Number of cases too small for reliability; shown for consistency only.

Sports Illustrated			Newsweek			Playboy		
%	(000)	C/M P4C	%	(000)	C/M P4C	%	(000)	C/M P4C
100.0	5,414	$ 2.23	100.0	6,454	$ 2.51	100.0	7,338	$ 3.20
64.7	3,505	3.44	59.1	3,814	4.26	67.4	4,943	4.74
9.3	503	23.99	9.9	637	25.48	14.1	1,032	22.72
23.4	1,266	9.53	19.4	1,250	12.98	24.2	1,778	13.19
16.5	894	13.50	18.7	1,205	13.47	16.0	1,177	19.92
49.2	2,663	4.53	47.9	3,092	5.25	54.3	3,987	5.88
15.6	842	14.33	11.2	723	22.45	13.0	956	24.53
1.4	**77	156.69	0.6	**41		1.6	**116	
9.7	524	23.02	8.9	574	28.28	10.1	744	31.52
1.5	**82	147.13	0.6	**40		2.6	** 189	124.07
3.0	*163	74.02	2.6	*169	96.04	4.4	*325	72.15
3.5	*187	64.52	3.6	**231	70.26	2.4	*177	132.49
3.5	*191	63.17	2.5	*159	102.08	1.8	*132	177.65
5.1	*277	43.56	4.3	278	58.38	8.6	633	37.05
3.0	*160	75.41	2.1	*133	122.03	3.5	*256	91.60
3.3	**178	67.78	5.3	*343	47.32	4.9	*357	65.69
0.4	**22		1.2	**77		1.1	**80	
1.3	**68	177.43	0.7	**44		2.2	**159	147.48
3.0	**162	74.48	3.2	*206	78.79	2.9	*214	109.58
24.9	1,347	8.96	21.9	1,413	11.49	19.3	1,416	16.56
1.5	**83	145.36	2.0	**130	124.85	2.2	**165	142.12

Table 7

AVERAGE-ISSUE ADULT FEMALE AUDIENCES
(SIMMONS 1966)

B-1 F - Beer - Domestic - Served in the Home - Usage and Brands

	U.S.		Post		
	%	(000)	%	(000)	C/M P4C
Total Adult Females	100.0	62,966	100.0	11,132	$ 3.61
Served — past month Beer — domestic	40.5	25,494	44.6	4,962	8.10
Number of glasses used in past week					
Heavy	6.1	3,816	7.1	792	50.72
Medium	14.7	9,233	14.5	1,614	24.89
Light	12.1	7,636	12.2	1,353	29.69
Total users	32.8	20,685	33.8	3,759	10.69
Nonusers	7.6	4,809	10.8	1,203	33.39
Brand used most often					
Ballantine	1.1	713	2.9	*322	124.75
Budweiser	3.9	2,432	4.1	458	87.71
Carling	1.4	873	1.5	*166	241.99
Coors	1.5	946	2.1	*237	169.49
Falstaff	1.6	1,024	2.1	*230	174.65
Hamms	2.3	1,465	2.1	*238	168.78
Miller	2.7	1,699	2.7	302	133.01
Olympia	1.8	1,137	2.8	309	130.00
Pabst	1.5	972	1.8	*195	206.00
Rheingold	1.0	600	0.5	**61	
Schaefer	0.8	515	0.6	**69	
Schlitz	2.1	1,341	2.2	*245	163.96
Other	17.1	10,784	16.8	1,869	21.49
Do not remember	1.7	1,086	2.5	276	145.54

Definitions: Heavy - 15 or more glasses in past week
              Medium - 5 to 14 glasses in past week
              Light - 1 to 4 glasses in past week
  * Projection relatively unstable because of small sample base.
**Number of cases too small for reliability; shown for consistency only.

	Look			Life			Sports Illustrated	
%	(000)	C/M P4C	%	(000)	C/M P4C	%	(000)	C/M P4C
100.0	14,926	$ 3.55	100.0	16,347	$ 3.32	100.0	1,106	$10.91
44.1	6,585	8.04	46.5	7,596	7.14	46.7	516	23.38
8.8	1,307	40.49	7.8	1,277	42.48	13.7	**151	79.90
14.7	2,200	24.05	16.0	2,619	20.71	14.6	*161	74.94
11.2	1,676	31.58	13.8	2,249	24.12	13.1	*145	83.21
34.7	5,183	10.21	37.6	6,145	8.83	41.3	457	26.40
9.4	1,401	37.77	8.9	1,451	37.39	5.4	*60	
1.6	*233	227.12	1.8	*300	180.33	0.5	**6	
3.4	513	103.16	3.1	507	107.00	3.4	**38	
1.5	219	241.64	2.0	329	164.89	2.8	**31	
1.9	279	189.68	1.8	301	180.23	5.9	**65	185.62
1.7	*253	209.17	1.4	*235	230.85	0.3	**3	
2.8	414	127.83	2.0	323	167.96	1.6	**18	
2.7	408	129.71	3.6	587	92.42	6.3	**70	172.36
2.0	297	178.18	2.5	416	130.41	1.4	**15	
1.7	253	209.17	1.7	272	199.45	5.1	**56	
0.6	*92		0.7	*108				
0.7	**111		1.0	*171		1.2	**13	
2.4	360	147.00	3.3	537	101.02	0.7	**8	
18.7	2,790	18.97	19.1	3,116	17.41	16.9	187	64.52
2.6	390	135.69	2.5	411	132.00	1.1	**12	

Table 7 (cont.)

	Newsweek			Playboy		
	%	(000)	C/M P4C	%	(000)	C/M P4C
Total Adult Females	100.0	3,670	$ 4.42	100.0	1,662	$14.11
Served — past month						
Beer — domestic	42.8	1,569	10.34	54.4	904	25.94
Number of glasses used in past week						
Heavy	6.4	235	69.06	9.9	*165	142.12
Medium	17.9	656	24.74	21.3	354	66.24
Light	12.4	455	35.67	9.9	164	142.99
Total users	36.7	1,346	12.06	41.1	683	34.33
Nonusers	6.1	223	72.78	13.3	221	106.11
Brand used most often						
Ballantine	1.2	**43		1.8	**30	
Budweiser	3.7	*134	121.12	5.5	*92	
Carling	1.1	**39		2.1	**35	
Coors	3.0	**111	146.22	3.5	**58	
Falstaff	1.1	**40		3.9	**65	
Hamms	1.5	**55		2.8	**46	
Miller	4.1	*150	108.20	4.2	**70	
Olympia	4.4	**161	100.81	1.9	**32	
Pabst	2.5	**93	174.52	3.6	**59	
Rheingold	0.9	**34		1.0	**16	
Schaefer	0.4	**13		0.5	** 8	
Schlitz	2.9	**107	151.68	6.1	**102	
Other	14.6	536	30.28	16.0	266	88.16
Do not remember	1.6	**58		2.0	**34	

Definitions: Heavy - 15 or more glasses in past week
Medium - 5 to 14 glasses in past week
Light - 1 to 4 glasses in past week
* Projection relatively unstable because of small sample base.
**Number of cases too small for reliability; shown for consistency only.

Consumer
Value Stores (B)

Media Scheduling Assignment

The advertising manager of a chain of discount drugstores must prepare a media schedule for the back-to-school promotion to be run by CVS stores in the Springfield (Massachusetts) area.

In addition to creating print and broadcast advertisements, one of the responsibilities of the advertising manager of Consumer Value Stores (CVS) was that of preparing specific media schedules for these ads. These schedules, along with a rationale supporting the expenditure considered necessary, had to be presented to other members of CVS management for approval before the ads could be run.

Consumer Value Stores was a chain of "health and beauty aid" stores operating in shopping centers and in neighborhood shopping areas throughout New England. CVS stores offered drugstore and proprietary products—e.g., aspirin, toothpaste, shampoo, vitamins, and the like—at discount prices. CVS was one of several such chains in New England; competitors included the Rexall, Rix, Wendy K, and Big L groups.

Approximately 60% of the 45 CVS outlets were located in Massachusetts. The sizes of stores varied, but all were modern, well-lighted, self-service operations. Although many stores devoted space to pet products, film, and school supplies, the heart of the business was health and beauty aids. Most CVS customers were women in the middle- and upper-middle-income brackets.

Consumer research had shown that in towns where CVS stores were located, better than half the women had heard of Consumer Value Stores. Of these more than two-thirds had seen CVS advertising, almost entirely in newspapers. This advertising had centered around the "good value" image the chain was trying to project. The newspaper ads typically had featured the weekly specials and the slogan, "You get it for less at CVS." Occasionally the chain had tried other media; for example, a recent institutional campaign had consisted exclusively of radio commercials.

In early July the advertising manager was in the process of preparing media schedules for the CVS back-to-school promotion. This campaign would be run during the last two weeks of August and the first two weeks of September. His immediate concern was to develop a schedule on behalf of the CVS stores in the Springfield-Holyoke-Chicopee (Massachusetts) trading area. Although the budget for this promotion was somewhat flexible, the ad manager knew it would be difficult to justify a total area expenditure for this promotion that was larger than $5,000.

Exhibits 1 to 4 contain rate-and-audience data for Springfield-Holyoke-Chicopee media in summary form. Appendices A and B reproduce promotional literature supplied by two of these individual media vehicles, illustrative of the additional information provided to the advertising manager by the media.

Exhibit 1

OUTDOOR ADVERTISING DATA

Springfield - Chicopee - Holyoke

	Metro Market		Metro County*	
Population—				
January 1968	382,300		552,700	
Size of Showing	# 100	# 75	# 100	# 75
No. of Illuminated				
Panels	26	20	26	20
No. of Regular				
Panels	26	20	49	36
Costs for One				
Month	$3,380	$2,600	$4,490	$3,368
Operator	Springfield Advertising Company			

Posting Dates: 5th, 10th, 15th, 20th, 25th of any month.

* Metro County includes Holyoke, Northampton, Springfield, Chicopee, Westfield, and balance of Hampden and Hampshire Counties.

Exhibit 2

NEWSPAPER ADVERTISING DATA

	Holyoke Daily Transcript-Telegram	Springfield Herald*	Springfield Union	Springfield Daily News	Republican
Publication times and dates	Evenings except Sundays and holidays	Thursday and Sunday	Mornings except Sunday	Evenings except Sundays and holidays	Sundays
City zone population	122,900**		353,975***	353,975***	353,975***
City zone occupied housing units	35,450		105,475	105,475	105,475
Average paid circulation – city zone	24,881		47,940	78,016	76,471
Retail trading zone population	95,050#		248,950##	248,950##	248,950##
Retail trading zone OHU's	26,625		70,925	70,925	70,925
Average paid circulation – retail trading zone	1,793		18,753	17,149	28,070
Total paid circulation ###	27,563		77,776	96,314	117,987
Line rate – black and white	$.15	$.25	$.39+	$.51	$.46
Rate for B/W and 1 color	B/W rate + 47%		B/W line rate plus $250		
Position charges	20% for a specific page		12-1/2% next to reading; 25% for full position; specific page not guaranteed		

* No data supplied by publisher.
** Includes Holyoke, Chicopee, South Hadley.
*** Includes Springfield, Chicopee, Westfield, plus half a dozen towns in Hampden County.
\# Includes Westfield City, West Springfield, Amherst, Belchertown, Easthampton, Granby, Hadley, Southampton.
\## Includes Holyoke, Northampton, approximately two dozen towns in Hampden, Hampshire, and Franklin Counties, plus four towns in Connecticut.
\### Total paid circulation includes some circulation beyond the retail trading zone.
+ Combination *Union* and *Daily News* ads can be used at a cost of $.63 per line. Such ads must start in the evening newspaper and be finished the following morning.

Exhibit 3

RADIO ADVERTISING DATA

Station	WACE	WDEW	WHYN	WHYN-FM	WMAS	WMAS-FM	WREB	WSPR	WTXL	WTYM
Watts of power	5,000	1,000	5,000	50,000	1,000		500	5,000	1,000	5,000
Location	Chicopee	Westfield	Spring-field	Spring-field	Spring-field	Spring-field	Holyoke	Spring-field	W. Spring-field	E. Long-meadow
Station Programming	some ehtnic music	m-o-r music, ethnic music, Yankees	pop music	m-o-r* music	m-o-r music, some sports		m-o-r music, some ethnic	pop music		show tunes, standards
Cost/Announcement "AA" time	below	below	60 30 6-10 A.M. 3-7 P.M.	60 all hours	60** 5:30-10 A.M. 3-7 P.M. (M-Sat)	30**	below	60 30 5:30-10 A.M. (M-Sat)	60 30 6-10 A.M. 4-7 P.M. (M-Sat)	below
1-6***			16.00 12.50	7.50	10.00	9.00		15.00 13.00	22 18	
7-13			15.50 12.00	7.25	9.50	8.50		14.00 12.00	20 16	
14-20			15.00 11.50	7.00	9.00	8.00		13.50 11.50	18 14	
21-27			14.50 11.00	6.75	8.50	7.50		13.00 11.00	17 13	
28+			14.00 10.50	6.50	8.00	7.00		12.50 10.50	16 12	
"A" time			10 A.M.- 3 P.M.		10 A.M.-3 P.M. (M-Sat) 8 A.M.-7 P.M. (Sun)	10 A.M.-3 P.M. (M-Sat) (Sun)		3-7 P.M. (M-Sat); noon-7 P.M. (Sun)	10 A.M.- 4 P.M. (M-Sat); (Sun)	
1-6			13.00 12.50		9.00	8.00		14.00 12.25	20 16	
7-13			12.50 12.00		8.50	7.50		13.00 11.25	18 14	
14-20			12.00 11.50		8.00	7.00		12.50 10.75	16 12	
21-27			11.50 11.00		7.50	6.50		12.00 10.25	15 11	
28+			11.00 10.50		7.00	6.00		11.00 9.75	14 10	
			7-12 P.M.		All Other Times			10 A.M.-3 P.M. (M-Sat)	All Others	

"B" Time

Times	60	30	60	30	60	30	60	30
1-6	11.00	10.50	7.00	6.00	13.00	11.50	15	12
7-13	10.75	10.25	6.50	5.50	12.00	10.50	13	10
14-20	10.50	10.00	6.00	5.00	11.50	10.00	12	8
21-27	10.25	9.75	5.50	4.50	11.00	9.50	11	7
28+	10.00	9.50	5.00	4.00	10.50	9.00	10	6

"C" Time

Times	12 P.M.- 6 A.M.	
1-6	5.00†	4.00†
7-13		
14-20		
21-27		
28+		

All Other Times

Times	60	30
1-6	9.50	8.25
7-13	8.50	7.25
14-20	8.00	6.75
21-27	7.50	6.25
28+	7.00	5.75

WDEW rates

Cost/Announcement

Times/Week	60	30
12	$6.00	$5.00
24	5.40	4.50
36	4.80	4.00
48	4.20	3.50

WACE rates

	"AA"		"A"	
	60	30	60	30
1 Time	$25.00	$19.50	$22	$18
26 Times	24.00	17.00	21	16

"AA" - 6-10 A.M. & 4-7 P.M.
"A" - 10 A.M.-4 P.M. & 7 P.M. - sign-off

WREB rates

One minute — $8.00 (less than 10 times)
30 seconds — 5.00 (less than 10 times)

Volume discounts

10 times	less 10%
20 times	less 20%
30 times	less 30%
40 times	less 40%

WTYM rates

	"AA"		"A"	
	60	30	60	30
12 Times	$14	$12	$11	$9
18 Times	13	11	10	8
24 Times	12	10	9	7

"AA" - 6-9 A.M. & 4-7 P.M.
"A" - 9 A.M.-4 P.M. & all other times

---

* Middle-of-the-road.
** Same rates apply to either AM or FM station.
*** Times per week.

Note: Rates for WACE, WTXL, and WTYM were extracted from SRDS and probably represent general rates. Retail rates, which are usually lower than general, were unavailable from these stations.

† Flat rate, no frequency discounts.

Exhibit 4

TELEVISION ADVERTISING DATA

	WWLP-TV	*WHYN-TV*
Network affiliation	NBC	ABC
Power — watts	1,000,000	250,000
Average daily TV homes*	152,700	132,900
Net weekly TV homes*	232,800	231,600
Color capability		
Network	Yes	Yes
Local	Yes	Yes

*Springfield Metro-Market only.

ANNOUNCEMENT RATES

WWLP-TV The following rates are for fixed position, non-preemptible one-minute announcements at all times and 30/20-second announcements from 7:30 P.M. to 10:30 P.M. The first announcement in any week costs $300; the second $270; the third $243. Additional announcements are as follows:

	4	*5*	*6*	*7*	*8*	*9*	*10*	*11*	*12*	*13*	*14*
Cost for Annemt. Number	$219	197	177	159	143	129	116	104	94	85	76

WHYN-TV

Class		*1 Time*	*26 Times*	*52 Times*	*ARB Rating*
"AA" Rates	60/30	$132.00	$125.00	$119.00	36,300*
(7:30 p.m.–	20 sec.	110.00	105.00	99.00	
11:00 p.m.)					
"A" Rates	60/30	73.00	70.00	67.00	33,800
(6:00 p.m.–	20 sec.	63.00	60.00	58.00	
7:30 p.m. &					
11:00 p.m.–					
11:30 p.m.)					
"B" Rates	60/30	46.00	44.00	42.00	31,300
(4:00 p.m.–	20 sec.	41.00	39.00	37.00	
6:00 p.m.)					
"C" Rates	60/30	36.00	34.00	32.00	16,100
(all other	20 sec.	30.00	29.00	28.00	
times)					

Additional discounts for 104, 156, and 260 times not shown here.

* Average number of viewing homes.

APPENDIX A

Springfield Union-News-Republican Promotional Material

Exhibit 4
RADIO ADVERTISING DATA

SPRINGFIELD

MASSACHUSETTS'
2nd LARGEST MARKET

THE NEW SPRINGFIELD NEWSPAPERS' MODERN PLANT

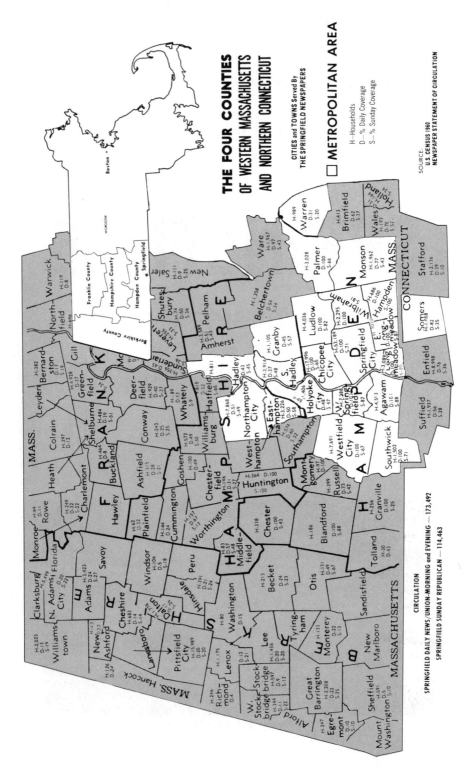

THE FOUR COUNTIES
OF WESTERN MASSACHUSETTS
AND NORTHERN CONNECTICUT

CITIES and TOWNS Served By
THE SPRINGFIELD NEWSPAPERS

☐ METROPOLITAN AREA

H—Households
D—% Daily Coverage
S—% Sunday Coverage

SOURCE:
U.S. CENSUS 1960
NEWSPAPER STATEMENT OF CIRCULATION

CIRCULATION

SPRINGFIELD DAILY NEWS/UNION-MORNING and EVENING — 173,492
SPRINGFIELD SUNDAY REPUBLICAN — 114,463

190

OUTSIDE OF BOSTON . . .
SPRINGFIELD NEWSPAPERS
REACH THE LARGEST NUMBER
OF MASSACHUSETTS FAMILIES
DAILY AND SUNDAY . . .

	Market Rank	Newspapers	Circulation Daily	Sunday
Boston	1	Record-American, Advertiser	433,372	432,963
		Globe	432,667	566,377
		Herald Traveler	216,305	298,557
Springfield	2	Union-News, Republican	172,482	113,754
Worcester	3	Telegram-Gazette	156,562	108,367
New Bedford	4	Standard-Times	71,238	62,154

COVERAGE ANALYSIS

March 1969

	Standard Metropolitan Statistical Area**	4-County Market*	A.D.I. 3 Counties
Population 1968	521,000	767,300	617,400
Households 1968	155,100	229,000	185,000
Circulations		(3/31/68 ABC Audits)	
Union-News (M&E)	143,675	161,148	155,606
Republican (S)	95,677	108,103	100,725
Household coverage			
Union-News (M&E)	93%	70%	84%
Republican (S)	62	47	54
Total Circulation		Milline	General Rate
(9/30/68 Publisher Statements)			
Union-News (M&E)	172,482	$3.59	$.63 Flat
Republican (S)	113,754	3.98	.46 Flat

  * Hampden, Hampshire, Berkshire and Franklin Counties
 ** Parts of Hampden, Hampshire and Worcester Counties
    Source: Population and Households–1968 Sales Management; ABC Estimates; SRDS and Census.
    Newspaper Circulations–As indicated.

SPRINGFIELD, MASS.

The DAILY Newspaper
Reaches **86.4%**
of <u>ALL</u> Households

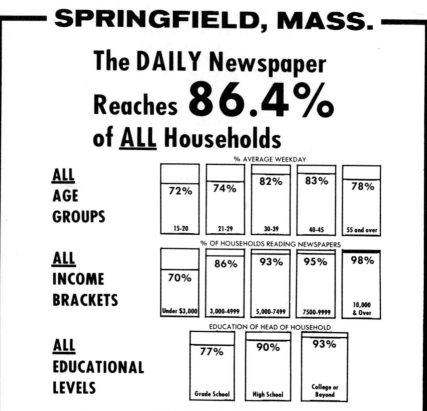

% AVERAGE WEEKDAY

ALL AGE GROUPS

72%	74%	82%	83%	78%
15-20	21-29	30-39	40-45	55 and over

% OF HOUSEHOLDS READING NEWSPAPERS

ALL INCOME BRACKETS

70%	86%	93%	95%	98%
Under $3,000	3,000-4999	5,000-7499	7500-9999	10,000 & Over

EDUCATION OF HEAD OF HOUSEHOLD

ALL EDUCATIONAL LEVELS

77%	90%	93%
Grade School	High School	College or Beyond

SOURCE: AUDITS AND SURVEYS INC.

READ THOROUGHLY . . . People who buy a newspaper read it thoroughly. 71% read the paper page by page, from front to back. Median reading time is 37 minutes per paper, and the average person reads 1.4 newspapers per day*.
*Source Audits and Surveys, Inc.

YEAR ROUND STABILITY . . . The Daily Newspaper changes with the seasons and adapts to all segments of the population, so the size of the audience is constant . . . no summer slumps.

AFFORDABILITY . . . Advertising is an investment, not an expense, when it produces more in profits than it costs. Local advertisers the kind of businessmen who expect an ad investment to pay quick dividends at the cash register favor the newspaper over all other media.
SOURCE: McCANN-ERICKSON

SPRINGFIELD RETAIL TRADING ZONE AREA
POPULATION 599,325 - OCCUPIED HOUSING UNITS 175,475 - COVERAGE 91.5%
SOURCE: AUDIT BUREAU OF CIRCULATIONS 3/31/68

SPRINGFIELD, MASS.
TV COVERAGE
Metropolitan Area

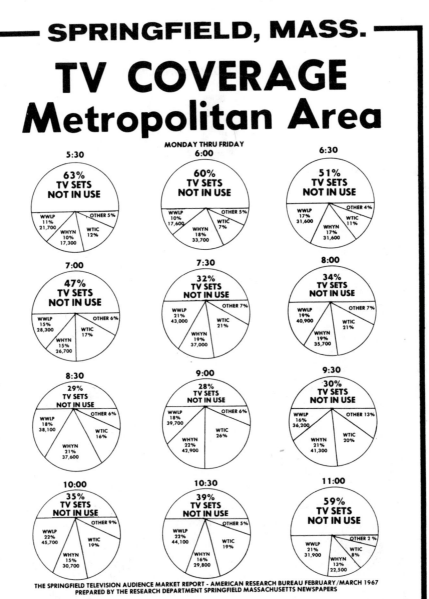

MONDAY THRU FRIDAY

5:30

63% TV SETS NOT IN USE

WWLP 11% 21,700 — OTHER 5% — WHYN 10% 17,300 — WTIC 12%

6:00

60% TV SETS NOT IN USE

WWLP 10% 17,600 — OTHER 5% — WTIC 7% — WHYN 18% 33,700

6:30

51% TV SETS NOT IN USE

WWLP 17% 31,600 — OTHER 4% — WTIC 11% — WHYN 17% 31,600

7:00

47% TV SETS NOT IN USE

WWLP 15% 28,300 — OTHER 6% — WTIC 17% — WHYN 15% 26,700

7:30

32% TV SETS NOT IN USE

WWLP 21% 43,000 — OTHER 7% — WTIC 21% — WHYN 19% 37,000

8:00

34% TV SETS NOT IN USE

WWLP 19% 40,900 — OTHER 7% — WTIC 21% — WHYN 19% 35,700

8:30

29% TV SETS NOT IN USE

WWLP 18% 38,100 — OTHER 6% — WTIC 16% — WHYN 21% 37,600

9:00

28% TV SETS NOT IN USE

WWLP 18% 39,700 — OTHER 6% — WTIC 26% — WHYN 22% 42,900

9:30

30% TV SETS NOT IN USE

WWLP 16% 36,200 — OTHER 13% — WTIC 20% — WHYN 21% 41,300

10:00

35% TV SETS NOT IN USE

WWLP 22% 45,700 — OTHER 9% — WTIC 19% — WHYN 15% 30,700

10:30

39% TV SETS NOT IN USE

WWLP 22% 44,100 — OTHER 5% — WTIC 19% — WHYN 16% 29,800

11:00

59% TV SETS NOT IN USE

WWLP 21% 31,900 — OTHER 2% — WTIC 8% — WHYN 13% 22,500

THE SPRINGFIELD TELEVISION AUDIENCE MARKET REPORT - AMERICAN RESEARCH BUREAU FEBRUARY/MARCH 1967
PREPARED BY THE RESEARCH DEPARTMENT SPRINGFIELD MASSACHUSETTS NEWSPAPERS

APPENDIX B

WHYN—AM PROMOTIONAL DATA

SPRINGFIELD HIGHLIGHTS

1.   59th SMSA with 522,000 people.

2.   There are 21 cities, towns and villages in this metropolis of Springfield-Chicopee-Holyoke.

3.   49% of all employees are engaged in manufacturing—a heavily industrial area.

4.   24% of all households earn $10,000 up, well ahead of the national average.

5.   70% (384,000) of the population resides outside central city.

6.   Springfield itself houses 44% of the manufacturing plants and businesses of the SMSA.

7.   Springfield is a transportation hub of the area being served by seven major air carriers, 4 railroads, 14 bus lines and 12 major motor freight carriers.

8.   Median age is 31.9 years. (U.S. average 29.5 years.)

9.   Within 100 miles, the population is 1.8 million.

10.   In 48% of all area households, there are 2 or more workers.

11.   Educational attainment corresponds almost exactly with the national average.

12.   Springfield is the Gateway to New England vacation and skiing resorts for those arriving from New Jersey, New York, and Connecticut.

13.   The city is almost equidistant from New York (135 miles) and Boston (100 miles).

14.   There is one car for every 3.7 persons.

15.   Leading food chain is A & P with 26% share of the total food sales.

WHYN–SPRINGFIELD
5,000 watts–560 kc

* Modern popular contemporary music.

* 5,000 watts . . . 560 kc . . . best signal and coverage in the area.

* Tight production with a modern top tune format and well-known personalities.

* The most heavily manned and most active news staff in the Market with 18 men. UPI, AP, UP Audio. WHYN is publicized as the "News Station."

* Winner of the UPI News Award 5 Consecutive years; 11 UPI awards total.

* Extensive merchandising program that includes:
(1) in-store displays; (2) personal calls; (3) jumbo mailings;
(4) marketing surveys.

* Six sport capsules daily with a wrapup of the top sports stories of the day.

* Personalities deeply involved in community events.

* WHYN broadcasts four agricultural reports each morning, 3:30-6 A.M. six days per week. They work closely with the University of Mass-achusetts and use wire service reports of UP and AP, to provide excellent material to the community.

53509

WHYN—SPRINGFIELD, MASSACHUSETTS
5,000 watts—560 kc

Monday thru Saturday

6: A.M.—10:00 A.M.—Bob Allen Show
    5-min. news on the hour
    News Headlines on the half hour
10:00 A.M.—2:00 P.M.—Lou Terri Show
    5-min. news on the hour
    News Headlines on the half hour
2:00 P.M.—6:00 P.M.—Bud Williams Show
    5-min. news on the hour
    News Headlines on the half hour
6:00 P.M.—10:00 P.M.—Ron Savage Show
    5-min. news on the hour
    News Headlines on the half hour
10:00 P.M.—2:00 A.M.—Bob O'Brady Show
    5-min. news on the hour
    News Headlines on the half hour
2:00 A.M.—6:00 A.M.—"Nite Train Show" with Norm Lambert
    5-min. news on the hour
    News Headlines on the half hour
    Farm Almanac Reports—4 between 3:30-5:30 A.M.

AVERAGE QUARTER-HOUR LISTENING ESTIMATES
PERCENTAGE SHARE OF MARKET*

Station Call Letters	WACE	WDEW	WHYN	WHYN-FM	WMAS	WMAS-FM	WREB	WSPR	WTXL	WTYM
Mon.-Fri.: 6-10 A.M.										
Total persons:	7.0	0.7	32.6	7.0	2.9	0.1	2.1	23.9	8.7	3.1
Teen	-	-	58.8	2.4	2.4	-	-	10.7	13.1	1.3
Men	8.1	0.5	27.1	6.8	2.9	-	2.9	23.6	6.9	4.8
Women 18-24	-	3.0	59.9	6.2	-	-	-	21.3	30.4	-
25-34	4.9	-	38.2	7.8	-	-	-	21.6	-	2.5
35-49	10.9	-	28.0	15.0	4.5	1.2	3.3	36.5	4.9	3.7
50-64	15.9	1.8	19.8	10.7	5.2	-	5.2	26.7	3.2	3.6
Total	8.2	1.0	29.2	8.6	3.1	0.3	2.0	28.2	8.9	2.1
Mon.-Fri.: 10 A.M.-3 P.M.										
Total persons:	5.7	0.6	24.5	7.4	5.6	0.8	4.1	16.3	8.2	4.4
Teen	1.3	-	42.3	1.3	1.3	-	1.3	5.0	9.9	1.3
Men	4.9	-	15.7	5.8	5.5	1.0	4.2	13.8	8.2	4.1
Women 18-24	-	-	47.5	9.2	7.9	3.0	-	23.3	21.3	-
25-34	-	-	30.4	17.7	-	-	-	20.1	-	6.4
35-49	9.3	3.7	23.9	12.6	1.2	1.2	3.7	25.0	7.4	7.4
50-64	15.5	1.8	18.5	10.7	5.0	-	8.4	13.9	3.2	5.2
Total	7.8	1.4	26.6	10.8	7.0	0.9	4.8	21.9	7.7	5.6

Station Call Letters	WACE	WDEW	WHYN	WHYN-FM	WMAS	WMAS-FM	WREB	WSPR	WTXL	WTYM
Mon.-Fri.: 3-7 P.M.										
Total persons:	7.7	0.6	24.5	8.1	3.8	1.1	1.0	13.0	6.6	3.8
Teen	2.0	-	53.5	3.0	1.0	-	-	4.0	14.9	-
Men	6.6	-	18.2	8.7	4.9	1.4	1.4	14.0	5.9	5.6
Women 18-24	-	1.9	55.8	1.9	-	3.8	-	7.7	19.2	-
25-34	9.1	-	29.5	4.5	-	2.3	-	22.7	-	-
35-49	9.2	2.0	18.4	19.4	1.0	-	1.0	18.4	1.0	7.1
50-64	9.0	1.3	9.0	10.3	3.8	-	1.3	12.8	2.6	2.6
Total	10.3	0.6	21.2	9.1	3.6	1.2	0.9	14.8	4.5	3.3
Mon.-Fri.: 7-12 P.M.										
Total persons:	-	-	22.8	14.4	6.9	2.7	-	9.6	9.3	-
Teen	-	-	64.6	1.5	6.2	-	-	3.1	12.3	-
Men	-	-	10.4	14.8	10.4	4.4	-	11.9	6.7	-
Women 18-24	-	-	26.3	10.5	-	7.9	-	13.2	34.2	-
25-34	-	-	30.0	10.0	-	-	-	20.0	-	-
35-49	-	-	7.0	44.2	7.0	-	-	7.0	2.3	-
50-64	-	-	6.9	6.9	6.9	-	-	10.3	-	-
Total	-	-	15.0	20.3	3.8	2.3	-	10.5	10.5	-

* Row percentages do not total 100. Stations outside the Springfield area and nonlisteners account for the remaining persons.
Note: These data were provided by the stations based on American Research Bureau reports.

WHYN - SPRINGFIELD, MASSACHUSETTS
5,000 WATTS - 560 KC

Newspaper Coverage of the Market

Newspaper	*City Zone*	*Retail Trad. Zone*	*City Zone & Retail Trad. Zone*	*% of Homes Not Reached By Newspapers*
Union (M)	46,454	18,939	65,393	
Penetration:	44.3%	26.8%	37.3%	62.7%
News (E)	76,407	17,294	93,701	
Penetration:	72.9%	24.5%	53.4%	46.6%
Families reached by newspapers	88,021	27,586	115,607	
Penetration:	84.0%	39.0%	65.9%	34.1%
Total families:	104,800	70,675	175,475	

QUESTIONS

1. Prepare a media schedule for the Springfield area back-to-school promotion.

2. What is the rationale behind your proposal?

Weyerhaeuser Company (B)

The company conducts a six-week test in eight market areas to help determine whether to shift its corporate identity advertising effort— which has been in print media since its inception—to television. Pre- and post-test attitude and awareness measures are used.

In July of 1967, Mr. Carroll O'Rourke, Director of Public Relations and Advertising at the Weyerhaeuser Company, was examining the results of a recently completed corporate advertising television test. These results were to serve as a major influence in his decision on whether to shift the company's corporate identity advertising campaign to television in 1968.

DEVELOPMENTS LEADING UP TO THE TV TEST

Weyerhaeuser, a leading forest products company, had traditionally relied entirely on print media to carry its corporate identity advertising campaign. The main thrust of this campaign since its inception in 1952 had been to make the general public aware of the company's ethical and responsible policies of forest management. However, as rapid growth and new product introductions radically changed the nature of the company's business during the 1960s, executives became increasingly concerned that the campaign was failing to convey a true picture of "Weyerhaeuser on the move." As B. L. Orell, Vice-President of Public Affairs, put it: "It was obvious that the advertising no longer reflected a true image of the company." Thus he directed a reexamination of the entire advertising program. As part of this reexamination the company's Marketing Research Department was assigned, along with the Weyerhaeuser account team at the Cole and Weber advertising agency, to design a test to determine how effectively the Weyerhaeuser corporate story could be told on television. [See Weyerhaeuser Company (A) for a more detailed account of the history of Weyerhaeuser corporate advertising and its role within the company.]

The test was conducted in early 1967, and its results reached Mr. O'Rourke in July of that year. Exhibit 1 contains the report which he received.

IMPLICATIONS OF THE TEST RESULTS

Print ads and TV commercials featured Weyerhaeuser's replanting of forests by helicopter seeding and hand planting. The agency creative team had attempted to make the print and TV versions as identical as possible. (See Exhibits 2 and 3 for the print and TV pair featuring the helicopter reseeding message.) Mr. O'Rourke wondered whether a different copy theme, placing greater emphasis on Weyerhaeuser's new products and related research activities, would have changed the results significantly and, if so, in what way. This concerned him, for he was anticipating this sort of copy emphasis in the 1968 Weyerhaeuser campaign regardless of the media choice.

Also of concern to him was the realization that the test assumed a television budget of $1.5 million. This $1.5 million represented the entire advertising budget, so the TV campaign would mean abandoning entirely the national print campaign. This campaign had become a virtual trademark for the company through its use of color paintings depicting the tranquility of wildlife in natural forest settings. (Exhibit 4.) Mr. O'Rourke commented on the trade-offs involved in this decision.

If we drop the wildlife format entirely we can probably count on one of our competitors picking it up. To prevent this we would have to keep about a quarter million dollars in the wildlife print campaign, which would make it possible to return to this format later if our experience with TV proved negative. However, our frustration during recent years in conveying an updated "Weyerhaeuser on the Move" identity in the wildlife campaign leaves many of us convinced that we must totally sever all ties with the past campaign to get this message across. Furthermore, anything less than the TV expenditure assumed in the test would detract from the test's predictive validity.

Exhibit 1

1967 CORPORATE ADVERTISING TELEVISION TEST

Table of Contents

5. Recall of Specific Message—Replanting by Hand or
Helicopter Seeding   13
6. Company and Source of Advertising—Hand Planting/
Helicopter Seeding   16

Appendix

Questionnaire

WEYERHAEUSER COMPANY
WOOD PRODUCTS GROUP
MARKETING RESEARCH DEPARTMENT

Peter Rosik

Marketing Research Report for
Public Affairs
Project No. 095-1027

July 7, 1967

Corporate Advertising
Television Test
Report No. 095-1027-1

JOB DESCRIPTION

A before and after survey of the adult (18 years of age and over) population in eight metropolitan areas.

OBJECTIVE

To determine the additional amount of Company recognition obtainable by using (1) program television, (2) spot television, or (3) increased magazine space, compared with the recognition obtained through the regular media schedule.

BACKGROUND

Weyerhaeuser corporate advertising is entirely in print media where its efforts have met with consumer recognition and numerous industry awards. The corporate advertising section has periodically evaluated its reliance on print and, to date, has found sufficient justification to continue to rely on it. They have, however, noted the sustained growth of television in terms of numbers of homes covered, the selectivity of audiences, and in the impact it has on its viewers. They have also recognized that the use of television could require an increase in advertising expenditures. Although television costs are generally lower than print costs on a per viewer versus per reader basis, the much greater number of viewers raises the absolute cost of television well over that of print. The recent rapid growth of color television programming and set usage gave a boost to their interest, for color has always been a significant part of the Weyerhaeuser message.

In order to gauge the probable impact of Weyerhaeuser's use of television more factually, the corporate advertising section, together with Cole & Weber, designed a testing program with four specific objectives:

— To measure the increase in recognition over the regular print schedule caused by a program-oriented television schedule.

— To measure the increase in recognition over the regular print schedule caused by a spot-oriented television schedule.

— To measure the increase in recognition over the regular print schedule caused by a magazine schedule raised to the dollar expenditure level of the television tests.

— To evaluate the results of each of the above tests in relation to the regular print schedule and in relation to each other.

Marketing Research was responsible for the design of the test, its control, and its final evaluation.

SUMMARY OF FINDINGS

The principal results of this study are shown in the figure below. It is a summation of data from the Detailed Findings and the Appendix tables. The figure shows:

1. Television usage significantly increased (1) Company recognition, (2) message penetration, and (3) association of the message with Weyerhaeuser. There is little doubt that this was caused by the use of a new medium and reaching, for the first time, a new audience.

2. Increased magazine expenditures significantly increased Company recognition; but since it is reaching an established audience, the amount of increase for a comparably increased expenditure was not so great as that of television. Additionally there was no significant increase in either message

penetration or association of the message with Weyerhaeuser derived from increased magazine usage at this expenditure level in the historical magazine format.

	Percentage Point Change Before-to-After Interviews			
	TV Program	*TV Spot*	*Increased Magazine*	*Control*
Recognition of Weyerhaeuser Co.	15.2*	23.6*	9.2*	.9
Recall of any Weyerhaeuser advertising	11.4*	17.1*	1.7	2.1
Recalled hand planting/helicopter seeding message	13.3*	20.7*	(.8)	(1.4)
Share recalling message who associated it with Weyerhaeuser	13.8*	28.3*	.5	2.6

* Indicates a statistically significant difference as measured by the chi-square test.

3. Increases in the television markets occurred more frequently among younger men and women and the lower income categories, probably the same people.

METHOD

For this test four pairs of markets, eight markets in all, were selected. The study hoped to have one of the pairs using regularly scheduled television programs, and a second pair using spot insertions on television so that spot *versus* program presentation could be compared. Spot purchases, however, are not fully controllable and were often actually presented in a program format. This muddied the waters of any clear-cut comparison, making it less valid than it would otherwise be. Therefore the differences noted between television spot and television program scores should be considered more as approximations than as sharp delineations. Within each category, however, the pre-post variations are accurate reflections of the impact of television.

The third market pair used increased magazine. The fourth pair of markets had only normal print exposure and were used as the control (the markets against which all changes were measured). The metropolitan-area markets selected for each purpose were:

TV Program	Madison, Wisconsin
	Salinas-Monterey, California
TV Spot	Wichita Falls, Texas
	Fort Wayne, Indiana
Increased Magazine	Denver, Colorado
	Cleveland, Ohio
Control	Atlanta, Georgia
	Cincinnati, Ohio

Measurement was based on interviewing matched samples of the adult population before and after the six-week test period. Identical questionnaires, a copy of which is in the Appendix, were used for all interviews. With the matched samples, whose demography is also shown in the Appendix, and identical questionnaires, differences between the pre-test and post-test interviews are attributable to the variable of the media.

The chi-square technique was used to test statistical significance, at a .95 confidence level (2 sigma). Thus any difference cited as statistically significant could have happened by chance up to five times out of a hundred. Conversely, if the same test were tried one hundred times the same results would occur at least ninety-five times.

Each test-market pair represents an increase over the current dollar expenditure of about $1 million on a national basis.

Interviewing centered around proven recognition of the Company name, advertising message, and source recall. Interviewing was conducted the week of January 23, 1967, followed by six weeks of commercial exposure, and then reinterviewing the week of March 13, 1967. All interviewing, coding, and tabulating was conducted by Market Dynamics, Inc., a subsidiary of Opinion Research Corporation, Princeton, New Jersey.

The result of the television tests apply only to an initial effort in that medium. The magazine-test results apply only to expanded magazine usage in the historical format. A major change in the format or message of the magazine advertising could have different results from those indicated by this study.

The tables presented in the Appendix are summations of the more important data contained in the computer run. The complete run will be maintained by Marketing Research for more detailed analysis as desired by the corporate advertising section or Cole & Weber.

DETAILED FINDINGS

Throughout the conduct of this study neither the interviewer nor the respondent knew the identity of the sponsoring firm. This was done to minimize the possibility of such knowledge causing either interviewer or respondent bias. In order to accomplish this, all questions requiring information about a specific company were asked for several firms. Where one item was volunteered, the interviewers asked about the others as well. Besides Weyerhaeuser, information was obtained on U.S. Plywood and Georgia-Pacific. Since these additional data do not directly relate to the issue under study, the result obtained about USP and G-P are not reported here. They are, however, on file with Marketing Research and available.

1. AWARENESS OF FOREST PRODUCTS COMPANIES–WEYERHAEUSER

(Appendix Table 1)

Respondents were asked to name as many companies in the forest products industry as they could. The sum of the aided and unaided mentions of Weyerhaeuser remained the same in the control market pairs, but increased significantly in the television spot markets, the television program markets, and the magazine markets.

AIDED AND UNAIDED AWARENESS OF WEYERHAEUSER

Market	Before	After	Change
TV Program	44.3%	59.5%	15.2*
TV Spot	25.3%	48.9%	23.6*
Magazine	30.1%	39.3%	9.2*
Control	26.8%	27.7%	0.9

☐ Before   ▨ After

* Denotes a statistically significant difference

INCREMENTAL DOLLARS IN THE TESTED AMOUNT RESULTED IN ABOUT TWICE AS MUCH AWARENESS INCREASE IN TELEVISION AS THEY DID IN MAGAZINE.

A. Awareness–Weyerhaeuser–by Sex   A significant increase in awareness of Weyerhaeuser occurred among men in each market pair except the control. Among women a significant increase occurred only in the markets exposed to television. In all cases, the awareness level began and ended at a higher level among men than among women.

| | *Point Difference – Pre- vs. Post-Test* | | | |
	TV Program	*TV Spot*	*Magazine*	*Control*
Men	13.1*	26.4*	15.6*	5.2
Women	17.7*	21.3*	3.1	(3.4)

* Denotes a statistically significant difference.

B.   Awareness—Weyerhaeuser—by Age   A significant increase in awareness of Weyerhaeuser occurred among each age group in TV spot market pair and three of the four (excluding 40-49-year-olds) segments in the TV program market pair. For those exposed to increased magazine promotion, increments of note occurred only in the 50-and-over age category. No significant increases are noted in the control group.

	Point Difference – Pre- vs. Post-Test			
	TV Program	*TV Spot*	*Magazine*	*Control*
Under 30	15.7*	49.8*	(2.1)	4.2
30-39	16.7*	21.4*	5.9	5.0
40-49	10.3	22.5*	16.0	.7
50 & over	16.7*	11.5*	12.4*	(3.2)

* Denotes a statistically significant difference.

C.   Awareness—Weyerhaeuser—by Income   Major increases are noted in all age groups after exposure in TV spot market pair. In the TV program market pair increases occurred only in the two lower income groups. No significant increases are noted in either the magazine or the control segments of the test.

	Point Difference – Pre- vs. Post-Test			
	TV Program	*TV Spot*	*Magazine*	*Control*
Under $6,000	21.6*	21.4*	3.1	(7.3)
$6,000-$7,999	18.7*	26.8*	7.9	10.3
$8,000-$9,999	11.1	28.6*	(3.0)	(4.4)
$10,000 or more	9.2	18.3*	12.2	(1.1)

* Denotes a statistically significant difference.

2.   WEYERHAEUSER INVOLVEMENT IN FOREST CONSERVATION

(Appendix Table 2)

All respondents claiming an awareness of Weyerhaeuser were asked about the extent of Weyerhaeuser's involvement with forest conservation. Of those who responded to the question, more than 95 out of 100 considered Weyerhaeuser involved to some extent. Those who consider the Company deeply involved increased significantly only in the TV spot market pair.

WEYERHAEUSER DEEPLY INVOLVED IN FOREST CONSERVATION

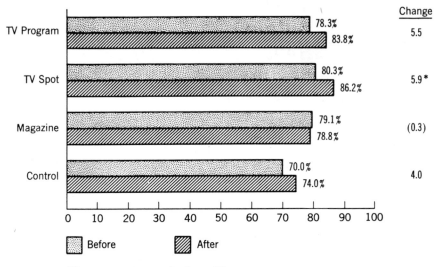

	Change
TV Program	5.5
TV Spot	5.9*
Magazine	(0.3)
Control	4.0

* Denotes a statistically significant difference

INCREMENTAL DOLLARS IN THE TESTED AMOUNT RESULTED IN AN INCREASE IN THE UNDERSTANDING OF WEYERHAEUSER'S COMMITMENT TO FOREST CONSERVATION WHEN SPENT IN TELEVISION BUT NOT WHEN SPENT IN MAGAZINE.

3. RECALLED WEYERHAEUSER ADVERTISING

(Appendix Table 3)

Respondents were questioned on their recall of Weyerhaeuser advertising on an unaided and aided basis. The unaided questioning asked about any advertising they could recall for forest products firms and who the firms were. If Weyerhaeuser was not then mentioned, the aided question asked if they recalled any advertising for the Weyerhaeuser Company.

Major increases in recalling advertising by Weyerhaeuser are observed in the TV spot market pair and the TV program market pair. No increase occurred in either the magazine or the control market pairs.

RECALLED WEYERHAEUSER ADVERTISING

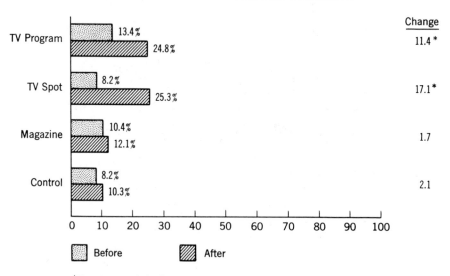

INCREMENTAL DOLLARS IN THE TESTED AMOUNT RESULTED IN SEVEN TO TEN TIMES AS MUCH INCREASE IN RECALL OF WEYERHAEUSER ADVERTISING IN TELEVISION AS THEY DID IN MAGAZINE.

Examining the changes in unaided and aided recall to learn where the total change occurred shows that the unaided recall, that is, where the name of the company was not provided, accounted for all the increase in the TV spot market pair and almost all of it in the TV program market pair.

RECALLED WEYERHAEUSER ADVERTISING

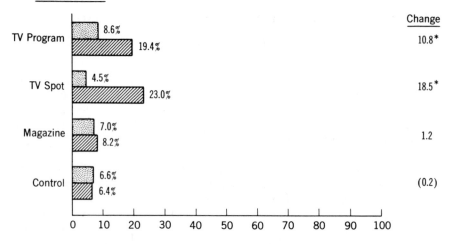

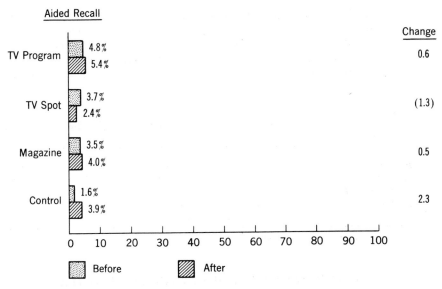

Aided Recall

	Change
TV Program 4.8% / 5.4%	0.6
TV Spot 3.7% / 2.4%	(1.3)
Magazine 3.5% / 4.0%	0.5
Control 1.6% / 3.9%	2.3

■ Before   ▨ After

* Denotes a statistically significant difference

A. Recalled Weyerhaeuser Advertising—by Sex The recall of advertising by Weyerhaeuser increased significantly among men and women in the market pairs using TV spots and TV programs, but not in the magazine or control pairs.

	Point Difference — Pre- Va. Post-Test			
	TV Program	*TV Spot*	*Magazine*	*Control*
Men	12.0*	19.0*	5.1	5.6
Women	11.2*	15.6*	(1.9)	(1.2)

*Denotes a statistically significant difference.

B. Recalled Weyerhaeuser Advertising—by Age No significant changes are noted by age groups for either the magazine or the control market pairs. Each age group increased significantly in the TV spot market pair; in the TV program only one group, the 40-49-year-olds, did not increase significantly.

	Point Difference — Pre- vs. Post-Test			
	TV Program	*TV Spot*	*Magazine*	*Control*
Under 30	11.2*	32.7*	1.9	2.5
30-39	21.2*	23.4*	(3.6)	5.8
40-49	.7	10.6*	7.4	3.6
50 & over	13.2*	8.0*	1.0	(.8)

*Denotes a statistically significant difference.

C. Recalled Weyerhaeuser Advertising—by Income　After exposure to the TV spots, each income group except the $10,000 or more significantly increased its remembrance of Weyerhaeuser advertising. Following exposure to TV programming, only the $8,000–$9,999 income category did not increase its recall. For magazine and control market pairs no significant increases are noted.

	Point Difference – Pre- vs. Post-Test			
	TV Program	TV Spot	Magazine	Control
Under $6,000	12.5*	19.5*	(1.7)	(1.5)
$6,000-$7,999	17.3*	19.1*	2.2	4.0
$8,000-$9,999	5.7	26.5*	(8.0)	2.9
$10,000 or more	13.1*	10.6	5.2	.7

*Denotes a statistically significant difference.

4. MESSAGE AND SOURCE OF WEYERHAEUSER ADVERTISING

(Appendix Tables 4 and 5)

All those who claimed recalling some advertising by Weyerhaeuser were asked what they remembered about it and where they saw or heard it.

In the television spot and the program market pairs the message created especially for these markets came through strongly. The magazine ad, showing a helicopter seeding a logged-over area, failed to register in its markets.

	Point Difference – Pre- vs. Post-Test			
Message:	TV Program	TV Spot	Magazine	Control
When a tree is cut down another is planted	14.4*	23.6*	3.3	3.8
Showed helicopter replanting	8.0*	18.9*	(2.0)	

*Denotes a statistically significant difference.

INCREMENTAL DOLLARS IN THE TESTED AMOUNT RESULTED IN FOUR TO EIGHT TIMES AS MUCH MESSAGE RECALL RELATED TO WEYERHAEUSER IN TELEVISION AS THEY DID IN MAGAZINE.

When asked where they saw or heard the Weyerhaeuser advertising, both television market pairs showed significant increases of highly unusual proportions, and the magazine market pair actually declined in its mention of magazines.

SOURCE OF WEYERHAEUSER ADVERTISING

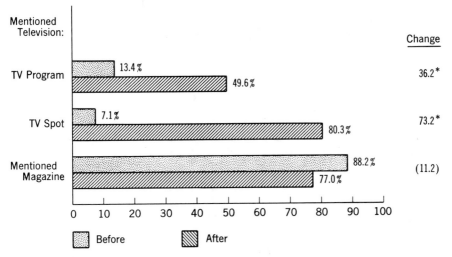

Mentioned
Television:

Change

TV Program — 13.4% / 49.6% — 36.2*

TV Spot — 7.1% / 80.3% — 73.2*

Mentioned Magazine — 88.2% / 77.0% — (11.2)

☐ Before   ▨ After

*Denotes a statistically significant difference

5. **RECALL OF SPECIFIC MESSAGE—REPLANTING BY HAND OR HELICOPTER SEEDING**
(Appendix Table 6)

RECALL OF HAND PLANTING/HELICOPTER SEEDING

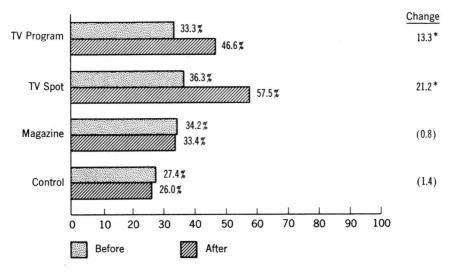

Change

TV Program — 33.3% / 46.6% — 13.3*

TV Spot — 36.3% / 57.5% — 21.2*

Magazine — 34.2% / 33.4% — (0.8)

Control — 27.4% / 26.0% — (1.4)

☐ Before   ▨ After

* Denotes a statistically significant difference

INCREMENTAL DOLLARS IN THE TESTED AMOUNT RESULTED IN A MAJOR INCREASE IN REGISTRATION OF A SPECIFIC MESSAGE IN TELEVISION, BUT NOT IN MAGAZINE.

All respondents who did not mention the emphasized message of the Weyerhaeuser ads—replanting by hand or by helicopter seeding—including those respondents who did not recall any Weyerhaeuser advertising, were asked specifically about this message. Adding their responses to the responses of those who previously played back the message shows significant increases in specific message recall within the TV spot and TV program market pairs, but none within the magazine or control market pairs.

A. Recall of Specific Message—By Sex Differences of a significant magnitude are noted among men and women from the before to the after interviewing in TV spot and TV program market pairs. No significant variations are noted in the magazine or the control markets.

| | *Point Difference – Pre- vs. Post-Test* | | | |
	TV Program	*TV Spot*	*Magazine*	*Control*
Men	17.2*	29.9*	1.5	-
Women	9.7*	12.3*	(3.4)	(2.7)

* Denotes a statistically significant difference.

B. Recall of Specific Message—by Age Markets exposed to TV spot commercials show significant increases in recall of the hand-planting/ helicopter-seeding message in all age groupings. In TV program markets significant gains are noted in each except the 30-39 age group; no significant increases are seen in either the control or the magazine markets.

| | *Point Difference – Pre- vs. Post-Test* | | | |
	TV Program	*TV Spot*	*Magazine*	*Control*
Under 30	12.2*	29.3*	(7.3)	5.6
30-39	4.8	29.9*	4.3	(5.3)
40-49	15.2*	15.8*	(.3)	(2.1)
50 & over	17.5*	15.2*	(1.9)	(3.4)

* Denotes a statistically significant difference.

C. Recall of Specific Message—by Income TV spot markets contain significant increases in each income group except that of under $6,000. Within TV program markets, increases occurred in the under $6,000 and the $6,000-$7,999 categories but not among the higher groupings. No significant variations occurred in either the magazine or the control market pairs.

| | Point Difference – Pre- vs. Post-Test | | | |
	TV Program	TV Spot	Magazine	Control
Under $6,000	19.0*	11.5	(2.6)	7.0
$6,000-$7,999	31.0*	34.3*	2.2	(12.7)
$8,000-$9,999	6.9	19.8*	(8.9)	.9
$10,000 & over	2.8	18.8*	.5	.9

* Denotes a statistically significant difference.

6. COMPANY AND SOURCE OF ADVERTISING– HAND PLANTING/HELICOPTER SEEDING

(Appendix Tables 7 and 8)

Those individuals who recalled any advertising about hand planting/ helicopter seeding were asked if they remembered the company connected with that advertising and the medium by which they had seen or heard it.

Recognition of Weyerhaeuser as the company putting out the message increased significantly within the TV spot and the TV program market segments, but not within the magazine or control markets.

ASSOCIATION OF MESSAGE WITH WEYERHAEUSER COMPANY

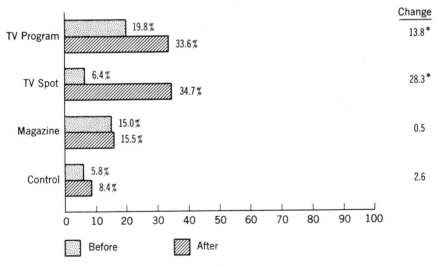

	Change
TV Program	13.8*
19.8% / 33.6%	
TV Spot	28.3*
6.4% / 34.7%	
Magazine	0.5
15.0% / 15.5%	
Control	2.6
5.8% / 8.4%	

☐ Before   ▨ After

*Denotes a statistically significant difference

INCREMENTAL DOLLARS IN THE TESTED AMOUNT RESULTED IN A MAJOR INCREASE IN ASSOCIATION OF A SPECIFIC MESSAGE WITH WEYERHAEUSER IN TELEVISION, BUT NOT IN MAGAZINE.

Recognition of the medium by which the message was delivered also increased significantly within the TV spot and TV program market areas, but not within the magazine or the control market pairs.

RECOGNITION OF MEDIUM

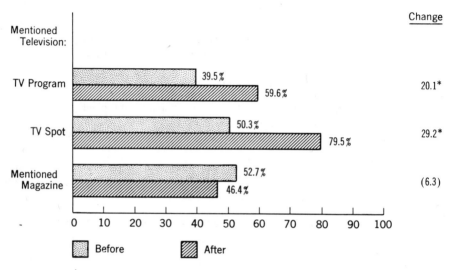

Before   After

*Denotes a statistically significant difference

Peter Rosik

PR/gb

MARKET DYNAMICS, INC.
Princeton, New Jersey

Hello. My name is _____. I'm an interviewer for Market Dynamics Research Company of Princeton, New Jersey. We're conducting a survey throughout the country and we'd like to ask you just a few questions. First...

		WEYERHAEUSER		
	U.S. PLYWOOD	GEORGIA PACIFIC	(Pronounced "Wear-Houser")	OTHERS (Specify)

1a. Would you please name as many companies as you can in the forest products industry? (PROBE: Any others?)

       1   2   3

(FOR EACH NOT MENTIONED, ASK):

       X NONE

b. Have you ever heard of a company called
_____?

	U.S. PLYWOOD	GEORGIA PACIFIC	WEYERHAEUSER
YES	1	5	9
NO	2	6	0
DON'T KNOW	3	7	X

(FOR EACH CIRCLED IN BOX ABOVE, ASK):

2. What are the principal products you associate with (COMPANY)? (PROBE: What others?)

U.S. PLYWOOD	GEORGIA PACIFIC	WEYERHAEUSER
Y DON'T KNOW	Y DON'T KNOW	Y DON'T KNOW

3. How involved would you say (COMPANY) is in programs of forest conservation? Would you say (COMPANY) is...

	U.S.PLYWOOD	GEORGIA PACIFIC	WEYERHAEUSER
DEEPLY INVOLVED------	1	1	1
SOMEWHAT INVOLVED----	2	2	2
SLIGHTLY INVOLVED or-	3	3	3
NOT AT ALL INVOLVED--	4	4	4
DON'T KNOW-	5	5	5

(ASK EVERYONE)

4a. Do you recall having recently seen or heard any advertising about forest products companies?   1 YES ——→ GO ON TO Q. 4b   2 NO ——→ SKIP TO Q. 6

b. What firm or firms was this advertising for? (PROBE: Any others?) _____

(FOR EACH FIRM MENTIONED, ASK):

c. Where did you see or hear the advertising for (COMPANY)?

TELEVISION	1	1
NEWSPAPERS	2	2
MAGAZINES	3	3
RADIO	4	4
OTHER (Specify)	_____	_____

d. What did the advertising for (COMPANY) say or show? (PROBE: What else?)

Continued.....

(IF WEYERHAEUSER NOT MENTIONED IN Q. 4b, ASK):

5a. Do you recall seeing or hearing any advertising for the Weyerhaeuser Company?

   1 YES ⟶ GO ON TO Q. 5b

   2 NO ⟶ SKIP TO INSTRUCTIONS
   3 DON'T KNOW   PRECEDING Q. 6

b. Where did you see or hear the advertising for Weyerhaeuser?

   1 TELEVISION   4 RADIO
   2 NEWSPAPERS   5 OTHER (Specify)
   3 MAGAZINES

c. What did the advertising for Weyerhaeuser say or show?

> IF "REFORESTATION BY HELICOPTER SEEDING OR BY HAND PLANTING" MENTIONED ANYWHERE, SKIP TO Q. 7. IN <u>ALL OTHER CASES</u>, GO ON TO Q. 6.

6a. Do you recall seeing or hearing any advertising that talked about the replanting of forests by hand planting or by helicopter seeding?

   1 YES ⟶ GO ON TO Q. 6b   2 NO ⟶ SKIP TO Q. 7a
                                        3 DON'T KNOW

b. Where did you see or hear this advertising?

   1 TELEVISION   2 NEWSPAPERS   3 MAGAZINES
   4 RADIO   5 OTHERS (Specify)

c. Can you recall whose advertising this was?

   1 YES ⟶ Whose advertising was it?
   2 NO

d. What can you tell me about this advertising? (PROBE: What else did the advertising say or show?

Now just a question or two for classification purposes only.

7a. Into which of these age groups do you fit? Are you...

   1 UNDER 20   2 IN YOUR 20'S   3 IN YOUR 30'S
   4 IN YOUR 40'S <u>or</u>   5 50 OR OVER

b. What is the occupation of the head of this household? (BE SPECIFIC)

                  (JOB)   (INDUSTRY)

c. Is your family's total yearly income...

   6 UNDER $7,500 ⟶ Is that..........   1 UNDER $5,000, <u>or</u>
                                   2 OVER $5,000

      <u>or</u>

                                   3 UNDER $10,000,
   7 OVER $7,500 ⟶ Is that..........   4 BETWEEN $10,000 AND $15,000, <u>or</u>
                                   5 OVER $15,000

d. INDICATE: 1 MALE   2 FEMALE

8a. May I have your name please?
b. And your telephone number?
c. City   State

THANK YOU VERY MUCH FOR YOUR COOPERATION

INTERVIEWED BY: DATE:

Table 1

AWARENESS OF FOREST PRODUCTS COMPANIES — WEYERHAEUSER

	TV Program			TV Spot			Magazine			Control		
	Pre	Post	Diff	Pre	Post	Diff	Pre	Post	Diff	Pre	Post	Diff
Total No. Interviews: %	501 100.0	504 100.0	-	515 100.0	501 100.0	-	489 100.0	503 100.0	-	500 100.0	503 100.0	-
Total	44.3%	59.5%	15.2	25.3%	48.9%	23.6	30.1%	39.3%	9.2	26.8%	27.7%	.9
Men	54.5	67.6	13.1	35.3	61.7	26.4	40.9	56.5	15.6	35.2	40.4	5.2
Women	33.8	51.5	17.7	14.7	36.0	21.3	19.9	22.0	2.1	18.4	15.0	(3.4)
Under 30	33.6	49.3	15.7	14.1	63.9	49.8	29.2	27.1	(2.1)	21.5	25.7	4.2
30-39	42.9	59.6	16.7	29.0	50.4	21.4	25.5	31.4	5.9	30.1	35.1	5.0
40-49	51.3	61.6	10.3	25.4	47.9	22.5	34.4	50.4	16.0	26.2	26.9	.7
50 & over	50.7	67.4	16.7	28.7	40.2	11.5	30.4	42.8	12.4	28.5	25.3	(3.2)
Under $6,000	35.6	57.2	21.6	22.0	43.4	21.4	26.0	29.1	3.1	22.7	15.4	(7.3)
$6-$7,999	36.9	55.6	18.7	26.7	53.5	26.8	22.4	30.3	7.9	15.7	26.0	10.3
$8-$9,999	48.6	59.7	11.1	25.0	53.6	28.6	39.3	36.3	(3.0)	29.4	25.0	(4.4)
$10,000+	62.1	71.3	9.2	32.1	50.4	18.3	40.1	52.3	12.2	40.5	39.4	(1.1)

QUESTION: WOULD YOU PLEASE NAME AS MANY COMPANIES AS YOU CAN IN THE FOREST PRODUCTS INDUSTRY? ANY OTHERS? HAVE YOU EVER HEARD OF A COMPANY CALLED _____?

Table 2

EXTENT OF WEYERHAEUSER INVOLVEMENT IN FOREST CONSERVATION

	TV Program			TV Spot			Magazine			Control		
	Pre	Post	Diff	Pre	Post	Diff	Pre	Post	Diff	Pre	Post	Diff
Total Aware of Weyerhaeuser: %	166 100.0	234 100.0	- -	81 100.0	181 100.0	- -	105 100.0	151 100.0	- -	90 100.0	108 100.0	- -
Weyerhaeuser is:												
Deeply involved	78.3%	83.8%	5.5	80.3%	86.2%	5.9	79.1%	78.8%	(.3)	70.0%	74.0%	4.0
Somewhat involved	12.1	13.2	1.1	12.3	8.8	(3.5)	11.4	11.3	(.1)	22.2	20.4	(1.8)
Slightly involved	7.2 97.6	2.6 99.6	(4.6) 2.0	4.9 97.5	3.9 98.9	(1.0) 1.4	5.7 96.2	7.3 97.4	1.6 1.2	5.6 97.8	2.8 97.2	(2.8) (.6)
Not at all involved	2.4	.4	(2.0)	2.5	1.1	(1.4)	3.8	2.6	(1.2)	2.2	2.8	.6

QUESTION: HOW DEEPLY WOULD YOU SAY WEYERHAEUSER IS IN PROGRAMS OF FOREST CONSERVATION? WOULD YOU SAY IT IS DEEPLY INVOLVED, SOMEWHAT INVOLVED, SLIGHTLY INVOLVED, OR NOT AT ALL INVOLVED?

Table 3

RECALLED WEYERHAEUSER ADVERTISING

	TV Program			TV Spot			Magazine			Control		
	Pre	Post	Diff	Pre	Post	Diff	Pre	Post	Diff	Pre	Post	Diff
Total	501	504	-	515	501	-	489	503	-	500	503	-
Interviews: %	100.0	100.0	-	100.0	100.0	-	100.0	100.0	-	100.0	100.0	-
Total	13.4%	24.8%	11.4	8.2%	25.3%	17.1	10.4%	12.1%	1.7	8.2%	10.3%	2.1
Men	18.4	30.4	12.0	12.5	31.5	19.0	13.9	19.0	5.1	11.2	16.8	5.6
Women	8.1	19.3	11.2	3.6	19.2	15.6	7.1	5.2	(1.9)	5.2	4.0	(1.2)
Under 30	11.7	22.9	11.2	5.4	38.1	32.7	9.2	11.1	1.9	6.9	9.4	2.5
30-39	5.1	26.3	21.2	14.0	37.4	23.4	14.3	10.7	(3.6)	8.6	14.4	5.8
40-49	25.2	25.9	.7	9.6	20.2	10.6	7.8	15.2	7.4	11.2	14.8	3.6
50 & over	11.5	24.7	13.2	5.8	13.8	8.0	10.6	11.6	1.0	7.0	6.2	(.8)
Under $6,000	8.5	21.0	12.5	2.5	22.0	19.5	8.0	6.3	(1.7)	4.2	2.7	(1.5)
$6-$7,999	6.0	23.3	17.3	10.0	29.1	19.1	3.9	6.1	2.2	3.4	7.4	4.0
$8-$9,999	20.0	25.7	5.7	8.3	34.8	26.5	18.0	10.0	(8.0)	5.4	8.3	2.9
$10,000+	19.7	32.8	13.1	15.5	26.1	10.6	16.5	21.7	5.2	17.4	18.1	.7

QUESTION: DO YOU RECALL HAVING RECENTLY SEEN OR HEARD ANY ADVERTISING ABOUT FOREST PRODUCTS COMPANIES? WHAT FIRM OR FIRMS WAS THIS ADVERTISING FOR?
DO YOU RECALL SEEING OR HEARING ANY ADVERTISING FOR THE WEYERHAEUSER COMPANY?

Table 4

PLAYBACK OF WEYERHAEUSER ADVERTISING RECALLED

		TV Program		
		Pre	*Post*	*Diff*
Total Recalling Any:	No.	67	125	58
	%	100.0	100.0	-
Special messages:				
When tree cut down another is planted		- %	14.4%	14.4
Replanting trees by hand		-	2.4	2.4
Showed helicopter replanting		-	8.0	8.0
Regular messages:				
Conservation/preservation of forests		29.9	12.0	(17.9)
Animals in ad, in Weyerhaeuser forest		19.4	12.8	(6.6)
Replanting the forests/trees		10.4	11.2	.8
Showed wood paneling		10.4	16.8	6.4
Pictured forests		9.0	12.0	3.0
About forest products; concerned tree industry		7.5	4.8	(2.7)
About their reforestation program		6.0	7.2	1.2
Harvest and ship lumber to industry		6.0	4.8	(1.2)
Pictured tree farms		6.0	4.0	(2.0)
A colorful ad/commercial		6.0	3.2	(2.8)
An attractive ad; a beautiful ad		6.0	3.2	(2.8)
Stressed importance of preventing forest fires		4.5	.8	(3.7)
Pictured houses; house plans		4.5	1.6	(2.9)
Manufacture all kinds of building materials		4.5	6.4	(1.9)
Showed forest/trees being cut down		3.0	1.6	(1.4)
Stressed various uses for lumber		3.0	3.2	.2
Pictured large tree; redwood tree		1.5	.8	(.7)
Showed mountain scene		1.5	.8	(.7)
Large, 2-page ad		1.5	.8	(.7)
Stressed quality of products		-	.8	.8
All other recall		11.9	12.0	.1
Don't know; recall name only		22.4	16.8	(5.6)

QUESTION: WHAT DID THE ADVERTISING SAY OR SHOW?

	TV Spot			Magazine			Control	
Pre	*Post*	*Diff*	*Pre*	*Post*	*Diff*	*Pre*	*Post*	*Diff*
42	127	85	51	61	10	41	52	11
100.0	100.0	-	100.0	100.0	-	100.0	100.0	-
- %	23.6%	23.6	- %	3.3%	3.3	- %	3.8%	3.8
-	8.7	8.7	-	-	-	-	-	-
-	18.9	18.9	2.0	-	(2.0)	-	-	-
16.7	15.0	(1.7)	15.7	19.7	4.0	7.3	13.5	6.2
4.8	3.1	(1.7)	17.6	9.8	(7.8)	7.3	9.6	2.3
16.7	24.4	7.7	17.6	6.6	(11.0)	9.8	3.8	(6.0)
11.9	6.3	(5.6)	11.8	9.8	(2.0)	9.8	19.2	9.4
9.5	4.7	(4.8)	13.7	13.1	(.6)	19.5	11.5	(8.0)
2.4	2.4	-	2.0	1.6	(.4)	4.9	3.8	(1.1)
4.8	4.7	(.1)	7.8	3.3	(4.5)	2.4	1.9	(.5)
-	10.2	10.2	-	-	-	2.4	-	(2.4)
-	2.4	2.4	3.9	3.3	(.6)	4.9	-	(4.9)
2.4	.8	(1.6)	-	4.9	4.9	-	1.9	1.9
4.8	1.6	(3.2)	2.0	3.3	1.3	4.9	5.8	.9
2.4	.8	(1.6)	-	-	-	-	3.8	3.8
9.5	1.6	(7.9)	5.9	4.9	(1.0)	19.5	5.8	(13.7)
7.1	10.2	3.1	3.9	1.6	(2.3)	2.4	7.7	5.3
7.1	6.3	(.8)	-	1.6	1.6	-	-	-
-	2.4	2.4	3.9	4.9	1.0	-	3.8	3.8
2.4	.8	(1.6)	2.0	3.3	1.3	2.4	3.8	1.4
2.4	1.6	(.8)	-	4.9	4.9	-	-	-
4.8	-	(4.8)	5.9	4.9	(1.0)	2.4	-	(2.4)
4.8	-	(4.8)	-	3.3	3.3	2.4	1.9	(.5)
2.4	8.7	6.3	17.6	14.8	(2.8)	7.3	9.6	2.3
35.7	10.2	(25.5)	17.6	31.1	13.5	26.8	34.6	7.8

Table 5

SOURCE OF WEYERHAEUSER ADVERTISING RECALLED

	TV Program			TV Spot			Magazine			Control		
	Pre	Post	Diff	Pre	Post	Diff	Pre	Post	Diff	Pre	Post	Diff
Total Recalling Any Weyerhaeuser Advertising	67	125	58	42	127	85	51	61	10	41	52	11
% Advertising:	100.0	100.0	-	100.0	100.0	-	100.0	100.0	-	100.0	100.0	-
Television	13.4%	49.6%	36.2	7.1%	80.3%	73.2	7.8%	6.6%	(1.2)	12.2%	9.6	(2.6)
Newspaper (incl. magazine section)	6.0	8.8	2.8	9.5	3.9	(5.6)	9.8	14.8	5.0	7.3	3.8	(3.5)
Magazines	89.6	52.0	(37.6)	78.6	21.3	(57.3)	88.2	77.0	(11.2)	80.5	76.9	(3.6)
Radio	1.5	1.6	.1	-	.8	.8	-	-	-	2.4	-	(2.4)
Mail	3.0	.8	(2.2)	2.4	-	(2.4)	-	-	-	2.4	-	(2.4)
Others	9.0	1.6	(7.4)	4.8	-	(4.8)	2.0	3.3	1.3	7.3	9.6	2.3
Don't remember	1.5	1.6	.1	4.8	3.9	(.9)	-	6.6	6.6	-	1.9	1.9

QUESTION: WHERE DID YOU SEE OR HEAR THE ADVERTISING FOR WEYERHAEUSER?

Table 6
RECALL OF ADVERTISING OF REPLANTING BY HAND OR HELICOPTER SEEDING

	TV Program			TV Spot			Magazine			Control		
	Pre	Post	Diff	Pre	Post	Diff	Pre	Post	Diff	Pre	Post	Diff
Total	501	504	-	515	501	-	489	503	-	500	503	-
Interviews: %	100.0	100.0	-	100.0	100.0	-	100.0	100.0	-	100.0	100.0	-
Total	*33.3%*	*46.6%*	*13.3*	*36.3%*	*57.5%*	*21.2*	*34.2%*	*33.4%*	*(.8)*	*27.4%*	*26.0%*	*(1.4)*
Men	38.0	55.2	17.2	35.0	64.9	29.9	39.2	40.7	1.5	30.4	30.4	-
Women	28.5	38.2	9.7	37.7	50.0	12.3	29.4	26.0	(3.4)	24.4	21.7	(2.7)
Under 30	29.2	41.4	12.2	31.5	60.8	29.3	36.9	29.6	(7.3)	23.5	29.1	5.6
30-39	30.6	35.4	4.8	29.0	58.9	29.9	29.6	33.9	4.3	25.9	20.6	(5.3)
40-49	33.9	49.1	15.2	43.0	58.8	15.8	37.1	36.8	(.3)	24.3	22.2	(2.1)
50 & over	38.5	56.0	17.5	38.8	54.0	15.2	34.3	32.4	(1.9)	32.6	29.2	(3.4)
Under $6,000	33.9	52.9	19.0	40.5	52.0	11.5	33.0	30.4	(2.6)	18.5	25.5	7.0
$6–$7,999	19.0	50.0	31.0	30.8	65.1	34.3	30.1	32.3	2.2	33.7	21.0	(12.7)
$8–$9,999	39.0	45.9	6.9	32.4	52.2	19.8	42.7	33.8	(8.9)	28.3	29.2	.9
$10,000+	43.9	46.7	2.8	41.7	60.5	18.8	40.9	41.4	.5	30.4	31.3	.9

QUESTION: WHAT CAN YOU TELL ME ABOUT THIS ADVERTISING? WHAT DID IT SAY OR SHOW?

225

Table 7

COMPANY ADVERTISING HAND PLANTING OR HELICOPTER SEEDING

	TV Program			TV Spot			Magazine			Control		
	Pre	Post	Diff	Pre	Post	Diff	Pre	Post	Diff	Pre	Post	Diff
Total	167	235	68	187	288	101	167	168	1	137	131	(6)
Recalling Any: %	100.0	100.0	-	100.0	100.0	-	100.0	100.0	-	100.0	100.0	-
Weyerhaeuser	19.8%	33.6%	13.8	6.4%	34.7%	28.3	15.0%	15.5%	.5	5.8%	8.4%	2.6
U.S. Plywood	2.4	2.1	(.3)	-	.7	.7	.6	.6	-	.7	3.8	3.1
Georgia-Pacific	4.8	1.7	(3.1)	2.1	1.0	(1.1)	1.2	3.0	1.8	2.9	3.1	.2
Others	.6	2.1	1.5	2.1	.3	(1.8)	1.2	1.8	.6	2.2	3.1	.9
Don't remember	73.7	62.6	(11.1)	90.4	64.2	(26.2)	82.6	79.2	(3.4)	89.1	82.4	(6.7)

QUESTION: CAN YOU RECALL WHOSE ADVERTISING THAT WAS?

Table 8

WHERE ADVERTISING OF HAND PLANTING OR HELICOPTER SEEDING WAS SEEN

	TV Program			TV Spot			Magazine			Control		
	Pre	Post	Diff	Pre	Post	Diff	Pre	Post	Diff	Pre	Post	Diff
Total	167	235	68	187	288	101	167	168	1	137	131	(6)
Recalling Any: %	100.0	100.0	-	100.0	100.0	-	100.0	100.0	-	100.0	100.0	-
Television	39.5%	59.6%	20.1	50.3%	79.5%	29.2	34.1%	31.5%	(2.6)	40.1%	37.4%	(2.7)
Newspapers (incl. magazine sec.)	15.6	10.6	(5.0)	10.2	4.2	(6.0)	14.4	16.1	1.7	13.9	14.5	.6
Magazines	50.9	36.2	(14.7)	41.2	22.9	(18.3)	52.7	46.4	(6.3)	43.8	36.6	(7.2)
Radio	5.4	3.8	(1.6)	4.3	2.1	(2.2)	5.4	3.6	(1.8)	5.8	5.3	(.5)
Mail	-	-	-	-	-	-	-	.6	.6	-	1.5	1.5
Others	.6	2.6	2.0	1.1	1.4	.3	-	3.0	3.0	2.9	5.3	2.4
Don't remember	4.8	2.6	(2.2)	5.3	2.4	(2.9)	3.0	9.5	6.5	5.1	7.6	2.5

QUESTION: WHERE DID YOU SEE OR HEAR THIS ADVERTISING?

Table 9

SAMPLE DEMOGRAPHY

	TV Program		TV Spot		Magazine		Control	
	Pre	Post	Pre	Post	Pre	Post	Pre	Post
By age:								
Under 20	2.8%	1.4%	1.9%	1.8%	.4%	1.8%	.2%	2.8%
20-29	24.6	26.4	15.9	17.6	12.9	14.3	20.2	20.5
30-39	19.6	19.6	19.4	21.4	20.0	24.1	23.2	19.3
40-49	23.0	22.2	22.1	23.8	23.7	24.9	21.4	21.5
50 & over	29.5	29.8	40.0	34.7	42.3	34.4	34.4	35.4
N.A.	.6	.6	.6	.8	.6	.6	.6	.6
By income:								
Under $6,000	23.6	23.6	31.7	29.9	20.4	15.7	23.8	21.9
$6–$7,999	16.8	17.9	23.3	17.2	21.1	19.7	17.8	16.1
$8–$9,999	21.0	21.6	21.0	13.8	18.2	15.9	18.4	14.3
$10,000 or over	26.3	24.2	16.3	23.8	26.0	31.2	27.6	31.8
N.A.	12.4	12.7	7.8	15.4	14.3	17.5	12.4	15.9
By sex:								
Male	50.9	49.6	51.1	50.1	48.5	50.3	50.0	49.7
Female	49.1	50.4	48.9	49.9	51.5	49.7	50.0	50.3
By occupation:								
Prof., tech.	13.4	10.1	10.9	11.4	14.7	14.5	12.4	9.7
Mgrs., off., prop.	16.8	10.1	12.4	14.8	12.1	15.3	14.2	14.5
Clerical & kind.	7.6	6.5	7.4	8.2	9.2	8.3	9.8	9.5
Sales	4.2	6.9	7.0	5.8	11.2	9.7	10.2	13.5
Craftsmen, foremen & kind.	20.8	21.0	22.5	21.4	16.4	20.7	19.0	17.1
Operatives & kind.	3.8	7.9	6.2	7.6	7.8	8.3	6.2	7.4
Service	6.6	6.3	7.4	7.0	7.4	5.6	7.6	6.0
Laborers	2.2	2.6	4.7	7.0	2.0	2.4	2.6	2.8
Farmers	1.2	2.4	1.0	3.0	.2	.2	.6	.2
Out of labor force	21.6	23.8	18.8	17.0	16.6	12.9	15.4	16.5
N.A.	2.0	2.2	1.7	1.6	2.5	2.0	2.0	2.8

Exhibit 2

PRINT AD USED IN 1967 TV TEST

Some days we seed a million trees before your morning coffee break.

Elk flee as a helicopter seeds a new forest on a Weyerhaeuser tree farm

The pages in this magazine came from a harvested tree. So did the milk cartons in your kitchen, the lumber in your home and the beautiful paneling in your den.

Replacing the trees you use is a man-size job. For you consume wood at an incredible pace.

Sometimes we sow seed from helicopters to speed the work along. In other cases, we leave seed trees close by to restock an area naturally. Or set out millions of young trees by hand.

We call it reforestation — restoring the trees on the scattered spots we harvest every year. This prompt reforestation keeps our land constantly covered with trees of all ages, from tiny seedlings to large, mature timber.

As a result, there always will be beautiful forests, water, wildlife and recreation for you and yours on our tree farms. Today. Tomorrow. Generation after generation.

If you'd like to know more about what we're doing to help keep America beautiful and still meet today's demand for forest products, just write us. Ask for "Tree Farm to You." It's free. Box A-36, Tacoma, Washington 98401.

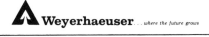

Weyerhaeuser . . . *where the future grows*

Exhibit 3
DESCRIPTION OF COMMERCIAL USED IN 1967 TV TEST

Video	*Audio*
Forest scene with deer grazing.	*Quiet of woods broken by calls of birds.*
Close-up of deer alert to sound. Deer bound away as helicopter draws near.	*Sound of helicopter first softly, as from a a distance, then louder and louder.*
Close-up of helicopter with foresters inside.	*Announcer*: These men are farmers of the forest. Their job . . . growing continuous crops of timber on Weyerhaeuser tree farms.
Camera closes in on seeds spewing from helicopter	They sow the seeds of tomorrow's trees with the promise of . . .
As helicopter pulls away, the lush forest below is revealed.	a harvest more bountiful than nature alone could ever produce.
Logging truck snakes down a mountain road.	[*Sound of helicopter fades into truck sound.*] These modern tree farms provide an endless supply of raw materials . . .
Shots of sawmill with slab being cut from giant log.	for Weyerhaeuser Mills . . . world wide producers of . . .
Carpenter putting exterior plywood on skeleton of house.	lumber and plywood . . .
School room scene.	paper . . .
Containers being loaded at dock.	packaging . . .
Arched beams at a construction site.	more than five thousand useful products made from trees.
Forest scene with tree farm sign.	Weyerhaeuser — the company that grows today's forests for tomorrow's needs.
Weyerhaeuser logo and name.	The mark of quality on products made from wood.

Exhibit 4

REPRESENTATIVE AD FROM FORESTRY CAMPAIGN

NEW TREES FOLLOW THE OLD on a Weyerhaeuser tree farm. Planned reforestation and careful management keep these lands continually productive ... insuring a permanent source of wood, water, wildlife and other important forest benefits.

From tree farm to you...a new home to enrich your life

Of all the benefits from Weyerhaeuser forestlands, none enriches the lives of so many as the wood itself—the continual flow of materials to build homes for our growing nation. For versatile wood continues to be man's favorite building material, practical and durable, yet radiant with nature's grown-in beauty of texture and color.

From strong, expertly dried structural materials to beautiful sidings, panelings and fine finish lumber, you'll find a Weyerhaeuser product for every home building need. And your builder will tell you that a well-designed home, carefully built with these materials, is your greatest assurance of achieving long-lasting value, comfort and convenience. He knows you can depend upon products bearing the Weyerhaeuser name—products made with the care and patience born of growing trees in century-long crops.

Make this the year to begin to enjoy better living in your new home. Send for a booklet on the benefits of new home ownership: Weyerhaeuser Company, Box A, Tacoma 1, Washington.

Symbol of quality in the world of wood **Weyerhaeuser**

Ad. No. 138: *Saturday Evening Post,* April 6, 1963.

QUESTIONS

1. *Appraise the media test carried out for Weyerhaeuser. What were the results?*

2. *What action should the company take now?*

Developing
and
Appraising
Advertising Messages

PART III

Consumer Value Stores (A)

Preparing an Advertisement

The advertising manager of a chain of discount drugstores must prepare a newspaper ad for the spring promotion.

In early March, the advertising manager of Consumer Value Stores (CVS) was looking over a list of merchandise sent to him by the merchandising promotion manager. (See Exhibit 1.) These items would be featured in all CVS outlets as the weekly specials from March 16 to March 21, and consequently were to be incorporated into the CVS March 15, 1,200-line (half-page) newspaper advertisements.

Consumer Value Stores was a chain of "health and beauty aid" stores operating in shopping centers and in neighborhood shopping areas throughout New England. CVS stores offered drugstore and proprietary products—e.g., aspirin, toothpaste, shampoos, vitamins, and the like—at discount prices. CVS was one of several such chains in the Greater Boston area; competitors included the Rexall, Rix, Wendy K, and Big L groups.

Of the 45 CVS stores, approximately 65% were located in central and eastern Massachusetts. Some twelve of these were in the Greater Boston area. The sizes of stores varied; but all were modern, well-lighted, self-service operations. Although many outlets devoted space to pet products, film, and school supplies, the heart of the business was health and beauty aids. Most CVS customers were women in the middle and upper-middle income brackets.

Consumer research had shown that slightly over half the women in the immediate Boston area had heard of Consumer Value Stores. Of these, some two-thirds had seen CVS advertising, almost entirely in newspapers. In some of the outlying towns, these figures were considerably higher: for example, over 90% had heard of CVS, of whom over 80% had seen its advertising.

This advertising had centered around the "good value" image the chain was trying to project. In the past, newspaper ads had featured the details of the weekly specials and the slogan, "You get it for less at CVS." Some ads had included a listing of store locations. However, management was not so committed to previous formats or content that other ideas would not be considered. In fact a recent CVS radio campaign had consisted of humorous institutional commercials that did not feature price specials or specific store locations.

Exhibit 1

PROMOTION ITEMS, MARCH 16-21

Item	Size	Mfr's Sug. List Price	CVS Sale Price
Adorn Hair Spray Regular	13.7 oz.	$2.25	$1.29
Adorn Hair Spray Hard to Hold	13.7 oz.	2.25	1.29
Aspergum Regular	16	.45	.29
Clairol Great Body Hair Conditioner	3.5 oz.	2.00	1.19
Crest Toothpaste Regular	5 oz.	.83	.57
Crest Toothpaste Mint	5 oz.	.83	.57
Dial Antiperspirant Spray Deodorant	5 oz.	1.19	2/.92
Kodak CX127 Film		1.25	.83
Kodak CX126-12 Film		1.40	.93
Prell Concentrate Shampoo	5 oz.	1.45	.79
Propa PH Liquid	6 oz.	1.69	.97
Schick SS Injector Blades	15	1.98	1.39
Zestabs Vitamins with free Adult Zestabs with Iron 25's	130	3.49	1.98

Exhibit 2

CVS LOCATIONS IN GREATER BOSTON

1322 Beacon Street, Brookline
37 Central Square, Lynn
427 Paradise Road, Swampscott
River City Shopping Center, Braintree
South Shore Shopping Center, Medford
Northgate Shopping Center, Revere
Hingham Plaza Shopping Center, Hingham
60 Leonard Street, Belmont
Natick Mall Shopping Center, Natick
Weymouth Shopping Center, Rte. 18, Weymouth
997 Watertown Street, West Newton

QUESTIONS

1. *Prepare a half-page ad suitable for CVS to run on Sunday, March 15.*
2. *What should a good CVS ad include? Emphasize?*

Exercise in Television Commercial Analysis

Television advertising campaigns are seldom produced in a creative vacuum. Underlying each commercial should be a carefully thought-out objective—an attempt to communicate a particular message to a specific audience. When a commercial "fails," the fault might be traced to either the objective or the execution.

The following storyboards and rationale statements are presented through the courtesy of the several advertisers of the Leo Burnett Company, the advertising agency that created the commercials.

General Motors Corporation (AC Sparkplug Division)	"Stunt Pilot"
The Pillsbury Company	"Crazy Crust Pizza"
Hadley School for the Blind	"Hadley School"
Vick Chemical Company (Clearasil)	"Oh No"
General Motors Corporation (Oldsmobile Division)	"It Could Happen"
Kellogg's of Battle Creek (Rice Krispies)	"Vesti"

Exhibit 1

AC SPARK PLUG – "STUNT PILOT"

This 60 second television commercial for the AC Spark Plug Division of General Motors is one of a new series utilizing unusual spark plug applications to demonstrate product reliability.

In this commercial, dramatic photography captures the excitement of a stunt pilot performing precision aerobatics. This action is designed to capture the viewer's attention and to establish the reliability of AC spark plugs. This product reliability is then transferred to the AC spark plugs used for automobiles, both visually and through the copy in the balance of this commercial.

LEO BURNETT COMPANY, INC.		GENERAL MOTORS - AC
AS FILMED AND RECORDED (5/70)	"Stunt Pilot"	C-62-AC-60

1. (Sound: music and engine roar)...

2. ...

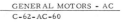

3. (Music under, Anncr VO) When you fly like this for a living...

4. ...your engine can't miss a beat...no matter how much it's tortured.

5. That's why stunt piolot Mike Dewey relies on...

6. ...AC Fire Ring Spark Plugs.

7. He knows AC's hot tip re- \sists fouling. So when Mike needs full power...he gets it.

8. And the same hot tip that's built into AC Aircraft Spark Plugs...

9. ...is built into the AC Fire Ring Spark Plugs that go into your car.

10. They fire hotter, burn cleaner. Next tune-up, insist on relaible AC Spark Plugs.

11. They're original equipment on all GM cars.

12. AC builds more parts for more cars...

13. ...than anyone else in the world.

14. (Singers VO) You go more carefree when you go with AC. AC keeps your car in action.

15. (Musical playoff)

Exhibit 2

PILLSBURY FLOUR – "CRAZY CRUST PIZZA"

Objectives:

(1) To build awareness of Pillsbury as the "Idea Flour" a contemporary product that fits both the needs and the desires of today's busy housewife.

(2) To create interest in and desire to try the "Crazy Crust Pizza" recipe and, thus, to create sales of the Pillsbury Flour product.

Strategies:

(1) Introduce the commercial with Poppin' Fresh presenting another "idea" recipe found inside the sack of Pillsbury Flour.

(2) Demonstrate this unique flour recipe for pizza. This recipe is novel because the pizza crust is poured; it is easy to prepare since there is no need to go through the traditional time-consuming steps of rolling and kneading to prepare it.

(3) Close with the Doughboy reminding consumers that the "idea" recipe can be found *only* in sacks of Pillsbury, the "Idea Flour."

 LEO BURNETT COMPANY, INC.

PILLSBURY

AS FILMED AND RECORDED (10/69)   "Pizza"   C-3218-PBF-30

1. (Mandolin music under) P. F.: And now a magnifico recipe...

2. ...from Pillsbury...the Idea Flour.

3. Crazy Crust Pizza.

4. (Anncr VO) Imagine! Pizza crust you pour. No rolling or kneading. Crazy!

5. Sprinkle meat and mushrooms on top, . . .

6. . . . and bake.

7. Spread on pizza topping, . . .

8. . . . and finish baking.

9. Mmmmm. . . Crazy Crust Pizza.

10. P. F.: The recipe's in sacks of Pillsbury. . .

11. . . . whoops! . . .

12. . . . the Idea Flour.

Exhibit 3

HADLEY SCHOOL FOR THE BLIND

Although this commercial mentions the name of a particular school in a particular city, it is also being shown—with appropriate changes—to benefit similar institutions in other cities throughout the United States. It was prepared by the Leo Burnett Company as a voluntary project to assist a worthy cause. Each year Burnett and many other advertising agencies voluntarily plan, write, and produce such commercials as a public service.

VIDEO:*

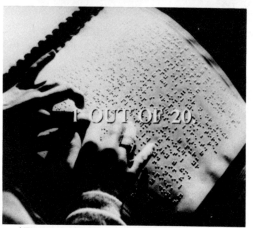

AUDIO: Once there was blindness that ended the sun, and the city, and the faces of friends. It ended a whole world that every man should own as long as he lives. Then came Braille. . .and the world came back. The blind could read. Doesn't that make you feel better? Don't feel too much better, because the gift of Braille is enjoyed by—how many do you think? Fifteen out of 20 blind persons; 10 out of 20? Stop dreaming! One out of 20 reads Braille. That's a shocker, because Braille books are free. Braille education is free. We provide both to all who ask. We are the Hadley School for the Blind, a non-profit organization. We exist on your donations, nothing else. Only 1 out of 20. Give to the Hadley School for the Blind, Winnetka, Illinois. Near the station. . .maybe you've seen it. Remember, our students never do.

*These are representative still shots from the filmed commercial.

Exhibit 4

CLEARASIL—"OH NO"

Empathy and believability are important factors when trying to sell a product to teenagers. This commercial execution dramatizes teenage frustration with acne by inventing a "disease" called the "Oh No's." "Oh No" is a typical human exclamation when pimples flare up—especially right before an important engagement or social situation. A strong degree of empathy is achieved from the several "frustrated" teens. A promise of relief is given by introducing Clearasil medication. Special product application shots and the promise of real medicine working for you is the product story. The commercial ends resolving to an emphatic "Oh Yes."

 LEO BURNETT COMPANY, INC.   VICK CHEMICAL (CLEARASIL)
AS FILMED AND RECORDED (1/70)   "The Oh, No's"   C-605-CLEAR-60

1. (Silent pullup)

2. GIRL: Oh, no! (Music figure)

3. BOY: Oh, no!

4. (Music figure)

5. BOY: Oh, no! (Music figure)

6. GIRL: Oh, no!

7. (Music figure, then music under, Anncr VO) The Oh No's--those...

8. ...frustrating, aggravating,...

9. ...infuriating acne blemishes.

10. Next time you get them, fight back with Clearasil. Clearasil Cream Medication contains...

11. ...the same blemish fighters many dermatologists use.

12. In fact, it's the most serious kind of blemish medicine you can get without a prescription.

13. Use Clearasil all over your face. Extra on the trouble spots. And don't quit. Fight those Oh No's every day...

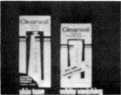

14. ...with Clearasil skin tone that hides or white vanishing. Clearasil gives your skin a fighting chance.

15. GIRL: Oh, yes! (Music figure to end)

Exhibit 5

OLDSMOBILE–"TORONADO–IT COULD HAPPEN"

The objective of this commercial is to project an image of unique prestige and luxury for Oldsmobile's Front Drive Toronado. The device used is an evocation of the magnificent classic cars of the past, which appear as ghost images, as a man and his wife drive along a deserted parkway after dark.

Great care was exercised in portraying the Duesenberg, the Packard, and the other classics as *unreal*, rather than as actual cars. In other words, they are images in the man's imagination. His wife is unaware of them. Executed in this way, there is a ruboff of prestige and glamour in associating the classics with the Toronado ("You're in good company when you own a Toronado"), and yet the relationship between truth and fancy is clearly maintained: the old classics belong to the past; their heir and successor, the Toronado, belongs to the present.

The commercial was shot in three nights at Stone Mountain, Georgia, on a closed stretch of parkway. The scenes of the old classics as viewed in the finished print are the result of "marrying" three separate pieces of film: one of deserted roadway, one of the classic car (or cars) traveling that same stretch of roadway, and one of the fog. This was necessary to achieve the "see through" or ghost effect and called for precise registration of camera and car positions and speeds.

LEO BURNETT COMPANY · INC.   GENERAL MOTORS − OLDSMOBILE

"Toronado − It Could Happen"

1. (Mood music mysterioso)
NARRATOR: After dark...on a road
you think you have all to yourself

2. it could happen.

3. The feeling...that the classic
cars of the past

4. are all around you.

5. It takes Toronado to weave
such a spell...

6. Toronado...successor to the
great ones of the past.

7. Deep reserves of coordinated
power in its big Rocket V-8 and
Turbo-Hydramatic transmission.

8. Emphatic stopping power with its
Tandem Power front disc brakes.

9. Proud and elegant styling.

10. Luxury and spaciousness...

11. ...uncommon freedom of movement
all around...down to a floor...as
flat as the floor in your living room.

12. The positive and incomparable
maneuverability and handling that's
yours only with Toronado's Front-Drive.

13. You're in good company...in a
Toronado.

14. Meet and drive one

15. at your Oldsmobile Dealer's.
Toronado by Oldsmobile!

Exhibit 6

KELLOGG'S RICE KRISPIES – "VESTI"

This commercial is one of a pool used in a Kellogg's Rice Krispies campaign titled "Great Moments at Breakfast." Rice Krispies' 20-year-old snap-crackle-pop theme is blended into familiar music from the world of opera and operetta. Besides the *Pagliacci* "Vesti Le Giubba" melody used in this commercial, there is another that takes off from the *Carmen* "Toreador" score, and a third inspired by the Romberg *Maytime* duet, "Wake Up."

A Kellogg official noted that

> "consumer and trade apathy can develop toward any cereal product that has been on the market as long as Rice Krispies—since 1928. It is with this thought in mind that Leo Burnett came up with a unique and highly visible idea—one that combines the world's most cultivated grain (rice) with highly cultivated music."

Because Kellogg's Rice Krispies has wide appeal as a cereal and as a recipe ingredient it is the third largest selling ready-to-eat cereal in the U.S.

"Great Moments at Breakfast" is aimed at only a portion of the TV audience. There are other commercials directed at younger viewers, using the Snap-Crackle-Pop characters and cast commercials on children's TV programs.

KELLOGG COMPANY
RICE KRISPIES

KELLOGG-C-3468-RK-60 (Color)
"VESTI"

LEO BURNETT COMPANY

1. (Music: establish "Pagliaci" theme)

2. (Anncr VO) Great Moments at Breakfast, presented by Kellogg's Rice Krispies. FATHER (sings): Barbara, ...

3. ...pass the Kellogg's Rice Krispies before it's all gone... ha-ha-ha-ha.

4. (Music)

5. No more Rice Krispies, ...

6. ...we ran out of Rice Krispies.

7. My tears will not stop...

8. ...(music)...

9. ...until I hear Snap! Crackle! (sob) Pop!

10. (Sound: knock at door) MOM-IN-LAW (sings): I've brought the Rice Krispies.

11. FATHER (recitatively): It's my mother-in-law.

12. MOM-IN-LAW: Enough to last at least two months. That's how long I'll be here.

13. FATHER: It's her fifteenth visit so far this year. (Sob-sob-sob-sob)

14. (Ha-ha-ha-ha)

15. (Sob-sob-sob-sob).

QUESTIONS

1. *Appraise each television commercial and its rationale. How sensible do you consider each approach and its execution to be?*

Weyerhaeuser Company (C)

The development of four commercials for a corporate identity TV advertising campaign is examined. Emphasis is on the method used to determine which specific settings best convey certain messages.

"This 'copy matrix' is certainly nothing brilliant or spectacular, but we have found it to be a sensible objective way of taking the things we want to say about Weyerhaeuser and determining the best possible ways in which to say them." Mr. Carroll O'Rourke, Director of Public Relations and Advertising at the Weyerhaeuser Company, was referring to the process by which the company and its advertising agency, Cole and Weber, determined the formats of the four television commercials to be run in the company's 1968 corporate identity advertising campaign.

BACKGROUND OF THE 1968 TELEVISION CAMPAIGN

Weyerhaeuser, a leading forest products company, began its corporate identity advertising effort in 1952 with full-color insertions in leading national publications. The format of the ads, featuring serene, tranquil scenes of wildlife in forest settings (see Exhibit 1) achieved wide acclaim for the company; and the series received over a dozen awards through 1967 for "distinguished advertising in the public interest." [See Weyerhaeuser Company (A) for a detailed account of the history of Weyerhaeuser corporate advertising and its role within the company.]

As the company expanded and introduced a number of new products during the early 1960s, the campaign attempted to convey a more up-to-date message of "Weyerhaeuser on the move." However, studies showed that although the company's identity as an ethical and responsible "protector of the forests" was well-established with the public, somewhat less had been successfully conveyed about Weyerhaeuser as a forward-looking, innovative, research-minded company. As a result, a reexamination of the entire advertising approach, including copy and media, was undertaken in the mid-1960s resulting, in part, in a 1967 research study to determine the extent to which the Weyerhaeuser corporate message could be conveyed on television. [See Weyerhaeuser Company (B) for a description of the TV test and its findings.] The test findings were sufficiently encouraging to bring about the decision to proceed into television in 1968. This decision left the company and agency account team with the tasks of determining the copy direction which the TV campaign should take to convey the desired corporate identity and the content of specific commercials.

DEVELOPMENT OF THE COPY MATRIX

The advertising group decided to first establish which corporate "qualities" should be conveyed, and then determine what settings or subjects could best convey the chosen qualities. After discussions with top management, the qualities identified by the group as important were:

Responsible
Ethical
Forward-looking
Innovative
Dynamic
Research-minded
Diversified

Executives believed that the sixteen years of the print campaign had effectively conveyed the message of Weyerhaeuser's commitment to ethical and responsible forest-management policies. Thus these qualities were, in essence, eliminated from the list, with the understanding that they would be preserved as a "halo" message inherent in some way in all commercials and would be emphasized in public relations activities. Priority was assigned to the remaining five qualities as major advertising thrusts; identifying Weyerhaeuser with these qualities became the major task of the campaign.

Since five qualities were regarded as too many to attempt to communicate simultaneously, the remaining task was divided into two parts. First, in selecting the settings for commercials all five qualities would serve equally as criteria, with audience appeal added as a sixth. Second, three qualities—forward-looking, innovative, and dynamic—would also receive emphasis in the consistent closing treatment for the commercials. Such a standard closing treatment would lend continuity to all ads used, and would serve as the theme of the entire campaign. (The closing line chosen was: "Weyerhaeuser...working on tomorrow's ideas today.")

THE COPY MATRIX

The "copy matrix" is presented in Exhibit 2. The subjects listed vertically came from many sources within the company. "Countless people have come up to us and suggested, 'Hey, why don't we do an ad on such and such?'" commented Mr.

O'Rourke. "We kept a record of these suggestions, and the subjects on the matrix represent what we regarded as the most promising of them."

Each subject was discussed by the advertising group as to how effectively the subject was believed able to convey each of the criterion qualities. A rating of 1 (low), 3 (moderate), or 5 (high) was then applied, with "audience appeal" receiving double weighting since, as one executive noted, "If the subject matter of the commercial isn't inherently interesting or appealing it's doubtful that the viewer will stay with it long enough to retain any of our messages." Mr. O'Rourke noted the rating method as "admittedly subjective, especially on audience appeal," but he believed that the system was justified if only because it "lends *some* order and is at least a serious attempt at rationality in a process which otherwise is done largely by intuition."

The four subjects chosen (marked by asterisks in Exhibit 2) were then taken by the agency's creative team to be converted into "mood boards" which would establish the general audio/visual progression of each 60-second commercial. "Mood boards are less precise and restricting than traditional storyboards," explained a member of the agency team. "By allowing the director of each commercial maximum freedom within the established message constraints, we believe that the tastefulness and aesthetic presentation which made the print campaign notable will be maintained in the TV commercials." Exhibits 3-6 contain descriptions of mood boards of the selected commercials.

FURTHER TESTING

The agency believed that the commercials as produced conveyed the specific messages which they were intended to convey. No further testing of the commercials was planned, primarily because of the high cost of producing a TV commercial of high technical quality for viewing by a test panel or a theater audience. The Weyerhaeuser advertising research group believed that a test commercial would need to be of reasonable technical quality to serve as a valid measure of the final commercial's effectiveness, particularly since the use of color and tasteful settings were believed to play such a significant part in determining the campaign's success.

The research group did intend, however, to conduct tests of each commercial's effectiveness after the campaign had run for several months. Weyerhaeuser Company (D) contains details on this research plan and the test results.

Exhibit 1

REPRESENTATIVE AD FROM FORESTRY CAMPAIGN

Raccoons on a Weyerhaeuser tree farm where tree crops are grown in endless cycles.

What is the greatest threat to America's forest lands?

☐ **Fire?**

☐ **Insects?**

☐ **Disease?**

☐ **Taxes?**

Fire, insects and disease are real hazards, but they are risks today's tree farmers are prepared to accept.

These are threats that usually can be controlled. And even though they'll always concern us they should not prevent tree farmers from keeping their forests green and growing, forever.

Taxes are another story. They must take into account that it may take 60 years or more for a tree to reach usable size. If they don't, taxes can make it impractical for tree farmers to reforest and pay

the costs of managing forests year in and year out.

When that happens, you lose because tree farms benefit everybody.

They provide a stable base for jobs and payrolls.

They provide opportunities for healthy outdoor recreation to millions of people from dry-fly purists to teen-age hikers.

Even if you never get closer to Mother Nature than a downtown park, you have a stake in tree farms.

They are one of the nation's most important

sources of raw materials for more than 5,000 products made from wood vital to our economy.

Fortunately, today's tax climate in most instances encourages reforestation.

Should the tax base fail to consider the long-term costs of growing timber as a crop it could mean a far greater threat to tomorrow's forests than fire, insects or disease.

For an informative booklet, "Plain Talk About Trees and Taxes," write Weyerhaeuser Company, Box A2, Tacoma, Washington 98401.

⋀ Weyerhaeuser
Pulp, paper, chemicals, packaging, lumber, plywood

This advertisement will appear in: *Look,* May 4, *Time,* May 14, *Saturday,* May 15, *The Atlantic* June.

Exhibit 2

"COPY MATRIX" FOR THE 1968 TELEVISION CAMPAIGN

Subject	Criteria						Total
	Forward-looking	Innovative	Research-minded	Dynamic	Diversified	Inherent Audience Appeal	
*Domed stadium	5	5	3	5	1	10	29
Paper – full line	1	1	1	1	5	2	11
Tomato carton	1	3	3	1	5	2	15
*High-yield concept	5	5	3	1	1	2	17
High-yield operations	5	5	3	5	1	6	25
Milk Carton	1	3	1	1	5	2	13
*Paneling	1	3	1	1	1	10	17
Drama – print	1	3	1	1	5	2	13
Polystone	1	3	3	1	5	2	15
*Product diversification**	5	3	1	3	5	1	18
*Geog. diversification**	5	1	1	3	5	6	21
Molded Doors	1	5	1	1	3	2	13
Milk Carton – Nonmilk	1	3	1	1	5	2	13

* Subjects chosen for commercials for the 1968-69 campaign.
** Both diversification themes were combined in the same commercial.

Exhibit 2 (cont.)

EXPLANATION OF COPY MATRIX SUBJECTS

Subject	*Explanation*
*Domed stadium	shows the design work done by the company in building a domed football stadium out of wood.
Paper—full line	in some way showing the full line of paper products made for commercial use.
Tomato carton	an illustration of the company's innovative practices in designing a shipping carton for fresh tomatoes.
*High-yield concept	shows the thinking in back of the High-Yield Forestry concept.
High-yield operation	showing some of the actual machinery and equipment used to put the High-Yield Forestry concept into use.
Milk carton	showing the work done in paperboard use for milk cartons.
*Paneling	emphasizes the beauty and economy of Weyerhaeuser home paneling.
Polystone	showing a new type of vinyl surface on cement block or other type of ceramics. Company was test-marketing this product through retail lumber dealers in 1968.
*Product diversification**	an attempt to show that Weyerhaeuser was more than a lumber company.
*Geographical diversification**	pointing out that the company had plants and locations all over the world rather than just in the Pacific Northwest.
Molded doors	showing a company product innovation to make complete door skins that are molded wood fiber rather than solid lumber.
Drama-print	a company trade name for four-color process printing on milk cartons for nondairy use.
Milk carton—Nonmilk	showing the increasing applicability of Pure-pak cartons for any noncorrosive materials such as coke syrup, mayonnaise, vinegar, etc., that can use this type of easy-pour carton and save the weight and storage requirements of glass.

*Subjects chosen for commercials for the 1968-69 campaign.
**Both diversification themes were combined in the same commercial.

Exhibit 3

MOOD BOARD FOR "DIVERSIFICATION-AIRPLANE" COMMERCIAL*

Video	*Audio*
Jet plane taking off. . .	ANNCR: In this fast-changing world nothing will ever be the same. And nobody knows that better than Weyerhaeuser. . . .
Aerial view of a partially completed development of houses,	the company that makes more than a thousand different building materials for homes. . .
a jet in flight, and aerial shots of farms and farmland	new packaging materials for farm produce, frozen foods, ice cream, and milk. . .
Aerial view of a jet,	the company that makes capacitor tissue for jets and space craft,
a complex highway cloverleaf,	giant plywood-concrete forms for highway construction. . .
a harbor,	industrial products for everything from boats. . .
railroad yards,	to boxcars. . .
the skyline of lower Manhattan,	papers with new properties for books, computers, and business.
a ship, and	And Weyerhaeuser cargo vans are helping revolutionize shipping—by sea, land,
an airplane with the Weyerhaeuser name and logo superimposed.	and air. Weyerhaeuser. . .working on tomorrow's ideas. . .today.

*"Mood boards" consist of artist's impressions (rough sketches) of the prospective video Portion of the color television commercial. These illustrations are intended to convey the mood of the advertisement, along with the prospective audio portion. For case purposes, because of reproduction problems, the video portion is reproduced in verbal form as above.

Exhibit 4

MOOD BOARD FOR "DOMED STADIUM - COLOSSEUM" COMMERCIAL*

Video	*Audio*
Overhead and interior shots of the ruins of the Colosseum. . .	ANNCR: (soft, deliberate) In ancient Rome, the Colosseum was the greatest amphitheater in all the world.
and a large, deserted bull-fighting arena.	In the New World the first great arenas were the "plaza de toros" of Mexico.
Exterior and interior views of a model domed stadium constructed of wood.	And for the stadium of tomorrow, a new design idea from Weyerhaeuser. A stadium that can be built of wood larger than the Astrodome, with giant laminated beams that would span three football fields and stand 250 feet high. And that, sport fans, is some stadium.

A man's hands remove the roof of the stadium, then replace it. . .with the Weyerhaeuser name and logo superimposed.	The stadium of tomorrow, another design innovation from Weyerhaeuser. . . working on tomorrow's ideas. . .today.

---

* See note on Exhibit 3.

Exhibit 5

MOOD BOARD FOR "PANELING - WOOD CARVER" COMMERCIAL*

Video	*Audio*
Craftsman working with wood. Close-up of his hands chiseling a design and polishing the finished piece, a jewelry box.	MUSIC: A single, mellow violin ANNCR: (soft, deliberate) Nature gave us a most remarkable material. . .wood. There's nothing like it in all the world. In skilled hands it can be turned into a thing of beauty that even nature herself wouldn't recognize.
Camera slowly pans over a lush interior scene. The room, decorated in warm tones, has paneled walls and several pieces of wooden furniture.	This same care goes into Weyerhaeuser paneling. Time was when quality like this was costly. Anything less was a compromise. But Weyerhaeuser's found a way to create paneling that looks as though it were crafted especially for your home, and it doesn't cost a fortune. So, if you've been putting off looking at paneling because you think it's expensive, visit your Weyerhaeuser dealer.
Camera closes in on the jewelry box on a shelf in the room, with the Weyerhaeuser name and logo superimposed.	He can probably change your mind. Weyerhaeuser. . .working on tomorrow's ideas. . .today.

---

* See note on Exhibit 3.

Exhibit 6

MOOD BOARD FOR "HIGH-YIELD OPERATION - FOREST" COMMERCIAL*

Video	*Audio*
Camera focuses on an evergreen twig, moves in to a close-up of a trout swimming near the surface of a stream, then to a nearby fawn.	ANNCR: (soft, deliberate) Forestry used to be a waiting game. But no more. America needs more wood today, tomorrow, and beyond.
The scene switches to various shots of the fir trees in a forest. The camera backs up to show the size of the trees.	Now Weyerhaeuser's found a way to actually speed up the forest. First we cultivate the land. . .plant young super trees. . .fertilize. . .and thin the forest. Result? One-third more wood per acre. . . per year. . .forever. It's called High-Yield Forestry. Even Mother Nature likes the idea.
A bald eagle takes off from its nest, soars through the treetops, then lands in the nest again. Weyerhaeuser name and logo superimposed.	So the next time someone says we're running out of trees, tell them about Weyerhaeuser High-Yield Forestry. Weyerhaeuser. . .working on tomorrow's ideas. . .today.

* See note on Exhibit 3.

QUESTIONS

1. Appraise the copy-matrix scheme which Weyerhaeuser used to develop TV commercial ideas.

2. Was the decision not to pretest a good one? Why? Why not?

Sodaburst (A)

The product manager for a new instant ice cream soda considers the
message strategy and product appeals to be used in advertising, in light
of research data and competitive information.

In early 1964, the Birds Eye Division of General Foods was readying its new
home ice cream soda, Sodaburst, for test marketing in Jacksonville, Florida. In the
course of developing marketing and advertising strategies for the product's introduction, Sodaburst's product manager and the advertising agency product group
were considering what message strategy and appeals should be employed.

For purposes of initial test marketing, Sodaburst was to be sold in 2-, 3-, and
4-soda sizes at retail prices of about 20¢ per soda. Retail carton size and price as
well as case size were to be evaluated as part of the test-marketing operation.

In trying to develop a clear and specific message strategy the group had available
extensive market research information, including background data on ice cream
soda consumption, results of Sodaburst's product testing, housewives' opinions on
the product's appropriateness for various occasions, its nutritional value, and so
forth.

Product and market research information follow.

BACKGROUND

Sodaburst is an instant ice cream soda consisting of a single unit made of ice
cream, syrup, and frozen carbonated water fused together and packaged in a
"miniature" cylindrical ice cream container. The ice cream soda is prepared by
slipping the single unit (ice cream, syrup, and frozen carbonated water) from its
cylindrical container into a large glass and adding tap water. On contact with the
tap water, the frozen carbonated water is released and mixes with the syrup. In one
minute, the soda is ready to serve.

At the time of the test marketing, the product was available in two flavors—
chocolate (vanilla ice cream with chocolate syrup) and strawberry (vanilla ice cream
with strawberry syrup). The product was to be sold from ice cream cabinets in the
retail outlet and had to be kept in the freezer section of the home refrigerator until
ready for use.

Research indicated that about 70% of housewives and other adults and 80% of teens/children drink ice cream sodas. Among adult ice cream soda drinkers, about two-thirds consume at least one per week in summer. Teens/children exceed this usage frequency, with about 85% reportedly drinking at least one per week in summer. In winter, usage levels drop, as indicated in Table 1.

Table 1
AVERAGE WEEKLY NUMBER OF ICE CREAM SODAS CONSUMED SEASONALLY BY FAMILY

	Total	Housewives	Other Adults	Teens/Children 8-18
Summer	2.63	2.05	1.97	3.56
Winter	.94	.87	.65	1.21

Research conducted in the course of Sodaburst's early product testing revealed that on a year-round basis housewives reported their own consumption of ice cream sodas at three per month; other family adults at three per month; children age 5-11 at three per month; and teens age 12-17 at five per month. Field checks at soda fountains in cities throughout the country confirmed the fact that ice cream sodas enjoyed a broad base of consumption not only among children/teenagers but also among adults.

CONSUMER REACTION

Several product formulations and product/package combinations were rated by consumers in a series of product use tests conducted in 1963. Table 2 summarizes the ratings of the winning product formulation and product/package combination by housewives, other adults, children under 12, and children 12-17. (These ratings

Table 2
FACIAL SCALE RATING OF SODABURST

	Housewives	Other Adults	Children under 12	Children 12-17
Winning product formulation	1.21	.90	1.98	1.60
Winning product/ package combination	1.44	1.14	1.99	2.12

may be compared with housewives' facial ratings, on the same scale, of established Jell-O flavors. These ratings ranged from .7 to 1.3.)

Further research, in the form of an extensive home-use test, was conducted in two cities in over 400 homes, representing a cross-section of families in various income, age, and educational strata. These tests consisted of one week's use of Sodaburst, at the conclusion of which users were questioned on possible uses and purchases of the product. Among these housewives, intent to buy was: High—64%, Moderate—31%, Low—5%.

These tests revealed no evidence that the appeal of the product would be limited to any particular geographic area or socioeconomic group. There was some tendency toward greater acceptance of the product in lower income/education households. (However, the fact that new product acceptance is historically higher among middle and upper income group would be expected to smooth out this tendency.) Respondents were asked: "If this product was sold in your supermarket, what would you expect to pay for a package of four sodas the same size as the ones you tried?" The average expected price per soda was about 17¢ ; however, Table 3 shows the wide range in expected price per soda.

Table 3
PERCEIVED COST PER SODA

Price	Percent
11 cents or less	10%
12—16 cents	45%
17—21 cents	30%
22 cents or more	15%

PRODUCT APPEAL AND APPROPRIATENESS

Those participating in the home-use test were also queried on their views of the product's appeal to adults, teenagers, and young children. Table 4 reports their responses, broken down separately for those housewives with and without children.

Early exploratory research had indicated that housewives did not see the product as a substitute for fountain ice cream sodas, particularly for themselves, because it could not furnish the highly valued "going-out" experience associated with consuming fountain sodas. Rather they saw the product as a family snack, competing with the whole spectrum of at-home snacks. Thus the housewives who participated in the home-use tests were asked about the product's appropriateness for various occasions. These results appear in Table 5.

Table 4

HOUSEWIVES' PERCEIVED APPEAL OF PRODUCT AMONG ADULTS, TEENAGERS, AND YOUNG CHILDREN

	Total	Housewives with Children	Housewives without Children
Base: Total housewives in each group	431	273	158
Housewives stating product would appeal to:			
Adults			
A great deal	29%	22%	42%
Somewhat	55	59	48
Not at all	16	19	10
	100%	100%	100%
Teenagers			
A great deal	73%	68%	81%
Somewhat	23	27	17
Not at all	3	4	1
Not stated	1	1	1
	100%	100%	100%
Young children			
A great deal	75%	71%	81%
Somewhat	20	21	18
Not at all	5	8	1
	100%	100%	100%

In earlier group interviews, after experience with the product, housewives had clearly indicated that because of its relative cost Sodaburst would not be bought simply to satisfy teenagers/children since "kids can be satisfied with much less." Alternative snacks were seen as "direct substitutes," such as homemade floats and sodas (10-13¢), as well as less expensive milk and cookies, soft drinks, ice cream novelties (e.g., Dixie Cups), etc. Many housewives explicitly stated that their interest in the product was influenced by the opportunity they saw for it in promoting "family sociability" in snack-eating situations.

SPECIFIC PRODUCT APPEALS

Since many instant products instill a "flavor distrust" among consumers, the flavor and taste of Sodaburst were areas of particular interest and inquiry in the home-use test research. The novelty and "magic" of the product were expected to raise doubts in some consumers' minds about its ability to provide a highly satis-

Table 5

HOUSEWIVES' OPINIONS REGARDING THE PRODUCT'S APPROPRIATENESS
FOR VARIOUS OCCASIONS

	Occasion						
	Afternoon Snacks	Dessert at Lunch	Dessert at Dinner	Evening Snacks	Children's Parties	Teens' Parties	Adult Guests
Very appropriate	54%	23%	19%	68%	81%	71%	22%
Fairly appropriate	34	35	25	24	11	20	30
Not appropriate	12	42	55	7	7	8	47
Not stated	-	-	1	1	1	1	1
	100%	100%	100%	100%	100%	100%	100%

fying ice cream soda. Such "flavor reservations" had been expressed by about 25% of the housewives during Sodaburst's early product testing.

In response to questions about what specific things they liked about Sodaburst, housewives, after the home-use test, cited four major areas: flavor/taste, convenience, ease of preparation, and packaging/storage. Responses to this question, further broken down by "intent to buy," appear in Table 6.

Table 6

SPECIFIC "LIKES" OF PRODUCT

| | Total | Intent To Buy | | |
		High	Moderate	Low
All flavor/taste mentions	*67%*	*78%*	*66%*	*54%*
Tastes like a real ice cream soda	21	32	22	7
Good ice cream taste	17	17	15	19
Good flavor, taste (general)	12	8	15	11
Good chocolate taste	11	12	12	8
Refreshing, cool	4	4	4	2
All other flavor/taste mentions	12	15	8	11
All convenience mentions	*61*	*70*	*67*	*43*
All ease of preparation comments	*57*	*58*	*68*	*43*
All packaging/storage mentions	*44*	*46*	*49*	*34*

Exploratory research had also revealed that ice cream sodas, in contrast to many other snack foods, are regarded as wholesome. Thus housewives in the home-use test were asked their opinions of the product's nutritional value. Approximately 68% thought the product was very or fairly nutritious, as shown in Table 7. These results are also broken down by "intent to buy."

Table 7

NUTRITIONAL VALUE AND INTENT TO BUY

| | Total | Intent to Buy | | |
		High	Moderate	Low
Perceiving Product As Very or Fairly Nutritious	68%	80%	70%	51%

COMPETITION

Several other manufacturers were in various stages of introduction of products considered potentially competitive with Sodaburst. Included were two products from Borden Foods Company, one from Pet Milk Company, and one from National Sugar Refining Company. Information on these products[1] is given below.

Borden's Milk Shake "The first ice cream-thick milk shake from a can." A refrigerated product, it is made with ice cream mix and whole milk. The use theme is: "Just shake! open! pour!" The shake comes in 10¼-ounce cans retailing at two for 39 ¢ . Each can is dated, and according to Borden's has a shelf-life of five months under proper refrigeration.

Borden's Moola Koola A ready-to-drink milk-based canned product, requiring no refrigeration. Promotion theme: "New soft drink that comes from a cow." Emphasis is on fun and flavor. Moola Koola retails for 29 ¢ for a 9½-ounce can. A 32-ounce family size is also offered. (Both Borden drinks are vitamin enriched and come in chocolate, strawberry, and vanilla flavors.)

Pet Milk's Big Shot A milk additive in an aerosol container designed to look like a soda jerk. The chocolate fudge-flavored syrup is offered as the "first self-mixing milk additive that needs no refrigeration."

National Sugar Refining's Jack Frosted A creamy chocolate milk-base additive that can make rich milk shakes and frosteds at the touch of a button. The product, in a 21-ounce aerosol can, is squirted into a glass and changes the ingredients to a shake.

QUESTION

1. *Develop a clear and specific message strategy statement based on the market research information available as of early 1964.*

---

[1] Information based on "New Products Marketing," *Printers' Ink,* July 24, 1964, p. 14.

Sodaburst (B)

Given a basic message strategy statement for a new instant ice cream soda, the product manager must decide which of several TV and print ads should be employed.

In early 1964, the product manager and advertising agency product group for Sodaburst were considering what message strategy and appeals should be employed on behalf of the product. Sodaburst was the Birds Eye Division of General Foods' new home ice cream soda. (For background, see SODABURST (A).)

After extensive discussion, the following message strategy statement was approved:

> Advertising copy will be directed to an all-family audience, with particular emphasis on housewives in homes with children aged 5-17.
>
> Copy will be designed to appeal to consumers in all geographic areas and among all socioeconomic groups except that no special effort will be made to assure appeal to members of lowest-income-quartile households.
>
> The principal objective of the advertising will be to announce that all the familiar taste enjoyment of an ice cream soda is now quickly and conveniently available at home with Sodaburst.
>
> A secondary objective will be to convince housewives of the product's quality/wholesomeness that makes it suitable for all-family consumption.
>
> The copy will dramatize the interest and excitement inherent in the totally new product concept Sodaburst represents.

The basic selling proposition submitted by the agency and agreed to by division executives was: "A real ice cream soda that makes itself at home in one minute cold." In support of this basic selling proposition, the agency submitted several television commercials and print advertisements. (See Exhibits 1 through 6.) In examining these proposed advertisements, the Sodaburst product manager and his staff wondered which ones best implemented the agreed-on message statement.

Exhibit 1

STORYBOARD FOR TELEVISION COMMERCIAL
COMMERCIAL # 1

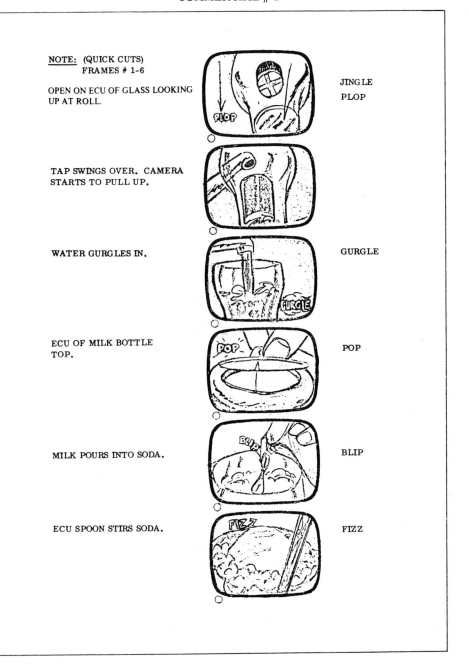

NOTE: (QUICK CUTS)
FRAMES # 1-6

OPEN ON ECU OF GLASS LOOKING
UP AT ROLL.

JINGLE
PLOP

TAP SWINGS OVER. CAMERA
STARTS TO PULL UP.

WATER GURGLES IN.

GURGLE

ECU OF MILK BOTTLE
TOP.

POP

MILK POURS INTO SODA.

BLIP

ECU SPOON STIRS SODA.

FIZZ

Exhibit 1 (cont.)

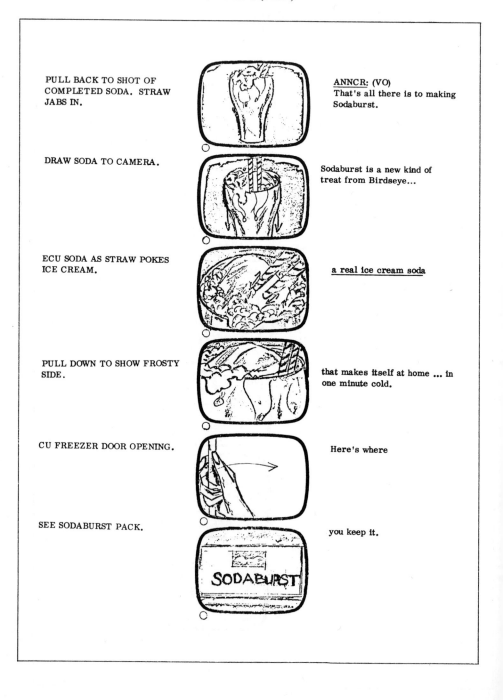

PULL BACK TO SHOT OF
COMPLETED SODA. STRAW
JABS IN.

ANNCR: (VO)
That's all there is to making
Sodaburst.

DRAW SODA TO CAMERA.

Sodaburst is a new kind of
treat from Birdseye...

ECU SODA AS STRAW POKES
ICE CREAM.

a real ice cream soda

PULL DOWN TO SHOW FROSTY
SIDE.

that makes itself at home ... in
one minute cold.

CU FREEZER DOOR OPENING.

Here's where

SEE SODABURST PACK.

you keep it.

SODABURST

Exhibit 1 (cont.)

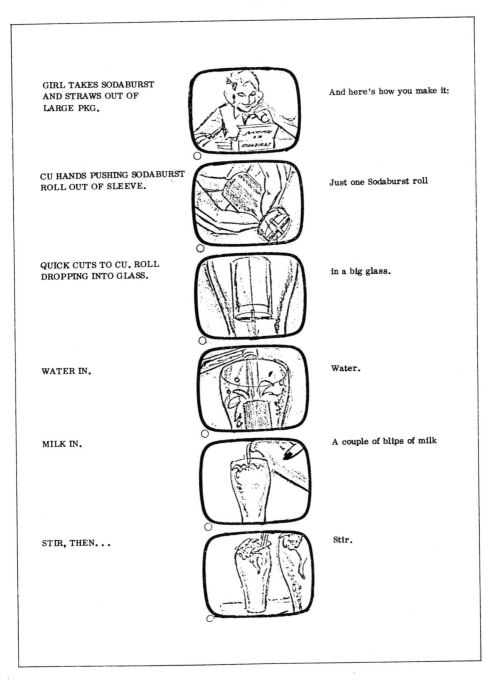

GIRL TAKES SODABURST
AND STRAWS OUT OF
LARGE PKG.

And here's how you make it:

CU HANDS PUSHING SODABURST
ROLL OUT OF SLEEVE.

Just one Sodaburst roll

QUICK CUTS TO CU. ROLL
DROPPING INTO GLASS.

in a big glass.

WATER IN.

Water.

MILK IN.

A couple of blips of milk

STIR, THEN. . .

Stir.

Exhibit 1 (cont.)

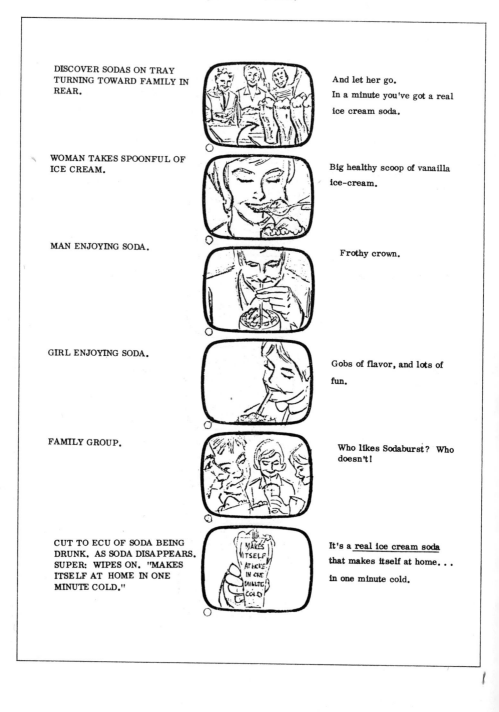

DISCOVER SODAS ON TRAY TURNING TOWARD FAMILY IN REAR.

And let her go.
In a minute you've got a real ice cream soda.

WOMAN TAKES SPOONFUL OF ICE CREAM.

Big healthy scoop of vanailla ice-cream.

MAN ENJOYING SODA.

Frothy crown.

GIRL ENJOYING SODA.

Gobs of flavor, and lots of fun.

FAMILY GROUP.

Who likes Sodaburst? Who doesn't!

CUT TO ECU OF SODA BEING DRUNK. AS SODA DISAPPEARS. SUPER: WIPES ON. "MAKES ITSELF AT HOME IN ONE MINUTE COLD."

It's a real ice cream soda that makes itself at home. . . in one minute cold.

Exhibit 1 (cont.)

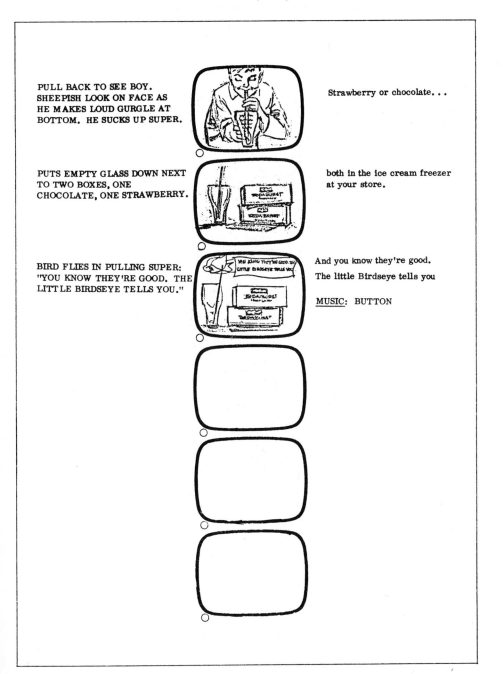

PULL BACK TO SEE BOY.
SHEEPISH LOOK ON FACE AS
HE MAKES LOUD GURGLE AT
BOTTOM. HE SUCKS UP SUPER.

Strawberry or chocolate...

PUTS EMPTY GLASS DOWN NEXT
TO TWO BOXES, ONE
CHOCOLATE, ONE STRAWBERRY.

both in the ice cream freezer
at your store.

BIRD FLIES IN PULLING SUPER:
"YOU KNOW THEY'RE GOOD. THE
LITTLE BIRDSEYE TELLS YOU."

And you know they're good.
The little Birdseye tells you

MUSIC: BUTTON

Exhibit 2

STORYBOARD FOR TELEVISION COMMERCIAL
COMMERCIAL # 2

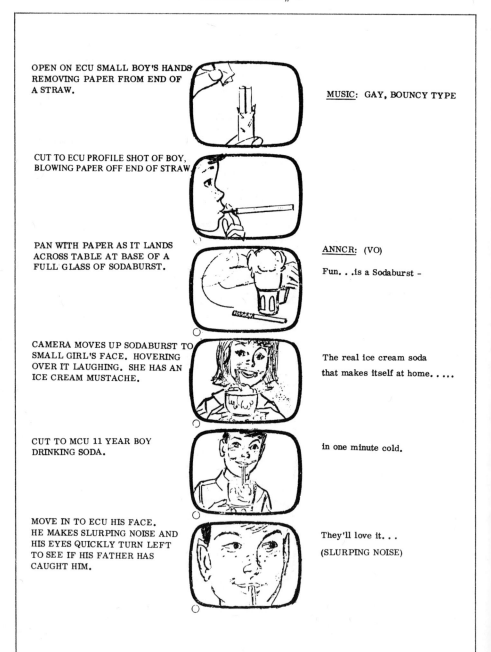

OPEN ON ECU SMALL BOY'S HANDS REMOVING PAPER FROM END OF A STRAW.

<u>MUSIC</u>: GAY, BOUNCY TYPE

CUT TO ECU PROFILE SHOT OF BOY, BLOWING PAPER OFF END OF STRAW.

PAN WITH PAPER AS IT LANDS ACROSS TABLE AT BASE OF A FULL GLASS OF SODABURST.

<u>ANNCR</u>: (VO)

Fun. . .is a Sodaburst –

CAMERA MOVES UP SODABURST TO SMALL GIRL'S FACE. HOVERING OVER IT LAUGHING. SHE HAS AN ICE CREAM MUSTACHE.

The real ice cream soda that makes itself at home. . ...

CUT TO MCU 11 YEAR BOY DRINKING SODA.

in one minute cold.

MOVE IN TO ECU HIS FACE. HE MAKES SLURPING NOISE AND HIS EYES QUICKLY TURN LEFT TO SEE IF HIS FATHER HAS CAUGHT HIM.

They'll love it. . . (SLURPING NOISE)

Exhibit 2 (cont.)

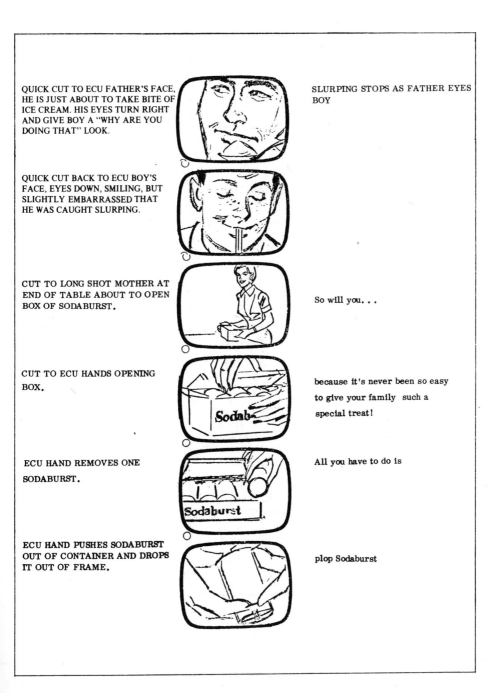

QUICK CUT TO ECU FATHER'S FACE, HE IS JUST ABOUT TO TAKE BITE OF ICE CREAM. HIS EYES TURN RIGHT AND GIVE BOY A "WHY ARE YOU DOING THAT" LOOK.

SLURPING STOPS AS FATHER EYES BOY

QUICK CUT BACK TO ECU BOY'S FACE, EYES DOWN, SMILING, BUT SLIGHTLY EMBARRASSED THAT HE WAS CAUGHT SLURPING.

CUT TO LONG SHOT MOTHER AT END OF TABLE ABOUT TO OPEN BOX OF SODABURST.

So will you. . .

CUT TO ECU HANDS OPENING BOX.

because it's never been so easy to give your family such a special treat!

ECU HAND REMOVES ONE SODABURST.

All you have to do is

ECU HAND PUSHES SODABURST OUT OF CONTAINER AND DROPS IT OUT OF FRAME.

plop Sodaburst

Exhibit 2 (cont.)

CU SODABURST IN GLASS.

into a big glass

CUT TO CU WATER POURING INTO GLASS.

add water

STAY ON GLASS AS SODABURST STARTS TO MAKE ITSELF.

and wait a minute for the frozen cube of bubbles to turn Sodaburst

DISSOLVE TO SODA ALREADY MADE.

into a real ice cream soda!

CUT TO CU MILK POURING INTO GLASS.

Now. . .a little milk

CU SPOON STIRRING.

a little
stir

Exhibit 2 (cont.)

SPOON DIGS INTO ICE CREAM.	and dig right in
ECU ICE CREAM ON SPOON.	to a mound of rich, creamy vanilla ice cream
CUT TO ECU MOTHER DRINKING SODA.	in a fresh fruit strawberry or a deep chocolate soda.
CUT TO BIRDS EYE LOGO ON SODABURST PKG.	Birds Eye has put 4 of them in a pkg.
PULL BACK TO SEE NAME SODABURST, TOO.	and dropped them
CONTINUE PULLING BACK SO YOU SEE ENTIRE SODABURST PKG.	in your grocer's ice cream freezer

Exhibit 2 (cont.)

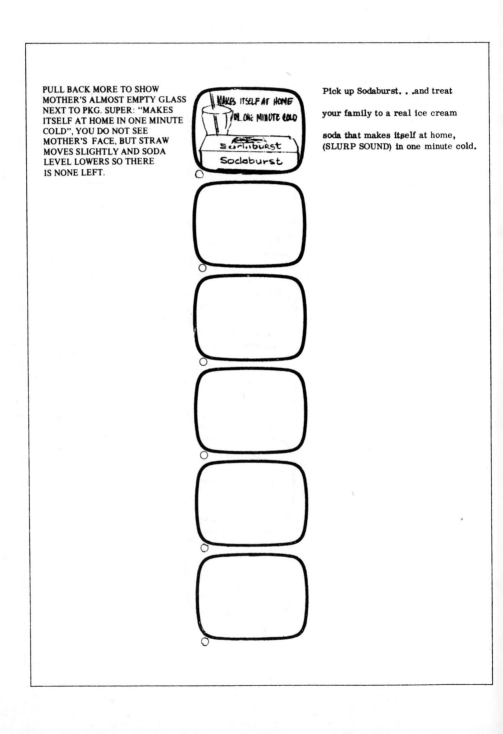

PULL BACK MORE TO SHOW
MOTHER'S ALMOST EMPTY GLASS
NEXT TO PKG. SUPER: "MAKES
ITSELF AT HOME IN ONE MINUTE
COLD", YOU DO NOT SEE
MOTHER'S FACE, BUT STRAW
MOVES SLIGHTLY AND SODA
LEVEL LOWERS SO THERE
IS NONE LEFT.

Pick up Sodaburst. . .and treat

your family to a real ice cream

soda that makes itself at home,
(SLURP SOUND) in one minute cold.

Exhibit 3

STORYBOARD FOR TELEVISION COMMERCIAL
COMMERCIAL # 3

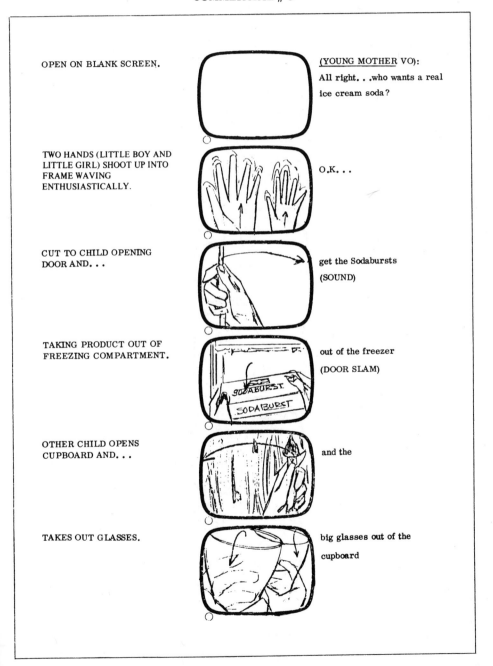

OPEN ON BLANK SCREEN.

(YOUNG MOTHER VO):
All right. . .who wants a real
ice cream soda?

TWO HANDS (LITTLE BOY AND
LITTLE GIRL) SHOOT UP INTO
FRAME WAVING
ENTHUSIASTICALLY.

O.K. . .

CUT TO CHILD OPENING
DOOR AND. . .

get the Sodabursts
(SOUND)

TAKING PRODUCT OUT OF
FREEZING COMPARTMENT.

out of the freezer
(DOOR SLAM)

OTHER CHILD OPENS
CUPBOARD AND. . .

and the

TAKES OUT GLASSES.

big glasses out of the
cupboard

Exhibit 3 (cont.)

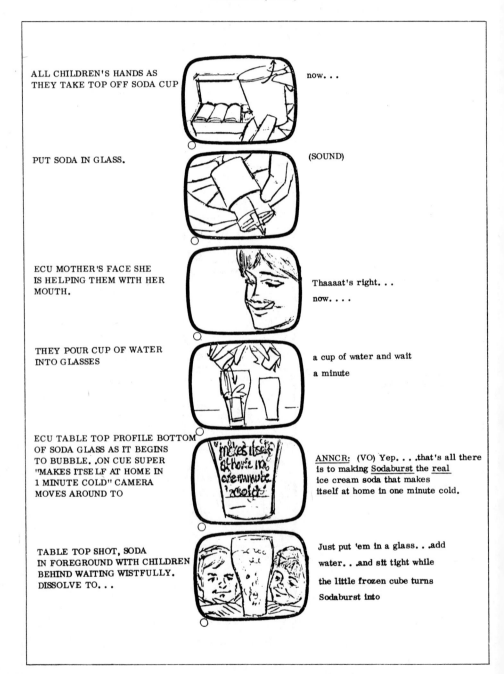

ALL CHILDREN'S HANDS AS
THEY TAKE TOP OFF SODA CUP

now. . .

PUT SODA IN GLASS.

(SOUND)

ECU MOTHER'S FACE SHE
IS HELPING THEM WITH HER
MOUTH.

Thaaaat's right. . .
now. . . .

THEY POUR CUP OF WATER
INTO GLASSES

a cup of water and wait
a minute

ECU TABLE TOP PROFILE BOTTOM
OF SODA GLASS AS IT BEGINS
TO BUBBLE. .ON CUE SUPER
"MAKES ITSELF AT HOME IN
1 MINUTE COLD" CAMERA
MOVES AROUND TO

ANNCR: (VO) Yep. . . .that's all there
is to making Sodaburst the real
ice cream soda that makes
itself at home in one minute cold.

TABLE TOP SHOT, SODA
IN FOREGROUND WITH CHILDREN
BEHIND WAITING WISTFULLY.
DISSOLVE TO. . .

Just put 'em in a glass. . .add
water. . .and sit tight while
the little frozen cube turns
Sodaburst into

Exhibit 3 (cont.)

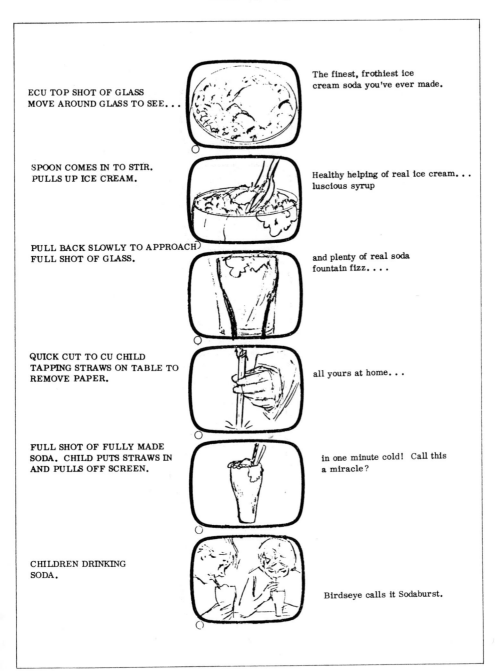

ECU TOP SHOT OF GLASS
MOVE AROUND GLASS TO SEE...

The finest, frothiest ice cream soda you've ever made.

SPOON COMES IN TO STIR.
PULLS UP ICE CREAM.

Healthy helping of real ice cream... luscious syrup

PULL BACK SLOWLY TO APPROACH
FULL SHOT OF GLASS.

and plenty of real soda fountain fizz. . . .

QUICK CUT TO CU CHILD
TAPPING STRAWS ON TABLE TO
REMOVE PAPER.

all yours at home...

FULL SHOT OF FULLY MADE
SODA. CHILD PUTS STRAWS IN
AND PULLS OFF SCREEN.

in one minute cold! Call this a miracle?

CHILDREN DRINKING
SODA.

Birdseye calls it Sodaburst.

Exhibit 3 (cont.)

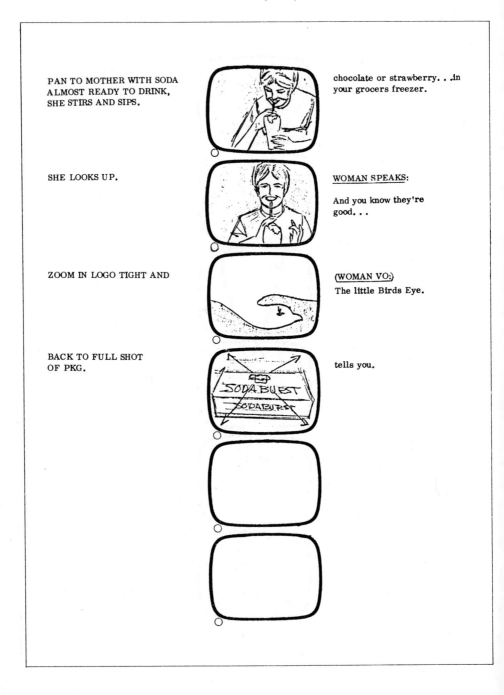

PAN TO MOTHER WITH SODA
ALMOST READY TO DRINK,
SHE STIRS AND SIPS.

chocolate or strawberry. . .in
your grocers freezer.

SHE LOOKS UP.

WOMAN SPEAKS:

And you know they're
good. . .

ZOOM IN LOGO TIGHT AND

(WOMAN VO:)
The little Birds Eye.

BACK TO FULL SHOT
OF PKG.

tells you.

Exhibit 4

LAYOUT OF PRINT ADVERTISEMENT: AD #1

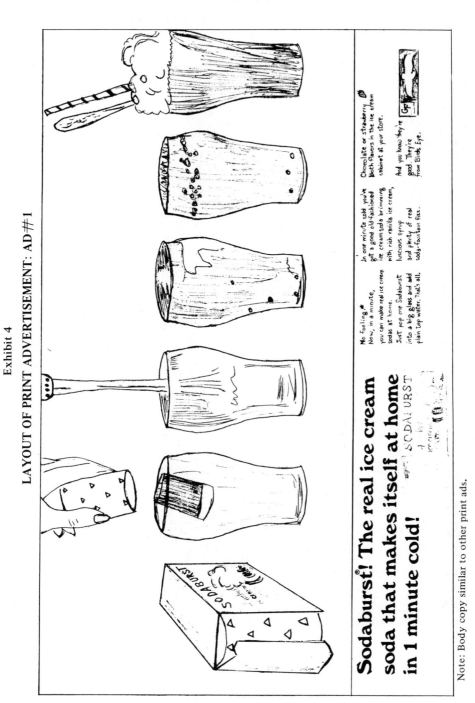

Note: Body copy similar to other print ads.

Exhibit 5

**LAYOUT OF PRINT ADVERTISEMENT
AD # 2**

You are looking at a real ice cream soda about to happen

see,
it happened!

No fooling!
Now you can make
real ice cream sodas
at home.
Just pop one
Sodaburst
into a big
glass

and add
plain tap water.
That's all.

In one minute
you've got a good
old-fashioned ice
cream soda,
brimming with rich
vanilla ice cream,
luscious syrup
and plenty
of real
soda
fountain
fizz.

Chocolate or
Both flavors
in the ice cream
cabinet at your
store.

And you know they're
good. The little
Birds Eye tells you.

SODABURST
A instant
ice cream
sodas

Sodaburst! The real ice cream soda
that makes itself at home in 1 minute cold!

Exhibit 6

LAYOUT OF PRINT ADVERTISEMENT: AD #3

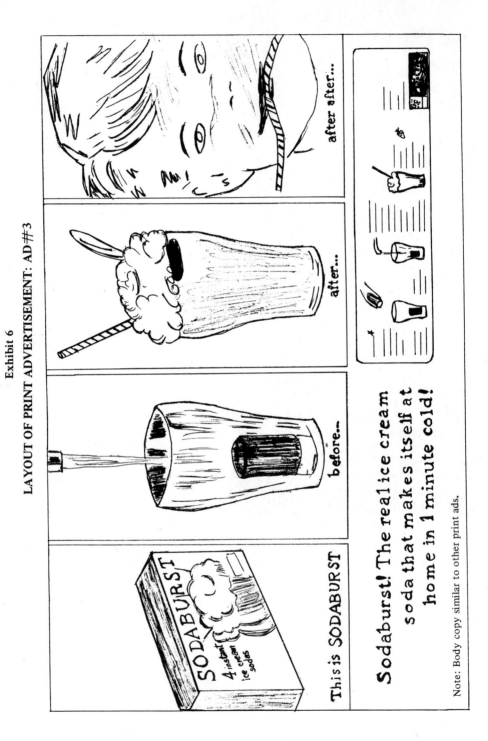

QUESTIONS

1. Which of the proposed TV commercials best implements the message strategy selected by the product manager?
2. Which is the best print execution?

Edgerton Company

> The account executive for Edgerton's spiced-meat product must decide whether to order a pretest to help in determining which of two magazine advertisements should be run. If he decides to test, he must specify the kind of research he wants carried out.

"Which of the 2 ads should we use?" The account executive for Edgerton Spiced Meat at the San Francisco office of the Twaddle and Herrling Advertising Agency wondered how to determine the answer to that question. The advertisements (see Exhibits 1 and 2) had been prepared by the agency for a one-half page, 4-color insertion in leading women's magazines. Both agency and company executives believed each ad was well conceived and well done. However, they thought that pretesting the 2 ads with consumers would yield information which could aid in deciding which would be more effective.

The William Edgerton Company, founded in 1872, was one of the Pacific Coast's oldest packers. The company packed and marketed a number of specialty foods, including spiced meat, Pacific sardines, dried cured beef, and anchovy paste. The firm employed about 100 people in its main plant and offices located in the waterfront area of San Francisco. Edgerton sales were estimated at over $10 million, of which the largest part was derived from Edgerton Spiced Meat, the company's oldest, major, and most extensively advertised product. Made from a beef and pork combination chopped and seasoned according to a traditional and closely guarded recipe, Edgerton Spiced Meat was first marketed in 1895. National advertising commenced in 1921. As had been the case for many years, Edgerton Spiced Meat was packed in 2 sizes, a 2½- and a 4½-ounce tin, labeled with a multicolored wrapper with the name Edgerton prominently printed in black. The small tin sold at about $.23, and the larger size at about $.45. Edgerton, like many other specialty food producers, distributed its products through food brokers; this had been Edgerton's practice since the early 1900s. Five Edgerton regional field sales managers worked with about 100 brokers, whose several hundred salesmen sold to chain supermarket headquarters, large independent supermarkets, and independent stores.

Edgerton's marketing activities were directed by the marketing vice-president, Wilbur Bowers, who had been with the company 10 years. His predecessor, John

Barnard, was now Edgerton's president. Barnard had had extensive experience in sales management, and had centralized the company's sales and marketing operations. Edgerton retained the San Francisco branch of Twaddle and Herrling for advertising and marketing services.

During the preceding 5-year period, Edgerton sales had increased over 40% and annual advertising expenditures had increased commensurately to over $600,000. In the face of steadily increasing advertising expenditures on behalf of food products in general, Edgerton had been able to increase its share of total retail food store sales during this period while maintaining constant its share of total food advertising.

The national market for spiced meat was relatively stable, with only a slight upward trend in total consumption. Sales were not seasonal in nature. However, there were strong regional patterns in the consumption of spiced meat; for example, the percentage of Pacific Coast families purchasing the product (20%) was 3 times the national family percentage. Pacific Coast residents also consumed the largest average number of tins of spiced meat. Family purchase was lowest in the South Atlantic and Deep South areas.

Edgerton's share of the spiced meat market had climbed from roughly 35% 10 years before to about 60% at present. Sales were highest in the Pacific Coast area, where about three-quarters of the spiced meat sold was Edgerton, while the brand's share was lowest, slightly over half the market, in the Midwest and Southeastern regions. Competition was chiefly from various national and regional meat packing firms, none of which had more than a tenth of the national market, although each had its regional centers of preference.

Spiced meat usage was highly concentrated. Users had been classified as heavy (over 24 tins annually); medium (12-24 tins); and light (1-12 tins) in a nationwide research study conducted for Edgerton. The study revealed that although only about a fourth of spiced meat users were classified in the "heavy" category, this group accounted for almost two-thirds of spiced meat consumption. Medium purchasers, numbering slightly under a third of the total, consumed about a fifth of the spiced meat sold. Light users, who constituted almost half of the product's consumers ate slightly over a tenth of spiced meat total. From this and other research,[1] the agency and company were able to construct a careful demographic profile of the Edgerton Spiced Meat purchaser. This information was of use in planning advertising and promotional strategy.

As mentioned above, Edgerton products were distributed through brokers to retail outlets. Three promotions were conducted annually in conjunction with the brokers. These involved in-store point of purchase displays and mats[2] for retailers to use for local advertising. In addition, stores were encouraged to offer multiple cans of Edgerton Spiced Meat in store promotions, e.g., 5 for $1.00. Promotions with the brokers had been increased from 1 to 3 per year 4 years before, and were

---

[1] Data on retail sales shares and consumer profiles were purchased by Edgerton.

[2] Mat(rice)s were papier-mache models used to reproduce a printing plate. Ads could be sent in this manner to be used at the retailer's discretion.

not envisioned as increasing beyond 4 in the near future. Coupons and self-liquidating premiums had also been employed at the local level from time to time. The broker-conducted promotions had been particularly helpful in the Middle Atlantic area over the past several years, during which time Edgerton had increased its share of market from only a small portion to over a half.

Because spiced meat was a specialty item, and relatively slow moving compared to most supermarket products, agency and company executives believed that there was a practical limit to the amount of promotion stores would give to Edgerton. Consequently, only about a fifth of the company's marketing efforts was devoted to this activity.

Company and agency executives believed that the role of the sales organization was to get the product to the store, that sales promotion and, to some extent, advertising moved spiced meat to the pantry, but that the major task of the Edgerton advertising program was to get people to use the product, rather than just be aware of it. Company and agency executives believed that many housewives purchased spiced meat "to have around the house." They thought that the demonstration of new and tempting methods of preparing and using spiced meat in advertising would lead housewives to use and then replenish their pantry stocks, and increase sales of Edgerton Spiced Meat.

Planned advertising expenditures for Edgerton products were based on a per case allocation. The preceding year's case sales, adjusted for sales expectations in the coming year, served as a planning base, and actual adjustments took place as the sales pattern for the year emerged. This manner of establishing the advertising budget had been followed by Edgerton for a number of years. No radical increases or decreases in advertising dollars had been tried.

Edgerton's media advertising had traditionally been concentrated in national magazines, which accounted for two-thirds of the media budget. The magazine schedule planned for the current year consisted of 21 half-page 4-color insertions, for which 7 individual advertisements were to be prepared. The schedule is detailed in Exhibit 3. Three women's magazines were to be used, one fewer than in prior years, because national network radio had been added to Edgerton's advertising program for the first time.

National radio advertising for Edgerton consisted of announcements on the morning Ted Lester program, beamed into 200 cities, over the XYZ Radio Network. Local (Pacific Coast) testing of radio announcements during the past 2 years had preceded the decision to put Edgerton into the medium. Although this area had registered the highest per capita consumption of spiced meat prior to the use of radio, the sales increase in that region was larger during the 2 years of radio than any that occurred elsewhere. The rise in sales was more than enough to offset the increased advertising cost. Further, it was subsequently discovered that the new sales level did not taper off. Hence, after 2 experimental years, local radio was discontinued and national network radio became part of the regular Edgerton advertising budget. While the magazine advertising was considered to have impact and broad reach for Edgerton, the radio advertising was seen as providing frequency as well as broad reach. The Ted Lester program was selected because of the strong personal relationship presumed to exist between the entertainer and his audience, and the atmosphere of confidence which was believed to surround that relationship. In the current year, about a third of Edgerton's media dollars were being spent on network radio. The Lester schedule consisted of one announcement per week.

In considering what individual advertisements for Edgerton should feature, the agency drew upon information derived from extensive product-use research. Such research among old and new spiced meat purchasers revealed that main-dish use of the product was secondary to its use as an ingredient. Sandwiches were the most popular way to eat spiced meat, with almost all families recording some sandwich use. Spiced meat on crackers, in hors d'oeuvres, or in party dishes was also popular. New users of spiced meat were found to be interested in "offbeat" ways to use it; unusual ideas for snack and fill-in meals employing spiced meat appealed to them.

As noted above, agency executives believed that advertising's major job was to promote uses for the product. "People have heard about spiced meat, but haven't thought about it. We use magazines which reach women who are thinking about food products. Ideas sell food, and our ads consist of ideas for using Edgerton Spiced Meat. In planning the content of individual advertisements, we try to give coverage of the many uses for the product, weighting by the use pattern but leaning toward the unusual dishes which appeal to new users. Attention is given to how much horsepower given appeals have for nonusers of spiced meat, as well as for present users." Hence, advertising tended to concentrate on uses of the product in cocktail snacks, with salad dressings, and so on. New ideas for sandwiches for home, work, and school were also presented frequently.

The dishes featured in the advertisements were linked to particular times of year (e.g., May magazine ads featured spiced meat at late spring and summer cookouts) or to a well-known dish (e.g., spiced meat as a major ingredient in a hash). Radio commercials also featured particular and often unusual uses for Edgerton Spiced Meat. One such commercial is reproduced in Exhibit 4, as it was delivered over the Ted Lester program.

In addition, "hitch-hikes" with allied products (such as joint promotions with mayonnaise manufacturers) were arranged not only to provide additional variety in the presentation of uses for spiced meat, but to extend the promotional activity in behalf of the product without overextending the advertising budget.

In planning consumer testing of the advertisements, the account executive knew that the Twaddle and Herrling research department could make arrangements to carry out interviews and analysis of test results, if necessary. However, a number of decisions had to be made prior to making such arrangements. Among them were determining the number and characteristics of the respondents to be tested, the geographic locations in which to conduct the test, and the way in which the test should be set up. In addition, the variables to be measured and the criteria by which effectiveness was to be judged had to be specified.

Exhibit 1

Just beat together a 2½ oz. can of Edgerton Spiced Meat, 2 eggs, chopped onion, chopped green pepper, 1 tbsp. milk, fry to golden goodness. Makes 2 sandwiches.

Enjoy a Fast Western made in minutes (and so delish) with Edgerton Spiced Meat!
Keep lots of these one-meal cans handy for dozens of meat-and-egg dishes — and snacks.

Made from pure lean meat!

FOR OTHER SNACK RECIPES WRITE: ELLEN EDGERTON. DEPT. 00, GOLD GATE LANE, PALO ALTO, CALIF.

Exhibit 2

"Spiced Meat" makes a dandy Western . . .

For a delicious Sunday night snack or noon-time treat, go Western at your house.

● JUST BEAT TOGETHER A 2¼ OZ. CAN OF EDGERTON SPICED MEAT, 2 EGGS, CHOPPED ONION, CHOPPED GREEN PEPPERS, 1 TEASPOON MILK, FRY TO GOLDEN GOODNESS. MAKES 2 SANDWICHES.

It's just one way this "spiced meat" goes great with eggs at any house. Edgerton Spiced Meat takes up so little space — keep plenty on hand for meat treats in a hurry!

DOES MOST ANYTHING MEAT CAN DO . . . AND JUST AS DELICIOUSLY, TOO!

Made from lean meats finely ground and deftly seasoned for a wonderful can't-be-copied flavor.

FOR OTHER SNACK RECIPES WRITE: ELLEN EDGERTON, DEPT. 00, GOLD GATE LANE, PALO ALTO, CALIFORNIA.

Exhibit 3

EDGERTON MAGAZINE SCHEDULE

Magazine*		Month										
	Jan.	Feb.	Mar.	Apr.	May	June	July	Aug.	Sept.	Oct.	Nov.	Dec.
Good Housekeeping	A	A**		B	C	D		E		F		G
Ladies Home Journal			B		C		D		E		F	G
Sunset***		A		B		C	D		E		F	G

*The combined space cost of a one-half page, 4-color insertion in each of these magazines was about $50,000.
**Letters indicate use of the 7 advertisements to be run during the year.
***A "shelter" magazine (like Better Homes & Gardens) oriented particularly to Western living.

Exhibit 4.

TED LESTER RADIO COMMERCIAL
(as recorded from actual broadcast)

10:32:12   LESTER: We have two—two—two sponsors, one of which is Cox Air Conditioners and the other is Edgerton Spiced Meat.

10:32:34   LESTER: Linda Wood has fixed up some of the most delicious Spiced Meat treats you have ever tasted. We're going to pass it around in a minute.

10:40:20   LESTER: Spicy Pecan Bites is a dish thought up by Miss Linda Wood and she has brought some here. I passed them among you folks.

Oh, boy! You know what she has done? She has taken a pecan—two halves of a pecan—and put some Edgerton Spiced Meat on one of them, you know, and then stuffed a toothpick through the two of them . . . on the end of my toothpick now I have two nuts between which is some Edgerton Spiced Meat and it is delicious, I think.

But wait a minute—let me hear what you say.

MAN. I love it!

LESTER. Tell me only the truth.

MAN. I love it!

LESTER. You cannot love Edgerton Spiced Meat.

MAN. I'm weird that way.

[*Laughter*]

LESTER. Win, how is it?

WIN. It's mighty good, but I bet it's got lots of calories because of the

pecan.

LESTER. Yes, you would bring that up.

WIN. Well, I'm sorry. I'm just conscious of it. They're awful good.

Awful good.

LESTER. That's why she ate ten in a row.

WIN. [*Laughs*] That's right.

LESTER. You feel anything different inside you, Roger?

ROGER. Yes, I think this is the third one I've had. He says he's not in love with them. Hear the story about the guy who goes up to a psychiatrist. He had a problem. After six months, the psychiatrist says, "I think I've solved it." And he says, "Well, what is it?" And he says, "Well, you're in love with your raincoat." The guy says, "You're out of your head! We're fond of one another but love! Never!"

[*Laughter*]

LESTER, Ingrid, when you ate it before, did you like it?

GIRL. Yes.

LESTER. You enjoy?

GIRL. Yes.

LESTER. Would you say Wunderbar!

GIRL. Wunderbar!

LESTER. Wonderful! But, oh, gee, you talk about Christmas time, huh. You always get nuts for Christmas don't you? What do you find in the bottom of your sock—an orange and nuts is what we used to get. And toothpaste. Not all mixed up, of course.

MAN. Makes a wild sandwich.

[*Laughter*]

LESTER. But really, this is a great idea—Spicy Pecan Bite. Take a pecan half, spread it with Edgerton Spiced Meat on one side, top it with another pecan half and spear the two together with a toothpick. Then when you get through you have a toothpick. Very practical idea, I think.

Do you use it in your house, Win, I hope, I hope, I hope?

WIN. Yes. Yes, I have occasionally. I don't have it in the pantry right now but I have used it and it is good.

LESTER. Well, this is something you should have on the pantry shelf at all times, because you never know when someone is going to drop in and want a little nuts.

WIN. I thought it was Edgerton that was sponsor.

[*Laughter*]

LESTER. Edgerton Nuts!

[*Laughter*]

LESTER. Edgerton Spicy Nuts. What does it say here? Doesn't it say "Spicy Nuts"? No, "Spicy Pecan Bite." I'm sorry. There's a difference.

Linda, bless her little heart, makes these things up for us. You haven't been around here for a long time. Come back, will you? I was getting thin without you.

[*Laughter*]

10:44:07   LESTER. Ingrid, will you be so kind as to get up and sing a little song.

Once a plan had been established for typical consumer ad testing research, the Twaddle and Herrling research department usually completed such studies within a few weeks.[3] A decision on which of the two advertisements to run was necessary in three weeks.

[3]Twaddle and Herrling undertook extensive advertising and marketing research in behalf of its client companies. Carrying out copy tests and advertisement testing such as that for which the problem is posed in this case was one of the many services which the agency performed for its accounts, including Edgerton. A description of some of these Twaddle and Herrling services is given in the Appendix to this case.

Appendix

Twaddle and Herrling's activity in behalf of its clients, as indicated, did not consist solely in preparing advertisements.

"We get involved in a wide variety of Edgerton's marketing operations—product research, store tests, opinion studies, as well as copy and advertising testing. Our job neither begins nor ends at creating ads." Mr. Grey Stevens, vice-president and regional director of the San Francisco office[4] of Twaddle and Herrling, thus summarized the agency's relationship with the William Edgerton Company of San Francisco.

Twaddle and Herrling provided a variety of marketing and advertising services for Edgerton. Over-all marketing plans for Edgerton were formulated annually and reviewed quarterly by company and agency executives. Edgerton's president and marketing vice-president met regularly with the agency's top management and account people.

Twaddle and Herrling executives believed that one of the agency's most important functions outside of creating individual advertisements and advertising campaigns was in the evaluation of the results of the advertising. Research information was regularly gathered for Edgerton in several areas—over-all campaign evaluation, media evaluation, and individual advertisement evaluation.

Evaluation of Edgerton campaigns as entities was accomplished in several ways. The achievement of over-all objectives, i.e., gains both in usage and users, was assessed by researching both retail movement and consumer percentage penetration of Edgerton Spiced Meat. Both the Nielsen Retail Index and the Market Research Corporation of America services were purchased by Edgerton. Mr. Stevens described this information as "necessary to fill the voids in order to make disciplined marketing decisions."

The Nielsen Retail Index yielded data on total sales, retail inventories and stockturn, wholesale and retail prices, retail displays, local advertising, and percentage of stores stocking various brands. This information, for both Edgerton and other brands of spiced meat, was broken down by territories, city size, and type and size of store, e.g., chain, large independent, and small independent. From MRCA, Edgerton and T&H received information on consumer purchases and share of market for each spiced meat brand. The data were also broken down by such consumer characteristics as age, sex, income, and region. The approximate cost for these two services was $30,000 per year paid by Edgerton directly.

Another gauge of the over-all effectiveness of Edgerton's promotional efforts was the trend in the ratings given the product and the brand name, versus other

---

[4]Twaddle and Herrling maintained 7 offices in the United States and Canada. The main office was located in New York. T&H clients included large national grocery and proprietary drug product manufacturers, a major automobile firm, and several large industrial products manufacturing companies. The San Francisco office of Twaddle and Herrling serviced the products of regional beer, dairy, candy, and soft drink concerns, as well as a local bank and several industrial firms, in addition to the Edgerton company.

sandwich fillings or spreads, on periodic consumer image studies conducted by Twaddle and Herrling.

Studies of media in which Edgerton Spiced Meat ads were or might be placed took two forms. Complete media analyses were undertaken annually by the agency's New York staff for each of T&H's client companies. This evaluation extended even to media not currently used by a client. For example, a study of television was included in the most recent media evaluation book, containing facts and trends on television coverage, audiences, programming, and cost trends. The magazine evaluation included information on circulation, costs, and advertising pages, with an additional section devoted to an analysis of Edgerton's magazine advertising expenditures. Advertising dollars were compared with sales, and indices constructed to show the changes in expenditures required to maintain position, based on increases in magazine costs and total advertising volume.

Longer-run media studies were also in progress to benefit all T&H clients. One such effort involved research on the question: "How many advertisements, of what size and frequency, are necessary over a period of several years in order to maintain continuity[5] at some 'proper' level?"

As noted above, magazines had been and were the primary medium carrying Edgerton Spiced Meat advertising messages, with about two-thirds of the media dollars devoted to magazine space. These advertisements were directed to housewives, more specifically to mothers with growing children, since this group was seen as most interested in the home and food. A number of magazines were examined, including general publications (e.g., *Life, Look*), women's service magazines (e.g., *McCall's, Ladies' Home Journal*), "store" magazines such as *Woman's Day,* and the "shelter" magazines such as *Better Homes & Gardens.*

Several criteria were employed in selecting the actual magazines used. Among these were:

(a)   Continuity of advertising within a magazine (and its audience), which limited the total number of publications which could be used.

(b)   Use of 4-color ads, limiting the minimum size of advertisements to one-half page, in turn limiting the total number of insertions.

(c)   Broad reach, which meant the use of large circulation magazines.

(d)   Trade interest, which called for magazines the use of which could be "merchandised" to the grocery trade.

In appraising individual magazines, the agency took into account (a) circulation size and growth, both of subscription and single copy sales, including the proportion of reduced rate subscriptions;[6] (b) total editorial and food editorial lineage, for an assessment of editorial climate; (c) total advertising and food advertising

---

[5]Continuity in advertising attempts to compensate for the curve of forgetting by maintaining a level of awareness through repeated advertising of the product and/or brand.

[6]From time to time, magazines solicited subscriptions on a less than full-price basis. Magazines were required to maintain records of the number of such reduced rate subscriptions.

pages, as a yardstick of advertiser confidence; and (d) an estimate of reader confidence in the magazine.

Further media experimentation was planned for the future, including the use of television (long deemed too expensive a medium) on an individual market basis, as had been done with radio. Market areas selected for such testing usually were ones in which Edgerton was already strong.

In local advertising media tests, Twaddle and Herrling conducted research to determine sales results. The agency would note the level of sales (through the broker) into the area prior to the advertising. By comparing this to the rates of shipments during and after the advertising, a measure of sales changes was recorded. In addition to this area-wide measure, the agency occasionally visited the larger supermarket chains to solicit their cooperation in obtaining a record of their inventory prior to the advertising's start and their Edgerton purchases during the campaign.

In addition, consumer interviews were undertaken to gain information on the appeals which the advertising had contained. Appeal memorability was assessed by asking housewives, after several preliminary "masking" questions, whether they recalled Edgerton advertising. If they did, they were asked what they remembered.

Individual advertisements for Edgerton Spiced Meat were created by T&H's copy department. Copy people were given the product consumption and use pattern for Edgerton, as well as the objectives for the specific campaign at hand. Research-derived information played an important part in determining the subject matter for the advertisements, as had been indicated in the description of Edgerton's advertising goals.

Ads were researched by Twaddle and Herrling prior to actual insertion. Tests gave a measurement of over-all impact of the advertisements as well as the impact of the component parts of the ads. This research was done by means of personal in-home interviews with the public. Through advertising pretests, 24 proposed individual advertisements had been reduced to the 7 selected for actual use in the current campaign.

In addition to advertising pretests, T&H used other criteria to evaluate the strength of Edgerton ads after they had appeared. One of these was the pulling power of the recipe offers contained in the Edgerton magazine and national radio ads. In much of the Edgerton advertising, such recipe offers were "hidden" relative to the main features of the ads. As a result, the response to recipe offers was considered a secondary measure of the relative effectiveness of ads. One reason that the Ted Lester radio commercials were considered valuable was the fact that recipe requests arising from two Lester commercials far outpulled those from two half-page magazine ads running at the same time. Over 200,000 recipe books were distributed in the previous year; and, judging by the current rate of requests, this year's figure was expected to exceed 250,000.

Starch ratings were also used to evaluate advertisements after they had appeared. Starch scores, reported by the Daniel Starch Company, indicated ratings on a specific advertisement with reference to its having been "noted," "seen-associated," and "read most."[7] Starch ratings were viewed by the agency as an additional trend indicator of advertising effectiveness when examined in comparison with Edgerton ads in other years, with other food ads of the same size (one-half page), and with all ads rated. No direct relationships between Starch scores and T&H's own pretest ad ratings had been determined.

Both the Twaddle and Herrling advertising pretests and the Starch studies were conducted at the expense of the agency. Twaddle and Herrling spent approximately $1,500 per year for Starch rating of Edgerton ads. T&H internal research costs for its work on the Edgerton account were not available.

Twaddle and Herrling worked on a number of other activities for Edgerton. A home economist's kitchen was built at the agency's San Francisco office, where product and use testing took place, e.g., agency-instigated studies of product flavor. Packaging studies were performed: these had led, two years ago, to a revision of the traditional Edgerton label to make it cleaner and more visible on supermarket shelves. Various new sizes of cans were store-tested under agency auspices. The agency carried out tests of product sampling,[8] both supported and unsupported by advertising, in several cities as a possible means of finding new customers. Special local promotions were prepared by the agency for target areas. The agency also conducted extensive product publicity for Edgerton with media, in home economics classes, and through tie-ins with related products. In some of these activities T&H served only as counsel; e.g., Edgerton contracted for the production of its own point of sale material after ideas and artwork had been developed by the agency. The agency was not involved with Edgerton's broker relations or with its day-to-day selling activities.

Twaddle and Herrling's policy was to provide services for its clients as the latter needed and wanted them. The agency derived its income from the usual 15 per cent commission received from media expenditures. In addition, the agency made charges for production work on ads and for certain collateral services such as publicity.

Both company and agency executives believed that the "partnership" was building better advertising and marketing programs and increased sales for Edgerton Spiced Meat.

QUESTIONS

> *1.   Which of the two ads should be used? Why?*
>
> *2.   What further information would you like? What research would you design to get it?*
>
> *3.   In Edgerton's product-market situation, what is the job of advertising? Of an individual ad?*

[7]"Noted" meant that the reader remembered that he or she had seen the particular ad in the particular magazine; "seen-associated" meant that the reader saw or read a part of the ad indicating the product or advertiser; "read most" meant that the reader had read over half of the copy in the ad. Starch data were gathered for advertisements as a whole and for component parts of ads, such as headlines, company symbols, or particular copy sections.

[8]Sampling consisted of distributing free samples of a product to households in an area, with the hope that housewives would purchase it based on favorable use experience.

On Exposure
to
Advertisements

This note explains the differences between opportunities for exposure to advertisements and actual exposure to advertisements based on conscious awareness.

One of the most frequent topics of discussion and debate among advertising men is that of the attention people pay to advertisements. Interest in how much people are exposed to advertisements encompasses the total extent of exposure, the extent of exposure to particular ads or types of ads, and the extent of exposure to ads in particular media or in specific media vehicles (e.g., *Life,* " Bonanza," etc.).

Businessmen, advertising men, and media representatives are interested in exposure as the first criterion of advertising effectiveness. If an advertisement can be made to coexist in time and space with the consumer, at least it has a chance of having some effect. The social critic has a similar interest in the extent of advertising exposure, although in general he places a different evaluation on the phenomenon and perhaps even regards it as a sort of "index of pollution" of man's world of sight and sound.

WHAT IS EXPOSURE?

The very concept of exposure is exceedingly difficult to pin down. In the above paragraph we used the phrase "coexist in time and space" as a sort of minimum condition for exposure, or, more properly, "opportunity for exposure." But a man in the same room or house with a magazine which contains an advertisement can scarcely be considered to be "exposed" to it. And is the woman engaged in a lively conversation with a friend while "watching" a TV commercial "exposed" in the same sense as the woman who is closely following the message?

One of the most vigorously pursued activities in the field of advertising research is the measurement of exposure. The measures begin with the simple notions of reach and frequency: What numbers of people are reached by a given TV program, magazine, newspaper, radio program, and how often does the same vehicle reach the same person? These tell only the numbers of people who are exposed to the *medium,* and how often they are exposed. (These we would define as *opportunities* for advertising exposure.) The criteria of exposure extend from measures of recall of advertisements employing varying degrees of rigor[1] to elaborate devices such as a camera mounted on the TV set (the Dynascope) which records those persons actually in a position to view the television screen at a given time.

Needless to say, each measure is based on a somewhat different conception of what "exposure" is, and each measure must of its nature produce a different set of figures. *Any figure for "exposure to advertising" is meaningless except in terms of the procedure by which it is attained.*

Nevertheless, many people talk about "the level of exposure to advertising" as though there is some *single* meaningful figure. In trying to understand what data on "exposure" mean, one should recognize *three distinct levels* of response to ads:

> 1) *Opportunity for exposure*—which involves only being in the physical presence of an ad.
>
> 2) *Conscious awareness*—which involves actually seeing or hearing an ad.
>
> 3) *Reaction beyond awareness*—which involves some expression of further reaction, e.g., a particularly strong feeling about the ad, impact such that the product or message in the ad is remembered, and so on.

The delineation of this "third level" of exposure (i.e., beyond conscious awareness) is an important and indeed in many ways a crucial one. Failure of people to react to ads at this "third level" is a reflection of circumstances of considerable interest to the advertiser (and also to the critic of advertising). In large measure it is a function of the product and/or brand advertised, the advertising presentation itself, and people's relationships to the product, the brand, or the ad. For example, some ads may never be very interesting; some may have been interesting once, but are later "old hat." Some people weary of ads sooner than do others. Some people are not interested in some products or in learning about them.

1,500 ADS A DAY

Both inside and outside the business community resides a figure for advertising exposure that has become an almost universally accepted part of advertising's folklore. According to this tradition, an "average" person is exposed in a normal day to approximately 1,500 advertisements. This figure apparently originated in a 1957 speech[2] by Edwin W. Ebel, then Vice-President and Marketing Director of General Foods Corporation.

---

[1]For example, is the person supposed to have seen or heard the ad, to remember the name of the product, to recall what the ad's message was, and so on? And, is this to be unaided or aided recollection, and if so, what kind of aid?

[2]Reported in *Advertising Age,* May 13, 1957.

Addressing the West Coast meeting of the Association of National Advertisers, Ebel discussed the amount of advertising the public is asked to observe. He constructed a "typical Metropolitan family" whose husband and wife would "spend the national average amount of time" with newspapers, magazines, home and car radio, and television. The number of actual ads was reconstructed for each of these media during the day: 510 display ads in three specific newspapers read by a commuting husband and active suburban wife; 53 radio commercials heard at breakfast, lunch, or in the car; 447 ads in two specific national magazines read by the wife; 64 TV commercials from dinner time to 10:30 P.M. To these were added 216 subway posters and car cards along the husband's route to work; 178 outdoor billboards along the wife's driving route; and 50 ads in comic books read by the couple's children. Total: 1,518.

We have gone into detail on Ebel's reconstruction to depict its obvious inadequacy as an estimate of *exposure*. That any given family could have paid attention to more than a fraction of these hypothetical 1,518 advertisements is patently absurd. That the family could be even more than passingly aware of the great majority of them is questionable. That only a fraction of these ads could make any meaningful impact on the individual family members seems certain.

What *does* this hypothetical 1,518 figure mean, particularly when translated into its current folklore form of "the average consumer is exposed to 1,500 ads a day"? Literally it means that a hypothetical typical big-city suburban couple may find about 1,500 *opportunities* to be exposed to ads in a given day in print, broadcast, and poster media. To repeat, the 1,500 figure represents *opportunities* for exposure, not exposures themselves; and it refers to *families*, not individuals. These opportunities obviously cannot be equated with the actual engagement of consumer attention whether the latter is by one's own choice or by the ad's intrusion.

The persistence of such a figure in the folklore of advertising is testimony to two things: (1) the looseness with which the concept of exposure is used, and (2) some idea of how densely the American environment is assumed to be saturated with advertisements. It is difficult to decide whether Ebel's figure of a family's 1,518 potential exposures to ads in the course of the day is a reasonable one. If it is assumed that each spouse is involved with only about half of the potential ads, Ebel's calculations suggest that the average adult is potentially exposed to about 750 ads daily. This is not an improbable figure, but could be either high or low, depending on such factors as whether to include all advertisements in a magazine or only those on pages which the person opened; and so on.

If a commonly agreed-on estimate of the average number of opportunities for potential advertising exposure existed, it certainly would be an interesting yardstick against which to calibrate other measures of exposure. Presumably one could reconstruct such data based on the average adult's daily hours of TV watching and radio listening; the average number of newspaper and magazine pages read; and the like. But having completed this task, one would probably be little better off than he is with the above estimate of 750 ads. The interest in such a figure is less in its use per se, than in the perspective it offers in terms of estimating the consumer's capacity to *ignore* opportunities to pay attention to advertisements.

RECENT EVIDENCE

Indeed, data from the recent American Association of Advertising Agencies' study of the consumer judgment of advertising shed important light on this latter point. Whatever one's estimate of opportunities for exposure to ads might be, the findings show that Americans effect a *vast reduction* in their potential opportunities to see, read, or listen to advertisements.

Space does not permit a detailed description here of the methodology of the portion of the study relevant to this topic. In brief, the manner in which a respondent registered "conscious awareness" of ads was via a hand counter pressed each time he or she saw or heard an ad in magazines, newspapers, radio, or TV. By this measure—and as is the case with other measures of the different levels of exposure, the results reflect in part the particular measures used—the average American consumer is aware of some 76 ads per day: 36.3 in the daytime, 39.6 in the evening.

The important finding is not the 76 ads as such, but the fact that this number—or even twice this number—of ads would still represent *a very small proportion* of ads in the average consumer's environment (i.e., "opportunities for exposure") that actually capture his conscious attention.

Once one has grasped the distinction delineated above between opportunity for exposure and conscious awareness, he may turn to the matters of *why* some ads generate different kinds of reactions beyond simply conscious awareness, and why some ads fail to generate such further reactions.

Samson
Brewing Company

**Executives ponder how to use industry research on consumer
attitudes toward beer to deal with their own specific product problems.**

Founded in 1874 by the immigrant brewmaster Eli Samson, the Samson Brewing
Company achieved early and continued sales success in its three-state marketing
area. Five generations of Samsons had inherited and maintained this upward sales
trend. Although in recent years Samson had been able to record increases in
physical and dollar volume, the company had not been able to hold its traditional
share of an expanding regional beer market.

Company executives attributed the sales rise to increases in the number of
people in the area reaching beer-drinking age. They charged the decline in market
share to an invasion by two supra-regional brands, backed by heavy merchandising
and promotional budgets within the preceding two years. This encroachment,
coupled with increased competition from other purely local brands and continuing
promotion by the major national premium beers, led to a realization by Samson
management that an "agonizing reappraisal" of its selling climate and marketing
activities was necessary for future growth.

The review was not undertaken with any sense of grave necessity for immediate
action. Rather, it was to proceed on an exploratory basis, examining several aspects
of Samson marketing strategy in an orderly manner. A series of informal meetings
for executives and outside personnel concerned with each particular phase of
Samson marketing activities was arranged. To date, two men, Sam Gaines (Samson's
sales manager) and Paul Samson III (assistant to and son of the Samson president),
had attended all of the marketing appraisal meetings.

PREVIOUS MEETINGS

Paul Samson acted as his father's executive assistant, preparing for eventual
ascension to the Samson presidency by learning all phases of the brewery's operations. Although very interested in these review meetings, the senior Samson had

been unable to attend any thus far. Young Paul had kept him up to date by preparing a number of memos for him to look over, summarizing the major findings at each session.

From the Meeting of 9/5   An analysis of Samson sales by geographic subsections within our distribution area failed to uncover any major trouble spots. Traditionally strong pockets of popularity for Samson have maintained sales volume in the face of the increased competition, while areas in which we have never achieved great sales success continue as such.

From the Meeting of 9/12   A study of Samson's distribution pattern did not reveal any weaknesses that the review conference would label as "major." Samson is carried by most of the major chain and independent supermarkets in the region, and virtually every package store sells Samson. As you know, draft beer business is not a significant portion of our sales, although Samson is on tap in some taverns in our top sales areas. Almost every tavern in the three-state region carries bottled Samson for bar and table sale.

From the Meeting of 9/29   Our pricing is right in line with the other local beer brands. The appraisal group feels that our retailer margins and prices are competitive. However, we learned that several of our local competitors have made occasional deals with large purchasers, or have instituted special price promotions— both practices we have been reluctant to try.

From the Meeting of 10/7   Right now, we are spending about $100,000 per year on promotion, mostly on point-of-purchase display and our cooperative deal for tavern and package store signs. Here's the committee's assessment:
Point of Sale   The committee thinks that our coverage of package stores and supermarkets is very good in those areas where Samson has always been popular. However, in some other parts of our territory retailers are reluctant to take our signs and banners because of crowding and "not enough back-up promotion."
Lighted Display Signs .   Our cooperative program for package stores and taverns is now four years old. With some variations, we are paying about half the costs of these signs, featuring both the retailer and Samson names. Many major package stores have our signs, and their modernizing effect is popular with the owners. Some committee members do not think that we can go much further with this device, as almost all of the stores we really want have either a Samson sign or their own, and are not interested in changing.
Media Advertising   Except for minor changes, Samson newspaper ads as well as radio and TV spots are still featuring our traditional themes—Samson is a local beer, brewed by men of long experience. In general the committee is pleased with the work that the agency has been doing for us, including the point-of-sale material.
There is one more point. The committee thinks we ought to discuss the possibility of expanding our limited advertising spending in response to the

increased activity by other beers. Increased advertising might provide something new for Samson. As you can guess, a number of previously undiscussed ideas came up—beyond the question of increasing the ad budget. We have scheduled another meeting to discuss whether or not Samson should continue with its traditional advertising themes, regardless of any change in expenditures. This meeting will probably get into our over-all approach to marketing Samson.

On 10/10 the following note was sent to those who had attended the last appraisal meeting:

MEMORANDUM

TO: *Advertising Session Participants, P. Samson, P. Samson III, Gaines, Agee*
FROM: *Al Mann, Advertising Mgr.*

Since we are going to devote the 10/14 session to discussing the content of our advertising, I thought that the attached research report might be of interest to you when thinking things over. No doubt we all have our own ideas as to what themes and appeals might be most effective for Samson, but maybe we can learn something from this report. It is a shortened version of a study sponsored back in 1951 by a major metropolitan newspaper. Our agency tells me that it represents the best research available on consumer attitudes toward beer. I think it provides a logical springboard for our discussion, since the meeting should concentrate on ways to appeal to the beer consumer through advertising.

Al/am
(*signed*)

THE MEETING

Though there was no formal chairman for the marketing review meetings, Sam Gaines, Samson's sales manager and the "elder statesman" of the Samson marketing executives, usually steered the meeting. A veteran of 20 years with Samson, Sam had worked his way up from driver salesman to promotion man to area sales manager to assistant sales manager, to his present job. Sam, now in his fifties, took great pride in the fact that he "still gets out with the boys and buys a few beers on a route just to keep in touch." Tieless and jacketless, Sam was the idol of the salesmen—their staunch defender—and was never known to hold his tongue when he had something to say.

Others at the table for the meeting were:

Al Mann   advertising manager of Samson since joining the firm three years ago. Al had been in promotional work since he majored in advertising and marketing at college. Now in his thirties, Al came to Samson from another small beer company when the separate position of Samson advertising manager was created.

Paul Samson III heir to the Samson brewery. Paul followed five generations of Samsons. During high school and college Paul worked summers at the brewery, doing everything from driving trucks to buying hops. Now in his late twenties, he was a prime force behind these marketing appraisal meetings.

Art Agee account executive at the local agency working for Samson for the past two years. Art joined the agency at the same time the Samson account did (Samson's agency had dropped the company because of low media expenditures).

Sam Gaines opened the meeting by recalling that in the previous sessions the pattern had been to concentrate on a review of policy and position, as well as new ideas. He hoped that this meeting would "get into the open the best possible approaches available for reaching consumers," should the budget be expanded to allow for a considerable amount of advertising.

SAM GAINES: This means that both "the *who* and the *what*" of our advertising appeals ought to be discussed. Al, you sent around the report . . .why don't you give us your comments first?

AL MANN: The subject of possible ad campaigns is not exactly a new topic for me to take up with you. (*Smiles.*) All that aside, I think that today is a chance for us to explore some possible campaigns and review our existing general strategy. I hope we can continue with the informal approach of the promotion meeting last week. About the only other thing I'd like to say is that if we *do* go into an advertising campaign, it's obvious that the payoff is going to be in the themes we use, and the people we direct those themes to. That's why I sent around the study.

SAM: That's a good point right there, Al. "Who we direct our ads to" is important. Let's face it. Most beer is drunk by people this report calls the "middle majority." They have a beer when they go out, or open one up when just sitting around the house. Beer tastes good to them, is a thirst quencher— the thing to drink when they feel like relaxing or enjoying themselves. These people are our repeat sales; they have it around all the time. They find a beer, like it, and stick with it. I think most of our Samson buyers right now are this kind of person . . . my salesmen are, and I guess I am too.

 When I get home at night, I take off my shoes, drop into a chair, open up a cold one, and enjoy it while my wife is getting supper. Most people who drink Samson are the same way . . . at home, going out, or when company comes over, our beer is around to help them enjoy themselves. On my rounds I think I meet more people who drink our beer than most of you do, and some of them tell me that they've been drinking Samson ever since they were stealing sips from their old man's buckets.

AL: What do these people think of our ads, Sam?

SAM: Well, I'm no researcher, but I think the ads we're running now are pretty sensible. They tell people that Samson's been made and sold here for over 80 years . . . that means it *must* be good. Besides, because it's made here, it doesn't cost as much as the big boys' products, even though it's certainly just as good. This makes a sensible pitch that has sold, does sell, and will sell our beer. And our package store display signs keep Samson in front of them day and night.

I've seen plenty of the ads that this report talks about . . . with fancy-dressed people holding beers—beers that they probably don't even drink. I think our approach is a lot more reasonable. If we do start more advertising—which I guess would certainly help us—I would say that probably just showing plain folks actual pictures and voices of people who have been drinking Samson for years would really hit this middle majority just right. It's like the Brewers' National Foundation says, "Beer belongs; enjoy it."

As I said before, I'm no professional researcher, but I think the people who did this study certainly confirmed *my* opinions about beer drinking! The only thing the report doesn't do is tell us enough about one real reason people buy a particular beer—price. And that's Samson's real advantage . . . it has the taste of big beer, is easy on the throat, and has a good price to boot. People watching their food bills aren't going out of their way to run up the beer tab—we don't need research to tell us that. My wife says that even if I didn't bring Samson home, she'd still go out and buy it. And that's what the middle majority housewife thinks too. I think the middle majority approach would pay off for us if we decided to go in for a big campaign. (*pause*)

But you know, I'm not sure if that would be a big change from what we are already doing. In fact, as Al was saying to me the other day, we've been using the same kind of appeal since before I worked on the advertising, and that was . . . ahh, about seven or eight years ago. We hit the middle majority with our ads then and still do. Right, Al?

AL: Well, you're right about the ads, at least from those I've found in the files. Now, I agree with this study too. We have to concentrate on basic appeals and motivations of beer drinkers. I think that's what you've been saying, Sam. This study shows what we can really do for Samson, and still take advantage of our old name and good reputation.

My idea would still appeal to the middle majority, but would do it by setting ourselves apart. I want to see us distinguish Samson from all the other local brands, and particularly from some of the new brands that have been invading our territory. We ought to be able to gain respect for Samson as a venerable member of the regional community. That would set us apart. We all know what a good theme some advertisers have by stressing the quality of their beer. Well, frankly, I'd like to think that Samson is the quality beer in this area to people who know our name.

PAUL SAMSON III (*interrupting*):   That's right, Al, and I'd like to push that point a bit further. I've been intrigued by parts of the report that *don't* talk about the "average man" theme. Now I'm not saying that we shouldn't concentrate on the middle majority primarily. But I do think people will respond to our special story—the one that no one else around here can tell . . . the fact that people know and respect our name.

Take the part of this study which talks about the *taste* of beer . . . "Beer ought to be talked about as a drink consistent in quality and satisfaction, clean and carefully made." Remember that people like to judge beer by its taste, or at least they like to think they do. We have a real story here.

When Eli Samson founded this brewery back in 1874, he wanted to make the best beer possible, in the old tradition. He hired the best brewery men he could, set up the best factory and processing equipment known for the time, and sold his beer as a quality brew. Even since then, Samson has never strayed from those original objectives. We've always tried for the best. I think that our product research, brewing process, quality control, and history would be very interesting to people, especially to those who like and drink Samson.

ART: Is that what people really want to know?

SAMSON: Sure, people are interested in what makes a beer a *good* beer. It doesn't have to be a scientific or overly technical presentation, but it should be information-oriented. We should sell product quality, and I think that this is the kind of story to set Samson apart as a product that has always been, and still is, concerned with consistent quality and uniform taste.

Why not show a television tour of our brewery, showing them the ingredients of beer, how they are put together, processed, how Samson is aged, our new and extra-sanitary bottling methods, and so on? That's one sure way in which we can capitalize both on our long years here and on our product.

I think the report indicates that people convince themselves that they judge beer by its taste. If we can *show* them why our beer tastes good, consistently good, then we can let them convince themselves that their taste tells them to drink Samson. This goes for the middle majority and the others as well.

Sorry to have interrupted, Al, but your "quality" comment really set me going. Have I followed up your idea, Al?

AL: Well . . . in a sense. But you know, there is a good chance that brewing processes and all the rest may go right over the head of the average beer drinker. I think we should relate Samson to the beer drinker in a more personal way, and try to avoid some of the pitfalls the study points to when using approaches that stress manufacturing.

In other words, I think we would have to tie the quality of Samson to the *pleasure* the drinker will get out of it. If people think that Samson will be fun, be enjoyable, our biggest job is done. Maybe we could try to link some of your ideas, Paul, to this pleasure approach. For example, we can say that Samson has always been, and still is, concerned with proper aging, best hops, careful processing, and so forth because *we believe* that is the best way to assure the kind of quality that will make Samson the most pleasant beer for them. That's our route to quality, and quality makes pleasure. There is a definite place for creativity here, but right now I find it hard to say exactly what I'm looking for.

It's not just "pretty" ads, high-status advertising, or stories about our past that I envision. They would all miss our target in the middle majority. What I'm looking for is more like a series of ads which try to make our beer a little more respected among the brands available to the beer-drinking public in this area. We have to be "creative"; or maybe I mean we have to give our ads a bit of "style"—within the limits of the pleasure theme, of course, I guess what I'm really after is to create a picture of "an upper class beer for the middle majority drinker."

ART: I'd like to break in a minute here, Al, as long as you've brought up this idea of being "creative." Now this study certainly does provide a lot of ideas to stimulate creative thinking; and it outlines a number of "do's and don'ts" at the same time. In fact, since the study has come out, a number of campaigns have been created with these admonitions in mind. This may be the real problem in trying to approach the middle majority.

The middle majority, that great beer-imbibing mass, has been assailed by hundreds of flannel-shirted, open-necked, clean-cut, athletic men enjoying their beers with wholesome women or wives in homey, panelled, do-it-yourself recreation rooms. I admit that I'm exaggerating, but I think that this sameness shows just how much room for a real creativity there is . . . much more than a quick glance at this report would indicate. This is probably because these findings have made their way into every nook and cranny of our industry. There's nothing like a research-built band wagon to jump on.

I agree that we should focus on an idea to attract attention to our beer—a creative idea, backed up by good beer when they open the bottle. Just think of the amount of beer advertising that goes on. People just won't see or hear all of it. If we want them to notice ours, we have to find a special hook to hang it on—something which is entirely Samson's.

One point that I find interesting in thinking about this report is that people probably rationalize a good deal about beer. That is, they probably attribute good qualities to their favorite beer and associate unpleasant qualities with those brands they don't use—whether these things are true or not. They'll make up their mind about the beer after we get them to taste it. What I think Samson needs, especially because we have never done too much straight media advertising, is a distinctive campaign which will enable people to recognize our name. This would create a broader base of people who would consider Samson the next time they buy or switch brands.

SAM: What do you mean by "distinctive"? We already have a fine old name.

ART: Well, put it this way: except for the few beers that people like or dislike strongly, most beer is just beer to them. This means that our big opportunity is to get the attention of people who have no opinion about Samson. I think we ought to be different, and my idea is to take a humorous approach. As long as our beer is just beer, we might as well be entertaining when we try to reach the public. I think you are all aware of how successful some of the humorous beer campaigns have been. So I guess I agree with the report, as far as it goes. But I don't think that the material in the report is going to give us the creative clue, the direction in which to be different, that we need. If people are willing to try a different beer, then I think that something new, out of the ordinary—"creative" if you like—is the most important element in advertising beer. Get them to remember Samson favorably the next time they are looking for that "something new."

I don't think that we have to be concerned about what the industry should do to sell more beer. This report is really directed more to the industry than to any one company. Our concern is with our own problems. We have to set ourselves apart, and our basic advertising theme will have to attract attention to Samson. That's what really has to be done.

I guess I've been a little overexuberant, but I don't think that I'm in total disagreement with anyone here. Let's chalk a lot of it up to the fact that I'd like a chance to do something creative for Samson. After all, we haven't really had a chance to do very much in the way of straight advertising since our agency started working with you.

SAM: Well, I think that we've had a good opportunity to give our own approaches to this problem. Why don't we get something to eat before we talk outselves into starvation? Kidding aside, I think this has been one of the most interesting of these review sessions—even if we've done nothing but get our own ideas off our chests.

At this point the conference room door opens, and Paul Samson, Jr., president of the Samson Brewing Company, enters.

PAUL SAMSON, JR.: Sorry to be late, but my train took longer than I expected. Looks as if I arrived just in time. I was able to read your memo and that report on the train this morning, Al. They certainly make a number of interesting points, and give some helpful clues on how to try to reach what I suppose is the most important segment of the beer-drinking market.

I guess I'm a brewmaster rather than a marketer at heart. I'm having some real trouble trying to understand some of the "why's" in this report . . . I'm sorry, have you all been over this?

SAM: Just a little. Keep going. We'd like to hear your ideas.

PAUL SAMSON, JR.: Well, just a couple of things. As I said, there are a few things in this study that worry me. The introduction says that it explores people's attitudes toward beer and beer advertising from the point of view of WHY? Now, I know that to get at the why's of behavior one doesn't need to get involved in a detailed, elaborate statistical presentation. And I realize as well that one doesn't need large numbers of people to get at them either. But I do wonder how the researchers came to some of their conclusions without reference to the "how many," and if *they* referred to "how many," why didn't they tell *us* how many?

I'm also interested in a couple of statements from the report itself: for example, how do you reconcile the finding that "beer is a congenial drink" with the immediately following idea that "solitary beer drinking is meaningful too"? Or what about the conclusion that men are the major market, but that women are important and increasing in importance?

I don't mean to imply by bringing up these examples that the report tries to straddle the fence when it comes to conclusions. On the contrary, these apparent ambiguities may indeed be the realities. What I have trouble doing is envisioning how the information from this report could be put into operation for us. How can we use this research in our own situation? But I suppose that's what you have been talking about all this time, so why don't you fill me in over lunch?

Consumer Attitudes toward Beer and Beer Advertising

The study[1] was undertaken to determine the real underlying attitudes and motives which people have toward beer, to determine any differences in these attitudes by social class levels, and to measure the impact of typical beer advertising on these different classes. Why do people drink beer? When? With whom? What advertising can cause them to switch brands?

METHOD

The findings in the study were based on over 350 psychological depth interviews with men and women of all social classes. The research question was basically: "*Why* do people do this?" rather than "*How many* do this?" Typical quotations revealing fundamental attitudes toward beer and beer advertising are cited in the report summary.

SOCIAL CLASS

This study accepts the concepts of social class in America developed by Dr. Lloyd Warner, based on studies of typical American communities. Social classes are not economic classes. Social status is determined by education, family background, type of occupation, type of home and neighborhood, not just amount of income.

The two major social class groupings important to the advertiser are the Upper Middle and Upper classes (15% of the population—the quality market), and the Middle Majority (65% of the population—the mass market). The Upper Middle and Upper classes are made up of the leaders of the community, businessmen, professional men, and their families. These people emphasize values of sophistication, self-reliance, and leadership. Their behavior marks them off from the "common man" by their ability to handle this world to their own social and economic advantage. The Middle Majority, in contrast, is made up of the large majority of working people—white-collar workers, semi-skilled and skilled laborers, and small businessmen. Their jobs

[1] Material is based on a study for the *Chicago Tribune* by Social Research, Inc.

mean everything to these people because they have few resources for saving and maintaining themselves in hard times. They emphasize highly conventional behavior. In their world, there is much less leeway for individual variation in social behavior.

With most products, the upper middles react most positively to advertising that caters to their higher status positions in society—which indicates through sophisticated language, prestige objects, and well-to-do settings that the advertiser feels that those who appreciate the finer things of life will use his product. In terms of copy and layout they prefer ads which are reserved, do not make extravagant claims, and which are often playful in their treatment of the product.

The middle majority, on the other hand, often react quite negatively to advertising that appeals to the upper middles. They feel that such advertising is too highflown, and they prefer advertising which is realistic in terms of settings and people, which sticks to practical details. They react most positively to advertising catering to their needs and interests, giving them information of use, and showing respect for the common man.

There is no real proof that middle majority families fall all over themselves to imitate high society. Some scientists have said that the greatest single motivation for an American is fear of being different from his own class.

By far the largest group of beer drinkers is in the middle majority, and the middle majority consumes the largest amount of beer per capita as well.

HIGHLIGHTS

Up and Down the Social Ladder, We Find Beer a Well-liked Drink   People have clear attitudes toward beer and its uses. They know what they want from beer; they get basic social and psychological satisfactions in drinking it.

WHEN DO PEOPLE DRINK BEER?

Beer Is a Congenial Drink   It oils the wheels to make a social gathering enjoyable, relaxing, and refreshing; it breaks down social barriers and lets people be democratic. ("A good drink for a get-together.") ("After a couple of drinks of beer, you feel like talking more.")

Solitary Beer Drinking Is Meaningful Too   Men drink it as an adjunct to other activities—puttering, reading, watching TV, working. Fewer women drink alone but some find beer enjoyable while they are doing housework or for a break in the day's routine.

WHEN IS BEER AN APPROPRIATE SOCIAL DRINK?

Beer Fits Best Where Equalitarian Relaxing Is In Order   People drink beer in all social classes and for similar reasons. Beer is considered to mark the absence of authority; it is an invitation to informality. Most drinking is done to be socially proper. What is appropriate differs from class to class.

In the Upper Middle Class (UMC)   People often speak, act, and dress to mark themselves off from the way of life of the middle majority. In drinking habits the mark of UMC status is the mixed drink or the fine wine, not beer. Only when the UMC person is emphasizing his commonality with others does he drink beer to show that he is a good fellow. When he wants to emphasize his membership in a higher status group, as is more often the case, he drinks something else.

In the Middle Majority (MM) There are fewer occasions when people wish to be formal, to "put on the dog." Most MM people take their "in-between" status for granted and have few needs to appear classier. They consider beer the drink of the Common Man. They insist that when those above them drink beer, they are bringing themselves down to the "like-me" level. Only on formal occasions (few in middle majority society) do they bring out the high status mixed drinks or wine. Cost also makes beer the drink of the middle majority.

GUIDES TO BEER DRINKING

Middle Majority Members Often Express Hostility at the Suggestion in Beer Advertising That They Should Be Guided by the Upper Classes (Said a 28-year-old clerk: "Those 'man of distinction' ads make me mad. My money will buy just as good liquor as anybody else's.") This feeling manifests itself toward testimonials too. While snob appeal is effective for some prestige items recognized as such, beer is not a prestige item.

WHAT MAKES BEER A GOOD DRINK?

At the Most Universal Level, the Pleasure of Beer Drinking Lies in the Throat Words used to describe beer are more descriptive of how it feels than how it tastes, e.g., "smooth."

Beer is Disliked When the Flavor Interferes With the Feel Beers are disliked because they taste bitter, sour, biting, or when they are "watery" and without texture.

Beer is Just Alcoholic Enough to Give the Drinker a Feeling of Relaxation and Lack of Inhibitions In socializing this enables him to feel more at home and more willing to be spontaneous. At the same time, there is little likelihood of losing control completely. Middle majority people, especially, are attracted to this quality; they fear drunkenness but need something to make them relax in social situations. ("I can drink beer for hours on end and still not overdo it.")

A Thirst Quencher There is almost complete agreement that beer is a good cooling drink, noticeably more thirst-satisfying than whiskey or wine.

HOW DO PEOPLE FEEL ABOUT BRANDS?

For Most People There Is "My Brand," "the Brand That Let Me Down," and "All Those Others" And people describe their favorite beer(s) with all the good words advertisers have taught them to apply to what a beer should be. With bad words they describe the beer that let them down, e.g., the beer they were drinking "that time the party was no fun." People usually know three or four good and bad beers; all the rest are just beers. Beer drinkers generally stick to a brand for an extended period; few people will drink *any* kind.

Generally speaking, many people feel that nationally advertised brands are more trustworthy than brands with less advertising or less extensive distribution. A large majority of the people do not believe beers from one city are better than another. ("Just because it's from Milwaukee doesn't make it a good beer.") Most people are quite willing to accept a less well-known beer once they've tasted it.

The consumer rationalizes his reasons for preferring a brand. There is no general consumer agreement as to the meaning of terms used to describe beer. The terms used to justify brand preferences actually are the emotional symbols expressing pleasure in beer drinking. The same positive admiring characteristics are applied to different beers which middle majority people like, and common negative descriptions are applied to those they do not like.

WHAT ARE THE COMMON APPEALS IN BEER ADVERTISING?

Most Beer Advertisers Don't Make Use of Favorable Attitudes toward Beer In place of advertising which harnesses these attitudes most successfully, much beer advertising falls into these main categories:

The prestige endorser theme—perhaps is the most popular theme among beer advertisers. This approach seeks to influence the beer drinker through endorsements by some prominent persons. There are at least three disadvantages:

—People do not believe it; they believe the endorsers are "insincere."

—The situation is usually impersonal; it has few connotations of a friendly relation.

—Many of the figures chosen are not meaningful to the audience, such as theater stars only vaguely known to the middle majority, or sports stars whom people believe should not endorse beer because the're in training and heroes to the young. ("Those big shots don't drink beer; you can't kid me.")

The high-class theme—in advertising communicates to the audience by dress, setting, and tone of copy that beer is a "high-class" drink. To the MM (and even the UMC) people this idea is distinctly inappropriate. For them beer is a universal drink, not the formal beverage of the wealthy or prominent. Typical reactions of ordinary beer drinkers indicated disbelief of and resentment toward this theme. (A 21-year-old Italian laborer said "looks like they might be drinking highballs instead, in a real ritzy place.")

The scientific proof theme—emphasizes technical phrases, information to prove that one brand of beer is better than others. People do not use technical reasons for their beer preferences. Most beer drinkers judge beer more by the satisfaction they get from it—simply by using it—and have little interest in technical information. (A 52-year-old housewife commented, "I don't care how beer is made as long as it tastes good.") Also, this theme is essentially impersonal and does not have the attention-holding power of ads which tie in with the social and personal meanings of beer. The scientific theme has reassurance value but is not a good attention-getter as a major ad appeal.

The average man theme—is not widely used, but, where it is, it receives a good deal of favorable attention from the audience. Such ads emphasize people who look "average" or slightly better in dress and surrounding and who are doing things which middle majority people commonly do or want to do. People feel that such ads "fit" with beer and the meanings it has for them. The ad is much more likely to arouse interest and a desire to have a beer. ("I get relaxed just looking at this—because I feel that way myself with a glass of beer in my hand, nice and relaxed.")

APPEALS THAT ELICIT RESPONSE

Appeals recalling, suggesting, and demonstrating pleasure are those to which people respond most. Beer is bound up with social and personal feelings—what it is used for, what pleasure it can give.

WE RECOMMEND THAT ADVERTISING:

Should be directed primarily at the middle majority since this is the mass market and the market in which more beer is consumed per capita.

Should take into account that men are probably the major market in terms of both consumption and brand selection, but that women are important and apparently increasing in importance.

Should embody and emphasize these appeals—

—Family and friends in informal gatherings.
—Relaxation and refreshment after work or exercise.
—Refreshment of spectators at appropriate sports gatherings.
—Equalitarian festivities such as lodge meetings and Fourth of July.
—Beer with meals.

Should use these kinds of people

—Hearty, active men of middle majority and upper middle class in informal clothing.
—"All-American girls" with emphasis on wholesomeness, not sexiness.

Should talk about beer as

—A cool, refreshing drink.
—A friendly, hospitable drink.
—A drink for equals, "for people like you."
—A drink which *feels good.*
—A drink consistent in quality, clean and carefully made.

DO'S AND DON'TS OF ADS

People should be

—Either man or woman at middle majority level.
—Interesting to middle majority.
—Someone who represents activity, "he-man" achievement, spectacular or romantic work.

People should not be

—Intellectuals or artists.
—Businessmen with a formal "man of distinction" manner.
—Merely sexy or glamorous.

Settings should be

—Casual and informal.
—Nice, clean but modest. Not a Hollywood version of an upper-class home, party, or table setting.
—Believable in terms of the kinds of people shown and the kinds of occasions at which beer is served.

Settings should not be

—Loaded with high-status symbols in location, furnishings, or activities.
—Unbelievable in terms of either people or serving beer.
—Extremely stiff or formal.

QUESTIONS

1. *How can Samson make use of the findings in the Social Research study?*
2. *What other consumer information would you like?*
3. *What message strategy would you recommend for Samson?*

American Sheep Producers Council (B)

The industry trade association conducts a qualitative study to investigate the high-cost image of lamb. The study classifies respondents into ten psychographic roles according to respondent's meat-buying attitudes and behavior.

American Sheep Producers Council (ASPC) executives agreed that the most predominant and recurring attitude regarding lamb which emerged from their 1964 consumer attitude study was that "lamb is expensive." [American Sheep Producers Council (A) presents the background of the Council, its marketing/advertising environment, and summary findings from the 1964 consumer attitude study.] For instance, the study uncovered the following:

— 52% of all respondents said that lamb compared with the same cuts of other meats generally has a higher price per pound.

— 21% of those who serve lamb less often at certain times per year said they do so because "it is too expensive."

— 18% of all respondents said that the way to change lamb so that they will serve it more often is to "make it less expensive."

— 13% of those who said lamb is *not* a good substitute for other meats gave as their reason "it's too expensive except when it's on sale."

— 12% of those who *never* serve lamb said they do not do so because "it is too expensive."

ASPC executives regarded these findings as particularly alarming, since the 1964-66 period was marked by extreme concern among American housewives regarding high food prices in general. For example, this period witnessed occasional boycotting of supermarkets throughout the country by housewives in protest of what they regarded as high prices. Executives believed that the high-price associations which surrounded lamb were largely unjustified and that, when comparing the amount of *usable* (edible) meat on a cut of lamb with the usable meat on other cuts of meat and poultry, lamb was competitively priced due to proportionately less fat and bones than certain other meats.

315

DEVELOPMENT OF THE COST-PER-SERVING CONCEPT

ASPC's Executive Director at the time was a former restaurant man. He recalled that in that business the relative economy of different meat purchases was determined on the basis of estimated *cost per serving* of the different meats rather than simply their prices per pound. He believed that this cost-per-serving concept could be as relevant a guide in *consumer* meat purchasing as it was in institutional procurement, and that if consumers could be educated to understand and accept this concept the high-price image of lamb might be reduced substantially.

To achieve this end, ASPC launched its "cost-per-serving" advertising campaign in all media in 1966 (see Exhibit 1) to convey to consumers that they should determine the actual cost of different cuts of lamb, pork, beef, and chicken on the basis of not only price per pound but also servings per pound. To help make this point, wallet-sized cards which explained the cost-per-serving concept were made available to inquiring advertisement readers. Exhibit 2 contains a cost-per-serving card. (This card was originally designed and made available by Ohio State University's Cooperative Extension Service as a guide to aid meat consumers in general. As such, ASPC executives regarded the servings-per-pound figure as objectively determined and containing no preference for lamb or any other meat.)

THE QUALITATIVE STUDY OF COST-PER-SERVING

After the cost-per-serving campaign had run for several months, ASPC commissioned an in-depth study to explore housewives' understanding of and reaction to the cost-per-serving concept, particularly as it applied to lamb. This study, conducted by Chase and Associates in late 1966, employed group interviews among housewives in four metropolitan areas. The study and its results are summarized in Appendix A.

Exhibit 1

COST-PER-SERVING AD

what do you MEAN... lamb costs no more than chicken?

Apricots to Zucchini

Of course, savings is only one reason for serving lamb often at your home. There's the tenderness that you get from such young meat. And the delicate flavor that is lamb's own. And lamb's compatibility with all the fruits and vegetables of the harvest. Once a week, every week . . . lamb, the tender surprise.

For FREE lamb recipes and a cost-per-serving chart for meats and poultry, write:

american lamb council

Dept. LX-166, 520 Railway Exchange Bldg.
909 17th Street, Denver, Colorado 80202

Why such a flap about a simple fact? U. S. Department of Agriculture studies* show it to be so—lamb costs no more than chicken, even though some cuts of lamb cost more per pound in the store. A little arithmetic will prove it to you. Suppose you pay 20¢ per pound more for bone-in shoulder of lamb than for ready-to-cook frying chicken. The chicken at 20¢ less per *pound* will cost you 5¢ more per equal *serving* of edible meat. That's because there's more bone, more waste in the chicken—more edible meat in the lamb. So you see—you can enjoy lamb, the prestige meat, whenever you want—with no qualms of conscience, no feeling that you're being "extravagant."

*Based on:
U.S.D.A., Agricultural Handbook 102, Food Yields Summarized by Different Stages of Preparation.
N. Y. State College of Agriculture, Cornell University, Handbook, Cost Per Serving.
Ohio State University, Marketing Information for Consumers.

Golden-Glazed Lamb Chops

4 LAMB SHOULDER CHOPS, ABOUT ¾ INCHES THICK
2 TABLESPOONS BUTTER
SALT AND PEPPER
½ TEASPOON POWDERED THYME OR FINELY CHOPPED MINCED FRESH THYME
4 SLICES CANNED PINEAPPLE
2 TABLESPOONS CHOPPED PARSLEY
1 TABLESPOON CUT CHIVES, IF DESIRED
¼ CUP OR MORE SYRUP FROM CANNED PINEAPPLE

Heat butter in skillet. Add chops and brown slowly on one side, turn, brown other side. Sprinkle chops with salt, pepper and thyme. Place a slice of pineapple atop each chop. Sprinkle with parsley and cut chives. Add ⅓ cup syrup from canned pineapple, more if liquid cooks low. Cover skillet tightly, and cook slowly until the chops are fork-tender, about 40 minutes for ¾-inch-thick chops.

Exhibit 2

COST-PER-SERVING CARD

A GUIDE TO COST PER SERVING FOR MEAT

When buying meat or poultry it's cost per serving that counts, not cost per pound: A high price per pound does not always mean a high cost per serving and vice versa. Differences in the amount of edible meat and therefore in the servings per pound should be considered. Use this guide to compare prices on a cost per serving basis. Remember that price relationships between different cuts of meat change often. So make comparisons each time you shop. Just fold and carry in your purse or billfold. Simple directions for use are on the back.

HOW TO USE

Let's assume chuck roast (bone-in), lamb shoulder roast, and Boston Butt (bone-in) are all 59 cents per pound. Which is the more economical choice? Reading the table under the 59 cents per pound column shows chuck roast at 30 cents per serving, lamb shoulder roast at 24 cents per serving, and bone-in Boston butt at 20 cents per serving. Just match the price per pound with the meat cut you are comparing. It's as easy as that! Servings are from 2½ to 3½ ounces of cooked lean meat.

   Marketing information for Consumers Cooperative Extension Service. The Ohio State University, Columbus, Ohio.

Exhibit 2 (cont.)

Meat

Retail Cut	Serv- ings Per Pound	Price Per Pound											
		29	39	49	59	69	79	89	99	109	119	129	139
		Cost Per Serving											
Beef													
Sirloin Steak	2½	12	16	20	24	28	32	36	40	44	48	52	56
Porterhouse, T-bone													
Rib Steak	2	15	20	25	30	35	40	45	50	55	60	65	70
Round Steak	3½	8	11	14	17	20	23	25	28	31	34	37	40
Chuck Roast, bone-in	2	15	20	25	30	35	40	45	50	55	60	65	70
Rib Roast—boneless	2½	12	16	20	24	28	32	36	40	44	48	52	56
Rib Roast—bone-in	2	15	20	25	30	35	40	45	50	55	60	65	70
Rump, Sirloin Roast	3	10	13	16	20	23	26	30	33	36	40	43	46
Ground Beef	4	7	10	12	15	17	20	22	25	27	30	32	35
Short Ribs	2	15	20	25	30	35	40	45	50	55	60	65	70
Heart, Liver, Kidney	5	6	8	10	12	14	16	18	20	22	24	26	28
Frankfurters	4	7	10	12	15	17	20	22	25	27	30	32	35
Stew Meat, boneless	5	6	8	10	12	14	16	18	20	22	24	26	28
Lamb													
Loin, Rib, Shoulder													
Chops	3	10	13	16	20	23	26	30	33	36	40	43	46
Breast, Shank	2	15	20	25	30	35	40	45	50	55	60	65	70
Shoulder Roast	2½	12	16	20	24	28	32	36	40	44	48	52	56
Leg of Lamb	3	10	13	16	20	23	26	30	33	36	40	43	46
Pork—Fresh													
Center Cut or Rib Chops	4	7	10	12	15	17	20	22	25	27	30	32	35
Loin or Rib Roast	2½	12	16	20	24	28	32	36	40	44	48	52	56
Boston butt—bone-in	3	10	13	16	20	23	26	30	33	36	40	43	46
Blade Steak	3	10	13	16	20	23	26	30	33	36	40	43	46
Spare Ribs	1 1/3	22	29	37	44	52	59	67	74	82	89	97	104
Pork—Cured													
Picnic—bone-in	2	15	20	25	30	35	40	45	50	55	60	65	70
Ham—fully cooked													
bone-in	3½	8	11	14	17	20	23	25	28	31	34	37	40
boneless and canned	5	6	8	10	12	14	16	18	20	22	24	26	28
shankless	4¼	7	9	12	14	16	19	21	23	26	28	30	33
center slice	5	6	8	10	12	14	16	18	20	22	24	26	28
Poultry													
Broiler, ready-to-cook	1 1/3	22	29	37	44	52	59	67	74	82	89	97	104
legs, thighs	3	10	13	16	20	23	26	30	33	36	40	43	46
breasts	4	7	10	12	15	17	20	22	25	27	30	32	35
Turkey, ready-to-cook													
under 12 lbs.	1	29	39	49	59	69	79	89	99	109	119	129	139
12 lbs. and over	1 1/3	22	29	37	44	52	59	67	74	82	89	97	104

APPENDIX A

Excerpts from "Lamb Cost-per-Serving Concept Study: A Qualitative Assessment" (1966)

PURPOSE OF THE STUDY

The major objective of the study was to explore, in depth, the attitudes and experiences of homemakers relating to the purchase and preparation of meats and to obtain their understanding of and reaction to the cost-per-serving concept, particularly as it applies to lamb. The study was designed to provide a qualitative assessment of salient attitudes and perceptions for the purpose of assisting in the design of an effective advertising campaign.

METHOD

The technique employed was the Intensive Group Interview in which eight or nine housewives, guided by a professional moderator, discussed together their feelings and experiences with meat and the cost-per-serving concept. Ten groups were conducted in different geographical areas in accordance with the following age specifications:

Denver, Colorado

Group 1   Younger Housewives under 25 Years of Age
Group 2   Older Housewives 26 to 40 Years of Age

Chicago, Illinois

Group 3   Younger Housewives under 30 Years of Age
Group 4   Older Housewives 31 to 45 Years of Age
Group 5   Mixed Housewives 25 to 45 Years of Age

Pasadena, California

Group 6   Younger Housewives under 30 Years of Age
Group 7   Older Housewives 31 to 40 Years of Age
Group 8   Mixed Housewives 25 to 45 Years of Age

Boston, Massachusetts

Group 9   Younger Housewives under 30 Years of Age
Group 10   Older Housewives 31 to 60 Years of Age

Although there was no screening to insure the inclusion of lamb consumers, each group contained women with favorable attitudes toward lamb and also women adverse to lamb. Only vegetarians or those opposed to all forms of meat were specifically excluded.

COMMENTS

Housewives' attitudes toward the cost-per-serving concept were discussed in only one of several sections of the report. A major section of the study dealt with the broader issue of consumers' attitudes toward the purchase and consumption of meat in general.

THE TEN SOCIAL ROLES

A psychologist at Chase and Associates, the firm that conducted the study, had identified in previous studies ten basic roles or personalities into which housewives can be classified with regard to their food-buying orientation. The following section is a classification of these ten basic orientations, expressed by homemakers during the group sessions of this study. It is taken intact from the Chase and Associates report.

1. The Well Organized This group, even though seemingly small in number, is admired by those with less talent in this direction. These people plan their purchases carefully, checking recipes, the household budget, and the store specials before deciding on the weekly meat menu. Usually alternatives are planned in the event the planned purchase looks less inviting at the store than anticipated.

A good buy in meat is described as economical with little unnecessary fat or waste. There is less emphasis on aesthetic or taste satisfactions, for the orientation is essentially utilitarian. They attain personal satisfaction by perceiving themselves as astute guardians of the family purse strings, efficient household managers and rather reluctant and parsimonious spenders.

As a consequence of this orientation, familiar dishes take preference over untried recipes and meat must be totally consumed—and stretched, if possible—to insure economy and astute management.

Typical of this group is the following comment:

> I plan my meals for the entire week, checking cookbooks, magazines and newspaper ads. I allocate my food budget to take care of each purchase I plan and try not to exceed it. I plan a roast to last three servings, supplemented by chops or chicken. I want to give my family what they need, and still stay within my budget.

2. The Versatile While expressing some concern that meat must be "stretched," these housewives indicate a strong desire to have a different kind of meat for each meal. Consequently their purchases are apt to be dominated by steak and chops, meats which can be consumed in their entirety at a single meal.

Relief from monotony through constantly changing vistas provides welcome variety and new experiences. A roast becomes the excuse for entertaining friends and relatives, and eating out is seen as almost a necessity.

These women particularly stress the need to disguise conventional cuts of meat by the liberal use of gravies or sauces. New recipes are of interest, provided no substantial increase of preparation time is required.

Special prices or sales are less important than unplanned impulse purchases. Although generally unwilling to take a chance on an entirely new cut of meat, they attempt to provide their families with a reasonable variety of familiar meats, frequently disguised by altering the appearance. In some cases a lack of knowledge of how to use leftovers differently results in both waste and dissatisfaction.

A typical comment by a member of this group is:

> I like to have a different meat dish every night. We don't like leftovers, and usually I end up throwing them away. Sometimes I don't try new cuts when I'm uncertain of how to prepare them. I just can't afford to take a chance.

3. **The Quick and Convenient** These housewives possess little real involvement with meat or other household food purchases. Essentially meal preparation is regarded as a chore, something rather disagreeable that somehow must be accomplished.

Meat that can be prepared quickly with a minimum of fuss and bother is most appreciated. If the preparation responsibilities can be transferred to the husband via the backyard barbecue, a major victory has been won.

Of special interest to the group are easily prepared foods such as steaks, precooked hams, and boneless roasts. Frozen, convenience dishes are frequently stocked to avoid prior planning and the necessity of elaborate preparation.

Since meal preparation is generally regarded as an intrusion, an unwelcome task to be quickly performed, very little consideration is given to cost of meat or to the use of leftovers. In the main, leftovers are unacceptable unless in the form of easily used ham, turkey, or chicken slices for sandwiches. The purchase of meat is apparently a haphazard affair with almost no preplanning or budgetary considerations. The emphasis is placed on personal convenience, and there is little involvement with the possible consequences.

Typical of this group is the following comment:

> I don't want to spend a lot of time preparing meals. I'm on too tight a schedule for that. Give me the convenience foods any day. I like to have a well-stocked freezer so I can decide at the last moment what to prepare. Often my husband will help me get it ready.

4. **The Experimenters** Like the *versatile*, these housewives are constantly looking for different kinds of meat. However, their basic satisfaction comes from

discovery of a new kind of meat or a new method of preparation. They generally enjoy shopping, the search for new recipes and, if necessary, will spend considerable time in planning and preparing a newly discovered meat dish.

This group especially enjoys the satisfactions derived from an appreciative husband or friends when a new dish is well received. Taste, a feeling of fullness, second helpings, and expressions of appreciation are the criteria of success.

To a considerable extent there is interest in meat quality, its appearance, and especially its final taste. Their reputation as "good cooks" is to a considerable degree dependent on their selection of proper cuts of meat to insure tenderness, flavor, good appearance, and eating satisfaction.

These adventuresome homemakers are continually looking for new recipes, new ways of preparing conventional meats, and new cuts with which to surprise their families. Conforming to a budget seems less important than personal relationships, and the frequent plaudits of family and friends provide ample reward for their unceasing efforts to please them.

A comment typical of this group is:

> I'm always on the lookout for new ways to serve meat. I enjoy an attractive table, it makes the dinner taste so good. When I shop, I look for bright red meat and I can usually visualize how it will look on my table. If everything turns out right, I enjoy receiving the compliments.

5. The Aesthetic These consumers judge meat primarily by its appearance. It must "look good" to be acceptable. The quality of the meat must appear tender, contain little unwanted fat, and red meat must appear "healthy." It must also smell good while it is cooking and when eaten.

This group is also concerned with what can be done with the meat, but essentially the orientation is how it will look on the table or plate. A pleasing appearance is equated to an emotionally satisfying eating experience.

Meat, the focal point of dinner, must conform to the decor of the dining setting. To make the meat more attractive it may be "dressed up" with paper handles or "feet" and served with proper complementary dishes. Considerable concern is expressed about the appearance of the meat when it is served, and there is obvious anxiety present when meat seems either overdone or too rare. The rest of the meal must complement the meat dish, so that each dish is chosen in accordance with the entire effect to be achieved.

Although the total cost of the meal might be a consideration, meat is perceived primarily in terms of narcissistic values rather than as a quickly consumed commodity. In this regard, the more attractive meats are those of color, such as red beef, pink ham, or browned turkey.

A comment typical of this group would be:

> Meat must be satisfying to make it worthwhile. I don't mind a lot of preparation if the result looks and tastes just right. You must serve the right things with each kind of meat to enjoy it—mint jelly with lamb, and pineapple sauce with ham. If it doesn't look right, it just doesn't taste as good.

6. The Child Stuffers Some women express considerable concern about serving the proper meats to their growing children. Some mothers buy "soft" or less expensive meats for their children on the basis of ease of chewing or their inability to distinguish expensive meat from the cheaper cuts; this group, however, seems dominated by two considerations: filling the children up with a sufficient amount of meat, and being certain that the meat is digestive and nutritious.

Provided it can meet these two requirements, meat is frequently seen as a bargain at any price. Healthy children are presumed to be well worth the cost of meat, and these mothers are genuinely pleased when a great deal is consumed for this indicates a continuation of healthy nutritious growth.

Since meat is viewed as the most important ingredient in the diet and therefore should be consumed in quantity, these women may be described as "stuffers." A large quantity of meat consumed by each member of the family provides assurance that the supplier's role has been adequately fulfilled.

There is a tendency for some members of this group to be concerned with food values, and meats are selected on the basis of providing maximum nutrition. Expensive meats are preferred to lower-priced meats because of the assumption that higher quality assures greater satisfaction and, therefore, increased consumption.

The following statement expressed by a member of this group is typical.

> My problem is filling up my children. If I don't serve enough meat, they'll be back later for soda pop and peanut butter sandwiches. I'd rather see them eat more meat. It will keep them healthy.

There are a number of subcategories which also distinguish purchaser motivations:

7. The Bountiful These people are contented only when there is ample meat on hand. Purchases are made in volume, both in terms of large cuts and amounts. Frequently, this orientation provides justification for a large upright freezer. While waste may prove a problem, a well-stocked freezer assures a satisfied family.

Typical of this group is the following comment:

> I buy in quantity so I won't have to bother about not having enough on hand. I know it's wasteful, because we don't always like some pieces.

8. The Above and Beyond These women display no interest whatever in meat. They frequently referred to eating as a "necessity" rather than a "pleasure." Since their primary interests lie elsewhere, this lack of involvement provides little opportunity to motivate this group in a specified or predetermined direction.

Typical of this group is:

> I couldn't care less about eating. I'm much more interested in my work and hobbies.

9. The Avoiders   Some homemakers consciously avoid certain kinds of meat because of prior conditioning, lack of knowledge concerning its preparation, or dissatisfaction with previous experiences. This group also includes dieters who are primarily concerned with consumption of low-calorie meats.

Representative of this group is the following comment:

> We just wouldn't consider lamb. I had it once, and it was stringy and tasted awful.

10. The Bargain-Hunters   These housewives seem to lack an ability to distinguish quality. Primarily their orientation is "the most meat at the lowest price" regardless of past experiences. The store specials provide the basis for the meat selection. Despite frequent disappointments, most meat is chosen in this manner.

The following comment was frequently expressed by members of this group:

> I select the best (cheapest) buys even if the quality is not so good. Then I have more money for other things.

ATTITUDES ABOUT LAMB
AND THE COST-PER-SERVING CONCEPT

The study also explored attitudes about lamb and other meats. Its conclusions verified findings of the 1964 "Lamb and the Consumer" study; namely, women were seldom neutral in their appraisal of lamb; their comments ranged from "the best meat you can ever have" to "I just wouldn't touch the stuff." Lamb was generally viewed as a "changeover" dish not served regularly, possessing numerous negatives in the attitudes and perceptions of consumers. In contrast, beef was seen as the nearly perfect meat and its few disadvantages emerged only under interviewer-probing.

The cost-per-serving concept came under wide criticism from housewives. Only about one-fourth of the group participants appreciated the cost-per-serving card (see case Exhibit 2) or indicated that they believed it would be useful in some instances. The remainder rejected the card for reasons ranging from "I can't see trying to figure it out every time I go shopping" and "serving amounts don't fit my family" to "it's not worth the trouble for the few pennies it might save."

In general, other factors, such as convenience and family happiness, seemed to be more important to housewives than budgetary considerations. Most tended to agree that the budget-conscious housewife is somewhat cold and archaic in today's affluent society. A young Boston housewife voiced a representative summary of what appeared to be the majority position.

> I buy whatever I see that looks good and I think my family will enjoy. I hardly ever look at the price, and I certainly can't try to figure out how much

it costs to serve each portion. I don't want to be like my grandmother—always concerned with using up every scrap of meat even though no one enjoyed eating those stews and casseroles. I want to have what we like to eat irregardless [sic] of how much it costs.

Even the admittedly budget-conscious housewives tended to describe their economy-mindedness in terms of "stretching" meats to serve several meals. In this respect, such meats as chicken, ground beef, and pot roast emerged as meats associated with lower costs per serving due to their high versatility. In contrast, lamb was perceived as possessing little versatility. Therefore participants agreed that it must be regarded as costly on a price-per-serving basis regardless of what appeared to be true on the basis of the cost-per-serving card.

QUESTIONS

1.   *What is the significance of these findings in terms of new directions for lamb consumer advertising?*
2.   *What are the implications of this study for the cost-per-serving consumer advertising theme? For an economy theme in general?*
3.   *What needs for further research arise as a result of these findings?*

American
Sheep Producers Council (C)

The lamb industry trade association conducts a study to further investigate the ten psychographic groups uncovered in an earlier qualitative study. This new research focuses on the relative sizes and demographic characteristics of the groups as well as their reactions to four test ads for lamb.

The ten social roles of food-purchasing orientation which emerged in the 1966 qualitative cost-per-serving study served as a basis for a number of subsequent studies commissioned by the American Sheep Producers Council (ASPC). [American Sheep Producers Council (A) contains background information on ASPC, a number of the Council's marketing and advertising problems in the mid-1960s, and a summary of a 1964 national study probing consumer attitudes regarding lamb. American Sheep Producers Council (B) summarizes the qualitative study undertaken in late 1966 to probe consumers' reactions to the cost-per-serving concept. This concept had been a major thrust in 1966 lamb advertising in an attempt to rid lamb of its high-price image.]

THE QUANTITATIVE COST-PER-SERVING STUDY

The first study to further investigate the nature and sizes of the social role groups was the quantitative cost-per-serving study undertaken in early 1967. Whereas the qualitative phase of the study had employed group interviews among housewives chosen against relatively rough criteria of age and lamb use, the quantitative phase featured personal at-home interviews among a carefully screened population sample from four major U.S. metropolitan areas. This study measured interviewee responses to specific print advertisements for lamb in an attempt to evaluate the relative ability of each ad to convey certain characteristics about lamb, and the relative sizes of the ten social-role groups identified in the qualitative phase.

Appendix A summarizes the quantitative cost-per-serving study and its findings.

APPENDIX A

Excerpts from "Lamb Cost-per-Serving Concept Study Advertising Assessment" (1967) (The Quantitative Cost-per-Serving Study)

PURPOSE:

This study covered the second part of a two-part study to evaluate the relative appeal of different advertising approaches for lamb and consumer reaction to the cost-per-serving concept. Phase I was a qualitative study designed to provide an assessment of salient attitudes and perceptions. [American Sheep Producers Council (B) focuses on the qualitative study.] Phase II was a quantitative assessment to measure response to specific print advertisements and to explore further the ten social-role groups identified in Phase I, including the relative importance of each as a target group for lamb advertising.

METHOD:

In four U.S. marketing areas—Boston, Chicago, Denver, and Los Angeles—403 personal at-home interviews were conducted among housewives. Probability samples were drawn from each area. Approximately 100 interviews were obtained in each area, and then composited into one sample to provide a cross-sectional response.

Four lamb advertisements and one control ham ad were used. Each respondent initially responded to one lamb ad and the control ad, and later was shown two of the other three lamb ads.

ADVERTISEMENTS USED

Control Ham Ad (Exhibit A-1)   The control ad was one that had appeared in *Family Circle* magazine. It showed a Rath smoked ham being covered with champagne. The background was dark and the headline said, "Now Rath has a different ham for every Sunday of the Month."

Barbecue Ad (Exhibit A-2)   The Barbecue ad showed children and young people gathered around a charcoal burner with lamb shishkabob on skewers. The headline said, "Come to our cookout—we're having Lamb."

Stretch Ad (Exhibit A-3)   The stretch ad showed a leg of lamb with small pictures below indicating different meals that could be obtained from it. The headline said, "How to stretch a leg of Lamb into four delicious meals."

Bones Ad (Exhibit A-4)   The bones ad showed six plates with chicken and lamb before cooking, after cooking, and the waste. The headline said, "Lamb gives you more eatin' meat for your money."

Cartoon Ad (Exhibit A-5)   The cartoon ad showed a pig and chicken discussing the relative price per pound of lamb, pork, and chicken.

COMMENTS:

A. Responses to Advertisements   The report first discussed the relative performances of the five ads used. All respondents were asked to state their favorite of the ads they were shown. As seen in the table below, the ham ad was the favorite by a wide margin on the basis of the percentage of those seeing the ad who chose it as their favorite, with the barbecue ad and the stretch ad scoring highest among the lamb ads. As seen in Exhibit A-6, the choice of ads varied considerably depending on whether respondents were lamb users or nonusers.

Table A-1

AD CHOICES - ALL RESPONDENTS

	Ham	Barbecue	Stretch	Bones	Cartoon
Number Seeing Ad	403	278	301	303	327
Number Choosing*	211	66	75	23	22
Percentage	52.4	23.7	24.9	7.6	6.7

* Six did not choose any ad.

Respondents rated each ad they saw on a five-point scale against a list of polar characteristics. Exhibit A-7 contains the average responses for all ads; Exhibit A-8 breaks down responses by users and nonusers for the two highest-scoring lamb ads. The study report noted that any average response outside the 2.5 to 3.5 "neutral zone" could be considered significantly different from neutral at the 95% level.

B. Social-Role Groups   A number of tables in the study attempted to determine how many and what sorts of people make up the different social-role groups identified in the previous qualitative study. Categorization of respondents into different social roles was a largely subjective process. Interviewers asked respondents to describe their orientation and motivation in food purchasing, and categorized them into one or more roles on the basis of their responses. As noted in Exhibit A-9, which shows the number of respondents exhibiting characteristics of each social role, the number of roles indicated averaged between two and three per respondent.

Additional tables investigated the following characteristics of respondents falling into the different social roles:

—frequency of lamb use (Exhibit A-10)

—age [Child Stuffers were the oldest (53.7% aged 40 and above); the Versatile group was the youngest (62.3% under age 40).]

— income (Exhibit A-11)

—number of children (The Bountiful group had the greatest percentage of respondents with four or more children, and the Child Stuffer and Experimenter groups had the greatest percentage with less than two children.)

—head of household occupation (The Versatile group had the highest percentage of blue-collar heads, and the Experimenter, Aesthetic, and Bountiful groups had the highest percentage of white-collar heads of household.)

Exhibit A-12 breaks down the ad choices by the different social role groups.

The report concluded by discussing marketing implications of the study findings. A final recommendation urged that the findings be used to bring more precise direction to ASPC's consumer lamb advertising: "Rather than attempt to reach all groups simultaneously, the best immediate opportunities stem from the selection of one or two groups as the basis for the advertising program."

American Sheep Producers Council (C)

LIST OF EXHIBITS

Exhibit	Contents
A-1	Control Ham Ad
A-2	Barbecue Ad for Lamb
A-3	Stretch Ad for Lamb
A-4	Bones Ad for Lamb
A-5	Cartoon Ad
A-6	Ad Choice by Lamb Use
A-7	Average Responses to All Ads
A-8	Average Responses to Two Ads by Lamb Use
A-9	Percentages of Respondents Exhibiting Characteristics of the Social-Role Groups
A-10	Lamb Use by Social Role
A-11	Income by Social Role
A-12	Ad Choice by Social Role

CONTROL HAM AD

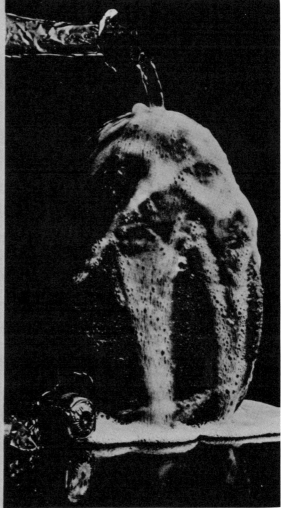

Now Rath has a different ham for every Sunday of the month.

Rath hickory-smoked ham has always been a special, Sunday kind of ham. Now it's even more so. Comes ready-fixed in a choice of elegant new ways. Glazed with honey, soaked with champagne, sauced with tropical fruits. Or straight hickory-smoked.

Here, to make your mouth water, is our champagne recipe: we take one of our hickory-smoked hams, drench it with genuine bubbly, then cook it to winey perfection. Voila! Serve it hot or cold.

Choose Rath Hawaiian, Honey Glazed, Champagne, Hickory-Smoked

Rath.

Come to our cookout...
we're having Lamb
Deliciously different — costs less, too!

It's true. The lamb that adds life to the party often costs
less* than other meats and poultry. That's because there's
less waste in the lamb. It's young meat with a light
bone structure. After the meal, you won't see plates piled high
with bones and fat. And it's so much fun to cook lamb
out-of-doors . . . to grill tender chops and steaks, to roast a fine

 leg of lamb on your rotisserie. Treat your family
and guests. Save money, too . . . with LAMB.

*U. S. Department of Agriculture Handbook 102

how to stretch a
leg of Lamb

STEAKS ROAST SANDWICHES STEW

into 4 delicious meals

Versatile . . . that's the word for leg of lamb. It can turn up at the table in many delectably different forms. Have your meat-man cut the leg into sections. Slices from the large end become steaks you can broil for a mid-week treat. Comes Sunday, roast the plump center section, and if there's any left after dinner, put it in the refrigerator for raiders' sandwiches. You still have the small end of the leg. Cut the meat from it and use it to make a hearty stew or exotic lamb kebabs or curry. That's stretching a leg of lamb. That's stretching your food budget. **LamB**

IN THE CIRCLE OF GOOD TASTE

For FREE lamb recipes, write:

american lamb council

520 Railway Exchange Building
Denver, Colorado 80202

LAMB
gives you more eatin' meat for your money

SEE HERE:

chicken --
uncooked

portion of cooked chicken
that is *edible*

waste – bone and fat –
from chicken

same weight leg of lamb –
uncooked

portion of cooked leg of
lamb that is *edible*

waste – bone and fat –
from leg of lamb

All meats are good buys and good for you—but compare the amount of "eatin' meat" in lamb with the meat that gets on your fork from chicken, pork, turkey, even beef. Compare the bones and fat left on plates or platter when it's time to do dishes. There's more good eatin' meat, less waste in lamb. U. S. Department of Agriculture studies prove it in cut after cut. * Lamb is young meat with a light bone structure. It's this *inside* story that so often makes lamb the real bargain. Don't wait another day to enjoy tender juicy lamb. And when you serve it to your family, you can even brag a bit about the money you saved!

*U. S. Department of Agriculture Handbook 102.

HOW TO ROAST A LEG OF LAMB

Place leg of lamb on rack in shallow roasting pan. Season. Roast at 325° for 35 to 40 minutes per pound or until meat thermometer registers 175° to 180°, depending upon desired degree of doneness. VARIATIONS: Baste the lamb while it's roasting with your favorite Italian dressing or any frozen fruit juice concentrate.

For FREE lamb recipes, write:

american lamb council

520 Railway Exchange Building
Denver, Colorado 80202

IN
THE CIRCLE
OF GOOD
TASTE

Exhibit A-5

CARTOON AD

Exhibit A-6

AD CHOICE BY LAMB USE

	Lamb Users	Lamb Nonusers	Total
Ham ad			
No. Seeing	241	162	403
No. Choosing	114	97	211
Percentage	47.3	59.9	52.4
Barbecue ad			
No. Seeing	167	111	278
No. Choosing	42	24	66
Percentage	25.1	21.6	23.7
Stretch ad			
No. Seeing	178	123	301
No. Choosing	58	17	75
Percentage	32.6	13.8	24.9
Bones ad			
No. Seeing	180	123	303
No. Choosing	13	10	23
Percentage	7.2	8.1	7.6
Cartoon ad			
No. Seeing	198	129	327
No. Choosing	11	11	22
Percentage	5.6	8.5	6.7

AVERAGE RESPONSES TO ALL ADS

Item	Averages					Item
	Ham	Barbecue	Stretch	Bones	Cartoon	
Young	2.2	1.9	2.7	2.7	2.5	Old
Light	2.9	2.4	3.1	3.2	3.4	Heavy
Tough	4.1	4.1	4.0	3.7	3.3	Tender
Inexpensive	3.6	3.1	3.3	2.8	2.9	Expensive
Indoors	1.7	3.2	2.0	2.3	2.1	Outdoors
Lean	1.6	2.3	2.3	2.0	3.0	Fat
Ordinary	3.9	3.0	2.7	2.2	2.6	Special
Little waste	1.4	2.2	2.2	2.3	3.1	Much waste
Tasteless	4.5	3.9	3.9	3.3	3.2	Tasty
Poor buy	3.9	3.1	3.7	3.5	3.4	Good buy
Little edible	4.6	3.8	3.9	3.8	3.5	Much edible
Light bone	1.9	2.3	3.1	2.3	3.0	Heavy bone
Can't do much	4.4	3.1	3.8	2.8	3.2	Versatile
One meal	4.6	2.4	3.9	2.7	3.4	Several meals
High cost per serving	3.0	2.8	2.7	2.9	3.4	Low cost per serving
Less cost than others	3.4	3.5	3.4	3.3	2.9	More cost than others
Plain	4.2	2.8	2.9	2.4	2.6	Elegant
Thrifty	3.2	3.2	3.0	3.0	2.5	Extravagant
Commonplace	3.6	2.9	2.9	2.1	2.8	Unusual
Not believable	4.0	4.1	4.4	4.0	3.1	Believable
Old-fashioned	4.4	4.1	3.0	2.9	3.4	Modern
Family	3.7	2.7	2.6	2.2	2.5	Guests
Special	2.3	3.0	3.0	3.8	3.5	Everyday use
Unattractive	4.4	4.0	3.9	2.8	2.7	Attractive
Not for me	3.9	3.1	3.0	2.7	2.5	For me
Avoid it	3.8	3.7	3.5	3.1	3.0	Try it
Skip it	3.8	3.3	3.2	3.0	2.7	Read it
Not buy	4.0	3.4	3.3	3.0	2.8	Like to buy

Scale Used: 1 2 3 4 5.

Exhibit A-8

AVERAGE RESPONSES TO TWO ADS BY LAMB USE

| | Averages | | | | |
| | Barbecue Ad | | Stretch Ad | | |
Item	Users	Nonusers	Users	Nonusers	Item
Young	1.8	2.1	2.4	3.1	Old
Light	2.2	2.8	3.0	3.2	Heavy
Tough	4.1	4.1	4.0	4.0	Tender
Inexpensive	3.1	3.1	3.4	3.2	Expensive
Indoors	3.1	3.4	2.2	1.7	Outdoors
Lean	2.1	2.7	2.1	2.6	Fat
Ordinary	2.9	3.2	2.8	2.6	Special
Little waste	2.1	2.4	2.4	1.9	Much waste
Tasteless	4.1	3.5	4.2	3.5	Tasty
Poor buy	3.2	2.9	3.7	3.7	Good buy
Little edible	4.0	3.4	3.8	4.0	Much edible
Light bone	2.2	2.5	3.2	3.0	Heavy bone
Can't do much	3.2	2.9	3.8	3.8	Versatile
One meal	2.4	2.4	3.9	3.9	Several meals
High cost per serving	2.7	3.0	2.8	2.6	Low cost per serving
Less cost than others	3.4	3.7	3.4	3.4	More cost than others
Plain	3.0	3.4	2.8	3.0	Elegant
Thrifty	3.2	3.2	2.8	3.3	Extravagant
Commonplace	3.0	2.7	2.9	2.9	Unusual
Not believable	4.3	3.7	4.4	4.4	Believable
Old-fashioned	4.2	3.9	2.8	3.3	Modern
Family	2.5	3.1	2.8	2.3	Guests
Special	3.1	2.8	2.9	3.1	Everyday use
Unattractive	4.0	4.0	3.9	3.9	Attractive
Not for me	3.6	2.0	3.7	2.1	For me
Avoid it	4.1	2.8	3.9	3.0	Try it
Skip it	3.5	2.9	3.6	2.7	Read it
Not buy	3.8	2.5	3.9	2.5	Like to buy

Scale Used: 1 2 3 4 5

Exhibit A-9

PERCENTAGES OF RESPONDENTS EXHIBITING CHARACTERISTICS
OF THE SOCIAL-ROLE GROUPS

Social Role*	Number**	Percentage
Experimenter	222	55.1
Well organized	165	40.9
Aesthetic	228	56.6
Versatile	85	21.1
Child stuffer	74	18.4
Bountiful	152	37.7
Quick and convenient	17	4.2
Above and beyond	28	6.9
Bargain hunter	13	3.2
Avoider	239	59.3

* See American Sheep Producers Council (B) for a discussion of the characteristics of these social roles.

** A person may exhibit characteristics of more than one social role. The average number of roles indicated was between two and three. There were 403 respondents in all.

Exhibit A-10
LAMB USE BY SOCIAL ROLE

Lamb Use	Social Role					
	Experimenter	Well Organized	Aesthetic	Versatile	Child Stuffer	Bountiful
Frequent	35 (15.8)	19 (11.5)	29 (12.7)	9 (10.6)	18 (24.3)	11 (7.6)
Once in a while	59 (26.6)	39 (23.6)	51 (22.4)	22 (25.9)	17 (23.0)	31 (20.1)
Seldom	50 (22.5)	39 (23.6)	62 (27.2)	17 (20.0)	13 (17.6)	43 (28.5)
Never	78 (35.1)	68 (41.2)	86 (37.7)	37 (43.5)	26 (35.1)	67 (44.1)
Total	222 (100.0)	165 (100.0)	228 (100.0)	85 (100.0)	74 (100.0)	152 (100.0)

Exhibit A-11

INCOME BY SOCIAL ROLE

			Social Role			
Income	Experimenter	Well Organized	Aesthetic	Versatile	Child Stuffer	Bountiful
Under $6,000	52	46	50	27	20	36
	(23.5)	(27.9)	(21.9)	(31.8)	(27.0)	(23.6)
$6,000– $8,500	67	51	70	28	24	43
	(30.2)	(30.9)	(30.7)	(32.9)	(32.4)	(28.5)
$8,500– $10,000	37	28	37	10	13	22
	(16.7)	(17.0)	(16.2)	(11.8)	(17.6)	(14.5)
Over $10,000	58	34	64	17	7	46
	(26.2)	(21.2)	(28.0)	(20.0)	(20.3)	(30.6)
Refused	8	6	7	3	2	5
	(3.6)	(3.6)	(3.1)	(3.5)	(2.7)	(3.5)
Total	222	165	228	85	74	152
	(100.0)	(100.0)	(100.0)	(100.0)	(100.0)	(100.0)

Exhibit A-12

AD CHOICE BY SOCIAL ROLE

			Social Role			
	Experimenter	Well Organized	Aesthetic	Versatile	Child Stuffer	Bountiful
Ham ad						
No. seeing	222	165	228	85	74	152
No. choosing	114	79	123	42	35	83
Percentage	51.4	47.9	53.9	49.4	47.3	54.5
Barbecue ad						
No. seeing	152	108	159	56	52	102
No. choosing	38	36	30	12	14	25
Percentage	25.0	33.3	18.9	21.4	26.9	24.5
Stretch ad						
No. seeing	170	131	171	62	55	104
No. choosing	48	29	48	17	15	22
Percentage	28.2	22.1	28.1	27.4	27.3	21.2
Bones ad						
No. seeing	168	128	171	67	52	113
No. choosing	10	9	13	7	4	10
Percentage	6.0	7.0	7.6	10.4	7.7	8.8
Cartoon ad						
No. seeing	176	128	183	70	63	116
No. choosing	10	11	12	6	6	8
Percentage	5.7	8.6	6.6	8.6	9.5	6.9

QUESTIONS

1. *What target groups should the Lamb Council try to reach?*
2. *What copy themes should be used?*
3. *What further research, if any, is called for?*

American
Sheep Producers Council (D)

The lamb industry trade association conducts a study testing three different headlines and copy approaches for the same advertising theme.

Following the qualitative and quantitative studies of the cost-per-serving concept as a meaningful theme for lamb advertising, in 1967 American Sheep Producers Council (ASPC) executives commissioned further research efforts in order to bring even greater copy direction to lamb consumer advertising. [American Sheep Producers Council (A) contains background information on ASPC and a summary of a 1964 national study probing consumer attitudes regarding lamb. American Sheep Producers Council (B) and (C) deal with, respectively, the qualitative and quantitative phases of the cost-per-serving study undertaken in late 1966 and early 1967. The cost-per-serving concept had been a major thrust in 1966 lamb consumer advertising in an attempt to rid lamb of its high-price image.]

THE PRODUCT AND AD IMAGE STUDY

The first study to follow the cost-per-serving studies was called the "Product and Ad Image Study." Undertaken in the spring of 1967, its aims were limited essentially to clarifying and expanding on certain of the findings of the cost-per-serving studies. For example, the study investigated the reasons for the success of the control ham ad in the quantitative study, concluding that its popularity resulted more from the product than the specific appeals or format of the ad. In addition, it found that many of the ad profile ratings for the barbecue and stretch lamb ads changed significantly when retested, possibly due to certain slight changes in these ads. (See Appendix A for selected findings from this study.)

REVIEWING THE RESULTS

Based on findings from the above and previous studies, ASPC executives concluded that the cartoon ad "never really got across the idea," and the bones ad (tested in the quantitative cost-per-serving study) seemed to come across as somewhat unappetizing to the average housewife. They did, however, believe the bones ad to be a meaningful presentation to home economists, and subsequently ran the ad in home economist trade publications.

The barbecue theme appeared to have greater overall appeal than the stretch concept. However, for certain target audiences, the stretch theme was still regarded as a valuable one to investigate further. In addition, it was thought to be an approach better suited for newspaper advertising and the colorful outdoors format of the barbecue ad was seen as being perhaps more applicable to magazine insertions.

HEADLINE AND COPY TEST

To attempt to determine the best possible way in which to present the basic stretch idea in consumer advertising, ASPC executives authorized a study conducted in mid-1967 entitled "Evaluation of Alternative Headlines and Copy for Leg of Lamb Ad." For this study, three ads were tested which employed different headline and copy variations to present lamb as a versatile meat worthy of the consideration of the budget-conscious housewife. Appendix B summarizes this study and contains selected findings.

American Sheep Producers Council (D)

LIST OF EXHIBITS

APPENDIX A

Excerpts from "Product and Ad Image Study"—May 1967

PURPOSE:

The study had the following objectives:

1) to determine to what extent the response to the Champagne Ham Ad used as a control in the quantitative cost-per-serving study was due to the product, the brand name, or particular aspects of the appearance of the ad;

2) to determine ad profiles for three revised lamb ads;

3) to determine the proportion of housewives who have tendencies as "avoiders";

4) to study the importance of time as opposed to cost in the "stretching" of meat for more than one meal;

5) to investigate budget-consciousness of housewives.

METHOD:

Three hundred personal at-home interviews were conducted in the Downey and Lakewood suburbs of Los Angeles. Respondents were chosen to match roughly the lamb user/nonuser percentage breakdown among Los Angeles area respondents in the previous quantitative cost-per-serving study. In each study the user/nonuser split was roughly half-and-half.

Four control ads and three lamb ads were used, to result in 12 possible control and lamb ad comparisons. All ads used were of the same size and reproduced in the same manner to insure comparability. A total of 36 area segments were used in the sample providing three interpenetrating replications of the possible ad comparisons.

Control Ads Used   The following four ads served as controls:

1) *Ham-Rath Ad* (Exhibit A-1)—This was the same ad used as a control in the quantitative cost-per-serving study. It showed a Rath smoked ham being covered with champagne.

2) *Ham Ad* (Exhibit A-2)—Identical to the Ham-Rath ad except that all reference to Rath was replaced or removed.

3) *Ham-Lamb-Rath Ad* (Exhibit A-3)—Identical to the Ham-Rath ad except that all reference to ham was replaced by lamb.

4) *Ham-Lamb Ad* (Exhibit A-4)—Identical to the Ham-Lamb-Rath ad except that all reference to Rath was replaced or removed.

Lamb Ads Used   The following three lamb ads were tested:

1) *Stretch Ad* (Exhibit A-5)—This was similar to the stretch ad used in the quantitative cost-per-serving study. The difference consisted in an actual leg of lamb being used rather than a model. The background was of a brighter color. The ad showed a leg of lamb with small pictures below indicating different meals that could be obtained from it.

2) *Cartoon Ad* (Exhibit A-6)—This ad differed significantly from the cartoon ad used in the cost-per-serving study. The illustration for this ad showed a large chicken and a small pig.

3) *Barbecue Ad* (Exhibit A-7)—This ad had a different scene and a larger piece of meat than the barbecue ad used in the previous study.

COMMENTS:

As seen in the table below, both ham-control ads did significantly better than the control ads in which the word "lamb" was substituted. (All differences termed significant may be considered so at the 95% level.)

Number and Percentages	Control Ads			
	Ham-Rath	*Ham*	*Ham-Lamb-Rath*	*Ham-Lamb*
No. seeing	158	154	146	142
No. choosing	93	84	68	59
Percentage	58.9	54.5	46.6	41.5

Among the lamb ads, the cartoon ad was definitely not as popular as the other two ads tested. The barbecue ad did significantly better than the stretch ad among users, but not among nonusers. (See Exhibit A-8.) Exhibit A-9 highlights the differences in the polar adjective scores for these two ads by including the scores for these ads as well as the scored achieved by the counterpart versions of these ads in the previous quantitative cost-per-serving study.

Exhibit A-10 lends support to respondent opinions voiced during the previous study to the effect that "budget-conscious" meat-buying behavior is defined primarily in terms of stretching meat for several meals or looking for cuts with a maximum amount of edible meat. Again, only moderate support was voiced for the cost-per-serving concept which was still being featured in national lamb-consumer advertising. Respondents were nearly evenly split in their replies when asked if they believed their friends would describe them as "budget-conscious" housewives (44.6% "yes," 43.0% "no," 11.7% "sometimes," 0.7% no answer). A considerable majority defined "budget-conscious" in terms of *money*, rather than *time*, saved. Exhibit A-11 contains replies to questions which probed for the meanings housewives attached to specific budget-conscious phrases.

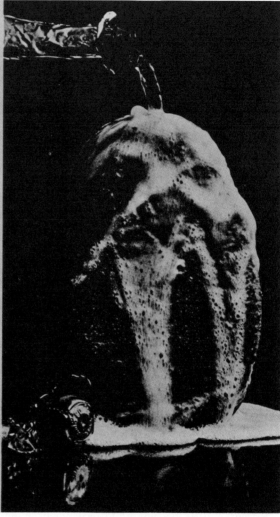

Now Rath has a different ham for every Sunday of the month.

Rath hickory-smoked ham has always been a special, Sunday kind of ham. Now it's even more so. Comes ready-fixed in a choice of elegant new ways. Glazed with honey, soaked with champagne, sauced with tropical fruits. Or straight hickory-smoked.

Here, to make your mouth water, is our champagne recipe: we take one of our hickory-smoked hams, drench it with genuine bubbly, then cook it to winey perfection. Voila! Serve it hot or cold.

Choose Rath Hawaiian, Honey Glazed, Champagne, Hickory-Smoked

Rath®

"Champagne" Ham. Hickory-smoked, of course.

Now a different kind of ham for every Sunday of the month.

Hickory-smoked ham has always been a special, Sunday kind of ham. Now it's even more so. Comes ready-fixed in a choice of elegant new ways. Glazed with honey, soaked with champagne, sauced with tropical fruits. Or straight hickory-smoked.

Here, to make your mouth water, is our champagne recipe: we take our hickory-smoked ham, drench it with genuine bubbly, then cook it to winey perfection. Voila! Serve it hot or cold.

Choose Hawaiian, Honey Glazed, Champagne, Hickory-Smoked

Rath "Champagne" Lamb. Hickory-smoked, of course.

Now Rath has a different kind of lamb for every Sunday of the month.

Rath hickory-smoked lamb has always been a special, Sunday kind of lamb. Now it's even more so. Comes ready-fixed in a choice of elegant new ways. Glazed with honey, soaked with champagne, sauced with tropical fruits. Or straight hickory-smoked.

Here, to make your mouth water, is our champagne recipe: we take our hickory-smoked lamb, drench it with genuine bubbly, then cook it to winey perfection. Voila! Serve it hot or cold.

Choose Rath Lamb...
Hawaiian, Honey Glazed,
Champagne,
Hickory-Smoked

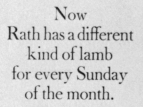

"Champagne" Lamb. Hickory-smoked, of course.

Now a different kind of lamb for every Sunday of the month.

Hickory-smoked lamb has always been a special, Sunday kind of lamb. Now it's even more so. Comes ready-fixed in a choice of elegant new ways. Glazed with honey, soaked with champagne, sauced with tropical fruits. Or straight hickory-smoked.

Here, to make your mouth water, is our champagne recipe: we take our hickory-smoked lamb, drench it with genuine bubbly, then cook it to winey perfection. Voila! Serve it hot or cold.

Choose Hawaiian, Honey Glazed, Champagne, Hickory-Smoked

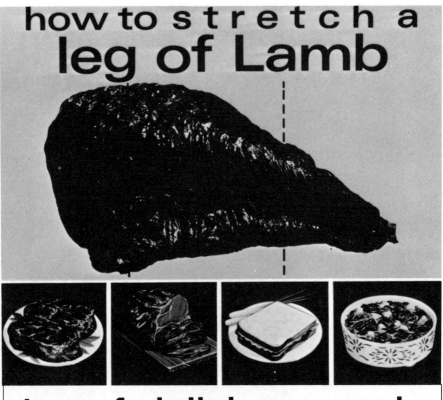

how to stretch a
leg of Lamb

into 4 delicious meals

Versatile . . . that's the word for leg of lamb. It can turn up at the table in many delectably different forms. Have your meat-man cut the leg into sections. Slices from the large end become steaks you can broil for a mid-week treat. Comes Sunday, roast the plump center section, and if there's any left after dinner, put it in the refrigerator for raiders' sandwiches. You still have the small end of the leg. Cut the meat from it and use it to make a hearty stew or exotic lamb kebabs or curry.

That's stretching a leg of lamb. That's stretching your food budget.

For FREE lamb recipes, write:

american lamb council
520 Railway Exchange Building
Denver, Colorado 80202

LAMB
IN
THE CIRCLE
OF GOOD
TASTE

It's true. While all meats are a good buy, it's lamb that is often the real bargaih! U. S. Department of Agriculture studies* prove it. Price-per-pound doesn't tell the whole story. It's the edible meat you get for your money—the meat that gets on your fork that counts. Pound-for-pound, a bone-in leg of lamb gives you 20% more edible cooked meat than a pork loin roast . . . *three times* as much edible meat as turkey, more than *twice* as much edible meat as broiler chicken. And lamb compares well with beef, too. The reason: Lamb is young meat with a lightweight bone structure. There's less waste—less bone and fat—in lamb. You can enjoy the variety that tender, juicy lamb brings to your family dinner table as often as you like—without feeling "extravagant."

For FREE lamb recipes, write:

american lamb council

520 Railway Exchange Building,
909 17th St., Denver, Colo. 80202.

Come to our cookout...
we're having Lamb
Deliciously different—costs less, too!

It's true. The lamb that adds life to the party often costs less* than
other meats and poultry. That's because there's less waste in the lamb.
It's young meat with a light bone structure. After the meal,
you won't see plates piled high with bones and fat. And it's so much fun
to cook lamb out-of-doors . . . to grill tender chops and steaks, to roast a fine

 leg of lamb on your rotisserie. Treat your family
and guests. Save money, too . . . with LAMB.

*U. S. Department of Agriculture Handbook 102

Exhibit A-8

RESPONDENT CHOICE OF THE THREE TEST ADS

A. ALL RESPONDENTS

Number and Percentages	Lamb Ads		
	Stretch	*Cartoon*	*Barbecue*
No. seeing ad	107	104	89
No. choosing ad	57	23	57
Percentage	53.3	22.1	64.0

B. AD CHOICE BY USE

Number and Percentages	Lamb Ads by Use			
	Stretch		*Barbecue*	
	Users	*Nonusers*	*Users*	*Nonusers*
No. seeing ad	55	52	42	47
No. choosing ad	29	28	31	26
Percentage	52.7	53.8	73.8	55.3

C. AD CHOICE BY CONTROL AD SEEN

Ads Seen	*Control Ad*	*Lamb Ad*	*No Choice*	*Total*
	No. Choosing (Percentage)			
Ham vs. Stretch	30	22	2	54
	(55.6)	(40.7)	(3.7)	(100.0)
Ham-Lamb vs. Stretch	15	35	3	53
	(28.3)	(66.0)	(5.7)	(100.0)
Ham vs. Barbecue	19	28	2	49
	(38.8)	(57.1)	(4.1)	(100.0)
Ham-Lamb vs. Barbecue	10	29	1	40
	(25.0)	(72.5)	(2.5)	(100.0)

Exhibit A-9

POLAR ADJECTIVE SCORES OF THE BARBECUE AND STRETCH ADS

| Item | Stretch Ad | | | | Barbecue Ad | | | | Item |
| | Users | | Nonusers | | Users | | Nonusers | | |
	C.P.S. Study*	This Study	C.P.S. Study*	This Study	This Study	C.P.S. Study*	C.P.S. Study*	This Study	
Young	2.4	2.6	3.1	3.0	1.9	1.8	2.1	2.2	Old
Light	3.0	2.8	3.2	3.1	2.3	2.2	2.8	2.4	Heavy
Tough	4.0	3.8	4.0	3.8	4.4	4.1	4.1	4.1	Tender
Inexpensive	3.4	3.0	3.2	2.8	3.3	3.1	3.1	2.6	Expensive
Indoors	2.2	2.4	1.7	2.6	3.6	3.1	3.4	3.7	Outdoors
Lean	2.1	2.4	2.6	2.4	2.0	2.1	2.7	2.1	Fat
Ordinary	2.8	3.2	2.6	3.0	3.8	2.9	3.2	3.6	Special
Little waste	2.4	2.6	1.9	2.5	2.1	2.1	2.4	2.3	Lot of waste
Tasteless	4.2	4.3	3.5	3.8	4.6	4.1	3.5	3.6	Tasty
Poor buy	3.7	3.8	3.7	3.3	3.7	3.2	2.9	3.8	Good buy
Little edible	3.8	3.8	4.0	3.6	4.1	4.0	3.4	3.9	Much edible
Light bone	3.2	2.7	3.0	2.8	2.8	2.2	2.5	2.5	Heavy bone
Can't do much	3.8	3.9	3.8	4.0	3.8	3.2	2.9	3.2	Versatile
One meal	3.9	3.8	3.9	3.9	4.0	2.4	2.4	3.5	Several meals
High cost per serving	2.8	3.1	2.6	3.4	2.9	2.7	3.0	3.2	Low cost per serving
Less cost than others	3.4	3.1	3.4	3.1	3.6	3.4	3.7	3.5	More cost than others
Plain	2.8	3.4	3.0	3.0	3.9	3.0	3.4	3.5	Elegant
Thrifty	2.8	3.0	3.3	2.9	3.3	3.2	3.2	2.7	Extravagant
Commonplace	2.9	3.3	2.9	3.1	3.4	3.0	2.7	3.5	Unusual
Not believable	4.4	4.3	4.4	4.4	4.3	4.3	3.7	4.2	Believable
Old-fashioned	2.8	2.8	3.3	3.1	3.7	4.2	3.9	3.9	Modern
Family	2.8	2.9	2.3	2.8	3.1	2.5	3.1	3.1	Guests
Special	2.9	3.3	3.1	3.0	3.0	3.1	2.8	2.7	Everyday use
Unattractive	3.9	3.9	3.9	4.0	4.5	4.0	4.0	3.9	Attractive
Not for me	3.7	3.9	2.1	2.4	4.0	3.6	2.0	2.1	For me
Avoid it	3.9	3.8	3.0	2.9	4.3	4.1	2.8	3.3	Try it
Skip it	3.6	3.7	2.7	3.1	3.7	3.5	2.9	3.0	Read it
Not buy	3.9	3.7	2.5	2.5	4.2	3.8	2.5	2.9	Like to buy

Scale Used: 1 2 3 4 5.

* Refers to the quantitative cost-per-serving study of February 1967, described in American Sheep Producers Council (C).

Exhibit A-10

MEANING OF THE TERM "BUDGET-CONSCIOUS"

In the purchase of food items for her family, Mrs. Smith is often described by her friends as a "budget-conscious" housewife.

MRS. SMITH

	Would Definitely	Would Probably	Would Most Likely Not	No Comment	Total
Look for the cheapest cuts of meat	54 (18.0)	119 (39.7)	124 (41.3)	3 (1.0)	300 (100.0)
Be guided in her meat selection by Advertised Sale Prices	174 (58.0)	101 (33.6)	23 (7.7)	2 (0.7)	300 (100.0)
Look for meat with lowest costs on a per-serving basis	123 (41.0)	106 (35.4)	67 (22.3)	4 (1.3)	300 (100.0)
Look for meat she could stretch to serve more than one meal	186 (62.0)	93 (31.0)	19 (6.3)	2 (0.7)	300 (100.0)
Reduce the portions of meat served to each member of her family if necessary to stay within her budget	26 (8.7)	94 (31.3)	177 (59.0)	3 (1.0)	300 (100.0)
Look for cuts of meat with the maximum amount of edible meat	235 (78.3)	48 (16.0)	14 (4.7)	3 (1.0)	300 (100.0)
Look for lowest priced meat on a per package basis	55 (18.3)	94 (31.3)	148 (49.4)	3 (1.0)	300 (100.0)
Look for lowest priced meat on a per pound basis	114 (38.0)	115 (38.3)	65 (21.7)	6 (2.0)	300 (100.0)

Exhibit A-11

MEANINGS OF SPECIFIC BUDGET-CONSCIOUS PHRASES

	1st Choice	2nd Choice
A. "STRETCHES INTO MORE THAN ONE MEAL" MEANS:		
I can reduce costs by using leftovers for two or more meals.	137	49
I can save time because I wouldn't have to shop tomorrow.	32	60
I can get more usable meat from my purchase.	87	110
The cost per serving will be lower.	17	62
I would have to contend with unwanted leftovers.	11	2
None of these—then what?	2	1
No answer.	14	16
Total	300	300
B. "MORE EDIBLE MEAT" MEANS:		
Less waste and a likely higher per-serving cost.	27	16
A lower per-serving cost because of less waste.	86	106
A greater amount of consumable meat for my money.	146	100
Lighter bone structure and therefore young and tender meat.	24	47
Meat that is easy to prepare and carve	9	24
None of these—then what?	3	0
No answer.	5	7
Total	300	300

C. "LEAN, LESS BONE, LESS WASTE" MEANS:

	1st Choice	2nd Choice
Meat that will probably be tough and tasteless.	5	1
Just what I'd like to serve my family.	118	92
More meat at a lower per-serving cost.	72	84
An expensive cut that I couldn't afford.	8	7
The type of purchase I'm always on the look out for.	91	106
None of these—then what?	1	2
No answer.	5	8
Total	300	300

APPENDIX B

Excerpts from Headline and Copy Test for Leg of Lamb Ad—June 1967

PURPOSE:

The purpose of the study was to evaluate three alternative headlines and copy for the leg of lamb stretch ad.

METHOD:

Three hundred personal at-home interviews were conducted among housewives in the Evanston and Berwyn suburbs of Chicago. As seen below, the distribution of frequency of lamb use matched almost perfectly with the distribution found in the Chicago area subsample in the quantitative cost-per-serving study.

| | *Frequency of Lamb Use — Chicago Area* | | | |
| | *Previous Study* | | *This Study* | |
Lamb Use	*No.*	*%*	*No.*	*%*
Frequently	24	24.0	64	21.3
Once in a while	22	22.0	73	24.3
Seldom	26	26.0	79	26.3
Never	28	28.0	84	28.1
Total	100	100.0	300	100.0

Each respondent was shown one of three test ads for lamb as well as a control ham ad. One of the three lamb ads (called **Ad** 1 in this study) was identical to the stretch ad tested in the June 1967 "Product and Ad Image Study." (See Exhibit A-5.) The other two test ads (called Ad 2 and Ad 3) are contained here as Exhibits B-1 and B-2. The control ham ad was the champagne ad in which all reference to Rath had been removed. (See Exhibit A-2.)

COMMENTS:

As in previous studies, respondents were asked to choose one of the ads presented to them. In this case the choice was between the control ad and the one lamb ad which each respondent was shown. Exhibit B-3 presents the ad choice findings by lamb use. The report noted that the subsample sizes were too small to attach significance to these figures.

A number of significant findings (95% level) did emerge, however, by analyzing changes in respondent opinions about lamb before and after seeing the test ads. Exhibit B-4 is representative of six tables which presented before-and-after data for users and nonusers for each of the three lamb ads. The changes that emerged in each of these tables were then summarized in the table shown here as Exhibit B-5. For lamb users, a 0.4 change was required to constitute a significant change; for nonusers a 0.6 change was necessary.

Exhibits B-6 and B-7 present the average responses to the same polar adjective pairs used in previous studies. Among users, no significant differences among the three lamb ads emerged. Among nonusers, Ad 3 came through as significantly younger than Ad 1 and lighter-boned than Ad 2. (A0.6 difference was required for significance in the findings for users; in findings for nonusers a 1.0 difference was required.)

Since there were few differences among the lamb ads, findings from all lamb ads were combined to arrive at a comparative ad profile for both lamb and ham. (See Exhibit B-7.) Individual ratings falling outside of the 2.5–3.5 range were considered significantly different from neutral.

The report of study findings concluded with a number of tables showing demographic differences between the lamb user and nonuser. These findings verified earlier ASPC studies which characterized the lamb user as more likely to be older than the nonuser and of a higher income; to have the head of the house a white-collar worker; to have fewer children at home; and not to be employed full time.

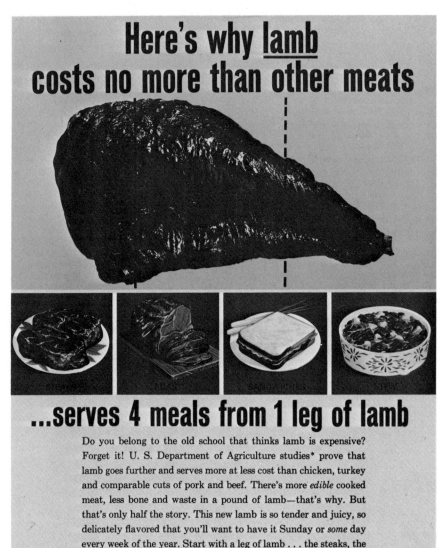

Here's why lamb costs no more than other meats

...serves 4 meals from 1 leg of lamb

Do you belong to the old school that thinks lamb is expensive? Forget it! U. S. Department of Agriculture studies* prove that lamb goes further and serves more at less cost than chicken, turkey and comparable cuts of pork and beef. There's more *edible* cooked meat, less bone and waste in a pound of lamb—that's why. But that's only half the story. This new lamb is so tender and juicy, so delicately flavored that you'll want to have it Sunday or *some* day every week of the year. Start with a leg of lamb . . . the steaks, the roast, the sandwiches and the stew. It's a promise—when you finish it off you'll be hooked . . . on lamb!

*U. S. Department of Agriculture Handbook 102.
For FREE lamb recipes, write:

american lamb council
520 Railway Exchange Building
Denver, Colorado 80202

LAMB
IN THE CIRCLE OF GOOD TASTE

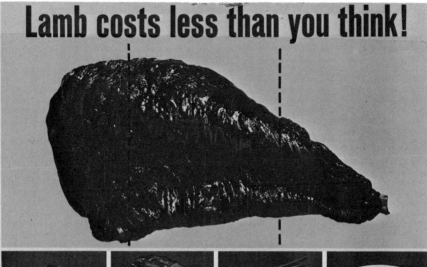

Lamb costs less than you think!

STEAKS   ROAST   SANDWICHES   STEW

4 delicious meals from 1 leg of lamb...

Enjoy the variety that tender, juicy lamb brings to your family dinner table without feeling "extravagant." Lamb costs less than you think . . . less than many other meats. U. S. Department of Agriculture studies* prove it. Pound for pound, a bone-in leg of lamb gives you *three times* as much edible cooked meat as turkey, *twice as much* as chicken, *20% more* than a pork loin roast. And lamb compares well with beef, too. The reason: Today's lamb is young meat with a light bone structure. There's less waste, less bone and fat, in lamb. Think about that next time you shop for meat. Take home a leg of lamb!

*U. S. Department of Agriculture Handbook 102

For FREE lamb recipes, write:

american lamb council

520 Railway Exchange Building
Denver, Colorado 80202

L**a**mB

IN
THE CIRCLE
OF GOOD
TASTE

L

Exhibit B-3

AD CHOICE BY LAMB USE

Ad Choice	Lamb Users	Lamb Nonusers	Total
"How To Stretch. . . . ." Ad No. 1			
No. seeing	82	32	114
No. choosing	45	12	57
Percentage	54.9	37.5	50.0
"Here's Why Lamb Costs No More. . ." Ad No. 2			
No. seeing	75	28	103
No. choosing	50	13	63
Percentage	66.7	46.4	61.2
"Lamb Costs Less Than You Think. . ." Ad No. 3			
No. seeing	59	24	83
No. choosing	41	7	48
Percentage	69.5	29.2	57.8
Ham Ad			
No. seeing	216	84	300
No. choosing	79	51	130
Percentage	36.6	60.7	43.3

RESPONDENT OPINIONS OF LAMB BEFORE AND AFTER SEEING AD NO. 1

Lamb Users - Ad No. 1 "How to Stretch. . . ."

Opinions	Lamb		Ham	
	Before	After	Before	After
For my personal enjoyment	2.1	2.1	1.9	1.9
Suitability for a family meal	2.0	2.0	1.9	1.9
A tasty and satisfying dish	2.0	2.0	1.8	1.9
Suitability for children	2.0	2.1	1.9	1.9
For an enjoyable gathering of friends	2.5	2.3	1.6	1.6
Low cost per serving	3.2	2.9	2.1	2.2
A good buy	2.7	2.4	2.0	2.0
Can be stretched to serve other meals	2.8	2.2	1.5	1.6
Costs less to serve than other meats	3.2	3.1	2.3	2.4
Always dependable	2.5	2.3	1.8	1.6
Versatile, can be served in many forms	2.6	2.1	1.7	1.6
Variety at a low cost	3.1	2.7	2.1	2.1
Little bone and waste	2.8	2.5	2.3	2.0
More edible meat than many other meats	2.7	2.5	2.0	1.9
Costs more than other meats	2.1	2.4	2.9	2.7
Can do a lot with it	2.8	2.1	1.8	1.6
Can be cut into several sections to be served in different ways	2.6	1.9	1.9	1.6
Young meat with a light bone structure	2.2	2.0	2.5	2.2
Number of Respondents	82			

Scale Used: 1 2 3 4 5.

Exhibit B-5

CHANGE IN AVERAGE RESPONSES OF LAMB AND HAM OPINIONS AFTER SEEING ADS

Opinions	Lamb Users			Lamb Nonusers			All Respondents	
	Ad No. 1	Ad No. 2	Ad No. 3	Ad No. 1	Ad No. 2	Ad No. 3	Lamb	Ham
For my personal enjoyment	.0	.0	.0	.2	.2	.3	.1	.0
Suitability for a family meal	.0	.2	.2	.4	.2	.7	.2	.0
A tasty and satisfying dish	.0	.1	(.1)	.2	.3	.1	.1	.0
Suitability for children	(.1)	(.1)	.0	.3	(.1)	.1	.0	(.1)
For an enjoyable gathering of friends	.2	.1	.6	.0	.2	.3	.3	.0
Low cost per serving	.3	.2	.2	(.1)	.4	.4	.2	(.1)
A good buy	.3	.2	.3	.1	.8	.7	.4	.0
Can be stretched to serve other meals	.6	.4	.4	.3	1.0	.8	.5	(.1)
Costs less to serve than other meats	.1	.3	.4	.0	.7	.5	.3	.0
Always dependable	.2	.0	.1	.1	.0	.3	.1	.1
Versatile, can be served in many forms	.5	.2	.2	.2	1.0	.4	.4	.1
Variety at a low cost	.4	.4	.4	.1	.6	.0	.3	.0
Little bone and waste	.3	.3	.5	.1	.9	.3	.4	.1
More edible meat than many other meats	.2	.4	.4	.3	.4	.3	.3	.2
Costs more than other meats	.3	.1	.2	.1	.6	.4	.3	(.1)
Can do a lot with it	.7	.3	.3	.5	1.1	.1	.5	.1
Can be cut into several sections to be served in different ways	.7	.2	.1	.5	1.5	.3	.4	.1
Young meat with a light bone structure	.2	.1	.3	.6	.6	(.3)	.2	.2
Favorable change	5.0	**3.5**	4.6	4.0	10.5	6.0	5.0	0.9
Unfavorable change	0.1	0.1	0.1	0.1	0.1	0.3	0.0	0.4
Net change	4.9	3.4	4.5	3.9	10.4	5.7	5.0	0.5

Notes: 1) Changes in parentheses are unfavorable.
2) For lamb users, a 0.4 change was required to constitute a significant (95% level) change; for nonusers, a 0.6 change was necessary.

Exhibit B-6

AVERAGE RESPONSES ON POLAR ADJECTIVE PAIRS AFTER SEEING ADS

Item	Ad No. 1	Lamb Users Ad No. 2	Ad No. 3	Item
Young	2.3	2.4	2.3	Old
Light	2.6	2.7	2.4	Heavy
Tough	4.1	4.0	4.3	Tender
Inexpensive	2.9	2.8	2.8	Expensive
Indoors	2.0	1.6	1.8	Outdoors
Lean	2.0	2.2	1.9	Fat
Ordinary	3.0	2.9	2.9	Special
Little waste	2.0	2.4	2.2	Lot of waste
Tasteless	4.5	4.3	4.3	Tasty
Poor buy	4.2	3.8	3.8	Good buy
Little edible	4.4	4.1	4.2	Much edible
Light bone	2.5	2.5	2.5	Heavy bone
Can't do much	4.2	4.3	4.1	Versatile
One meal	4.2	4.0	4.0	Several meals
High cost per serving	3.2	3.2	3.2	Low cost per serving
Less cost than others	3.2	3.0	3.3	More cost than others
Plain	3.4	3.0	3.1	Elegant
Thrifty	3.0	2.9	2.7	Extravagant
Commonplace	3.2	2.7	2.8	Unusual
Not believable	4.5	4.3	4.4	Believable
Old-fashioned	3.7	3.2	3.5	Modern
Family	3.0	2.4	2.5	Guests
Special	3.3	3.6	3.7	Everyday use
Unattractive	4.2	4.0	4.0	Attractive
Not for me	4.1	4.2	4.2	For me
Avoid it	4.2	4.2	4.3	Try it
Skip it	4.2	3.8	4.1	Read it
Not buy	4.3	4.2	4.2	Like to buy

Scale Used: 1 2 3 4 5.

Exhibit B-6 (cont.)

Item	Ad No. 1	Ad No. 2	Ad No. 3	Item
		Lamb Nonusers		
Young	3.2	2.9	2.1	Old
Light	3.2	3.2	2.8	Heavy
Tough	3.5	3.3	4.1	Tender
Inexpensive	3.5	3.4	3.5	Expensive
Indoors	2.4	2.3	2.1	Outdoors
Lean	2.2	2.4	2.1	Fat
Ordinary	2.7	3.0	3.0	Special
Little waste	2.6	2.7	1.9	Lot of waste
Tasteless	3.0	2.6	3.5	Tasty
Poor buy	3.1	3.1	3.3	Good buy
Little edible	3.4	3.7	3.8	Much edible
Light bone	3.0	3.4	2.4	Heavy bone
Can't do much	3.6	3.0	3.5	Versatile
One meal	3.8	3.6	3.7	Several meals
High cost per serving	2.8	2.9	2.4	Low cost per serving
Less cost than others	3.5	2.8	3.6	More cost than others
Plain	3.1	2.8	3.2	Elegant
Thrifty	3.2	3.1	3.5	Extravagant
Commonplace	3.1	2.9	2.8	Unusual
Not believable	4.1	4.0	4.2	Believable
Old-fashioned	3.2	3.3	3.8	Modern
Family	3.3	3.1	3.5	Guests
Special	3.1	3.5	3.2	Everyday use
Unattractive	3.8	3.2	3.7	Attractive
Not for me	2.9	2.1	2.1	For me
Avoid it	3.4	2.8	3.2	Try it
Skip it	3.4	2.6	3.0	Read it
Not buy	3.1	2.3	2.7	Like to buy

Scale Used: 1 2 3 4 5.

Exhibit B-7

AVERAGE RESPONSES ON POLAR ADJECTIVE PAIRS FOR LAMB AND HAM AFTER SEEING ADS

Item	All Respondents		*Item*
	Lamb	*Ham*	
Young	2.5	2.4	Old
Light	2.7	2.9	Heavy
Tough	4.0	4.1	Tender
Inexpensive	3.0	3.2	Expensive
Indoors	1.9	2.0	Outdoors
Lean	2.1	2.2	Fat
Ordinary	2.9	3.2	Special
Little waste	2.2	2.1	Lot of waste
Tasteless	4.1	4.3	Tasty
Poor buy	3.8	4.0	Good buy
Little edible	4.1	4.3	Much edible
Light bone	2.6	2.7	Heavy bone
Can't do much	4.0	4.3	Versatile
One meal	4.0	4.4	Several meals
High cost per serving	3.1	3.4	Low cost per serving
Less cost than others	3.2	2.9	More cost than others
Plain	3.1	3.4	Elegant
Thrifty	3.0	3.0	Extravagant
Commonplace	2.9	2.9	Unusual
Not believable	4.3	4.1	Believable
Old-fashioned	3.5	4.1	Modern
Family	2.8	3.4	Guests
Special	3.4	2.9	Everyday use
Unattractive	3.9	4.2	Attractive
Not for me	3.7	4.2	For me
Avoid it	3.9	4.2	Try it
Skip it	3.7	3.8	Read it
Not buy	3.9	4.2	Like to buy

Scale Used: 1 2 3 4 5.

QUESTIONS

1. Based on the findings of the May 1967 study, which aspects of the barbecue and stretch ads would you incorporate into lamb advertising?

2. Are there limitations to the usefulness of these data (in Appendix A)?

3. Assuming that the "stretch" idea does have merit, which of the ads tested in June 1967 is best for the Lamb Council? Why?

American

Sheep Producers Council (E)

Pupillary Reactions As
A Measure Of Advertising Impact

The trade association uses a method of "pupillary responses" to test seven lamb ads. The research findings include pupillary responses, verbatim responses, and ad choices by user/nonuser and other demographic respondent breakdowns.

In the mid-1960s American Sheep Producers Council (ASPC) executives commissioned a series of research studies in an effort to bring greater copy direction to the Council's national consumer advertising for lamb. It was believed that carefully formulated copy themes aimed specifically at high-priority consumer groups would ultimately result in the greatest possible increase in the United States consumption of lamb. American Sheep Producers Council cases (A) through (D) outline the background of ASPC, its marketing/advertising environment, and the results of five separate studies conducted during the 1964-67 period. These studies as a group were conducted nationally and within selected metropolitan areas, employed personal at-home interviews and in-depth group interviews, classified respondents according to demographic and psychographic dimensions as well as according to user/nonuser categories, and elicited responses from subjects ranging from opinions, attitudes, and beliefs about lamb/meat buying to choices of specific test lamb advertisements.

In early 1967, the Council commissioned Lawrence M. Krueger, a Purdue University psychologist, to conduct a study of a nature considerably different from previous ASPC studies. This study would assess the relative effectiveness of seven lamb advertisements on the basis of the *differing pupillary responses* evoked by the ads among consumers.

PUPILLARY REACTIONS TO ADVERTISEMENTS

The following is taken from a preliminary report from Professor Krueger to ASPC:

Hess [*Scientific American*, April 1965] has shown that an increase in pupil size is related to interest or preference, oftentimes on a subconscious level, while decrease or constriction is related to dislike or unpleasantness. Although many studies have been conducted using advertising as stimulus materials, very little of this work has been published. However, those studies published show a positive correlation between pupillary change and some criterion [sales, coupon returns, recognition, recall scores, etc.]. These correlations have been attained in some cases where the correlation between verbal response and the criterion was low.

For the ASPC study, each respondent was seated in a booth and shown a series of slides consisting of control (blank) slides and different lamb advertisements. As subjects were shown the slides, a 16 mm. movie camera recorded any changes taking place in their pupils. Since the control slides were matched in brightness to the advertisement slides, any pupillary change that took place was assumed to be attributable to a factor other than light.

Only the pictorial sections and headlines of the lamb ads were used. The entire copy was not included, since the primary purpose of this method was regarded to be to measure the visual impact of the ad on the subject. Appendix A summarizes the findings of this study.

APPENDIX A

Excerpts from Pupilometric Study, June 1967

PURPOSE:

The purpose of the study was to measure the relative impact of seven lamb advertisements on the basis of pupillary reactions to the advertisements by subjects.

METHOD:

Fifty women, selected at random from Lafayette, Indiana, served as subjects. Of these, 20 were lamb users and 30 were nonusers. Each subject viewed all seven lamb advertisements tested. Advertisements were presented in the form of slides. Interspersed among the lamb slides were a number of control (blank) slides, which were matched in brightness to the advertisement slides to assure that any pupillary change taking place would be due to a factor other than light.

As subjects were presented the ads, a 16 mm. movie camera recorded all pupillary changes in their eyes. The resulting 22,000 16 mm. film frames were measured individually and the changes in pupillary size from the control slides to the advertisement slides were computed. The women were also subjected to semidepth interviews to obtain specific favorable and unfavorable comments on the ads, as well as their ranking of which ads they liked best.

The ads tested are included here as Exhibits A-1 through A-7. For test purposes, however, the copy portion of each ad was not included, since the pictorial sections and headlines of the ads were regarded as the primary determinants of advertising visual impact.

COMMENTS:

Each ad was actually evaluated against three separate measures: pupillary reactions, the relative number of favorable versus unfavorable comments, and an index based on the subjects' ranking of the ads. Exhibit A-8 summarizes the pupillary changes resulting from the ads tested. As can be seen, 11 different ads were actually tested, since black-and-white and color versions of three of the ads were used in addition to two caption-print styles for another. For only two ads—the black-and-white version of the steer ad (No. 4) and the "More Eatin' Meat" ad (No. 7)—were the differences between users and nonusers significant at a 95% level. All other differences were not significant, although for some a clear trend was evident which, the report noted, might assume significance with a larger sample size. Exhibit A-9 breaks down the pupillary reactions according to income groups. No significance tests were performed on these differences.

After viewing the seven ads, subjects were asked for opinions on each ad. All comments were recorded and classified as either favorable, unfavorable, or indifferent. The table below summarizes these comments for the entire sample.

	Advertisement	% Favorable Comments	% Unfavorable Comments	% Indifferent Comments
No. 5	Cookout	72	19	9
No. 7	More eatin' meat	69	29	2
No. 3	How to stretch	68	30	2
No. 1	Lamb chops and peaches	62	34	4
No. 4	Steer	52	40	8
No. 6	Chicken with pig	42	50	8
No. 2	Study proves	40	53	7

These comments were then analyzed in detail for each advertisement. In each case responses were broken down according to respondent age, income, and lamb use. Exhibit A-10 contains such data for one of the test ads.

As a final measure, subjects were asked to rank the seven ads according to their first, second, third, and last choice. Exhibit A-11 contains details on these ratings.

American Sheep Producers Council (E)

LIST OF EXHIBITS

Exhibit	Contents
A-1	Ad # 1: Lamb Chops and Peaches
A-2	Ad # 2: "How to stretch"
A-3	Ad # 3: "Study Proves"
A-4	Ad # 4: Steer
A-5	Ad # 5: Cookout
A-6	Ad # 6: Chicken with Pig
A-7	Ad # 7: "More Eatin' Meat"
A-8	Summary of Pupillary Reactions to the Test Ads
A-9	Pupillary Responses by Income Groups
A-10	Comments on Ad # 5 (Cookout Ad)
A-11	Verbal Preferences for Lamb Ads

AD # 1: LAMB CHOPS AND PEACHES

STUDY PROVES Merchandising of New Netted Lamb Roasts Pays Off in Sales.

Test Market Report #291 Spring, 1966
Bryan and College Station, Texas

A 7-store study by Market Development Section
Dept. of Agricultural Economics and Sociology
Texas A & M University

376

LAMB...boneless, netted rolled roasts score a hit with customers!

On the first weekend of the promotion the Ramada Inn at College Station, Texas, offered new netted lamb on its popular Sunday buffet, and served 90 portions of the boneless, rolled roasts to its patrons. There were so many questions..."Where can I buy lamb like that?" ...that the chef posted a sign on the buffet table directing dine-out housewives to their supermarket meat counters!

THE FIRST WEEK, LAMB SALES IN 7 TEXAS STORES WENT UP 271%!

Average Weekly Sales, in Pounds, of Regular Lamb Cuts and Boneless Lamb Roasts

PERIOD	BONE-IN LAMB CUTS	BONELESS LAMB ROASTS				ALL LAMB CUTS
		Shoulder Roast	Leg Roast	Scotch Roast	Total	
Pre-Promotion (5 weeks)						
Average Per Store	43	—	—	—	—	43
Total All Stores	302	—	—	—	—	302
Sales Index	100	—	—	—	—	100
Promotion (2 weeks average)						
Average Per Store	50	37	24	16	77	127
Total All Stores	347	257	165	110	532	879
Sales Index	115	—	—	—	—	291
PRICE IN THE MEAT COUNTER:	na*	$1.19 per lb.	$1.39 per lb.	59¢ per lb.	na*	na*

*na—not applicable.

4 WEEKS AFTER THE PROMOTION, LAMB SALES ARE STILL UP A GOOD 62%!

PERIOD	LAMB AVERAGE	7-STORE TOTAL
5 weeks prior to promotion	100*	302 lbs.
2 weeks promotion	291	879 lbs.
4 weeks after promotion	162	488 lbs.

*302 lbs. = 100

In addition, the new netted lamb roasts renewed consumer interest in ALL lamb. Four weeks after the two-week promotion ended, half of the 62% increase in lamb sales was in *regular* cuts of lamb...the other half in new netted products.

IT'S AS EASY AS 1-2-3 TO PROCESS LAMB THIS POPULAR AND PROFITABLE NEW WAY!

PROCESSING LAMB IN ELASTIC NET
Bone and trim the lamb to be processed. Lightly coat all inner seams and bone cavity with Salmonella-free powdered egg white – a binder that is tasteless, color-less, accepted by the USDA. Shape the lamb into a roll with the hands. Roll the shoulder or leg so that it may be carved across the grain. (Make Scotch roast by stuffing breast evenly and fully with lean ground lamb. No egg white is needed.) Cut elastic net approximately 1" longer than the roll. Slip over small end of tube, allowing some overlap. Now, using plunger, push lamb through tube into net. Hand or machine tying is eliminated. In 10 seconds – a compact roast. Binder holds lamb together for easy carving.

what
do you
MEAN...
lamb
costs
no more
than
beef?

All red meats are a good buy. But U. S. Department of Agriculture studies* show that lamb is often the *best* buy of all. Lamb is not as expensive as you might think. You *can* afford to buy lamb and let its delicately different taste bring new variety to your menus. Take two comparable cuts of the same size, for example. A lamb shoulder roast and a beef chuck roast. U. S. D. A. tests prove there is 25% more edible lean meat for your fork in the lamb than there is in the beef. You could pay almost one-fourth more for the lamb, if there were such a price difference in the store, and save money with the extra servings of lean edible meat you'd get from the lamb. You pay just as much per pound in the package for bone, fat and waste as you pay for lean edible meat. You get *less* bone, *less* fat, *less* waste . . . in lamb! Think about that next time you ask yourself "What can I fix for dinner tonight?" Think lamb.

*Based on:
U.S.D.A., Agricultural Handbook 102, Food Yields Summarized by Different Stages of Preparation.
N. Y. State College of Agriculture, Cornell University, Handbook, Cost Per Serving.
Ohio State University, Marketing Information for Consumers.

Lemon-Cranberry Lamb Shoulder

4 to 5 pound pre-carved square shoulder of lamb*
Salt and pepper to taste
1 large lemon
1 cup jellied cranberry sauce
½ teaspoon nutmeg
Parsley

*Have meatman pre-slice lamb on band saw and tie. Place lamb on rack in shallow roasting pan. Sprinkle with salt and pepper to taste. Bake in slow oven (325°) 1½ hours. Drain off drippings. Meanwhile, cut lemon into thin slices; cut each lemon slice in half. Combine cranberry sauce and nutmeg. Cook over low heat, stirring constantly, until melted. Pour cranberry mixture over lamb. Arrange lemon slices in lamb slits. Bake 30 minutes, or until meat thermometer registers 175°-180°, depending upon desired degree of doneness. Baste lamb with cranberry mixture frequently during cooking period. Garnish with parsley.

Low-cost Lamb Riblets star in this Super Supper Dish

4 pounds lamb riblets
2 tablespoons butter or margarine
1 package (1½ ounces) dehydrated onion soup mix
1 cup water
1 large tomato, chopped
1 large green pepper, chopped
¼ teaspoon pepper
Salt to taste
1 package (10 oz.s) frozen cut green beans
Cooked rice

Brown riblets on all sides in melted butter or margarine. Drain off excess drippings. Combine water and soup mix. Add soup mix, tomato, green pepper and pepper to riblets. Salt to taste. Cover and cook over low heat about 45 minutes. Add green beans, cover and cook 10 to 15 minutes longer or until beans and lamb are tender. Serve over cooked rice.

For FREE lamb recipes and a cost-per-serving chart for meats and poultry, write:

american lamb council

Dept. LX-466, 520 Railway Exchange Building
909 17th Street, Denver, Colorado 80202

Come to our cookout...
we're having Lamb
Deliciously different—costs less, too!

It's true. The lamb that adds life to the party often costs
less* than other meats and poultry. That's because there's
less waste in the lamb. It's young meat with a light
bone structure. After the meal, you won't see plates piled high
with bones and fat. And it's so much fun to cook lamb
out-of-doors . . . to grill tender chops and steaks, to roast a fine
leg of lamb on your rotisserie. Treat your family
and guests. Save money, too . . . with LAMB.

La**mb**

IN
THE CIRCLE
OF GOOD
TASTE

*U. S. Department of Agriculture Handbook 102

AD # 6: CHICKEN WITH PIG

It's true. While all meats are a good buy, it's lamb that is often the real bargain! U. S. Department of Agriculture studies* prove it. Price-per-pound doesn't tell the whole story. It's the edible meat you get for your money—the meat that gets on your fork that counts. Pound-for-pound, a bone-in leg of lamb gives you 20% more edible cooked meat than a pork loin roast . . . *three times* as much edible meat as turkey, more than *twice* as much edible meat as broiler chicken. And lamb compares well with beef, too. The reason: Lamb is young meat with a lightweight bone structure. There's less waste—less bone and fat—in lamb. You can enjoy the variety that tender, juicy lamb brings to your family dinner table as often as you like—without feeling "extravagant."

For FREE lamb recipes, write:

american lamb council

520 Railway Exchange Building,
909 17th St., Denver, Colo. 80202.

LAMB
gives you more eatin' meat for your money

SEE HERE:

chicken -- uncooked

portion of cooked chicken that is *edible*

waste – bone and fat – from chicken

same weight leg of lamb – uncooked

portion of cooked leg of lamb that is *edible*

waste – bone and fat – from leg of lamb

All meats are good buys and good for you—but compare the amount of "eatin' meat" in lamb with the meat that gets on your fork from chicken, pork, turkey, even beef. Compare the bones and fat left on plates or platter when it's time to do dishes. There's more good eatin' meat, less waste in lamb. U. S. Department of Agriculture studies prove it in cut after cut. * Lamb is young meat with a light bone structure. It's this *inside* story that so often makes lamb the real bargain. Don't wait another day to enjoy tender juicy lamb. And when you serve it to your family, you can even brag a bit about the money you saved!

*U. S. Department of Agriculture Handbook 102.

HOW TO ROAST A LEG OF LAMB

Place leg of lamb on rack in shallow roasting pan. Season. Roast at 325° for 35 to 40 minutes per pound or until meat thermometer registers 175° to 180°, depending upon desired degree of doneness. VARIATIONS: Baste the lamb while it's roasting with your favorite Italian dressing or any frozen fruit juice concentrate.

LAMB american lamb council

For FREE lamb recipes, write:

520 Railway Exchange Building
Denver, Colorado 80202

IN THE CIRCLE OF GOOD TASTE

Exhibit A-8

SUMMARY OF PUPILLARY REACTIONS TO THE TEST ADS

	Advertisement	% Pupillary Change		Total	Significance Level*
		Users	*Nonusers*		
No. 1	Chops and Peaches (b&w)	+1.64	+1.01	+1.80	.001
No. 5	Cookout (color)	+2.51	+1.18	+1.68	.001
No. 5	Cookout (b&w)	+1.39	+1.51	+1.45	.005
No. 4	Steer (color)	+1.77	+1.10	+1.37	.001
No. 7	"More eatin' meat" (color)	+1.92	+0.11	+0.84	.10
No. 4	Steer (b&w)	+1.50	+0.10	+0.72	.05
No. 3	"How to stretch" (color)	+0.67	+0.15	+0.32	N.S.
No. 2	"Study Proves" (bold print)	+0.35	-0.10	+0.19	N.S.
No. 1	Chops and Peaches (color)	+0.62	-0.22	+0.12	N.S.
No. 6	Chicken with Pig (color)	-0.03	-0.77	-0.35	N.S.
No. 2	"Study Proves" (fine print)	+0.92	-1.47	-1.16	.01

* Applies only to the per cent changes for the total sample. A significance level of .001 indicates that the probability of this difference occurring by chance alone is less than 1 in 1,000.

Exhibit A-9

PUPILLARY RESPONSES BY INCOME GROUPS

	Advertisement	Monthly Take-home Pay		
		Less than $500 (n-26)	*$502-$700 (n-13)*	*Over $700 (n-11)*
No. 1	Chops and Peaches (b&w)	+2.15	+1.00	+2.27
No. 5	Cookout (color)	+1.12	+0.84	+2.93
No. 5	Cookout (b&w)	+2.17	+1.28	+1.30
No. 4	Steer (color)	+1.23	+0.57	+1.90
No. 7	"More eatin' meat" (color)	+0.89	-0.11	+2.27
No. 4	Steer (b&w)	+1.04	-0.08	+1.17
No. 3	"How to stretch" (color)	+1.18	-0.59	+1.26
No. 2	"Study Proves" (bold print)	+1.11	-0.52	-0.18
No. 1	Chops and Peaches (color)	-0.28	-0.16	+0.85
No. 6	Chicken with Pig (color)	+0.40	-1.50	+0.52
No. 2	"Study Proves" (fine print)	+0.23	-1.79	-1.45

COMMENTS ON AD NO. 5 (COOKOUT AD)

		Users		
		By Income		0-29
	High	Med.	Low	
Favorable Comments				
Looks good, delicious, colorful, love it	6	11	17	3
Fun, refreshing, love to be there	9	7	14	3
Pleasant surprise, didn't know about lamb bbq.	7	4	-	-
Appeals to youth, adults, children	2	5	-	-
I like the "Circle" idea	1	3	-	-
Thought of lamb as for adults only	-	1	-	-
Subtotal	25	31	31	6
	(78%)	(62%)	(69%)	(30%)
Neither Favorable Nor Unfavorable				
Add sub-title "Come to Our Lamb Cook-out"	-	-	1	1
Emphasize Lamb more — "Lamb-K-Bob"	-	-	2	1
Add a picnic table setting	-	-	2	-
All meats on skewer haven't same cooking time	1	-	-	-
Meat pieces too large for shishkabob	-	2	-	-
Portray some adults in swimsuits	1	1	-	-
This ad is just fair	-	1	1	1
Other	-	-	-	-
Subtotal	2	4	6	3
	(6%)	(8%)	(13%)	(15%)
Unfavorable or Critical				
Don't like circle	2	6	3	4
No impact — needs more color	-	6	3	4
Print too small — too hard to read	1	1	-	1
More expensive than chicken	-	2	-	-
Need more information on lamb bbq'ing	2	-	2	2
Hard to tell what's being advertised	-	-	-	-
Other	-	-	-	-
Subtotal	5	15	8	11
	(16%)	(30%)	(18%)	(55%)
Grand Total	32	50	45	20
	(100%)	(100%)	(100%)	(100%)

Note: Multiple comments were recorded for most respondents.

Exhibit A-10 (cont.)

By Age		Nonusers					
			By Income			By Age	
30-49	50+	High	Med.	Low	0-29	30-49	50+
20	11	11	5	33	30	17	2
16	12	6	12	38	32	21	1
7	4	-	1	6	5	2	-
6	1	2	-	-	1	1	-
4	-	-	2	5	5	2	-
1	-	-	-	1	1	-	-
54	28	19	20	83	74	43	3
(71%)	(85%)	(73%)	(75%)	(75%)	(75%)	(74%)	(60%)
-	-	-	-	-	-	-	-
-	1	-	-	-	-	-	-
2	-	-	1	-	-	1	-
1	-	-	-	-	-	-	-
2	-	-	1	1	-	2	-
2	-	-	-	1	-	1	-
1	-	1	-	4	5	-	-
-	-	-	-	3	2	1	-
8	1	1	2	9	7	5	0
(10%)	(3%)	(4%)	(7%)	(8%)	(7%)	(9%)	(0%)
7	-	3	-	7	7	4	-
4	2	2	2	6	6	4	-
-	1	-	1	-	-	1	-
2	-	-	-	-	-	-	-
1	1	1	-	3	3	1	-
-	-	-	1	1	1	-	1
-	-	-	1	-	-	-	1
14	4	6	5	17	17	10	2
(19%)	(12%)	(23%)	(18%)	(17%)	(18%)	(17%)	(40%)
76	33	26	27	109	98	58	5
(100%)	(100%)	(100%)	(100%)	(100%)	(100%)	(100%)	(100%)

Exhibit A-11
VERBAL PREFERENCES FOR LAMB ADS

	Advertisement	1st Choice	2nd Choice	3rd Choice	Last Choice	Index of Rankings*
No. 5	Cookout	13	13	6	0	81
No. 1	Chops and Peaches	16	15	13	1	67
No. 3	"How to stretch"	11	9	12	1	58
No. 4	Steer	1	10	3	5	32
No. 7	"More eatin' meat"	3	4	4	5	13
No. 6	Chicken with Pig	4	5	6	18	-26
No. 2	"Study Proves"	2	3	1	20	-57

* Based on percentage of subjects' rankings for the ad which were first or second placings minus the percentage of last place rankings.

QUESTIONS

1. What is the value of the pupillary response data relative to other research findings?

2. If a year-round theme must be used, which ad would you select as best? Why?

Evaluating
Promotional Programs

PART IV

Weyerhaeuser Company (D)

The company conducts a Gallup and Robinson theater test of the four TV commercials used in its national corporate identity advertising campaign. The results must be used to help assess the relative effectiveness of the commercials in conveying predetermined characteristics about the company.

In January of 1969, Mr. Carroll O'Rourke, Director of Public Relations and Advertising of the Weyerhaeuser Company, and Mr. B.L. Orell, the company's Vice-President of Public Affairs, were examining the results from a recent Gallup and Robinson advertising research study. The study analyzed the relative performance of the four television commercials which Weyerhaeuser had been running in its national institutional advertising campaign for some four months on "Wide World of Sports" and NCAA football "Games of the Week." (Weekly spots had also been placed on regional telecasts of NFL football games in Oregon and Washington.)

Weyerhaeuser executives had awaited the study results with particular anticipation, since the TV campaign instituted in the Fall of 1968 had represented a radical departure from the company's traditional institutional advertising strategy. Since its inception in 1952, the campaign had run solely in print media—predominantly in leading national magazines—featuring scenes of wildlife in forest settings. (See Exhibit 1.) Studies had indicated that the campaign had successfully helped to convey a distinctive corporate identity for Weyerhaeuser as an ethical and responsible manager of the nation's forest lands. However, it was believed to have had somewhat less success in recent years in communicating the variety of ways in which the company was growing, diversifying, and looking to the future through research and innovation. Thus, in the mid-1960s, it was decided to reexamine all aspects of the institutional campaign including the traditional commitment to print media. [See Weyerhaeuser Company (A) for a detailed history of the Weyerhaeuser print advertising campaign.]

After a six-week TV test in eight selected U.S. market areas in 1967 [Weyerhaeuser Company (B) presents the TV test and its results] executives decided to shift the bulk of the company's $1.2 million institutional advertising budget from print to TV in 1968. Four commercials were then developed which, although still concerned with presenting Weyerhaeuser as ethical and responsible, had the primary objective of communicating five additional qualities about the company. These were:

Innovative
Forward-looking
Diversified
Dynamic
Research-minded

[Weyerhaeuser Company (C) discusses the development of these four commercials.] Exhibits 2-5 contain descriptions of "mood boards" for the four commercials used.

As Mr. O'Rourke and Mr. Orell studied the Gallup and Robinson report (excerpts from the report are contained here as Appendix A) they weighed its implications with regard to the four commercials studied and the future direction of the entire Weyerhaeuser institutional campaign.

Exhibit 1

REPRESENTATIVE AD FROM WILDLIFE CAMPAIGN

new timber crops replace each tree farm harvest...

Natural-finish wood is used for an endless variety of beautiful home interiors. It affords a warmth and distinctive personality which blend perfectly with a broad range of decorating themes.

There are more than 4,000 different lumber, pulp, fiber and chemical products which are made from wood. They all play an important part in our everyday life. Both people and industry use these products . . . which come from *today's* timber harvest. To provide an abundance of such products for use in the future, new tree crops must be grown again and again on harvested lands. By managing timber as a continuing crop, tree farmers can supply wood needed for today *and* tomorrow.

Tree farms are privately owned areas of commercial forestland . . . land better suited for growing trees than any other crop. Tree farm owners are growing a perpetual wood supply by long-range forest management plans under supervision of more than 4,500 graduate industrial foresters. They are also decreasing timber losses from fire, insects and disease.

Today, nearly 5,400 tree farms are operated by private owners on more than 31 million acres of tax-paying timberland all across America. All Weyerhaeuser Timber Company forestlands are managed as certified tree farms. *For the full story of modern industrial forestry, write us at Box A, Tacoma, Washington for our colorful free booklet,* **Tree Farming in the Pacific Northwest.**

Weyerhaeuser Timber Company

This advertisement appears in *The Saturday Evening Post,* September 11; *U.S. News,* September 10; and *The Farm Journal,* October, 1954.

Exhibit 2

MOOD BOARD FOR "PANELING–WOOD CARVER" COMMERCIAL*

Video	*Audio*
Craftsman working with wood. Close-up of his hands chiseling a design and polishing the finished piece, a jewelry box.	MUSIC: A single, mellow violin ANNCR: (soft, deliberate) Nature gave us a most remarkable material. . . wood. There's nothing like it in all the world. In skilled hands, it can be turned into a thing of beauty that even nature herself wouldn't recognize.
Camera slowly pans over a lush interior scene. The room, decorated in warm tones, has paneled walls and several pieces of wooden furniture.	This same care goes into Weyerhaeuser paneling. Time was when quality like this was costly. Anything less was a compromise. But Weyerhaeuser's found a way to create paneling that looks as though it were crafted especially for your home, and it doesn't cost a fortune. So, if you've been putting off looking at paneling because you think it's expensive, visit your Weyerhaeuser dealer.
Camera closes in on the jewelry box on a shelf in the room, with the Weyerhaeuser name and logo superimposed.	He can probably change your mind. Weyerhaeuser . . . working on tomorrow's ideas . . . today.

* "Mood boards" consist of artist's impressions (rough sketches) of the prospective video portion of the color television commercial. These illustrations are intended to convey the mood of the advertisement, along with the prospective audio portion. For case purposes, because of reproduction problems, the video portion is reproduced in verbal form above.

Exhibit 3

MOOD BOARD FOR "HIGH-YIELD OPERATION–FOREST" COMMERCIAL*

Video	*Audio*
Camera focuses on an evergreen twig, moves in to a close-up of a trout swimming near the surface of a streat, then to a nearby fawn. The scene switches to various shots of the fir trees in a forest. The camera backs up to show the size of the trees.	ANNCR: (soft, deliberate) Forestry used to be a waiting game. But no more. America needs more wood today, tomorrow, and beyond. Now Weyerhaeuser's found a way to actually speed up the forest. First we cultivate the land. . .plant young super trees. . .fertilize...and

	thin the forest. Result? One-third more wood per acre. . .per year... forever. It's called High-Yield Forestry. Even Mother Nature likes the idea.
A bald eagle takes off from its nest, soars through the tree tops, then lands in the nest again. Weyerhaeuser name and logo superimposed.	So the next time someone says we're running out of trees, tell them about Weyerhaeuser High-Yield Forestry. Weyerhaeuser... working on tomorrow's ideas... today.

* See note on Exhibit 2.

Exhibit 4

MOOD BOARD FOR "DOMED STADIUM—COLOSSEUM" COMMERCIAL*

Video	*Audio*
Overhead and interior shots of the ruins of the Colosseum...	ANNCR: (soft, deliberate) In ancient Rome, the Colosseum was the greatest amphitheater in all the world.
and a large, deserted bull-fighting arena.	In the New World the first great arenas were the "plaza de toros" of Mexico.
Exterior and interior views of a model domed stadium constructed of wood.	And for the stadium of tomorrow, a new design idea from Weyerhaeuser. A stadium that can be built of wood, larger than the Astrodome, with giant laminated beams that would span three football fields and stand 250 feet high. And that, sports fans, is some stadium.
A man's hands remove the roof of the stadium, then replace it...with the Weyerhaeuser name and logo superimposed.	The stadium of tomorrow, another design innovation from Weyerhaeuser. . .working on tomorrow's ideas...today.

* See note on Exhibit 2.

Exhibit 5

MOOD BOARD FOR "DIVERSIFICATION–AIRPLANE" COMMERCIAL*

Video	*Audio*
Jet plane taking off...	ANNCR: In this fast-changing world, nothing will ever be the same. And nobody knows that better than Weyerhaeuser. . .
Aerial view of a partially completed development of houses,	the company that makes more than a thousand different building materials for homes. . .
a jet in flight, and aerial shots of farms and farmland,	new packaging materials for farm produce, frozen foods, ice cream, and milk. . .
aerial view of a jet,	the company that makes capacitor tissue for jets and spacecraft. . .
a complex highway cloverleaf,	giant plywood-concrete forms for highway construction. . .
a harbor,	industrial products for everything from boats. . .
railroad yards,	to boxcars. . .
the skyline of lower Manhattan,	papers with new properties for books, computers, and business.
a ship, and	And Weyerhaeuser cargo vans are helping revolutionize shipping–by sea, land,
an airplane with the Weyerhaeuser name and logo superimposed.	and air. Weyerhaeuser...working on tomorrow's ideas. . .today.

* See note on Exhibit 2.

APPENDIX A

Excerpts from Gallup and Robinson Analysis of Impact Patterns of Four Weyerhaeuser Commercials

I. Introduction

PURPOSES

Survey purposes were twofold—one: to evaluate the relative Impact levels of four Weyerhaeuser commercials one against the other and against appropriate on-air norms; two: to evaluate the total "campaign" effect in terms of established image goals.

The four commercials selected were:

"Paneling-Wood Carver" (Exhibit 2)

"High-Yield Operation-Forest" (Exhibit 3)

"Domed Stadium-Colosseum" (Exhibit 4)

"Diversification-Airplane" (Exhibit 5)

RESEARCH DESIGN

1. **The Facility** The Mirror of America[1] —a technique employing a captive-audience approach wherein respondents are exposed to commercials within the body of a filmed TV program.

2. **The Program Vehicle** An appropriate film was selected, *Michelangelo— The Last Giant*, to provide a proper program atmosphere for the commercials and to adhere to the Weyerhaeuser goal of sponsoring programs "related to public concerns and interests."

3. **The Program Format** Within the film, six commercials, four Weyerhaeuser commercials and two AISI[2] control commercials, were spliced at 10-minute intervals.

In each of the eight sessions, the Weyerhaeuser commercials were rotated in order.

4. **Sample Selection** The sample was drawn so that a minimum of 100 men and 100 women would be provided for delayed recall measurement bases.

Respondents were selected so to provide a sample weighted to upper income, middle-aged (30 to 50) households drawn from the suburbs of Philadelphia. (See Exhibit A-1.)

Adequate samples were drawn to provide additional respondents for taped discussions (not included in delayed recall sample).[3]

5. **The Test Atmosphere** For each session, a sample was invited to attend a viewing of a film of a television program.

Throughout the session *no mention is made of advertising.*

On their arrival, the audience is asked to fill out a respondent identification card and demographic questionnaire.

The audience is presented with the idea that they are to view the program as they would any TV show, but with the thought that they will be asked to express their opinions about the *show* at the conclusion.

---

[1] "Mirror of America" was a name used by Gallup and Robinson for this type of theater-testing format.

[2] American Iron and Steel Institute.

[3] Respondents were not paid directly for participating in the viewing. However, they were traditionally drawn from groups and organizations that received remuneration, the amount of which depended on the number of group members who participated.

6.   The Testing Technique At the conclusion of the program, the audience is asked to complete a questionnaire dealing with their opinions of the show and viewing habits.

Based on their demographics, a small number of respondents is selected for the taped discussions that take place while the "show" questionnaire is being administered.

The day following exposure telephone interviews are conducted with those who viewed, to determine for each commercial:

> Perception
> Idea communication
> Attitudinal patterns

Special questions are administered at the conclusion of the standard questionnaire. Exhibit A-2 contains the standard questionnaire. Exhibit A-3 contains the special impact questionnaire.

7.   Measurement Definitions   Perception—Remember Commercial

The per cent of exposed viewers who can recall, on an unaided basis, and accurately describe the commercial content and/or execution.

Idea Communication

The playback of copy points and attitudes of those who recall the commercial(s)
> — Verbatim testimony
> — Idea registration profiles

Favorable Attitude

The rate of expression of favorable attitudes toward the company by those who recall the commercial.

8.   Computation of On-Air Performance Prediction

> —Owing to captive audience situation, perception levels are inflated.
> —On-air measurement of control commercials compared with scores in captive test situation provides inflation ratio.
> —Inflation ratio provides adjustment factor for on-air prediction of test commercial perception level.

II.   Scale Ratings of Corporate Image Semantics

To each respondent who recalled one or more Weyerhaeuser commercial(s), the day following exposure, a special questionnaire was administered whereby respondents were asked to assign a quantitative value, on a scale from "0" to "10," that best fits their impression of three advertisers:

A.   Weyerhaeuser
B.   Alcoa
C.   Steel Industry

Before being asked to respond on Alcoa and the Steel Industry, each respondent was required to have indicated prior awareness of the company or industry.

CORPORATE IMAGE PROFILE SCALE RATING

	Weyerhaeuser Image	
	Men	*Women*
Modern	9.2	9.4
*Innovative	9.2	8.7
*Forward-looking	9.1	9.2
*Research-minded	9.0	9.1
*Responsible	8.7	8.6
Fast-growing	8.5	8.3
*Dynamic	8.4	7.8
*Diversified	8.3	8.6
*Ethical	8.2	8.4
Friendly	7.4	7.5

* Explicit Weyerhaeuser corporate goals.

COMPARATIVE CORPORATE IMAGE PROFILE SCALE RATING

Men

Items on which Weyer-haeuser was ranked:	*Corporate Image Rating*		
	Weyer-haeuser	*Alcoa*	*Steel Industry*
First:			
*Innovative	9.2	8.6	8.4
Modern	9.2	9.0	8.8
*Forward-looking	9.1	8.9	9.0
*Responsible	8.7	8.4	8.5
Fast-growing	8.5	8.2	8.1
*Ethical	8.2	8.0	8.0
Friendly	7.4	7.2	7.2
Second:			
*Research-minded	9.0	9.3	9.0
*Dynamic	8.4	8.8	8.1
Third:			
*Diversified	8.3	9.3	8.4

* Explicit Weyerhaeuser corporate goals.

**COMPARATIVE CORPORATE IMAGE PROFILE
SCALE RATING**

Women

Items on which Weyer-haeuser was ranked:	Corporate Image Rating		
	Weyer-haeuser	Alcoa	Steel Industry
First:			
Modern	9.4	9.3	9.2
*Forward-looking	9.2	9.2	9.2
*Responsible	8.6	8.6	8.1
*Ethical	8.4	8.2	8.0
Friendly	7.5	7.5	7.3
Second:			
*Research-minded	9.1	9.1	9.4
*Innovative	8.7	8.6	8.9
Third:			
*Diversified	8.6	9.0	9.1
Fast growing	8.3	9.0	9.0
*Dynamic	7.8	8.3	8.7

* Explicit Weyerhaeuser corporate goals.

III.   Impact Patterns

A. COMMERCIAL RECALL

Predicted on-air performance patterns indicate the following:

When compared with appropriate corporate norms for 60 second commercials—

	Men	Women
"Paneling—Wood Carver"	Above Average	Above Average
"High-Yield Operation—Forest"	Above Average	Below Average
"Domed Stadium—Colosseum"	Above Average	Average
"Diversification—Airplane"	Below Average	Below Average

	Per Cent Who Remember Commercial			Points Above/
	Men	*Women*	*Norm*	*Below Norm*
"Paneling—Wood Carver"	22		14	+ 8
		21	13	+ 8
"High-Yield Operations—Forest"	20		14	+ 6
		9	13	- 4
"Domed Stadium—Colosseum"	18		14	+ 4
		12	13	- 1
"Diversification—Airplane"	7		14	- 7
		2	13	-11
Base (people):	100	133		

B.   CORPORATE CONCEPT REGISTRATION

	% Respondents	
	Men	*Women*
"Paneling—Wood Carver"		
(Refer to innovative concept)	5	-
"High-Yield Operations—Forest"		
(Refer to forward-looking concept)	39	37
"Domed Stadium—Colosseum"		
(Refer to forward-looking concept)	27	38
"Diversification—Airplane"		
(Diversified company)	30	3
(Concerned with future)	25	4

C.   FAVORABLE ATTITUDE—TO WEYERHAEUSER

	% Respondents		
	Men	*Women*	*Norm**
"Paneling—Wood Carver"	53	75	28
"High-Yield Operations—Forest"	57	78	28
"Domed Stadium—Colosseum"	61	59	28
"Diversification—Airplane"	35	-	28

* Combined norm.

D. FAVORABLE ATTITUDE–TOWARD COMMERCIAL

	% Respondents		
	Men	Women	Norm*
"Paneling–Wood Carver"	40	37	14
"High-Yield Operations–Forest"	53	50	14
"Domed Stadium–Colosseum"	49	26	14
"Diversification–Airplane"	10	–	14

* Combined norm.

IV. Verbatim Comments

A. "PANELING–WOOD CARVER"

SUMMARY OF VERBATIM COMMENTS

	% Respondents			
		Men		Women
Base (people):		57		73
One or more ideas		88%		95%
Beautiful/attractive/elegant		47		56
Versatility of paneling		58		52
Variety of uses	45		44	
Variety of types/colors	17		8	
Economical		44		33
Only expensive looking	19		5	
Reasonably priced	10		21	
Practical	5		–	
Used for interior decorating		17		20
Good quality		10		20
Easy/quick to install		7		12
Progressive company		5		–
Dependable/reliable		4		3

REPRESENTATIVE VERBATIM TESTIMONY[4]

MEN

"They showed a paneled room. It was furnished and looked very nice. It looked like a professional job. They said that Weyerhaeuser paneling wasn't as expensive as it looks. And if you are interested, contact the company. They

[4]Included in all verbatim testimony are excerpts from both telephone interviews one day after viewing and taped interviews immediately following viewing.

said it was easy to put up. They showed some panels and they said they have a special way for processing it. They showed some nicely finished panels. I got the impression that if you wanted to finish a room, it is a good idea. I thought about the paneling itself. I was thinking that the price is not too high, and I thought about the way the room looked. I was impressed because it looked so nice."

"They were making authentic beams for your house and different types of wall coverings or panelings. They had a fellow carving a jewelry box out of wood. He finished it up and shellacked it and put it on the mantelpiece. They were narrating this, again saying what can be made out of Weyerhaeuser wood handicraft, and again bringing to mind that beautiful things can be made out of wood. I imagine they were trying to get to the home decorator or homeowner himself, who was thinking of decorating rather than with imitation or photographed paneling. If I did any paneling in my house, I would consult Weyerhaeuser, being a name brand, as to how to go about it and what I would use. I would say that the different types they had amazed me—the variety of wood. I think it was very well done—the way it was set, the settings of the paneling, and the way they had it decorated, and everything in the living rooms."

"It started out with a steel chisel. A man was holding the chisel. Then it showed a piece of art out of a piece of wood. They talked about steel and wood together and then they went off on Weyerhaeuser Wood Paneling. The idea that they were trying to get across was that a piece of art can be made out of a piece of wood. I thought they missed a chance to connect this to the theme of the show—the art work with the chisel. It was worth remembering how beautiful the wood was. They made a strong case, but it could have been better. They could have saved about ten seconds of the commercial to connect it with the theme of the show."

"They showed a man carving wood, then the inside of a home made from lumber. It was a beautiful home, and most of the rooms were paneled. They have a red color scheme in the room and the paneling in the background. They said that when you buy, ask for Weyerhaeuser Paneling and Building Materials. The paneling did look beautiful, and I'd look into it. I thought this paneling and grain looked real different. If I would panel, I'd look into this paneling. I would keep the name in mind. I was impressed by the color schemes and decorations and furnishings."

WOMEN

"The commercial showed a man working with wood. It was a craftsman chipping at some wood. He came out with a beautiful piece of wood carving. They showed that before you needed only a skilled craftsman to get your good wood, but today you can go and buy the same quality. I thought it was interesting. I had never seen anybody do this before. In the Weyerhaeuser wood commercial, I was just impressed with the quality of the wood. They got their point across just because they were effective and you learned something."

"They show this beautiful paneling in a room. It was Weyerhaeuser Paneling. The color made it look very expensive, but they said anyone could afford it. They show how easy it was to put up. It had a very rich look. I think the idea the advertiser was trying to get across was the many uses of wood and the way you can use more of it in decorating your home. You didn't see the holes and knots in the paneling that you see in some. It was a good quality. I was thinking that I liked the way it looked, and wouldn't mind having it myself. The point worth keeping in mind was the beautiful paneling and how easy it is to install. They did make a strong case. Being in color, the idea got across better. It brought out the beauty of the product."

"There was a man carving wood. It was something to hang on a wall, but I don't remember what it was. I think it was a jewel box. I'm not swayed by the commercial, which was about wood paneling. I don't enjoy them, and I don't listen to them either, so I don't know anything about it."

"This showed the man carving the wood. It looked like some sort of a box with a musical instrument—a decorative box. I think it was a violin. They referred to nature's greatest gift to man, and said that man himself could do more with it. Nature wouldn't recognize it in its finished product. I can't remember the name of the company, but it was wood. The advertiser was showing the use of wood in the home. It doesn't necessarily have to be a metal or alloy of any sort. In enhancing the beauty of the home, you could use wood products. I was thinking that I just liked the Spanish room they were showing. The warm overall appearance of the room was what I liked. It was very warm and comfortable-looking. They put this little box that the man had carved in it. That was used as a decoration. The beauty of it was worth remembering. I appreciate the beauty of wood. They did make a strong case because it was presented very interestingly."

"I just remember looking at the paneling. It was Weyerhaeuser Paneling. I think they had the recreation room paneled. The point the advertiser was trying to get across was that they make the best paneling, I assume. Nothing went through my mind. It is worth remembering that they have wood for paneling. They did make a strong case, because it was presented nicely."

B. HIGH-YIELD OPERATIONS—FOREST"

SUMMARY OF VERBATIM COMMENTS

	% Respondents		
	Men		Women
Base (people):		52	32
One or more ideas		100%	97%
Concerned with conservation		65	66
Replant/will not deplete	46		50
Benefits wild life	8		10
Method of increasing yield		48	63
Promotes rapid growth	17		13
Uses fertilizers	14		16
Trees weeded	12		6
Concerned with future		39	37
Insures future forests	27		13
Thoughtful/farsighted	10		16
Good quality lumber		17	10
Research-minded		4	-

REPRESENTATIVE VERBATIM TESTIMONY

MEN

"Well, this just made a point that there will not be a shortage of wood. It was an aerial shot of a great forest—nothing but trees. You see younger trees coming up, the saplings. Some of the ground was washed away, and Weyerhaeuser makes sure that this is replenished. The commercial mentioned the fact that they are interested in the conservation of wood, and said not to be afraid to use it because there will be plenty around. I learned that they are conservation-minded, and I appreciate their being that way. Also, it helps the game. They had the animals running through the woods; they showed deer running. I think they made a strong case. They mentioned it a couple of times, and showed water running down and washing trees out. They came along and replenished them."

"The commercial was about forestry and how Weyerhaeuser prolongs the life of trees and practices conservation. I just remember a lot of green—a lot of forests. I just got the impression that the company was sharp on land conservation, and they made their point well. It was very interesting. That was all I remember. They were just telling the importance of land conservation, and how Weyerhaeuser participates in it, and its importance. I learned about the various ways in which a big company goes in for conservation and its importance. I just thought that the point was well made."

"They said there was six times as many trees as there was years ago. The Weyerhaeuser Company plants new trees to replace the ones they use and they take good care of them. They grow at a very rapid rate. It looks like we'll never run out of wood. They want you to know that wood is plentiful and beautiful. They said it wasn't very expensive to use. I thought it was a very instructive commercial."

"The commercial was about the conservation program that Weyerhaeuser has. They told about planting seedlings. I thought it was a good commercial—not ordinary. I think it increased my interest."

"They showed the forest. They showed the number of trees and how much wood was in the forest. They also showed the scenery; it was beautiful with the tall, old trees. The Weyerhaeuser Company was trying to show where their products come from—the forest. I wish I was where the scenery was. I was thinking about the tall trees and the heights were really something to look at. I think they made a strong case. I know they were a lumber dealer and were showing the forest."

"It kept switching back to the forest and comparing it. The commercial showed how they conserved the forests and yet kept the trees growing in good condition to be used. I would assume that the purpose of the commercial was to show you the manner and the diversification of the Weyerhaeuser Company and to fulfill needs in a responsible manner. I thought that the name would stand out and the level was solid and dignified. The general attitude is that it is a responsible company. Their image and intelligence and the manner were in very fine fashion. I think they made a strong case because it was made on a high level and was very favorable."

"They showed how they farmed their trees—Weyerhaeuser. They cut the trees out to give the remaining ones more room to grow, and they fertilize them so that they get one-third more lumber. That's the only thing I remember. They brought out that they employ conservation methods to increase the supply of lumber faster. I didn't think of anything in particular. They did make a strong case. I like their ideas on the preservation of our forests."

"There were scenes of planting trees, and it told about scientifically improving the yield of forests by careful use and good management. They showed various methods of Weyerhaeuser conservation and scenes of forests. They got across that Weyerhaeuser not only makes uses of the wood in the forests—they try to replace as much, or even more, than they're using, and the importance of doing this. They mentioned that they're something more than just a lumber firm that's stripping the country of its resources, and how important this is. I was reminded how important conservation is and I agree with this—it's terribly important. Everything was worth remembering. The conservation of forests is terribly important. They definitely made a strong case. It was well presented, and made a very strong impression on me. It's an important thing, and I feel everyone should be made aware of it."

"It showed land and more land and lots of woods with young trees, and how they plant the young trees after they take out the older trees. Their main point was that there is one-third more wood now—more and better wood. I don't know what I learned. I thought it was a good ad. The ad was really just to educate the public."

WOMEN

"They were showing a new method of having the trees grow faster. They told how they fertilized the forest to inspire growth of trees. The advertiser made the point that the idea of destroying the forest, which people have complained about, is not a new argument. They insisted that they now inspire the growth of trees scientifically enough so that there need not be any concern about the trees. I am not sure whether this is a fallacy or not. It was not made especially clear to me. It was worth remembering how they say they have a new method of inspiring the growth of trees. They did not get their point across. It was not especially clear to me, and I am not sure I believe it."

"This commercial showed that they grew their own forests, and they yielded one-third more production per year per acreage. They fertilized it and cultivated it and showed that the forest aided nature by assisting the animals in living. There was a picture of a deer and an eagle. There was a running narrative. It was for Weyerhaeuser wood. I felt that they weren't destroying forests. They were replanting and cultivating. I thought, 'They care.' I thought the whole general theme was good and worth remembering. I was interested because they showed they cared."

"In this commercial, they showed the forest and how much timber they have. Weyerhaeuser has a plentiful supply of timber. The forest was in the mountains. They just tried to get across the idea that they have a plentiful supply of timber. I thought they were beautiful mountains. It was worth remembering that there is a plentiful supply of timber. I don't know whether the commercial was effective or not. It didn't impress me."

"They showed a lot of scenery and forests. It was the Weyerhaeuser forests. I wasn't interested. I didn't pay too much attention, I guess. It was just a lot of forests. I have no idea what the sales points were. I don't remember what went through my mind. Nothing was worth remembering—I didn't pay any attention, I guess. I don't know whether they made a strong case or not."

"They showed how they grow their own trees to make the Weyerhaeuser wood. They said that the fertilizer and care they give the trees help them grow faster and better. They also showed some wildlife like deer and rabbits, and how they survive in their forests. I got the idea that they are trying their best to produce a good product that lasts and will take punishment of children and other people that put hard wear on it. The preservation of the forest and the wildlife was worth remembering. They did make a strong case, but I don't know in what way."

"All I can remember is that it was about the forests. They showed them cutting down trees and planting them. They were talking about how rapidly they're using the trees they have, and also that they are replacing them at the same rate. It is about the Weyerhaeuser uses of lumber. I got the idea that they have the people's welfare in mind as well as their own, because they are replacing them. It occurred to me that they're not just another money-making company because they have the people's welfare in mind. I got nothing definite out of it. The commercial was effective. I remember I was impressed at the time because of the things they are now using wood for, but I can't remember what the commercial was about."

C.   "DOMED STADIUM–COLOSSEUM"

SUMMARY OF VERBATIM COMMENTS

| | *% Respondents* | |
	Men	*Women*
Base (people):	49	42
One or more ideas	94%	85%
Stadium constructed of wood	92	74
Versatility of wood	47	52
Wooden beams	35	7
Laminated	20	7
Company concerned with future	27	38
Plan future buildings	20	38
News	33	—
Stadium built of wood	29	—
New ideas	10	—
Good quality/durable	20	14
Economical	16	5
Research-minded	4	2

REPRESENTATIVE VERBATIM TESTIMONY

MEN

"They showed a stadium, so I was interested, I guess. I like sports. It was a picture of this different type of stadium they'd be putting up in the future. They showed how it would be built. They showed this model and took the roof off and showed the structure inside, and then put the roof back on. They told how big it would be, that it would be three times the size of present day stadiums. They explained about the structure of it. I don't remember, I had a hard day today. I don't know really what the advertiser's aim was. It was kind of—I guess you'd call it soft sell, I don't really know. I was thinking about construction, I guess, and how it will be done in the future. This commercial was for Weyerhaeuser. It was interesting to watch. As I said, I'm interested in the idea of a stadium, and seeing it built and how it's done. That was worth keeping in mind. They got their point across, if I were interested in a product of that type. It was nicely done, and as I said, soft sell. I like that."

"In this commercial they explain how wood is used in making domes for roofs. They are used in arenas. The sales point was that they are safer. I think when you see a structure that size, you can't help but remember the name of the manufacturer. I thought the commercial blended so well with the program. I didn't mind seeing them at all. What I got out of it was that wood is still an important product. These were the Weyerhaeuser Dome Tops. This is a construction that is considered by the layman as fantastic, but for large cities it is a future must. But in any case, their ideas were great and made a strong impression on me at least."

"In this one I think they showed the construction, and they laminated the wood in order to get the length of the beam. No one piece of wood is that long. It was Weyerhaeuser—different things made of wood. It was mostly just pictures. There was one fellow who did the mock-up. We could see his hands. They were narrating that they were making more things out of wood, taking the place of other items. Then they showed the inside of the stadium, looking up to the roof. They opened it up, and you could see the football field inside. I imagine they were talking to the bigger business people and engineers. Their aim was to get them into wood rather than steel. What amazes me is what they can do with wood today. People would never dream that they would make a stadium out of wood. The potential in wood was really worth remembering. It's more comfortable, and at home it's warmer than steel, I think. I do think they made a strong case by bringing to light that wood can be used in more useful things than we think."

"This commercial showed the Weyerhaeuser building—a new stadium—that seemed to me to be very similar in design to the Astrodome. It was a large round stadium with a removable roof. They showed how it was built and its capacity, and the surprising ways that wood was used in its construction, and various new ideas about building with wood. The advertiser's aim was to emphasize how versatile and how good it is to use in construction. Also, it told of the modern ways of using it in construction by showing the building of this stadium. I thought that it was very interesting to see the methods of constructing things with wood. Some of the ideas of building with wood were very interesting and informative. The modern methods of construction were worth keeping in mind. They made a strong case by showing an extremely modern utilitarian building that was also quite attractive to look at, and it was built with wood."

"They spoke of wood and its uses, that's all. I remember something else—Weyerhaeuser Stadium made with wood—that was new to me. I didn't think they used wood any more for stadiums. They were pointing out the diversification of wood, I guess. I can't think of anything else. I think they made a strong case because they were emphasizing the products of tomorrow in the world today."

"They showed the Weyerhaeuser Stadium that was constructed completely of wood—no steel. I was amazed because I didn't think this was possible. I never saw anything like it before. The stadium shown was a model, and they showed the large beams made of wood and other parts of the stadium, too—also made all of wood. Like I said, this was all new to me, and I enjoyed seeing it. I didn't know they built completely of wood in such a large building. I enjoyed the commercial very much, and think Weyerhaeuser is a good name in wood."

WOMEN

"I believe that was the one about the stadium with the removable top. It showed the stadium and talked about the type of wood Weyerhaeuser was going to use in building this. It went over my head. I thought the commercial was really excellent, and I enjoyed learning about their products very much. I enjoyed it and was impressed."

"In the Weyerhaeuser Wood commercial they showed how reliable and durable wood was and they also had a stadium molded with wood. It showed homes made out of wood. They brought out the idea that the wood company isn't only interested in building better wood products, but showed how they are looking to the future. I thought that was an excellent idea. It occurred to me that it probably was a very good program. They were not only taking care of themselves now in their modern approach but they were planning for the future. I think they made a strong case because they were looking ahead."

"That was sort of tied in with the story that went along. They showed the Roman Colosseum and other buildings, and said Weyerhaeuser Laminated Wood was used for these buildings. The explanation was that this was thicker and stronger wood. The sales point was that it is wood that has unusual strength. They just mentioned it was one of the products put into these buildings. I thought it was interesting information to pick up. There was nothing offensive about it. You hardly knew it was a commercial. I don't know what was worth keeping in mind. I just thought it was interesting to know that wood would be used in important buildings. They made a strong case, I thought to myself. It was interesting to me."

"First they showed you a stadium in Michelangelo's time and then the stadium through history and ended up with stadiums of today. In the Weyerhaeuser commercial they showed the one in Houston and the one in Pittsburgh with the covers that come off the stadium. I learned that tops on stadiums can fold back. The commercial was half over before I realized it was a commercial. It said that stadiums with tops are the coming thing."

"They were showing how they used laminated wood to make a huge stadium three times the length of a football field. They said that this stadium would be bigger than any other stadium. It was a commercial for the Weyerhaeuser new type of stadium. The main point was the way they laminate the wood, it would last longer than any other wood. It seemed very improbable to me. There was nothing worth keeping in mind. I don't think they made a strong case. I didn't understand it, and I am not interested in stadiums."

"In the commercial for building materials there was a picture of a stadium. It was too modern for me—too far in the future. It has durability, I suppose. It was put over quite nicely, I thought. The roof did slide off. I think it rolled back. That's about all. I can't remember more about it at all."

"In the Weyerhaeuser commercial they talked about the future design. They referred to the ancient Colosseum, then to the stadium in Mexico, and then to the Astrodome of the future. Their aim was to show how well their product would fit into the plans of the future. I just thought of the future of sporting events and how comfortable it would be. How nice it would be to have a fine-looking stadium with a cover! It was important to remember the fact that they were looking at the future. I was impressed because they were concerned for the comfort of the people and also the beauty of the stadium." "There was a stadium with a roof that came off in the Weyerhaeuser commercial. It was round. They showed how they built it. I'm really not interested in building a stadium. They told how to build a stadium—how they do it. I have no idea. There was not much worth keeping in mind."

D. "DIVERSIFICATION—AIRPLANE"

SUMMARY OF VERBATIM COMMENTS

	% Respondents	
	Men	Women
Base (people):	20	6
One or more ideas	100%	5%
Versatility of wood	75	4
Housing projects	50	1
Crates/boxes for shipping	45	1
Airplane products	25	2
Paper products	20	—
Highways	10	1
Diversified company	30	3
Concerned with future	25	4
Good quality products	25	—
News	20	—
Diversification of Weyerhaeuser	5	—
Uses of wood	5	—

REPRESENTATIVE VERBATIM TESTIMONY

MEN

"It showed that they make milk cartons and shipping boxes. It mentioned how many ways Weyerhaeuser wood can be used and how sturdy it is. I learned that wood can be used in small or large jobs or products. It did not interest me."

"They showed the many uses of wood. They showed the forms used to pour concrete on highways. It seemed to be aimed at the commercial uses of wood and the advantages of using it in construction because it's inexpensive. I was surprised at how much wood was used in construction."

"This one concerned many ways in which Weyerhaeuser wood can be used. They showed how airplanes can be stored, and there were these new types of box cars for shipping. I would say that all of the commercials were actually a followup of the actual film of Michelangelo because of his construction of the Sistine Chapel so as to compare the cost of those days to the present time."

"It was construction, I remember—a big development going up. There were no specific items. I took it that way. They just had some shots of this big development. I don't remember what they were trying to get across. I learned nothing. I think I was distracted. I can't recall any more. I'm not in this line."

"The commercial showed houses—many types of houses. It also showed a great many ways to use wood. This was a Weyerhaeuser Company commercial."

"I don't remember so much about these, just which was which. I think there were several things in one commercial. I remember these big boat crates and the highway forms. They showed shots of highway building and then the finished product. I was more interested in the different ways of using the Weyerhaeuser wood than thinking about buying and I didn't notice any of that. I just didn't notice the sales points, I guess."

WOMEN

"They showed all the things that this company, Weyerhaeuser, does for the world and for industry. There is a picture of jet planes. Then they show the New York skyline. There was just so much. There were cartons of milk, and jet planes, and I guess just about everything. You saw planes taking off, and the bodies of planes. They seem to be doing everything. They tried to get across the idea that this company is thinking of the future, and how everything is changing. They are trying to be right there with it. You know, thinking of the future. They do this by showing how they're doing all these things for industry and everything with an eye to the future. I was thinking how fast everything is changing, and how different the world will be for our kids, and how much it's changed in my life. There is really nothing for me to keep in mind. These aren't personal things. They are kind of, you know, too big to think about. I'm not involved with construction and all. It just kind of happens, but I don't keep it in mind. I guess they got their point across. I guess I was impressed by it. I had never even heard of this company before last night, so I guess they impressed me."

"They showed different things made from Weyerhaeuser wood. They showed boats and trailers for boats made from their product. I felt that they are expanding and had many things in mind for the future. I thought it was a nice commercial and I haven't seen too many of them. Just the name 'Weyerhaeuser' was worth keeping in mind. I don't really think they made a strong case. The commercial didn't impress me as much as the commercial on the steel industry."

Exhibit A-1

SELECTED DEMOGRAPHIC INFORMATION ON "MIRROR OF AMERICA" AUDIENCE COMPOSITION

	Men	*Women*
Sex		
Male—169		
Female—171		
Age		
21–34	21%	45%
35–49	46	40
50 or over	32	14
No answer	1	1
Education		
Grammar school	6%	5%
High school	51	73
College	42	21
No answer	1	1
Income		
Under $7,000	9%	8%
$7,001–$10,000	29	37
$10,001–$15,000	28	26
Over $15,000	28	10
No answer	6	19

Exhibit A-2

STANDARD QUESTIONNAIRE USED FOR TELEPHONE INTERVIEWS

Standard Questionnaire Used for Telephone Interviews

Time this interview started _____   Respondent's Name _____
                                                Respondent's Number _____
GALLUP & ROBINSON, INC.   Respondent's Telephone _____
                                                Interviewer _____
Fill out an envelope for each name that
you are assigned even though an interview   Number of calls placed to this respondent
is not obtained.   1 2 3 4 5 6 7 8 9 10 11 12
                                                        Could not reach respondent

                                                Reason _____

Introduction:

      HELLO, MY NAME IS _____. I AM AN INTERVIEWER FOR THE MIRROR
      OF AMERICA. I WOULD LIKE TO ASK YOU SOME ADDITIONAL QUESTIONS ABOUT
      LAST NIGHT'S PROGRAM.

A.   WHILE AT THE MIRROR YOU SAW A TELEVISION PROGRAM. PLEASE TELL ME
      BRIEFLY WHAT THEY DID ON THIS SHOW. (WHO WAS ON IT? WHAT WAS THE
      PLOT?) Interviewers: Indicate probes with ⓅP . Write all answers in the respon-
      dent's own words. _____

      _____

      _____

B.   WHAT DID THEY ADVERTISE ON EACH OF THE COMMERCIALS ON THE PROGRAM
      LAST NIGHT?

	BRAND	PRODUCT	
WHAT ELSE?	_____	_____	□ DK
WHAT ELSE?	_____	_____	□ DK
WHAT ELSE?	_____	_____	□ DK
WHAT ELSE?	_____	_____	□ DK
WHAT ELSE?	_____	_____	□ DK
WHAT ELSE?	_____	_____	□ DK
WHAT ELSE?	_____	_____	□ DK

Allow the respondent several minutes in which to recall commercials. Do not leave
Question B until you feel sure the respondent has had adequate opportunity for recall.

After you have completed questions A and B copy each of the commercials recalled in
Question B to the yellow area of a playback sheet. Then take playback on each commercial
mentioned. Be sure that all answers are in the respondent's own words. Probe carefully
for full details. Indicate probes with Ⓟ.

SPECIAL NOTE: After all playback has been completed, ask all respondents:

C.   WERE YOU ANTICIPATING THIS FOLLOW-UP INTERVIEW AS A RESULT OF ANY
      PREVIOUS INFORMATION?   □ YES   □ NO

      If "Yes," why? _____

Time interview completed _____   Date of interview _____

SPECIAL IMPACT QUESTIONNAIRE

Special Impact Questionnaire

INSTRUCTIONS TO INTERVIEWERS:

>   TO BE ADMINISTERED TO ALL RESPONDENTS WHO RECALL ONE OR MORE
>   WEYERHAEUSER COMMERCIALS AND HAVE BEEN FIRST INTERVIEWED ON
>   THE STANDARD IMPACT QUESTIONNAIRE.

1. As you think about the commercials you saw yesterday, I would like you to give me
   your impression of the Weyerhaeuser Company. I'll read you some phrases and I'd
   like you to tell me how well the phrase fits your impression of the Weyerhaeuser
   Company. To do this, give me a number from "0" to "10." The more a phrase fits
   your impression of the company, the bigger the number you would give it. The less
   it fits your impression, the smaller the number you give it.

INSTRUCTIONS TO INTERVIEWER:

>   READ EACH OF THE PHRASES BELOW, ONE AT A TIME, AND THEN ASK THE
>   RESPONDENT TO CHOOSE A NUMBER FROM "0" to "10."
>
>   WRITE IN THE NUMBER SELECTED BY THE RESPONDENT OPPOSITE EACH
>   PHRASE. ASK EACH RESPONDENT ABOUT ALL 10 PHRASES.

	Q.1 Weyerhaeuser	Q.2 ALCOA	Q.3 Steel Industry
Friendly			
Fast-growing			
Ethical			
Dynamic			
Responsible			
Modern			
Innovative			
Diversified			
Forward-looking			
Research Minded			

2. Have you heard of the Aluminum Company of America (ALCOA)?

   ☐ Yes   ☐ No
   > If "yes": Based on what you have heard and using the
   > same rating system as you just used for Weyerhaeuser,
   > please tell me your impressions of ALCOA.
   >
   > (REPEAT EACH OF THE PHRASES AND RECORD UNDER Q. 2)

3. Have you any knowledge of the Steel Industry?

   ☐ Yes   ☐ No

   > If "yes": Based on what you have heard about the Steel Industry, please
   > give me your impressions of the industry.
   >
   > (REPEAT EACH OF THE PHRASES AND RECORD UNDER Q. 3)

RESPONDENT'S NAME: _____   Resp. Sex: ☐ Male ☐ Female

QUESTION

*1. What action should the company take now regarding media?
Message content?*

Florists'
Telegraph
Delivery Association (A)

Testing Media Effectiveness

Executives of the Association and its advertising agency attempt to design a research test to determine the sales effectiveness of various media considered for FTD advertising messages.

The Florists' Telegraph Delivery Association was founded in 1910 to provide a means whereby flowers could be sent from one city to another. An individual could order flowers from an FTD-affiliated florist in one city, and the bouquet would be delivered in the destination city. The florist in the originating city (depending on the speed required) wired, wrote, or telephoned an FTD member florist in the destination city who then delivered the flowers and the accompanying message. The charge for a rapid delivery bouquet was typically the cost of the flowers plus the wire cost plus, after 1957, a 50¢ service charge. Payments to originating and fulfilling florists were effected via a central clearing house where records of all FTD "flowers-by-wire" orders were maintained. FTD member florists were grouped in over 90 local organizations throughout the country. Florist association members displayed the FTD Mercury Symbol on their windows.

FTD membership in the United States and Canada numbered approximately 11,000 florists in 1960. Growth had been rapid in the post-World War II era. FTD had little in the way of direct competition in the service of sending flowers by wire. Only one relatively small competitor existed, which did virtually no advertising. FTD sales increased from $10 million to $56 million during the years 1943-1958. Floricultural trends and FTD sales and membership data for selected years are given in Exhibits 1A and 1B. Advertising expenditures by the FTD had been over $1 million annually since 1952, and the total promotional budget was estimated at about $1.8 million per year for 1960. Total media advertising was about 3% of sales. Advertising traditionally had been most heavily in print media, featuring magazines, daily newspapers, and Sunday newspaper supplements.[1] In 1959 and 1960 television and radio were also used. Advertising usually was concentrated in periods prior to "florists' holidays" such as Mother's Day, Easter, Valentine's Day, and Christmas.

In 1958 the association sponsored on an alternate-week basis the regularly scheduled television program "Person to Person," and put virtually all its advertising dollars into television. A breakdown of advertising expenditures in major media, 1954-58, is presented in Exhibit 2.

In August 1958, the Florists' Telegraph Delivery Association selected a new advertising agency, Keyes, Madden & Jones, Inc., of Chicago. As one of its first jobs for the FTD, the agency conducted a motivation-research study with the objective of aiding the development of an effective creative platform for FTD advertising.

Interviews were conducted with users and nonusers of the FTD Service. Nonusers were selected by calling on neighbors of the users, a device which the agency felt would equate for social-economic status. The study showed few differences between users and nonusers of the FTD service with reference to age, income, occupation, education, and so on. However, psychological probing revealed that flowers had a set of particular meanings for those who sent them. To these people, flowers were sent in order to create an emotional impact rather than just to try to fill a need. Flowers thus had a symbolic meaning which transcended their practical value. Based on the findings of this study, Keyes, Madden & Jones developed an advertising campaign with primary emphasis on the emotional aspects of sending flowers and secondary emphasis on the flowers themselves.

The Keyes, Madden & Jones campaign for the FTD for 1959 was built around the newly developed theme of "Something warm and human and wonderful happens when you send flowers by wire." It was believed that the appeal lent itself to presentation in all media; consequently FTD advertising in 1959 appeared in newspapers, magazines, television, radio, outdoor billboards, and business papers. A large part of the budget went into radio, a medium previously little used by the FTD. A musical theme representing the "sound of flowers" was devised, and vignettes depicting women receiving flowers were woven into commercials for that medium.

Television spot announcements utilizing the overall FTD theme were used at Easter and Mother's Day. The FTD placed advertisements in magazines prior to Christmas, Easter, and Mother's Day. Advertisements to promote the use of flowers for congratulations and thank you's were inserted in various trade magazines. A sample 1959 advertisement appears in Exhibit 3. Advertising expenditures in major media for 1959 are summarized in Table 1:

[1] National feature magazine sections, distributed by local newspapers in Sunday editions, e.g., *This Week, Parade.*

Table 1*

FTD ADVERTISING EXPENDITURES

(in 000's)—1959

Magazines	$ 191
Newspapers	179
Radio	665
Television	138
Business Papers	4
Outdoor	174
	$1,351

* *Printers' Ink*, 1961 Marketing Guide.

FTD sales for 1959 rose 11% from the preceding year.

In considering its advertising plans for 1960, the Florists' Telegraph Delivery Association believed that it would be helpful if more knowledge were available concerning the effectiveness of the various media employed by the FTD. Keyes, Madden & Jones was asked to conduct appropriate research.

Company and agency executives hoped that an experimental plan could be developed which would enable them to determine the return obtained by the FTD for advertising expenditures in any particular medium. Although a number of interim criteria of media usefulness existed, the executives sought to devise a plan that would give clues on the *sales* effectiveness of various media for the association. It was thought that through testing, it would be possible initially to find the *single* medium yielding the most FTD sales per advertising dollar invested. Eventually it was hoped to discover the most effective *combination* of media for the FTD advertising messages.

In late 1959, the executives approached the problem of designing a media effectiveness test to yield the most satisfactory data.

QUESTION

1. Design a media research study to test the sales effectiveness of FTD advertising.

Exhibit 1A

FTD AND FLORISTS' SALES
SELECTED YEARS

Year	Retail Flower Sales (000,000)	FTD Orders (000,000)	FTD % of All Sales	FTD Members (000)	FTD % of All Florists
1929	$176	$ 8.0	4.5%	5.4	57.4%
1935	99	4.9	4.9	6.7	59.6
1939	149	7.5	5.0	6.9	42.8*
1948	510	29.0	5.7	8.3	38.1
1954	661	41.2	6.2	9.9	42.4
1958-59	750	60.7	8.1	11.0	43.5

* The Telegraph Delivery Service (TDS) was founded in 1935. Its membership was usually about 20% of all florists.
Source: M.T. Fossum, "Performance of FTDA...1929-1959."

Exhibit 1B

TRENDS IN U.S. FLORICULTURE
TEN-YEAR GROWTH PATTERN—SELECTED ITEMS

Item	% Increase 1949-1959
Population	20%
Industrial production	54
Floricultural crop production	50
Per capita disposable income	52
All kinds of retail trade	53
Consumer expenditures with floriculture	54
Retail sales of florists	47
Number of FTD orders	84
Value of FTD orders	112
Average value per FTD order	16
All consumer prices	23
All wholesale prices	20

Source: M.T. Fossum, "Trends in U.S. Floriculture and Related Business Factors," January 1961.

Exhibit 2

1954-58 FTD ADVERTISING EXPENDITURES IN MAJOR MEDIA*

(000's)

	Total	Magazines	Newspapers	Network TV	Spot TV	Business Papers	Outdoor	Sunday Magazines**
1958	$1,008	$ 85	$ -	$807	$55	$ -	$60	$ -
1957	1,202	647	494	52	-	9	-	174
1956	1,168	541	627	-	-	-	-	169
1955	1,097	499	519	79	-	-	-	-
1954	1,003	531	448	23	-	-	-	-

* *Printers' Ink*, Guide to Marketing, 1960.
** Included in newspaper expenditure.

Exhibit 3

Something warm and human and wonderful happens when you send <u>flowers-by-wire</u>

In times of cheer, and times of sorrow—hearts open right up to flowers-by-wire. They speed love and hope and faith across the miles as no other gift can. They touch people so deeply, you almost *feel* the glow come back. They're the next best thing to having you *there*. Next time you can't be there, say it with flowers-by-wire. It's easy. It's fast. Just phone or visit your FTD florist—listed in the phone book Yellow Pages. Beautiful selections as low as $5. Delivery *anywhere*.

This Emblem Guarantees Quality and Delivery —or your money back

FLORISTS' TELEGRAPH DELIVERY

Advertisement no. FTD-5936-RI, 1 page; B & W, 7 x 10 in; Religious Publications, December 1959.

Florists'
Telegraph
Delivery Association (B)

Evaluating Media Effectiveness Test

FTD and agency executives evaluate the design and results of a recent media effectiveness test run in a number of FTD markets.

In 1960, Keyes, Madden & Jones, advertising agency for the Florists' Telegraph Delivery Association, conducted a test of media effectiveness at the request of the client. The objective of the test was to determine which single medium would yield the greatest volume of FTD business per dollar of advertising investment. The agency developed a creative theme which had been used in a number of media during 1959 when the FTD recorded substantial sales increases. [See Florists' Telegraph Delivery Association (A).]

Numerous aspects of the FTD situation were considered in planning and designing the media effectiveness experiment. Among the questions that had to be resolved were:

    a) what media to test;
    b) where to test them;
    c) what time period and duration to select for the experiment;
    d) how large an advertising budget to use for the test period;
    e) how to control against possibly invalid test results;
    f) what measure(s) of effectiveness to employ;
    g) how to derive the measure(s).

420

MEDIA AND AREAS FOR FTD EXPERIMENT

It was decided to confine the testing to specific markets. Four media were selected for testing—radio, newspaper, television, and outdoor. Because only several test cities were to be employed, magazine advertising was not included in the test; its scope was too broad. Test cities were selected from three different sections of the country, and each medium was to be used exclusively in one city in each of the three sections. The cities for each of the media are shown in Table 1:

Table 1

TEST MARKET CITIES–1960 FTD TEST

	TV	*Radio*	*Newspaper*	*Outdoor*
West	Spokane	Bakersfield	Fresno	Tacoma
South	Wheeling-Steubenville	Charlotte, N.C.	Charleston, W. Va.	Columbus, Ga.
Midwest	Madison	Grand Rapids	Wichita	Des Moines

It was believed that the selected cities were not unusual in terms of any unique monthly flower-purchasing pattern, any over- or underpurchase of flowers in general, or any peculiarities in flower retailing. Only national advertising had been run by the FTD in these cities prior to the 1960 test. The groups of markets were selected so as to be roughly comparable in geographic location, population, number of households, effective buying income per household, number of FTD members, and FTD sales per household. The data for each group of markets, in terms of these characteristics, are given in Table 2, and characteristics for each city in Exhibit 1.

Three additional cities were selected, comparable to the groups used for the media testing. In these cities, the national FTD media mix was to be run. Characteristics of these cities are given in Exhibit 2.

The six-month period from January to June 1960 was selected for the duration of the test. Two major florist holidays (Easter and Mother's Day) and one secondary holiday (Valentine's Day) would occur during these months.

The advertising expenditures during the test were to be based on the system normally employed in determining the national budget. Budgets were based on a percentage of 1959 sales in each group of cities, and were, therefore, roughly equal for each group. The actual amounts spent were between $4,500 and $5,000 for each set of cities over the six months, divided as follows:

Television markets	–	$4,790
Radio markets	–	$4,620
Newspaper markets	–	$4,710
Outdoor markets	–	$4,517

Table 2

FTD TEST MARKET CITIES—1960

Attribute	TV Markets	Radio Markets	Newspaper Markets	Outdoor Markets	Average
Population	860,300	907,300	1,014,100	932,400	903,522
Households*	257,700	264,600	304,800	238,400	266,375
E.B.I. per household**	$ 6,155	$ 6,196	$ 5,733	$ 6,327	$ 6,103
No. of FTD members	51	50	57	42	50
FTD sales per household (1958)	$ 1.16	$ 1.20	$ 1.12	$ 1.15	$ 1.16

* A "household" included all persons occupying a dwelling with the exception of institutional residents.
** Effective buying income was equivalent to "disposable personal income." It included both cash and noncash (e.g., imputed rentals of owner-occupied homes) income.

ADVERTISING PROGRAM

The advertising in the test cities was tied to the timing of the national FTD schedule. The national program during the test months included use of magazine and newspaper space, and radio and television time. Radio and newspaper were bought on an individual city basis. The magazine schedule for the first six months is detailed in Exhibit 3. Two operas were sponsored by the FTD over NBC-TV in 1960, prior to Valentine's Day and Easter.

For each test market group, preholiday advertising schedules were made up utilizing the FTD theme "something warm and human and wonderful happens when you send flowers by wire." Exhibits 4-7 contain a copy of the 1,000 line FTD newspaper advertisement, the script of the FTD one-minute radio commercial, the FTD television one-minute script, and a reproduction of the FTD outdoor color poster.

The television and radio schedules of one-minute advertisements purchased approximately 100 rating points in each market.[1] Newspapers carrying the 1,000-line black-and-white advertisement covered approximately 75% of the families in their city areas. The color outdoor posters covered 75% of the traffic flow in each market area. The schedules for each medium are outlined in Table 3:

Table 3

FTD MEDIA TEST SCHEDULES—JAN.-JUNE 1960

Medium	Time	Advertisement	Cost
Television:	Easter	9 announcements	$4,790
	Mother's Day	9 announcements	
Radio:	Easter	35 announcements	$4,620
	Mother's Day	35 announcements	
Newspapers:	Valentine's Day	1,000 lines	$4,710
	Easter	1,000 lines	
	Mother's Day	1,000 lines	
Outdoor:	Easter	75 showing*	$4,517
	Mother's Day	75 showing	

* A number 100 showing consisted of a sufficient number of poster panels in the market area to produce an efficient repetitive frequency and provide adequate coverage of the various traffic patterns in the area. A number 75 showing provided 75% of this coverage.

A breakdown of the advertising for each individual city is shown in Exhibit 8.

[1] One rating point equalled 1% of the ratio or television homes in the area. An announcement scheduled between programs with 10 and 13 ratings respectively was considered to have an 11.5 rating, or 11 1/2% of the radio or television homes tuned in.

MEASURE OF EFFECTIVENESS

Both the FTD and the agency were interested in measures that would yield data on the sales effectiveness of the various media. Because each FTD order cleared through a central clearing house in order to make proper payments to the florists involved, extremely accurate sales data were available.

The criterion selected was the *rate of sales increase* during the January to June 1960 period, compared with the same months in 1959. In making the measurements the national rate of increase was given an index value of 100, and experimental and control market increases were to be compared to the national figures. FTD orders during this period rose in number about 3½% and in value about 6½%.

From each group of cities, the number and value of FTD sales were computed. Index figures were derived for the number and value of the orders for each group of cities. These figures are presented in Table 4.

Sales volume during the six-month period were considered to reflect only the normal fluctuation pattern of FTD orders. Figures showing the index changes for each city are given in Exhibit 9. No unusual advertising or sales promotion on the part of non-FTD florists was noted during the test period.

Table 4

RATE OF FTD SALES INCREASE

(Total U. S. Rate of Increase—100)

| | Rate of Change—Jan.-June 1960 vs. Jan.-June 1959 | |
	Number	*Value*
All FTD sales	100	100
Three selected control markets	99	95
Test Markets:		
Outdoor	179	131
Radio	102	101
TV	42	46
Newspaper	37	63

Exhibit 1

TV TEST MARKETS

	Spokane, Wash.	Madison, Wisc.	Wheeling, W. Va. Steubenville, Ohio
Population 1/1/59	286,100	214,100	360,100
Households 1/1/59	93,500	60,500	103,700
Effective buying income per household 1958	$ 5,786	$ 6,904	$ 5,776
FTD members 1958	14	7	30
Sales per household	$ .91	$ 1.05	1.45

RADIO TEST MARKETS

	Bakersfield, California	Grand Rapids, Michigan	Charlotte, N.C.
Population 1/1/59	284,300	348,000	275,000
Households 1/1/59	84,500	106,300	73,800
Effective buying income per household 1958	$ 6,260	$ 6,015	$ 6,312
FTD members 1958	15	21	14
Sales per household	$ 1.03	$ 1.09	$ 1.59

NEWSPAPER TEST MARKETS

	Fresno, California	Charleston, W. Virginia	Wichita, Kansas
Population 1/1/59	341,800	339,500	332,800
Households 1/1/59	104,300	91,100	109,400
Effective buying income per household 1958	$ 5,724	$ 5,906	$ 5,569
FTD members 1958	21	15	21
Sales per household	$ .80	$ 1.22	$ 1.32

Exhibit 1 (cont.)

OUTDOOR ADVERTISING TEST MARKETS

	Columbus, Ga.	Tacoma, Wash.	Des Moines, Iowa
Population 1/1/59	247,800	319,900	264,700
Households 1/1/59	57,100	95,500	85,800
Effective buying income per household 1958	$ 6,855	$ 5,943	$ 6,182
FTD members 1958	7	18	17
Sales per household	$ .91	$ .99	$ 1.50

Exhibit 2

OTHER TEST MARKETS

	Brownsville, Harlingen, Tex.	Albuquerque, New Mexico	Tulsa, Oklahoma	Total
Population 1/1/59	374,100	238,500	381,000	993,600
Households 1/1/59	88,500	66,900	120,500	275,900
Effective buying income per household 1958	$ 4,405	$ 6,279	$ 5,708	$ 5,463
FTD members 1958	9	7	30	46
Sales per household	.60	1.21	1.73	1.24

Exhibit 3

FTD MAGAZINE ADVERTISING–JAN.-JUNE 1960

Publication	April	May	Total Cost
Business Week	One page		$ 5,660
Esquire		One page	9,200
Holiday	One page	One page	18,300
House Beautiful	One page	One page	15,200
National Geographic	One page	One page	27,486
New Yorker	One page		4,500
Newsweek	One page		11,155
Presbyterian Life	4th Cover	4th Cover	9,460
Town and Country	One page	One page	4,600
All advertisements in four colors.			$105,561

Source: Publishers Information Bureau, Leading National Advertisers, 1960.

Exhibit 4

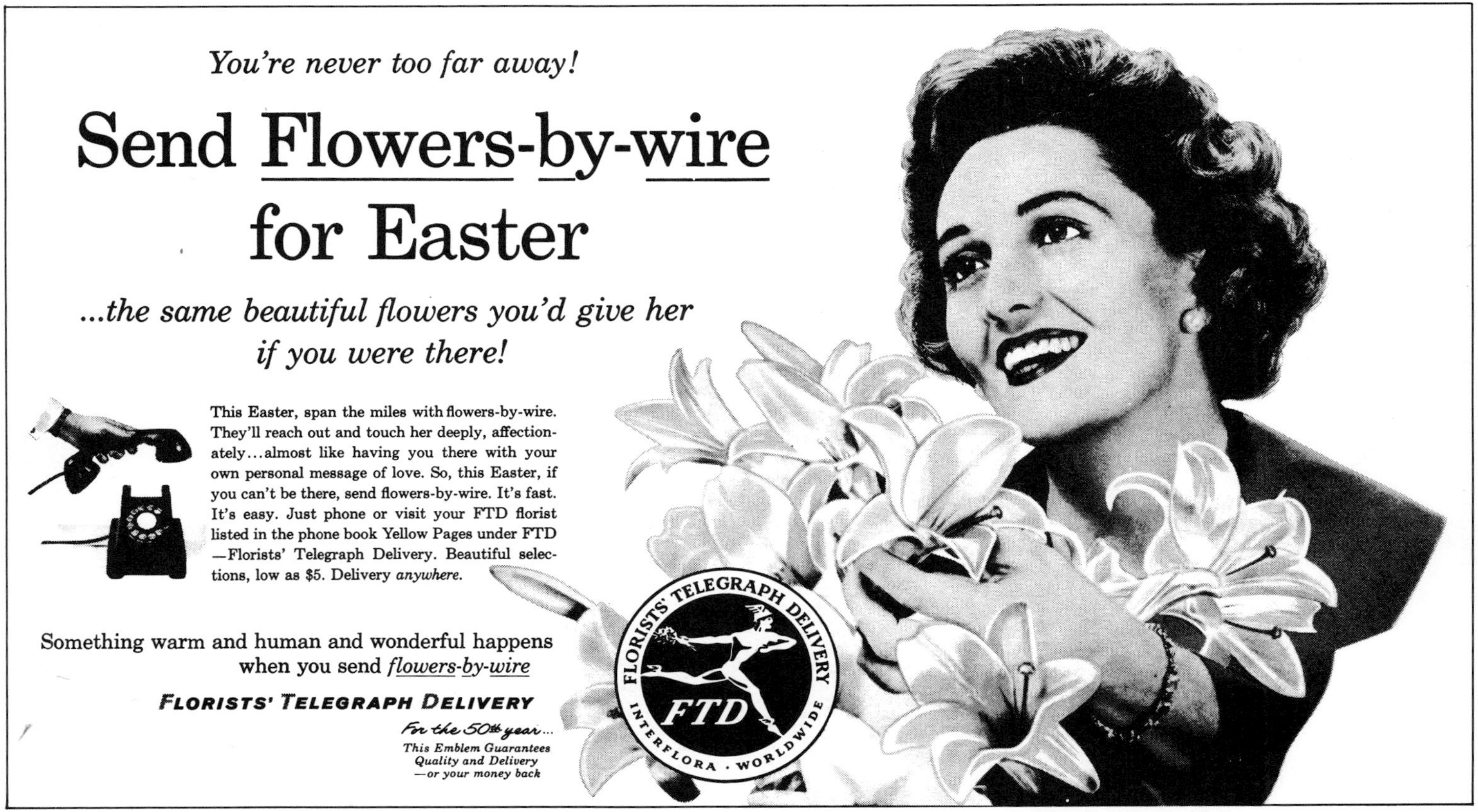

You're never too far away!
Send Flowers-by-wire for Easter
...the same beautiful flowers you'd give her if you were there!
This Easter, span the miles with flowers-by-wire. They'll reach out and touch her deeply, affectionately...almost like having you there with your own personal message of love. So, this Easter, if you can't be there, send flowers-by-wire. It's fast. It's easy. Just phone or visit your FTD florist listed in the phone book Yellow Pages under FTD—Florists' Telegraph Delivery. Beautiful selections, low as $5. Delivery anywhere.
Something warm and human and wonderful happens when you send flowers-by-wire
FLORISTS' TELEGRAPH DELIVERY
For the 50th year...
This Emblem Guarantees Quality and Delivery —or your money back
FLORISTS' TELEGRAPH DELIVERY
FTD
INTERFLORA · WORLDWIDE

Ad. no. FTD-6020: 1000 li., newspapers; *Bee*, Fresno, Cal., April 13, 1960; *Eagle*, Wichita, Kansas, April 13, 1960; *Gazette Daily Mail*, Charleston, W. Va., April 13, 1960.

Exhibit 5

RADIO SCRIPT, MOTHER'S DAY

Keyes, Madden & Jones
60-Second Radio E.T.

Production Date   Cont. No. KR
Feb. 27, 1959   10-4-60

Special Mother's Day
                    (as recorded)

FTD-5917

ANNOUNCER: This is the sound of a Mother's Day flower . . .

MUSIC: *Statement of theme (in 4 seconds): pizzicato strings*

ANNOUNCER: This is the sound of a *bouquet* of Mother's Day flowers.

MUSIC: *Restatement (in 6 seconds) of same theme with bowed strings*

ANNOUNCER: And *this* . . . is the sound of a mother . . . who received Flowers-by-Wire for her special day.

YOUNG WOMAN: Flowers . . . so fresh and sweet! Almost like having the children here.

MUSIC: *Flowers-by-Wire theme softly under*

ANNOUNCER: Yes . . . something *warm* and *human* and *wonderful* happens when you send *flowers by wire.* So easy . . . just phone or visit your FTD florist.

He'll guarantee you quality and delivery or your money back. So . . . if you can't be there on Mother's Day . . . make sure something *warm* and *human* and *wonderful* happens.

MUSIC: *Fade out under last line above*

ANNOUNCER: Send a bouquet of Mother's Day flowers.

MUSIC: *Restatement by bowed strings of theme (6 seconds)*

ANNOUNCER: Look up your FTD florist now in the phone book Yellow Pages . . . under FTD—Florists' Telegraph Delivery.

Exhibit 6
TELEVISION SCRIPT
Keyes, Madden & Jones-
10-1-60B

Length: 60 Sec. Film TV
Production Date: Nov. 14, 1958

Video	*Audio*
1. Full screen close-up of double plate glass doors to smart flower shop. On right half is FTD emblem. On cue "starts here," doors swing open (away from camera, as music comes in under) revealing florist behind counter writing up FTD order for customer. (dissolve to):	1. ANNCR.: (*off camera–low key*) It all starts here. (*pause*) *MUSIC: Establish as glass doors swing open and then hold under announcer:* ANNCR.: (*continues off-camera*) When you send flowers by wire. . . .especially at Easter. . . . .
2. MCU of woman (about 50) at door of middle-class home receiving box of flowers from FTD delivery-man. (dissolve to):	2. . . . .it's like reaching out a hand to someone far away. . .(*pause for music*). . .
3. MCU of woman inside house opening flowers. She lifts them up, holding them at arms' length, and regards them fondly. Then she reaches for card and reads it to herself. (Camera moves in slowly.) Then she crushes flowers to her face and half closes her eyes in deep emotion. (dissolve to):	3. Flowers are so personal. . .almost like sending part of yourself. (*pause*) When you send flowers by wire. . .something warm. . . and human. . .and wonderful happens! *MUSIC:* *Button up*
4. MCU announcer in shop beside floral display. On wall over his shoulder is FTD emblem. (On counter is an easel card.) On cue he indicates emblem on wall. (dissolve to):	4. ANNCR.: (*on camera*) It's so easy through Florists' Telegraph Delivery. Get acquainted with the florist near you who displays this emblem. . . He's listed. . .
5. ECU: insert of yellow pages listing. Finger points to "Florists Retail" then to FTD emblem and list of members. (dissolve to):	5. ANNCR.: (*off camera*). . .in the Yellow Pages. . .under "Florists Retail." He'll give you special attention. . .for the FTD emblem guarantees you quality and delivery—or your money back. *MUSIC: In under*
6. MCU: same woman at table graciously set for two, arranging flowers into center-piece. FTD emblem zooms up over scene from infinity on cue: "FLORISTS' TELEGRAPH DELIVERY" and fills screen. Hold FOR RUN-OFF FOOTAGE.	6. . . .so. . .this Easter. . .if you can't *be* there, make something warm and human and wonderful *happen* there. . . .Say it with flowers by wire . . .through Florists' Telegraph Delivery. . .FTD. . . . *MUSIC: Button up*

Exhibit 7

OUTDOOR POSTER

Exhibit 8

INDIVIDUAL CITY ADVERTISING SCHEDULE
TEST MARKETS
TV–JANUARY THROUGH JUNE 1961

Rates (per minute)

	Day	*Night*
Spokane	$ 65.00	$210.00
Madison	70.00	200.00
Wheeling-Steubenville	50.00	140.00
	$185.00	$550.00

Schedule and Cost

	7 *Minutes* *Day*	*2* *Minutes* *Night*	*Total*
Week preceding Easter	$1,295	$1,100	$2,395
Week preceding Mother's Day	1,295	1,100	2.395
Total	$2,590	$2,200	$4,790

Exhibit 8 (cont.)

RADIO – JANUARY THROUGH JUNE 1961

Rates (per minute)

Bakersfield	$ 8.00
Grand Rapids	16.00
Charlotte	42.00
Total	$66.00

Schedule and Cost

Week preceding Easter	$2,310
Week preceding Mother's Day	2,310
Total	$4,620

NEWSPAPERS–JANUARY THROUGH JUNE 1961

Rates

Line Rates

Fresno	E	$ .41	S	$ .41
Charleston, W. Va.	M & E	.56	S	.50
Wichita	M & E	.60	S	.45
		$1.57		$1.36

Schedule and Cost

1,000 Line Ads

Preceding Valentine's Day	$1,570
Preceding Easter	1,570
Preceding Mother's Day	1,570
Total	$4,710

Exhibit 8 (cont.)

OUTDOOR—JANUARY THROUGH JUNE 1961

Rates (75 showing)

	Number of Panels		
	Unilluminated	*Illuminated*	*Cost Per Month*
Columbus, Ga.	6	6	$ 396.00
Tacoma	8	9	885.00
Des Moines	11	12	977.50
Total	25	27	$2,258.50

Schedule and Cost

	52 Panels
Month preceding Easter (March 15-April 15)	$2,258.50
Month preceding Mother's Day (April 15-May 15)	$2,258.00
Total	$4,517.00

Exhibit 9

INDEX OF FTD SALES MOVEMENT
TEST MARKETS

Rate of Change—Jan.-June 1960
vs. Jan.-June 1959
(total U.S. rate of increase = 100)*

	Number	*Value*
All FTD sales	100	100
TV markets		
Spokane	-204	-122
Madison	239	197
Wheeling	198	128
Radio markets		
Bakersfield	-187	- 50
Grand Rapids	114	102
Charlotte	245	180
Newspaper markets		
Fresno	172	152
Charleston	160	145
Wichita	- 67	- 12
Outdoor markets		
Columbus	356	178
Tacoma	236	178
Des Moines	67	82
Selected markets		
Brownsville	350	214
Albuquerque	70	79
Tulsa	67	84

* E.g., 200 = twice as much percentage increase as national average increase; -100 = as much decrease as national average increase.

QUESTIONS

1. *Appraise the FTD media effectiveness test.*

2. *Using your analysis of the test results, what recommendations would you make to FTD?*

A.T.&T.
Princess Telephone

Level of Spending
Media Test

Executives responsible for the introduction of the Princess telephone appraise the results of a recent research study. Advertising recall and sales information are given for each of the four media treatments used in the test.

Before introducing the Princess telephone on a national basis, the Market Development Division of the American Telephone and Telegraph Company, in cooperation with participating operating companies of the Bell System, conducted a 4-month, full-scale marketing test of the new telephone in 4 "reconnaissance" areas. These areas were Colorado, Georgia, Illinois (excluding Chicago), and Central Pennsylvania. They were selected because they were considered representative of the Bell System's operating companies in terms of size, demonstrated sales ability, and adequate advertising media with a minimum of overlap into adjoining areas.

The principal objective of this test was to acquire information on the effects of different total amounts of advertising support and of varied media use patterns in behalf of the Princess. It was hoped that this information could be used to determine the most effective and economical level of advertising and media combination for the new telephone when national marketing commenced in 1960. Another major objective of the marketing test was to determine the approximate size of the market for the Princess in order to aid Western Electric in setting up final production schedules prior to the national introduction. Other areas in which information would be available from the 4-area test included pricing (slight variations in the initial and monthly recurring charges were to be employed in some areas), the effect of the Princess on sales of other equipment, and the characteristics of families that bought the Princess telephone.

The study plan was worked out by the Princess working committee in the New Product Planning section; this committee comprised representatives from AT&T's advertising agency and staff members from AT&T's advertising, marketing, and statistical groups. The study was carried out by advertising and statistical people in the participating operating companies. The 3 major dimensions of the advertising test were the specific locations in which the test was to be conducted, the media to be included, and the advertising expense levels to be tested (total and per customer). Background information on management's thinking on these points is contained in this excerpt from a memorandum prepared by the Market Development Division's working committee.

THE MEMORANDUM

Concerning how much should be spent on advertising to support the Princess, estimated expenditures on telephone extension advertising for 1959 may serve as a guide. (Telephone extension advertising was considered the previous marketing program most comparable to that envisioned for the Princess.)

	Total	Per Customer Household
For the system	$9,000,000	$.30
For the 4 participating companies	2,000,000	.24

Using the System expenditures as being most representative, for 4 months (the length of the proposed four-area test period) an average expenditure per customer household for extension advertising would be about 10 cents.

What are the principal advertising media that will be used in the test area?

1. Television
2. Newspapers
3. Radio
4. Bill inserts
5. Displays
6. Cards
7. Posters

News of the new telephone will be spread also by publicity and word-of-mouth.

National advertising on a full scale will not appear until after the end of the test period.

The principal media to be employed, following the telephone extension advertising pattern, would be newspapers (35%) and television (25%); other media would receive 40% of the budget.

Applying this distribution to the System figure of 30¢, for the year produces the following result:

	For Year	For 4 Months	
Newspapers	$.11	$.04	⎫ $.06
TV	.07	.02	⎬
All other	.12	.04	
Total	$.30	$.10	

For purposes of setting up the research plan, the following assumptions have been made:

1. That the principal advertising variables will be the amount spent on TV and newspaper advertising.

2. That as a *minimum,* the amount to be spent on these two media during the test period should probably be somewhat higher than the 6¢ figure above. Considering that the Princess is a new product and the heavier promotion on extensions is normally done in the fall of the year, we might assume for purposes of illustration that 10 ¢ would be a reasonable minimum.

3. That in some locations, for test purposes, it will be desirable to spend perhaps as much as two or three times this amount.

4. That the relative expenditures between TV and newspapers should be varied considerably in some places in order to provide some measure of the relative effectiveness of these two media.

5. That, although radio is a major medium, its use will be held relatively constant in all areas, as will the use of other media.

TEST DESIGN

The basic pattern for varying expenditures in newspapers and TV between different areas was as shown in Exhibit 1.

In planning the actual design of the advertising test, the AT&T group concentrated on how the areas designated in Exhibit 1 should be defined. One possibility considered was to have each of the 4 reconnaissance areas *in toto* correspond to a test area. Under this plan, however, the group believed that differences in Princess buying rates might not be a function of advertising expenditures alone. Rather, differences among the areas in other characteristics (such as economic status, rate level) might affect sales more than the advertising level or media pattern. The group believed that establishing 4 test cities in each of the areas, one to test each advertising-media treatment, would best allow for control of the advertising variables. This plan meant that advertising expenditures among the different participating companies would be reasonably well-equalized, and no one of the 4 areas would carry an especially light or heavy advertising program. Outside of the 16 test cities, participating operating companies were free to use whatever media, ad themes, and so on, they chose, providing that the test cities were not exposed to any variations.

The major criteria for city selection were that duplication of television coverage between cities be avoided, that the test cities have economic stability and balance, and that they be geographically spread. The cities selected and the advertising treatments for them are given in Exhibit 2.

The expense levels of Exhibit 1 were translated into numbers and frequencies of television commercials and newspaper insertions for a test period of 15 weeks' duration. These levels were defined by the test design group as follows:

Definitions of High and Low TV and Newspaper Levels   HIGH TV—12 spot announcements per week per TV station in the test city, with 5 spots in A (prime) time, 2 in B time, and 5 in C time. Spots in A were 20 seconds, since longer spots were seldom available. Spots in B and C time were generally 60 seconds.

LOW TV—4 spots per week per TV station with 2 in A time and 2 in C time.

HIGH NEWSPAPER—24 ads per newspaper in the 15-week period, in sizes ranging from 1,600 lines to the size normally used for telephone extension advertising by each company. The total linage was about 20,000 lines for each high city.

LOW NEWSPAPER—8 ads per newspaper during the same period, with the same size range. Total linage was about 6,000 lines.

All ads were in black and white only, since ROP color was not available in all newspapers.

Applying these television and newspaper purchase definitions in the actual test cities resulted in more accurate estimates of the per household expenditures for each of the test situations. These estimates are given in Exhibit 3.

To insure that the same basic selling appeal was used in all the test cities, the participating companies and AT&T agreed that the material be produced by AT&T. The actual advertisements employed in the campaign were built around the theme "It's little, it's lovely, it lights." This theme emphasized the major product features of the Princess, concentrating on the instrument's unique size, styling, and innovative dial-night light. Information on the Princess' major appeals had been sought throughout the course of the various customer reaction and sales tests conducted by AT&T for the Princess. These features had drawn the greatest attention during the earlier tests. The actual ads were tested by the advertising agency in conjunction with AT&T statisticians. Reproductions of representative newspaper and television advertisements from the introductory campaign for the Princess appear as Exhibits 4 and 5.

RESEARCH AND RESULTS

Recall studies of the Princess telephone advertising were made in all test cities in October and again in November, 1 and 2 months, respectively, after the advertising had been initiated. A group of 300 customers, randomly selected, were interviewed by telephone in each city in each study. These studies were conducted by professional interviewers under the auspices of the participating operating companies. The questionnaire focused on determining how fast and how well the advertising in each test city did its work in telling the Princess story. Customers were first given a chance to recall the Princess advertising unaided; if they did not, they were given cues in order to get a measure of aided recall. Unaided recall was in response to questions on whether the respondent had recently seen or heard any telephone company advertising. Aided recall was in response to questions about advertising for a "new telephone named the Princess." Recall was checked by asking respondents to describe the advertising and to tell in what media they had seen or heard it. In addition to percentage recall data, information was gathered on the most influential appeals of the Princess based on the reactions of those who had seen the advertising, and on the family size, telephone service, and so on, of those who had seen the advertising.

The statistical people at the New York headquarters compiled the recall data for each of the test cities and for each of the 4 advertising-media treatments employed in the test for both October and November. Summary information on the media to which recall was attributed was also prepared for each month. Based on the recall information, the expenditures for households covered and reached for each month were then computed for each medium. This information was then combined in order to show the total expense per household reached for each media treatment and to note any relationships between the expense per household reached and the recall level. In addition, data relating the advertising recall information to actual Princess sales were prepared. A final analytic approach involved a comparison of sales, recall, and advertising expenditure. This information appears in Exhibits 6-13.

In addition to the special advertising recall telephone interviews, questionnaires were administered in connection with every residence installation in the 16 test cities during the test period. Data from these interviews are presented as Exhibits 14 and 15.

Exhibit 1

EXPENDITURES PER CUSTOMER HOUSEHOLD
FOR 4-MONTHS' TEST PERIOD

	TV	News-papers	Total
Low TV—low newspaper	$.05	$.05	$.10
Low TV—high newspaper	.05	.10	.15
High TV—low newspaper	.10	.05	.15
High TV—high newspaper	.10	.10	.20

Exhibit 2

TEST CITIES SELECTED FOR THE PRINCESS STUDY

	Colorado	Georgia	Illinois	Pennsylvania
Low TV—low newspaper	Denver	Savannah	Danville	Altoona
Low TV—high newspaper	Greeley	Albany	Peoria	Scranton
High TV—low newspaper	Pueblo	Atlanta	Decatur	Harrisburg
High TV—high newspaper	Colorado Springs	Macon	Springfield	Lancaster

Exhibit 3

ESTIMATED ADVERTISING EXPENSE (CENTS PER HOUSEHOLD)

	Colorado	Georgia	Illinois	Pennsylvania	All Four States	
Low TV—	$.05	$.09	$.04	$.02	$.04	$.09
low newspaper	.06	.05	.05	.05	.05	
Low TV—	.05	.23	.08	.01	.04	.22
high newspaper	.21	.23	.13	.26	.18	
High TV—	.14	.31	.07	.13	.20	.24
low newspaper	.09	.02	.06	.05	.04	
High TV—	.14	.27	.07	.11	.12	.27
high newspaper	.13	.14	.15	.19	.15	

Exhibit 4

NEWSPAPER AD

PRESENTING

The Princess phone

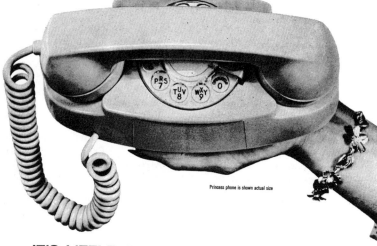

Princess phone is shown actual size

IT'S LITTLE, IT'S LOVELY, IT LIGHTS!

Here's a new extension phone that's dramatically different in size and styling from any you've ever seen before.

It's small—to take up less room on table or desk —lets you have an extension where space is limited.

It's modern—for the modern taste that asks for beauty with simplicity. Its low, lovely lines will grace any setting in your home.

The dial lights up. It glows in the dark so you can find it quickly and, when you lift the receiver, lights up brightly to make dialing easy.

You can choose from five popular colors— white, beige, pink, blue and turquoise. To enjoy the modern convenience of the Princess phone, just call your local telephone business office. Or ask a telephone serviceman.

(This space will be left blank for local insertion of company signature)

The Princess phone goes beautifully as an extension...

...in the bedroom where the light-up dial is handy...   ...in your kitchen to help you run your home...   ...in a teen-ager's room to give privacy...   ...in the living room by your favorite chair

The Princess phone with dial and night lights built in costs only pennies a day after a one-time charge. Your choice of five colors.

Exhibit 5

60-SECOND TELEVISION STORYBOARD AND COMMERCIAL

TV COMMERCIAL

AMERICAN TELEPHONE & TELEGRAPH COMPANY

SUBJECT: PRINCESS PHONE
THEME: EXTENSION SALES (ONE MINUTE)
PROD.: #8-10-329-B-60

video

1. OPEN ON CU OF PRINCESS PHONE ON SMALL TABLE WITH VASE OF FLOWERS. FADE IN "THE PRINCESS" AT BOTTOM OF SCREEN.

2. DISSOLVE TO VAN DERBUR WITH HAND ON PHONE. SHE IS DRESSED RATHER GLAMOROUSLY.

3. MOVE IN TO CLOSER SHOT OF VAN DERBUR AND PHONE.

4. CUT TO CU OF PHONE, LIT FOR NIGHT. WOMAN'S HAND LIFTS RECEIVER AND PHONE LIGHTS UP.

audio

1. MUSIC: PRINCESS THEME, INSTRUMENTAL INTRO, THEN FADE TO BG

   MARILYN VAN DERBUR:

   Introducing -- the Princess phone -- an exciting new extension telephone.

2. I'm Marilyn Van Derbur and this is the new Princess phone. It's so little -- (picks up phone) fits almost any place you'd like to put an extension phone.

3. Lovely, isn't it? So gracefully compact -- with clean lines and attractive color.

4. And it lights up for easy phoning in the dark.

Exhibit 5 (cont.)

AMERICAN TELEPHONE & TELEGRAPH COMPANY

SUBJECT: PRINCESS PHONE
THEME: EXTENSION SALES (ONE MINUTE)
PROD.: #8-10-329-B-60

TV COMMERCIAL

video

audio

5. DISSOLVE TO WOMAN IN BED. SHE PICKS PHONE OFF BEDSIDE TABLE AND STARTS TO DIAL.

5. The Princess phone is so light to pick up and hold -- so handy when you want to telephone in the comfort and quiet of your own room.

6. DISSOLVE TO CU OF PHONE. MAN'S HAND COMES TO PHONE ON STEP TABLE BESIDE COUCH.

6. It takes up so little space --

7. PULL BACK TO SHOW MAN ON COUCH TALKING ON PHONE.

7. in your living room, kitchen, -- or anywhere at home where you do a lot of telephoning.

8. DISSOLVE TO VAN DERBUR HOLDING PHONE.

8. The new Princess phone comes in five attractive colors -- that will complement any color scheme in your home.

Exhibit 5 (cont.)

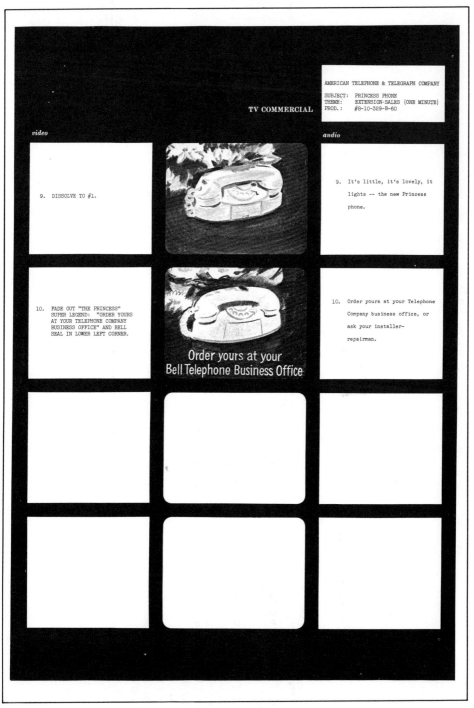

AMERICAN TELEPHONE & TELEGRAPH COMPANY

SUBJECT: PRINCESS PHONE
THEME: EXTENSION·SALES (ONE MINUTE)
PROD.: #8-10-329-B-60

TV COMMERCIAL

video

audio

9. DISSOLVE TO #1.

9. It's little, it's lovely, it lights -- the new Princess phone.

10. FADE OUT "THE PRINCESS" SUPER LEGEND: "ORDER YOURS AT YOUR TELEPHONE COMPANY BUSINESS OFFICE" AND BELL SEAL IN LOWER LEFT CORNER.

Order yours at your
Bell Telephone Business Office

10. Order yours at your Telephone Company business office, or ask your installer-repairman.

Exhibit 6

COMBINED AIDED AND UNAIDED RECALL OF PRINCESS ADVERTISING FOR TEST CITIES

	Georgia	Pennsylvania	Illinois	Colorado
High TV–high newspaper	Macon	Lancaster	Springfield	Colorado Springs
October	80%	82%	70%	86%
November	90	81	74	86
High TV–low newspaper	Atlanta	Harrisburg	Decatur	Pueblo
October	82%	75%	74%	89%
November	86	78	84	90
Low TV–high newspaper	Albany	Scranton	Peoria	Greeley
October	58%	64%	82%	72%
November	81	82	83	70
Low TV–low newspaper	Savannah	Altoona	Danville	Denver
October	69%	59%	45%	67%
November	72	67	49	75

Exhibit 7

**COMBINED AVERAGE AIDED AND UNAIDED RECALL
FOR 4 TEST ADVERTISING-MEDIA TREATMENTS**

	High TV– high NP	High TV– low NP	Low TV– high NP	Low TV– low NP
October study	80%	79%	69%	61%
November study	83	85	79	66

Exhibit 8

MEDIA RECALL* FOR 4 ADVERTISING-MEDIA TREATMENTS

	High TV– high NP	High TV– low NP	Low TV– high NP	Low TV– low NP
October study				
TV	64%	64%	47%	39%
Newspaper	34	28	38	27
November study				
TV	70%	74%	61%	46%
Newspaper	38	30	44	30

* Results for the groups mentioning both TV and newspapers in combination were added to both groups. This preserved the balance between the 2 although it inflated the results somewhat.

Exhibit 9

ADVERTISING COSTS (CENTS PER HOUSEHOLD)*

Television	High TV– high NP	High TV– low NP	Low TV– high NP	Low TV– low NP
First month—expense				
all households	$.04	$.05	$.01	$.01
households reached	.06	.08	.02	.03
Second month—expense				
all households	.04	.06	.01	.01
households reached	.06	.08	.02	.03
Newspapers				
First month—expense				
all households	$.09	$.01	$.10	$.02
households reached	.26	.05	.26	.07
Second month—expense				
all households	.04	.01	.04	.01
households reached	.09	.03	.08	.03

* Based on actual media purchases.

Exhibit 10
ADVERTISING EXPENSE AND RECALL SURVEY

	High TV– high NP	High TV– low NP	Low TV– high NP	Low TV– low NP
First month				
Expense–households reached*	$.32	$.13	$.28	$.10
Recall–October	80%	79%	69%	61%
First two months				
Expense–households reached	$.47	$.24	$.38	$.16
Recall–November	83%	85%	79%	66%

* Cents per household

Exhibit 11
ADVERTISING RECALL AND SALES

City	Inward Princess Movement over Total Inward Movement (November)	Recall (November study)	Average Recall
Savannah	28.1%	72%	
Atlanta	27.8	86	
Harrisburg	25.8	78	
Lancaster	24.3	81	
Greeley	24.2	70	78%
Altoona	24.0	67	
Colorado Springs	22.5	86	
Scranton	22.0	82	
Denver	21.3	75	
Pueblo	19.6	90	
Decatur	18.9	84	
Springfield	17.5	74	
Macon	16.8	90	78%
Danville	15.6	49	
Peoria	14.7	83	
Albany	13.4	81	

Exhibit 12

ADVERTISING RECALL AND REPLACEMENT SALES

City	Princess replacements as % of residence main phones (October & November)	Recall (November study)	Average recall
Atlanta	1.3%	86%	
Harrisburg	1.3	78	
Savannah	1.2	72	
Albany	1.0	81	
Greeley	1.0	70	80%
Lancaster	.9	81	
Macon	.8	90	
Decatur	.8	84	
Scranton	.7	82	
Denver	.7	75	
Altona	.7	67	
Colorado Springs	.6	86	
Springfield	.6	74	76%
Pueblo	.4	90	
Peoria	.4	83	
Danville	.3	49	

Exhibit 13

ADVERTISING RECALL, HOUSEHOLD SALES, AND HOUSEHOLD ADVERTISING COSTS

City	Sales per household (annual basis)	Recall (November study)	NP & TV costs per household
Colorado Springs	$.65	86%	$.27
Greeley	.61	70	.18
Denver	.59	75	.05
Atlanta	.53	86	.18
Harrisburg	.42	78	.12
Savannah	.40	72	.08
Albany	.36	81	.30
Lancaster	.29	81	.23
Decatur	.29	84	.09
Macon	.28	90	.27
Altoona	.28	67	.04
Pueblo	.26	90	.12
Scranton	.24	82	.22
Springfield	.24	74	.13
Danville	.20	49	.06
Peoria	.18	83	.11

Exhibit 14

MEDIA RECALL OF PRINCESS ADVERTISING BY PURCHASERS

City and treatment*		TV only	NP only	TV & NP	Media recalled TV, NP etc.**	TV, etc.	NP, etc.	Etc. only	Approximate number of questionnaires
Altoona	A	30%	5%	26%	28%	5%	1%	5%	686
Danville	A	16	16	14	17	13	8	16	876
Denver	A	25	7	21	25	10	4	8	20,331
Savannah	A	22	3	17	41	10	3	8	3,458
Scranton	B	17	15	27	24	4	9	4	1,385
Peoria	B	25	7	29	27	5	3	4	3,966
Greeley	B	18	12	25	25	8	4	8	1,063
Albany	B	14	9	28	33	7	3	6	645
Harrisburg	C	32	4	15	29	11	2	7	3,624
Decatur	C	26	5	26	26	8	3	6	2,131
Pueblo	C	31	4	23	27	10	2	3	1,751
Atlanta	C	36	3	17	28	12	1	3	18,385
Lancaster	D	21	9	32	23	7	2	6	955
Springfield	D	21	6	26	29	9	3	6	1,830
Colorado Springs	D	30	5	22	24	9	4	6	2,867
Macon	D	29	3	24	35	5	2	2	2,551

* Treatments: A—Low TV, low newspaper   C—High TV, low newspaper
              B—Low TV, high newspaper   D—High TV, high newspaper

** Etc.—other media.

Exhibit 15

INFLUENCE ATTRIBUTED TO ADVERTISING BY PURCHASERS

City and treatment*		Respondents indicating advertising most influential	Approximate number of questionnaires
Altoona	A	32%	686
Danville	A	28	876
Denver	A	30	20,331
Savannah	A	28	3,458
Scranton	B	34	1,385
Peoria	B	46	3,966
Greeley	B	24	1,063
Albany	B	20	645
Harrisburg	C	41	3,624
Decatur	C	41	2,131
Pueblo	C	43	1,751
Atlanta	C	36	18,385
Lancaster	D	39	955
Springfield	D	40	1,830
Colorado Springs	D	38	2,867
Macon	D	29	2,551

* Treatments: A—Low TV, low newspaper C—High TV, low newspaper
    B—Low TV, high newspaper D—High TV, high newspaper

QUESTIONS

1. What are the objectives of AT&T's testing?

2. Is the test well designed? How would you improve it, given the current objectives?

3. Was the design well executed?

4. What do the test results tell you? Given this information, what marketing actions would you take?

Brown-Forman
Distillers Corporation

The marketers of Old Forester bourbon must decide whether (and, if so, how) to continue a program of substantially-increased advertising expenditures in selected market areas.

In late 1967, advertising and sales executives of Brown-Forman Distillers Corporation were reviewing the recently completed five-year "push" campaign on behalf of Old Forester bourbon whiskey. The campaign, which essentially consisted of substantially increased advertising expenditures in specific areas, had been conducted in 18 selected United States markets. Among management's considerations in evaluating the program were whether or not to continue the stepped-up advertising level in the selected markets, and/or to extend it to still further market areas.

The "push market" campaign had been initiated in 1959 to bolster sales of Old Forester, which, along with the firm's other major bourbon, Early Times, had for several years not been performing up to management's expectations. As an integral part of the campaign, Brown-Forman had introduced a new Old Forester 86 proof brand in 1962 to complement the established 100 proof bottled-in-bond Old Forester brand.

THE UNITED STATES LIQUOR INDUSTRY

a) **The Market** The years after 1954 were ones of growth for the liquor industry, following some years of declining per capita consumption of distilled spirits. Exhibit 1 shows that in contrast to the rather stable consumption pattern of the 1947-1954 period, gallonage and per capita use increased after 1954. Total distilled spirit-dollar expenditures are also given in Exhibit 1. By 1963 it was estimated that there were 52.8 million consumers of distilled spirits of which 31.9 million were men and 20.9 million were women. (See Exhibit 2 for a breakdown by selected population segments.)

Industry sources attributed this marked increase in liquor consumption after

1954 largely to an increasing adult population, a period of relatively uninterrupted economic growth, and changing social patterns that made alcoholic beverages a more acceptable part of American life. Affecting the types of liquor consumed were greater diversity of available products and consumer tastes, as well as changing "fashions" in drink recipes as in other parts of American life.

b) The Product The liquor industry is composed of three general product categories: distilled spirits, beer, and wine. The distilled-spirits category is further broken down into two general classificiations (whiskeys and nonwhiskeys) made up of ten different product types as follows:

Whiskeys	*Nonwhiskeys*
Blends	Gin
Straights	Vodka
Bonds	Rum
Canadian	Brandy
Scotch	All other

Each product type is manufactured under federal standards (see Exhibit 3) and close federal supervision. However, these federal standards are sufficiently loose to allow wide variations in quality and distinctiveness of taste, not only among product types but particularly within any given category. Although the manufacturing process and liberal federal standards lead to these variations, the average consumer finds it difficult to differentiate between certain product types, e.g., blends and Canadian whiskeys. Within a given product type, it is particularly difficult for the average consumer to detect even some of the wide variations in taste and quality.

Total distilled spirit case sales and market shares for the seven major types of distilled spirits are given in Exhibit 4. Historically, blends and straight whiskey have dominated the market with blends controlling as much as 60% of sales during the short-supply World War II period. However, the previously noted changing consumer patterns in the early 1950s brought about significant shifts in market share. Although the desire for diversity on the part of consumers affected sales of all distilled spirits types, the increasing status associated with an imported label resulted in relatively faster growth of Scotch and Canadian whiskeys. Furthermore, the move toward "lightness" in liquor taste caused significant shifts as evidenced particularly in the growth of vodka's popularity.

c) The Industry Structure The distilled spirits industry had traditionally been dominated by the "Big Four"—Seagrams, National, Schenley, and Hiram Walker. Together the Big Four controlled more than 60% of industry sales; each firm marketed a full line of nationally known brands in every product category, and, with the exception of Hiram Walker, had diversified to a significant degee outside the liquor industry. The depth and breadth of their product line was substantial; the Big Four, nevertheless, derived their strength primarily through concentrating on one or two product types. For example, Seagrams possessed the first, third, fourth, and fifth top selling blend brands; and National controlled the first, sixth, seventh, and eighth top-selling bourbon brands. (See Exhibit 5.)

Several medium-sized companies competed directly with the Big Four on the basis of nationally known brand names. These firms included Brown-Forman, Heublein, and Jim Beam. Despite the fact that some of these companies carried a full line of nationally known brands, they derived their strength almost solely by concentrating on one product type. Even though they were significantly smaller in size, they were somewhat more successful than their Big Four competitors on the basis of profits as a percentage of sales. (See Exhibit 6.)

In addition to the above, a large number of smaller national or regional firms competed mainly on the basis of price through private labels, or by multilabels with little or no advertising. These firms made up a highly competitive segment of the industry; industry analysts considered the influence of these firms only minor, despite their significant growth, particularly among private labels.

d)   Advertising   Despite some price competition, notably by local labels, competition for volume and profits within the distilled spirits industry was primarily on the basis of establishing nationally known brand names. Hence national advertising became one of the industry's prime competitive tools. By industry agreement no firm advertised distilled spirits on television or radio, forcing distilled spirits advertising to communicate entirely through printed media— magazines, newspapers, and billboards. The dominance of liquor advertising in these media is evidenced by the fact that in 1965 liquor advertising surpassed automobile advertising as the largest single category in *Time* magazine.

Advertising expenditures were heavily concentrated among a few brands (see Exhibit 7) and generally corresponded with the concentration of sales. For example, the top 8 blend brands represented 67% of total blend sales; the top 6 Scotch brands made up 70% of total Scotch sales; the top 2 Canadian brands comprised 70% of total Canadian sales. Industry folklore held that heavy advertising afforded an established brand a 10% to 20% price advantage for some 5 to 10 years, depending on the product category.

e)   Distribution   Advertising performed a key marketing function, but distribution also played a vital role. The system of distribution within the distilled spirits industry was a complicated one, geographically covering local areas with extremely diverse backgrounds, customs, and attitudes toward liquor.

The most important distinction was that between the "open states" and "control states." In the 32 open states distribution followed the traditional form of manufacturer to wholesaler to retailer. Since hundreds of different brands passed through this distribution system to some 215,000 retailers (1966 estimate) the wholesaler was depended on not only for physical facilities but also for development and expansion of retailer contacts. Owing to rising costs and a trend toward retail supermarket chain ownership the number of wholesalers had been declining, with a consequent increase in the power of the remainder. In the 18 control states, state agencies controlled the distribution of liquor to the extent that in certain cases state employees operated the retail liquor stores. In the control states a variety of laws affected marketing activity—for example, limits on the amount of point-of-sale promotion, limits on the number of total brands carried within the state, a common price floor for brands sold in the state, and bars on the mention of price in advertisements. These regulations varied from state to state.

THE BOURBON MARKET

Bourbon dominated the American liquor market until the short-supply situation during World War II greatly increased the popularity of blends. With the replenishment of stocks after the war, bourbon began to regain its market dominance. The trend toward lightness in liquor taste during the middle 1950s, which caused a shift away from bonded whiskey, also retarded somewhat the advance of the bourbon category as a whole. Each of the relatively few "bottled-in-bond" bourbon brands responded to this shift in consumer taste by introducing a lower proof, lower price straight under the same brand name. *The Liquor Handbook* commented on this situation:

> Those fortunate enough to have top-selling higher-priced bonds in their lines are fully aware that maintaining prestige has an essentiality going beyond case sales. This prestige is readily transferred to 86 proof versions of famous bonds, as witness the striking success of Old Crow 86 proof, and the quite rapid market progress made by Kentucky Tavern, Old Taylor, I. W. Harper, and Old Grand-Dad when introduced in the mid-Fifties as 86 proof straight whiskeys. They were joined by famed Old Forester in 1959. Old Fitzgerald, the only major "hold-out," introduced a straight version in 1964.[1]

Within the straight bourbon whiskey category which represented 90% of bourbon sales in 1966, there were a wide variety and number of brands ranging in price from roughly $3.00 to $5.50 per fifth. The nationally known volume brands such as Old Crow, Jim Beam, and Early Times, generally commanded prices in the $5.00 to $5.50 per fifth range. The established premium "bottled-in-bond" bourbon brands such as Old Grand-Dad, Old Forester, Old Taylor, I. W. Harper, and Old Fitzgerald, ranged in price from $6.50 to $7.50 per fifth.

[1] *The Liquor Handbook,* 1967 edition, page 142.

BROWN-FORMAN–COMPANY BACKGROUND

The Brown-Forman Distillers Corporation was founded in 1870 by George Garvin Brown. Throughout the late 1800s and early 1900s Brown-Forman remained small in size, producing bourbon whiskeys centered around the brand name of Old Forester. Prohibition then brought about a complete curtailment of production of Brown-Forman products for general consumption; however, the firm continued to produce small quantities of whiskey for medicinal purposes. With the repeal of Prohibition in 1933, the company immediately joined the many distillers who attempted to satisfy the pent-up consumer demand.

As before, the company's production centered around the bottled-in-bond whiskey, Old Forester. Sales were light during the immediate post-Prohibition era but began to expand rapidly due to the increasing success of Old Forester and the market's acceptance of Early Times, a straight bourbon whiskey acquired by Brown-Forman during Prohibition. For many years Old Forester had been a leading bottled-in-bond whiskey; during the 1940s and early 1950s Early Times also came to be the nation's leading straight bourbon. During this period Brown-Forman offered also a number of minor brands, most of which were sold on a regional basis. These labels included Kentucky Dew, Bottoms Up, L&G (all straights) and King (a blend) among others.

BROADENING THE PRODUCT LINE

As Brown-Forman continued to experience success through the early 1950s with its bourbon product line, management believed that it should diversify into other product lines in an attempt to take advantage of the changing consumer patterns that were occurring in the 1950s. Leading the list of acquisitions Brown-Forman made in the 1950s was that of the Jack Daniels Distillery in Lynchburg, Tennessee. Jack Daniels, makers of a Tennessee sour-mash whiskey of the same name, became a wholly owned but independently operated subsidiary of Brown-Forman. The other acquisitions made during this period were Usher's Green Stripe Scotch whiskey, Bols Liqueurs, Veuve Clicquot Champagne, and Cruse and Anheuser wines. Continued success encouraged the company to diversify further during the 1960s. First, Oertel's Brewery—a regional producer of real-draft beer—was acquired, followed by the acquisition of Chequers Scotch, and Korbel Champagne and Brandy through the Jack Daniels Distillery. A new Canadian whiskey brand, Gold Pennant, was introduced in 1964. Ambassador Scotch and Old Bushmills Irish Whiskey were acquired in 1967.

Although by 1967 the company was represented in almost every product category, throughout this period the long-established brands of Old Forester and Early Times remained the mainstay of the company's product line. The other well-known brand, Jack Daniels, played an increasingly important role in the company's sales and profits during the late 1950s and early 1960s.

MARKETING ORGANIZATION

Brown-Forman maintained parallel advertising and sales department organizations, meeting at the top under the Director of Marketing who was also an Executive Vice-President of the company. The Sales and Advertising Departments were organized geographically owing to the pressing need to adjust marketing efforts to local conditions. A vital function served by field-sales representatives was to convey local conditions to the home office in addition to their tasks of implementing company promotion and merchandising as well as working with the distributor's salesmen.

Similarly Brown-Forman's advertising program featured extensive utilization of local media and point-of-sale support for the national campaign. The majority of the company's various marketing campaigns were not only originated and planned by the Sales and Advertising Departments but also usually implemented by them. This factor seemed to stem from Brown-Forman's strong drive to expand sales, although the 200 field sales representatives were continually reminded of the ultimate importance of profits.

ADVERTISING PHILOSOPHY

The national portion of Brown-Forman's advertising was composed entirely of insertions in leading national magazines; this program also served as an umbrella for the additional local advertisements. Management believed that a national magazine advertisement should get the attention of the consumer as well as reinforce in his mind Brown-Forman's already well-established brand names.

The criteria used for selecting media and messages in the national campaigns were to place in prestige magazines four-color ads with a "class" appearance, featuring use or implied use of the product. Media selection focused on reaching people over 35 years of age with incomes over $7,500, who were heavy consumers of liquor. A typical magazine schedule was that for Old Forester in 1966 as summarized below from Publisher's Information Bureau records:

Publication	Insertions	Cost
Newsweek	9	$163,115
Saturday Evening Post	5	180,993
Sports Illustrated	9	121,255
Time	10	296,696
Town and Country	5	16,400
True	3	57,338
U.S. News and World Report	3	36,855
Venture	2	7,331
Total		$879,983

Sixty percent of the national ad budget was spent during the last four months of the year, the period during which the bulk of liquor sales traditionally came.

The local portion of Brown-Forman's advertising consisted of newspaper and outdoor media, as well as point-of-sale material. The purpose of this advertising was more specific than the national campaign in that it was designed not only to reinforce Brown-Forman's established brand names but also to carry the consumer further toward the purchase decision—although executives were reluctant to claim that advertising actually could create sales.

Local advertising typically featured special announcements such as those regarding bottle sizes and prices. The use of local advertisements emphasizing price was seen as particularly important, since several states' regulations on price in liquor advertising limited treatment of this subject on a national magazine basis. Local advertising and promotion were planned in close conjunction with field sales personnel in order to adapt to local conditions in general and to coordinate with current sales programs.

THE PUSH MARKET CAMPAIGN

While Brown-Forman was extensively strengthening and expanding its product line in the late 1950s, management was somewhat concerned over adverse trends in the sales of its bourbon line of Old Forester and Early Times. The slowing trends were accentuated by the above mentioned consumer tendency to favor "lighter taste" in liquor.

As a reaction to this development, in 1959 Brown-Forman followed the lead of all but one of the prestige bottled-in-bond brands by introducing an 86 proof straight bourbon under the prestigious Old Forester label. The lower proof was intended not only to serve the changing consumer tastes toward lightness, but also to offer a lower-priced bourbon on the market. The 86 proof brand did not, however, yield sales gains comparable to those achieved by competitive lower-proof brands which had been introduced throughout the mid-1950s. Therefore, in 1962, Brown-Forman executives were faced with a downward trend in Old Forester bond sales and only a moderate improvement by the new 86 proof brand.

At this point the Sales Department suggested the idea of a major "push market" campaign for the Old Forester brand, and the 86 proof version in particular. The concept of push markets was an old one within Brown-Forman. It had first been used in several control states in an effort to keep the state regulatory officials from eliminating a particular Brown-Forman brand from the authorized list of brands to be sold within that state. Later, the push market idea had been employed in both "open" and "control" distribution systems, but always utilized a very limited number of states as push markets. Therefore the 1962 proposal represented the first application of the concept on a relatively large scale.

CAMPAIGN OBJECTIVES

In terms of overall objectives for the push market campaign, Brown-Forman considered it essential that growth in Old Forester's sales should exceed that of the liquor market in general, and of the faster-growing straight bourbon category in particular. To accomplish this growth, management decided to emphasize the new 86 proof version and utilize the full prestige of the Old Forester bond name even though bond sales might suffer somewhat as a consequence of some consumers merely shifting from the bond (100 proof) to the 86 proof version. The threat of such prospective shifts was a calculated risk executives were prepared to take in order to stimulate overall Old Forester sales.

Management hoped to obtain the desired growth without excessive merchandising and advertising expenditures; thus the minimization of costs became another objective. Although company executives were willing to expand the push market concept to the point of a large-scale campaign, they did not want to initiate a national undertaking at this time.

In addition, despite the fact that retail distribution was well established throughout the country for Old Forester 100 and the new 86 proof brand (management estimated in the 80% to 90% overall range) the push market campaign was also aimed at creating excitement among the trade in order to assist the field representatives in their job of motivating distributor salesmen. Finally there was the explicit desire to learn from the "campaign" in terms of aiding the planning of future marketing programs.

SELECTING THE PUSH MARKETS

With these objectives as a framework, the Advertising and Sales Departments set out to formulate the details of the program. Together they developed criteria for selecting individual markets to be included in the campaign. First, they agreed that selected markets must display a strong 86 proof potential as reflected by such factors as previously successful introductions of 86 proof labels by other prestigious bonds—such as Old Forester's principal competitor, Old Grand-Dad. This was believed to be largely a matter of those geographic areas which had traditionally been bourbon-oriented. Second, the Old Forester brand name had to have an excellent history in each market. Third, Brown-Forman needed to be working from a position of marketing strength within each of the selected markets, those in which the field sales force, the advertising climate, and the distribution system were sufficiently effective to allow the company to take full advantage of its resources allocated to the campaign. Using the above criteria, 18 markets—representing about half the brand's sales—were selected to be included in the Old Forester push market campaign beginning in fiscal 1962. (See Exhibit 8 for the names of the 18 markets.)

DESIGNING THE CAMPAIGN

Following selection of the individual markets, the Brown-Forman advertising and sales executives turned to planning the specifics of the campaign. First, it was decided to treat the push market campaign as an investment over 5 years. Under this plan advertising expenditures in the push markets would be substantially increased over previous levels in the early years (1962-63) and held at the higher level, anticipating a modest return during the middle period (around 1964) and a considerable return of profits during the latter years (1965-66). This was in contrast to the perhaps more traditional approach of increasing marketing expenditures gradually—as sales grew—over the entire period of 5 years. Management favored their approach, since it featured a "big splash" right from the beginning, which they believed would result in a distinct competitive advantage and justify itself through greater profits at the end. In the nonpush markets it was agreed to attempt to maintain advertising expenditures at the existing per case levels during the five-year period.

In considering the part advertising would play in the campaign, advertising executives recognized that the marketing plan for the 18 push markets primarily involved the local component in Brown-Forman's dual local/national advertising approach. However, in view of the importance of this campaign and the large segment of the national market represented by the 18 territories, it was decided that the Old Forester national advertising should be closely tied to local advertising presenting the same theme exposure that was to be used in the 18 individual markets. Thus not only would the level of expenditures in national magazines be increased slightly, but the same advertising format would be used in both the national and local media.

After determining this relationship between national and local advertising, executives then turned to a consideration of the crux of the push market campaign—local advertising. The approach developed centered around the question "What does it take to do the job in each push market," from which several guidelines evolved. First, Old Forester should be the most heavily advertised bourbon in the dominating medium in each market. Second, a continuity must be maintained within each market throughout the five-year period to obtain sufficient frequency but avoid overspending in any one year. Third, dramatically new techniques should be tried whenever possible, such as the use of Spectacolor in newspapers. Fourth, the local advertising must be carefully related to the sales effort given by the Sales Department in each push market. Finally, although intermarket uniformity was an objective, flexibility *within* any given market remained desirable. Management thought it optimal to treat each push market with an individualized approach.

CAMPAIGN IMPLEMENTATION: 1961-64

Even though they used the above guidelines as a general framework, management evaluated each market independently to determine the level of expenditures and the market's media mix. Exhibit 9 shows the widely varying degrees by which Old Forester advertising expenditures were increased in the 18 push markets during the campaign, particularly in 1962, although expenditures in all markets were considerably boosted.

Similarly, different media patterns were employed in different markets. In the Georgia market, for example, two Atlanta newspapers were used without outdoor billboard support; in the Maryland market, three Baltimore newspapers were used with outdoor support; in the Louisiana market five cities received Old Forester newspaper advertising with outdoor support. (See Exhibit 10 for a summary of 1964-65 Old Forester media expenditures in the Maryland market.) By treating each market individually, the advertising department thought it could best utilize its experience. As one executive put it:

> We knew these markets very well so we ended up treating each one individually, trying to apply what was right in each particular situation. In addition, we had the advantage of some hindsight from observing Old Grand-Dad's introduction of an 86 proof.

The level of expenditures and the media mix for each market was determined by that market's particular strengths and weaknesses, but the content of Old Forester's advertisements was essentially the same throughout the country in the push markets and in the nonpush markets. The similarity between the national magazine messages and the local campaign messages was present throughout the campaign, and especially so during the program's early years when both were virtually identical. Exhibits 11 and 11A and 12 and 12A illustrate this close relationship between national magazine and local newspaper advertising. Exhibit 11 is an example of the "announcement copy" magazine ad used early in the campaign, in which the 100 proof and the 86 proof labels received about equal emphasis; the follow-up ads were similar in appearance (Exhibit 11A is a newspaper "follow-up" ad) but placed major emphasis on the Old Forester brand name, with minor attention directed to the 100 proof and 86 proof bottles. This major emphasis on the brand name represented an intermediate step toward an almost complete emphasis on the Old Forester 86 proof label during most of the campaign. Exhibits 12 (magazine) and 12A (newspaper) are typical of the ads run during the bulk of the campaign.

In general, the Old Forester ads emphasized the 86 proof bottle; this was in contrast to the Old Grand-Dad approach of several years before, in which alternate advertisements had featured, in turn, the 100 proof and the 86 proof labels. However, Brown-Forman management thought that the great impact created by the high level of spending at the outset of the campaign justified their decision to place principal emphasis on the 86 proof label during the bulk of the campaign.

CHANGE IN STRATEGY: 1965-66

Although the messages in the ads during the latter years of the push market campaign continued to be centered around Old Forester 86 proof, Brown-Forman's management believed that the program's maturity by 1965 necessitated a slight change in strategy. During most of the campaign the consumer's attention was directed primarily toward the new product's lower proof and therefore lighter taste. Little was said about such factors as the lower price of the 86 proof or the variety of bottle sizes available. However, during the latter years, local advertising began to emphasize more frequently "specials" which were run in 1965 and 1966. (See Exhibits 13 and 14.) During the same period, the national campaign became less closely tied to local newspaper advertisements, retaining a more general theme. (See Exhibit 15.)

An additional change instituted in 1965 was the substantial increase in local advertising expenditures highlighted in Exhibit 9. The declining advertising cost per case in 1964, caused by expanding sales in the push markets, justified this hike in the eyes of Brown-Forman management.

RESULTS OF THE PUSH MARKET CAMPAIGN

In reviewing the push market program during 1967, Brown-Forman's management believed that the campaign had proved to be a great success. Much of their enthusiasm was based on case sales of Old Forester, which had increased by 45% during this period, while the total bourbon market had grown by only 11%, and the straight bourbon category by 14%. (See Exhibit 16 for data on the case sales of Old Forester and its principal competitors.)

In achieving this performance, the 18 push markets clearly represented the crucial factor. From 1962 to 1966 combined Old Forester sales in these markets had increased by over 60%. During the same period, Old Forester case sales in the nonpush markets had advanced by about 25%. In examining the campaign's results (Exhibit 17 gives 1962-66 case sales in each of the 18 push markets) Brown-Forman's management was particularly pleased with the consistency of the campaign's impact. In 16 of the 18 markets the growth of Old Forester case sales exceeded that of the total bourbon market as well as that of the faster growing straight category. Furthermore, in 11 of the 18 markets, the growth of Old Forester case sales exceeded that of Old Grand-Dad, its principal competitor. Company executives regarded this growth as especially notable, since they believed that Old Forester advertising expenditures were considerably less than those of competing labels. Finally, although Brown-Forman's management had anticipated gains for Old Forester 86 proof as a direct result of the campaign, they were pleasantly surprised to see that Old Forester 100 proof sales had reversed its previous downward trend and even experienced a slight improvement over the sales level of several years before. (See Exhibit 18.)

Executives thought that the push market campaign had gone exceedingly well, especially in view of the fact that this was the first time Brown-Forman had undertaken the push market concept on such a large scale. They considered the advertising plans to have been well conceived and well implemented. However, they questioned whether the push market concept should be continued in the 18 key markets and extended to all markets, or cut back. Naturally they were anxious to maintain the advertising momentum behind the brand which the push market campaign had established. They also pondered how, if at all, they should react to the estimated 30% increase in local ad spending undertaken by Old Grand-Dad in 1966.

Brown-Forman Distillers Corporation

LIST OF EXHIBITS

Exhibit	*Contents*
1	Apparent Distilled Spirit Consumption in the United States: 1934-1966
2	Percent of United States Adult Consumers of Distilled Spirits by Selected Population Segments – 1963
3	Distilled Spirits: Product Characteristics and Federal Standards
4	Consumption of Distilled Spirits by Types: 1962-66
5	Case Sales and Producers of Leading Brands within the Major Product Types – 1966
6	Financial Information on Selected Firms in the Liquor Industry: 1961-66
7	Advertising Expenditures for Selected Leading Brands of Distilled Spirits – 1966
8	Brown-Forman Push Markets in the 1962-66 Campaign
9	Advertising Expenditures by Individual Push Markets: 1961-66
10	Summary of Media Expenditures, Maryland Market: 1964-65 (12 months)
11	1963 Color Magazine Ad
11A	1963 Newspaper Ad
12	1965 Color Magazine Ad
12A	1965 Newspaper Ad
13	1965 Newspaper Ad Featuring 86 Proof Bottle and Price
14	1966 Newspaper Ad Featuring Half-gallon, 86 Proof Bottle and Price
15	1966 Color Magazine Ad Featuring 86 Proof Bottle
16	Total Case Sales of Selected Leading Bourbon Brands: 1962-66
17	Old Forester Case Sales by Individual Push Markets: 1961-66
18	Old Forester Case Sales (Combined, 100 proof, 86 Proof) for the Combined 18 Push Markets: 1961-66

Exhibit 1

APPARENT DISTILLED SPIRIT CONSUMPTION
IN THE UNITED STATES: 1934-1966

Year	Total Consumer Expenditures (in millions)	Wine Gallons (in millions)	Per Capita Consumption (gallons)
1966	$8,630	308.9	1.58
1965	8,160	294.2	1.52
1964	7,715	275.9	1.44
1963	7,300	259.0	1.38
1962	6,900	253.7	1.37
1961	6,360	241.5	1.33
1960	6,185	234.7	1.31
1959	5,920	225.5	1.28
1958	5,615	215.5	1.24
1957	5,490	212.1	1.25
1956	5,230	215.2	1.29
1955	4,835	199.6	1.21
1954	4,600	189.5	1.18
1953	4,545	194.7	1.23
1952	4,410	183.7	1.18
1951	4,320	193.8	1.26
1950	3,955	190.0	1.26
1949	3,690	169.6	1.14
1948	3,900	171.0	1.17
1947	4,560	181.7	1.27
1946	5,060	231.0	1.65
1945	4,400	190.1	1.44
1944	3,850	166.7	1.26
1943	3,200	145.5	1.09
1942	2,685	190.3	1.42
1941	1,980	158.2	1.19
1940	1,675	145.0	1.10
1939	1,510	134.7	1.03
1938		126.9	0.98
1937		135.4	1.05
1936		122.1	0.95
1935		89.7	0.70
1934		58.0	0.46

Source: *LBI Facts Book*, 1967 edition, pp. 32, 34.

Exhibit 2

PERCENT OF UNITED STATES ADULT CONSUMERS OF DISTILLED SPIRITS BY SELECTED POPULATION SEGMENTS–1963

Total	46.7%
Sex	
Men	58.0
Women	36.3
Age (by age of household head)	
18-24	40
25-34	51
35-44	48
45-54	42
55-64	33
Over 65	20
Annual household income	
Under $2,000	22.3
$2,000-$2,999	35.8
3,000-3,999	43.8
4,000-4,999	46.7
5,000-6,999	58.8
7,000 or more	61.4

Source: *The Liquor Handbook*, 1964 edition, pp. 67-78.

Exhibit 3

DISTILLED SPIRITS: PRODUCT CHARACTERISTICS AND FEDERAL STANDARDS

Product Type	*Standards*
Straight Bourbon Whiskey	Fermented from corn, rye and barley (51% corn by law) distilled at no more than 160 proof, and aged in new white oak charred barrels for not less than 2 years. The comparatively low distillation proof and the aging process produce the full-bodied taste of the product.

Exhibit 3 (cont.)

Product Type	Standards
Bonded Straight Bourbon Whiskey	A straight bourbon whiskey with the added requirements of being 100 proof and aged not less than 4 years, which produces a somewhat fuller-bodied taste.
Blended Whiskey	Law requires that by volume blended whiskeys be at least 20% straight whiskey, the rest being unaged grain neutral spirits (a tasteless product). In practice straights or a mixture of straights represent a much larger percentage of the volume, but the addition of neutral spirits makes the product extremely light-bodied.
Canadian Whiskey	Fermented from an equal mixture of corn, rye, and wheat, with malt added and distilled at a high proof, and aged for not less than 2 years, producing a light-bodied, clean-tasting product.
Scotch Whiskey	Barley dominates the fermented mixture and largely accounts for Scotch's smoky taste. The heaviness or lightness of taste depends on the mixture of low proof and high proof distillates from different regions. Aged not less than 2 years.
Rum	A distilled spirit derived from fermented sugar cane, resulting in light (Puerto Rico) and dark (Jamaica) rums. Aged in white oak barrels.
Gin	Grain neutral spirits (a tasteless product) are redistilled primarily with juniper berries and other botanical flavorings at high proofs to minimize flavor transference. (Not aged.)
Vodka	A product of grain neutral spirits (a tasteless product) which is typically filtered through charcoal to further eliminate any taste. (Not aged.)

Note: Proof is equal to twice the alcoholic content of a product; i.e., 100 proof equals 50% alcoholic content.

Exhibit 4

CONSUMPTION OF DISTILLED SPIRITS BY TYPES: 1962-66

	1966	1965	1964	1963	1962
Total Consumption in Cases (000's)	116,083	110,670	104,334	97,925	96,139
Product Type					
Blend	23.9%	24.8%	25.9%	27.1%	28.3%
Straight	23.6	23.8	24.9	25.0	25.1
Scotch	11.0	11.0	10.2	9.8	9.4
Gin	10.2	10.2	10.3	9.8	9.6
Vodka	10.2	9.8	9.3	8.9	8.5
Canadian	7.1	6.7	6.2	5.9	5.6
Bond	2.5	2.6	2.9	3.2	3.5
All others (Rum, Brandy, etc.)	11.5	11.1	10.3	10.3	10.0
Total	100.0	100.0	100.0	100.0	100.0

Source: *The Liquor Handbook*, 1967 edition, pp. 42, 44.

Exhibit 5

CASE SALES AND PRODUCERS OF LEADING BRANDS WITHIN THE MAJOR PRODUCT TYPES—1966

Brand Name	Producer	Approximate Case Sales (000's)
Blends		
Seagram's 7 Crown	Seagram	7,750
Imperial	Hiram Walker	2,225
Calvert Extra	Seagram	2,100
Kessler	Seagram	1,525
Four Roses	Seagram	1,375
Fleischmann Preferred	Fleischmann	1,275
Schenley Reserve	Schenley	1,200
Corby's Reserve	Hiram Walker	1,150
Bourbon		
Old Crow*	National	2,325
Jim Beam	Beam	2,275
Early Times	Brown-Forman	1,750
Ancient Age	Schenley	1,500
Ten High*	Hiram Walker	1,450
Old Taylor*	National	1,350
Old Grand-Dad*	National	1,075
Old Sunny Brook	National	900
Bourbon Supreme	American	725
Old Forester*	Brown-Forman	725
Scotch		
Cutty Sark	Buckingham	1,650
J&B	Paddington	1,650
Johnnie Walker Red	Canada Dry	925
Dewar's	Schenley	750
Black & White	Fleischmann	675
Ballantine's	21 Brands	650
Canadian		
Seagram's VO	Seagram	3,000
Canadian Club	Hiram Walker	2,800
Vodka		
Smirnoff	Heublein	2,750
Gilbey's Vodka	National	550
Tovarisch/Tvarscki	American	550
Wolfschmidt	Fischel	500
Gin		
Gordon's Gin	Renfield	2,350
Gilbey's Gin	National	1,925
Fleischmann's Gin	Fleischmann	1,300
Seagram's Gin	Seagram	950
Beefeater	Kobrand	825
Hiram Walker Gin	Hiram Walker	675

* Available in 100 and 86 proof.
Source: *Business Week*, February 18, 1967, p. 87.

Exhibit 6

FINANCIAL INFORMATION ON SELECTED FIRMS IN THE LIQUOR INDUSTRY: 1961-66
(SALES IN MILLIONS)

	Seagrams			Schenley			National			Hiram Walker		
	Sales	Profits	EPS	Sales	Profits	EPS	Sales	Profits	EPS	Sales	Profits	EPS
1966:	$1,104.4	4.1%	$2.57	$477.9	4.3%	$3.98	$898.3	4.5%	$3.09	$565.3	6.7%	$2.21
1965:	1,005.1	4.1	2.34	460.8	5.2	4.69	829.0	3.8	2.37	529.6	6.5	2.01
1964:	897.1	4.2	2.15	405.8	2.8	2.16	810.9	3.3	2.02	498.2	6.5	1.87
1963:	864.5	4.0	3.90	400.4	2.6	1.69	766.9	3.0	1.67	478.8	6.2	3.45
1962:	820.4	3.9	3.60	370.5	2.0	1.17	775.1	3.1	1.76	469.3	5.9	3.22
1961:	794.2	3.9	3.53	405.9	3.0	2.01	748.1	3.1	1.67	449.9	5.9	3.05

	Brown-Forman			American			Beam			Glenmore		
	Sales	Profits	EPS	Sales	Profits	EPS	Sales	Profits	EPS	Sales	Profits	EPS
1966:	$ 154.1	6.7%	$1.38	$120.5	2.4%	$2.91	$100.8	7.0%	$2.68	$ 68.4	0.9%	$0.60
1965:	137.5	6.2	1.13	113.7	2.5	2.76	92.4	6.7	2.25	72.0	1.5	1.02
1964:	123.7	6.2	1.25	111.9	2.5	2.73	87.8	6.6	2.05	70.6	1.9	1.31
1963:	119.6	5.8	1.79	110.1	2.5	3.01	86.5	6.8	2.50	67.8	1.8	1.19
1962:	108.8	5.8	1.62	104.9	2.5	2.82	85.1	6.4	2.37	65.5	1.3	0.85
1961:	101.8	4.6	1.19	97.2	2.6	2.60	82.5	5.9	2.11	68.8	2.2	1.46

Source: *The Liquor Handbook*, 1967 edition, p. 103, and 1964 edition, p. 81.

Exhibit 7

ADVERTISING EXPENDITURES FOR SELECTED LEADING BRANDS OF DISTILLED SPIRITS—1966
(figures in thousands)

Brand Name	Magazine	Newspaper	Outdoor	Total
Blends				
Seagram's 7 Crown	$2,518	$2,612	$2,022	$7,153
Calvert Extra	1,625	2,369	906	4,900
Four Roses	1,115	1,256	592	2,963
Schenley Reserve	154	549	750	1,453
Bourbon				
Old Crow	1,726	1,030	779	3,535
Jim Beam	529	758	99	1,486
Early Times	867	913	NA	1,780
Ancient Age	416	575	550	1,541
Ten High	386	415	NA	801
Old Taylor	1,294	565	17	1,875
Old Grand-Dad	1,726	841	181	2,748
Old Sunny Brook	23	417	318	758
Old Forester	880	894	290	2,064
Scotch				
Cutty Sark	858	401	NA	1,259
J&B	1,226	NA	18	1,244
Dewar's	668	410	375	1,453
Black & White	847	1,125	130	2,102
Ballantines	1,134	169	NA	1,303
Canadian				
Seagram's VO	2,426	1,206	724	4,455
Canadian Club	2,292	1,416	NA	3,708
Vodka				
Smirnoff	1,931	1,916	883	4,729
Gin				
Gordon's Gin	1,114	622	147	1,883
Gilbey's Gin	922	437	353	1,711

Source: *The Liquor Handbook*, 1967 edition, pp. 218-23, 234-44, 253-4.

Exhibit 8

BROWN-FORMAN PUSH MARKETS IN THE 1962-66 CAMPAIGN

Brown-Forman Push Markets (18)

Metro New York	South California
Maryland	Chicago
Florida	Indiana
Georgia	Michigan
Kentucky	North Carolina
Louisiana State	Virginia
South Carolina	Arkansas
Tennessee	Missouri
North California Bay	South Texas

Other Brown-Forman Markets (39)

Alabama	New Jersey
Alaska	New Mexico
Arizona	North California Valley
Colorado	North Dakota
Connecticut	North Nevada
Delaware	North Texas
District of Columbia	Ohio
Hawaii	Oklahoma
Idaho	Oregon
Illinois	Pennsylvania
Iowa	Rhode Island
Kansas	South Dakota
Maine	South Nevada
Massachusetts	Upstate New York
Minnesota	Utah
Mississippi	Vermont
Montana	Washington
Nebraska	West Virginia
New Hampshire	Wisconsin
	Wyoming

Source: Company records.

Exhibit 9

ADVERTISING EXPENDITURES
BY INDIVIDUAL PUSH MARKETS: 1961-66

Market	1966	1965	1964	1963	1962	1961
Metro New York	$127,500	$ 81,300	$ 86,500	$ 78,400	$ 85,000	$ 43,500
Maryland	118,000	114,000	64,500	66,500	56,500	32,000
Florida	105,000	91,500	66,500	71,500	69,000	34,000
Georgia	47,500	36,900	21,600	16,150	17,450	7,800
Kentucky	37,300	35,000	33,800	35,500	42,400	16,500
Louisiana	103,000	91,000	64,500	67,500	55,500	32,000
South Carolina	16,800	13,100	5,850	3,750	3,650	900
Tennessee	47,500	42,000	29,700	31,000	31,200	14,600
North California Bay	47,000	45,500	35,500	33,800	30,500	13,400
South California	176,500	166,500	160,000	203,000	83,500	42,900
Chicago	310,000	310,000	163,000	154,000	143,000	59,000
Indiana	23,200	23,000	21,500	26,500	24,500	12,300
Michigan	23,600	25,000	16,800	7,800	17,700	12,700
North Carolina	800	1,200	500	120	50	-0-
Virginia	38,000	39,000	22,000	20,500	20,500	10,800
Arkansas	34,500	23,000	13,000	12,300	9,900	9,300
Missouri	54,500	63,500	34,700	41,500	44,500	16,500
South Texas	98,000	92,500	74,000	75,000	75,000	26,200
Total Push Market Advertising	$1,408,700	$1,294,000	$913,950	$944,820	$809,850	$384,400

Source: Company records.

Exhibit 10

SUMMARY OF MEDIA EXPENDITURES, MARYLAND MARKET: 1964-65 (12 MONTHS)

	Morn. or Eve.	Circulation	Line Rate	Frequency	Lines per Ad	Total Expenditures
Newspaper						
Baltimore						
News-American	Eve.	218,439	$0.85	25	600	$13,515
Sun	Both	400,401	1.15	25	960	41,369
				2	Full Page	
Salisbury						
Times	Eve.	25,327	0.16	25	405	1,717
Outdoor						
Baltimore		4 painted billboard locations for 12 months; 1 for 1 month				15,275
		Special 30 poster preholiday showing				4,200

Source: Summarized from company records.

Exhibit 11

1963 COLOR MAGAZINE AD

Enjoy bourbon's favorite flavor
OLD FORESTER, at either proof

86 proof
light-hearted bourbon

100 proof
mellow bottled in bond

Among Kentucky's great bourbons, Old Forester continues to stand out as the unchanging standard of perfection. Enjoy its unsurpassed flavor at either mellow 100 proof or light-hearted 86 proof. Whichever you choose, you'll recognize the rare pleasure offered only by this finest of fine bourbons.

Promised on every label:

"There is nothing better in the market"

KENTUCKY STRAIGHT BOURBON WHISKY · BROWN-FORMAN DISTILLERS CORPORATION · AT LOUISVILLE IN KENTUCKY

As appearing in *Gourmet*, February, March; *Social Spectator*, Winter Editions; *Time*, March 13, April 10; *Town & Country*, January, February, March, April; *U.S. News & World Report*, January 30, February 27, March 27, April 24, 1961.

Among Kentucky's great bourbons, Old Forester continues to stand out as the unchanging standard of perfection. Enjoy its unsurpassed flavor at either mellow 100 proof or light-hearted 86 proof. Whichever of the two proofs you choose, you'll recognize and enjoy the rare pleasure offered only by this finest of fine bourbons.

Ad No. 8661G: (C1727A), 4 col. x 266 lines (1064 lines), Newspapers, 1961.

Exhibit 12

1965 COLOR MAGAZINE AD

Enjoy the brightest taste in bourbon

Old Forester's deep, dazzling flavor
highlights quiet get-togethers.
Makes moments like this a brilliant idea.

OLD FORESTER

At 86 or 100 proof, "There is nothing better in the market."

© 1965. KENTUCKY STRAIGHT BOURBON WHISKY • 86 PROOF • 100 PROOF BOTTLED IN BOND • BROWN-FORMAN DISTILLERS CORPORATION • AT LOUISVILLE IN KENTUCKY

Ad. No. 10701-52003: this advertisement appears in magazines.

Enjoy the brightest taste in bourbon

Old Forester's deep, dazzling flavor
highlights quiet get-togethers.
Makes moments like this a brilliant idea.

OLD FORESTER

At 86 or 100 proof, "There is nothing better in the market."

© 1965. KENTUCKY STRAIGHT BOURBON WHISKY • 86 PROOF • 100 PROOF BOTTLED IN BOND • BROWN-FORMAN DISTILLERS CORPORATION • AT LOUISVILLE IN KENTUCKY

Ad No. 10701-51005-E: 300 lines (3 col. x 100 lines); this advertisement appears in newspapers.

Exhibit 13

1965 NEWSPAPER AD FEATURING 86 PROOF BOTTLE AND PRICE

OLD FORESTER

$5 35 4/5 qt.

86 PROOF

OLD FORESTER

KENTUCKY STRAIGHT BOURBON WHISKY

© 1965. BROWN-FORMAN DISTILLERS CORPORATION • AT LOUISVILLE IN KENTUCKY

Ad No. 10701-51002-U: 600 lines (4 col. x 150 lines); this advertisement appears in newspapers.

Exhibit 14

1966 NEWSPAPER AD FEATURING HALF-GALLON, 86 PROOF BOTTLE AND PRICE

Make it an Old Forester kind of party, with the money saving, Party Size Half Gallon. 64 ounces of great bourbon flavor. (43 generous drinks.) And the little conveniences too: built-in pourer to control the flow; and special side grooves to ensure your grip. So—invite 'em all...and save a little. **$14⁴⁰** 86 PROOF

At 86 or 100 proof, "There is nothing better in the market."

KENTUCKY STRAIGHT BOURBON WHISKY • 86 PROOF • 100 PROOF BOTTLED IN BOND • BROWN-FORMAN DISTILLERS CORPORATION • AT LOUISVILLE IN KENTUCKY ©1966.

Ad. No. 10701-61026: 600 lines (4 col. x 150 lines); this advertisement appears in Alabama newspapers.

Exhibit 15

1966 COLOR MAGAZINE AD FEATURING 86 PROOF BOTTLE

Ad No. 10701-62004: this advertisement appears in magazines.

Exhibit 16

TOTAL CASE SALES OF SELECTED
LEADING BOURBON BRANDS: 1962-66

Old Forester

	1966:	725,000
	1965:	650,000
	1964:	550,000
	1963:	525,000
	1962:	500,000

Old Grand-Dad

	1966:	1,075,000
	1965:	975,000
	1964:	875,000
	1963:	775,000
	1962:	750,000

Old Crow

	1966:	2,325,000
	1965:	2,300,000
	1964:	2,225,000
	1963:	2,225,000
	1962:	2,225,000

Old Taylor

	1966:	1,350,000
	1965:	1,300,000
	1964:	1,250,000
	1963:	1,200,000
	1962:	1,200,000

Source: *Business Week*; February 23, 1963; February 22, 1964; February 20, 1965; February 19, 1966; February 18, 1967.

Exhibit 17

OLD FORESTER CASE SALES
BY INDIVIDUAL PUSH MARKETS: 1961-66

Market	1966	1965	1964	1963	1962	1961
Metro New York	25,500	23,100	23,000	24,700	24,700	24,700
Maryland	32,200	32,000	30,900	26,900	23,100	20,200
Florida	29,100	23,500	19,900	18,800	19,300	18,800
Georgia	19,200	13,700	9,200	6,700	4,900	4,000
Kentucky	14,300	12,900	11,600	11,300	12,200	12,100
Louisiana State	40,100	32,800	28,300	26,400	25,400	24,100
South Carolina	13,300	8,100	4,800	3,500	2,600	2,900
Tennessee	25,300	14,100	10,500	8,600	8,100	7,100
North California Bay	14,500	13,700	12,800	11,700	11,100	8,500
South California	41,800	41,200	36,400	35,700	33,100	29,300
Chicago	78,300	63,200	54,400	47,100	46,100	42,900
Indiana	10,100	8,600	7,900	7,600	8,600	8,600
Michigan	9,500	8,300	6,400	5,700	5,400	6,100
North Carolina	10,900	9,000	7,700	6,500	5,800	5,500
Virginia	19,200	16,100	12,200	9,700	6,600	8,300
Arkansas	20,300	12,800	6,000	4,400	3,800	3,500
Missouri	18,500	18,400	16,400	15,300	16,400	16,100
South Texas	46,800	38,200	33,400	27,600	27,700	N.A.
Total	468,900	389,700	331,800	298,200	284,900	242,700
						(incomplete)

Source: Company records.

Exhibit 18

OLD FORESTER CASE SALES
(COMBINED, 100 PROOF, 86 PROOF)
FOR THE COMBINED 18 PUSH MARKETS: 1961-66

Combined Old Forester		
	1966:	468,902
	1965:	389,706
	1964:	331,795
	1963:	298,244
	1962:	284,880
	1961:	276,867
Old Forester, 100 Proof		
	1966:	144,732
	1965:	144,963
	1964:	141,646
	1963:	N.A.
	1962:	N.A.
	1961:	201,559
Old Forester, 86 Proof		
	1966:	324,170
	1965:	244,743
	1964:	190,139
	1963:	N.A.
	1962:	N.A.
	1961:	75,308

Source: Company records.

QUESTIONS

1. How successful has the "push" campaign been? Why?

2. Should a stepped-up level of advertising be continued in the selected markets? Should it be extended to still other markets?

3. What changes, if any, should be made in Old Forester's advertising program? Why? Treat particularly your views of the mix between national and local media.

Abex Corporation

The manufacturer of industrial controls equipment directs a nine-week institutional TV/newspaper advertising campaign at the financial community in selected metropolitan areas following a corporate name change. The effectiveness of the campaign is judged by pre- and post-measures of attitudes toward and awareness of Abex.

In August 1968, Mr. J. Paul Carroll, Director of Public Relations at the Abex Corporation, a diversified manufacturer of industrial controls equipment, reviewed the results of a nine-week institutional advertising campaign which had been conducted in nine selected metropolitan areas during the previous spring. He studied the findings with special interest since the campaign represented a significant departure in media selection from past Abex advertising. Specifically television commercials and local newspaper advertisements had been employed by Abex for the first time in an attempt to create in the financial community an awareness of Abex as "a controls company."

COMPANY HISTORY

In 1902, the American Brake Shoe and Foundry Company was formed through the merger of five small foundries into a new company that made products, mostly brake shoes, for the railroad industry. As the growing firm prospered, it expanded into production of other railroad products; in 1910, a subsidiary was organized to manufacture manganese steel castings for the mining and construction industries as well as for the railroad industry. The company continued to expand, entering the steel forging business in 1920 and the bronze bearing business in 1928. Eventually a division was formed to manufacture and sell automotive brake linings.

World War II saw the company's production expanded manyfold to meet military and essential civilian needs. With the return of production to normal levels during the postwar years, company management recognized a need to intensify diversification efforts due to technological advances which posed problems of obsolescence for some of the major product lines; in addition, sales to the railroads were beginning to decline. Thus, in 1955, the firm entered the hydraulic equipment business through the purchase of the Denison Engineering Company, a well-established manufacturer of hydraulic pumps, presses, and controls. Expanding from the Denison nucleus, hydraulic products for aerospace and industrial applications soon became an important segment of the company's business. In 1959, the firm formed an international company in Europe. During the 1960s, penetration was extended in the friction materials and hydraulics segments of the business through further acquisitions and internal growth. By 1968 the company had grown to nine divisions, operated plants in four European nations as well as in Mexico, Canada, and Japan, and employed over 14,000 people. (Exhibit 1 contains selected financial data for the years 1958-1967.)

AMERICAN BRAKE SHOE BECOMES ABEX

The first corporate name change took place in 1943, when the American Brake Shoe and Foundry Company became the American Brake Shoe Company. Then, as company management took a number of steps during the postwar years to become less dependent on the highly cyclical railroad business, it became increasingly apparent that there was little in the name "American Brake Shoe" to reflect the diversity and scope of the company's operations. Further problems arose as the firm broadened its international operations and the name posed translation difficulties in a number of languages. In addition, management discovered that two or more divisions would at times be unknowingly competing to sell similar products to the same customer; all divisions and subsidiaries determined their own names, and essentially had no tie with each other or with the parent company.

To deal with all these problem areas, management set about to create a new corporate identity emphasizing the strength of the parent company. At the center of this new identity was to be a new corporate name that could encompass all corporate operations. Three criteria were formulated against which to evaluate each proposed name:

1. It must be satisfactory to all countries.
2. It must be unidentifiable with any particular product as well as sufficiently flexible to allow for corporate growth into unknown product lines in the future.
3. It must connote the "right" (modern, forward-looking) image and generally "sound good."

Mr. Carroll emphasized the particular need of the company to create the "right" corporate identity:

> We're not selling a 25-cent item . . . *reliability* is a huge factor in selling industrial products like ours, and this makes a strong central name a great asset—I would say much more so than in consumer marketing. We especially need a strong dependable corporate identity, since our products are diffused through usage in *other* industrial products. We serve a small number of large

customers in highly concentrated industries such as automobiles and railroads . . . to these people the supplier's reputation is particularly important.

In 1963 the company hired Lippincott & Margulies, marketing consultants who had gained a wide reputation for their expertise in corporate image and name-change programs. Lippincott & Margulies narrowed down an original list of over 1,000 proposed names to 20, on the basis of how well each proposed name was believed to meet the established criteria. Fifteen of these 20 were eliminated due to conflicts with other firms. Of the remaining 5, "Abex" was preferred as the "cleanest-sounding" and also because it was already owned by the company (as a trademark used by one of the divisions). Lippincott & Margulies was especially pleased with Abex because of its simplicity and resultant ability to serve as both corporate name and trademark; in addition, they believed the name to be extremely graphically exploitable. (See Exhibit 2 for the Lippincott & Margulies design for the new name.)

After a careful screening for possible overseas conflicts or unfavorable foreign-language connotations, Abex was adopted as the corporate trademark in mid-1965. At the time it was estimated that a three-year transition period would be necessary to achieve sufficient recognition of the new name before it could be officially adopted as the legal corporate name.

Reaction throughout the company to the new name was generally even more favorable and rapid than had been anticipated. Thus, in response to pressure, primarily from divisional marketing personnel, the transition period was accelerated and the American Brake Shoe Company legally became the Abex Corporation on April 26, 1966.

CORPORATE ADVERTISING
IN CONJUNCTION WITH THE NAME CHANGE

Prior to 1965, the company had never had a consistent corporate advertising program. The great bulk of its advertising featured products and was handled individually by the separate divisions. Management, however, viewed the corporate name change as merely one aspect of a broader movement to create a new corporate identity in which the parent company's reputation for quality, dependability, and good management would be dominantly linked to all its subcorporate parts. Since a national advertising program was regarded as essential to the successful implementation of the new identity, in 1965 the company retained the J. M. Mathes advertising agency to develop a corporate advertising campaign.

The Mathes agency stated the primary audiences of the campaign to be the customers and prospects of Abex, its stockholders, the general financial community, dealers, distributors, and suppliers.

The first ads developed by the agency emphasized the great diversity of American Brake Shoe products and their behind-the-scenes contributions to worldwide progress. The corporate signature on these ads read: "Abex—American

Brake Shoe Company." (See Exhibit 3.) The six-month 1965 ad budget was $300,000. Insertions were placed in regional editions of *Time* and *Newsweek* as well as in national *Wall Street Journal* and *Business Week* editions. In addition, certain publications directed to the financial community were selected. (Exhibit 4 gives a breakdown of the 1965 corporate advertising schedule.)

Mr. Carroll commented on the role of advertising and the criteria for media selection:

> . . .we. . .needed a way. . .to give Abex fast acceptance among the many publics important to our company. Advertising was the answer—but it would take a wider, more general effort than we could accomplish in trade media. We wanted exposure on a broad scale, but with concentrated impact where it would do our business the most good.

Mr. Fred Dixon, Vice-President of the Mathes agency in charge of the Abex account, explained the use of selected geographical editions of national publications:

> By combining regional and metropolitan editions we were able to come up with a campaign that was still within our budget. Our strategy was to penetrate those sections of the country where Abex customers were most heavily concentrated, and where major financial and business decisions are made.

In 1966, the ad budget was increased to $700,000 for the full year; the same publications were selected as in 1965. Immediately following the corporate name change in April, "announcement copy" ads explained the name change. (See Exhibit 5.) During the remainder of 1966, company ads continued the 1965 theme of emphasizing Abex's diversity through presentations of the end products of their customers, although the corporate signature was changed to read: "Abex Corporation—Formerly American Brake Shoe Company." (See Exhibit 6.)

In 1967, the ad budget of $750,000 supported a campaign that was essentially a continuation of the 1966 campaign in both copy and media selection. By this time the corporate signature had become simply "Abex Corporation." (See Exhibit 7.) By mid-1967, the corporate advertising campaign, which had featured the "Abex" logo for two years, was deemed by Abex executives to be a success. This belief was based principally on reports from field sales personnel ("our marketing sensors," in the words of a top marketing executive) of favorable acceptance of the new name by customers and prospects. In addition, corporate executives and other employees as well as stockholders indicated generally favorable response to the name. Furthermore, Starch readership "noted" scores had, since the ad campaign's inception in 1965, shown Abex ads to be consistently more effective in evoking awareness than most other ads in the issues in which Abex ads appeared. (See Exhibit 8.)

THE OPINION RESEARCH CORPORATION STUDY

Despite a general belief that the corporate campaign had successfully conveyed the desired image for Abex and achieved high recognition of the new name in the marketplace, Abex executives were uncertain of what impact, if any, the campaign had had on the financial community. Thus, in August 1967, Abex executives agreed to participate in a study conducted by Opinion Research Corporation of Princeton, New Jersey, the purpose of which was to determine the attitudes held by the financial community toward a number of diversified companies. In addition, the study planned to gather information on the factors which financial analysts considered most important in appraising stocks. Abex executives were particularly hopeful that the study would provide insights as to why the company's price/ earnings ratio stood at about 10 in 1967; Abex executives thought this to be low, compared with the average Dow Jones industrial P/E ratio of approximately 15 and P/E ratios of over 25 for some diversified "growth" firms. Ninety-three security analysts participated in the study.

The study results indicated that the majority of the analysts knew very little about Abex; of those who were able to comment on the firm, the majority regarded it as a conservative, old-fashioned company which manufactured "unexciting" products. (Selected excerpts from this study are presented in Appendix A.)

1968 ABEX CAMPAIGN TO THE FINANCIAL COMMUNITY

After reviewing the results from the Opinion Research Corporation study, Abex executives concluded that the advertising approach the company was using had apparently done little to create even an awareness of the new corporate name in the financial community. They believed that a fresh advertising program was necessary.

The Abex account team at the Mathes agency determined that only the company, through its policies and performance, could appreciably influence its stock's P/E ratio. They believed that the only realistic objective for an advertising campaign would be to create in the financial community an awareness of Abex as a controls company. The agency hoped to maximize the campaign's impact in two ways. First, an overall campaign theme was developed to identify Abex as "The Controls Company." The creative implementation showed a variety of natural forces such as weather, weight, and baldness, which Abex *cannot* control. Second, the media strategy was changed drastically. All space in general business publications was canceled. In its place Abex used television commercials in five major financial market areas, and newspaper insertions in the same five markets, plus four other leading financial markets. New York City was given the heaviest coverage of all cities because of the heavy concentration of financial and investment activity there. The local market saturation was to be supported by a continuation of the national print campaign in selected financial journals and the national edition of the *Wall Street Journal.*

The local campaigns were to take place in two 10-week spurts—one from mid-April through June, and the other from September to mid-November. The local campaigns were compressed into these periods for three reasons:

a) Executives believed that the frequency allowed by such spurts would result in greater impact than would be possible if the campaigns were spread over the entire year.

b) This plan avoided the low-viewing summer and holiday seasons.

c) April was the earliest possible time that the campaigns could be instituted, since the decision to proceed with the revised campaign was not made until March 1968.

Exhibit 9 summarizes the agency's media proposal for the local segment of Abex's 1968 campaign. Total 1968 local and national advertising expenditures were planned at approximately $1 million, of which over $100,000 was spent during the first quarter for general business publication insertions.

Some 70% of all security analysts in the United States worked in the 9 markets chosen. There were also in these markets significant proportions of other groups in the American financial community:

- 34% of all New York Stock Exchange member offices.
- 40% of the 50 leading insurance companies.
- 55% of the 500 leading industrial companies.
- 28% of all shareholders.
- Over half of the New York Stock Exchange stock volume traded on an average day.

Newspaper insertions were to be full-page ads positioned as closely as possible to the financial sections. The 30-second TV spots would run in local evening-news shows, positioned as closely as possible to stock market reports. Newspapers and TV news programs were regarded as particularly desirable media during 1968, owing to what Abex executives saw as the immediacy of the coverage in these media of world and national affairs (e.g., the political campaigns) in addition to financial news, which were believed to be of interest to the target audience groups. (Exhibit 10 contains a 1968 newspaper ad. Exhibit 11 contains the TV storyboard of an Abex ad.)

EVALUATION OF THE FINANCIAL COMMUNITY CAMPAIGN

Splitting the campaign into two distinct seasonal segments provided the agency with a natural opportunity for evaluation. By examining the results of the spring campaign, Mathes and Abex executives would then have some basis on which to decide whether or not to continue with TV and newspaper usage in the fall. Abex executives were especially anxious for early feedback on the campaign since it represented such a radical departure from the former media strategy.

The study designed by the agency hoped to measure the impact of the spring campaign on financial analysts in terms of their:

- awareness of the Abex company,
- association of Abex with "The Controls Company" theme,
- rating of Abex on specific company profile factors believed to influence an analyst's overall appraisal of a company (factors which emerged as important from the Opinion Research Corporation study of 1967).

Two rounds ("waves") of telephone interviews were made in New York, Chicago, and Los Angeles—the three cities receiving TV and newspaper coverage during the spring campaign. Wave I was conducted immediately prior to the campaign among a scientifically selected sample of 402 financial analysts in the three cities. Wave II interviews took place immediately after the spring campaign; although 402 different individuals were selected for the second survey, the respondent sample for the follow-up study was similar in all respects to the Wave I sample. The physical aspects of sampling, field interviewing, and tabulating were handled by Market Dynamics, Inc., a subsidiary of Opinion Research Corporation.

The results of the study, which are summarized in Exhibit 12, reached Mr. Carroll at Abex in August of 1968. The Mathes account team expressed great satisfaction with the results, claiming that the gains were especially significant considering that only ten weeks separated the Wave I and Wave II surveys, and that the campaign admittedly had relatively long-run objectives. In further support of the campaign's effectiveness were the data summarized in Exhibit 13, which the agency team had compiled. Although prior to the campaign the agency group had taken care to explain that effecting an increase in the market value of Abex's common stock was not a realistic objective for this (or any) advertising campaign, they believed that the Exhibit 13 data gave undeniable indications that the spring campaign had actually done just that.

As Mr. Carroll reviewed the campaign results, he wondered to what extent he should agree with the conclusions of the Mathes account team. He had to decide: a) whether to carry through with the fall segment of the proposed campaign, and b) the directions which Abex advertising should take in 1969.

Abex Corporation

LIST OF EXHIBITS

Exhibit	Contents
1	Selected Financial Data: 1958-1967
2	Graphic Presentation of the Corporate Name
3	1965 Color Ad
4	1965 Media Schedule (Six months)
5	1966 Announcement Copy Ad
6	1966 Color Ad
7	1967 Color Ad
8	Color Campaign Starch Scores ("Noted" vs. Norms): 1965-67
9	Proposed Media Coverage of Leading Financial Markets
10	1968 Newspaper Ad
11	1968 TV Commercial Storyboard
12	Summary of Results of the Financial Analysts Study: Spring 1968
13	Movement of Abex Common Stock before and during the Spring 1968 Campaign

Exhibit 1

SELECTED FINANCIAL DATA: 1958-1967

	1967	1966	1965	1964	1963	1962	1961	1960	1959	1958
Shipments (in millions)	274.8	277.4	260.2	241.5	214.7	194.9	165.5	164.6	168.0	138.0
Net earnings (in millions)	11.27	12.83	11.10	9.76	7.44	6.95	5.37	5.67	7.68	4.78
% of shipments	4.1	4.6	4.3	4.0	3.5	3.6	3.2	3.4	4.6	3.5
per common share*	3.05	3.49	3.01	2.64	2.00	2.13	1.64	1.74	2.36	1.48
Dividends paid (in millions)	5.91	5.80	5.27	4.64	4.45	3.91	3.91	3.90	3.88	3.87
per common share*	1.60	1.575	1.425	1.25	1.20	1.20	1.20	1.20	1.20	1.20
% of net earnings	52.4	45.2	47.5	47.6	59.9	56.3	72.9	68.9	50.5	80.9
Common stock selling price range*, **	27-35	26-36	28-35	25-30	24-29	21-27	19-26	18-26	23-29	17-24

* Adjusted for 2-for-1 stock split in 1966.
** Figures rounded off.
Source: Annual Report.

Exhibit 2

GRAPHIC PRESENTATION OF THE CORPORATE NAME

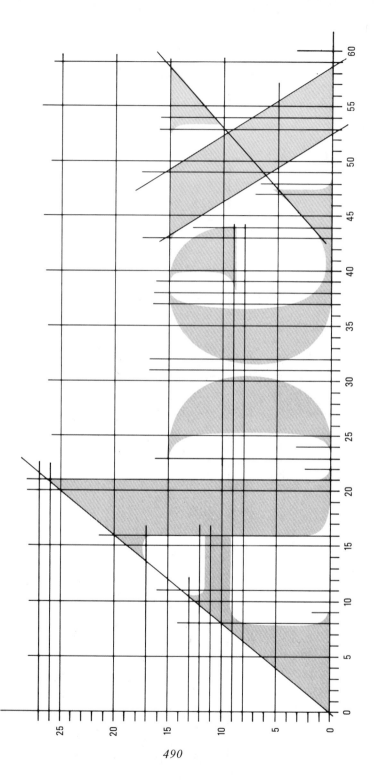

Exhibit 3

1965 COLOR AD

Today somebody will stop a truck, plow a field, catch a fish:

with a little help from Abex

Take 20,000 pounds of truck, load it with 40,000 pounds of timber, and head it down a steep hill. Several miles of hill, with brakes on practically all the way.

It's a real problem in braking. And the truck gets help from our Friction Products Group: thick brake blocks like this. It's one of the many types of friction products made by American Brake Shoe in shapes and forms to control and retard almost anything that moves — from automobiles to freight trains and even jet planes.

On farms, we're helping make sure that the land is always plowed on time. Forged steel parts like this power shaft bevel gear from our AmForge Division are providing more strength to farm equipment.

We're making it easier to bring fish to market, too. Compact hydraulic power units, like the one on the right developed by our Denison Engineering Division, are pulling up nets, providing power steering, lowering costs.

In fact, you'll find American Brake Shoe almost everywhere you go with its hydraulic equipment, friction products, castings and forgings, and railroad products. All helping people travel, farm, mine, ship goods and manufacture materials and products that contribute to progress throughout the world.

Abex

American Brake Shoe Company
530 Fifth Avenue, New York, N.Y. 10036

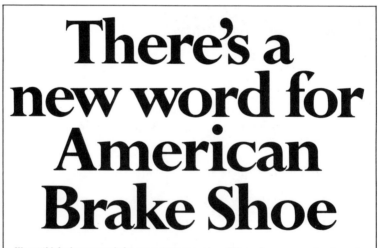

Exhibit 6

1966 COLOR AD

Exhibit 7

1967 COLOR AD

If every man, woman and child wielded a pick and shovel, we still couldn't build all the roads we need.

Get cut off from a road and you die. Places die. Ideas die.

In Appalachia there are people frozen in the eighteenth century. Because there's no easy way to get in or out.

There is hope. Roads are being built. We at Abex make things for roadbuilding machinery. Hydraulic equipment for muscle. Friction products for brakes and clutches. Dippers that move thousands of shovelsful of earth in a gulp.

Just what kind of company is Abex? We're a diversified company on the grow. Through cast metals, hydraulic equipment, friction and railroad products we're involved in a lot of industries.

We help make many things—from glass to concrete, from fertilizer to plastics.

Like to know more about us? Write Dept. PR for our latest brochure.

Abex
CORPORATION

530 Fifth Avenue, New York, 10036

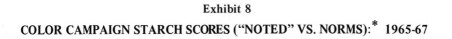

Exhibit 8

COLOR CAMPAIGN STARCH SCORES ("NOTED" VS. NORMS):* 1965-67

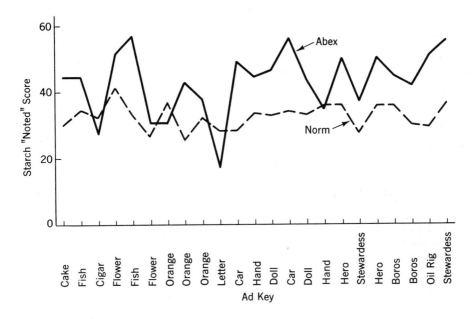

*Norm = average Starch "noted" score for all full-page ads in the issue.

Exhibit 9

PROPOSED MEDIA COVERAGE OF LEADING FINANCIAL MARKETS,

Spring 1968 (Mid-April–June 30th)

National Program (1/2 of year)	$115,000
Full Penetration (10-Week Program)*	
New York	
Newspaper: *Times* – 5 Full-page ads	$ 32,160
Television: WNBC – 50 Commercials (30 seconds)	55,000
	$ 87,160
Chicago	
Newspaper: *Tribune* – 5 Full-page ads	$ 23,385
Television: WMAQ – 50 Commercials (30 seconds)	25,000
	$ 48,385
Los Angeles	
Newspaper: *Times* – 5 Full-page ads	$ 22,200
Television: KNXT – 50 Commercials (30 seconds)	75,000
	$ 97,200
Total Effort–3 Areas	$232,745
Two Full-Page Ads in:	
Boston–San Francisco–Detroit–	
Washington, D.C.–Philadelphia–	
Cleveland	$ 41,670
Total Space and TV Cost	$389,415

* The spring campaign as actually instituted covered only 9 weeks.

Fall 1968 (September–Mid-November)

National Program (1/2 of year)	$115,000
Full Penetration (10-Week Program)	
Boston	
Newspaper: *Globe* – 5 Full-page ads	$ 16,920
Television: WBZ – 50 Commercials (30 seconds)	45,000
	$ 61,920
New York	
Newspaper: *Times* – 5 Full-page ads	$ 32,160
Television: WNBC – 50 Commercials (30 seconds)	55,000
	$ 87,160
San Francisco	
Newspaper: *Chronicle* – 5 Full-page ads	$ 27,090
Television: KPIX – 50 Commercials (30 seconds)	40,000
	$ 67,090
Total Effort–3 Areas	$216,170
Two Full-Page Ads in:	
Detroit–Chicago–Los Angeles–	
Washington, D.C.–Philadelphia–	
Cleveland	$ 51,844
Total Space and TV Cost	$383,014

Exhibit 10

1968 NEWSPAPER AD

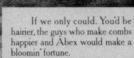

Exhibit 11

1968 TV COMMERCIAL STORYBOARD

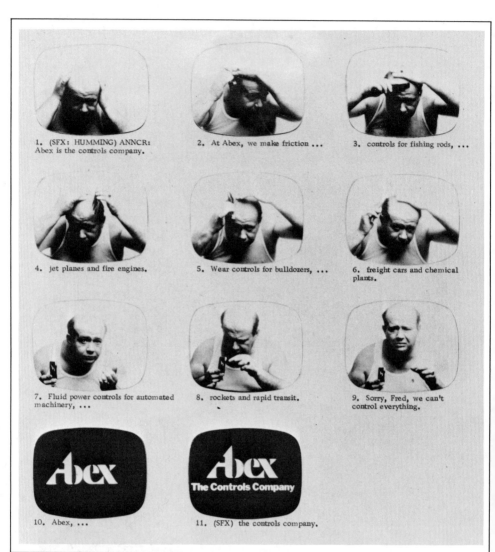

1. (SFX: HUMMING) ANNCR: Abex is the controls company.

2. At Abex, we make friction ...

3. controls for fishing rods, ...

4. jet planes and fire engines.

5. Wear controls for bulldozers, ...

6. freight cars and chemical plants.

7. Fluid power controls for automated machinery, ...

8. rockets and rapid transit.

9. Sorry, Fred, we can't control everything.

10. Abex, ...

11. (SFX) the controls company.

Exhibit 12
SUMMARY OF RESULTS OF THE FINANCIAL ANALYSTS STUDY, SPRING 1968
A. Degree of Familiarity

QUESTION: I'D LIKE TO MENTION THE NAMES OF FOUR LISTED COMPANIES. AS I MENTION EACH, PLEASE TELL ME HOW FAMILIAR YOU ARE WITH THE COMPANY. HOW ABOUT (COMPANY)—WOULD YOU SAY YOU ARE (READ SLOWLY)...VERY FAMILIAR WITH THE COMPANY... SOMEWHAT FAMILIAR WITH THE COMPANY...FAMILIAR WITH THE NAME ONLY, OR UNFAMILIAR WITH THE COMPANY?
COMPANY NAMES: ABEX, ELTRA, HOWMET, NORTON.

	Total		New York		Chicago		Los Angeles	
	Wave I	Wave II	Wave I	Wave II	Wave I	Wave II	Wave I	Wave II
Base:	(402)	(402)	(200)	(201)	(126)	(126)	(76)	(75)
Abex								
Very familiar	5%	9%	5%	8%	2%	5%	8%	20%
Somewhat familiar	20	28	14	28	28	32	25	21
Familiar with name only	28	31	26	32	30	29	29	32
Unfamiliar	47	32	55	32	40	34	38	27
Total	100%	100%	100%	100%	100%	100%	100%	100%
Eltra								
Very familiar	7%	8%	8%	8%	2%	3%	8%	13%
Somewhat familiar	27	28	35	34	19	20	21	27
Familiar with name only	26	32	22	30	32	39	29	27
Unfamiliar	40	32	35	28	47	38	42	33
Total	100%	100%	100%	100%	100%	100%	100%	100%
Howmet								
Very familiar	16%	18%	20%	18%	8%	11%	16%	28%
Somewhat familiar	43	34	40	36	44	29	50	39
Familiar with name only	22	32	20	32	29	38	18	20
Unfamiliar	19	16	20	14	19	22	16	13
Total	100%	100%	100%	100%	100%	100%	100%	100%
Norton								
Very familiar	9%	12%	11%	13%	6%	9%	8%	13%
Somewhat familiar	36	38	37	42	39	32	28	39
Familiar with name only	29	26	30	28	27	27	33	21
Unfamiliar	26	24	22	17	28	32	31	27
Total	100%	100%	100%	100%	100%	100%	100%	100%

Exhibit 12 (cont.)

B. Association with Theme "The Controls Company"

QUESTION: NOW I WOULD LIKE TO READ A SLOGAN USED BY ONE OF THESE COMPANIES AS A MEANS OF IDENTIFICATION IN THEIR ADVERTISING. WOULD YOU PLEASE TELL ME, IF YOU CAN, THE COMPANY YOU ASSOCIATE WITH THE SLOGAN: "THE CONTROLS COMPANY."

	Total		New York		Chicago		Los Angeles	
	Wave I	Wave II	Wave I	Wave II	Wave I	Wave II	Wave I	Wave II
Base:	(402)	(402)	(200)	(201)	(126)	(126)	(76)	(75)
Abex	7%	25%	10%	28%	5%	19%	4%	25%
Eltra	5	6	5	7	6	3	6	11
Norton	2	4	2	2	2	5	1	7
Howmet	1	1	1	1	2	1	1	1
Don't know	85	64	82	62	85	72	88	56
Total	100%	100%	100%	100%	100%	100%	100%	100%

C. Rating of Abex on Specific Attributes

QUESTION: I WOULD LIKE TO READ THREE STATEMENTS TO YOU, AND ASK YOU TO RATE ONE COMPANY ON THESE STATEMENTS. WE'RE ASKING EACH FINANCIAL ANALYST ABOUT A DIFFERENT COMPANY. IN YOUR CASE, WE'D LIKE YOU TO RATE ABEX. AS I MENTION EACH STATEMENT, SIMPLY TELL ME, FROM WHATEVER YOU KNOW OR ANY IMPRESSIONS YOU HAVE, WHETHER THE STATEMENT IS PARTICULARLY TRUE OF ABEX, SOMEWHAT TRUE OF ABEX, NOT VERY TRUE OF ABEX OR NOT AT ALL TRUE OF ABEX IN THAT RESPECT.

HOW ABOUT (STATEMENT)—WOULD YOU SAY THAT IS (READ SLOWLY). . .PARTICULARLY TRUE. . .SOMEWHAT TRUE. . .NOT VERY TRUE. . .OR NOT AT ALL TRUE OF ABEX?

STATEMENTS:

A.   A COMPANY THAT HAS PRODUCT APPLICATIONS IN MANY DIFFERENT FIELDS.

B.   A COMPANY THAT IS ACTIVE IN THE ADVANCEMENT OF MODERN TECHNOLOGY.

C.   A COMPANY THAT IS BROADENING ITS SCOPE OF OPERATIONS.

Exhibit 12 (cont.)

	Total		New York		Chicago		Los Angeles	
	Wave I	Wave II	Wave I	Wave II	Wave I	Wave II	Wave I	Wave II
Base:	(402)	(402)	(200)	(201)	(126)	(126)	(76)	(75)
A company that has product applications in many different fields:								
Particularly true	18%	23%	15%	17%	19%	25%	24%	33%
Somewhat true	14	23	13	29	17	17	12	19
Not very true	3	2	2	2	5	1	1	3
Not at all true	–	1	–	1	–	1	–	2
Don't know	18	19	15	19	19	22	25	16
Unfamiliar with Abex	47	32	55	32	40	34	38	27
Total	100%	100%	100%	100%	100%	100%	100%	100%
A company that is active in the advancement of modern technology:								
Particularly true	9%	13%	6%	11%	14%	12%	8%	21%
Somewhat true	17	22	15	21	17	20	24	27
Not very true	5	7	3	8	8	7	4	8
Not at all true	*	3	1	4	–	1	–	–
Don't know	22	23	20	24	21	26	26	17
Unfamiliar with Abex	47	32	55	32	40	34	38	27
Total	100%	100%	100%	100%	100%	100%	100%	100%
A company that is broadening its scope of operations:								
Particularly true	24%	30%	21%	26%	25%	29%	30%	43%
Somewhat true	11	18	8	19	17	14	7	18
Not very true	1	1	–	2	2	1	1	–
Not at all true	*	*	–	*	–	–	1	–
Don't know	17	19	16	21	16	22	23	12
Unfamiliar with Abex	47	32	55	32	40	34	38	27
Total	100%	100%	100%	100%	100%	100%	100%	100%

* Less than 0.5%

Evaluating Promotional Programs

Exhibit 13

MOVEMENT OF ABEX COMMON STOCK
BEFORE AND DURING THE SPRING 1968 CAMPAIGN

Abex

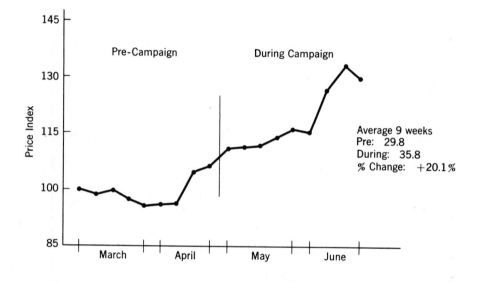

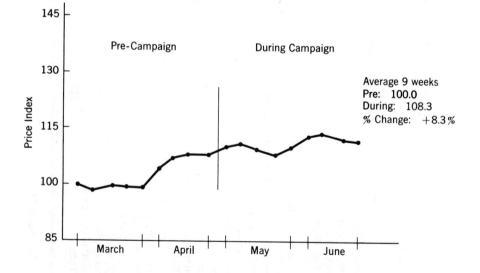

Standard and Poor Industrials

Exhibit 13 (cont.)

Abex

*Percent Change
Pre vs. During*

Average trading-day volume

9 Weeks Pre-Campaign
(Week ending March 1–April 26, 1968) = 4,114 shares

9 Weeks During Campaign
(Week ending May 3–June 28, 1968) = 7,293 shares

+77%

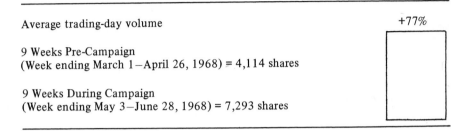

New York Stock Exchange

*Percent Change
Pre vs. During*

Average trading-day volume

9 Weeks Pre-Campaign
(Week ending March 1–April 26, 1968) = 11,466,533 shares

9 Weeks During Campaign
(Week ending May 3–June 28, 1968) = 14,045,315 shares

+23%

APPENDIX A

Excerpts from Opinion Research Corporation Study of August 1967

(A. SUMMARY OF FINDINGS)

MOST ANALYSTS ARE NOT FAMILIAR WITH ABEX CORPORATION

Several factors point up analysts' unfamiliarity with Abex:

— None of the analysts interviewed has made any recommendation in the past year as to the investment attractiveness of Abex.

— Virtually none (1%) has had occasion to contact a member of top management in the last year or so.

— Over three analysts in four (77%) select no image profile items which describe the company.

— About half the analysts are unable to rate Abex on financial communications, management, growth potential, or investment quality.

In view of the lack of familiarity with the company, it is not surprising that very few or no analysts select Abex from among the comparison companies as doing an outstanding job in these specific areas of communications or marketing:

— Annual report.
— Interim reports or other printed material.
— Handling of analysts' inquiries.
— Appearances before Analysts' Society meetings.
— Telling analysts of company plans and goals.
— Development of new products.
— Expanding and widening markets.

Following is the evaluation of Abex by analysts who feel they know the company.

COMMUNICATIONS

Among the 51% of analysts who rate Abex on communications, nearly two-thirds consider their program average in effectiveness; one analyst in three is inclined to be critical.

There is little or no specific criticism, however, from analysts rating the company's annual report, the accessibility of important people, or the adequacy of information provided by the company.

MANAGEMENT

Among the 48% of analysts who can rate Abex on management, the vast majority think it is about on a par with the quality of management of the other comparison companies.

GROWTH POTENTIAL

Nearly three-fourths of those 52% of analysts who rate the company on growth potential consider its prospects no better than average; one analyst in four rates them less than average.

INVESTMENT QUALITY

Among those 53% who rate the investment quality of the company stock, opinion is divided somewhat evenly as to whether Abex is suited to income portfolios, speculative portfolios, or none at all at the present time.

INVESTMENT IMAGE PROFILE

Those who feel they know the company credit Abex with having a good dividend policy and good corporate advertising, but criticize it for not doing enough research.

The picture one gets of the company from the comments of analysts who describe it in their own words is that Abex is in a rather dull situation with its prospects tied to the cyclical swings of the economy. As yet there appears to be only scattered recognition of the company's efforts to diversify.

(B. SELECTED DATA REGARDING HOW ANALYSTS APPRAISE COMPANIES)

MOST USEFUL INFORMATION SOURCES

"HERE IS A LIST OF SOURCES OF INFORMATION CLASSIFIED UNDER GENERAL COMMUNICATIONS, SPECIAL COMMUNICATIONS, and NONCOMPANY COMMUNICATIONS. LET'S TAKE THEM ONE AT A TIME. FIRST, WITHIN THE CLASSIFICATION OF GENERAL COMMUNICATIONS, WHICH SEVERAL ON THE LIST ARE MOST USEFUL TO YOU IN APPRAISING COMPANIES?"

Financial Analysts

Annual reports to shareholders	95%
Copies of presentations made by management to analysts in other cities	80
Quarterlies; interim statements	71
Supplementary statistical material for analysts	61
Press releases	34
Reports on annual meetings of shareholders	28
Newsletters, bulletins	16
Company magazines	5
Institutional advertising	2
Other	4
None; no opinion	0

"NEXT, WHICH SEVERAL SPECIAL COMMUNICATIONS ARE MOST USEFUL TO YOU IN APPRAISING COMPANIES?"

Financial Analysts

Personal conversations with company officials	75%
Informal give-and-take discussions between company officials and small groups of analysts	68
Attending management presentations made to formal groups of analysts	61
Tours and other special events planned by the company for analysts	51
Correspondence with company officials	23
Attending annual meetings of shareholders	9
Other	4
None	4
No opinion	0

"LASTLY, WHICH SEVERAL NONCOMPANY COMMUNICATIONS ARE MOST USEFUL TO YOU IN APPRAISING COMPANIES?"

Financial Analysts

Written reports of analysts in other firms	81%
Conversations with analysts in other firms	76
News, business, financial and professional publications	59
Information filed with the S.E.C.	46
Industry trade magazines	29
Other	4
None; no opinion	0

FACTORS CONSIDERED IN ANALYZING STOCKS

ANALYSTS PLACE WEIGHT UPON A WIDE VARIETY OF FACTORS WHEN THEY
ANALYZE THE INVESTMENT ATTRACTIVENESS OF STOCKS.

Of primary importance to nearly all analysts are projected earnings, management
competence, and the price-earnings ratio of a stock they are appraising. Yet beyond
these are a whole range of factors which analysts take into account in making their
judgments as indicated by the high proportions of analysts selecting many of the
specifics listed below.

"HERE IS A LIST OF FACTORS WHICH ANALYSTS MIGHT CONSIDER WHEN EVALU-
ATING THE INVESTMENT ATTRACTIVENESS OF VARIOUS COMPANIES. PLEASE
READ THROUGH THE LIST, AND TELL ME THE NUMBERS OF THOSE FACTORS TO
WHICH YOU GIVE THE <u>MOST</u> CONSIDERATION WHEN YOU ANALYZE STOCKS."

Financial Analysts

Estimate of future earnings	94%
Competence of management	90
Stock price in relation to current earnings	87
New product development	76
Potential of markets for company products	76
Outlook for the national economy	73
Past earnings record	68
Competition from other companies	66
Operating efficiency	65
Company's capitalization, financial resources	60
Quality of company products or service	59
Depth of management	56
Aggressiveness in marketing	55
Diversification of products	42
Proportion of earnings derived from foreign business	29
Company's financial communications	24
Stock price in relation to current dividend	24
Outlook for interest rates	19
Relations with employees or labor unions	17
Effectiveness of advertising	8
No opinion	1

(C. SELECTED DATA FROM ANALYSTS' APPRAISALS)

LITTON STANDS OUT FROM THE OTHER COMPANIES IN TERMS OF THE EFFECT-
IVENESS OF ITS OVERALL COMMUNICATIONS WITH ANALYSTS.

Slightly over three analysts in four think that Litton is doing an outstanding job
of communicating with the financial community. Textron ranks second with almost
half the analysts rating its communications program outstanding. Most of the other

companies on the list tend to be rated average in communications. Large proportions of analysts are apparently not well enough acquainted with most of these companies' communications efforts to express an opinion about them.

OVERALL FINANCIAL RELATIONS AND COMMUNICATIONS

"INSOFAR AS ESTABLISHING EFFECTIVE COMMUNICATIONS AND GOOD RELATIONS WITH THE FINANCIAL COMMUNITY IS CONCERNED, HOW WOULD YOU RATE THE COMPANIES ON THE LIST? PLEASE TAKE THEM ONE AT A TIME AND INDICATE FOR EACH COMPANY WHETHER YOU THINK IT IS DOING AN OUTSTANDING JOB, AN AVERAGE JOB, OR A SOMEWHAT LESS THAN AVERAGE JOB OF COMMUNICATING WITH THE FINANCIAL COMMUNITY."

| | *Financial Analysts* | | | |
	Out-standing	*Average*	*Somewhat Less than Average*	*No Opinion*
Litton Industries	78%	10%	0%	12%
Textron	47	29	1	23
Gulf & Western	41	27	10	22
TRW, Inc.	39	38	2	21
LTV	32	29	7	32
Teledyne	27	40	3	30
Automatic Sprinkler	24	33	12	31
Walter Kidde & Company	20	40	11	29
Eaton Yale & Towne	19	44	7	30
Rockwell-Standard	17	50	9	24
Borg-Warner	16	52	6	26
Amsted Industries	12	32	14	42
ACF Industries	10	45	15	30
General American Transportation	9	46	15	30
Hoover Ball & Bearing	6	41	15	38
Timken Roller Bearing	5	46	18	31
Westinghouse Air Brake	4	55	12	29
Budd Company	2	47	20	31
Abex Corporation	1	33	17	49

MANAGEMENT QUALITY

"WHICH OF THESE COMPANIES WOULD YOU SAY HAVE OUTSTANDING MANAGEMENTS, WHICH HAVE AVERAGE MANAGEMENTS, AND WHICH HAVE SOMEWHAT LESS THAN AVERAGE MANAGEMENTS?"

	Financial Analysts			
	Out-standing	Average	Somewhat Less than Average	No Opinion
Litton Industries	89%	2%	0%	9%
Textron	68	13	0	19
Teledyne	47	26	2	25
Gulf & Western	45	25	10	20
TRW, Inc.	42	34	2	22
LTV	38	33	2	27
Automatic Sprinkler	35	32	3	30
Walter Kidde & Company	34	36	3	27
Eaton Yale & Towne	22	46	4	28
General American Transportation	17	49	9	25
Borg-Warner	15	53	10	22
ACF Industries	14	49	10	27
Rockwell-Standard	12	57	9	22
Amsted Industries	10	42	4	44
Timken Roller Bearing	6	51	9	34
Westinghouse Air Brake	5	56	12	27
Budd Company	4	46	20	30
Hoover Ball & Bearing	2	53	6	39
Abex Corporation	1	40	7	52

WITH THE EXCEPTION OF LITTON AND TELEDYNE, MOST OF THE COMPANIES ON THE LIST ARE NOT CREDITED BY ANALYSTS WITH DOING AN OUTSTANDING JOB IN THE AREA OF NEW PRODUCT DEVELOPMENT.

Once again, Litton tops the list. The second ranking company is Teledyne, named by over four analysts in ten.

NEW PRODUCT DEVELOPMENT

"WHICH SEVERAL COMPANIES ON THE LIST WOULD YOU RATE AS PARTICULARLY OUTSTANDING IN THE DEVELOPMENT OF NEW PRODUCTS?"

	Financial Analysts
Litton Industries	60%
Teledyne	43
TRW, Inc.	28
Borg-Warner	17
LTV	16
Textron	16
Eaton Yale & Towne	11
Automatic Sprinkler	10
General American Transportation	9

	Financial Analysts
Timken Roller Bearing	8
ACF Industries	5
Gulf & Western	5
Rockwell-Standard	5
Walter Kidde & Company	5
Budd Company	4
Hoover Ball & Bearing	4
Westinghouse Air Brake	3
Amsted Industries	1
Abex Corporation	0
None	9
No opinion	10

ANALYSTS OVERWHELMINGLY THINK LITTON IS DOING THE BEST JOB OF EXPANDING AND WIDENING ITS MARKETS.

Eight analysts in ten think Litton Industries is doing the best job of any of these companies in the area of market expansion. Textron, Gulf & Western, Teledyne, LTV, and Walter Kidde also receive a relatively high rating.

MARKET EXPANSION

"WHICH OF THESE COMPANIES HAVE DONE THE BEST JOB IN EXPANDING AND WIDENING THEIR MARKETS?"

	Financial Analysts
Litton Industries	80%
Textron	55
Gulf & Western	45
Teledyne	41
LTV	38
Walter Kidde & Company	34
TRW, Inc.	28
Automatic Sprinkler	25
Eaton Yale & Towne	22
Rockwell-Standard	12
Borg-Warner	9
General American Transportation	9
ACF Indistries	4
Abex Corporation	2
Budd Company	2
Timken Roller Bearing	2
Westinghouse Air Brake	2
Amsted Industries	1
Hoover Ball & Bearing	1
None	0
No opinion	5

(D. ILLUSTRATIVE VERBATIM COMMENTS ABOUT ABEX)

ABEX IS PICTURED AS A DULL SITUATION BY THOSE FEW ANALYSTS WHO FEEL
FAMILIAR WITH THE COMPANY.

Only a small minority of analysts (about one in four) are able to give any
summary of their impressions of Abex. As indicated by the selected comments
below, the company is viewed as rather unexciting.

"IN YOUR OWN WORDS, HOW WOULD YOU SUMMARIZE YOUR IMPRESSIONS OF
ABEX?"

ILLUSTRATIVE VERBATIM COMMENTS

"I think it's a cyclic industry where the management has to cope with existing business conditions. They are affected by the ups and downs of the
general trend of the economy and will show a fluctuating earning trend."

"Dullsville."

"It's a fairly large company with an unexciting product mix in a not particularly rapid growth area."

"It is a highly cyclical company at best. It has never done more than hold its
own. Its stock is unattractive except for income."

"A company that is in a rather nonexciting field. Have some diversification
in electronics but are basically in railroad heavy equipment. They have
technology so if prosperity should return for the railroads—they would go to
town."

"They produce a bunch of uninteresting junk."

"It is a company that is seeking to diversify and broaden its product line."

"It is a diversified company with heavy dependence on capital goods spending."

"It is a much improved company over the last four years since getting rid of
cyclical stigma and registering consistent earning growth through diversifi-
cations."

ANALYSTS CITE LOW GROWTH AND CYCLICAL CHARACTERISTICS AS ABEX'S
WEAKNESSES.

There were so few comments by analysts on the weaknesses of Abex that
they are reproduced in full below.

"WHAT ARE ABEX's MAJOR WEAKNESSES?"

"It is involved in the areas of activity in which it lacks growth to such a degree that the company is apparently attempting to overcome its weakness by diversifying into areas offering prospects for growth. This is most difficult to do with success."

"The market it's in is not a rapid growth area."

"Its dependence on military and capital areas which are both subject to wide variations."

"I can't think of any."

"It's always a bridesmaid and never a bride."

"Uninteresting product on the market."

" Overconservative management, highly cyclical product base, too dependent on capital goods demand for industries."

"Principal markets are not growing very rapidly."

"It is basically unknown."

"Many products that are highly competitive."

"The business that it's in is not one of substantial growth."

"It has none. But it still has a long way to go, though."

"The growth of its markets is below average and somewhat cyclical, thus the major weakness is its difficulty of maintaining consistent earning growth."

"The industry it serves—that is it in a nutshell—you have a big capital investment business and relative high labor cost—a typical heavy industry situation."

(E.   IMPLICATIONS OF THE STUDY FOR ABEX)

The fact that the vast majority of analysts appear to be unfamiliar with Abex brings to mind several important questions.

ARE ANALYSTS AWARE OF THE RECENT NAME CHANGE?

At no time during the interview was Abex identified as "formerly American Brake Shoe Company." The findings therefore suggest that the company may not yet be widely known by its new name. If the company had been so identified in this study, there would have been no way of knowing whether or not the new name was known to the financial community.

At the present time company policy appears to be to include "Formerly American Brake Shoe" in small print under the name Abex Corporation on their stationery, reports, etc. *If continued identification with the former name is desired,* this practice should be followed until the new name has achieved wider recognition.

WERE THE RIGHT ANALYSTS INTERVIEWED?

When a company registers low in visibility or in performance on a study of this kind, it is only natural for management to wonder if the results might have been different if some other group of analysts had been interviewed. In this instance firms were asked to provide the names of analysts who appraised diversified companies such as those being compared in the study.

If Abex had been compared with railroad equipment companies by a group of analysts specializing in the transportation industry, it could be argued that results might well have been different. What the findings of this study show is that *at the present time* Abex does not appear to be appraised by the same analysts who review such companies as Litton and Textron, both of which are well known to respondents.

QUESTIONS

1. Appraise the Abex plan and execution of its 1968 corporate advertising program.

2. Was the 1968 campaign successful? Why? Why not?

3. More generally, how do you think such corporate advertising campaigns should *be evaluated? Should they be undertaken?*

Irish

Tourist Board

(Bord Failte Eireann)

The marketing manager of the Irish Tourist Board reviews his advertising-research activities, including campaign theme development, pre–testing of specific advertisements, post–testing of specific ads and media, and measuring campaign effectiveness in general.

In mid-1969, Mr. Robert Irvine, Marketing Manager for the Irish Tourist Board (Bord Failte Eireann) pointed to the stack of research studies on his desk and commented, "This collection is certainly not complete, but it is a good representation of the variety of types of research we undertake to attempt to make our advertising as effective as possible. Some studies, such as our *Survey of Travellers,* focus on appraising *past* efforts. Others, such as the Tavistock psychological study and the attitude studies, probe more deeply into the needs of the tourist and the extent to which Ireland can satisfy those needs. These findings aid us in determining the direction of our *future* advertising efforts."

In the course of his review of ITB's overall approach to advertising research, Mr. Irvine outlined four major areas in which studies were undertaken:

a)   Theme development.
b)   Pre-testing of specific ads.
c)   Post-testing of both ads and media.
d)   Reactions to ITB's overall effort by relevant groups of end-consumers (tourists) and by travel agents.

He weighed the appropriateness of the entire research "package" for ITB in the years to come, as well as the "fit" of each individual study within the overall research effort.

ITB–HISTORY AND OBJECTIVES

The Irish Tourist Board (Bord Failte Eireann)[1] was established as a public enterprise to perform two basic tasks—first, to *develop* Ireland's resources in such a way as to make the country as appealing as possible to tourists and, second, to *promote* Ireland as a tourist destination. Bord Failte (or ITB, as it will be called for the remainder of the case) assumed its present form in 1955. ITB was financed by an annual government grant which rose progressively from £384,000[2] in 1956-57 to £4,800,000 in 1969-1970. A small amount of revenue was also derived from hotel and guesthouse registration fees, advertising in ITB's glossy magazine *Ireland of the Welcomes* (distributed mainly to subscribers overseas) and the sale of photographs. A total ITB staff of about 350 was spread among the head office in Dublin and sales offices representing ITB in five cities in the United Kingdom[3] (Belfast, London, Manchester, Birmingham, and Glasgow); five cities in North America (New York, Chicago, San Francisco, Toronto, and Montreal); and two cities in Continental Europe (Paris and Frankfurt).

ITB and its subsidiary agencies moved in a wide variety of ways to make Ireland as attractive to tourists as possible. Its typical activities "at home" ranged from encouraging festivals to promoting and subsidizing the expansion and improvement of tourist accommodations to improving facilities for outdoor sports such as angling and game shooting.

In addition to these activities, ITB's combined sales and publicity efforts promoted Ireland as a tourist destination to its United Kingdom neighbors (see Exhibit 1 for a map of Ireland and neighboring countries) and to other selected areas around the world. In carrying out its marketing program, ITB distributed holiday literature, photographs, and films; advertised in numerous periodicals; encouraged (and sometimes financed) travel agents and travel writers to see Ireland for themselves; took steps to enhance Ireland's attractiveness to travel agents as part of packaged tours; and conducted research market planning and consultancy to assist the Irish tourist industry (especially hoteliers and car-hire firms.)

By the mid-1960s income from tourists (including payments by nonresidents of Eire to the nation's carriers) made vacations the Republic's most valuable single export. Earnings from tourism in 1966 totaled £77.7 million, of which £12.6 million represented payments to Irish carriers by tourists.

---

[1] The Republic of Ireland (Eire) is officially bilingual, the two languages being English and the native Gaelic tongue.

[2] For all figures given in the case, one pound £, = $2.80 U.S.; following devaluation in November 1967, £ = $2.40. Currency: 12 pence = one shilling; 20 shillings = one pound.

[3] The United Kingdom is composed of Britain (England, Wales, and Scotland) and Northern Ireland. Northern Ireland is an autonomous province of the U. K., with a government in Belfast. The Republic of Ireland or Eire (capital Dublin) is an independent sovereign state. Populations (1965 estimates): England 45.1 million; Wales 2.7 million; Scotland 5.2 million; Northern Ireland 1.5 million; Irish Republic 2.9 million (Republic of Ireland figure based on 1966 census).

OVERALL MARKETING/ADVERTISING CONSIDERATIONS

A number of factors combined to determine the general direction of ITB's promotional efforts. Among these considerations were:

a)   Nature of the product.
b)   Major market areas.
c)   Relevant market segmentation.
d)   Primary/secondary demand considerations.
e)   Ireland's "niche" in international tourism.

A)   The Nature of the Product   Mr. Irvine commented:

With a product as abstract as a holiday and as large as a country, some special marketing approaches are called for. Essentially, though, we attempt to employ a number of traditional concepts of product- and marketing-mix which are usually thought of as applying to more traditional tangible products. Once we can regard Ireland in terms of a *recognizable product concept,* then we can systematically determine the optimal implementation and interrelationships of such factors as advertising, merchandising, product development, pricing, personal selling, channels of distribution, and so on. For instance, by thinking this way, we have discovered the need to do a better job of "getting our product on the retailers' shelves." This translates to mean that we must develop and publicize to travel agents a variety of Irish tour packages[4] which will interest them sufficiently so that they will then have something specific to offer to the inquiring tourist.

Naturally, to a certain extent ITB's "product"—consisting of Ireland's 2,000 miles of coastline, its countryside, other natural resources, people, and weather—is a "given." However, Mr. Irvine noted that ITB did act, as noted earlier, on a number of fronts to make the product more accessible and appealing to the tourist. For instance £ 1,750,000 had been spent through 1966 on the improvement of resorts and resort areas, with another £ 750,000 approved for further resort development. About £ 120,000 had been expended through 1968 on the development and promotion of waterways for pleasure craft. Some 48,000 bilingual signposts had been erected by 1969. Many golf courses, wishing to modernize their clubhouse facilities, received a subsidy to help them do so.

Hotels and guesthouses could not legally be termed as such unless registered by ITB. Only through maintenance of ITB-enforced standards would a guesthouse or hotel be entitled to listing in ITB's internationally distributed tourist guide and to other promotional assistance. And, as much as possible, ITB encouraged towns and villages to provide and maintain public toilets and other tourist conveniences.

[4]Tour packages appealed to many tourists because, with only one initial expenditure, they could have the great bulk of their expenditures in a country (including travel, accommodations, meals, and various sightseeing options) paid for.

B) Major Market Areas   Irish tourism's three major geographic market areas were Northern Ireland, Britain, and the United States. (See Exhibit 2.) Other markets, such as Continental Europe, Canada, Southern Africa, and Australia, were regarded by ITB executives as potentially less lucrative than the first three, although they were by no means ignored. Northern Ireland presented a particularly unusual marketing situation, since over 95% of the tourists from there were "daytrippers" (i.e., stayed in Eire one day or less). In contrast, because of the distance involved, the great majority of visitors from the United States and Britain stayed for several days, and thus spent more per capita than the travelers from Northern Ireland. (See Exhibit 3 for details on per capita tourist expenditure by home country.)

The traveler from Northern Ireland was considered unique. In the words of Mr. Irvine: "People there tend to think they know all about Eire, and so are less easily *persuaded* to come." Because of this, and also because ITB management believed potential tourist gains to be greatest in the British and U. S. markets, a major proportion of ITB research was undertaken in these latter two markets. The remainder of the case thus focuses exclusively on ITB's promotional and research efforts in Britain and the United States.

One striking difference between the American and British tourist was the extent to which each relied on a travel agent to arrange his holiday in Ireland. Typically less than one quarter of all British tourists to Ireland contacted a travel agent to arrange their trip, and over half of all U. S. tourists made arrangements in this manner. Furthermore, most British tourists to Ireland who *did* make arrangements through a travel agent booked only transport, and American tourists tended to book transport *and* accommodations through agents.

This led ITB executives to believe that a U.S. tourist booking through an agent tended to seek advice from the agent regarding possible destinations; whereas most British tourists appeared to make use of the agent simply to place an order. As a result, ITB placed a heavy promotional emphasis in the U. S. on "getting its product on the shelves" of travel agents through personal sales efforts to agents and arranging desirable travel packages for agents to offer inquiring tourists. In Britain, the emphasis was much more on consumer advertising.

C)   Relevant Market Segmentation   ITB segmented its prospective consumers along a number of different dimensions, among which are the following:

1)   *International travel experience*—A number of studies had revealed that a person's experience with traveling abroad heavily influenced his attitudes about travel and how he arranged and spent his holiday. For instance, in a 1966 United States study, when asked whether they would consult a travel agent for advice on which countries to visit in the event of a European trip, 43% of respondents who had *never* traveled to Europe answered "yes" as compared with 30% of those who had traveled to Europe *once*, and 19% of those who had made the trip *twice or more*. Of the "never traveled" group, 43% claimed that they would consult an agent for an all-inclusive tour compared with 29% and 16% in the latter two groups. (Appendix A discusses this study in greater detail.)

A 1966 British survey categorized respondents as to whether they had traveled abroad for a holiday within the last three years (Sample A) or had not (Sample B). A significantly greater proportion of Sample B claimed that they would spend their next main holiday with their families than was the case for Sample A respondents (53% versus 35%). Sample A respondents noted "sun/climate/good weather" (45%) and "a change of scenery or people . . . different life, atmosphere, or customs" (36%) as their most frequent responses to a question asking what they look for on their holiday. In contrast, Sample B respondents most frequently mentioned "quiet" (37%) followed by "beaches" (25%) "different" (24%) and "sun" (21%). Sample A respondents indicated interest in spending holiday evenings in such activities as drinking, dancing, and eating, and Sample B respondents made predominant mention of some activity involving the children. (See Appendix B for further details on this study.)

2) *Geographic* (country of residence)—In addition to the distinction already noted regarding relative dependence on a travel agent, the U. S. and British tourist were found to be different in a number of other respects. Exhibit 4 summarizes some of these differences. In addition, more than one survey found that a substantial majority of British residents regarded Ireland as "home" rather than "abroad." Mr. Irvine believed that this was probably in large part due to the related currency and the lack of any passport or travel restrictions between the two countries. He commented on the "typical" U. S. tourist:

> Our American tourist is typically older and wealthier than the British visitor, which is to be expected since it costs him more to get over here. [In a 1963 survey, 47% of respondent U. S. families traveling to Europe earned over $15,000 annually, compared with 8% of all U. S. families in this income category.] However, there has been movement in both of these countries with regard to age and income of the "typical" tourist.
>
> Looking first at the situation in the U. S., the 21-day excursion economy fares which the airlines have offered since 1964 on trans-Atlantic travel have made Europe available to more Americans than ever before, and Shannon Airport makes Ireland the most economical point-of-entry to Europe from the U. S. As a result, even though we continue our high-quality advertising push to tell the executive that the beauty of Ireland and its warm people make it an ideal holiday choice, we believe that his secretary and other more economy-minded travelers will hear of his great vacation and now have the means to make the trip—although in some cases maybe not for another two or three years. We think that this phenomenon is already taking place on the basis of the declining figures in average length of stay and per-capita expenditures for U. S. visitors. This trend raises some fears regarding whether Ireland will possibly become too "trippery" for the discriminating traveler.

Mr. Irvine summarized ITB's approach in the United States:

> In the U. S. we have essentially a dual objective. First, we want to make Ireland sufficiently appealing to both travel agent and traveler so that the holiday-maker will include Ireland as a major stop on his next holiday in

Europe. Second, we hope to make the "21-day traveler" sufficiently aware of and interested in Ireland to remain with us for at least a few days after landing in Shannon rather than traveling on directly to the European "glamour" centers.

In contrast to the trend toward more economy-minded, shorter-staying tourists from the U. S., the British tourist to Ireland was tending to become increasingly affluent and higher-spending. Mr. Irvine believed that this trend resulted from an intensive recent advertising push in "prestige" British print media having a concentration of readership among upper-income population groups. To these experienced British travelers, Ireland was presented as a unique land in which to "make" a rewarding holiday. (See Exhibit 5.) Meanwhile, other media were used to reach those population segments who typically spent holidays within Britain; the message conveyed was that Ireland could be reached more easily and economically than they may have thought possible. (See Exhibit 6.) Implicit also to this group was the message that a holiday in Ireland is, in a sense, a logical transition to future holidays abroad since Ireland *is* abroad, yet offers a number of advantages (e.g., English speaking, economical, no currency or travel restrictions) not found in most other foreign countries.

3) *Demographic and psychographic breakdowns*—The predominant emphasis in the U. S. and Britain was toward the upper-income, older, more sophisticated traveler. Media selection and copy direction were aimed primarily to reach this target audience. Apart from strict demographic criteria, ITB executives believed that Ireland's strongest appeal lay with the "holiday makers"; that is, with those travelers who seek (in Mr. Irvine's words) "more than the traditional sun, sea, and sex" which the more casual "holiday *takers*" were believed to pursue.

D) Primary/Secondary Demand Considerations   Data such as those found in Exhibit 4 revealed to ITB executives the great preponderance of first-time visitors among U. S. travelers, as compared with the significant portion of British visitors who had made the journey to Ireland a number of times. In response to these findings, a number of steps were taken. In Britain, as previously mentioned, advertising emphasis shifted to create a distinctive "prestige" image for Ireland; this was to appeal more directly to the affluent British tourists who would spend more during their stay than those tourists from Britain visiting relatives, and would continue to spend more on repeat visits.

In the U. S., the primary task was still believed to be one of gaining favor with the growing segment of the population to whom European travel was becoming economically feasible. Mr. Irvine wrote in the 1965 *Marketing Plan for Irish Tourism:*

> Expansion of travel to Europe in the immediate future will be affected by the rate of growth in the numbers with incomes exceeding $15,000, but the $10,000 to $15,000 group also is clearly important. For instance, two-thirds

of repeat travellers to Europe by air were in 1963 within this category, which is expanding rapidly. Twenty-one percent of United States families had yearly income exceeding $10,000 in 1963, and the number of such families should have trebled by 1975. . . .

Most increased revenue for the rest of the present decade will be secured from the growing $10,000 to $15,000 income group (now comprising eight million families) but cheaper travel could enable really significant expansion of the market into the $7,500 to $10,000 group (currently composed of ten million families) which will be joined by more and more of the fifteen million families who are now receiving between $5,000 and $7,500 per annum. A truly mass market for European travel will be available in the early 1970s, when well over 2.5 million United States residents should come to Europe each year.

Mr. Irvine commented that ITB promotional activity in the U. S. was directed toward attracting *younger* travelers than those who were now visiting Ireland, since this would imply a higher long-run return in the form of more repeat visits. In general, relatively little advertising emphasis was directed towards the *repeat* visitor to Ireland since numerous surveys assured that tourists nearly unanimously enjoyed their holiday in Ireland after having made the initial decision to vacation there. Believing that the country itself would continue to satisfy visitors, bring them back, and bring their friends over on the strength of word-of-mouth recommendations, ITB executives considered their primary task to be to continue to attract the first-time visitor. This meant influencing the first-time traveler to Europe to include Ireland in his itinerary, and convincing the experienced traveler that Ireland had something to offer him for his next overseas holiday.

   E)   Ireland's "Niche" in International Tourism   Although agreement among ITB executives was less than unanimous, most of them believed that the Republic could not realistically hope to compete for tourists on the same grounds as such major tourist "powers" as Italy, France, and England. As Mr. Irvine noted in the 1965 *Marketing Plan for Irish Tourism:*

>   Although [Ireland's] verdant, limpid beauty and temperate climate are balm to residents of most of the United States, it lacks the spectacular qualities of Rome and Paris; quietly distinctive Ireland is most appreciated at the commencement of an itinerary. Should the tourist have experienced, for instance, the Italian cities and the more equable climate of north-western Continental Europe, this country will not evoke superlatives, and some tourists going home after three or four hectic weeks will regard the last country (and Ireland will be the last visited at the end of an itinerary) with a jaded detachment, even impatience. Nevertheless, many Americans who are already in Europe and without tight schedules can be persuaded to stop for a few days in Ireland on their way home.

Following this line of thinking, Mr. Irvine recommended that ITB advertising in the U. S. impress on the traveler "... that he will enjoy himself with a fun-loving, warm, friendly people, who will make him feel right at home and completely relaxed on what may be his first visit abroad." (See Exhibit 7 for examples of ITB advertising in the U. S.) Most ITB executives believed their ultimate objective to be that of creating a distinctive, favorable identity for Ireland as a leader among those nations with *secondary* tourist appeal; that is, to regard as competition such countries as Scotland, Greece, Portugal, and the Scandinavian countries, and attempt to establish the Republic at the forefront of these countries. As such, the first-time visitor to Europe would hopefully be convinced to spend a few days in Ireland in addition to his "must" stops in Rome, Paris, and London, and the repeat traveler to Europe might regard Ireland as a different place to spend his entire vacation or a major part thereof.

In British advertising (see Exhibits 5 and 6) the "people emphasis" was similar to that employed in U. S. ads, although here the relevant competition was regarded to be Britain itself. Thus the underlying advertising objective in the British campaign was to stress various qualities which the British traveler could find in Ireland but not in Britain, emphasizing at the same time how easy it is to "come on over" to Ireland. Among qualities emphasized were uncrowded roads, fresh food, easy-going people, various outdoor activities such as fishing and golf, and the fact that Ireland's high moral standards make it ideal for family holidays.

ADVERTISING AND ADVERTISING RESEARCH

In its 1968-69 fiscal year ITB budgeted £ 936,000 for its worldwide sales and publicity efforts. Of this amount, sales (merchandising and personal selling) represented £ 186,000; publicity (consumer advertising, editorial publicity, and brochures) represented £ 750,000. A total of £ 264,000 was spent on consumer advertising. As seen in Exhibit 8, the bulk of this amount was spent in Britain and North America. In Britain and the U. S. (spending in Canada was relatively minor) the predominant media dependence was on print—daily and weekly newspapers, Sunday color supplements, and magazines.

ITB traditionally scheduled the majority of its advertisements in both countries during the winter and spring months, when it was believed that travelers began planning their summer holiday. There was an historical peak of traffic in July and August. However, the seasonal pattern of advertising placement was shifting somewhat in the late 1960s as increased business was being secured in May and June and ITB executives attempted to stimulate tourist traffic for months other than the four summer months. For instance, a midsummer campaign was run in the U. S. to promote travel to Ireland during the autumn. Nevertheless, winter and spring advertising placements continued to predominate. (Exhibit 9 contains a representative British media schedule.) In the U. S., among the media typically used were *Esquire, The New Yorker, Saturday Review, Holiday, Sunset, Venture, The New York Times,* and the *Chicago Tribune.*

The particularly vital role played by travel agents in the travel decisions of U. S. travelers had resulted in a special emphasis to this audience by ITB. Regular advertising support in trade publications supplemented ITB's personal sales efforts to agents. (Exhibit 10 contains an ad directed specifically at the American travel agent audience.)

ITB's research program was a continuing process, drawing on three sources for data: desk research, commercial intelligence, and field surveys.

Desk research consisted of the day-to-day process of investigating and analyzing all written sources of information, such as statistical and related analytical studies, complaints, inquiries, requests, etc. *Commercial intelligence* was mainly the product of discussions held with travel agents and tour operators in the markets and when brought to Ireland for familiarization. Information from desk research and commercial intelligence served as the basis for more formal *field surveys* which sought to provide answers unattainable by either of the first two methods.

These field surveys were undertaken to measure the effectiveness of past ITB efforts as well as to provide answers regarding desirable future advertising/promotional directions for ITB. A number of studies served a dual purpose; for instance, biennial surveys of consumer attitudes indicated the current state of these attitudes (to help guide future advertising direction) and the movements in these attitudes in comparison with past studies (to help measure ITB effectiveness). Other studies were more specifically designed for one purpose or the other.

Field surveys, in addition to providing the above "pre" and "post" information on the overall ITB effort, served a similar function on the level of individual advertisements. Furthermore, media were regularly being evaluated. Thus the ITB field research effort can be categorized under four major headings:

    a)   Theme development for an entire campaign.

    b)   Pre-testing of specific ads.

    c)   Post-testing of specific ads and media.

    d)   Evaluation of the entire ITB effort in terms of reactions by both trade and consumers.

A) Theme Development   Nearly every study undertaken provided possible directions for the campaign to pursue. However, three specific surveys in Mr. Irvine's possession in 1969 were most directly oriented toward theme development. These were:

    1)   Market Facts, Inc.—U. S. consumer attitude survey.

    2)   Market Investigations Ltd. (M.I.L)—British consumer attitude survey.

    3)   Tavistock Institute—In-depth study of the social and psychological aspects of "The Holiday."

The first two studies had generally similar aims, namely, to examine consumers' attitudes about travel in general and to Ireland specifically. The Tavistock study was undertaken as a result of Mr. Irvine's skepticism regarding whether (a) people are actually conscious of what they truly seek in their holiday; and (b) if so, whether they will verbalize these feelings in a standard personal interview. An in-depth psychological study was believed to be the most effective way to explore these issues.

Since its focus was at the psychological level, executives tended to regard the findings of the Tavistock study as more applicable to the holiday maker in general, whatever his country of residence, than was the case with other attitude surveys and interview data. The latter findings were usually regarded as relevant only to the country in which the particular study was conducted. Mr. Irvine elaborated:

> We have to be quite cautious, for the most part, in making any attempts to generalize research findings across national boundaries. However, when considering the basic needs served by a holiday, it seems to me that we might be speaking about drives that are common to all men, or all of Western civilization, let us say. For instance, we have incorporated into our British *and* U.S. campaigns more emphasis on intake of good things and less emphasis on emptiness as a result of the Tavistock findings despite the fact that these findings were based on British respondents only.

Appendices A, B, and C contain excerpts from these three studies.

As an example of an additional study that was only secondarily concerned with theme development, the *Survey of Travellers* may be cited. This study, conducted every two years among travelers leaving the Republic, grouped findings according to the country of residence of the traveler. It sought primarily to determine information about the traveler along a number of basic dimensions, such as those contained in Exhibit 4, as well as the following: publicity noted, means of transportation while in Ireland, interests, regions visited, and what pleased the traveler most. Of these, one in particular—what tourists enjoyed most—related fairly explicitly to theme development. For instance, among travelers from the U. S. and Britain, the friendliness of the Irish people and the scenic beauty of the country were cited as the two top sources of enjoyment.

Although ITB marketing executives considered the data from these studies to be valuable, they naturally assessed the numbers in light of findings from other sources and their own judgment. For example, with regard to the above mentioned findings concerning friendliness and scenic beauty, the following interpretive comment was made on the research report:

> Each successive survey has indicated our main attractions to be people and scenery, but these are probably factors which tourists to many other countries would mention. The relaxed holiday atmosphere and traffic free roads which were often mentioned may be less common attributes.

B) Pre-testing of Specific Ads From the various studies concerned with general theme development for the ITB advertising campaign a number of prospective specific advertisements were created. These ads were often tested among sample populations before being released for general exposure as part of the ITB campaign. A study representative of this type of testing is the 1966 Market Investigations, Ltd. British study already noted in Appendix B. The final section of this study dealt specifically with interviewee reactions to seven ads prepared for use in ITB's British campaign. (Appendix D summarizes this section of the study.)

C) Post-testing of Advertisements and Media Two basic types of measures—analysis of coupon replies and readership studies—were undertaken to help appraise the effectiveness of specific ads or media used in ITB print campaigns.

1) *Coupon response analysis*—Analysis of coupon returns was made possible by ITB's standard practice of including in print ads a coupon which the reader could cut out and send in to ITB to receive printed material on holidays in Ireland. By coding coupons in a certain way, analysis of returned coupons could show the varying degrees of response pulled by the same advertisement in different media or by different ads run over a period of time in the same publication. The resulting cost per reply figures (cost of placing the insertion in the publication divided by the total number of replies resulting from that insertion) would then indicate the relative effectiveness of, respectively, different media or different ads.

Appendix E discusses a 1967 study undertaken to attempt to convert the traditional cost per reply (cost per completed coupon) figures into terms of cost per actual visit to Eire. In other words, "conversion factors" for each publication were derived specifying the percentage of the coupon respondents for that publication who actually took a holiday in the Republic. (See Exhibit E-2.)

The ultimate "cost per holiday taken" figures (Exhibit E-4) were believed by ITB executives to lend a significant new dimension to the evaluation of media effectiveness, although crucial questions remained unanswered. For instance, the publication drawing the largest number of completed coupons (Reader's Digest) was the only one in which a postage-paid reply postcard was made available. (Insertions in all other publications required the inquirer to cut out the coupon and mail it in a stamped envelope at his own expense.) Although a subsequent insertion in this publication without a reply-paid postcard produced a comparatively insignificant response, doubts remained regarding to what exact extent the high response achieved by the publication may have been due to the medium itself as opposed to the use of the reply-paid postcard or the positioning of the ad within the magazine. The first *Reader's Digest* ad was placed inside the front cover; the later insertion was on an inside page. Furthermore, executives noted with interest that the trip/inquiry conversion rate was the lowest of all for the first *Reader's Digest* insertion, indicating that possibly a relatively greater proportion of casual inquiries was encouraged by the lack of effort required to send in the postage-paid card as opposed to the standard coupon.

Executives thought it also significant that the trip/inquiry conversion rate for all respondents—21% (Exhibit E-2)—was in marked contrast to a figure determined in a 1965 mail survey. In the 1965 study, questionnaires had been mailed to every tenth coupon respondent; the survey generated a 30% return rate. Of those who completed the questionnnaire, 46% claimed to have taken a holiday in Ireland in 1965.

2) *Readership studies*—Readership studies were undertaken regularly to obtain feedback on the performance of specific advertisements in comparison to other ads in the same issue of the publication, other ITB insertions in earlier issues of the publication, and the same ad in other publications. Appendix F discusses the method and format of readership studies and contains excerpts from a representative study undertaken in Britain in 1968.

D) Evaluation of Campaign Effectiveness A variety of different measures attempted to appraise ITB's general advertising and promotional effectiveness. At a broad level, revenue intake from export tourism was plotted annually against ITB's marketing expenditure for the year. (See Exhibit 11.) In addition, tourist revenue growth for Ireland was compared with the growth in tourist revenue for other Northern European countries (Exhibit 12). Although measures of this sort were regarded by ITB executives as helpful in providing a rough indication of the effectiveness of ITB's efforts, they were seen as suffering from two major limitations:

1) Certain uncontrollable factors influenced tourist revenue, such as the general level of the world economy, political climate, and strikes among important labor groups (the 1966 British seamen's strike is one example).

2) The time lag between advertising impact and the actual tourist expenditure was not known precisely. Executives thought that one to several years elapsed between the time when some individuals' interest in visiting a country was aroused and when their trip to that country actually took place. Thus the effectiveness of increased promotional expenditure or a certain advertising theme in a particular year could not be fully appraised by "head count" or revenue measures in the same year.

Consequently other measures were undertaken in an attempt to determine more directly the effectiveness of specific ITB policies and decisions. For instance, the number of United States citizens indicating on their passport applications that they *intended* to visit Ireland was plotted in relation to ITB's promotional expenditures in North America, as shown in Table 1 for the years 1959-1967:

To supplement the above information, a number of attitude and awareness studies were undertaken to determine the conscious effect of different ITB actions on both travel agents and travelers. Two studies are representative of those conducted among travel agents:

1) Market Facts, Inc.,—"A Study Among Travel Agents on Irish Travel" (U.S.).

2) Martech Consultants, Ltd.,[5]—"A Study of the Attitudes of Travel Agents" (Britain).

The Market Facts, Inc., study (a separate study from the Market Facts, Inc., study described in Appendix A) is described in Appendix G.

Table 1

PLANNED VISITS TO IRELAND BY UNITED STATES CITIZENS

Year	Expenditure* on Promotion by the ITB in North America (Year Ended 31st March)	Numbers of Citizens Planning Visits to Ireland, Estimated by U.S. Passport Office (Calendar Year)
1959	£ 58,039	69,520
1960	£ 66,347	80,530
1961	£ 66,595	80,920
1962	£ 81,466	125,290
1963	£ 92,518	209,520
1964	£109,450	310,360
1965	£213,497	211,900
1966	£315,714	196,230
1967	£226,230	N.A.

* The larger part of it on publicity rather than sales effort.
Source: Robert Irvine, "Measuring the Promotional Effectiveness of National Tourist Organizations," p. 19.

As was often the case, the study provided ITB executives with an opportunity to compare results with those from another study. For example, when asked "What would you say are the main reasons that some of your clientele chose to visit Ireland?" agents gave the replies summarized in Exhibit G-4. ITB executives noted a heavy preponderance of "visiting relatives/ethnic ties" answers, which directly contradicted traveler responses to an equivalent question in the 1964 *Survey of Travellers*; in the latter study of actual American visitors to Ireland, just under one-fifth of all respondents indicated that the purpose of their visit was to visit relatives. ITB executives interpreted this discrepancy as indicative that agents had not made a full adjustment to the declining influence of ethnic traffic, pointing up the need for a more concentrated ITB personal selling effort to U. S. travel agents.

Attitudinal information among actual and prospective travelers, which was gathered for the purposes of measuring ITB's effectiveness, came from many sources. As earlier noted, certain findings regarding consumer attitudes and awareness about travel in Ireland could be looked at as a guide for theme develop-

[5]Now known as Metra Consulting Group, Ltd.

ment (attitudes in need of change) and a measure of ad campaign effectiveness (extent to which attitudes had been changed by *past* campaign themes). As such, several studies already noted as instrumental in theme development, such as the *Survey of Travellers,* the 1966 Market Facts, Inc. study described in Appendix A, and the 1966 Market Investigations, Ltd., study discussed in Appendices B and D, also served to help appraise advertising effectiveness. Selected findings from the sections of these studies dealing with advertising effectiveness are presented in Exhibit 13.

RESEARCH PROBLEMS AND ISSUES

The following are representative of statements made by Mr. Irvine regarding areas of particular concern to him in his attempts to measure ITB's promotional effectiveness:

> On a broad level, we face the obvious problem that factors beyond our control, such as weather, the political climate, and general travel trends, prevent us from gaining meaningful knowledge by plotting tourist revenues against promotional expenditures. We *have* given thought to the possibilities of this sort of technique as applied to promotion of a *specific* type of holiday—say, fishing, golf, or motoring. Over a period of several years we could hopefully determine the extra tourist revenue generated per £100 spent on promoting each type of holiday. An equation might then be formed to arrive at the optimal budget "mix" by type of holiday. This amounts to a familiar operations research programming exercise, but drawbacks arise in collecting data. For instance, dividing expenditures between capital and current items would present considerable difficulty since any expenditure tends to have both short-term and long-term effects.
>
> Another "mix" problem we face involves arriving somehow at the optimal allocation among our two basic promotional components [*publicity* (which includes advertising) and *sales,* in the forms of merchandising and personal selling]. We believe that consumer advertising is relatively influential in Britain while personal selling to the travel agent is more crucial in the States, but we haven't really been able to find out *what particular combination* of promotional activities is actually *optimal* in a certain market.
>
> A third "mix" problem is a geographic one. Comparing the effectiveness of our efforts in the States versus Britain versus anywhere else is an apples and oranges proposition for a host of reasons. Our office in New York is more expensive than the London office. Owing to a less concentrated population, few truly national media, and distance from Ireland, an ad in the U. S. must—other things being equal—be more expensive in terms of the number of prospects reached than its equivalent in Britain. The attitudes toward advertising in general differ between the two countries. I could go on, but the point is that we run into trouble when we try to say that we are doing better or worse in the States than in Britain and adjust our budget allocations accordingly.

As a final point, Mr. Irvine discussed his research budget:

> I guess we could call this another "mix" question, since I essentially have to determine which combination of research studies and surveys represents an optimal allocation of my research budget over the long run. I must continually ask myself: "What is the value of the information provided by a study compared to its cost? How does it relate to other studies we have undertaken or are planning?" This type of thinking is required to arrive at a general idea of how often certain studies are called for, but it would certainly seem possible to make the whole process more systematic in some way.

Costs of all research studies discussed in the case are contained in Exhibit 14.

Irish Tourist Board

LIST OF EXHIBITS

Exhibit	*Contents*
1	Ireland and Neighboring Countries
2	Targets for Revenue in 1970 in Relation to Recent Performance by Sources of Revenue
3	Sources of Receipts from Tourists, 1962-66
4	Selected Comparative Data on Tourists from Britain and the U.S.
5	1965 British Color Magazine Ad
6	British Newspaper Ad
7	Selected U.S. Magazine and Newspaper Consumer Ads
8	Ad Budgets by Geographic Area: 1964-68
9	Advertising Schedule — Britain
10	1967 Magazine Ad to U.S. Travel Agents
11	Total ITB Marketing Expenditures and Ireland's Receipts from Export Tourism: 1957-1966
12	Expenditures by U.S. Tourists in Ireland Compared with Expenditures in Other countries in Northern Europe: 1957-1966
13	Selected Findings from Consumer Studies of Advertising Effectiveness
14	Costs of Selected Research Studies
A-1	Influences in Favor of Visiting Ireland
A-2	Desirability of Various Factors about a Country among Those of 18-34 Years of Age Who Have Never Traveled to Europe

Exhibit 1

IRELAND AND NEIGHBORING COUNTRIES

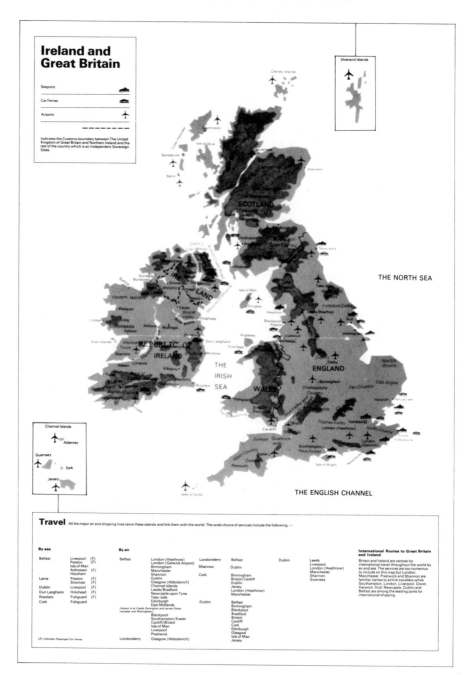

Exhibit 2

TARGETS FOR REVENUE IN 1970 IN RELATION TO RECENT PERFORMANCE
BY SOURCES OF REVENUE
(£ '000,000. 1960 VALUES)

	Britain	Northern Ireland	North America		Continental Europe	Other Areas	Air Carriers	Total
			U.S.	Canada				
					Combined			
Total target								
1970	27.1	25.0	13.8	1.0	6.2	2.8	12.5	88.4
1960, actual	19.1	10.5	4.3	0.2	5.6		4.5	44.2
Target growth,								
1960-1970	8.0	14.5	9.5	0.8	3.4		8.0	44.2
1964, actual	19.1	21.6	6.0	0.3	1.5	1.1	7.8	57.4
Actual change,								
1960-64	No change	11.1	1.7	0.1	-3.0		3.3	13.2
Required growth,								
1964-1970	8.0	3.4	7.8	0.7	6.4		4.7	31.0

Note: The above division of target revenue sources is presented as a guide only, since present shortcomings in the official statistical data create anomalies. Latest indications are that the targets for Britain and the United States in 1970 may well be surpassed in actual performance.
Source: *The Marketing Plan for Irish Tourism*, 1965, p. 6.

531

Exhibit 3

SOURCES OF RECEIPTS FROM TOURISTS, 1962-66

Markets	Tourists, '000s*			Total Revenue*, 1960 Values			Revenue Per Capita, 1960 Values		
	1962	1964	1966	1962	1964	1966	1962 (Apr/Sept)	1964 (Apr/Sept)	1966 (May/Oct)
				£M.	£M.	£M.	£	£	£
Britain	N.A.	966	999	N.A.	19.3	21.4	20.3	22.2	22.9
Northern Ireland	N.A.	10,329	15,309	N.A.	21.9	18.5	N.A.	1.8	N.A.
Daytrippers	N.A.	9,810	14,842	N.A.	12.5	11.3	1.0	1.2	N.A.
Nondaytrippers	N.A.	519	467	N.A.	9.4	7.2	10.3	12.8	N.A.
North America	N.A.	120	150	N.A.	6.4	8.7	48.3	56.2	51.8
Continental Europe	N.A.	45	60	N.A.	1.5	2.0	19.7	35.0	29.8
Other countries	N.A.	37	20	N.A.	1.1	0.7	21.9	35.9	36.1
All markets	7,206	11,497	16,538	42.6	50.2	51.3	23.2**	26.6**	26.6**
National carriers				7.1	8.5	10.0			

* January–December
**Excluding Northern Ireland
Source: All totals: Central Statistics Office, Dublin
By market estimates and per capita figures: ITB

Exhibit 4

SELECTED COMPARATIVE DATA ON TOURISTS FROM BRITAIN AND THE U.S.

| | *All Tourists: April–September* | | | |
| | *Britain* | | *U.S.* | |
	1964	*1966*	*1964*	*1966*
Purpose of visit:				
Holiday	50%	39%	75%	70%
Visiting relatives	42	53	19	25
On business	7	8	4	5
Other—not indicated	1	-	2	-
Size of party:				
One	27%	27%	28%	31%
Two	40	38	53	50
Three	13	14	10	10
Four and above	20	21	9	9
Sex:				
Male	48%	50%	38%	39%
Female	52	50	62	61
Age:				
Under 20	21%	23%	8%	9%
20-29	13	18	17	17
30-44	31	26	23	14
45-59	28	27	40	38
60 and over	7	6	12	22
Percent Irish born	43.8%	35.6%	15%	17%
Average length of visit (in days)	11.5	12.7	11.9	10.6
Average expenditure (per capita)	£ 26	£ 29	£ 65	£ 65
Proportion on first and other visits:				
1st	31%	23%	71%	65%
2nd	11	12	15	15
3rd	6	8	5	6
4th and above	42	55	9	14
Not indicated	10	2	0	0
Type of accommodation:				
Hotels	25%	21%	71%	65%
With relatives	41	51	16	19
Guesthouses	18	14	4	6
Other	16	14	9	10

Source: *ITB Survey of Travellers,* 1964 and 1966

Exhibit 5

1965 BRITISH COLOR MAGAZINE AD

Motoring as it was in the 30's—on the roads of the 60's

Photo: John Sadovy

REDISCOVER THE JOYS OF MOTORING IN IRELAND
(Now it's easier than ever to get there)*

YOU'VE GOT THE ROADS TO YOURSELF—or so it seems. The reason?—Ireland is the least crowded country in Europe, but it has 20,000 miles of good smooth roads, with every village and town signposted. You'll see few cars outside the towns. You choose your speed—fast, to see a lot of Ireland; or slower, to relish a small area. You drive on the left, petrol and oil cost about the same as in Britain, and documentation is kept to a bare minimum. Ferry your own car over, or hire one in Ireland. Come on over. Driving, even with a caravan, is still a pleasure in Ireland. Just as it was before the war.

IT'S A SHORT WAY TO TIPPERARY—and everywhere else

Ireland is compact. The only big thing about it is the variety of its scenery. Nowhere can you be more than 80 miles from the sea, with 2,000 miles of beaches and rocks to explore. Want to picnic? You can pull in, or turn off, almost anywhere you like. Ten to one, you'll find a ruined castle or a shimmering lake to eat beside. Want to stop for the night? You'll find excellent hotels and comfortable guest houses almost everywhere in Ireland. All are inspected by us annually. You and your family will be warmly welcomed—the Irish are great spoilers of children. In fact, you may not want to leave your hotel at all. But force yourself! There are many more welcomes ahead.
2,000 miles of coastline to explore

Killarney—one of Ireland's 209 golf courses

WHERE SHOULD YOU GO? Everywhere— it's so easy

Ireland itself is beautiful and easy to get to—and so is every county of the four provinces. How could you miss serene Killarney, the jewel of Ireland's landscape? Or the 'Ring of Kerry'—one of the most grandiose tours a car can take you on? Could you miss wild, wide Connemara, or the rugged softness of Mayo? Or the memorable beauty of Donegal, and Sligo with Yeats's Lake Isle of Innisfree? You could motor through all of them in a week, though each deserves a week's stay. Less than one hour's drive from Dublin takes you to the heart of Wicklow, the 'Garden of Ireland,' a microcosm of the whole beautiful land.

THE IRISH ARE PLEASED TO SEE YOU —and they show it!

Don't spend all your time behind the wheel —get out and stretch your legs if you want to meet the Irish. We Irish want to see you enjoying yourself, for hospitality is one of our pleasures. When you're hungry, we have the best home-grown food in the world. And throughout the day, you'll join in some of the liveliest conversation a man could wish to share. We're interested without curiosity, friendly without being interfering. As you'll find out for yourself.

A SHORT TALL STORY

(It's all lies and that's the truth!)

Every square inch of Ireland is covered in four-leaved shamrocks. The land is emerald green because it rains every fifteen minutes for a quarter of an hour. The Irish, who live entirely on murphies and black stout, resolve the slightest dispute with a shillelagh. The men, who are all called Paddy, are dishonest horse traders. The women, or colleens, wear shawls and smoke clay pipes. Every Irish child is spirited off at birth by the Little Folk, to kiss the Blarney Stone. They spend the rest of their lives frittering away the gift of eloquence on such remarks as 'Begob, sure and it's another wee drop of the hard stuff I'll be after taking, begorrah!'

It's all lies! Come on over and see for yourself

*New Drive-on, Drive-off British Railways Car Ferry

Starting in July, British Railways will operate a new drive-on, drive-off car ferry between Holyhead and Dun Laoghaire (Dublin). Three-and-a-quarter pleasant, carefree hours on a brand-new ship and you have the freedom of Ireland's peaceful roads, where another car is a rarity. Send for free magazine on Holidays in Ireland, and full information on British Railways Car Ferry. Book through your local Travel Agent; he will be pleased to help you. So come on over!

WHAT CAN I LOSE?
Since you're all so eager to get me over to Ireland, send me the free colour magazine on Holidays in Ireland straight away, and I'll think it over.

NAME

ADDRESS

C *Post (unsealed envelope, 3 d. stamp) to:—*
C.L.3
IRISH TOURIST BOARD, P.O. BOX 273, DUBLIN, IRELAND

You'll get on famously in *Ireland* —come on over!

Irish Tourist Board Offices in Britain:—150/1 New Bond St., London, W.1.; 16 Mount St., Manchester. Tel: Deansgate 5981; 11 Bennett's Hill, Birmingham. Tel: Midland 3882; 35 St. Enoch Sq., Glasgow. Tel: Central 2311.

Exhibit 6

BRITISH NEWSPAPER AD

Photographer wanted.

Come on over for a holiday in Ireland. It's a sight for sore lenses. You'll need plenty of film (it's considerably cheaper in Ireland) to record it all—the rugged grandeur, the mellow softness, your new Irish friends, the pleasure that you and your family took in it all. **Bargain-hunters wanted** to enjoy our bargain holidays. Take our

May Plan: 31 days hath May, and in Ireland four will cost thee nothing. One day in seven is free, a gift from Irish Tourist organisations. There's no £50 limit either in sterling area Ireland. And we devalued too, so an Irish pound goes just as far but buys more pleasure. **Beauty-lovers wanted.** Ireland's beauty opens up like a spring

flower. You can see it all on our conducted tours. Great castles, monasteries, country houses and the noble terraces of Dublin. Mountains and lakes, rolling valleys, sandy beaches. Ireland has to be seen. And even then it's hard to believe.

Ireland

Apply here.

Ireland, I'm the very man you're looking for. Send me your free colour brochures on holidays in Ireland.

Name:

Address:

Post to Irish Tourist Board, P.O. Box 273, Baggot Street Bridge, Dublin, Ireland.

Irish Tourist Offices in Britain:
150 New Bond St., London, W.1. 01-493 3201,
16 Mount St., Manchester 2. Deansgate 3981/2/3,
11 Bennett's Hill, Birmingham. Midland 3882/3/4,
35 St. Enoch Square, Glasgow. Central 2311

DT.7

You'll get on famously in *Ireland* come on over!

Exhibit 7

SELECTED U.S. MAGAZINE AND NEWSPAPER CONSUMER ADS

Just looking at people in Ireland is a delightful form of cultural exchange. You look at them. And they look at you. One look leads to another—and if you respond to their "Good Day" with one of your own, you'll probably be invited to tea. And end the day singing your head off in the back room of a pub, promising to look up somebody's third cousin in Boston on your way home to California, But if you're too shy to explore on your own Ireland's greatest attraction, its people, you can make arrangements to meet

the Irish through the Irish Tourist Board. They'll match you up with your particular brand of Irish human interest. (Nature and Guinness will do the rest.)

Trip over a stone in Ireland and you will be imagination-deep in Archaeology. Lose your way in a cobble-stoned alley and you'll find your way to a stone castle. There's so much to look at in Ireland it doesn't matter where you look first. Just keep your camera clicking and illustrate your story book memoirs of Georgian Dublin, Frisco-perched Cork City, me-

dieval Kilkenny and the green-marbled heights of Connemara, the Irish countryside and the cliffs diving into the sea and remember forever the soft-spoken Irish weather that makes palm trees feel at home (Irish weather is so photogenic). You can see it all via bus (a seven-hour day of scenic, guided touring only $2.15, with plenty of Irish wit), or hop aboard a delightful Radio Train (plush comfort, hostesses, music and a lively commentary on the passing scene, lunch, high tea). You can rent a car ($26 a week off-season, mileage included) and scoot off on traffic-free roads. Bikes can be had for practically nothing or you can strike out on your own Irish blackthorn walking stick (make sure you walk off with this souvenir of Ireland). But do get lost, whenever possible. Because finding your way in Ireland is such a stimulating social activity. Proof, as they say, that half the fun of going there is getting there.

If you're interested in travel bargains, we've got the juiciest ones, from October to the end of April. Here's a sampling:

Two weeks in Ireland, visiting 21 fascinating places. Comfortable hotels everywhere, breakfasts, Abbey Theater, medieval banquet at Bunratty Castle. Car with 50 free miles. $275. (Week in Britain, $88 extra, car with unlimited mileage, choice of five cities including London and Edinburgh.)

15 days touring Ireland, Edinburgh and London by luxury motorcoach. Limerick, Killarney, Ring of Kerry, Cork and Blarney Castle, Waterford, Dublin — nine sparkling Irish days. Two days in Edinburgh, four in London, finest hotels, inclusive air fare from New York, most meals, entertainment, touring. $470.

15 days in Ireland, escorted. Limerick, Killarney, the Ring of Kerry, Cork, the Blarney Stone, Waterford, Wexford, Dublin, Sligo, Galway, Connemara. Abbey Theater, Irish cabaret, medieval ban-

quet at Bunratty. Finest hotels with bath, most meals, motorcoach. Grand tour including jet airfare from New York, $405.

If time is running short and you want to see Ireland fast (pity) at off-season bargain prices, even more of a bargain at today's devalued pound, we suggest these stop-off package tours:

Three days in Dublin. Two nights in one of Dublin's finest hotels, bath and breakfasts, sightseeing, dinners, ticket to famous Abbey Theater, Irish cabaret, transfers. $26.

One day medieval tour. Be our guest at the Medieval Banquet at Bunratty Castle, where you'll be wined, dined and entertained like an Irish lord. $18. November-February.

IRELAND
IRISH TOURIST BOARD

AFTER BRITAIN, COME TO IRELAND
If you're touring Britain, take a breather in Ireland. Our air is the freshest, our people the friendliest. If you'd like our detailed tour package, see your travel agent or write to: Irish Tourist Board, Dept. 00, P.O. Box 238, Madison Square Station, New York, New York 10010.

Name_____
Address_____
City_____
State_____Zip_____

536

Exhibit 7 (cont.)

The Irish people speak the most fascinating foreign language of them all... English.

(You don't have to take a quickie course at Berlitz to understand it.)

The Irish never speak in a straight line. They go up a sentence a few words and a bit, stop in their tracks for reflection, ruffle the edges of a phrase. And end up with a punch line every time. Monotony of speech or manner is not their particular thing. Ask them whether you can drink the water, and they'll tell you it's as pure as the Guinness in the Long Hall Pub. (And to prove their point, they'll offer you a sample of Guinness.)

So if you're a nervous American who has been thoroughly forewarned not to drink foreign water or swallow fresh vegetables and fruits, forget it. Practically everything Irish is edible and drinkable. Fish grow big and tasty in Irish waters. Vegetables are naturally seasoned in Irish soil. Livestock has all that green stuff to chew on. You can eat like a rich American in Ireland on fresh smoked salmon, native shrimp, steak, lamb, and wait till you taste that all-American Irish breakfast of ham or bacon and eggs with whole meal brown bread. (Help yourself to lunch, **picture number 1.**) Gourmet dinner of prawns from Dublin Bay, steak with an Irish sizzle, Fruit Trifle Chantilly for dessert...**$2.40.** Hearty Appetite. Breakfast super de luxe, on the house, with every bed. So eat, eat, children. That's part of the fun of traveling.

Now if you're looking for all the comforts of home in a foreign setting, Ireland will serve you well. Old-world luxury hotels with new world plumbing, streamlined motels, guest houses brambled with roses, farm houses with expert riding instruction. (Plenty of horses, even Charley, **picture number 2.**) Swimming pools in season, golf year round. And the most up-to-date ancient castle resorts. At today's devalued pound, creature comforts will cost you less than ever. A night in a first class hotel where you can dream the most impossible dream, private bath, breakfast, for two...**$15.62.**

Now we know you didn't come to Europe just to eat and sleep. What's travel without some really first class ruins, churches and museums? Ireland has plenty of these attractions, too. Ancient castles with drawbridges and moats are part of the landscape. Do come for dinner some night to the Medieval Banquet in Bunratty, Dunguaire, Knappogue or some other authentically restored castle. You'll see a most unusual floor show of Irish minstrels, dancers and actors, gorge on Irish delicacies like Everlasting Syllabub, Mead, eat with your hands and wipe your greasy fingers on your bib. Medieval Banquet...**$6.25.**

After you've toured Georgian Dublin, paid your respects at Dunganstown, the ancestral home of John F. Kennedy, done the Ring of Kerry and Killarney bit, climbed the cobble-stoned hills of Cork City and kissed, if you insist, the Blarney Stone, twisted over the scenic coastal route to Galway and green-marbled Connemara in your own little rented car...**$6.62** per day. **$46.30** per week (mileage included) it's time to get down to the business of pure, unadulterated pleasure, especially during the early and late season, May, June and September.

Park your guidebooks and relax. You're in Ireland, where nature provides golf courses, seas and lakes for fishing, (prize catch, **picture number 3**) and ideal terrain for riding, and phenomenal horses for riding, hunting and betting. The most expensive American sports cost practically nothing in Ireland. Take heed: A full day's golf, including green fees, lunch and very high tea...**$3.60.** Salmon or sea trout fishing...fishing license, **$2.40** for 7 days. Other fish, absolutely free. Tennis court...35¢ a day per person. Horsing around: Admission to race track...**$1.20.** Ladies free. Putting on the dog: Greyhound racing, 60¢ admission. Pleasure cruise down the Shannon: Rent your own fully equipped boat. **$44** a week per person, party of four. (See picture number 4.)

If you like to take your vacation on an island fringed with palm trees, the island of Ireland will be happy to accommodate you. The south is warmed by the Gulf Stream year-round. Irish climate is never too cold, never too hot.

After a hectic day of relaxing, it's time for the evening's entertainment. The Abbey Theater for a blast of O'Casey, Behan, Shaw...front row center, **$1.50.** Some of the greatest Irish performances are impromptu. (Ever know an Irishman who can't sing, dance, fiddle, mimic or recite poetry?)

If you'd like to know how to get the most out of Ireland (or out of life) for the least amount of money, fill out the enclosed coupon or call your travel agent. Pan Am will jet you over in less than 6¼ hours from New York. (See picture number 5.)

1. Irish food is definitely not for thought.

2. Pony trekking at Foulksmills, great old horsey farmhouse.

3. Sea angling bears instant fruit.

4. A Shannon river boat for two or three or four.

5. Pan Am makes the going great.

IRELAND
IRISH TOURIST BOARD

Please tell me about Pan Am's round trip economy mid-week excursion fare New York-Shannon, $264.00 as well as airline schedule, rates and accommodations in Ireland during May, June and September.

Name

Address

City

State   Zip

Irish Tourist Board
Dept. PA
P.O. Box 238, Madison Square Station
New York, N.Y. 10010
Or pick up your phone and call

537

Exhibit 7 (cont.)

"Food may be good for thought
but 'tis the liquid stuff that interferes
less with conversation."

"He was that cute
if there were any flies on him,
you can be sure they were
paying taxes."

"If Irish milk were any fresher,
it would be grass."

"To go to Ballicooley,
follow the tarred road for a bit, turn left,
or go back the way you're after coming. If I were you,
I wouldn't start from here at all."

"He was the greatest idiot
in the southern parishes and
couldn't be trusted with a
burnt out match."

Exhibit 7 (cont.)

Bring Us Your Ears To Ireland.

You'll hear words hand-loomed like Irish tweed from the raw material of the English language. Words illuminated like Waterford Crystal. Distilled like Irish whiskey.

You can bring home tweeds, linens, crystal, fishermen's sweaters and whiskey, all at bargain-lover's prices. But words, the true native craft of Ireland, are yours for the collecting, absolutely free. Bring us your ears.

Come hear Ireland during the most eloquent time of the year. Now through Spring. When the Irish people have more time for a chat. And even the crisp, clear Irish air seems to be listening. (In February, supposedly the coldest month of the year, Spring is up and sprouting. Perfect listening weather.)

Hear the Irish talk back to the rough in their favorite year-round sport: golf. (Try matching your skill to their wit.) Hunt the fox with the horse. Chase the hare with the beagle (pronounced bagel.) Join the throngs at Croke Park for a Gaelic football game. Whatever the Irish do, you're welcome to do with them. (The fun is in the listening as well as the doing.)

Hear Ireland in the Abbey Theatre, original blasting-off ground of O'Casey, Behan, Shaw. You'll even hear words in the Irish pantomime theater (the Irish can't keep quiet)—a glittering blend of children's fairy-tale magic and grown-up satire. And do hear the Irish stage their greatest impromptu performances off-stage in their pubs, homes or wherever two Irishmen get together.

Take A Talking Tour Of Ireland At Come Hear Prices: from one day to three weeks.

Samples: two eye-and-ear-filled weeks in Ireland. Self-drive car to visit Cork, the Blarney Stone, Waterford, Wexford, New Ross, Dublin, then to Sligo, Galway. Hotel rooms, breakfasts, only $275. Or two full weeks gallivanting around Ireland, with unlimited train and bus transportation, all rooms with bath and breakfasts at first-class hotels, Abbey Theatre, tour of Dublin. $310. Round trip airfares are included via Irish International Airlines, Pan American or Trans World Airlines.

For $405., you can fly to Ireland via Irish International Airlines or TWA and travel all over by luxury motorcoach, for 15 days. Rooms with bath, most meals, guide-lecturers, Medieval Banquet at Bunratty Castle, Jury's Cabaret, Abbey Theatre, entertainment en route.

For $65. *more,* you can travel by escorted luxury motorcoach for 15 days in Ireland and Scotland, with a grand finale in London. Finest hotels with bath, most meals, Medieval Banquet, Abbey Theatre, London Theater. Round trip airfare included via Pan Am. Grand total: $470.

Thirteen other tours to choose from, including Stop-Off Mini Tours. One-day Medieval Tour featuring Medieval Banquet at Bunratty Castle to four days all over Ireland.

Also: Special Walkie-Talkie St. Patrick's Week Tour. (St. Patrick's Day takes a whole week in Ireland.) March with your own group, be our guest at the Lord Mayor's Luncheon and Ball, join the festivities everywhere in Ireland.

Special departures for participation in St. Patrick's Week are available from $285. including air fare.

If you'd like to bring home the true picture of Ireland, call your travel agent or send us the coupon above.

My ears are twitching at the prospect of hearing Ireland. Do send me your booklet of Off-Season Tours.

NAME_____

ADDRESS_____

CITY_____

STATE_____ZIP_____

Irish Tourist Board, 590 Fifth Avenue
New York, N.Y. 10036

It takes more than a camera to bring home the picture of Ireland.

The Grand Detour of Ireland

Even though our road maps point the most precise directions, we urge you to read between the lines. And get lost, whenever possible, when you're driving about Ireland. Take the road that gets you nowhere. And if you're properly absent-minded, it might lead you to Grianan Aileach, the stone fort on top of the mountains of Grianan with its three spectral terraces (visible only to people who see with their imaginations). Or to the enchanted valley of Fore where an ancient monastery still sits on a quaking scraw. And the ash tree that overhangs the wall bears only three branches. And the water in the well cannot be brought to a boil.

If you'd like to see all the secret places in Ireland, that people who go by the book never see, take the Grand Detour of Ireland. Our Ireland Motour gives you fourteen free-spirit days in your private car. Only $345 from New York including round trip air fare to Shannon by Pan Am Jet Clipper. (Tour operator: Thos. Cook & Son, Inc.) Fall through Spring. If you'd like to get the most out of Ireland at lower-than-ever prices, see your travel agent, call or write the Irish Tourist Board, 135 South La Salle Street, Chicago 60603. Tel. 726-9358.

For Rent: One Clockless Day.

After the razzle and frazzle of your European tour, you might just be wanting a brief snatch of time to catch up with yourself.

Our one day medieval tour is designed for people who want to take one long, deep breath before they're catapulted back into the Twentieth Century. We'll personally escort you to the Medieval Banquet at Bunratty Castle where you'll taste and see things that ordinary mortals don't.

So do squeeze one day from your European trip. TWA will drop you in Shannon at no extra charge. One day medieval tour, only $18. ($23.50 during October.) Tour operator: Castle Tours, Shannon Free Airport Development Co. or C.I.E. (Ireland's Transport Co.) And we'll give you a long stretch for your money. For full details of our Stop Off Mini Tours at the miniest prices, see your travel agent, or call or write the Irish Tourist Board, 135 South La Salle Street, Chicago 60603. Tel. 726-9358.

English is spoken here– in three different languages.

There's English-Irish. English-Scotch. And English-English. So if you speak English-American, you'll have no trouble at all in making yourself understood in Ireland, Scotland, or England. Or will you? From Fall through Spring, you can meet three English-speaking peoples at prices that would even impress the Scotch.

Ireland, Scotland and England Leisurely Tour—15 day escorted motorcoach tour, including round trip economy air fare via Pan Am Jet Clipper. First class hotels, with private bath. Ireland, Edinburgh, London. $470. from New York. (Tour operator: Thos. Cook & Son, Inc.) See your travel agent, call or write the Irish Tourist Board. 135 South La Salle Street, Chicago 60603. Tel. 726-9358.

To share: a private island: $30

We're a little country. Surrounded by lots of sky and sea and sunsets. Which makes us see ourselves in the right perspective. As a private people. Inclined more to the art of conversation than to the crass of commerce. We prefer fresh air to hot air. And the color of grass is our national color. We like our past to live with us in the present. So you might find us a bit slow on the skyscrapers but reasonably fast on the uptake.

If your body and soul feel the need for the big refreshment that comes from small, intimate encounters, visit us during the private season of the year. Fall through Spring. THREE DAY STOP OFF MINI-TOUR. Irish International Airlines will fly you into Dublin at no extra charge, for your Dublin and Medieval Tour—includes Abbey Theater, Medieval Banquet in Castle. All rooms with bath, most meals, evening entertainment. $30. Tour operator: C.I.E. (Ireland's Transport Co.) October to April 15, when prices hit a new low. For reservations, see your travel agent, call or write the Irish Tourist Board, 135 South La Salle Street, Chicago 60603. Tel. 726-9358

GHOSTS FOR HIRE.

Irish ghosts are like the Irish people. A bit on the shy side. Therefore, the management cannot undertake to guarantee their appearance. But if you approach them properly with a friendly eye and a not over-glib tongue, materialization is more than likely.

Come to Ireland during the relaxed time of year when the tourists go home and the Irish are at home. (Even the ghosts are more relaxed.) Our King of the Castle Tour—two improbable days starting in Dublin, ending in Kilkea Castle, Ireland's newest, ancient castle resort (with your own private ghosts, if you're lucky).

Irish International Airlines will waft you into Dublin on your trip to or from Europe at no extra charge. Fall through Spring, two days, room with bath, $39.50. (Tour operator: Lissone-Lindeman USA Inc.) See your travel agent, call or write the Irish Tourist Board, 135 South La Salle Street, Chicago 60603. Tel. 726-9358.

Exhibit 8

AD BUDGETS BY GEOGRAPHIC AREA: 1964-68
(£'000s)

Financial Year	*Total*	*Northern Ireland*	*Britain*	*North America*	*Western Germany*	*France*	*Australia*
1968/1969	264	17	90	85	25	37	10
1967/1968	123	4	50	43	8	14	4
1966/1967	100	6	50	32	4	4	4
1965/1966	218	9	94	70	20	20	5
1964/1965	130	8	60	44	7	7	4

Note: Following devaluation in November, 1967, £1 = $2.40 U.S. (compared to $2.80 prior to devaluation).
Source: ITB records

Exhibit 9

ADVERTISING SCHEDULE—BRITAIN

Week Ending Saturday Dated 1966

Publication	Size of space	Schedule (Jan.–July 1966)	Address / Rate
Sunday Times Magazine / Sunday Times / Sunday Times	1 page full colour / 6" x 2 columns / 1" x 4 columns		Thomson Newspapers Ltd., Thomson House, 200 Gray's Inn Road, London, W.C.1. Standard Rate: £26 per 1".
Observer Magazine / The Observer / The Observer	1 page full colour / 6" x 2 columns / 1" x 4 columns		160 Queen Victoria Street, London, E.C.4. Standard Rate: £18.
Daily Telegraph Magazine / Daily Telegraph / Daily Telegraph	1 page full colour / 6" x 2 columns / 1" x 4 columns		135 Fleet Street, London, E.C.4. £17 per 1".
Sunday Express / Sunday Express / Sunday Express	13" x 5 columns / 6" x 2 columns / 1" x 4 columns		Fleet Street, London, E.C.4. £35 per 1".
Daily Express	6" x 2 columns		Fleet Street, London, E.C.4. £30 per 1".
Daily Mail / Daily Mail / Daily Mail	13" x 5 columns / 6" x 2 columns / 1" x 4 columns		Northcliffe House, London, E.C.4. £22 per 1".
Radio Times	½-page		35 Marylebone High Street, London, W.1. Rates on application.
Glasgow Sunday Post / Glasgow Sunday Post	3 columns / 6" x 2 columns		144 Port Dundas Road, Glasgow. £10 per 1".
Scottish Daily Express	13" x 5 columns		Albion Street, Glasgow, C.1. £4 per 1".
The People	6" x 2 columns		Long Acre, London, W.C.2. £43 per 1".
Readers Digest	full page		25 Berkeley Square, London, W.1. Rates on application.
Punch	page full colour		10 Boverie Street, London, E.C.4. £10 per 1".
Country Life	page full colour		Southampton Street, London, W.C.2. £4.10s. per 1".
Field	page full colour		8 Stratton Street, London, W.1. Rates on application.
Scottish Field	page full colour		65 Buchanan Street, Glasgow, C.1. £3.10s. per 1".
Lancs Yorks/ Cheshire Life	page full colour		Thomson House, Withy Grove, Manchester 4. Rates on application.
Angling Times	8" x 2 columns		Newspaper House, Broadway, Peterborough. £4 per 1".
The Scotsman	13" x 5 columns		20 North Bridge, Edinburgh. £3.10s. per 1".
Glasgow Herald	6" x 2 columns		65 Buchanan Street, Glasgow, C.1. £3.10s. per 1".
Glasgow Citizen	6" x 2 columns		Albion Street, Glasgow, C.1. £4 per 1".
Birmingham Post	6" x 2 columns		38 New Street, Birmingham, 2. £2.5s. per 1".
Bristol Evening Post	6" x 2 columns		Silver Street, Bristol, 1 £2 15s per 1".
Cardiff Western Mail	6" x 2 columns		Thomson House, Cardiff. £2.10s. per 1".
Leeds Yorkshire Post	6" x 2 columns		Albion Street, Leeds, 1. £4.5s. per 1".
Liverpool Echo	6" x 2 columns		P.O. Box 48, Victoria Street, Liverpool. £5 per 1".
Newcastle Journal	6" x 2 columns		Thomson House, Great Market, Newcastle-on-Tyne, 1. £1.15s. per 1".
Plymouth Western Morning News	6" x 2 columns		Harmsworth House, Plymouth. £1.3s. per 1".
Sheffield Star	6" x 2 columns		York Street, Sheffield, 1. £3 per 1".
Television Weekly	6" x 2 columns		64 Fleet Street, London, E.C.4. £4.10s.
Angling	full page		167 Fleet Street, London, E.C.4. Rates on application.
Creel	full page		8 Shepherd's Walk, London, W.1. Rates on application.
Fishing	full page		Newspaper House, Broadway, Peterborough. £1.10s. per 1".
Trout & Salmon	full page		Newspaper House, Peterborough. £1.10s. per 1".
Horse & Hound	8" x 2 columns		96 Long Acre, London, W.C.2. £3.15s. per 1".
Motor	full page		Bowling Green Lane, London, E.C.1. £3.17.6d. per 1".
Autocar	full page		Dorset House, Stamford Street, London, S.E.1. £6.10s. per 1".
Universe & Catholic Times	6" x 2 columns / 3" x 1 column		21 Fleet Street, London, E.C.4. £4.10s. per 1".
Catholic Herald Group	6" x 2 columns		67 Fleet Street, London, E.C.4. £2.10s. per 1".
Catholic Pictorial	6" x 2 columns		92 Fleet Street, London, E.C.4. 18 6 per 1".

NOTE: The above schedule is subject to changes which may be made without time to notify all possible advertisers. Please mark your orders 'To appear as near as possible to, and on the same date as the Irish Tourist Board insertion.' In this way the publications will amend your order to tie in with the altered schedule.

As appearing in *Travel Weekly*, November 7 and December 5, 1967; *Travel Trade*, November and December, 1967; *Travel Agent*, November 6 and December 4, 1967.

Exhibit 10

1967 MAGAZINE AD TO U.S. TRAVEL AGENTS

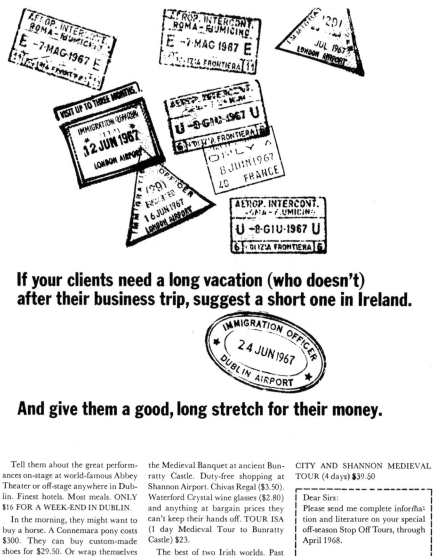

If your clients need a long vacation (who doesn't) after their business trip, suggest a short one in Ireland.

And give them a good, long stretch for their money.

Tell them about the great performances on-stage at world-famous Abbey Theater or off-stage anywhere in Dublin. Finest hotels. Most meals. ONLY $16 FOR A WEEK-END IN DUBLIN.

In the morning, they might want to buy a horse. A Connemara pony costs $300. They can buy custom-made shoes for $29.50. Or wrap themselves in Irish hand-woven tweeds and Irish charm (the latter is free). At night, in the Abbey Theater, they can hear the Irish speak the most lyrical language of all. English. TOUR 3SD (THREE DAYS IN DUBLIN) $26.

Castles with ghosts, singing pubs, the famous Bunratty Castle Singers at the Medieval Banquet at ancient Bunratty Castle. Duty-free shopping at Shannon Airport. Chivas Regal ($3.50). Waterford Crystal wine glasses ($2.80) and anything at bargain prices they can't keep their hands off. TOUR ISA (1 day Medieval Tour to Bunratty Castle) $23.

The best of two Irish worlds. Past and present. With all modern conveniences. TOUR 3SH (Dublin City and Medieval Tour) 3 days $28.

More time to get to know the Irish in their natural habitat: heaven. In Dublin City, Limerick City, Ennis. Medieval Banquet in Bunratty Castle. Irish Cabaret. TOUR 4DS DUBLIN CITY AND SHANNON MEDIEVAL TOUR (4 days) $39.50

Dear Sirs:
Please send me complete information and literature on your special off-season Stop Off Tours, through April 1968.

Name_____

Address_____

City_____

State_____Zip code____
Irish Tourist Board, Ireland House, 590 Fifth Avenue, New York, N.Y. 10036.

CPV, ITB, Regd. No. 22423; *Glasgow Herald, Dundee Courier, Scotsman:* 13 x 9½.

Exhibit 11

TOTAL ITB MARKETING EXPENDITURES AND IRELAND'S
RECEIPTS FROM EXPORT TOURISM: 1957-1966

Year	Total Marketing Expenditure by the I.T.B. (year ended 31st March)		Receipts from Export Tourism (Calendar Year)	
	£ m. (1960 values)	Index 1957=100	£ m. (1960 values)	Index 1957=100
1957	0.283	100	35.5	100
1958	0.292	103.2	36.3	102.3
1959	0.304	107.4	39.6	111.5
1960	0.341	120.5	44.2	124.5
1961	0.325	118.4	48.2	135.8
1962	0.376	132.9	49.0	138.0
1963	0.443	156.6	51.8	145.9
1964	0.453	160.1	56.7	159.7
1965	0.634	224.0	63.6	179.2
1966	1.013	357.9	61.3*	172.7*

* Decline caused partly by British seamen's strike.
Source: Robert Irvine, "Measuring the Promotional Effectiveness of National Tourist Organisations," paper delivered to European Society for Opinion Surveys and Market Research Seminar on Travel and Tourism, Rigi-Kaltbad, November 23-25, 1967, p. 2.

Exhibit 12

EXPENDITURES BY U.S. TOURISTS IN IRELAND
COMPARED WITH EXPENDITURES IN OTHER COUNTRIES
IN NORTHERN EUROPE*: 1957-1966

Year	Expenditure in Northern European Countries Except for the Irish Republic		Expenditure in the Irish Republic		
	£ m.** (1960 values)	Index 1957=100	£ m*** (1960 values)	Index 1957=100	Share of Total in Northern Europe, Percent
1957	70.7	100	4.5	100	5.9
1958	83.6	118	4.6	104	5.2
1959	87.9	124	5.4	120	5.7
1960	100.0	141	4.3	96	4.1
1961	83.9	118	4.5	101	5.1
1962	83.9	118	5.3	118	5.9
1963	88.6	125	5.2	116	5.5
1964	92.9	131	6.1	140	6.1
1965	92.5	131	7.5	168	7.5
1966	98.6	139	8.4	188	7.8

* United Kingdom, Netherlands, Belgium, Luxembourg, Western Germany, Denmark, Norway and Sweden. Figures for Finland and Iceland are not available.
** Current prices deflated by the average consumer price index for Northern European countries other than Ireland, 1957-1966. The individual national indices were obtained from the U.N. Statistical Yearbook, 1957-1966.
*** Current prices deflated by the Consumer Price Index, Central Statistics Office, Dublin.
Source: Robert Irvine, "Measuring the Promotional Effectiveness of National Tourist Organisations," p. 19.

Exhibit 13

SELECTED FINDINGS FROM CONSUMER STUDIES OF ADVERTISING EFFECTIVENESS

A) Whether British Visitors Had Seen Any Publicity on Ireland before Making the Trip

Answer	%
Yes	42
No	34
Don't know	1
Not indicated	23
	100

B) What Publicity Was Noted by Those Responding "Yes" Above

Publicity	%
ITB advertising	38
Irish Airline advertising	6
Travel agent advertising	16
Press or magazine articles	30
Film shows	2
Radio or TV	3
Other	5
	100

Source: ITB Survey of Travellers, 1964, p. 19.

C) Image of the Irish Holiday Visitor among British Respondents

Q: CAN YOU THINK FOR THE MOMENT OF THE TYPICAL TRAVELLER TO IRELAND. DO YOU IMAGINE A TYPICAL TRAVELLER TO IRELAND ON HOLIDAY AS BEING:

	Sample A*	Sample B*
Total informants	526	502
More prosperous	13%	20%
Someone similar	71	72
Someone less prosperous	12	6
Upper class	4	4
Middle class	58	63
Working class	24	23
With Irish relatives	36	36
With Irish friends	8	7
(Certain other answers, including "don't know," have been omitted)		

*Sample A respondents had taken a holiday outside Britain and Ireland within the last three years; Sample B respondents had not.
Source: Market Investigations Ltd., "Holidays in the Republic of Ireland—Attitudes of British Holidaymakers," April, 1966, p. 42.

Exhibit 13 (cont.)

D) Definite Intentions among U.S. Respondents of Visiting Specific Countries in Europe

	Total	Traveled to Europe		Never Traveled			Sex		Prospects for Irish Travel	
		Once	Twice or More	Total	18-34 Yrs.	35 Yrs & Over	Male	Female	Good	Poor
Italy	50%	50%	46%	50%	43%	53%	46%	52%	53%	49%
England	48	55	57	44	47	43	50	45	60	36
France	48	44	43	51	47	53	48	50	48	49
Switzerland	40	44	39	40	40	41	38	43	50	35
Spain	30	38	32	29	33	26	31	30	35	28
Sweden	24	31	38	21	23	20	25	23	39	16
Republic of Ireland	21	28	22	19	19	20	21	21	55	-
Denmark	19	31	25	15	13	17	19	19	28	12
Scotland	19	26	27	16	16	16	20	18	36	9
Netherlands	18	24	21	16	13	18	17	19	27	11
Greece	16	25	22	13	14	12	12	20	19	14
Portugal	14	24	16	12	12	12	12	17	20	11
Wales	11	15	14	10	7	12	11	12	21	5
Number of respondents	(880)	(150)	(95)	(635)	(251)	(378)	(424)	(456)	(335)	(366)

Note: This table shows the percent of respondents with various characteristics who, when asked about their chances of visiting various countries when they go to Europe, answered that they "definitely would visit" the country.
Source: Market Facts-New York, Inc., "A Study of Attitudes toward Travel to the Irish Republic and Other Countries in Europe," July 1966, p. 24.

E) Awareness among U.S. Respondents of Countries as Places to Visit

| | | Prospects for Irish Travel | |
	Total	Good*	Poor*
European Countries			
France	65%	59%	70%
Italy	57	49	65
England	56	59	50
Spain	32	26	36
Germany	31	34	29
Switzerland	29	32	30
Sweden	19	22	18
Denmark	15	17	11
Greece	13	10	14
Republic of Ireland	12	30	**
Norway	12	15	9
Other United Kingdom countries	6	11	4
Non-European Countries			
Mexico	21	19	20
Israel	16	9	22
Canada	13	12	13
Number of respondents	(880)	(335)	(366)

* "Good" prospects were those claiming a definite intention to visit Ireland within the next two or three years. Poor prospects were all others.
** Less than 0.5%
Source: Market Facts-New York, Inc., "A Study of Attitudes Toward Travel to the Irish Republic and Other Countries in Europe," July, 1966, p. 15.

Exhibit 14

COSTS OF SELECTED RESEARCH STUDIES

Description of Study	Case Appendix	Cost*
ITB Survey of Travellers (Eire, points of exit)	-	£1,500
Market Facts Consumer Attitude Survey (U.S.)	A	$10,000
M.I.L. Attitude Survey (Britain)	B,D	£6,000
Tavistock Institute Psychological Study (Britain)**	C	£1,095
M.I.L. Coupon Conversion Rate Study (Britain)	E	£7,700
Social Surveys (Gallup) Readership Report (Britain)	F	£ 325***
Market Facts Travel Agent Survey (North America)	G	$10,000

* All studies except the Social Surveys (Gallup) Readership Report preceded devaluation of the pound. Note that all figures are in pounds except for the two Market Facts studies, costs for which are given in U.S. dollars.
** A non-profit making organization
***Total cost of £650 was shared with the *Daily Telegraph*.
Source: ITB Records

APPENDIX A

Market Facts, Inc.—U.S. Consumer Attitude Study (1966)

STATED OBJECTIVE:

To obtain from European travel prospects, awareness and attitudinal information which will be helpful in the development of more effective advertising and promotion for travel to the Republic of Ireland.

RESPONDENTS:

A total of 800 adult men (344) and women (456) who indicated they might visit Europe within the next two or three years were chosen from middle and upper income area census tracts in the metropolitan areas of New York, Los Angeles, Chicago, Dallas, and San Francisco.

METHOD:

Personal interviews.

COMMENTS:

The following were subject areas in which findings were given:

- Top-of-the-mind awareness of European countries.
- Awareness of places to visit in Ireland and other countries.
- Intentions to visit Ireland and other specific countries in Europe.
- Favorable/unfavorable influences for/against visiting Ireland and other countries.
- Desirability of various characteristics in a country.
- Beliefs about Ireland and other countries.
- Potential effectiveness of alternative strategies for promoting Ireland

Findings were broken down in a variety of ways. Throughout the study, findings for "good prospects for Irish travel" (those who claimed a definite intention to visit Ireland within the next two or three years) were compared with those for "poor prospects for Irish travel." (See for example, Exhibit A-1.) For certain findings more detailed breakdowns were undertaken, such as by sex, age, and number of previous trips to Europe. (See Exhibit A-2.)

Respondents were asked for attitudes and beliefs on three general levels: first, with regard to Ireland specifically (Exhibit A-3); then for Ireland, in comparison with other countries (for instance, data in Exhibit A-1 was presented in similar fashion for a number of other countries as seen in Exhibit A-4); and finally for "a country" in general, i.e., desirable characteristics for an ideal country to visit (Exhibit A-2).

To assess the potential effectiveness of alternative advertising themes, the replies of respondents with regard to nineteen descriptive statements which could be applied to any country were analyzed in the following manner: First the *desirability* of various factors for a tourist country in general was studied, focusing specifically on the desirability of factors among a target audience of poor prospects for Irish travel. A second step studied the extent to which factors were believed to be true about *Ireland,* with the objective of finding those factors which were believed by good prospects for Irish travel but were *not* believed by poor prospects. This second step was explained in the report:

> . . . if virtually everyone agrees strongly that a certain attitude is true about Ireland, it would not pay to try to convince the very few who do not believe Ireland has this particular characteristic. On the other hand, if comparatively few agree strongly that Ireland offers a particular benefit there may be considerable resistance to the idea. Additionally we can compare beliefs among prospects who indicate a high likelihood of visiting Ireland, and those who have little or no intention of visiting Ireland.
>
> If the difference in belief level is relatively high on an important characteristic, this characteristic will have high gain potential for improving attitudes toward visiting Ireland. Not only is the benefit offered important, but it discriminates between good and poor prospects for Ireland.

Each characteristic was then rated according to its desirability among the target audience of poor prospects for Irish travel, and its ability to discriminate between good and poor Irish travel prospects in terms of believability. Exhibit A-5 demonstrates how these two components of desirability and belief change potential were multiplied to arrive at a final index of the potential effectiveness of alternative advertising themes.

Exhibit A-1
INFLUENCES IN FAVOR OF VISITING IRELAND

	Prospects for Irish Travel		
	Total	*Good*	*Poor*
Countryside, rural beauty	36%	51%	23%
Charming, friendly people	19	27	11
Irish heritage, folklore	11	13	10
Have Irish ancestors, Irish lineage	7	15	1
History, historical sights	6	7	5
The Blarney Stone	5	6	3
Specific items of Irish manufacture	5	5	4
Dublin	4	5	3
Visit friends, relatives	4	9	1
Castles, ruins	3	3	3
Just interested in the country	3	3	2
Villages, towns	2	2	1
Literary and theatrical associations	2	1	2
Hear the language	2	3	1
Visit Irish pubs	2	3	1
Sports and sporting events	2	2	1
Other Irish cities	1	2	1
Architecture, quaint houses	1	2	*
Costs less	1	1	*
Convenient to England, to itinerary	2	3	3
None, not interested in Ireland	17	3	33
Don't know of anything	12	3	19
All other	5	7	4
Not reported	1	*	1
Number of respondents	(880)	(335)	(366)

* Less than 0.5%
Source: Market Facts—New York, N.Y., "A Study of Attitudes toward Travel to the Irish Republic and Other Countries in Europe," July 1966, p. 30.

Exhibit A-2

DESIRABILITY OF VARIOUS FACTORS ABOUT A COUNTRY
AMONG THOSE 18-34 YEARS OF AGE WHO HAVE NEVER TRAVELED TO EUROPE

	Extremely Desirable	Fairly Desirable	Slightly Desirable	Neither Desirable nor Undesirable	Undesirable
People of the country are warm and friendly to tourists	64%	26%	6%	3%	1%
The shopping is good; there are good bargains or interesting things to buy	38	29	18	14	1
There is much local color in the country and quite different from the U.S.	70	23	5	2	-
There are outstanding historical and cultural attractions	68	22	4	5	1
Many lively, exciting or unusual things to do in the country	64	28	6	2	*
Opportunity for a quiet, restful vacation	11	19	21	18	31
Pleasant climate	39	38	12	10	1
Good food	56	31	10	3	-
Outstanding scenery, has places of great beauty	72	22	3	3	-
Inexpensive to travel through the country	55	32	8	4	1
Good fishing, hunting or golf	12	15	16	32	25
Clean, efficient accommodations for tourists	70	17	8	4	1
People speak and understand English	28	34	24	13	1
Has places off the beaten path where few tourists go	37	32	16	10	5
Popular with tourists who know a lot about travel	28	27	24	16	5
Popular with U.S. tourists	24	31	20	18	7
Popular with young, lively tourists	42	25	18	11	4
Popular with cultured, well-educated tourists	34	32	20	12	2
Popular with tourists who have to travel on a tight budget	30	20	17	18	5
Number of respondents (251)					

* Less than 0.5%

Source: Market Facts-New York, N.Y., "A Study of Attitudes toward Travel to the Irish Republic and Other Countries in Europe," July 1966, p. 44.

Exhibit A-3
BELIEFS ABOUT IRELAND AMONG POOR PROSPECTS FOR TRAVEL TO IRELAND

	Agree Strongly	Agree Somewhat	Neither Agree nor Disagree	Disagree Somewhat	Disagree Strongly
People of the country are warm and friendly to tourists	25%	23%	44%	5%	3%
The shopping is good; there are good bargains or interesting things to buy	17	17	56	6	4
There is much local color in the country and quite different from the U.S.	33	28	31	6	2
There are outstanding historical and cultural attractions	24	24	36	12	4
Many lively, exciting or unusual things to do in the country	10	16	53	12	9
Opportunity for a quiet, restful vacation	35	25	35	4	1
Pleasant climate	6	23	42	16	13
Good food	9	15	58	11	7
Outstanding scenery, has places of great beauty	32	31	32	3	2
Inexpensive to travel through the country	9	22	58	6	5
Good fishing, hunting or golf	9	16	68	5	2
Clean, efficient accommodations for tourists	20	21	53	5	1
People speak and understand English	56	23	17	3	1
Has places off the beaten path where few tourists go	26	22	44	4	4
Popular with tourists who know a lot about travel	14	23	41	18	4
Popular with U.S. tourists	18	17	49	10	6
Popular with young, lively tourists	5	9	48	22	16
Popular with cultured, well-educated tourists	15	23	43	12	7
Popular with tourists who have to travel on a tight budget	14	21	53	8	4
Number of respondents (366)					

Source: Market Facts - New York, N.Y. "A Study of Attitudes toward Travel to the Irish Republic and Other Countries in Europe," July 1966, p. 61.

Exhibit A-4

INFLUENCES IN FAVOR OF VISITING DENMARK

	Total
The people	24%
Beauty of countryside	22
Customs, way of life	14
Food, cheese	9
Copenhagen	7
Just interested in the country	7
Clean country	6
Danish manufactured items	6
Tivoli Gardens	4
Have friends, relatives in Denmark	3
Have Danish ancestry	2
Historical interest	2
Beaches, seaside resorts	2
Museums, art objects	2
Ballet, theatre	2
Governmental system (socialism)	2
Sports	2
Peaceful, quiet country	1
Hans Christian Andersen home, etc.	1
Palaces, castles	1
Pleasant climate	1
Not expensive	1
Don't know of anything	†9
All other	11
None, not interested in Denmark	10
Not reported	*
Number of respondents	(430)

* Less than 0.5%
Source: Market Facts-New York, N.Y., "A Study of Attitudes toward Travel to the Irish Republic and Other Countries in Europe," July, 1966, p. 32.

Exhibit A-5

POTENTIAL EFFECTIVENESS
OF ALTERNATIVE ADVERTISING STRATEGIES

	Target Group (A)	*Belief Change Potential (B)*	*Index (A x B)*
Outstanding scenery, places of great beauty	80	36	2376
Much local color	74	31	2294
People are warm and friendly to tourists	66	31	2046
Outstanding historical and cultural attractions	73	24	1752
Clean, efficient accommodations	72	21	1512
Many lively, exciting or unusual things to do	58	15	870
Popular with cultured, well-educated tourists	41	20	820
Popular with tourists who know a lot about travel	31	23	713
Good food	48	12	576
Inexpensive to travel through the country	48	12	576
Places off the beaten path where few tourists go	35	16	560
Good shopping	37	12	444
Pleasant climate	37	11	407
Popular with tourists who have to travel on a tight budget	31	13	403
People speak and understand English	36	11	396
Popular with young, lively tourists	30	13	390
Popular with U.S. tourists	26	10	260
Good fishing, hunting or golf	9	12	108
Opportunity for a quiet, restful vacation	11	9	99

Target Group: Percentage (among persons who probably or definitely *will not* visit Ireland) rating benefit "extremely desirable" for any country.

Belief Change Potential: Difference (between poor prospects and good prospects for visiting Ireland) in "agree strongly" ratings of Ireland on this dimension.

Source: Market Facts–New York, N.Y., "A Study of Attitudes toward Travel to the Irish Republic and other Countries in Europe," July 1966, p. 69.

APPENDIX B

Market Investigations, Limited—
British Consumer Attitude Study (1966)

STATED OBJECTIVES:

1)   To establish what the British holiday maker was looking for when he went on holiday;

2)   To establish the extent to which he thought that what he was looking for was available in the Republic of Ireland;

3)   To present information to ITB which would aid it and its advertising agency in the formulation and content of its advertising policy.

RESPONDENTS:

A total of 1,028 adults, aged 16 and over, were chosen from throughout Britain (excluding Northern Ireland); 526 respondents (Sample A) had taken a holiday outside Britain and Ireland in the last three years, and the remaining 502 respondents (Sample B) had not taken a holiday abroad in the last three years. Both samples were matched in terms of age, social class, sex, and regional distribution.

METHOD:

Personal interviews.

COMMENTS:

The study was composed of four sections:

1)   General Patterns of Holiday Making—how holidays have been spent in the past, likes/dislikes about holidays in general, specific countries, and Ireland.

2)   Choosing a Holiday—"what do you look for," holiday activities, types of accommodation, how a typical day on holiday is spent, children on holiday, booking a holiday.

3)   Image of Ireland—the country and people, image of the Irish holiday visitor, climate, what there is to see and do in Ireland, Ireland and the motorist, etc.

4)   Advertising—pretest of seven advertisements later used in the 1966 ITB advertising campaign. See Appendix D for a more detailed discussion of this section of the study.

Nearly all replies were analyzed according to Sample A and Sample B respondents. As in the 1966 Market Facts, Inc., attitude study in the United States, interpretive text accompanies all tables. (See Exhibits B-1, B-2, and B-3 for selected findings from the survey.)

An additional question asked respondents whether they regarded Ireland as being "abroad." Only 24% of Sample A and 27% of Sample B respondents answered in the affirmative.

A number of implications and recommendations were noted throughout the study. However, no scheme was included that compared alternative advertising schemes in a similar manner with that attempted in Exhibit A-5.

Exhibit B-1

COMPOSITION OF HOLIDAY PARTY

Q.12A: THINKING OF YOUR NEXT MAIN HOLIDAY, WILL YOU PROBABLY BE SPEND-ING IT _____?

	Sample A*		Sample B*	
	No.	%	No.	%
Alone	19	4	16	3
With one other person	180	34	116	23
With your own family	184	35	265	53
With one other family as well	34	6	30	6
Or with a group/party	60	11	39	8
Don't know yet	31	6	30	6
Other	18	3	9	2
All informants	526		502	

The main difference emerging between the two groups of informants lies in the proportion who said that they plan to spend their next holiday with their own family; 53% of those who have not been abroad in the past three years gave this reply compared with only 35% of those who had taken a holiday abroad in the last three years. It should also be noted, however, that the proportion of Sample A taking a holiday with one other person was greater than for Sample B—not surprisingly when the difference in sample structures on the issue of family composition is remembered. Perhaps the most significant factor is that for both samples approximately three-quarters of all informants expected to spend their next holiday either with one other person or with their family.

* Sample A respondents had taken a holiday abroad within the past three years; Sample B respondents had not.
Source: Market Investigations Ltd., "Holidays in the Republic of Ireland Attitudes of British Holidaymakers," April 1966, p. 7.

Exhibit B-2

WHAT IS LOOKED FOR ON HOLIDAY

Q. 6: NOW ON YOUR TYPICAL HOLIDAY, SAY LIKE THE ONES YOU HAVE TAKEN IN
RECENT YEARS, WHAT EXACTLY WERE YOU LOOKING FOR WHEN YOU DECIDED
TO GO THERE?

	Total	*Sample A*		Total	*Sample B*	
		Have Visited Eire	*Would Like to Visit Eire*		*Have Visited Eire*	*Would Like to Visit Eire*
Total Informants	526	121	78	502	50	91
Different things to do	13%	16%	13%	13%	14%	12%
Few people	9	12	10	20	18	21
Sport/fresh air	8	8	8	10	14	10
Beaches, sea, weather	15	9	15	16	20	16
Sun and nightlife	30	27	22	13	16	9
Caravan/villa etc.	5	4	1	10	8	14
Holiday camp	1	1	1	4	2	1
At sea/cruise	5	6	6	4	2	3
Motor Touring	12	13	19	9	6	14
Camping	3	2	4	2	-	-
Don't know	**	1	-	-	-	-

* Sample A respondents had taken a holiday abroad within the past three years; Sample B
respondents had not.
** Less than 0.5%.
Source: Market Investigations Ltd., "Holidays in the Republic of Ireland Attitudes of British
Holidaymakers," April, 1966, p. 21.

Exhibit B-3
BELIEFS ABOUT IRELAND

Q. 18A: HERE IS A LIST OF ADJECTIVES THAT SOME PEOPLE HAVE USED CONCERNING IRELAND. WOULD YOU SAY WHETHER YOU AGREE OR DISAGREE THAT THESE WORDS APPLY TO IRELAND OR GOING TO IRELAND ON HOLIDAY OR TO THE PEOPLE YOU'D MEET THERE. WOULD YOU PLEASE SAY WHETHER YOU FEEL THAT THEY APPLY 'DEFINITELY,' 'SOMEWHAT,' 'YOU ARE NOT SURE,' OR 'DEFINITELY DOES NOT APPLY' TO IRELAND AND THE IRISH -

	Applies Definitely Sample*		Somewhat Sample		Not Sure Sample		Does Not Apply Sample	
	A	B	A	B	A	B	A	B
Total Informants	526	502	526	502	526	502	526	502
Religious	82%	79%	12%	14%	3%	6%	3%	2%
Unspoilt	71	65	17	21	7	7	5	7
Hospitable	70	70	16	15	13	12	2	3
Likeable	67	67	20	24	7	5	6	5
Healthy	65	66	19	19	12	12	5	3
Fit	62	63	20	21	13	12	5	4
Hilly	45	45	39	40	9	10	7	6
Poor	41	39	39	42	11	11	9	8
Lazy	19	17	25	34	21	17	35	32
Bleak	18	18	30	30	14	18	38	35
Drunken	16	17	31	35	21	21	33	27
Grey	15	11	14	13	19	24	53	52
Primitive	15	13	28	31	16	19	41	36
Dull	13	9	11	13	16	21	59	57
Flat	10	7	28	26	13	19	49	49
Expensive	10	8	13	14	22	24	55	55
Dirty	8	5	17	22	20	20	54	53
Hostile	5	5	18	20	16	19	61	55
Grasping	5	7	6	9	27	24	62	60
Insolent	5	6	11	13	17	21	67	61

* Sample A respondents had taken a holiday abroad within the past three years; Sample B respondents had not.
Source: Market Investigations Ltd., "Holidays in the Republic of Ireland Attitudes of British Holidaymakers," April, 1966, p. 42.

APPENDIX C

Tavistock Institute—In-Depth Study of the Social and Psychological Aspects of "The Holiday" (1965)

STATED OBJECTIVES:

To discover:

1) the reasons for taking holidays at all;
2) the feelings and attitudes that lead to the choice of one holiday destination rather than another; and
3) attitudes toward Ireland as a holiday destination.

RESPONDENTS:

A total of 82 British respondents were seen either in groups or in individual interviews. The interviewees represented a variety of social classes, and it was ensured that "a proportion" had actually been to Ireland for a holiday.

METHOD:

Eight groups, accounting for 59 interviewees, were composed as follows:

1) Eight unmarried men aged 17-26.
2) Eight unmarried women aged 17-23.
3) Seven unmarried men aged 21-30.
4) Four married couples without children aged 20-30.
5) Four married couples with children aged 30-40.
6) Four married couples with children aged 40-60.
7) Five fathers aged 30-40.
8) Seven mothers aged 29-46.

In addition to the group discussions an additional 18 interviews were held, five of which were with married couples while 13 were with individuals, to account for the remaining 23 respondents.

COMMENTS:

It was hoped by ITB executives that this study would probe beneath the motives for taking a holiday which emerged in other studies and surveys of a more traditional nature to uncover the deeper, often unconscious associations of holidays and the psychological needs served by a holiday.

The study was entirely qualitative in nature; at no point were any findings presented in graphical, tabular, or any other quantitative form. The format of the report was essentially representative quotes with interpretive text.

The actual interview findings were preceded by an overview of the role which the holiday has assumed throughout history. Proceeding to the subject of the role of the modern holiday, the study concluded:

> Fundamentally a person goes on holiday for the same reason that in ancient times he went on a pilgrimage: to enrich himself internally. . . . A successful holiday results in an internal sense of well-being, of having imbibed from the destination in a number of ways something which enriches the individual both physically and, more important, psychologicially. . .what is crucial is that something should be taken in and brought back afterwards, something which is both perceptible to the person concerned and demonstrable to others. . .hence, the importance. . .for example. . .of a tan or photographic evidences of vitality. . . .

> When people talk about eating and drinking on holiday, about breathing in the fresh air, soaking in or worshipping the sun, absorbing the peace and quiet, they are expressing in these various ways the same basic needs for internal replenishment and repair.

The different roles played by the holiday with different age groups were then analyzed. This section carefully plotted an individual's "holiday career" from childhood, during which time holiday decisions are dominated by the parents; through adolescence (when a holiday independent of parents symbolizes new-found maturity); through the early years of marriage (when the desire to take a holiday together clashes with a couple's wish to establish a firm financial base for their home); through middle-age and finally to the retirement years, when the holiday can represent either secure serenity or an opportunity to explore new adventures.

The section that followed explored the different associations of different social classes with regard to the holiday. The following is representative of the analysis in this section:

> The upper classes show the same kind of tendency on holiday to atavism and regression to more primitive forms of enjoyment, but whereas the lower classes tend to do this by projecting into and identifying with the children and perhaps enjoying more childish activities. . .at the upper end of the middle-class there seems to be more of an emphasis on being able to get away from the children so that parents can regress in their own way. While the children are around it forces the parents into taking a parental role; when the children are away the parents can let their hair down.

The study then focused on detailed aspects of the holiday, including influences on the choice of destination, accommodation, and both daytime and evening activities. The following passages are typical of this analysis:

> A satisfactory holiday destination means, for most people, a place that is manifestly different from the one where they live. Geographical distance in

itself is not so important as what might be described as perceived psychological distance. To cross the sea, for example, is an event that symbolized the necessary break with one's usual environment. Holidays abroad tend to be seen as potentially more adventurous and rewarding than holidays in Britain, and those who do take their holidays in Britain often tend to be defensive about what they feel is an unadventurous choice. . . .

The more ordinary, or nonspecialist, holiday maker needs to have (sightseeing) made meaningful for him by guides, guide books, or some such device that acts as a reassurance that the sight is meaningful and genuine. . . .

The presence of water in itself is often of considerable symbolic importance on a holiday in its most obvious form in the sea or in terms of lakes and rivers. What does vary between people is the degree of intimacy of their contact with such natural elements. . . .

. . .whereas the day is by and large destination oriented the evening is more activity oriented. . . .What is feared (about the evening) is a feeling of blankness, a shutting down after the evening meal.

As the study proceeded to investigate specific feelings about Ireland, the following passages emerged:

The emptiness and solitariness that thinking of Ireland evokes was also a source of ambivalence. This came up particularly over the matter of the empty beaches. On the one hand, for some people an empty beach may be a source of delight but at the same time it can be a source of anxiety. . .there may be a kind of sneaking suspicion that the people who are not there have in fact travelled to a better destination. The presence of at least a few other couples on the beach seems to be some kind of reassurance, especially for those with a family. . . .

There was some fear that everything would shut down in the evening. . . .

The Irish were also seen as often likely to be drunk, where this drunkenness seemed to have two aspects. On the one hand, the Irish were thought when drunk to get fighting drunk and to want to pick fights both with each other or preferably with any English who were in the vicinity; but, on the other hand, they were perhaps more often felt to get benignly drunk. They were seen to be feckless and in some ways incompetent and careless and unconcerned for visitors.

A number of advertising and marketing recommendations concluded the study. For example:

It would seem to make sense as a marketing policy to attempt to influence the potential Irish holiday goer to choose Ireland from among its competitors rather than to attempt to convert those who are against Ireland into potential visitors. . . .

Present advertising tends to lay stress on the emptiness of beaches and roads. . . .To say that the environment is empty. . . .can. . .arouse unconsciously the suspicion that one will return from holiday empty oneself. . . .

What seems to be necessary also is that advertisements should stress the sort of experiences that one can have in Ireland that one can have nowhere else. . . .Thus, the uniqueness of Ireland and its historical separation from England might be stressed.

APPENDIX D

Market Investigations, Limited—
Pretest of Seven Advertisements (1966)

STATED OBJECTIVES:

1) To examine the extent to which certain advertisements to be used in the Board's advertising campaign in Britain during the course of 1966 did or did not fit the image of Ireland previously held by the respondent.

2) As a relative comparison of the effects of these advertisements on informants and attitudes, each respondent was asked whether the advertisements shown tempted him to go to Ireland on holiday or not, and whether they had increased his chances of going to Ireland on holiday.

RESPONDENTS:

Same total respondent group as described in Appendix B. (This study was Section 4 of the study described in Appendix B.)

METHOD:

Each of the 1,028 respondents was shown one of the seven ads randomly. With 14 respondent subsamples (Sample A and Sample B groups for each of the seven ads) approximately 75 respondents in each subsample were questioned on their reaction to any one of the seven ads.

COMMENTS:

Respondents were shown a black-and-white reproduction of an ad (the ads used are included here as Exhibits D-1 through D-7) and asked a number of questions about the specific appeals of the ad. For example, Exhibit D-8 summarizes replies to a question about "Advertisement E" included here as Exhibit D-5.

After answering questions specifically related to the ad, each respondent was then asked whether the ad tempted him to go to Ireland on holiday and whether his chances of going to Ireland on holiday were increased as a result of discussing Ireland and seeing the ad. Exhibit D-9 summarizes the responses to these two closing questions for all seven ads.

Home-made bread, creamy butter and lobster fresh from the sea — let the Irish remind you what food is

 You're sitting face to face with home-made bread in which every crumb is an individual and tastes like it; Irish butter, and lobster fresh from the sea . . .

Don't wait. You're in Ireland and you're on holiday. A tourist marches on his stomach, and in Ireland he marches well.

Because Ireland's the sort of place where you can admit you enjoy eating and drinking and so on. The Irish do. If you're in Donegal and you're staying with Mrs. O'Donnell for Bed-and-

In a Dublin Hotel.

Breakfast, she'll expect you to appreciate the food she cooks for you: fresh farm eggs for breakfast, fresh spring lamb for dinner, and tea all the time, good tea. (In return she'll tell you about her eleven children and show you her second daughter's wedding photos).

Or you might be staying in one of Dublin's modern hotels where everything is so up-to-date it crackles. But the bacon you get for breakfast (in bed) has a delicious Irish curl in the taste. (There's a bit of an Irish twist in

the hotel service, too. 'God bless you lady', says the hall porter at Killarney's haughtiest hotel; and they'll look up your bus for you before you've decided to go by bus).

And of course, you wouldn't miss the most important hospitality of all—the Irish pub. Because it isn't just creamy stout and Irish coffee and whiskey and so on that you get there, it's the Irish tilt on life.

So 'Slainte', come on over and relax—get the Irish tilt on life. But cut out this coupon first.

you'll get on famously in *Ireland* 🍀 come on over!

Ireland is only an hour or so away when you fly Aer Lingus or BEA. You can fly from any of eleven points in Britain to Dublin, Cork or Shannon, so wherever you live you can't be far from a plane to Ireland. Aer Lingus can fly your car over with you too. Fill in this coupon and learn more.

TELL ME MORE ABOUT IRELAND

Please send me the FREE colour Holiday Pack about Ireland and details of BEA and AER LINGUS flights, straight away.

NAME ....

ADDRESS ....

....

B   *Post (unsealed envelope, 3d. stamp),*
IRISH TOURIST BOARD, DEPT. WT.3, BOX 273, DUBLIN, IRELAND

fly **BEA** or 🍀 **AER LINGUS**

IRISH TOURIST BOARD OFFICES IN BRITAIN: 16 Mount Street, Manchester. Tel: Deansgate 5981. 11 Bennett's Hill, Birmingham. Tel: Midland 3882. 35 St. Enoch Square, Glasgow. Tel: Central 2311
The new London office is at: Ireland House, 150 New Bond Street, W.1. Tel: Hyde Park 3201

Come and learn how to take it easy
from the experts — the Irish

 You arrive in Ireland, your face shining like china with earnest tourism, all eager to see the sights. But the Irish are starting on you. On the way from the airport you stop off at a pub where you meet a man who knows a horse...

Then on the second day you don't get up and plough through three churches, you have breakfast in bed and get up at noon.

Ireland's got you. Changed you in two days from a tourist into a human.

So you begin to look around and enjoy life at the Irish pace.

You potter round a lake in a little boat, not exactly fishing. You climb a hill in Kerry (most of a hill), and then you sit on it for a long time watching the cloud shadows and the sheep.

Even when you go on proper excursions, you don't rush. Say you drive from Cork to Blarney. Your car saunters along the road, and on the way you notice a cowherd asleep under the trees, a tinker's caravan by the side of the road, and long green weeds in the river.

And when you're feeling sociable (you do, in Ireland), you might

stroll into a pub in the Wicklow Mountains (only 15 miles from Dublin), where you'll meet a shepherd who has just been offered £10 for his dog. 'But what's the use of £10 if I've to run after the sheep myself?'

Even in Dublin, you find the Irish leave time for living as well as working. Dublin's delicate Regency atmosphere has not been crushed by traffic, and O'Connell Street is always full of Irish enjoying themselves.

Come and learn how to take it easy from the experts—the Irish. Fill in this coupon or see your travel agent now.

you'll get on famously in *Ireland* come on over!

Ireland is only an hour or so away when you fly Aer Lingus or BEA. You can fly from any of eleven points in Britain to Dublin, Cork or Shannon, so wherever you live you can't be far from a plane to Ireland. Aer Lingus can fly your car over with you too. Fill in this coupon and learn more.

fly **BEA** or **AER LINGUS** IRISH INTERNATIONAL AIRLINES

TELL ME MORE ABOUT IRELAND

Please send me the FREE colour Holiday Pack about Ireland and details on BEA and AER LINGUS flights, straight away.

NAME ....

ADDRESS ....

B IRISH TOURIST BOARD, DEPT. OM6, P.O. BOX 273, DUBLIN 2, IRELAND

IRISH TOURIST BOARD OFFICES IN BRITAIN: 16 Mount St., Manchester 2. Tel: Deansgate 5981. 11 Bennett's Hill, Birmingham 2. Tel: Midland 3882. 35 St. Enoch Sq., Glasgow C.1. Tel: Central 2311
The new London office is at: Ireland House, 150 New Bond Street, W.1. Tel: Hyde Park 3201

This could be you.

Leopardstown evening meeting.

The only crowds on Irish rivers are fish

If you've only fished on the crowded rivers and coasts of England, the Irish fishing will lift your heart.

There's lots of water in Ireland, and a lot of fish, but not so many anglers. Sea fishing is free (tope and ray and shark, in plenty and waiting for you), coarse fishing is unrestricted and the finest game fishing (salmon, sea-trout and brown trout) can be had for comparatively small sums by English standards.

But fishing isn't the only sport that's uncrowded and fresh in Ireland.

You're a golfer. You're on a championship course and you just walked in, no restrictions. You paid less than 30/- for the day (including lunch), yet you're almost alone on the course. There are 200 golf-courses in Ireland, all as peaceful as grass.

But the races, that's where the crowds are. The Irish invented steeple-chasing, they've bred and trained most of the world's winners, and they know how to enjoy a race. (Once at the Galway Races a dog wandered on to the track and everyone cheered and bet on the dog and the dog won.) The Irish race 150 days a year, especially at the Irish Derby on July 2nd. You're off.

Or you will be if you can get your family over with you for an Irish holiday. (Get your travel agent to tell them about the empty roads, the empty beaches, Irish hospitality and the soft wild hills.) Or just slip over by yourself. They won't miss you for a few days. You could be in Ireland in an hour or so.

Peaceful.

you'll get on famously in *Ireland* come on over!

Ireland is only an hour or so away when you fly Aer Lingus or BEA. You can fly from any of eleven points in Britain to Dublin, Cork or Shannon, so wherever you live you can't be far from a plane to Ireland. Aer Lingus can fly your car over with you too. Fill in this coupon and learn more.

fly **BEA** or **AER LINGUS IRISH**

IRISH TOURIST BOARD OFFICES IN BRITAIN: 16 Mount Street, Manchester. Tel: Deansgate 5981. 11 Bennett's Hill, Birmingham. Tel: Midland 3882. 35 St. Enoch Square, Glasgow. Tel: Central 2311
The new London office is at: Ireland House, 150 New Bond Street, W.1. Tel: Hyde Park 3201

There are lots of sandy beaches just lying around in Ireland. Come and get one of your own.

An unclaimed part of the 60 miles of beach on the Irish east coast.

You can have a gentle beach with grass right down to the sand. No buildings, no shrill concrete, just empty sand and the occasional cow.

Or a Connemara beach with a wild white light in the sky and white marbly rocks round your sand.

Or a Kerry beach, with rhododendrons.

There are 2,000 miles of coastline in Ireland and beaches are tucked in all along it. They're all kinds, wild or domesticated. All you do is cruise along and take your pick.

Say you drive south from Dublin. You'll find sixty miles of more or less continuous beach. Stop the car anywhere you like and stake a claim. There's no-one to argue. Or, if you're feeling sociable, come along to Bray or Greystones. They'll give you a good time without crowding you out.

Nearly all Irish beaches have the right kind of sand for castles and footprints. So come on over with your family and sit on your beach and watch the sea.

Or sail in Celtic seas. Just sail out quietly round the Irish coast. It's empty, the beaches glimmer, and you sail through a mythology of mountains and islands. You'll find the Irish fishing harbours are excellent.

All you do is come to Ireland. If you'll fill in this coupon and send it to us, we'll get you started.

you'll get on famously in *Ireland* come on over!

Ireland is only an hour or so away when you fly Aer Lingus or BEA. You can fly from any of eleven points in Britain to Dublin, Cork or Shannon, so wherever you live you can't be far from a plane to Ireland. Aer Lingus can fly your car over with you too. Fill in this coupon and learn more.

fly **BEA** or **AER LINGUS**

HOW DO I GET MY IRISH BEACH?

Please send me the FREE colour Holiday Pack about Ireland and details of BEA/AER LINGUS flights, straight away.

NAME ....

ADDRESS ....

B IRISH TOURIST BOARD, DEPT. P.1.   P.O. BOX 273, DUBLIN 2, IRELAND

IRISH TOURIST BOARD OFFICES IN BRITAIN: 16 Mount Street, Manchester. Tel: Deansgate 5981. 11 Bennett's Hill, Birmingham. Tel: Midland 3882. 35 St. Enoch Square, Glasgow. Tel: Central 2311. *And the new London office at:* Ireland House, 150 New Bond Street, W.1. Tel: Hyde Park 3201.

ADVERTISEMENT E

Children in Connemara

The Irish don't like children

(they love them, welcome them at hotels, make them feel at home, understand about baby-sitting and rainy days, offer them miles and miles of safe sandy beaches and donkey-carts and Connemara ponies).

Taking children on holiday can mean barricaded hotels and haughty faces. But there's a whole country just across the sea that welcomes children: Ireland.

Most hotels and guesthouses cater for your children. And the staff are friendly, full of talk, and kindly disposed when there's a crisis.

A child needs a good sandy beach, with no crowds to get lost in.

In Ireland you can sit around and talk

Ireland has 2,000 miles of coastline just bursting with beaches, most of them empty and safe for swimming.

Ireland will keep them interested (and you). Hire ponies and go trekking across the fresh Irish hills. Rent a bright red gipsy caravan; chug about Irish rivers in a boat; take them sailing, walking, fishing. Show them Dublin, Celtic crosses, round towers. And they'll notice for themselves the original little bits of Irish living—donkeys, tinkers, spry old bicycles, priests on scooters and women in black shawls.

Travel without tears in Ireland. You'll find family motoring a pleasant surprise because the roads are empty and excellent. You can easily rent a car in Ireland or bring your own. Cut this coupon and you're practically on your way.

you'll get on famously in *Ireland* 🍀 come on over!

Burns & Laird Lines overnight-ship direct from Glasgow can add another day to your holiday. You can save money if you travel midweek from May to october. And they'll ship your car over for you to enjoy Ireland's quiet roads. Post this coupon for details of Burns & Laird Lines. And have a good time in Ireland.

IRISH TOURIST BOARD OFFICES IN BRITAIN: 16 Mount Street, Manchester. Tel: Deansgate 5981. 11 Bennett's Hill, Birmingham. Tel: Midland 3882. 35 St. Enoch Square, Glasgow. Tel: Central 2311. *The new London office is at:* Ireland House, 150 New Bond Street, W.1. Tel: Hyde Park 3201

CPV, ITB, Regd. No. 22423; *Glasgow Herald, Dundee Courier; Scotsman*: 13 x 9 1/2

In Ireland the open road is really open— just what the car is longing for

At first you can't understand where the traffic is. You're driving on these excellent roads, and the

You can relax.

last car you saw was seven miles back.

But there is no traffic in Ireland, or hardly any. There are 20,000 miles of road and only 4 million Irish (and lots of them ride gnarled bicycles).

So you drive out of Dublin and in twenty minutes you're in the Wicklow Mountains where you meet five sheep, a donkey cart, a donkey by itself, some cows being chivvied by a black and white dog, and one car.

You can drive right across Ireland in three or four hours, if you want to.

But you won't want to. You'll wander about and explore:

Walking home after First Communion.

Peak holiday rush in County Wicklow.

You're driving round the Ring of Kerry (if you got off the B.R. ferry at Rosslare you'd be near Kerry), and you're looking at the hills and the wild beaches across the bay that seem to move as the light moves. You find a lane you like the look of, and you end up spending two days there.

Or you're bowling along the main road from Dublin to Galway

when you see a ruined tower on the stretches of grass and water near Galway. You stop the car.

So when your holiday's over you find you haven't seen Sligo, the Yeats country; or Donegal, or Connemara with its wild white light; you only had a glimpse of Tipperary and you'd like more time on that beach near Dublin.

you'll get on famously in *Ireland* ☘ come on over!

British Rail will ferry you and your car across to Ireland by Holyhead—Dun Laoghaire or Fishguard—Rosslare. Both routes have car-carry trains from London in summer. And when you get to Dun Laoghaire you're practically in Dublin; at Rosslare you're ideally placed for the whole of southern Ireland, with its beaches, mountains and lakes. Fill in this coupon and learn more.

British Rail

TELL ME MORE ABOUT IRELAND
Please send me the **FREE** colour Holiday Pack about Ireland, straight away.

NAME

ADDRESS

Post (unsealed envelope, ³d ·tamp),
H IRISH TOURIST BOARD, DEPT. WT.1, P.O. BOX 273, DUBLIN, IRELAND

IRISH TOURIST BOARD OFFICES IN BRITAIN: 16 Mount Street, Manchester. Tel: Deansgate 5981. 11 Bennett's Hill, Birmingham. Tel: Midland 3882. 35 St. Enoch Square, Glasgow. Tel: Central 2311 *And the new London office at:* Ireland House, 150 New Bond Street, W.1. Tel: Hyde Park 3201.

ADVERTISEMENT G

Kinvarra Castle. Hardly anyone knows about it

The Cliffs of Moher, Co. Clare

Ballad-singing in an Irish pub

There are no tourist traps in Ireland

(except the Irish light and Dublin and high crosses and race meetings and real folk singing and theatre festivals and film and beer and oyster festivals)

In Ireland things aren't ticketed and docketed.

You'll find ruined abbeys that are still ruined and have long grass and rooks instead of tourists.

You'll find carved crosses a thousand years old that no-one sees but the cows.

You'll wander into a whole rash of beauty spots that no-one's told you about: thundering great headlands, wide beaches and cloudy mountains that the Irish haven't bothered to name on the map. Why should they? There's so much of it.

Not that the Irish don't know how to give you a good time, though.

They'll take you racing like a flash (they invented steeplechasing), and you'll find it hard to miss an Irish festival. There are lots of them because festivals are the friendly sort of thing that suits the Irish. You get the Festival of Kerry, 27th Aug. – 4th Sept. Waterford Light Opera Festival, 11th – 25th Sept. Cork Film Festival, 18th – 25th Sept. Dublin Theatre Festival, 3rd – 16th Oct. and the Wexford Opera Festival 22nd – 30th Oct. Ask your travel agent about it all.

Come on over and forget all that tourist blarney. (Come and visit Blarney.)

you'll get on famously in *Ireland* ❧ come on over!

Ireland is only an hour or so away when you fly Aer Lingus or BEA. You can fly from any of eleven points in Britain to Dublin, Cork or Shannon, so wherever you live you can't be far from a plane to Ireland. Aer Lingus can fly your car over with you too. Fill in this coupon and learn more.

TELL ME MORE ABOUT IRELAND

Please send me the FREE colour Holiday Pack about Ireland and details on BEA and AER LINGUS flights. Straightaway.

NAME..

ADDRESS..

....

B IRISH TOURIST BOARD, DEPT. OM9 P.O. BOX 273, DUBLIN 2, IRELAND

IRISH TOURIST BOARD OFFICES IN BRITAIN: 16 Mount Street, Manchester 2. Tel: Deansgate 5981. 11 Bennett's Hill, Birmingham 2. Tel: Midland 3882. 35 St. Enoch Square, Glasgow C.1. Tel: Central 2311. *The new London Office is at:* Ireland House, 150 New Bond Street, W.1. Tel: Hyde Park 3201

Exhibit D-8

REACTIONS TO ADVERTISEMENT E

Q. 49: THIS ADVERTISEMENT WHERE THE CHILDREN ARE IN THE PONY/JAUNTING CART. WHAT IS YOUR REACTION TO THAT?

	Sample A*	Sample B*
All who saw Advertisement E	72	72
Children look happy	26%	26%
Good advertisement	15	24
The Irish *do* like children	11	21
Others favorable	11	10
Doesn't appeal	15	6
Not a good advertisement	15	8
Looks dangerous/not safe	7	6
Negative	10	8
Others neutral	8	3
Don't know	1	3

* Sample A respondents had taken a holiday abroad within the past three years; Sample B respondents had not.
Source: Market Investigations Ltd., "Holidays in the Republic of Ireland Attitudes of British Holidaymakers," April 1966, p. 84.

Exhibit D-9

RELATIVE EFFECTIVENESS OF EACH OF THE SAMPLE ADS

Q. 52A: THE ADVERTISEMENT YOU HAVE JUST SEEN; WOULD YOU SAY IT TOLD YOU SOMETHING ABOUT IRELAND THAT MIGHT TEMPT YOU TO GO TO IRELAND ON HOLIDAY OR NOT?
Q. 54: WE HAVE SPENT A LITTLE TIME NOW TALKING ABOUT GOING TO IRELAND ON HOLIDAY AND YOU HAVE ALSO SEEN AN ADVERTISEMENT FOR IRELAND. WOULD YOU SAY ALL THIS HAS INCREASED THE CHANCES OF YOUR GOING TO IRELAND ON HOLIDAY?

	Total Informants		Q. 52A Tempted	Q. 54 Chances	
				Increased	Decreased
Sample A*					
Advertisement A (Ex.D-1)	80	%	30	30	1
B (" D-2)	75	%	40	24	3
C (" D-3)	79	%	33	23	1
D (" D-4)	72	%	32	22	1
E (" D-5)	72	%	36	26	6
F (" D-6)	73	%	48	22	1
G (" D-7)	75	%	55	24	4

Exhibit D-9 (cont.)

	Total Informants Sample B*		Q. 52A Tempted	Q. 54 Chances Increased	Q. 54 Chances Decreased
A (Ex.D-1)	69	%	49	31	3
B (" D-2)	75	%	40	32	3
C (" D-3)	57	%	40	28	7
D (" D-4)	74	%	45	31	3
E (" D-5)	72	%	50	30	3
F (" D-6)	75	%	63	35	4
G (" D-7)	79	%	51	29	4

* Sample A respondents had taken a holiday abroad within the past three years; Sample B respondents had not.
Source: Market Investigations Ltd., "Holidays in the Republic of Ireland Attitudes of British Holidaymakers," April, 1966, p. 72.

APPENDIX E

Market Investigations, Limited (M.I.L.)–Study of Advertisement Coupon Inquirers (1967)

STATED OBJECTIVES:

The study, carried out in Britain among a sample of people having completed coupons to apply for brochures from ITB, sought to determine:

(1)   The extent to which individuals completing such coupons are making a genuine inquiry which is likely to result or has resulted in a visit to Ireland;

(2)   Inquirers' opinions of the literature they receive as a result of such inquiries and the extent to which they consider what they received to have covered the information they had hoped or expected to receive; and

(3)   The extent to which advertisements in different media may exhibit different conversion rates (i.e., the proportion of inquiries resulting in a visit to Ireland).

RESPONDENTS:

Nearly 100,000 completed coupons from British consumer advertisements were available from which to select the sample. These were sorted according to the medium or media group from which they came; the number of coupons available from each medium or media group ranged from 22,000 to less than 3,000. The selection of actual interviewees was then made in such a way as to yield a minimum of 120-130 interviews for each medium or media group. This selection was made at random except that, in order to keep fieldwork costs to a reasonable level, any town from which fewer then ten coupons had been returned was omitted from the sample.

METHOD:

Personal interviews. At the tabulation stage appropriate weights were applied to the results from each media group in order to give each the same proportion of the total sample as it had of the total number of coupons returned. The weights applied were as follows:

Publication	Number of Interviewees	Weight
Reader's Digest (British edition)	176	9.70
Daily Telegraph Magazine (Weekend)	124	6.53
Observer Magazine (Sunday)	160	6.15
Sunday Times Colour Supplement	136	6.65
National Dailies	167	4.61
Scottish Press	148	1.67
Radio Times	174	1.65
Motoring Magazines	126	1.06
Fishing Magazines	130	1.00
English Sunday Newspapers	116	2.10

The findings were then adjusted to account for these weightings.

COMMENTS:

Interviewees were grouped into seven major categories regarding the extent to which they had been serious in requesting ITB literature. As seen in Exhibit E-1, approximately two-thirds of the sample could be regarded as serious inquirers although only about one-third of this group had actually visited Ireland.

Findings were given in a number of general areas also covered in other research studies commissioned by ITB. For instance, characteristics of visitors and non-visitors to Ireland were compared; visitors were asked how they had arranged their holiday, the importance of certain holiday events and activities, and their willingness to return to Ireland; nonvisitors were asked why they had not made the trip; and all respondents were asked for opinions on the quality of ITB literature. Findings which were more unique to this study were those related to the third stated objective above, namely, to investigate the differences among the ten media or media groups in which ITB placed its British print advertising.

Exhibit E-2 summarizes the extent to which inquirers from different publications either visited Ireland during 1966, or seriously considered doing so. Exhibit E-3 is representative of a number of additional tables which compared inquirers from different publications on dimensions such as length of holiday, composition of holiday party, and type of accommodation chosen on holiday (regardless of where they spent their holiday). Exhibit E-4 represents the synthesis of traditional cost per reply data, and the conversion rate data contained in Exhibit E-2, to arrive at a "cost per holiday taken" measure of media effectiveness.

Exhibit E-1

EXTENT TO WHICH INQUIRERS FOR ITB LITERATURE WERE SERIOUS

Informants interviewed were grouped into the following categories:

i) Recalled requesting literature and visited Ireland.	19%
ii) Recalled requesting literature and seriously considered visiting Ireland.	42
iii) Did not recall requesting literature and visited Ireland.	2
iv) Did not recall requesting literature and seriously considered visiting Ireland.	2
v) Recalled requesting literature and thought might visit Ireland.	6
vi) Recalled requesting literature without any serious intentions.	15
vii) Did not recall requesting literature and neither visited nor considered visiting Ireland.	14

Source: Market Investigations Limited, "A Study of Advertisement Coupon Enquiries," May 1967, p. iv.

Exhibit E-2

PROPORTION FROM EACH MEDIUM WHO VISITED OR WHO SERIOUSLY CONSIDERED VISITING IRELAND IN 1966

	Visited	*Seriously Considered*
Total	21%	43%
Scottish Press	29	40
Fishing Magazines	26	33
Radio Times	26	43
National Dailies	26	45
Observer Magazine (Sunday)	25	49
Sunday Times Colour Supplement	25	49
English Sunday Newspapers	24	37
Motoring Magazines	19	38
Daily Telegraph Magazine (Weekend)	16	50
Reader's Digest	16	35

Source: Market Investigations Limited, "A Study of Advertising Coupon Enquiries," May 1967, pp. 1, 20.

Exhibit E-3

TYPE AND COST OF HOLIDAY

	Total	Reader's Digest	Daily Telegraph Magazine	Observer Magazine	Sunday Times Supplement	Media Group National Dailies	Scottish Press	Radio Times	Motor Magazines	Fishing Magazines	English Sunday Newspapers
All holidays—actual	1694	164	137	194	156	197	180	199	154	146	146
weighted	6987	1591	895	1195	1036	908	301	328	163	146	307
Spent holiday											
In one place	58%	62%	64%	57%	50%	60%	57%	61%	54%	70%	56%
Part in one place											
and part another	10	6	11	12	12	7	14	10	10	5	9
Touring	32	32	26	30	38	32	29	29	36	25	36
Cost of holiday											
Up to £25	14	13	12	13	16	14	18	13	19	20	12
£ 26.- 50.	24	23	29	24	17	24	29	27	32	29	27
£ 51.- 75.	13	11	10	12	10	14	19	21	14	16	18
£ 76.- 100.	14	12	12	13	15	12	12	16	12	14	18
£101.- 150.	10	9	8	12	10	12	9	5	9	7	10
£150.- 200.	3	5	1	3	4	2	3	4	1	1	3
Over £200.	2	1	-	4	4	2	3	1	3	1	3
Refused	1	-	4	-	1	2	1	1	1	-	1
Don't know	19	24	23	18	21	19	5	14	9	12	8

Source: Market Investigations Limited, "A Study of Advertisement Coupon Enquiries," May 1967, Table 10.

Exhibit E-4

COST PER HOLIDAY TAKEN

	No. of Enquirers	Cost per Reply	Cost per Holiday Taken
Total	91,833	£0.16. 9	£3.18. 6
Scottish Press	2,558	2. 3. 2	7. 8. 6
Fishing Magazines	2,051	13. 6	2.12. 0
Radio Times	3,593	18. 8	3.12. 6
National Dailies	12,039	13. 6	2.12. 0
Observer Magazine	12,687	1. 2. 3	4. 9. 0
Sunday Times Colour Supplement	13,775	1. 4.11	5. 0. 0
English Sunday Newspapers	5,749	6. 0	1. 5. 0
Motoring Magazines	1,916	10. 7	2.16. 0
Daily Telegraph Magazine (Week-end)	14,713	1. 6. 1	8. 3. 0
Reader's Digest (Britain edition)	22,752	4.10	1.10. 0

Source: "Measuring the Promotional Effectiveness of National Tourist Organisations," R.E. Walpole, seventh page (Paper following that given by Robert Irvine to ESOMAR market research seminar on travel and tourism, Rigi-Kaltbad, November 23-25, 1967).

APPENDIX F

Gallup Readership Report on 1968 British Ad

Gallup Readership Reports are similar to the Starch Readership Reports which are widely used by U.S. advertisers. Briefly, respondents are asked to recall the extent to which they noticed or read each page of a publication including the page on which the client's ad is placed. Interviewing takes place in the homes of respondents shortly after the publication has been read.

The advertiser receives from Gallup a copy of the publication accompanied by an interpretive report. Each page of the publication contains "page traffic" figures for men and women readers, which specify the per cent of each group which recalled noticing the page. For every advertisement, an additional two figures are given for men and women: "NN," which indicates the percentage of readers who recalled noticing the name of the advertiser, and "R," or the percentage reading two or more sentences of the ad. Exhibit F-1 contains an ITB ad and its scores. The ad, a full-page color insertion, was run in January 1968, in *The Daily Telegraph Magazine* which is a color supplement accompanying the Friday edition of *The Daily Telegraph* newspaper.

Exhibit F-2 contains selected test excerpts from the Gallup report which interpreted the performance of the ad. Exhibit F-3 contains a table from the report that summarizes the performance of the ad in comparison with other ads in the magazine and previous ITB ads in color magazines.

ITB's Publicity Department and advertising agency had aimed the ad specifically at women and young married couples with children; many of the criticisms in the Gallup report were thus regarded as unjustified. Moreover, ITB executives considered the figures for noting, noting name, and reading to be quite high.

FULL-PAGE COLOR AD FROM JANUARY 12, 1968, ISSUE OF THE DAILY TELEGRAPH MAGAZINE

Exhibit F-2

SELECTED EXCERPTS FROM GALLUP READERSHIP REPORT

SUMMARY

This advertisement did well in attracting the notice of women readers. But in all other respects it did badly:

— Few of the women went on to read
— Few of the men stopped to look, let alone to read

The fault lies in the advertisement itself, not in the medium. *The Daily Telegraph Magazine* consistently pulls higher reading and noting for travel and holiday advertisements; the position in the issue was favourable.

The montage illustration concentrated on women and children. This initially attracted women to the advertisement, but tended to confuse these women as well as the men with consequent lack of follow-on readership.

The headline: "Let your kids loose in Ireland" probably added to the confusion. In conclusion:

a)   Two checks on advertisements using the montage approach have each shown disappointing results. Unless the montage can be simplified and the individual pictures given the logical storytelling relationship of a strip, a single illustration will probably do better.

b)   The headline must be made to work harder and appeal to a wider audience.

c)   The test needs simplifying and the "product plusses" need systematic presentation which make it easy for the reader to assimilate.

WHY HAS THE ADVERTISEMENT FAILED TO GET PEOPLE TO READ IT?

The publication and media position cannot be faulted. The *Daily Telegraph Magazine* is an extremely effective magazine for travel advertisements, probably the best of all the colour magazines for travel and holiday advertising. The advertisement has been given a very good position in the issue—a left-hand page opposite a very clean page of right-hand editorial offering the minimum of distraction.

The trouble lies in the advertisement itself.

The advertisement formula is very similar to that employed in the Irish Tourist advertisement in the *Sunday Times,* 10 September, 1967. In only one respect does it escape the criticisms made of that ad in the Gallup Assessment on that advertisement.

We faulted the *Sunday Times* advertisement for the fact that "the photos mainly display masculine activities. . . ." This contributed to the low Noting score with women. The current *Daily Telegraph Magazine* advertisement has done very much better in getting women into the advertisement, because as already observed it uses illustrations with women and children in them.

In spite of a promising beginning, the current advertisement has failed to get women to read the text. The fault is probably in:

a)   the confusion of the montage
b)   the headline.

The headline "Let your kids loose in Ireland" is too exclusive. A large number of women do not have children, let alone "kids." Moreover, many who do have them will not, perhaps, welcome the idea of letting them "loose." For the majority, this is not the prime consumer benefit they are looking for on their holidays.

It is worth recalling that the *Sunday Times* advertisement in September did relatively well with reading scores, above the average for travel and holiday advertisements with both women and men. This reading was concentrated in a list of factual information headed "Some other happenings." In holiday advertisements, as in virtually every other type of advertising, facts systematically displayed almost invariably get high reading. The current advertisement scatters the facts in a mass of prose. It is difficult for the reader to systematise them.

The basic fault, though, in the *Sunday Times* advertisement, and given in paragraph five of that Summary remains:

"a)   the montage effect"
"b)   putting the headline in three tiers, which does not make it easy for the reader. There is no penalty for a headline which covers the width of the paper in a single line"
"c)   the small illustration does not add to the advertisement—it again makes it difficult for the reader to know where to start."

The headline on this occasion has only two lines, but still suffers from the disjointedness which is the underlying weakness of unjustified and multiline headlines.

The Aer Lingus advertisement in the *Sunday Times,* 4 April, 1965, was the best Irish advertisement ever checked by the Gallup Field Readership Index. It scored 76 per cent Noting, both with men and with women: 49 per cent Noting Name with men, 42 per cent with women, and 49 per cent Reading text with women, 40 per cent with men.

This advertisement illustrated some of the features of travel advertisements which pay off in terms of Noting and Reading:

a)   A single picture which not only avoids the inevitable disruption of the montage effect but gave the advertisement a magnificent unity. The horse riders, the hedge boundary, and the seating of the crowded stands, all led down from the picture into the headline, into the copy, into the advertiser's name.
b)   The sort of picture into which people could project themselves and instantly realise "consumer benefit," i.e., the pleasure of being there.

c) A very simple one-line headline: "This is the Dublin horse show."

d) Very simple text, short sentences; one typeface.

e) Maximum reader identification obtained by reference to familiar places; e.g.: Birmingham, Blackpool.

f) Clear invitation—"you should come."

g) The advertiser's name "Aer Lingus" is where it should be, used like the signature at the end of a letter. (It would be even better if the logo were simpler, uncluttered by artifice.)

This is the basic formula from which the advertiser departs at his peril. Why should he? It is the formula that permits almost infinite variation and scope for imagination.

Source: Gallup Advertising Research, "Irish Tourist Board Advertisement," February 1968.

Exhibit F-3

COMPARATIVE DATA ON PERFORMANCE OF ITB AD

	Noting		Noting Name		Reading	
	Men	Women	Men	Women	Men	Women
This advertisement	55	71	11	18	13	19
Full page colour advertisements in the Daily Telegraph Magazine						
Average:						
All products	53	57	27	29	20	21
Travel and holidays	65	69	31	32	26	29
Highest scoring ads:						
All products	85	92	67	61	59	57
Travel and holidays	82	83	69	60	59	47
Previous Irish Tourist Advertisements in colour magazines						
Sunday Times (10.9.67)	53	60	20	9	32	33
Daily Telegraph (5.2.65)	56	67	35	36	30	29
Daily Telegraph (5.3.65)	47	61	21	23	24	27
Jersey						
Half page colour advertisements in same issue	55	62	NN	NN	16	16

All figures are percentages; 100 per cent equals all readers.
Note: The figures underlined are higher than the current Irish Tourist ad scores
Source: Gallup Advertising Research, "Irish Tourist Board Advertisement," February, 1968.

APPENDIX G

Market Facts, Inc. Study Among North American Travel Agents (1966)

STATED OBJECTIVE:

This was a study of the activities and attitudes of travel agents in leading North American cities with respect to Irish travel. Its basic purpose was to provide information that will be helpful in assessing problems and detecting opportunities for increasing travel to Ireland.

RESPONDENTS:

Of 234 randomly selected registered travel agents in six North American cities (New York, San Francisco, Los Angeles, Chicago, Toronto, and Boston) approximately 60% of the agents in the study had visited Ireland.

METHOD:

Personal interviews.

COMMENTS:

This study was essentially oriented toward improving ITB's promotional relationship and sales methods used with travel agents through investigating agents' attitudes regarding travel in Ireland, including arrangements and facilities for Irish travel. Questions were asked about the desirability of certain tours, the relative merits of air carriers serving Ireland, the profitability of booking Irish travel, and related issues. Exhibits G-1 and G-2 contain selected findings in these areas.

In addition, certain findings related quite specifically to measuring advertising effectiveness. For example, agents were asked to rate the advertising and promotions of ITB and Irish International Airlines compared with other European tourist offices and transatlantic carriers, resulting in the following pattern of replies:

Attitude toward Advertising and Promotions	*Total*
Excellent	39%
Good	39
Fair	14
Poor	4
Not reported	4
Number of respondents	234

Exhibit G-3 details the specific reasons why agents held the above attitudes. Exhibit G-4 gives agents' views of why their clients visit Ireland.

Exhibit G-1

AGENTS' PREFERENCE FOR ROUTING CLIENTS TO IRELAND

	Total
Prefer to route clients to Ireland:	
On the way to Europe	34%
On the way back from Europe	30
Both on the way to Europe and on the way back	1
No preference	30
Clients travel only to Ireland	3
Not reported	2
Number of respondents who booked travel to Ireland in the past year	204
Total sample	234

FROM THE QUESTION: "DO YOU PREFER TO ROUTE YOUR CLIENTS TO IRELAND ON THEIR WAY TO EUROPE OR ON THE RETURN JOURNEY?"

Source: Market Facts–New York, Inc., "A Study among Travel Agents on Irish Travel," May 1966, Table 27.

REASONS FOR AGENTS' PREFERENCES

	Routing Preference		
	On the way to Europe	*On the way back from Europe*	*No routing preference*
Logical starting point	24%	- %	- %
Good start	21	-	-
More convenient to schedule	19	7	2
Better to end tour on a high tempo	11	-	-
Short flight	10	-	-
Depends on season, warm weather	10	8	15
Begin tour in an English-speaking country	7	-	-
Depends on client's itinerary	6	7	46
Availability of transportation	4	3	13
Only a stopover	3	7	2
Duty-free shopping in Shannon	-	41	5
Restful place to stop	-	28	2

	Routing Preference		
	On the way to Europe	*On the way back from Europe*	*No routing preference*
Depends on means of transportation	-	3	3
It makes no difference	-	-	10
All other reasons	12	10	2
Not reported	5	3	13
Number of respondents preferring each routing	70	61	61

FROM THE QUESTION: "WHY IS THAT?"

Source: Market Facts–New York, Inc., "A Study among Travel Agents on Irish Travel," May 1966, Table 28.

Exhibit G-2

AGENTS' SUGGESTIONS FOR PROMOTIONAL HELP.

	Total
More materials should be available to agents	18%
More advertising (general)	14
More advertising in magazines, newspapers, etc.	8
More ads on TV, radio	7
More films, better films	6
More displays, posters	4
Make more package tours available	4
Invite agents to Ireland, European tours	3
Put emphasis on castles, historical sights	3
Emphasize scenic beauty, lakes, mountains	3
Renovate hotels, more modern facilities	3
Lower rates (general)	3
Build image of Ireland as a new and different place, unusual	3
All others	19
Satisfied with advertising as it is	12
Don't think there is anything they can do	5
Not reported	11
Number of respondents	234

FROM THE QUESTION: "EVERYTHING CONSIDERED, WHAT DO YOU THINK THE IRISH TOURIST OFFICES IN THIS COUNTRY MIGHT DO TO HELP YOU GET MORE BUSINESS FOR IRELAND?"

Source: Market Facts–New York, Inc., "A Study among Travel Agents on Irish Travel," May 1966, Table 33.

Exhibit G-3

TRAVEL AGENT COMMENTS ABOUT ITB AND IRISH INTERNATIONAL AIRLINES ADVERTISING AND PROMOTIONS

	Overall Opinion about Irish Advertising and Promotions			
	Excellent	*Good*	*Fair*	*Poor*
Printed material good	20%	15%	3%	- %
Ads (any type) eye-catching, appealing	17	3	-	-
Keep agents up to date with material	13	6	-	-
Just started, improved lately	7	13	9	-
Good personnel—goodwill ambassadors helpful	7	6	-	-
TV commercials good	6	8	3	-
Ads (any type) informative	6	6	-	-
Radio commercials good	4	3	3	-
Honest, unpretentious ads	4	-	-	-
Needs more promotion (general)	3	9	21	1
Do not stress proper points of interest	2	6	15	2
Need more displays, posters	2	2	-	-
Working on limited budget, do not spend enough, lacking in funds	-	7	6	1
Not enough materials sent to agents, not kept up to date	-	4	18	3
Brochures, posters, films unattractive, unappealing	-	1	3	1
Not as frequent as others	-	-	12	3
Ads confined to Irish-American publications, Irish people, Irish born, etc.	-	-	6	1
Good (general)	25	26	6	-
Poor (general)	-	2	-	1
All other comments	15	9	6	1
No comments reported	10	14	15	-
Number of respondents expressing each opinion	91	91	33	9

Source: Market Facts-New York, Inc., "A Study among Travel Agents on Irish Travel" May 1966. (Table 19.)

Exhibit G-4

AGENTS' REPORTED REASONS WHY CLIENTS VISIT IRELAND

	Total
To visit relatives	42%
Ethnic ties	37
Beautiful scenery	26
To see another country	22
Irish history, historical places, things	18
Warm people of Ireland	17
Duty-free port, shopping at Shannon	9
It's a restful place	9
Sporting activities	9
It's inexpensive	7
Heard a lot about the country	7
Sporting events	7
Irish customs, folklore	7
To see the Blarney Stone	5
Just want to see Ireland (general)	5
English-speaking country	3
To sketch or paint scenery	3
Curiosity	2
All other reasons	9
Number of respondents who booked travel to Ireland in the past year	204

FROM THE QUESTION: "WHAT WOULD YOU SAY ARE THE MAIN REASONS THAT SOME OF YOUR CLIENTELE CHOSE TO VISIT IRELAND?"

Source: Market Facts–New York, Inc.,"A Study among Travel Agents on Irish Travel," May 1966, Table 9.

QUESTIONS

    A.   Case only (without reference to the Appendix material)

        1.   What is ITB's task? What should it be?

        2.   Who are the relevant target audiences for ITB's efforts?

        3.   What is the competition?

        4.   What kinds of research on ITB's advertising-marketing efforts would you consider necessary? Desirable?

    B.   Appendix material

        1.   In light of Appendices A through G, assess ITB's present advertising research program. What specific research do you now *consider necessary? Desirable?*

2. *What are the significant findings of each Appendix?*

3. *How transferable are these findings to other countries and other target groups?*

4. *Develop an advertising evaluation system for ITB.*

Advertising-Agency
Relationships

PART V

Lake Michigan
Bank and Trust Company

The advertising manager of a moderately large Chicago bank must decide whether or not to recommend that the bank drop its full-service advertising agency in favor of a new "creative boutique."

In the fall of 1970, Fred Rothermel, Advertising and Promotion Manager of Lake Michigan Bank and Trust Company, reflected on the luncheon conversation he had had with his boss Allen Davis, Director of Marketing for the bank. Rothermel had set up the meeting with Davis specifically to discuss the possibility of moving Lake Michigan's advertising account to a new agency. As he thought about Davis's comments on the proposal, however, Rothermel began to have doubts about the wisdom of such a move.

BACKGROUND

Founded in 1923, Lake Michigan Bank and Trust Company had experienced moderate but steady growth as a full-service bank. With total deposits in mid-1970 of nearly $190 million, Lake Michigan was among the larger of the over 200 different banks in Chicago and the surrounding suburbs. Lake Michigan's office was located in the Loop section of downtown Chicago. This was the bank's only location because of a strictly enforced Illinois law prohibiting branch banking. One consequence of this law was heavy reliance on banking by mail.

Within the bank, marketing was a small staff operation. In addition to advertising and promotion, the department was responsible for public relations, business development, and marketing research, although relatively little of the latter was done. Mr. Davis, head of the department, reported to the senior vice-president for operations; however, most requests for marketing assistance came directly to Davis from the operating departments desiring it.

The advertising efforts of Lake Michigan had been handled for the past fifteen years by the Chicago office of a large, full-service New York agency. Prior to that time, the work had been done internally. By 1970 the advertising budget had reached $225,000 annually; nearly half of this amount went into newspaper advertising.

THE LUNCHEON MEETING

When Rothermel and Davis got together for lunch that day, Rothermel explained what was on his mind. In almost every issue of *Advertising Age* there was news of another small advertising agency being formed. Many of these were the so-called ad boutiques—small "shops" that specialized in creativity, usually without accompanying services such as market research, merchandising, etc., offered by the traditional agencies and sometimes with limited media-buying capability. Examples of the new shops (and their clients) included Kurtz, Kambanis, Symon (Hudson Pulp & Paper Co.); Scali, McCabe, Sloves (Volvo); Freberg, Ltd. (Heinz); Della Femina, Travisano & Partners (Sea & Ski); Lois Holland Callaway (Magnavox).

The growth of creative boutiques was being facilitated by the concomitant appearance on the advertising scene of independent media-buying firms and the increase in the number of firms providing research services for advertisers (and agencies). With the use of independent marketing-advertising research firms and media-buying services, along with such traditionally available outside services as film production, an agency could indeed choose to be small and to focus on being "creative consultants."

ROTHERMEL: I never really paid much attention to this swing toward small shops and the importance of creativity until a few days ago. Then I read something about American Motors in *Business Week,* and it really hit home. By using Wells, Rich, Greene (generally considered to be one of the original boutiques) American Motors magnifies the impact of its small ad budget through the distinctiveness of its ads. They've got "the most recognizable ads in Detroit."[1]

DAVIS: What are you getting at, Fred?

ROTHERMEL: It'll soon be time for us to start putting our 1971 advertising plans together. Before the agency gets started, I wanted to talk with you about the possibilities of a change for Lake Michigan.

DAVIS: You mean switch *our* account to one of these hot-shot New York boutiques?

ROTHERMEL: No, not New York. There are a couple of small creative shops here in Chicago—and none of them has a bank client as yet.

DAVIS: That doesn't surprise me! Anyway, what's wrong with our present agency? They've done all right by us for fifteen years. And it's a well-known firm.

ROTHERMEL: Let's say I'm not dissatisfied with their work, Al. But the banking business around here is as competitive as hell. We open earlier and close later to please the customer. There are gifts for initial depositors, and

[1] *Business Week,* October 3, 1970, p. 17.

periodic premiums for regular depositors to compensate for the fixed interest rates. Some banks offer such a wide variety of services that they've begun to look like financial supermarkets. I think, in the face of all of this, we could use some advertising with a little more pizzazz.

DAVIS: I'm not sure that Lake Michigan is ready for anything *too* creative. Besides, what makes you think we couldn't get something jazzier out of our present agency if we asked for it?

ROTHERMEL: Too many old men stifling the creativity at that place. There's another reason for thinking about a change. The smaller shops tend to be low overhead operations—no top-heavy management structure, and no expensive additional services like merchandising and public relations. By working on a fee system, they sometimes save money for their clients.

DAVIS: That sounds like a stronger selling point for top management than the creativity bit. You know . . . I recall that one of those "expensive services" we've used in the past was help in preparing our annual advertising and marketing plans.

ROTHERMEL: I think we could get along without it.

DAVIS: Perhaps. Look, Fred, why don't you give this matter some further thought—and I will too. If you still think it's a good idea, let's write it up for presentation to top management.

QUESTIONS

1.   *Should Rothermel recommend a change of advertising agencies? Why? Why not?*

2.   *Under what conditions would your answer be different?*

Cramer
Food Corporation

The vice-president of marketing for a large diversified food manufacturer must decide whether and, if so, how to implement a formal system of advertising agency evaluation proposed by his assistant.

Martha Sherman, assistant to the vice-president of marketing at Cramer Food Corporation (CFC), was reviewing the final draft of her report on "Advertising Agency Evaluation—A Systematic Approach." The report was to be turned in to her boss before the end of the week. Miss Sherman, a student in the MBA program of a well-known eastern business school, had been specifically hired by CFC for the summer to work on this project, so she wanted to be certain that the report represented her best efforts.

COMPANY GROWTH

The Cramer Cracker Company was founded by E.G. Cramer in 1921 to produce and distribute a line of crackers and cookies within the Middle Atlantic States. Company growth came, first, by expanding distribution, and then by increasing share of market in the new territory. Cramer crackers and cookies were available throughout the eastern half of the United States by 1931, and nationwide by 1943.

By 1950, Mr. Cramer's son Walter had become active in the firm. The younger Cramer saw little opportunity for continued growth in the cracker and cookie business. Consequently, after a few years of learning the business, he began to search for ways to expand through acquisition of companies with related product lines. Thus, in 1954, Cramer purchased Ponzetti Company, a maker of pasta products (spaghetti, macaroni, noodles, etc.). Retail distribution of the Ponzetti product line was limited to the Midwest at the time of the purchase, but it was expanded as soon as production capacity was increased.

In 1957, the company changed its name to Cramer Food Corporation when it purchased a producer of dry dog food sold exclusively under the private labels of two regional supermarket chains. The following year, CFC also began to market the product nationally under the brand name Pet-agree. Two years later CFC introduced Pet-agree dog snacks and Pet-agree dry cat food.

The final period of expansion for CFC began in 1963, when the company introduced the first of its line of snack foods. The Smackers line grew to include six different items in a variety of flavors (potato sticks, corn puffs, wheat crisps, etc.). Smackers were distributed through grocery stores and through lunch shops. Consolidated sales for CFC in the fiscal year just ended were a little over $165 million, with earnings of $12 million.

MARKETING AT CFC

Each of the four major product groups operated as a semiautonomous division with its own marketing personnel. The marketing director for each division was assisted by advertising, product development, market research, and retail distribution managers. In addition four different advertising agencies, each independently selected by the individual divisions, performed work for the established CFC brands. The vice-president of marketing at the corporate level coordinated the marketing efforts of the various divisions, including new product development. One new product idea would be ready for test marketing within a few months. A fifth advertising agency was handling this assignment.

Sales were distributed among the four divisions as follows: pet food, 35%; crackers and cookies, 24%; snacks, 22%; and pasta, 19%. Although none of the CFC brands was the leader in its product category, each brand was among the top ten in national share of market. CFC's advertising budget averaged a modest 3.6% of sales, but there were some variations by product line. Sales of the Pet-agree products were supported by the largest advertising budget within the corporation ($2.4 million) in absolute terms and in terms of the A/S ratio. Smackers products had allocated $1.4 million for advertising during the previous year. The Cramer division, which marketed the original product line of CFC, had spent $1.1 million for advertising; and $1.0 million had been spent by Ponzetti.

It was because of the increasing expenditures for advertising—and the growing number of agencies involved—that the Vice-President of Marketing had hired Miss Sherman for the summer. Her assignment was to develop a procedure for evaluating the agencies presently used by CFC. Hopefully, a modification of this procedure might be used to select new agencies as the need for them arose. Although Cramer divisions had changed advertising agencies from time to time, all the present agencies had been on their assignments for at least five years. CFC's agencies were aware of Miss Sherman's work; in fact, she had met them all at various times during the summer. A synopsis of her report is contained in Appendix A.

APPENDIX A

Advertising Agency Evaluation—A Systematic Approach[1]

I. Background

Cramer Food Corporation spent approximately $5.9 million last year for product-related advertising. This is an amount equal to nearly half of its profit after taxes, and is certainly an expenditure over which management ought to maintain some control. Yet control is more difficult in a decentralized operation, and CFC is decentralized. There is no advertising staff at corporation headquarters. Rather there are four different advertising managers in four different cities and five separate advertising agencies working on CFC accounts.

Right now there is no orderly way of comparing the results of these agencies' efforts. What is needed is a control system that will help CFC to provide its agencies with the kind of feedback that will encourage the development of effective advertising.

II. Objectives of a Formal Evaluation System

Although a certain amount of informal agency evaluation goes on in the course of the day-to-day contacts between CFC and its agencies, there are definite benefits to be gained from formalizing the process. In the first place, a formal system provides an opportunity to involve top management more deeply in the advertising function. Additionally, a formal procedure should help to accomplish the following objectives:

1. To systematically and objectively appraise the performance of the agency on *predetermined* factors. Areas to consider should include creative, media, research, costs, and account management.

2. To identify areas of agency strength so that CFC can make fuller use of them; and potential problem areas so that they can be corrected before a crisis occurs. (For example, twice in recent years the agency handling the Ponzetti line has made single-recommendation creative presentations later than promised. These ads have met with approval in the past, but perhaps at some future time this will not be the case. The late timing and the one-program aspects might make it necessary to develop another advertising theme under crisis conditions. Such a situation might necessitate carrying an old campaign into the new season while the alternative programs were being developed and approved.)

---

[1] This material is based in part on "Considerations in Adopting a Formlized Procedure for the Evaluation of Advertising Agency Performance," published by the ANA Advertising Management Committee (April, 1970).

3. To regularly provide an opportunity to discuss with the agency all aspects of the CFC/agency relationship. This discussion should include feedback from the agency on ways in which CFC can improve its organization and operation and can make the agency's job easier. (One agency, which prefers to remain anonymous at present, suggested that it was looking forward to the day when the advertising manager did not come running back for new ideas every time the marketing director questioned something he had already approved.)

4. To compare agency performances so that product reassignments and new product assignments can be more easily determined.

III. Proposed Evaluation Procedure[2]

A. ADVERTISING MANAGER

Since the advertising managers have the most contacts with the agencies, the greatest burden of evaluation should fall on them. Therefore the ad manager should complete annually for the agency with which he deals an evaluation form on the account executive, the creative group, the media group, and personnel from other agency services used by CFC.

This preliminary appraisal should be based on the objectives set for each product and the agency's ability to meet those objectives. Hence the appraisal is basically *performance*-oriented rather than personality-oriented. However, the ad manager is also responsible for noting instances of people problems which may hinder the attainment of performance goals. (Although there apparently has been no actual personal conflict involved, one example of a personnel problem can be found with the Smackers situation. No account executive has been kept on that assignment for more than eighteeen months. Consequently the ad manager spends almost as much time getting to know the new men as he does getting problems solved.)

While noting areas of agency strength, the ad manager's evaluation also should point out weaknesses and recommend improvement. Following the completion of these preliminary evaluations, the manager should meet with the account executive to review the results and perhaps to revise them.

Suggested factors include:

1. Account Executive—assistance in setting advertising and marketing objectives; maintenance of cost control; use of all agency resources on behalf of CFC; ability to meet deadlines.

2. Creative—development of thoughtful alternative strategies; use of market research; TV, radio, and print execution of themes.

3. Media—development of alternative plans within budget constraints; use of market and media research; execution of plan for each medium.

4. Other services—as appropriate.

[2] Samples of proposed detailed evaluation forms are not included in the case.

B. MARKETING DIRECTORS

The marketing directors serve as a second source of evaluative material. Each director, independent of the ad manager, should rate the overall performance of the agency on his brand. This evaluation should note, where the opportunity exists, any differences among performances on various products within the line (e.g., dog food vs. cat food). In addition, the marketing director should appraise the work of the account supervisor at the agency. Where problems or potential problems are discovered, suggested changes should be included in this report too. At the same time that he meets with the account supervisor to discuss these two forms, he should review with the account supervisor the ratings done by the advertising manager. Following this session, the marketing director may want to revise his evaluations before passing them up the line.

The evaluation forms used by the marketing director should give him the opportunity to appraise the following:

1. Account Supervisor—responsiveness to problems; supervision of account executive; ability to involve agency resources and management on behalf of CFC. (The problem in the cracker and cookie division represents the sort of thing that should come out here. When the ad manager complained about "stale" creative efforts, he was told by the account executive that that was the best his (the account man's) creative group could come up with. At the same time, the agency's top management was making presentations to potential clients touting the agency's award-winning airline campaign.)

2. Overall Performance—general effectiveness of account executive, creative group, media group, other services; completeness of facilities to meet CFC's needs; cost consciousness and fairness in billing.

C. VICE-PRESIDENT OF MARKETING

The vice-president of marketing stands in the unique position of being able to look in a general way at the overall performance of each agency handling a CFC product line and of being able to compare the individual ratings of all agencies. In addition he, or someone designated by him, should complete a thorough appraisal of the work being done by any agency having a new product assignment. This latter appraisal would follow the procedures outlined above in (A).

At the time that the vice-president reviews his evaluation of an agency (subject to revision) with its top management, he also should discuss the rating of the account supervisor done by the appropriate marketing director. Finally he should compare the ratings of all CFC's agencies, and, in consultation with the marketing directors, make any changes in assignment that may be deemed necessary. (Note: Ordinarily no changes would be made on the basis of one round of poor evaluation unless it seemed unlikely that corrective action could or would be taken.)

Forms used by the vice-president of marketing should include space for appraising the following:

1. Overall Performance—ability of each agency group (creative, media, etc.) to accomplish objectives and meet deadlines; quality of account management; quality and amount of top management involvement; depth of resources to service CFC's needs; cost consciousness.

2. New Product Advertising—see (A) above.

IV. Action Recommended

At this point it is suggested that everyone potentially involved in the agency evaluation procedure (including the advertising agencies themselves) should have an opportunity to read and comment on this report. Comments should focus on, first, approval of or objections to the basic ideas covered in the report and, second, specific modifications which might be incorporated into the individual evaluative forms.

QUESTIONS

1. Does this appear to be a reasonable approach to agency evaluation for CFC? For the agencies involved?

2. Is the proposed system an operable one?

3. What should the role of corporate-level vs. product-group personnel be in the evaluation?

Promotion
and
Social Issues

PART VI

What Americans
Think About Advertising

This article summarizes the results of a recent study dealing with consumers' views of advertising as an institution and of advertisements themselves.

INTRODUCTION

This "Highlights" material presents a brief summary of the major findings of a comprehensive four-year research inquiry into what the American public thinks about advertising and advertisements. The full-length edition of *Advertising In America: The Consumer View* (published by the Harvard Business School Division of Research) by Professors Raymond A. Bauer and Stephen A. Greyser contains 474 pages and over 100 tables and exhibits. The original research was based on in-home interviews with a cross-section of 1,846 American adults. These interviews, conducted by the Opinion Research Corporation in 1964, were supplemented by an additional 524 interviews carried out in late 1967 to update certain key findings of the study. Financial support for the research was provided by the American Association of Advertising Agencies with the understanding that the researchers would have a free hand in the study itself and its publication. An academic review committee, composed of Harvard and MIT faculty members, oversaw the research phase.

RESEARCH ON ATTITUDES TOWARD ADVERTISING

Advertising is peculiar in that it is many things to many people—individual ads and ad campaigns, an economic force, part of the social fabric of our culture, and so on. This peculiarity is compounded by the paradoxes surrounding advertising, paradoxes that helped generate the study. On the one hand are the continuing streams of criticism of advertising on economic, social, aesthetic, or ethical grounds. But on the other hand, accompanying this criticism, is the ever-increasing use of advertising and corporations' greater reliance on it as a tool of business. Businessmen, social critics, government officials, and others who allege to speak on behalf of the public often do so with little true knowledge of what the public's opinions are. So it has been with advertising: the public's views have often been hypothesized, seldom explored. This study proceeded from the belief that the public itself was the best source of information on "what the public thinks." At the same time, the researchers recognized that the issues being explored were not matters to be settled by "a majority vote." Indeed, opinions other than those of the public at large are relevant and *any*one's opinions are subject to independent evaluation as "right" or "wrong" in terms of a given set of value judgments.

The purpose of the research was to provide an objective examination, comprehensive and systematic, of public attitudes toward advertising and advertisements and the reasons for these attitudes. The study reflected concern for finding out the facts about public opinion on advertising as well as appreciation of the relevance of public opinion on such a complex many-faceted topic.

HIGHLIGHTS

The following highlights summarize how Americans feel about *advertising as an institution,* i.e., as an economic and social force in American society, and about *advertisements themselves*—the individual ads consumers see and hear in their daily lives.

Among the specific questions treated are:

— How does advertising "fit into" the average consumer's life as compared with other aspects of our society?

— What are Americans' basic attitudes toward advertising? Why do they like or dislike it?

— What do Americans think about advertising's role in the economy? Its social impact?

— Do different kinds of Americans—in terms of education, income, age, etc.—have different attitudes toward advertising?

— How do Americans react to advertisements? What do consumers like and dislike most about the ads they see and hear? Why do many ads that attract consumer attention get no further reaction?

— What are the product groups whose ads please and displease consumers most?

— How are reactions affected by the product itself, the creative presentation in its ads, and the amounts spent on advertising?

— How do nonusers of a product react to that product's ads? Are people who like a brand more favorable to its ads?

— Do Americans feel differently about ads in print versus broadcast media?

— How do people's life situations shape their reactions to advertisements?

— Are people's overall attitudes toward advertising related to their reactions to advertisements?

— Have attitudes toward advertising changed much in recent years?

Following the highlights are summaries of some of the many implications of the study. Among the areas covered are:

— The screening process and the "defenseless consumer."
— The public's expectations from the advertiser—and vice versa.
— The relationship between *effectiveness* and *pleasantness* in advertising.
— The "communications gap" between advertisers and their critics.

How Advertising "Fits Into" Americans' Lives When asked, almost all Americans feel qualified to comment on advertising. However, the subject, when compared with other aspects of American life, does not rank as a burning issue for Americans of the mid-1960s. In the words of the authors: "Advertising seems to be a topic people enjoy complaining about but not seriously. . . . To the social critic concerned over the extent to which 'everybody is upset about advertising,' these data would indicate that this concern is largely misplaced."

Of ten aspects of American life explored, advertising ranks in last place as an issue on which people are likely to say they have strong opinions. People are most likely to have strong opinions on religion, bringing up children, family life, and public education.

Nevertheless, about one in seven Americans (15%) think that advertising needs immediate attention and change. Of these, about 10% would favor a ban on advertising for products seen as harmful or dangerous; about 35% aim their criticism not at advertising alone but at advertising as it is linked to the broadcast media; and about 7% of this group (or about 1% of all respondents) spontaneously say that advertising is in need of more government regulation.

Basic Attitudes Toward Advertising When asked about their overall attitudes toward advertising, 41% of Americans indicate they are favorable toward it, 34% have mixed opinions, 14% are unfavorable, 8% are indifferent, and 3% are unclassifiable. These overall attitudes are very clearly reflected in consumers' later reactions (see below) to advertisements themselves.

a) The main reason Americans say they *like* advertising in general is its informational role . . . it tells people about products and services and how to use and get them. Relatively few people say they like advertising because it is enjoyable. However, when later responding to individual advertisements, the public sees the entertainment value of ads as an element of equal importance with information value.

b) The main reason Americans say they *dislike* advertising in general is that it is intrusive. Negative reactions to advertising are primarily on the grounds that it is unpleasant, although advertising's failure in its informational role is the second biggest reason. When reacting to the ads themselves, consumers again cite unpleasantness as the main reason for their unfavorable reactions.

Economic and Social Distinctions Irrespective of overall attitudes, Americans draw clear distinctions about what they like and dislike about advertising. Nearly everyone approves of advertising's role in the economy, but many are critical of its social impact and the ways in which it impinges on the individual. For example:

— 78% of Americans agree that advertising is essential.

— 71% of Americans agree that advertising helps raise the standard of living.

— 74% of Americans agree that advertising results in better products for the public.

However:

— 65% of Americans agree that advertising persuades people to buy things they shouldn't.

— 43% of Americans think that most advertising insults the intelligence of the average consumer.

— 53% of Americans disagree that most advertisements present a true picture of the product advertised.

In the words of the authors: "Even those favorable to advertising call into question its social impact, and those unfavorable to advertising generally approve of its economic impact." Another way the authors characterize this is that "people appear to approve of advertising in principle, and criticize it in practice."

Demographic Similarities Attitudes toward advertising do not vary much among different demographic groups. However, college-educated people take a more mixed position toward advertising than do other groups, largely reflecting their ability to articulate both sides of any issue, including advertising. The group unfavorable toward advertising tends to be more highly educated than the group that is favorable toward it. On economic aspects, the college group has the most favorable attitudes among all educational groups, e.g., 89% agree that advertising is essential, 77% agree that advertising raises our standard of living, and 82% agree that advertising results in better products. But on social questions the college graduates shift to a more critical stance, e.g., of all educational groups, they are *least* likely to say that advertising seldom persuades people to buy things they shouldn't (22%); and only 51% (vs. 58% average) say advertising's standards are higher than they were ten years ago.

Reactions to Advertisements Themselves Of some 9,325 ads to which Americans react particularly favorably or unfavorably 36% are considered as enjoyable, 36% as informative, 23% as annoying, and 5% as offensive. Americans react to more ads favorably than unfavorably; but when they do react negatively to ads, their negative reactions are stronger than their positive reactions.

With regard to individual ads:[1]

---

[1] Percentages total more than 100% because of multiple responses.

a) When Americans consider ads *informative,* the chief reasons they do so are:

1)   They learn something personally from the ad (87%).
2)   The ads create personal involvement of the consumer with the ad situation or product (34%).

b)   The chief reasons Americans consider certain ads *enjoyable* are:

1)   The advertising treatment itself, that is, specific elements such as music, humor, performers, and so on (73%).
2)   People "derived vicarious enjoyment from the situation depicted" (21%).
3)   People enjoyed the product itself (20%).

c)   The chief reasons Americans consider ads *annoying* are:

1)   The ad's stimulus qualities, including (a) intrusiveness—seen or heard too often, too long or too loud; (b) insults the intelligence—silly, unreal or patronizing; (c) boring, depressing (73%).
2)   Informational failure, including disbelief of claims, misleading, false, dishonest (36%).
3)   Moral concern, including product shouldn't be advertised, ad is bad for children (10%).

d)   The chief reasons Americans consider ads *offensive* are:

1)   Moral concern (50%).
2)   Stimulus qualities of the ad (40%).
3)   Informational failure (31%).

Although estimates of the average consumer's *opportunities* for advertising exposure vary (the folklore figure is 1,500; a 1970 BBDO study puts the number at 305) the authors say that it seems clear that Americans effect a vast reduction in potential opportunities to see, read, or listen to ads. A still further filter occurs between those ads to which the consumer pays conscious attention, and the relatively few to which he reacts particularly favorably or unfavorably.

Why this lack of further reaction? The chief reasons why consumers react neither favorably nor unfavorably to certain ads are:[2]

1)   Lack of distinctiveness (39%).
2)   Lack of interest in the product or brand (20%).
3)   "Tired" ad, e.g., seen or heard before (11%).

___

[2]Percentages total more than 100% because of multiple responses.

The authors report: "Some of what the public sees as chaff represents poor creative concepts or performances in ads; some is due to the inevitable lack of fit between any one ad and some portion of the public."

Different Products, Different Reactions   Consumer reactions to ads vary greatly over product categories. For instance:

a) The product groups whose ads were categorized as most "annoying" or "offensive" by consumers were liquor (69% of these ads rated annoying or offensive); soaps and detergents (59%); dental supplies and mouthwashes (50%); depilatories and deodorants (51%); and cigarettes (56%).

b) In the case of liquor ads, the people who consider these ads offensive are largely nonusers who believe the product should not be advertised at all.

c) Those product groups whose ads rate high as "informative" include major appliances (79%); tires (75%); insurance (69%); and household furnishings (65%).

d) Those product groups whose ads rate high as "enjoyable" include soft drinks (70%); toilet soaps (69%); wine (68%); and cigars and tobacco (63%).

e) Some ads for virtually every product group (and for different brands within product groups) are seen positively and negatively.

Presentation vs. Product Related Criticism   An analysis of annoying and offensive ads shows that the ratio of criticism directed against the ad's presentation (i.e., its creative elements) as opposed to those directed against the product itself is 8:1 for annoying ads, 4:1 for offensive ads. In other words, the reason an ad is categorized as offensive is twice as likely to be product-related (versus the presentation) than the reason for an ad considered annoying.

Advertising Expenditures and Reactions to Ads   In general, those products with heavy advertising expenditures have disproportionately higher percentages of negatively categorized ads than do other products. But this is not an across-the-board finding: some frequently advertised products (such as in the food field) have very favorably evaluated ads, and some products not heavily advertised (e.g., movies, underwear, and foundation garments) generate very unfavorably evaluated ads.

Product Use and Brand Preference   Both product use and brand preference *markedly increase* the likelihood of an ad being favorably evaluated. People seem to transfer their feelings about brands to ads for those brands. For example, only 7% of the ads for "my favorite brand" are considered annoying or offensive compared with 76% of ads for "brands I wouldn't buy." Nonuse of a product is also associated with less favorable reaction. For instance, 87% of the liquor advertisements categorized by nonusers of liquor were reacted to negatively; this figure drops to 18% for ads categorized by users, and to 14% when users react to the ads for the particular liquor brands they like. Figures are not as divergent for "less controversial" products but the trend is still there.

Media Differences   Consumers find fewer annoying ads in newspapers and magazines than in the broadcast media. Broadcast ads, especially those on TV, seem to command a great deal more attention than do print ads; but a far higher percentage of broadcast ads are seen as annoying, particularly because of their intrusive elements. Specifically, of the ads to which Americans react favorably or unfavorably 27% of television ads and 24% of radio ads are considered annoying, compared with 9% of magazine ads and 12% of newspaper ads. Newspaper ads have the highest proportion of informative categorizations (59%) and 31% of television ads are considered informative.

Demographics   None of the standard demographic categories bears much relationship either to people's attitudes toward advertising or their reactions to specific ads. There are, however, *some exceptions,* especially people's life situation.

a) *Age*—Older people report more favorably evaluated ads than do younger people. In addition, there is an indication that older people tend to see advertising as needing less attention and change than do younger Americans. Older people tend to see ads as more informative than do younger people. For instance, 78% of those 50-64 years of age see ads as informative or enjoyable, and 64% of those 18-24 see them as informative or enjoyable. Likewise 31% of the younger age group (18-24) see ads as annoying, and 19% of the older age group (50-64) see them as annoying. Specifically, older age groups show a higher preference for print media.

b) *Sex*—Women, though they tend to patronize media (radio and television) with more annoying ads, are more favorable toward ads than men. However, men are 4% more favorable toward *advertising* than are women. Single women and married women with no children find ads more informative than married women with children.

Life Situation   A person's life situation is perhaps the most important factor in shaping his relationship to particular products and (presumably) to ads for these products. For example, women categorize and react more favorably to food ads than do men. Moreover, women are about twice as likely to consider such ads informative as men and are considerably less likely to call them annoying or offensive. The same elements in one's life situation, however, are not equally important from product to product, nor do they operate in the same direction for all products. In responding to food ads, for instance, sex and marital status are relevant. For household cleaning products, alcoholic beverage ads, and automobile ads, the sex role is most important but in different ways. For cigarette ads, marital and family status is most relevant.

Attitudes toward Advertising and Reactions to Ads   One's overall attitudes toward advertising are definitely reflected in one's reactions to individual advertisements. The tendency to report favorable reactions to ads is strongest for the group with favorable overall attitudes; the mixed and indifferent groups are next; and people unfavorable to advertising report the lowest proportion of enjoyable and informative ads, although still over half. Specifically, those Americans favorable to advertising categorize negatively 23% of the specific ads they react to particularly favorably or unfavorably. But those Americans unfavorable to advertising categorize negatively 41% of the ads they react to particularly favorably or unfavorably. People who question advertising's truthfulness, its propensity to insult intelligence, or its standards, all react more negatively than the average person to actual advertisements.

Attitude Trends In general, the authors conclude that overall attitudes toward advertising as well as attitudes toward the several institutional issues associated with advertising appear to have been rather stable over the past 30 years. This conclusion was reinforced by a 1967 supplementary study that replicated the attitudes portion of the original research. Although no comprehensive research on the public's attitudes toward advertising in American life had been done until this one, the authors analyzed a variety of data from individual past studies to develop their historical analysis.

With regard to criticisms of advertising, the authors identify three basic streams:

> "The first stream attacks advertising's basic economic function and its business role. This particular stream was at a high tide during the depression years, and it linked the idea of advertising as an economic waste and a cost that the American public could not afford, to more general ideological condemnation of business, branded goods, and so on. . . .
>
> "A second stream relates to the techniques of advertising as an extension of selling, incorporating displeasure over any partisan advocacy of a product and concern over possible manipulation of consumers by propagandists and persuaders. . . .
>
> "The third stream is criticism of advertising content and the amount of advertising. This criticism has been among the most persistent of all, focusing on advertising's ethical aspects (the truth issue) and its aesthetic aspects (the taste issue)."

IMPLICATIONS

(Chapters X and XI of the full-length volume discuss these and other areas in considerable detail.)

a) The Screening Process and the "Defenseless Consumer" Both defenders and attackers of advertising have been blind to the filtering mechanisms which people *must* use to survive—people of every age and every society. The more stimuli in one's environment, the more stringent one must be in selecting those one will attend.

The critic of advertising, of the mass media—and of the modern world—often bewails the increase of such stimulation, without perspective. For example, the individual may simplify his task by ruling out whole categories of messages, including using TV commercial time as an opportunity to engage in a variety of other activities.

In any event, the present study reinforces what students of communication and advertising already know: "The consumer is no helpless passive target of communications. He is an active defender of his time, energy, attention and interest . . . just as the social critic should not worry that the vast mass of the public will be helplessly inundated by the advertisers' messages simply because they are being sent out, so should the advertiser not hope that his messages will receive the avid attention of all the people, or that he and his advertising agency are inept if this does not take place." Indeed, the authors anticipate that as the total number of advertising messages increases, "the filters in the public's perceptual screen will grow finer and messages in general will have a more difficult task of getting through."

b) Advertiser's Goals and Responsibilities   Can an advertiser be expected to advise consumers of the limitations of his product? It seems to the authors "clearly untenable to expect him to do so voluntarily in the absence of some clear sanction. Such a sanction may be from the marketplace, such as the complaints of irate customers who expected the product to do something for which it was not designed. Or, it could be from beyond—such as the threat of legal action or the existence of a government regulation that certain information must be included routinely. If the concept of 'full information' is incorporated in one's notion of truth in advertising, then we must face up to the fact that the major purpose of advertising is and must be to sell products or services. It is completely unrealistic to expect that the individual advertisers will spontaneously include information that will lessen the probability of his selling his product."

c) Effectiveness and Pleasantness   While issues of advertising effectiveness were *not* objectives of the study, there remains the interesting question of whether the pleasantness or unpleasantness of advertisements is related to the effectiveness of ads in selling products.

Many admen consider the first job of an ad as that of attracting attention. This may call for the reader, listener, or viewer to be jarred from the medium's context. A further job of many ads is to instill the consumer with brand name reminders; this too can call for intrusiveness. Clearly then, effectiveness and pleasantness cannot always walk hand in hand. For example, over 50% of categorized soap and detergent ads were considered annoying or offensive. Yet presumably these ads perform the selling job since the manufacturers continue to use them.

Nevertheless, there is a correlation between a person's liking an advertisement and both his using the product and his preferring the brand being advertised. People tend to like ads for products and brands they also like. Perhaps they like the ads because they like the products, or perhaps they prefer to buy the products of ads that please them. The data cannot tell the direction of the causation.

Further exploration of the relationship will give the adman better guidance on how to be more effective without being offensive and will give the public a more realistic idea of what it can expect or demand from the adman.

d) "Communications Gap" between Marketers and Their Critics   According to the authors, there is a lack of communication between marketers and their critics, particularly in government. This misunderstanding grows from different perceptions of the consumer world, and is rooted in different definitions of several key words. Specifically:

1)   "Competition." To the critic, competition generally means price competition; to today's marketer it usually means product differentiation.

2)   "Product." To the critic, a product typically has a primary function only (e.g., an auto as transportation); to a marketer, a product's secondary functions may be the major means of product differentiation (e.g., an auto's looks, power, and so on).

3)   "Consumer Needs." To the critic, needs correspond to a product's primary function (e.g., transportation, nutrition); to the marketer, needs are any consumer lever he can use to differentiate his product.

4)   "Rationality." To the critic, a rational consumer decision is one that efficiently matches needs and products; to the marketer, consumers are the best judge of their own needs, so almost any decision is rational.

5)   "Information." To the critic, "good" information helps bring about the rational matching of product function and consumer need; to the marketer, information is anything (true) that presents a product favorably in the context of the consumer's own buying criteria.

QUESTIONS

1.   What are the aims (and non-aims) of the study, its methodology, and the major findings?

2.   What are the implications of the study findings for individual practitioners in companies and agencies? For those in advertising who are concerned with its broader impacts?

3.   What questions and issues concerning advertising bother you most as an individual?

The FTC
and
Aspirin Advertising

"Headaches for All"

Students must consider the implications of the FTC's 1967 proposals regarding aspirin advertising. A marketing/advertising analysis of current aspirin advertising and advertisements is included.

On July 6, 1967, the Federal Trade Commission proposed new and stricter rules governing the advertising of nonprescription analgesic remedies for pain relief, of which aspirin is the most common. In essence, the proposed rules (described in detail below) would ban advertising containing competitive claims for "greater effectiveness" or the advertising of unnamed "secret ingredients." The new rules also would severely limit the list of ailments for which analgesic manufacturers could claim effectiveness.

In issuing the rule proposal the Commission stated: "It appears that each of the various analgesic products now offered to the consuming public is effective to essentially the same degree as all other products supplying an equivalent amount of analgesic ingredient or combination of ingredients."[1] The Commission did not single out any individual companies, but did state that it was aiming at ". . . unfair and deceptive advertising practices which the Commission has reason to believe are being used." However, at the same time, the Commission had deceptive advertising cases pending against the manufacturers of four of the most widely known analgesics. These companies and their leading analgesic products were: Bristol-Myers Company (Bufferin and Excedrin); American Home Products Company (Anacin); Plough, Inc. (St. Joseph Aspirin); and Sterling Drug Company (Bayer Aspirin).

---

[1] *The New York Times,* July 6, 1967, p. 33.

THE ANALGESIC DRUG MARKET[2]

The ancient Greeks were known to recommend salicylates in the form of willow leaves for pain relief. Modern analgesics can be traced to the discovery of the pain-killing power of acetylsalicylic acid in Germany in 1898. The drug was named "aspirin" and patented by the Frederick Bayer Company. Aspirin was first sold in the United States in 1915. Anacin, introduced shortly thereafter, added caffeine and phenacetin, a secondary pain reliever, to the basic formula. (Phenacetin was removed in 1962 when evidence indicated that it could cause kidney damage.) In 1921, following World War I seizure of Bayer property in the U.S., aspirin was ruled a generic term, and brand proliferation began. Today, aspirin is marketed under several nationally advertised brand names and literally hundreds of regional and private labels.

Various recent estimates state that nonprescription analgesics represent an annual retail market of $400 to $450 million. A large variety of products compete for these sales, using different product formulations and consumer appeals. These include aspirin, buffered aspirin (e.g., Bufferin), and multiple-compound remedies (e.g., Anacin); "extra-strength" formulas such as Excedrin; and headache plus stomach-upset remedies like Alka-Seltzer. There are specific formulas for children (e.g., Liquiprin); and for females with menstrual distress (e.g., Midol). There are sustained-release formulas (e.g., Measurin); and formulas purporting to help induce sleep (e.g., Sominex). Despite the product proliferation and multitude of brands, over half of total sales are made by five products. The top three, with annual sales ranging from $50 to $60 million each are Bayer Aspirin, Anacin, and Bufferin. Close behind the "big three" is Alka-Seltzer, although the principal use for this product is the relief of upset stomach rather than headache alone. Fifth in sales, at an estimated $30 million, is Excedrin, introduced in 1961.

A closely related market is that for cold remedies, with annual sales estimated at $75 million. Marketers of the general-purpose analgesics have long promoted their use in relieving cold discomforts. However, the cold pills, particularly the newer varities, perform different functions than do the analgesics although they usually include analgesic compounds in their formulas. The market is dominated by a relative newcomer, Contac, made by the Menley & James Laboratories Division of Smith, Kline & French Laboratories, Inc. Introduced during 1961, Contac now claims about 40% of the cold-remedy market, with approximately $30 million in sales. Schering Corporation's Coricidin has about 22% of the market, and Whitehall Laboratories' Dristan has about 13%.

ADVERTISING EXPENDITURES

In 1966, according to estimates made by *Printers' Ink,* approximately $128 million was spent on national brand advertising for headache and cold remedies.

---

[2]Portions of this section are based on material in *Printers' Ink,* "Battle of the Brands," July 14, 1967.

The analgesics accounted for over $90 million of this sum, and the five products of the four manufacturers under current FTC attack accounted for $62 million alone. Most of this $62 million went into television, with $43 million on network TV and the remainder in local television (spot). Print media and radio accounted for the remaining expenditures. Exhibit 1 shows estimated consumer media expenditures for headache and cold remedies for 1965 and 1966.

RECENT GOVERNMENT-INDUSTRY INTERACTIONS

As indicated above, heavy consumer advertising has been a vital part of the marketing mix for major analgesic manufacturers. Much of the advertising has been of the hard-sell variety, and competitive claims have frequently been employed. These claims have been the subject of FTC and FDA (Food and Drug Administration) attention for at least the past seven years. The 1967 FTC rules mark the opening of another round in a continuing battle between the government agencies and the "big four" analgesic advertisers.

In 1961, after determining that each of these advertisers was claiming his product to be the fastest and/or most effective, the FTC issued deceptive advertising complaints against them stating that they obviously could not all be fastest or best simultaneously. The cases were dropped in 1965, when the Commission staff acknowledged that the hearings would produce a barrage of conflicting and inconclusive clinical evidence. In attempting to gather conclusive evidence on its own, the Commission sponsored a clinical study of the effectiveness of the five products. The study, performed in Baltimore city hospitals, compared Bayer Aspirin, St. Joseph Aspirin, Bufferin, Anacin, and Excedrin. The results, published in the *Journal of the American Medical Association,* December 19, 1962, showed no significant differences in pain-relieving ability among the five preparations. The findings did show that all of them were better than a sugar-pill placebo in relieving pain, and also that Excedrin and Anacin seemed to result in a somewhat higher incidence of stomach upset that did the other three compounds. Summary sections of the study are shown in Exhibit 2.

Immediately following publication of these results, advertisements for Bayer Aspirin and St. Joseph's Aspirin began to reflect the relatively favorable findings for their brands. For example, Bayer advertisements contained such phrases as: ". . . government supported medical team" whose findings were ". . . reported in the highly authoritative *Journal of the American Medical Association* . . . had found the Bayer product equal to the higher-priced pain reliever." In addition, Bayer advertising claimed that Bayer would not upset the stomach, was as gentle as a sugar pill, and was as gentle to the stomach as any analgesic containing more than one ingredient. The FTC issued a complaint against Sterling Drug Company, and asked for a temporary injunction restraining the company from making the above claims in its Bayer Aspirin advertising. The federal court denied the injunction and ruled that the claims did not misrepresent the Baltimore findings.

The new FTC actions against the "big three" analgesic manufacturers' advertising are based, in part, on Food and Drug Administration guidelines promulgated under

1962 legislation. These laws, revisions of the food and drug acts previously in force, were passed in the aftermath of the Kefauver drug industry hearings and the thalidomide incident. They provide, among other things, that the FDA has the absolute authority over what can be claimed on the label of any drug marketed since 1938. In April 1967, the FDA promulgated guidelines limiting label claims for over-the-counter analgesics to the following:

1)   Relief of simple headaches.

2)   Temporary relief of minor aches and pains associated with rheumatism, arthritis, bursitis, sprains, or neuralgia.

3)   Temporary relief of minor aches or pains associated with overexertion or fatigue, sinusitis, and the common cold or flu.

4)   Temporary relief of toothache.

5)   Temporary relief of minor cramps associated with the menstrual period.

The guidelines specifically forbade any labeling statement indicating such products are useful in treating such symptoms as fever, jittery nerves, irritability, lumbago, migraine, sciatica, sleeplessness, and tension headache.

In issuing its new advertising guidelines, the FTC took the position that any advertising claim which goes beyond what the FDA allows on the label can be assumed false. This avoids the problem faced by the FTC in its earlier round of complaints, i.e., proving its charges clinically. At the same time the burden of proof of the validity of competitive statements is now placed on the advertiser. In its July 1967 guidelines, the Commission stated that the following practices constituted unfair and deceptive advertising:

a)   Making effectiveness or safety claims that exceed or contravene those appearing on the label.

b)   Making comparative claims of superior speed, strength, or duration of relief unless a significant difference exists because the product has a greater amount of analgesic. (Note: The FDA presently limits the amount of analgesic ingredients allowed in a single dosage of an over-the-counter product.)

c)   Making claims for beneficial effects of specific or "secret" ingredients, unless the ingredient is identified by its common name and its effects explained. (Note: The FTC recently issued similar orders against marketers of various preparations for hemorrhoid relief, specifically aimed at the "mystery ingredient" claims.)

Examples of recent headache product advertisements appear in Exhibit 3. These ads ran prior to the FTC proposal.

Exhibit 1

ADVERTISING EXPENDITURES FOR HEADACHE AND COLD REMEDIES, 1965 AND 1966

(all figures in thousands of dollars)

	Total 1966	Spot TV 1965	Spot TV 1966	Network TV 1965	Network TV 1966
American Home Products					
Anacin	18,820	1,712	1,760	14,050	14,070
Dristan	7,331	928	1,046	5,827	5,989
B.C. Remedy Co.					
B.C.	3,122	1,431	1,482	-	-
Bristol-Myers					
Bufferin	12,724	4,481	2,994	8,975	9,270
Citrisun	1,806	184	422	-	1,069
Congespirin	1,489	-	-	738	1,393
Clinicin	399	129	399	-	-
Excedrin	9,962	2,118	2,306	6,262	6,453
4-Way	368	593	1	522	367
Resolve	5,541	135	2,169	13	3,035
Chesebrough-Pond's					
Measurin	2,998	224	1,568	-	1,430
Lever Brothers					
Stendin	603	83	557	-	-
Menley & James					
Contac	10,506	3,115	2,606	5,001	4,981
Miles Laboratories					
Alka-Seltzer	19,162	6,131	9,016	9,374	10,037
Pharmaco					
Aspergum	875	142	3	300	872
Plough					
St. Joseph (regular)	3,308	751	637	-	-
St. Joseph (children's)		436	792	782	848
Stanback Co.					
Stanback	674	384	399	-	-
Sterling Drug					
Bayer (regular)	17,444	2,649	2,020	8,284	10,606
Bayer (children's)		192	68	1,627	1,430
Cope	4,568	1,018	560	1,004	3,962
Vanquish	5,104	238	857	-	3,587
Warner-Lambert					
Anahist	452	-	-	-	-
Bromo-Seltzer	2,803	2,051	2,005	771	720

Source: Television Bureau of Advertising/N. C. Rorabaugh; Leading National Advertisers/Broadcast Advertisers Reports; Bureau of Advertising, ANPA; Publishers Information Bureau; Radio Advertising Bureau. Reproduced with permission from *Prir ters' Ink*, July 14, 1967.

Exhibit 1 (cont.)

	Magazines (general and farm)		Newspapers (including supplements)		Spot Radio		Network Radio	
	1965	1966	1965	1966	1965	1966	1965	1966
American Home Products								
Anacin	1,363	1,143	-	-	973	1,682	-	165
Dristan	-	49	108	125	81	-	-	122
B.C. Remedy Co.								
B.C.	77	65	-	-	2,513	1,575	-	-
Bristol-Myers								
Bufferin	937	422	-	-	339	38	-	-
Citrisun	-	267	53	48	-	-	-	-
Congespirin	39	96	-	-	-	-	-	-
Clinicin	10	-	-	-	9	-	-	-
Excedrin	1,302	880	1	-	-	216	-	107
4-Way	-	-	-	-	-	-	-	-
Resolve	-	267	-	-	-	47	-	23
Chesebrough-Pond's								
Measurin	-	-	-	-	-	-	-	-
Lever Brothers								
Stendin	15	46	-	-	-	-	-	-
Menley & James								
Contac	1,221	1,911	624	144	386	735	377	129
Miles Laboratories								
Alka-Seltzer	47	109	15	-	-	-	-	-
Pharmaco								
Aspergum	-	-	-	-	-	-	-	-
Plough								
St. Joseph (regular)	-	- } 385	78	130	567	516	-	-
St. Joseph (children's)	471							
Stanback Co.								
Stanback	62	54	-	-	127	221	-	-
Sterling Drug								
Bayer (regular)	1,087	1,139 } 570	905	681	22	35	1,154	895
Bayer (children's)	536							
Cope	-	46	12	-	1	-	-	-
Vanquish	39	386	44	274	-	-	-	-
Warner-Lambert								
Anahist	550	452	54	-	-	-	-	-
Bromo-Seltzer	14	52	54	-	23	26	-	-

Exhibit 2

EXCERPT FROM THE *JOURNAL OF THE AMERICAN MEDICAL ASSOCIATION*

COMMENT

On the basis of this study, it seems that, within the limits of generalization permitted by the population studied, there are no important differences among the compounds studied in rapidity of onset, degree, or duration of analgesia.

It also appears that, as far as gastrointestinal side-effect liability is concerned, Excedrin and Anacin may cause a higher incidence of gastric upset than Bufferin, Bayer Aspirin, and St. Joseph Aspirin. The latter three drugs were not significantly different from one another in this respect.

These observations are somewhat contrary to previously published laboratory findings, which have stressed the importance of blood concentrations of salicylates. It is our belief that the only criterion by which the rapidity of onset or degree of analgesia can be judged is the clinical response to the administration of the drug.

The difference in the retail purchase price of the five drugs is not reflected in the effectiveness and comfort of the treatment, and the over-all performance of the less expensive agents in the group compares favorably with that of the more expensive ones.

SUMMARY

Anacin, Bayer Aspirin, Bufferin, Excedrin, and St. Joseph Aspirin were compared with a placebo and with each other, from the point of view of analgesic efficacy and incidence of gastrointestinal distress. The analgesic effects were studied in postpartum patients, while the gastrointestinal side-effect study was performed in elderly infirmary patients. There was no striking difference among the agents so far as rapidity of onset, peak effect, or duration of analgesia was concerned. There was no difference between the incidence of gastrointestinal effects seen after the placebo and that after Bayer Aspirin, Bufferin, or St. Joseph Aspirin. The incidence of such side effects was higher after Anacin or Excedrin.

Source: "A Comparative Study of Five Proprietary Analgesic Compounds," by Thomas J. De Kornfeld, MD, Louis Lasagna, MD, and Todd M. Frazier, ScM, *JAMA,* Dec. 29, 1962, p. 78.

Exhibit 3

GREY ADVERTISING, INC. TELEVISION

CLIENT: BRISTOL-MYERS COMPANY   COMM'L # 90–60   60 (SECS.)
PRODUCT: BUFFERIN   TITLE: "HOUSE HUNTING"

1. 1ST MAN: (VOICE FADES IN) a little tour of the house. 2ND MAN: Wow, you can set . . .

2. our whole apartment in this living room. WOMAN: I guess so.

3. 2ND MAN: Is something wrong, honey? So far, it looks perfect.

4. WOMAN: Oh, it's just this darn headache. 2ND MAN: You had that headache . . .

5. when we left the apartment. Did you take anything? WOMAN: Aspirin, but it still hurts.

6. 1ST MAN: (VOICE FADES IN) the bedroom. 2ND MAN: That headache's still bothering you, isn't it, honey?

7. Maybe we should come back tomorrow. WOMAN: No, don't worry.

8. 1ST MAN: Mrs. Barkley, I've got some aspirin in my desk. WOMAN: Thanks, . . .

9. but I can't yet. I'm not supposed to take any more for another hour or so.

10. ANNCR: Next time, take Bufferin. Because compared with simple aspirin, right at the start, . . .

11. Bufferin gets more of the pure pain reliever going against a headache. More pure pain . . .

12. reliever, faster than plain aspirin tablets, without the stomach upset plain aspirin can cause.

13; Next time, take Bufferin. It's faster, more effective than plain aspirin tablets.

14. With Bufferin, . . .

15. you've got more going for you against pain.

Exhibit 3 (cont.)

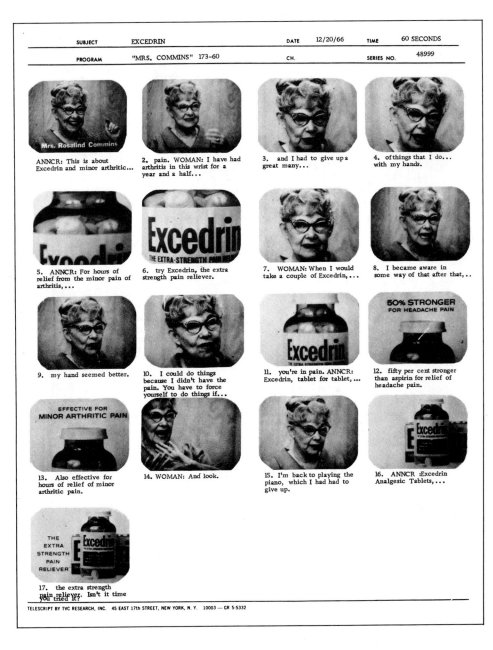

TELESCRIPT BY TVC RESEARCH, INC.   45 EAST 17th STREET, NEW YORK, N. Y.   10003 — GR 5-5332

| SUBJECT | EXCEDRIN | DATE | 12/20/66 | TIME | 60 SECONDS |
| PROGRAM | "MRS. COMMINS" 173-60 | CH. | | SERIES NO. | 48999 |

ANNCR: This is about Excedrin and minor arthritic...

2. pain. WOMAN: I have had arthritis in this wrist for a year and a half...

3. and I had to give up a great many...

4. of things that I do... with my hands.

5. ANNCR: For hours of relief from the minor pain of arthritis,...

6. try Excedrin, the extra strength pain reliever.

7. WOMAN: When I would take a couple of Excedrin, ...

8. I became aware in some way of that after that, ..

9. my hand seemed better.

10. I could do things because I didn't have the pain. You have to force yourself to do things if...

11. you're in pain. ANNCR: Excedrin, tablet for tablet, ...

12. fifty per cent stronger than aspirin for relief of headache pain.

13. Also effective for hours of relief of minor arthritic pain.

14. WOMAN: And look.

15. I'm back to playing the piano, which I had had to give up.

16. ANNCR :Excedrin Analgesic Tablets, ...

17. the extra strength pain reliever. Isn't it time you tried it?

617

Exhibit 3 (cont.)

QUESTIONS

1. *In your own view, was the FTC proposal justified? Why? Why not?*
2. *What are the implications of the proposal for analgesic manufacturers? Their advertising agencies? The public?*

The Nassau County
Election, 1967[1]

This case looks at the anatomy of a political campaign (for county commissioner) with focus on the candidate's marketing and advertising.

In late November 1967, Republican leaders of Nassau County, New York, were reviewing the election campaign of Sol Wachtler, the recently defeated Republican candidate for the office of County Executive of that populous Long Island county. Of particular interest in the course of the campaign had been the carefully planned marketing program mounted on behalf of Wachtler. The program, employing market research and considerable advertising, had been developed by the New York public relations firm of Harshe, Rotman & Druck.

Wachtler, who was little known to voters at the start of the campaign, was generally considered to have made an exceptionally strong showing in the election against the more well-known Democratic incumbent Eugene Nickerson. Nickerson's final margin was less than 3,000 votes—about one-half of 1% of the 542,000 ballots cast.

CAMPAIGN BACKGROUND

Nassau County is the nation's eleventh most populous county, with a population of 1,500,000, of whom 800,000 are qualified voters. The county is a suburban area on the outskirts of New York City. Exhibit 1 gives additional information concerning Nassau's electorate and its voting patterns.

In an election on November 7, 1967, Nassau County voters were to decide who would occupy the office of County Executive. The term of office is three years, with an annual salary of $30,000. The County Executive is charged with the responsibility of administering the county budget of $215 million a year, and determining who will receive $10 million in personal service contracts awarded

[1] This case is based on material originally developed by the Columbia Broadcasting System for its "Campaign American Style" telecast, *CBS Reports,* May 28, 1968. That program was written and produced by Jay McMullen. This version was adapted from that material, and is reproduced with the permission of CBS.

without competitive bidding. He supervises 14,000 county employees, and controls some 5,700 patronage jobs.

THE CANDIDATES

Eugene Nickerson, the Democratic incumbent, was a 49-year-old Roslyn, Long Island, lawyer who had served as County Executive since 1961. In 1966, Mr. Nickerson had made an unsuccessful bid for the Democratic gubernatorial nomination. In the 1967 election he was seeking a third term as County Executive. Mr. Nickerson was the candidate of both the Democratic and Liberal parties.

Sol Wachtler, his Republican opponent, was relatively unknown to the majority of the Nassau electorate. At the time of his nomination at the State Republican Convention in March 1967, he was Supervisor (equivalent to mayor) of North Hempstead, the smallest of three towns in Nassau County. According to public opinion polls, he had a local reputation as an able administrator and attorney, but was unknown to two-thirds of the total county's voters.

Nevertheless, the Republican organization that selected Wachtler thought that several factors were in his favor. Wachtler was young, personable, financially secure, and he and his family possessed considerable local social standing. In addition, Wachtler was a willing candidate and able to devote eight months to active campaigning. Wachtler's Jewish religion was also considered an asset. About one-third of Nassau's voting population is Jewish, and has traditionally voted Democratic; with Wachtler as their candidate, the Republican Party hoped to be able to appeal to the Jewish vote. (No Jew had previously sought the County Executive post.) Finally Wachtler's ability to raise money for the campaign was an important factor in his selection, since exposure, principally via advertising, would be a vital part of the campaign in such a large area.

By the time of the election, over $700,000 had been raised to aid Wachtler's campaign. He and his family had invested some $72,000 of their own money in the campaign. In addition, through a finance committee headed by a local garment manufacturer, the candidate had raised another $134,000 through a series of parties given for potential contributors. The Republican party organization also raised money (about $500,000) for the Wachtler campaign with a series of fund-raising dinners, luncheons, and breakfasts.

DEVELOPING AN IMAGE

Sol Wachtler and other members of the Republican organization believed that their first job was in creating a political image for the candidate. To assist in this job, they retained—for a fee of $75,000—Harshe, Rotman & Druck, a large New York public relations firm experienced in the marketing field.

Harshe, Rotman & Druck assigned Don Kellerman to coordinate the marketing of the candidate. Kellerman's first task was to determine the "proper" image for the candidate to project. Kellerman's personal view was that Wachtler communicated an impression of an extremely articulate and personable young man. But Kellerman was concerned that Wachtler seemed perhaps too perfect in manner. Kellerman thought that Sol Wachtler would be misunderstood if this element of his personal appearance were not eliminated from his political image; hence informality was incorporated into the projection of the Wachtler image. In addition Kellerman sought to project Wachtler's dynamism and youth, a concept Kellerman saw as allied to vigorous movement. Thus the campaign theme, a "Walk with Wachtler." The candidate was to be photographed walking in every community in Nassau County, talking to people about the issues. Accompanying Wachtler would be his wife, projecting the image of "his active partner in life."

THE VISIBILITY CAMPAIGN

To communicate this image for Wachtler, the public relations agency developed materials to promote "the visibility factor." Posters, billboards, newspaper advertisements, bumper stickers, buttons, and other materials were employed. Exhibit 2 summarizes the principal marketing-advertising costs of the campaign, including the expenditures made as part of the visibility campaign. These materials were devised to reflect the image which had been chosen for the candidate. For example, they showed Wachtler, along with his wife and young son, all informally attired, walking vigorously in various Nassau County areas. Later in the campaign, the same "Walk with Wachtler" theme would be used in the development of television and radio advertisements for the candidate.

An important aspect of obtaining visibility for the candidate was the role of the press. Wachtler cultivated the attention of the news media from the start of the race. The candidates were closely followed by reporters of the major Nassau County daily newspaper, *Newsday. (Newsday's* circulation was 428,500.) Wachtler and Kellerman were concerned that *Newsday* be provided each day with a story about their candidate's campaign activities. They thought that if they did not provide a story, *Newsday* would choose to run material about their opponent, Eugene Nickerson. It was their goal to obtain at least as much "favorably slanted" press copy as did the opposition. Nickerson, however, ultimately received the editorial endorsement of *Newsday, The New York Times,* and the *Long Island Press.*

Many of Nassau County's small weekly newspapers were found to have a "business interest" in the campaign for County Executive. These weeklies were believed to solicit political advertising on the unspoken understanding that if the candidate bought advertising in the paper, the paper would reciprocate by running the candidate's picture and a story. Therefore weekly newspapers were employed as part of Wachtler's visibility campaign.

In addition, radio and television interviews were arranged for the candidate and his wife. Harshe, Rotman & Druck also assisted in this task by arranging for coverage, sometimes supplying the interviewers with questions to ask, and assisting the candidate and his wife in preparing for the interviews.

MARKET RESEARCH

At a meeting of party leaders in early September, the president of Harshe, Rotman & Druck said that Wachtler's "visibility factor" had improved considerably since the start of the campaign. At this point, however, it was considered important to decide what positions Wachtler and the party should take on various campaign issues. For this purpose, the public relations agency had prepared a series of position papers for the candidate.

These papers were based on $10,000 worth of market research, public opinion polls, and analysis designed "to find out what the candidate should say, where he should concentrate his campaign, and what prominent figures should be asked to campaign for him." Wachtler and his advisers decided that the candidate should very closely follow the recommendations suggested by analysis of this research. It was their opinion that the candidate should not allow himself to become so committed to a position contrary to the thinking of the people as revealed in the polls that he would be unable to withdraw or modify his thinking.

The polls were important in that they indicated to the candidate and his advisers which issues were of salience to the Nassau County public. In Wachtler's personal opinion, for example, a very critical issue involved the planned revision of the Charter of the county government. The polls indicated, however, that the public was not interested in this issue; consequently Charter revision was not a major subject of the Wachtler campaign.

The polls were useful in setting general themes for the campaign. They indicated that voters believed that Nickerson had failed to resolve some county problems. Wachtler therefore stressed that his administration could—and in his words—"serve as a crucible for the testing of new ideas and new concepts." The polls indicated that Wachtler should appear "as a man who would move ahead," who would indicate that "the time for dreaming is over." Wachtler employed these themes. To reach independent voters, the polls indicated that Wachtler "should describe himself as an independent thinker and cite examples where he may have differed from his own party." Wachtler stated that he did not support a proposed new State Constitution although New York State's Republican Governor Rockefeller advocated a "yes" vote on this issue.

Market research was also useful in pointing to those areas of Nassau County where Wachtler should concentrate his effort. Research showed, for example, that the Republican party was "strongest among the large middle class", which led to a recommendation of "walking tours in middle class developments." The polls further indicated that "both Republican strength and undecided voters could be found among men," which led to a recommendation that the candidate "tour bowling alleys when men's leagues were in session." Wachtler followed these recommendations.

With regard to who should campaign on Wachtler's behalf, the poll analysis said that the Nassau County voter saw New York State's Republican United States Senator Jacob Javits as "slightly more liberal than himself," but the recommendation was made to seek help from Javits. In addition, poll analysis noted that "Governor Rockefeller had held his own in Nassau County," leading to the recommendation that Rockefeller's endorsement should be sought. Both Javits and Rockefeller campaigned for Sol Wachtler.

The market research analysis also guided the candidate's thinking with regard to specific issues. The poll analysis indicated that the Nassau County voters were concerned about taxes—Wachtler promised to cut taxes. The polls indicated that a State Bond Issue to improve transportation would carry in Nassau County —Wachtler came out strongly for approval of the Bond Issue. Most voters were found to be opposed to interdistrict school bussing—Wachtler opposed bussing.

Beyond local issues, the polls showed a decline in the popularity of President Johnson in Nassau County. The following question had been asked:

"In your opinion, is there any relationship between the Democratic Administration in Washington, D.C., and the Democratic Administration of the County Executive in Nassau County?"

Of those polled, 40% said yes, 31% said no, and 29% did not know. These results caused the Wachtler forces to devise a strategy that would associate the Democratic Administration in Washington with the Nassau County Democratic Administration in Mineola, Long Island. Consequently Wachtler criticized Nickerson, calling him "the big spender in Mineola" and comparing him to "the big spender in Washington."

THE TELEVISION CAMPAIGN

As the campaign continued, executives of the public relations firm proposed a saturation advertising campaign of TV commercials for Sol Wachtler. The agency suggested a total of about 200 60-second spot announcements averaging about 20 to 22 a week in September, with a somewhat heavier concentration in October. Although these television spots were considered prospectively very helpful to Wachtler in increasing his visibility and in enabling him to express his views on the campaign issues, Republican county leaders were concerned that a television campaign would be uneconomical. Nassau County lies outside of New York City, and does not have its own television station. Thus the Wachtler commercials (the time cost for which was as much as $4,500 a minute) would be reaching millions of people in New York City who would be unable to vote for the candidate. The public relations firm acknowledged that the Republican organization would be paying for waste viewership, but nevertheless believed that television was "probably the single most effective buy for Wachtler because over 98% of homes in Nassau County have television sets" and that television would make the difference in a Wachtler win. The recommendation for television was approved. Eventually 242 TV commercials were run at a total cost of $187,000.

The television commercials were prepared by Harshe, Rotman & Druck after consultation with the candidate and his Republican advisers. The group was concerned with finding a key line for these commercials to serve as a Wachtler trademark. They sought to express Wachtler's personality in a way that would be natural, but at the same time to stress his dynamism. After some discussion they agreed on the theme: "Wachtler will make things happen again in Nassau." Some of the commercials developed around this theme utilized a hard-sell approach, showing Wachtler speaking about substantive issues such as high taxes. Other commercials ostensibly consisted of spontaneous question-answer sessions.

THE FINAL DAYS OF THE CAMPAIGN

The campaign became more intensive and more acrimonious as Election Day drew near. The Wachtler approach had been to hit hard at Nickerson's county administration. Wachtler had informed voters that the last person indicted in Nassau County for land speculation was a Democratic Committeeman who had been appointed as a Deputy County Attorney by Nickerson. Wachtler had also accused the Democratic administration of waste in government. A Wachtler TV commercial, for example, pointed out that there were six photographers on the county payroll, implied that their only job was to follow Nickerson around, and linked this expense to the high tax level in Nassau.

Eugene Nickerson complained about the Wachtler campaign in testimony before a New York State Legislative Committee investigating high campaign costs. The Wachtler campaign, he asserted, contained all the elements of a big-money campaign. In testimony he described the Wachtler campaign and his reactions to it as: "Fraudulent commercials, an inexperienced prepackaged candidate mouthing the cliches of grey flannel ghostwriters."

As the campaign progressed, the charges and countercharges of scandal and fraud increased. Two weeks before the election, a Wachtler aid resigned after admitting he paid a spy to steal confidential documents from the Democrats.

One week before the election, the public opinion polls of the Republicans and Democrats showed Wachtler gaining in the race for County Executive. Nickerson stepped up the pace of his counterattack. First he requested and received endorsement and campaign aid from New York State's Democratic United States Senator Robert F. Kennedy. In the final week of the campaign, Nickerson followed Wachtler by promising a tax cut. Nickerson also purchased a very substantial amount of television time. Nickerson, like Wachtler, employed a public relations firm to plan, produce, and place his TV commercials. In the single week before the election, Nickerson spent $107,000 for a saturation campaign of TV advertisements.

THE ELECTION

On November 7, 1967, approximately 542,000 Nassau County voters cast their ballots for the office of County Executive. Eugene Nickerson was returned to office for a third term. His margin over Wachtler was 2,863 votes, about one-half of 1% of the total vote.

Exhibit 1

VOTING RECORDS AND REGISTRATION

Nassau County Voting Totals

Presidential elections

1960	Kennedy (Dem.-Liberal)	263,303
	Nixon (Rep.)	324,255
	Total	587,558
1964	Johnson (Dem.-Liberal)	382,590
	Goldwater (Rep.)	248,886
	Total	631,476

Elections for County Executive

1961	Dill (Rep.)	208,465
	Nickerson (Dem.)	216,096
	Liberal Candidate, name unknown	7,056
	Total	431,617
1964	Burns (Rep.)	264,925
	Nickerson (Dem.-Liberal)	358,475
	Total	623,400
1967	Wachtler (Rep.)	238,233
	Nickerson (Dem.-Liberal)	241,096
	Pleus (Conservative)	57,065
	Holwell (Peace)	5,295
	Total	541,689

Nassau Voter Registration—November 1967

	Republican	330,384
	Democratic	220,134
	Conservative	4,133
	Liberal	4,078
	Independent	54,123
	Total	612,852

Exhibit 2

CAMPAIGN EXPENDITURES

CANDIDATE EUGENE NICKERSON (DEMOCRAT)

The total cost of the Nickerson campaign exceeded $285,000. Of this amount, $107,000 was spent for a TV saturation campaign during the one week immediately preceding Election Day.

CANDIDATE SOL WACHTLER (REPUBLICAN)

The total cost of the Wachtler campaign exceeded $700,000. Traceable marketing and advertising expenditures are shown below:

Harshe, Rotman and Druck, fee	$ 75,000
Market research and opinion polling	10,000
Visibility campaign:	
Posters (20,000)	2,800
Billboard space	10,000
Newspaper space	25,000
Mailing and postage	30,000
Buttons	18,000
Brochures	15,000
Matchboxes and trinkets	10,000
Car stickers and signs	8,000
TV campaign:	
242 60-second commercials, averaging	
20-22 per week in September, heavier	
in October. Individual spots cost	
up to $4,500 per minute	187,000
Radio Spots	40,000
Total traceable marketing and	
advertising expenditures	$430,800

QUESTIONS

1. *Overall, was this a well-developed campaign?*
2. *What target groups is Wachtler trying to reach? Whom should he be trying to reach?*
3. *What basic message was/should have been employed?*
4. *Was the media plan appropriate?*

Advertising Acceptability- Practices and Problems

Magazine publishers and editors discuss their policies and problem areas regarding the standards of acceptance they use for advertisements.

Relatively few magazines consider policies and practices in the area of advertising acceptability to be among their major management problems. Most magazines now have rather clearly developed policies or procedures concerning whether specific ads are acceptable for publication. Nevertheless, for an increasing number of magazines the advertising acceptability area has presented headaches and occupied considerable discussion time largely because so many of the decisions are subjective ones where written guidelines don't provide clear-cut answers. Indeed, the guidelines—whether written or not—often seem to serve only to *identify* the problems, not to *resolve* them.

Interest in this topic led to the questioning of magazine publishers and editors concerning their own policies, practices, and problems with regard to advertising acceptability. Certain key issues stand out, namely:

1. What policies and criteria does the magazine use to determine the acceptability of particular ads or types of ads?

2. Who is involved in the acceptability process—e.g., editorial as well as business people?

3. What kinds of problems are encountered in applying these policies and criteria? Are any particular types of ads—e.g., product groups, copy themes, illustrations—especially difficult to evaluate?

4. Has the decision to accept or reject specific ads resulted in any serious disagreements or complaints *internally* from *advertisers* or from *readers?*

5. Do multimagazine companies have similar or different advertising acceptance policies? Does consistency or lack of it cause any problems?

6. If this area is *not* a problem, in what ways has it been kept from becoming one?

When asked for their views on these many aspects of advertising acceptability, magazine executives offered a variety of comments. The following are representative opinions expressed on the subject.

ACCEPTABILITY CODES AND CONCEPTS

We do have published standards in regard to advertising acceptance, viz.: Advertising standards are established to fulfill these policies:

to maintain the readers' confidence in, and respect for the publication as a whole;

to maintain readers' confidence in advertising as a believable, dependable, and essential means of communicating product availability and buying information to the market;

to maintain readers' confidence in the integrity and dependability of all advertisers in the publication;

to ensure impartial treatment of advertisers; that is, to do for all what would be done for any one advertiser.

To fulfill these policies, the publisher reserves the right to review any piece of advertising copy submitted for insertion, and to require that it conform to those reasonable standards of clean business, fair competition, and good taste which recognize and conserve the paramount interests of the reader, the advertiser, and the publisher. Although each doubtful case will be decided on its own merits, certain types of advertising which our publications will not accept, include:

Negative, unfair, or unprovable statements or claims about competitive products;

Fraudulent or misleading advertising;

Advertisements that make false, unwarranted, or exaggerated claims;

Advertisements that are vulgar, suggestive, repulsive, or offensive;

Attacks of a personal character; advertisements that make uncalled for reflections on other advertisers or their goods;

Medical advertising of products containing habit-forming or dangerous drugs; offers of free medical treatment; advertisements that claim to cure;

"Bait" advertising—where the reader is denied a fair opportunity to purchase the goods advertised.

[The above is typical of published codes.]

We do not have a formal written policy listing exclusions. However, here are some examples:

Dangerous products—guns sold by mail capable of firing live ammunition; explosives; lockblade and switchblade knives; drug and medical products sold by mail; courses in hypnosis, etc.

Products of questionable value—automotive attachments claiming to increase mileage, produce greater power, etc.; products making bold, unsubstantiated claims such as insect traps claiming effectiveness in large areas; nursery products claiming superior growth or producing characteristics for the items such as trees, flowering bushes, etc.

Products or advertising in bad taste—illustrated books on sex; motion picture films offering "exciting, hard-to-get entertainment which you can show in your own home."

Our main concern is protection of our subscribers and our publisher. Specifically, we do not accept advertising from the following:

Medical products not approved by the American Medical Association.

Savings and Loan Associations whose deposits are not insured by the Federal Government.

Former advertisers, particularly direct mail, whose products were reported to be shoddy or defective, or where the service to purchasers left something to be desired.

Advertisements which in the opinion of the publisher do not appear to be in good taste and in keeping with the character of our publication.

We do follow certain guidelines including. . .that the appearance of the advertisement itself is not patterned after our editorial appearance.

We insist that products advertised in our pages be available at least in a representative number of first-class stores, and have sufficient national distribution that they can be found by our readers. We do not accept advertising which might affront the feelings of our readers, especially on racial and religious subjects. For that reason, restricted resorts are out; and a year or so ago we told the Union of South Africa that we would no longer accept their travel advertising.

Among our policies, . . .we aim to exclude the advertising of any product that we believe to be harmful to the consumer. Products in the drug and cosmetic classifications about which we have any doubt are referred to an independent chemical laboratory for analysis and report regarding their safety and merit, and sometimes physicians are consulted.

Alcoholic beverages and tobacco advertising are not acceptable, nor is "Make Money for Your Group" advertising. Certain other categories, such as proprietary medicines and feminine hygiene, are treated on an individual basis but are not covered by clearly stated policies.

We have no *written* policy on the acceptability of particular ads or types of ads. Each one is judged individually on (1) good taste and appearance, (2) product and quality of product, (3) reliability of advertiser. We turn down at least $100,000 a year in objectionable ads, mostly mail order.

Every advertisement should be clearly identified as to who the advertiser is. For example, we requested that Volkswagen put "Volkswagen of America" on their recent automotive jungle ad so that there would be no question as to who the advertiser was. Ads that simulate editorial material are also not acceptable.

Low advertising volume in a particular issue or issues occasionally forces acceptance of advertisements containing questionable copy and/or illustration, for example, bath oil or brassieres.

In addition to normal criteria such as good taste, validity of claims, appearance of advertising, we strive to keep advertising within the bounds of compatability with our stated editorial purpose. Since we are firm in our conviction that the editorial matter and the advertising must be complementary to each other, we strive to avoid the appearance of any advertising which will jar the reader from the euphoric mood and climate created by the editorial concepts. Thus in addition to rejecting the obvious, such as acne cures, trusses, hemorrhoids, etc., we try to avoid ads which might call the reader's attention to shortcomings on various levels. We won't take ads which tell him he is too thin or too fat or losing his hair. We do not accept ads for correspondence schools or home-study courses for the purpose of filling gaps in a reader's education, nor for opportunities to supplement his income by engaging in work which is not related to his career, or in other ways suggesting that his income is inadequate. This is not a new policy.

We have a presumably highly sophisticated audience, and on that basis we have occasionally allowed advertising to go through which we might not have printed if we were publishing *Boys' Life* or *Reader's Digest*. But we have decided that we have at least a small minority of extremely vocal readers who are surprisingly prudish. . .and so every once in a while we are astonished at their reaction.

DECISION PROCESS

Our advertising manager has prime responsibility for screening ads. In the case of new advertisers, he checks FTC bulletins and contacts the BBB. If still in doubt, he asks the prospective advertiser for sample products and/or a list of the other places where the product is advertised currently. Once an ad has appeared, any complaints from readers are followed up assiduously. Editorial people sometimes are consulted on whether they know of a particular company or have had dealings with it in the editorial line.

Most copy acceptance problems are easily resolved by following the written ground rules. Occasionally, however, there are matters which the three-person advertising acceptance group and advertising management cannot agree upon. These are referred to the publisher's office for a final decision. If editorial simulation is involved, they may also be submitted to the managing editor.

We used to have a copy censorship department, but since we could establish no guidelines, now the people who receive proofs and read ads are instructed to call the publisher's attention to anything that appears even a little bit out of the ordinary. Quite often the latter rejects such copy out of hand. If in doubt, he discusses it with the editor; ultimate authority rests with the editor, because of his direct concern for our readers.

Editorial as well as business people do get involved, particularly where the specialized editors are themselves the technical experts capable of judging the acceptability of products.

Editorial people are consulted only if the problem is taste or product type, and only then if we feel their advice is needed.

The "public duty team" at *Good Housekeeping* (represented by the Good Housekeeping Institute) is constantly under a challenge from the "private enterprise team" (represented by a fine advertising sales organization) to modify product acceptance requirements. As "Advertising Editor," I serve as a referee in this working relationship between the "public duty team" and the "private enterprise team." This provides me with a most unusual opportunity to view from the middle the constant efforts of both teams. It puts me in a position where I must myself look at *Good Housekeeping* advertising as a *consumer.*

As editor, it is my custom to send all reader-criticisms in connection with advertising to the advertising department where they are handled with personal letters to the complainants. The criteria, kinds of problems, and recent experiences as to acceptances or rejections of specific ads, are known only by the man in charge—our advertising director.

Although the editorial staff is not formally involved in the matter of advertising acceptability, the editors have from time to time protested the character of certain advertisements—specifically the large number of mail-order ads that afflict the back of the book. These have often been criticized for their double entendre, vulgarity, and general sleaziness. This criticism has resulted in the rejection of numerous ads although the general quality of mail order advertising remains low. In the past year about two dozen ads have been rejected, mostly in the mail order category.

The editorial department does not become involved except in three specific areas: (a) Advertising which they believe looks like editorial is unacceptable, unless identified as being advertising; (b) copy which encloses editorial by some device, as when an advertiser might buy 2 outside columns on a 3-column page and have a headline beginning on the left column and ending on the right column; (c) the editors will not allow advertising which takes over the editorial function. In other words, when the advertiser does not sell a product or idea about his company but rather promotes some other thought. A typical example of that would be the _____ Company ads which criticize government practices, taxing policies, and so on. However, the editorial department seldom comes into the picture even here since we screen these out in advance.

Editorial does get involved in determining whether a certain ad should be accepted, and we do exercise control over the placement of ads in relation to editorial content. This is particularly important in a magazine of our type where often there is a very close relationship between the content and advertising. For example, we may have an editorial on how to cook with frozen vegetables and we would certainly wish to avoid running this opposite an ad for frozen vegetables. The business department is always a little sad when editorial raises the question of acceptability of a certain advertisement or copy proof. By and large, they do understand our position in the main and do try to be as objective as they possibly can. They will approach the agency and/or advertiser and try to get changes made so that the ad would be acceptable to editorial.

We run classified advertising in our publications, and we have a department that purchases from all these ads as a spot check to determine whether they are shipping the proper merchandise and whether the merchandise is properly priced. In fact most of this is purchased in advance through dummy names, so that the advertiser cannot ship good material to us and then ship improper material to a reader.

PROBLEM AREAS

We do not have many problems on acceptability—in relation to our volume of advertising. Those causing us the most trouble are:

Sex Books. Many of these are good medical books, and *The New York Times* accepts these without question. In our magazine, however, because of our former image, they tend to become "dirty" books so we reject them.

Overly Sexy Ads on any product. Again, because of our former image, some advertisers seem to feel they can go almost the nude route or use the audacious headline and are often surprised when we reject their ads.

Mail-Order Ads from companies with a bad reputation at the Better Business Bureau. We will not accept mail-order ads for guns.

Ads on "fag" clothes or copy that tends to attract "fag" customers.

Hemorrhoid Remedies. Simply because they do not enhance the overall appearance of our magazine.

"Black Nightgown" advertising, because it appeals to the type of reader we do not want.
Overly Competitive Ads, particularly those drawing comparison by naming other brands.
Ads involving the words "Sale" or "Wholesale" or "Discounts."
Chain-Store Clothing Advertising.

The application of our stated criteria can be largely a matter of personal taste or opinion, so unanimity is not always possible. For instance, if Avis says, "We are only No. 2, so our ash trays *have* to be clean," does this not imply that Hertz's ash trays are *not* clean, or at least not always clean? (Even though the implication is there, we accept Avis' advertising because in our opinion the whole campaign has been handled in a tasteful way.)

Always a problem area is determining the boundary lines of good taste, both in copy and in illustration, in a society whose standards are rapidly undergoing change. Thus the acceptance of copy lines or copy themes which might be regarded as suggestive or having double meanings, or the use of nudity in advertising, must be weighed in relationship to liberalized community standards as well as the important fact that ours is a magazine addressed primarily to a male audience and is not a family vehicle.

By all odds, the most difficult kind of decision to make is in the area of taste. For example, we were offered the advertising of a men's cologne called "Piping Rock." The illustration showed a girl in a nightgown lying on a rumpled bed with a dreamy look on her face. She is quoted in the headline as saying: "Was it him or his Piping Rock?" To us, that was totally offensive and we thought it would be so to our readers. Yet it appeared in at least one other highly respected publication.

Taste is the most difficult area in terms of definition. Many ads that might be suitable for *Playboy,* for instance, we find undesirable in our pages, particularly in the men's apparel and toiletries categories. A double entendre, intentional or not, can be read by some people while not noticed by others. For this reason, when an ad is deemed by us to be unacceptable because it is in poor taste we simply note that "the copy acceptance group does not find your ad acceptable" in an effort to avoid argument over what does or does not constitute good taste.

The problem is one of obtaining agreement on what is objectionable. This is somewhat related to the censorship of books or movies. What is considered to be pornographic by one group is looked upon as art by another.

The ads which bother us most, if that is the correct word, are those amateurish ads which try to use *sex.* We usually try to reason with the agency or the advertiser on the basis that the kind of advertising probably does not do a good job of representing the company's image. If this is handled carefully, it usually works. As advertising agencies are becoming more and more professional and sophisticated, they are not anxious to involve themselves in ads that cause dispute.

In the past two years there has been a dramatic increase in the number of *new personal and feminine hygiene products.* Since these products are not generally promoted on radio or television, magazines are almost always included in their media plan. There is always a major question as to the degree to which these advertisers can "hard sell" their product in a publication like ours. Also, intimate apparel advertisers have recently tended to move toward a more exotic advertising platform, frequently showing and posing models in such a way that the advertisement has "sexual overtones." Furthermore, cosmetic advertisers have employed the same approach as the intimate apparel advertisers and frequently push our ethics to the limit with the use of such copy devices as the double-entendre.

Although we are the publishers of dozens of magazines and annuals we actually have relatively few problems in the area of advertising acceptability, with the exception of the technical problems which are pretty well covered in the postal manual.

Some problems of consequence arise at [a photography magazine]. Because photography encompasses things which could border on the obscene or the pornographic, the staff has to be constantly on the alert to preclude any such material getting in the magazine—both editorial and advertising. Thus they have set up a rule which states that if an ad is running in the magazine that is selling artistic or glamour photography, and they approve it after having previewed the material that is going to be sold, then the advertiser may use any of his material in his ad to indicate what the person will be receiving. In that respect, a nude may appear in an ad. However, if you are selling photographic equipment such as cameras or movie projectors, etc., they will not permit nudes to appear with such equipment because the people are not selling nude material, they are selling equipment. They have lost a great deal of advertising in the past year or so because of this very strict rule; and they have also received reader objections to nude photography that does appear in the magazine, which they consider in very excellent taste. So they are sort of in the middle between trying to do the right thing in either direction—being fair to the artistic photographer who is working with nude photography, and being very strict with the person who is trying to profit on the pornographic aspect of it.

The question of sex in advertising is one that requires careful consideration these days. Standards of public acceptance of dress have changed radically, and a degree of nudity, for example, that would not have been acceptable five to ten years ago seems to be acceptable today. The Tenneco Corporation recently chose to introduce a name change by dressing a model in a skimpy bikini, plentifully adorned with the new company logo. We determined to accept this advertisement since the bikini now is a fairly acceptable costume at resorts, whereas ten years ago we probably would have rejected it.

The "personal products" category, including birth control and hygienic products, still has to be watched very carefully in terms of certain state laws, product claims, and good taste and decency in the headline, illustration and copy approach. Advertisers and agencies are aware of this, however, and probably because our magazine goes to single and engaged young women 18 to 24 years of age they usually call us to ask about the acceptability of a headline, etc. We request a proof of the ad before finally accepting it. If the proof does not meet our "standards," we will ask for a meeting with the agency to discuss the matter and in almost every case modifications are made, with some give and take on both parts in order to secure an acceptable ad. One of the most effective and attractive ads we have ever carried was a four-page, full-color "family planning" advertisement from Mead Johnson; so we do not always have problems in this category.

Public opinion, that is, the feelings of our readers, was and is an important factor in this area. When we first accepted the advertising of Emko three years ago, we received a bit of unfavorable reader mail. However, more and more articles on sex education and birth control have appeared on TV and radio, and in newspapers and magazines; and as government has moved into this area domestically and abroad, we have found that our reader mail in the form of complaints about this type of advertising is practically nil. In fact our editors cover the subject of marital adjustment regularly in every issue, and our reader research tells us that 1) our readers want this type of editorial service and 2) that articles of this type score very high on cover lines and inside the magazine.

There are grey areas even in our written copy rules. For example, we are now considering an ad for a well-known aspirin. Is this a patent medicine, or is aspirin a worldwide panacea? Our rule was adopted to keep out ads for laxatives, hemorrhoid remedies, trusses, and the like.

The most troublesome kind of advertisements are those in which comparative claims are made between the advertiser's product and his rival's. For example, an ad which showed a particular brand of Scotch also showed photographically numerous other brands by other distillers. The ad claimed that X Scotch was the *real* Scotch. This is a common enough advertising cliche. Nevertheless, it was done so badly that we felt it was offensive to our readers and competitive distillers. We try to discourage this kind of advertising, especially if it is done in such a heavy-handed manner. Volkswagen, of course, as well as Avis and Hertz have handled this kind of claim with some wit and therefore we feel their ads are not offensive to our readers.

An area of change in what is becoming acceptable is that of competitive claims. The Hertz-Avis case is well known, and it seems to have created a climate where companies will directly compare their products with a competitor's. We judge each advertisement of this type on its merits to determine whether what is said is true and whether it is defamatory. In each case that we accept what we consider to be a marginal advertisement, we let the advertiser know that we feel that he is getting close to unfair advertising and competitive practices. Sometimes this comment is enough to cause the advertiser to change his copy approach or modify it. This type of advertising seems to be prevalent today in the office-machine and office-copier area, to cite one major example.

Another area of difficulty is that of highly competitive copy between two large and reputable companies. This can be a real stickler. Obviously you do not want to carry copy from one good advertiser that will offend another good advertiser; but we have found it very difficult to arbitrate these conflicts, and usually have carried the copy on the premise that we are a "medium" which puts us squarely in the middle. We have asked complaining advertisers to settle the matter between themselves, and in almost all cases have had no real trouble. Legally, of course, we cannot be held accountable; but it does create some difficult sales situations.

Any normal buying or selling situation involves comparison, direct and indirect, with other products or services. Without comparing values there is no way to determine which one of two or more choices is the best buy, and therefore it seems to us hypocritical to prohibit straight-out comparisons and mention of specific names. What seems to us to be completely controlling in such a situation is that the comparison must be honest and fair—in the sense that it not only tells the facts, but tells them in such a way as to prohibit distortion of their meaning.

In the area of fraudulent and exaggerated claims, I think book publishers and weight-reducing advertisers are the most flagrant violators. Book publishers frequently advertise books that claim to improve brain capacity, reduce your weight, and stop your smoking. The books themselves never make as flagrant promises as do the ads.

Interestingly enough, I have seen more serious difficulties encountered over the problems of the use of superlatives in the advertising of well-known products than we have encountered in policing the many thousands of products which appear in our magazines each month.

An area that occasionally gives us problems is the area of inserts. It has been our sad experience to have had to turn down an entire campaign because of inserts which violated the spirit of the postal regulations. Even though they might have been acceptable under a loose interpretation of the letter of the regulations, we felt that our position in the field dictated that we reject the advertising.

Our advertising acceptability practices are probably peculiar to the type of magazine we are, and I'm not sure particularly pertinent to the kind of discussion you will be conducting. Our problem basically is to fight shy of "kookie" advertisers, including a lot of fringe and hate elements. To do so, we finally set up a blanket category of "political advertising" and announced we would not take any ads of that sort. This we found easier than telling Mr. A. that his ad was okay, and Mr. B., who was advertising the same kind of thing, that his ad was not okay.

RESULTING DISAGREEMENTS

I can't say that in the past few years we have had any serious disagreements either inside or outside the company.

There is no doubt that an advertiser, whose ad has been left out, cries bitterly. There is also no doubt that readers who find ads offensive complain and cancel their subscriptions. The circulation people naturally take the readers' point of view, and the advertising people are much more likely to be liberal in their interpretation of what is acceptable.

Internally we have had only minor disagreements, and these have usually stemmed from highly subjective opinions of junior editors. With advertisers we have had one major disagreement over a statement which implied that competitors' products were unacceptable "imitations." We refused to accept the advertisement, although the advertiser had run with us for years. The advertiser refused to change his copy. After a period of almost a year, the advertiser relented and is now running copy acceptable to us. We don't have many reader complaints about advertising. There is, of course, the usual quota of teetotalers who are horrified at our acceptance of liquor advertising, and the bigots who object to our carrying Knights of Columbus advertising. But we pay no attention to either of these small groups.

We rejected about $50,000 worth of advertising from some insurance firms after we had carried the ads for several years. Some were for hospitalization policies which paid a few hundred dollars—a drop in the bucket considering hospital costs—and lulled policyholders into thinking that they were protected. Among our readers were the insurance commissioners for two states who objected that the policies were inadequate. When we rejected these ads, the companies complained in turn. They said that other magazines took such ads and that our rejection of them was a reflection on the caliber of the insurance company. But we've kept them out.

The most recent disagreement we have had with readers has been our refusal to carry advertising for the play *MacBird* which we felt to be immoral, vicious, and libelous. Our refusal was given wide coverage in the newspapers, on radio, and even in magazine stories. We received a great many letters; I would guess about two-thirds of them were in favor of our stand, and one-third against.

Our relationship with advertisers and agencies, though, is often strained because of our policies. A specific case was our refusal to carry the advertising of a very well-known product, the distribution of which was confined entirely to discount houses. The agency and account could not understand why we didn't wish to use our readers as a lever to help force distribution of this product into better stores. It's rather obvious that the rejection of advertising does not make friends for us.

The decision to accept or reject specific ads has occasionally resulted in substantial problems with advertisers and occasionally from readers. Naturally we have lost the revenue from the advertising we did not accept, and sometimes have been penalized by multiproduct advertisers for not accepting *one* of their products.

Naturally a publication worries whether it might offend an advertiser, or an agency which might be placing other business with it; but in the case of a "strong" magazine like ours, this is usually overcome. In one case, however, where we will not accept a proprietary drug from an advertiser, he has openly stated that if we are to get other business from him we must accept this product first. We have not done so.

We have had complaints from advertisers about our acceptance of certain ads such as for a "bust developer."

Recently we received some reader complaints about an advertisement that revealed too much of the feminine form in the eyes of some of our readers. It was, and remains, our view that although the ad might offend a few people, it really is not offensive. We feel the complaints are not justified.

We have received complaints from readers in the past two years, primarily about advertisers who fall into the feminine-hygiene and cosmetic categories. Most of these advertisers have been most understanding of our concern over taste because, in most cases, they receive an equal number of complaint letters. Since our readers are their customers, they don't want to offend them any more than we do and, in many instances, they have seized the initiative and have toned down the copy before we requested that they take such action.

The question of advertising "birth-control" products is very interesting. We went into this matter at great length with one of the leading drug companies, and after testing advertising in limited markets we have now permitted them to extend the promotion of their product into sizeable regional sections of our circulation.

There has been only one ad that we misjudged, and we quickly notified the agency and advertiser that we could not accept this particular ad again or any one like it. Since this particular advertiser was well identified in the advertisement, they had also heard from our readers and made a similar decision before we called.

Even with all our careful procedures, we occasionally offend our readers. A good example is the recent Ponder and Best (Vivitar) camera advertisement, which drew several hundred letters protesting its appearance in our magazine. The letters did not come from bluenoses or prudes but from obviously intelligent and reasonably broad-minded people. I think we made a mistake in accepting this piece of copy.

Readers are continually commenting on the advertising in the magazine, and seem to be particularly distressed with liquor and cigarette advertising, but only in general rather than with specific ads. Policies have not been changed recently.

As for reader complaints about advertising, there always are a few who object to advertising in principle, or to specific advertisements. Some of these people continue to write letters month after month.

"FAMILY" PRACTICES

Advertising acceptance policies are the same for all magazines in our company.

With regard to multimagazine companies, the fact that we are guided by our company's "Practices and Procedures" manual keeps problems of consistency to a minimum. I cannot recall that any difficulty has arisen in recent years.

Our company permits each magazine pretty much to establish its own policy with regard to the screening of ads. In the case of our five major magazines, ad policies vary considerably but this variance has not caused problems.

Most advertisers seem to accept the fact that each publication is entitled to its own policy, and occasionally there can be a difference in opinion between two magazines in spite of the fact that both are owned by the same corporation.

We are associated with a multimagazine company and, even though the overall policies are the same, problems do arise from time to time. Advertising that would be acceptable to a woman's magazine may not quite be our cup of tea. Women especially seem to approach our male-female dual audience magazine with a different attitude than they do a woman's magazine as such. Some years ago, we accepted an ad which showed a nude female figure in back of a translucent glass shower door. The woman's husband was shaving in the same bathroom. This brought a few letters from our readers. I am sure this ad in a woman's magazine would not have had the same kind of response.

Some foundation-garment advertising which might be perfectly consistent with the women's audience and with the general fashion and psychological climate of *one* of our company's magazines, would not be acceptable within the pages of two others. Yet in that same magazine—which would accept foundation-garment ads—cigarette and tobacco advertising would not be consistent with the general atmosphere of the magazine, although both others do accept such advertising.

Individual magazines may on occasion decide not to accept a particular advertisement that is agreeable to another magazine in our company.

Most questions of advertising acceptability are resolved by the publisher and/or advertising manager of our magazine, although the editor-in-chief is frequently consulted and occasionally the opinion of our editorial department head is also sought in making a decision in a "grey" area. If the case also affects 'other magazines in our family, the corporate advertising director or the executive vice-president may suggest a course of action, or reach a decision which would apply to all our magazines, or to one or more publications but not to others, depending on the circumstances.

PROBLEM PREVENTION

We attempt so to present the case for not handling an advertisement that the advertiser is grateful to us for calling to his attention a possible future difficulty and helping him to avoid it. We at all costs try to avoid the role of the bluenose or censor. Thanks to this attitude on our part, we have not experienced any serious difficulty with advertisers in recent years.

It should be emphasized that the magazine does not set itself up as a board of censors. As the tastes of the country change, so do the kinds of ads that are presented to us. In contrast to our editorial policy, in which we attempt to remain to some degree in advance of public taste and to break new ground, we are in no great rush to push advertisers in such a direction. In fact our hope is that advertising will remain within a fairly predictable area so that it will not impinge on our editorial ideas or features.

Copy problems are probably no more or less numerous than they were 10 or 20 years ago. However, the kinds of problems that arise today are much more subtle in nature and therefore make decisions more difficult. As an example, a "snake oil" that claimed to cure all ills, and which was manufactured by a relatively unknown company, was quite easy to deal with. In contrast, today we are dealing with whether or not a large reputable cosmetic company can show the model's navel in their advertisement.

The area of copy censorship is always a touchy one; but we have been able to persuade advertisers to change copy that we thought required it, pointing out it was to their advantage. We really don't have too much trouble.

QUESTIONS

1. What general reactions do you have to the comments of those quoted in the case?

2. What are your own views on the key issues listed on page 627?

3. What, to you, is the most important area of concern with respect to advertising acceptability for magazines? For advertising in general?

The Whirlpool Corporation

The director of corporate and public affairs must decide whether or not to make a major investment in a public relations campaign. The program, developed in response to the growing consumerism movement, had received unfavorable crticism from distributors of the company's appliances.

In August 1969, Juel Ranum, Executive Director of Corporate and Public Affairs of the Whirlpool Corporation, was reviewing his plans for the Care-A-Van show, a noncommercial live musical designed to inform consumers on the purchase, use, and service of electrical household appliances. The show was an attempt on the company's part to dramatically respond to the growing consumerism movement in the United States.

Parts of Care-A-Van had recently been presented to several groups of company distributors and had elicited a wide range of comments, most of them critical. Disturbed by this unfavorable response to the previews, Ranum wondered whether or not the Care-A-Van project should be continued. In view of the sizeable amount of management time and the roughly $100,000 which had already been committed to the show, Ranum was reluctant to drop the project at this point. However, he also recalled the arguments of executives in other departments who had thought that the funds allocated to the Care-A-Van show could be better spent on the direct promotion of Whirlpool products and the Whirlpool name.

COMPANY BACKGROUND

The Whirlpool Corporation is one of the leading U.S. manufacturers of household appliances. The company was founded shortly after the turn of the century, and for several decades had concentrated its activity on the manufacturing of private-label washing machines for Sears, Roebuck & Company.

This pattern had remained unchanged until the end of World War II when Whirlpool began to sell to the general market under its own trade name, although Sears continued to be its major customer. A distribution agreement with the Radio Corporation of America facilitated the establishment of a wide network of retail outlets for Whirlpool products. Another major development after the war had been the company's development into a full-line manufacturer of major appliances and home entertainment products through a number of mergers and acquisitions. (The term "major appliances" excludes small household appliances like mixers, toasters, can openers, and so on.)

In 1969 the company's product line comprised a wide range of consumer goods such as laundry equipment, air conditioners, kitchen ranges, refrigerators, freezers, vacuum cleaners, dehumidifiers, and trash compactors. Whirlpool also manufactured commercial products, e.g., central heating and cooling systems, equipment for coin-operated laundries, icemakers, and bulk milk coolers.

Consolidated net sales had shown growth above average industry rates for a number of years. Sales in 1968 were $1.02 billion, with net after-tax earnings of $36.2 million. (Exhibit 1 presents a review of sales, earnings, and other company data for the ten-year period 1959 to 1968.)

Sales made to Sears under the "Kenmore," "Coldspot," and "Silvertone" brand names accounted for about two-thirds of Whirlpool's total volume in 1968. Roughly one-sixth of the remainder came from service and component sales to other manufacturers, and the rest from sales of appliances under the Whirlpool brand. (Exhibit 2 depicts the growth of Whirlpool brand sales compared with industry sales for the period from 1958 to 1968.)

Appliances carrying the Whirlpool brand name moved through about 35 distributors and 13 factory branches to roughly 13,000 retail outlets such as appliance dealers, department stores, discount stores, furniture dealers, and hardware stores. More so than other manufacturers, the Whirlpool Corporation relied on traditional appliance dealers for the distribution of its branded products. Although these appliance dealers (in 1968) still accounted for the major part of Whirlpool product sales, they were decreasing in importance and gradually were being replaced by mass merchandisers. Some executives watched this trend with concern; they believed that the shift to mass merchandisers would be accompanied by a deterioration of customer service in the stores.

Management of the Whirlpool Corporation described the company as the largest manufacturer of major appliances in the United States. One executive observed: "In terms of total sales—that is, Whirlpool brands and Sears brands combined—we are first in the appliance industry. However, if we take just sales under the Whirlpool brand, we are second after General Electric, with Frigidaire and Westinghouse probably in third and fourth place in terms of major appliance sales. People often don't recognize our size. G.E. and Westinghouse get much more attention because of their activities in many fields other than appliances. We are only in appliances, and naturally are perhaps more interested in trends affecting the appliance industry than are firms that don't have all their eggs in one basket."

CONSUMER ORIENTATION

Shortly after Elisha Gray II had become Whirlpool's Chairman of the Board in 1958, he made a statement which came to represent the basic philosophy of the Whirlpool Corporation in the succeeding years: "The future of our company depends on consumer satisfaction after the sale. . . . The desire to please our customers is paramount from the time a product starts on the drawing board— through engineering, manufacturing, testing, distribution—and continues while the product is in use in a customer's home or business. Our standards are not thought of in terms of competition's standards. . . . Our aim is to provide the best appliances that can be imagined for a particular purpose." Several moves subsequently were made to implement this philosophy, many of which had received wide publicity.

A Consumer Services Division was formed in 1959.[1] This division was responsible for coordinating all company activities having a potential influence on the degree of consumer satisfaction, such as product design, quality control, warranty service, installation, maintenance, and the handling of complaints. (Exhibit 3 presents a partial organization chart of the Whirlpool Corporation.)

Within the Consumer Services Division, the Customer Assurance Department contacted several thousand consumers each year in order to learn about their likes and dislikes regarding existing appliances. In turn, this information was analyzed and guidelines developed for future production. Based on the consumer surveys, complaints, and service incidents as well as other feedback from consumers, the department had developed a set of standards against which new products had to be measured through all phases of product development, production, and marketing. Some of the major standards established concerned product life expectancy, noise level, consumer ease of use, product safety, installation, and serviceability. (Exhibit 4 gives an example of the nature of these standards.)

Customer Relations—another department of the Consumer Services Division— reacted to letters from customers and kept records of all correspondence. Management emphasized that it was company policy to answer all letters from consumers within 48 hours of receipt; letters directed to the president were said to be answered by wire the same day; complaints from customers were to be resolved within a maximum of two weeks of receipt. Management reported that in 1968 there had been only 13 complaints which the company had not been able to close out within this two-week period.

The late 1950s witnessed a growing number of appliances in private homes and the emergence of mass merchandisers who provided only minimal customer service. In light of these developments, management believed that the traditional service policies of the appliance industry were becoming inadequate to guarantee consumer satisfaction after the sale. Hence a network of about 1,300 franchised service outlets was established by Whirlpool under the trade name of "Tech-Care." About two-thirds of these outlets did maintenance and repair work only, whereas the rest also sold Whirlpool appliances.

Technicians employed by a Tech-Care outlet had to be trained by Whirlpool in a training center established especially for that purpose at company headquarters. Furthermore, Tech-Care outlets had to meet company standards regarding the

---

[1] Formed as the Customer Quality and Services Department in 1959, incorporating the customer assurance, field service, and parts departments, the department's name was revised to Consumer Services Division in 1968, headed by a vice president.

quality of their equipment and facilities and the size of their parts inventories. Attendance at refresher courses was made a requirement for the annual franchise renewal. Tech-Care outlets were required to complete service on 80% of Whirlpool customer requests within 24 hours; all service was to be completed within 72 hours subject to availability of parts. Whirlpool controlled the quality of service rendered by contacting users of Tech-Care Service and asking them what they liked or disliked about the service they had received. As a general rule, Tech-Care outlets had to maintain a "satisfactory" or better rating on competence, courtesy, and dependability from at least 95% of customers surveyed.

Management of the Whirlpool Corporation believed that the fulfillment of appliance warranties was of paramount importance for the achievement of customer satisfaction. To assure that the free labor specified in most warranties was provided, even when the product was moved out of the selling dealer's territory, Whirlpool created a department (in 1964) to administer funds to pay for required warranty service. A sum of money was set aside for each product sold for the purpose of paying any dealer or service agent anywhere in the United States his full retail service charge for performing warranty labor on Whirlpool appliances. This system made the Whirlpool warranty valid any place the customer might move with the product within the United States, at the same time assuring all dealers and service outlets their full share for warranty work performed.

Management was also concerned about the deterioration of customer assistance given in the retail stores. "There is a general trend that salesclerks are becoming less and less knowledgeable, and also less and less interested in customers," one executive remarked. "We try to overcome this problem by inviting our dealers to attend our sales-management courses here at headquarters."

Another move to provide better assistance to the consumer in making his purchase decision had been the creation of the so-called Consumer Buy Guide in 1968, an information tag attached to almost all appliances.[2] (See Exhibit 5 for an example of a Consumer Buy Guide.) An executive explained:

> We always had a sales sticker on our appliances, but this sticker didn't really do much for the consumer. It was just another piece of promotion emphasizing how good we thought we were and what a marvelous product we had. So we replaced the old sales sticker with a Buy Guide which contains only realistic, factual information about the respective appliance. A number of people in our organization were opposed to the change from the sales sticker to the Buy Guide. Some people in the sales department still think that it wasn't a particularly good idea. They argue that the sales sticker was important because there is less sales push these days in the self-service stores.
>
> More important, perhaps, than the Buy Guide was another step we took in early 1968 to provide our customers with better information. Even before Betty Furness [formerly Special Assistant to President Johnson for Consumer Affairs] began making speeches about the gobbledygook in appliance

---

[2]Except air conditioners, for which separate booklets were provided, because there was no convenient place to attach them to the product itself.

warranties, we had started revising our warranties. Historically our warranties resembled all others. They were written by lawyers for the express purpose of protecting us, the manufacturer, against unreasonable demands from the consumer. Since they were written by lawyers, consumers were often unable to understand what they meant. And then came consumerism; and with it consumer advocates such as Betty Furness, who expressed public dissatisfaction with the complexity and the legalese of most major appliance warranties. We realized that here was an opportunity for us to use the work we had already done on the simplification of our warranties as a marketing plus. So we took a radical step, and revised our warranty from the conventional certificate format to a friendly letter style which told the consumer in plain English what protection she could expect and what she could not. [Exhibit 6 shows an example of Whirlpool's simplified warranty letter.]

The very favorable response this step received from Betty Furness and other consumer activists was an indication for us that we were on target. We placed full-page ads in magazines such as *Life* and *Look*, announcing our conversion to the "friendly letter warranty." We feel that our product-acceptance across the nation was enhanced by this small but timely refinement. Interesting to note is the fact that this step was preceded by heated debates with our lawyers, who thought that we were giving the company away.

The establishment of direct communication via direct telephone service between the corporation and the owners of its products was described as another notable achievement by members of Whirlpool's Consumer Services Division management. One executive said:

If you are interested in establishing customer loyalty, you have to talk to your customer. We realized that there is a communication gap between appliance manufacturers and the consumer. Normally the retailer is the only one who has direct contact with the consumer. With the deterioration of sales service in the stores, however, consumers often experience difficulty in finding somebody to talk to about their troubles with appliances. In particular, consumers frequently don't know where to get good service for their appliances when they move to a new town. We began to think about what we could do to fill this communications gap. It had to be something newsworthy and also obviously effective.

In September 1967, we opened the "Cool Line," that is, a toll-free telephone service which enables customers to call the factory, free, from anywhere in the United States 24 hours a day to get answers to questions about the operation of their equipment, its maintenance, or the need to locate a service source for it. The Cool-Line number is now listed in all instruction books and warranty letters, and we publicize it in our magazine advertising. We get over a thousand calls per month. A record is made of all incoming calls for the information that may be provided to factory personnel. We believe that the Cool Line has helped our sales. . .although by how much we can't measure. Actually after we publicized it, we received a number of calls from consumers who wanted to know where they could buy Whirlpool products in their area.

In October 1968, we made another move to open direct channels of communication between the consumer and Whirlpool. We placed two-page ads headlined "Here is your chance to fight City Hall." The ads invited customers to tell our vice-president of Consumer Services what they thought—good or bad—about our products, and then provided a full page for their replies. We got more than 2,500 replies which, of course, have been evaluated by design and production staffs. [Exhibit 7 reproduces a copy of this ad.]

THE CARE-A-VAN SHOW

In the late 1960s, consumerism—a trend toward growing public support of policies, programs, and laws designed to provide greater protection to the consumer in the market place—was gaining momentum. Among the criticisms directed against business by consumer advocates was that consumers were not being provided with sufficient and truthful information by manufacturers to make intelligent choices among the increasing number of products offered.

It was against the background of the growing consumerism movement that Gray approached Ranum in early 1969 with the following questions:

— How can we demonstrate in a dramatic and forceful fashion Whirlpool's concern for the consumer?

— How can we prove to consumer activists that Whirlpool and the appliance industry are engaged in effective programs that are responsive to consumer needs and wants?

— How can we bridge the so-called information gap that consumers and consumer activists claim exists between manufacturers and users of appliances?

Ranum said:

It was our feeling within the company that a lot of useful information was already available to consumers, like our Buy Guides and the Cool Line. The trouble is that housewives often don't know about information such as this that is available from us or from other manufacturers. . .or they are just not interested. Therefore we concluded that if the consumer was unaware of the wealth of information existing in the marketplace, any move to close the information gap would have to be something very imaginative to catch the attention of the public.

A committee was formed, including William Breninghouse, Director of Public Relations; Ronald Gow, Manager of Public Relations; and John Helsley, Manager of Service Communications and Planning. They were given the task of developing answers to the questions posed by Gray. At this stage, no budgetary constraints were imposed on the committee.

Among the early thoughts discussed by the committee were the placement of more institutional advertisements, emphasizing Whirlpool's concern for the consumer; the training of home economists for lectures at women's clubs; and the production of educational movies to be shown to consumer organizations and in schools. Another suggestion was to place a series of one-minute educational announcements on network TV, to sponsor an entire TV show on consumer protection and appliance buying. Most of these early ideas were discarded fairly quickly. "The industry has been doing many of these things for a long time," Ranum explained, "but conventional means of reaching the consumer with information have obviously become ineffective."

Breninghouse, who had a background in the production of stage shows and movies, then came up with the idea of a live musical combining consumer education with entertainment. It would tell the consumer with songs, skits, and dances where and how to buy appliances, how to use and care for them, and where to get service if needed. Ranum said:

> The idea of a live show for consumer information was something new and appealing. That's why we liked it. By utilizing the modern medium of entertainment as a vehicle for this information, we felt that we could spark greater consumer knowledge in appliances.

The proposal for the show was presented to Gray and other members of top management in May 1969, and met with their enthusiastic support. Working with Jam Handy Productions, a film production firm in Detroit, Breninghouse then began to write and design a 90-minute rock musical, named Care-A-Van, which also included a short movie, slides, psychedelic lights, and opportunities for audience participation. Although geared primarily to first-time appliance buyers—homemakers in their twenties—the show was also intended to appeal to women of all age brackets and social strata. Although no formal consumer research was conducted to determine what information should be included by the show, considerable time and effort were devoted to the matter by consumer specialists, educators, and government representatives working closely with Whirlpool personnel.

The objectives of developing the show were set forth specifically as follows:

> 1. To demonstrate to consumer activists, especially at governmental and quasigovernmental levels that Whirlpool is striving to be responsive to the needs of the consumer, especially in the field of consumer information.
> 2. To produce an outstanding presentation in keeping with the times that would stimulate writers, editors, home economists, educators, and opinion leaders to write and speak positively about consumer education.
> 3. To produce a vehicle that will assist Whirlpool's public affairs efforts to make Whirlpool a household word. In fact, the advent of consumerism

provides a striking opportunity for us to establish a meaningful and unique "care" image. Public affairs efforts have initiated the warranty letter, the "Cool Line," and a positive, cooperative approach to consumerism. Care-A-Van adds momentum to the total effort.

4.   To determine the extent of the American homemaker's personal concern for closing the so-called "information gap" between herself and the appliance manufacturer.

"None of our competitors has thought of taking such initiative," Gow commented. "They are all waiting for some industry action through our trade association."

Regarding the content of Care-A-Van, the executives noted:

We haven't quite finished writing Care-A-Van, but we have a pretty good idea what the show will be like when it is completed. We plan to staff the show with three well-known actor-singers from Broadway. The first cast member is "Leslie Paige," a bright, vibrant, witty lady acting as the appliance industry's spokesman. She knows how to shop, what to look for, and she talks truth. Leslie's advice repeatedly helps "The Young Woman," who represents the viewpoint of today's young homemaker. The third cast member is "The Young Man," who at different times represents a husband, a salesman, or a narrator-spokesman for the industry.

Meaningful information is conveyed to the consumer in nine scenes, plus a 15-minute movie. [See Exhibit 8.] The show is stuffed with facts. . .such as why a lock is important on a freezer. . .the need for rinse water cool-down for permanent press. . .why you should always use an aluminum pan on a range's thermostatic burner. It ends with Leslie Paige pointing out that homemakers will always have questions, and when they go unanswered they feel that nobody cares. Because it is impossible to answer the audience's questions we intend to let Leslie Paige refer to a postage prepaid letter addressed to her, which consumers can pick up at the exit and mail with their questions.

The show will be free, of course. . .there will be no tickets or reserved seats. We will also give each consumer a free booklet summarizing the Care-A-Van's lessons. As an added incentive to attend, consumers will have the chance to win a top-of-the-line Whirlpool appliance used on stage.

Ranum said:

It is important to note that no one speaks for Whirlpool in the show; there is no attempt to sell the company or Whirlpool products. Naturally the products used to illustrate the various points on the stage are Whirlpool, and most consumers will be aware or can easily find out that Whirlpool sponsored the show. But this is never stated outright. We have deliberately made the show noncommercial. The American public is sick and tired of commercial puffery, and any attempt to use Care-A-Van directly as a promotional tool would discredit our honest attempt to demonstrate to consumers and to legislators in Washington that the appliance industry really understands the consumer's product needs and product problems. . .and really cares.

A special budget amounting to $1 million was allocated to the Department of Corporate and Public Affairs for the show. Of this amount, $800,000 was to be used for the production, exhibiting, and promotion of Care-A-Van during the second half of 1969 and the first half of 1970. The remaining $200,000 was to be reserved for the production of a movie version of the show in 1970, if Care-A-Van turned out to have the desired success. Compared with the company's annual advertising expenditures, which industry sources estimated at $5 million, the budget allocated to Care-A-Van represented a sizable investment for the Whirlpool Corporation.

It was planned to show Care-A-Van in New York, Washington D.C., Chicago, and other major cities. Management realized that the total number of performances which could be produced within the limits of the budget would very much depend on local conditions in the cities where Care-A-Van was to be presented. It was expected, though, that roughly $500,000 would be spent in 1969 for approximately 40 performances.

The company hoped that Care-A-Van would draw between 500 and 1,000 consumers per show. No detailed plan for attracting consumers to the show had as yet been developed, but management was hopeful that local newspaper and radio advertising, television announcements, and personal contacts with schools, clubs, consumer organizations, and Better Business Bureaus would produce sufficient consumer interest in the show. [Exhibit 9 presents a sample advertisement which was to be used for the announcement of Care-A-Van in local newspapers. Exhibit 10 shows a sample mailer to be sent to households.] Although Whirlpool had planned to make wall banners available to its dealers announcing the Care-A-Van show, the company did not intend to rely greatly on the retail outlets for the promotion of Care-A-Van. "It would smack too much of commercialism," Gow said. "Besides, the typical appliance dealer probably is only slightly aware of consumerism."

After the concept for the Care-A-Van show was firmly established it was presented to other departments within the Whirlpool organization. Ranum reported their reactions:

> Of course not everybody in our company agreed that this was the right approach. Our director of retail marketing liked the idea; he thought that it would enhance our image among retailers. The advertising people, however, said: "Give *us* the $1 million you have budgeted for Care-A-Van. That money will buy us 20 full-page ads in *Life*, or 20 one-minute network TV spots, which will make a direct contribution to our sales growth." They also thought that the use of rock music and psychedelic effects would limit our audience to youngsters. The sales people argued: "If we could use the $1 million for the reduction of our prices we would certainly sell more ranges and refrigerators than we can ever hope to sell as a result of Care-A-Van." We

admit we have no idea as to what, if any, impact Care-A-Van will have on our sales. Care-A-Van is frankly an experiment in communications designed to bridge the information gap between the industry and the consumers. If the signals we have got from Washington are right, if consumerism is here to stay, we have to prove that the appliance industry is responsive to consumers' complaints.

So far, we have made no formal presentation of the Care-A-Van concept and technique to any groups outside the company. We feel confident, however, that consumer activists will be impressed with the noncommercial posture of Care-A-Van and its modern handling of consumer information, and that once we get the show running it will receive a tremendous amount of publicity in the press designating Whirlpool as the industry leader in closing the information gap.

The opening "performance" for Care-A-Van had been scheduled for September 29, 1969. Although the work on the script and the final form of Care-A-Van were still not completed, management decided to test the concept by putting together a 15-minute preview for presentation to company distributors at the regular Distributor Sales Conventions which were held in Washington D.C., San Francisco, and Chicago during the month of August 1969. The preview included an opening movie and some of the songs, dances, and skits which had already been written and were presented by actors who had been hired only for the three short performances. Executives said:

> The effect of the previews ranged from audience apathy to complete disaster. In spite of our high expectations, to the distributors the show was like a bucket of cold water poured over them. They didn't like the music. They thought it was too mod and drowned the dialogues. They didn't like the dancing. They thought there was too much entertainment and too little education and selling. The whole idea of the show wasn't appealing to them. Some of the distributors argued that in spite of all the interest and enthusiasm consumer protection leaders might show, we would have a hell of a time attracting sizeable crowds to see Care-A-Van. Housewives would rather watch soap operas on TV than come to a musical dealing with appliances. And even if they came, how much of the information on a broad range of appliances as well as on warranties, repairs, and so on, would the audience retain?
>
> One mistake we may have made is that we didn't prepare our distributors for the show—we didn't tell them what it was all about and what to expect. They didn't like it because they couldn't see what benefit they would derive from a noncommercial thing like this. Besides, we may have picked the wrong parts of the show for them to see. Also the previews lacked the degree of professionalism we want to achieve in the real performances. Finally, Care-A-Van aims primarily at the young homemakers or future homemakers and we're just not sure that our distributors talk the same language and have the same preference for music as these young women do.

SUMMARY

It was against this background that Ranum had to decide what action to take with regard to the future of Care-A-Van. He realized that a decision had to be reached soon, since the reservations for auditoriums, the hiring of musicians, and the preparation of local promotional campaigns for Care-A-Van had to be made well in advance. He was aware that if he did decide to go ahead with the Care-A-Van program, he would also have to develop some ways of assessing its impact once it was under way.

The Whirlpool Corporation

LIST OF EXHIBITS

Exhibit	Contents
1	10-Year Statistical Review: 1959-1968
2	Growth of Whirlpool Brand Sales and Industry Sales
3	Partial Organization Chart—1969
4	Sample of Customer Assurance Standards
5	Sample of a Consumer Buy Guide
6	Simplified Warranty
7	Reproduction of October 1968 Advertisement
8	Scenes of the Care-A-Van Show
9	Sample Advertisement
10	Sample Mailer for the Announcement of Care-A-Van

Exhibit 1

10-YEAR STATISTICAL REVIEW: 1959-1968

	1968	1967	1966	1965
Operations				
Sales	$825,820	$773,717	$704,816	$630,745
Earnings before Income Taxes	$ 74,223	$ 64,072	$ 69,019	$ 68,660
Per Cent to Sales	8.99%	8.28%	9.79%	10.89%
Net Earnings	$ 36,223	$ 33,272	$ 36,219	$ 35,860
Per Cent to Sales	4.39%	4.30%	5.14%	5.69%
Per Share of Common Stock**	$ 3.10	$ 2.86	$ 3.12	$ 3.13
Earned on Stockholders' Equity	16.5%	16.6%	19.6%	21.6%
Dividends Paid	$ 18,708	$ 18,619	$ 18,563	$ 13,834
Per Share of Common Stock	$ 1.60	$ 1.60	$ 1.60	$ 1.20
Per Share of Preferred Stock	$ -0-	$ -0-	$ -0-	$ .85
Depreciation of Plant and Equipment	$ 9,739	$ 8,256	$ 10,426	$ 9,070
Amortization of Tooling	$ 11,926	$ 9,832	$ 9,255	$ 7,188
Net Additions to Property,				
Plant, and Equipment	$ 15,552	$ 24,905	$ 22,652	$ 16,359
Net Additions to Tooling	$ 14,365	$ 11,038	$ 11,790	$ 8,335
Balance Sheet				
Working Capital	$117,907	$104,106	$114,603	$112,036
Ratio of Current Assets to				
Current Liabilities	1.94 to 1	1.75 to 1	2.20 to 1	2.40 to 1
Property, Plant, and Equipment—Net	$ 95,566	$ 90,856	$ 74,207	$ 61,980
Tools—Net	$ 12,172	$ 8,630	$ 7,424	$ 4,890
Long-Term Debt	$ 65,000	$ 67,200	$ 69,400	$ 36,595
Stockholders' Equity	$219,776	$200,293	$184,640	$166,296
Number of Common Shares				
Outstanding (in thousands)	11,722	11,658	11,616	11,575
Book Value Per Share	$ 18.75	$ 17.18	$ 15.90	$ 14.37
Non-Financial				
Number of Employees (Year-End)	19,690	20,868	19,474	15,545
Number of Stockholders (Year-End):				
Common Stock	11,836	12,291	12,569	12,334
Preferred Stock	-0-	-0-	-0-	-0-

* After deduction of special item, $9,244,000 (equivalent to $.87 per share) as reflected in financial statements. Before special item, per share earnings were $2.22.
** Based on average shares outstanding during each year restated to reflect the two-for-one split of the common stock effective May 14, 1965.

Exhibit 1 (cont.)

	1964	1963	1962	1961	1960	1959
Operations						
	$590,777	$538,704	$465,257	$436,865	$446,378	$430,497
	$ 58,127	$ 32,535	$ 37,843	$ 28,000	$ 31,589	$ 42,215
	9.84%	6.04%	8.13%	6.41%	7.08%	9.81%
	$ 29,327	$ 15,050*	$ 18,643	$ 13,500	$ 15,689	$ 20,715
	4.96%	2.79%	4.01%	3.09%	3.51%	4.81%
	$ 2.65	$ 1.35*	$ 1.48	$ 1.02	$ 1.20	$ 1.61
	20.5%	12.3%	16.2%	10.2%	12.2%	17.0%
	$ 10,991	$ 9,247	$ 9,162	$ 9,475	$ 9,443	$ 7,546
	$ .95	$ .80	$ .70	$ .70	$ .70	$ .55
	$ 3.40	$ 3.40	$ 3.40	$ 3.40	$ 3.40	$ 3.40
	$ 8,455	$ 8.276	$ 8,022	$ 8,121	$ 7,949	$ 8,125
	$ 7,075	$ 5,322	$ 7,978	$ 8,100	$ 5,479	$ 3,790
	$ 12,927	$ 6,888	$ 1,926	$ 4,655	$ 5,811	$ 2,513
	$ 6,595	$ 6,158	$ 4,686	$ 5,626	$ 10,140	$ 3,920
Balance Sheet						
	$100,500	$ 80,067	$ 72,885	$ 87,431	$ 79,075	$ 85,221
	2.42 to 1	2.25 to 1	2.38 to 1	3.03 to 1	2.82 to 1	2.49 to 1
	$ 54,691	$ 50,219	$ 51,607	$ 57,703	$ 61,169	$ 63,367
	$ 3,743	$ 4,223	$ 3,387	$ 6,679	$ 9,153	$ 4,432
	$ 38,800	$ 40,800	$ 42,800	$ 44,800	$ 46,678	$ 48,798
	$143,026	$122,438	$114,781	$132,852	$128,164	$121,735
	10,876	10,700	10,563	12,523	12,448	12,427
	$ 11.61	$ 9.83	$ 9.23	$ 9.23	$ 8.91	$ 8.41
Non-Financial						
	15,437	14,737	12,647	12,998	13,670	13,318
	11,703	10,977	12,505	13,426	13,958	13,164
	1,919	2,008	2,108	2,174	2,270	2,350

Exhibit 2

GROWTH OF WHIRLPOOL BRAND SALES AND INDUSTRY SALES

1958 = 100

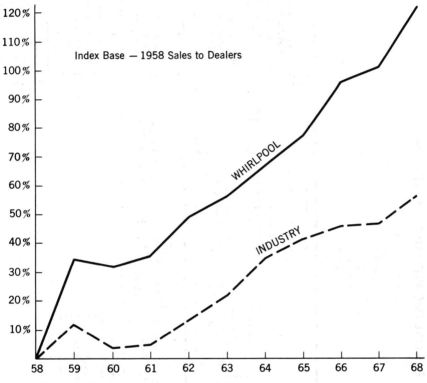

Index Base — 1958 Sales to Dealers

Source: Company records.

Exhibit 3

PARTIAL ORGANIZATION CHART — 1969

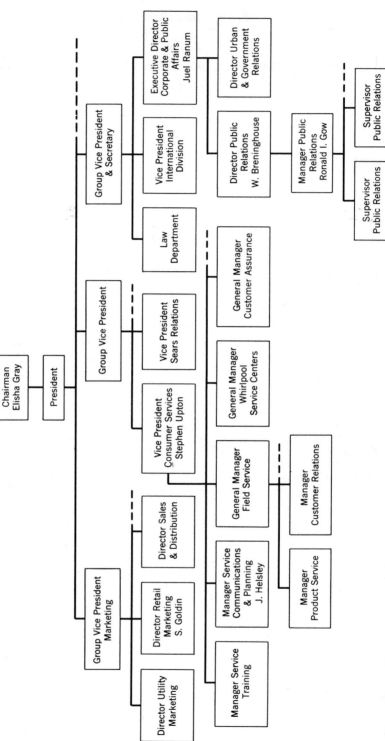

Source: Drawn from company records.

Exhibit 4

SAMPLE OF CUSTOMER ASSURANCE STANDARDS

1 INSTALLATION
(including required accessories and instructions)

2 SERVICEABILITY

NOTE: It is absolutely necessary for the basic goal of reduced "Cost of Ownership" to be applied in the very concept stages of product development.

Scope: This section covers the overall goal of minimum customer service cost.

1 INSTALLATION

Product will be designed and manufactured to allow installation by the various trades normally involved, including customers, without undue risk of malfunction or substandard performance.

Accessories — All accessories normally required for product installation (except normal tools) should be a part of the product, or packaged with the product in a manner which will not allow loss or misplacement.

Instructions — All installation instructions must accompany the product, and be prepared in a simple, concise and clear form. All installation instructions should be prepared from observation of actual product installation.

Installation adjustments — All products will be shipped adjusted for operation upon installation; in those exceptions where adjustment must be made to match local conditions (e.g., gas calorific content and specific gravity), such adjustments should be accessible and understandable by the installer.

2 SERVICEABILITY

All products should be designed and assembled for maximum service accessibility without moving the machine from its normal position where possible.

Serviceability of major components — All components or subassemblies of major components which are subject to failure, and

3 SERVICE PARTS AND PARTS INTERCHANGEABILITY

4 WARRANTY POLICY

which are field repairable, will be established as service parts. The elements of major components which fail most frequently, rendering the component inoperable, should be constructed and assembled so that the element is replaceable.

Consistent fasteners — All screws and other fasteners should be specified so that a minimum number of standard tools are required for servicing; i.e, should not have Phillips head and slotted head screws to be removed for only one service operation.

Product changes — All changes or modifications made to product should render the product more, rather than less, serviceable.

3 SERVICE PARTS AND PARTS INTERCHANGEABILITY

All service parts must be available for shipment from parts depot at the date of first product shipment or before.

Parts literature — Necessary Engineering Bills of Material should be available prior to production to allow production of service parts lists, order and schedule parts and all other related functions.

Parts finish — Finish on service parts should be such that the customer is not left with the impression that seconds or rejects are used as spare parts.

Interchangeability — Any component change or modification should be considered for interchangeability. The comparative economics of stocking and handling non-interchangeable parts should be considered at each component change or modification. Subsequent design should consider parts and components already in the system.

4 WARRANTY POLICY

At periodic product reviews, existing warranty policy should be examined to determine adequacy to cover any changes made in either product, merchandising concepts, or distribution.

Source: Company records.

Exhibit 5

SAMPLE OF A CONSUMER BUY GUIDE

Consumer buy guide

Whirlpool

2-SPEED FRONT LOADING PORTABLE DISHWASHER

MARK I MODEL SVF-100

2-Speed...High water pressure in Super Wash, Rinse Hold, Rinse Dry and Short. Lower water pressure in Gentle Wash and China Crystal

Wash system...full-size jet spray arm under each basket

Self-cleaning filter...prevents redeposit of food particles

Food-warmer ....normal warming temp. 170°

Controls ....6 cycle pushbuttons

Wash chamber ....porcelain enamel

Baskets ....vinyl-coated, full extension

in-the-door silver basket...opens for loading; removable for unloading

In-the-door cutlery basket

Dispensers..dual detergent and 1 rinse conditioner

Thermostatic-Hold .....Raises final rinse to 145°

Signal light ....Indicates when operating

Top ....reversible solid maple with juice ring

Pull bar ....full-width, built into panel

Stabilizer front panel...prevents tipping when door is open and rack extended

Faucet connector..pressure relief to prevent splash

Water flow...allows you to use faucet while dishwasher is operating

Cord reel ......automatically rewinds power cord

Separate recessed hose and power cord storage

Heater ....800 Watts

Operating time...10 to 60 min. depending on cycle

Water consumption ......range from 4.6 gals. for RINSE-HOLD to 13.8 gals. for SUPER WASH

Water pressure...operates on line pressures from 15 to 120 p.s.i.

Water temperature .....recommend 140° to 160°

Electrical system...120-volt, 12.6 amps, 1435 watts, 0.86 KWH per cycle

Motor...⅓ hp., 60-cycle, 3450 r.p.m., 6.0 amps, 635 watts, permanently lubricated

Food Warmer .....120 volt, 1.0 amps., 120 watts

Dimensions...height 36⅜", width 24⅛", depth 24¾", depth including hardware 26¼"

Net Weight ....165 lbs.

Listed ....Underwriters' Laboratories, Inc.

Whirlpool
HOME APPLIANCES

Part No. 717697   Printed in U.S.A.

Exhibit 6

SIMPLIFIED WARRANTY

Dear Customer:

Good performance. That's what this letter is all about.

We know that you expect good performance from your Whirlpool dryer, and we aim to see that you get it. Here's how its performance is protected.

YOUR WARRANTY

During your first year of ownership, all parts of the appliance (except light bulbs) which we find are defective in materials or workmanship will be repaired or replaced by Whirlpool free of charge, and we will pay any labor charges.

During the second year, we will continue to assume the same responsibility as stated above, except you pay any labor charges.

This protection is yours as the original purchaser for your home use, and requires that all service be performed by a service organization authorized to service Whirlpool products. Naturally, it doesn't cover damage by accident, misuse, fire, flood or acts of God. But it does cover you wherever you live in the United States. . .even if you move.

Now about servicing. Let's face it. Sometimes even the best products need service. So, if that's ever true of your Whirlpool dryer, there is a way to get action fast. Just call your servicing Whirlpool dealer or a Whirlpool Tech-Care agent. He is trained to make whatever's wrong right. We do not pay for service calls that only involve instructing you on how to use your new Whirlpool appliance.

On the other hand, we do offer a unique telephone information and assistance service. If you have any questions about operating, maintaining or servicing any Whirlpool appliance, just dial (800) 253-1301*. Free. From anywhere in the continental United States. We'll give you, day or night, the name and number of the authorized Whirlpool Tech-Care serviceman nearest your home.

We suggest you keep this letter with your sales slip and Operating Instructions. It's nice to know you'll have protection, even though you may never need it.

Sincerely,

WHIRLPOOL CORPORATION

Exhibit 7

REPRODUCTION OF OCTOBER 1968 ADVERTISEMENT

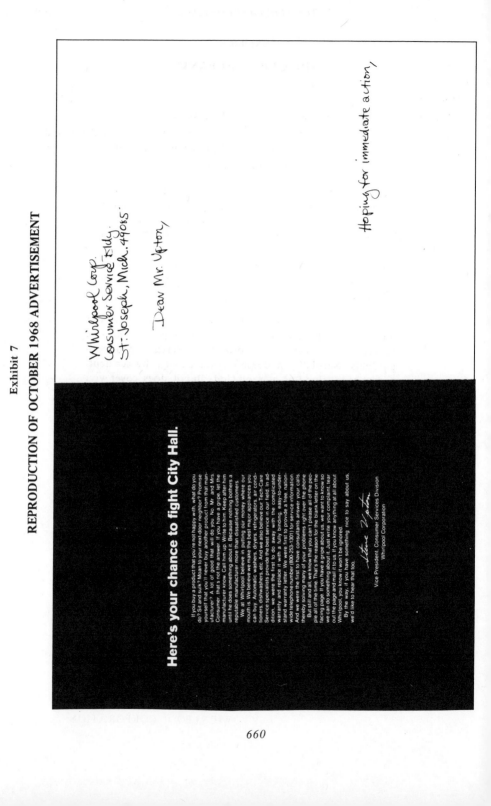

Whirlpool Corp.
Consumer Service Bldg.
St. Joseph, Mich. 49085

Dear Mr. Upton,

Hoping for immediate action,

Here's your chance to fight City Hall.

If you buy a product that you're not happy with, what do you do? Say and sulk? Moan to your next-door neighbor? Promise yourself that you'll never buy another product from that manufacturer? A lot of good that will do you. No. Mr. and Mrs. Consumer, that's not the answer. If you have a gripe, let the manufacturer know. Call him up. Write to him. Keep after him until he does something about it. Because nothing bothers a reputable manufacturer more than dissatisfied customers.

We at Whirlpool believe in putting our money where our mouth is. We believe we make the best major appliances you can buy. Automatic washers, dryers, refrigerators, air conditioners, dishwashers, etc. And we also believe our Tech-Care Service specialists provide the best service in our field. In addition, we were the first to do away with the complicated warranty and replace it with a fully binding, easy-to-understand warranty letter. We were first to provide a free, nationwide telephone number (800-253-1301) for service information. And we were the first to have consultants answer your calls, thereby solving many of your problems right over the phone.

But still and all, we know that you can't please all of the people all of the time. That's the reason for the blank letter on the facing page. If you have a gripe about us, we want to know so we can do something about it. Just write your complaint, tear out the page and mail it to us. If you know anything at all about Whirlpool, you know it won't be ignored.

By the way, if you have something nice to say about us, we'd like to hear that too.

Steve Upton

Vice President, Consumer Services Division
Whirlpool Corporation

Exhibit 8

SCENES OF THE CARE-A-VAN SHOW

SCENE 1: The World We Live In
SCENE 2: The Homemaker's Dilemma
(Out of all the machines available, which one fits my needs?)
   Song: "Who Cares?"
SCENE 3: How to Buy Appliances
(Find the refrigerator to fit shopping habits and family size.)
SCENE 4: The Dishwasher Story
(How to get dishes really clean.) \
   Song: "Out of Sight, Out of Mind."
SCENE 5: The Washer and Dryer Story
(How to care for permanent press.)
   Song: "Doing Your Laundry Thing."
SCENE 6: Warranty and Service
(What warranties cover and how to get service.)
SCENE 7: The Refrigerator-Freezer Story
(What's the value of an ice-maker?)
   Song: "Lady, Don't Lose Your Cool."
SCENE 8: The Range Story
(How to get the most out of your range.)
   Song: "What's Cooking, Baby?"
SCENE 9: How to Buy Air Conditioners
(How to match capacity to need.)
   Song: "That's a Lot of Hot Air."
SCENE 10: Movie: *Home Is What You Make It*
FINALE: Reprise, "Who Cares?"

Exhibit 9

SAMPLE ADVERTISEMENT

Presenting a new musical about a refrigerator, a washer, a range and an air conditioner.

(With a message)

This may sound like a lot of fun, but it's about some pretty serious business; consumer protection. Or, more specifically consumer protection as far as major household appliances go.

It's being presented as a public service (admission free, of course) to educate you, the consumer, on how to buy, use and service appliances.

The title of this hour and a half presentation is Care-A-Van. And, it will blend music, comedy skits and even a short film, to tell you some pretty important things in some pretty entertaining ways. (There will also be a few major appliances given away as door prizes).

Care-A-Van is being sponsored by the Whirlpool Corporation. However, the show won't be about Whirlpool appliances but appliances in general.

As we said before it's a part of this whole consumerism movement to arm people with the knowledge they need to get a fair shake.

If you can at all make it that day, please do. We can't promise Care-A-Van will be the funniest show you've ever seen. But it may very well be the most helpful.

[Time — Date — Place]

Exhibit 10

SAMPLE MAILER FOR THE ANNOUNCEMENT OF CARE-A-VAN

Presenting a new musical about a refrigerator, a washer, a dryer, a dishwasher, a range and an air conditioner.

Care-a-van is a live stage show to be performed all over the country before consumers like you.

If you've recently bought or intend to buy any major household appliance, here's your chance to get hip on the latest features, how to buy an appliance, how to live with it, how to cope with uptight topics like warranties and service.

You'll pick up plenty of appliance savvy and, at the same time, enjoy a fast-moving ninety minutes of multi-media entertainment.

Care-a-van has a talented cast of professional performers . . . original music and lyrics . . . a psychedelic light show . . . movies, slides . . . and more than a few laughs in it for you.

So, mark the date and come to Care-a-van. You'll be missing more than a good time if you don't make it.

You don't buy anything at Care-a-van, not even a ticket—*There's no charge for admission.* And, you just might win a valuable door prize (major appliance). Bring friends, if you like!

Care-a-van is presented as a public service in the interest of consumer information

QUESTIONS

1. What action should Mr. Ranum take regarding the Care-A-Van promotion? Why?

2. How would you attempt to evaluate a program such as this in the context of Whirlpool's overall communications efforts?

3. Who is the prospective consumer of the Care-A-Van program? To what consumer problems is the program addressed?

4.   What is the difference between, and the relative roles of, advertising and consumer information in Whirlpool's situation?

5.   What is your assessment of Whirlpool's overall efforts in greater consumer orientation and communication? Does this program fit well within these efforts?

6.   What problems and opportunities does consumerism pose for the home appliance industry in general? For Whirlpool in particular?

Index of Cases